THE WORLD OF GREAT COMPOSERS

OTHER BOOKS BY DAVID EWEN

The Complete Book of 20th Century Music
The Home Book of Musical Knowledge
Panorama of American Popular Music
Complete Book of the American Musical Theater
A Journey to Greatness: *The Life and Music of George Gershwin*
Richard Rodgers
The World of Jerome Kern
The Encyclopedia of the Opera
The Encyclopedia of Concert Music
Milton Cross' Encyclopedia of Great Composers and Their Music
(with Milton Cross)
Music for the Millions
Dictators of the Baton
Music Comes to America
The New Book of Modern Composers
Leonard Bernstein
The Story of America's Musical Theater

THE
WORLD
OF
GREAT
COMPOSERS

Edited by David Ewen

Prentice-Hall, Inc., Englewood Cliffs, New Jersey

EDITOR'S PREFACE

The World of Great Composers was conceived to present a four-dimensional study of thirty-seven great composers—from Palestrina in the 16th century to Debussy on the threshhold of the 20th. Each composer is discussed in four sections. First, a brief biography provides the basic facts of the composer's life. This is followed by an intimate portrait of the composer as a man, usually by a contemporary or friend, but sometimes by later writers who have been remarkably skilful in separating the man from his music. An eminent musicologist then provides a critical analysis of the composer's work. Each section concludes with the composer speaking for himself—and sometimes about himself—bringing the reader an even more penetrating insight into the genius under discussion.

Since each composer lives most vibrantly in his music, the heart of the book lies in the critical evaluation of each composer's work. For this purpose, the editor has gathered into a single volume—and for the first time—some of the foremost musical scholars of the world. Usually, collective biographies of the great composers are written by a single critic, and are thus subject to the strengths and weaknesses, the penchants and prejudices of that writer. Since no single musicologist or critic—however capable—is sufficiently equipped, or for that matter sufficiently catholic in his tastes, to discuss every composer of the past with equal penetration, such one-man efforts often suffer appalling lapses of critical insight. After all, the Bach scholar is not likely to do as well by Tchaikovsky, nor is the Mahler authority usually able to do equal justice to Massenet. The editor, consequently, decided to have each of the thirty-seven composers discussed by the critic best suited by scholarship and temperament to do so. Bach is discussed by Charles Sanford Terry; Handel, by Rolland; Monteverdi, by Henri Prunières; Mozart, by W. J. Turner; Beethoven, by Paul Bekker; Weber, by Alfred Einstein; Schubert, by Sir Donald Francis Tovey; Mendelssohn, by Sir George Grove; Wagner, by Prof. Edward J. Dent; Mussorgsky, by Gerald Abraham; Verdi, by F. Bonavia. Each musicologist chosen is an undisputed authority on the subject he is discussing; each gives an interpretation and appreciation of the individual genius of the composer that is based on lifelong research and scholarship.

But this volume goes even further than simply gathering some of the best writing in existence on some of the world's greatest composers.

A second dimension to each composer is provided by an intimate, informal portrait, usually by someone who knew that composer well. Thus we are given singularly revealing personal insights into Beethoven by Franz Grillparzer and Anton Schindler; into Rameau by Chabanon; into Haydn by Dies; into Mozart by Michael Kelly and Schlichtegroll; into Schubert by Anselm Hüttenbrenner; into Mendelssohn by Eduard Devrient; into Meyerbeer by Heinrich Heine; into Chopin by George Sand and Franz Liszt; into Liszt by Countess Marie d'Agoult; into Franck by Vincent d'Indy; into Tchaikovsky by his sister-in-law, Mme. Anatol Tchaikovsky; into Mahler by his wife, Alma. All these writers have drawn their material from many years of personal contact. Some of the other personal portraits, however, come not from contemporaries but from later writers: Deems Taylor tells us about Wagner; Slonimsky about Mussorgsky and Rimsky-Korsakov; Rolland about Gluck and Saint-Saëns; Geiringer about Brahms; Oscar Thompson about Debussy.

The editor felt that still another dimension was needed to give a well-rounded and complete study of each composer, and that dimension comes from the composer himself in comments derived from letters, diaries, note books, published writings, and occasionally from well-authenticated conversations. Sometimes the composers discuss aesthetic aims and purposes; sometimes they record their ideas about music in general or the creative impulse; sometimes they plumb deep within their own emotional and personal lives to present such poignant human documents as Beethoven's letter to his immortal beloved and his "Heiligenstadt Testament," or Schubert's revealing allegory about a dream.

The appendices that follow the text include a listing of all the principal works of each composer and, for further reading, a select bibliography of works written in English.

CONTENTS

GIOVANNI PIERLUIGI DA PALESTRINA *(c. 1525–94)*   1
The Man, *Zoë Kendrick Pyne*   2
The Composer, *Hugo Leichtentritt*   4
Palestrina Speaks   7

CLAUDIO MONTEVERDI *(1567–1643)*   9
The Man, *David Ewen*   9
The Composer, *Henri Prunières*   11
Monteverdi Speaks   16

JEAN-PHILIPPE RAMEAU *(1683–1764)*   18
The Man, *Michel-Paul-Guide Chabanon*   19
The Composer, *Bernard Champigneulle*   20
Rameau Speaks   23

ANTONIO VIVALDI *(1669–1741)*   25
The Man, *Marc Pincherle*   26
The Composer, *Donald Jay Grout*   28
Vivaldi Speaks   33

JOHANN SEBASTIAN BACH *(1685–1750)*   34
The Man, *Johann Nikolaus Forkel, Albert Schweitzer*   35
The Composer, *C. Sanford Terry*   38
Bach Speaks   52

GEORGE FRIDERIC HANDEL *(1685–1759)*   54
The Man, *Charles Burney, Newman Flower*   55
The Composer, *Romain Rolland*   58
Handel Speaks   73

CHRISTOPH WILLIBALD GLUCK *(1714–87)*   74
The Man, *Romain Rolland*   75
The Composer, *William Foster Apthorp*   77
Gluck Speaks   85

CONTENTS

JOSEPH HAYDN *(1732–1809)*   87
    The Man, *Albert Christoph Dies*   88
    The Composer, *W. Oliver Strunk*   91
    Haydn Speaks   102

WOLFGANG AMADEUS MOZART *(1756–91)*   104
    The Man, *Michael Kelly, Adolph Heinrich von Schlichtegroll*   106
    The Composer, *W. J. Turner*   108
    Mozart Speaks   119

LUDWIG VAN BEETHOVEN *(1770–1827)*   122
    The Man, *Anton Schindler, Franz Grillparzer*   124
    The Composer, *Paul Bekker*   127
    Beethoven Speaks   141

KARL MARIA VON WEBER *(1786–1826)*   146
    The Man, *André Coeuroy*   147
    The Composer, *Alfred Einstein*   150
    Weber Speaks   153

FRANZ SCHUBERT *(1797–1828)*   155
    The Man, *Anselm Hüttenbrenner*   156
    The Composer, *Donald Francis Tovey*   158
    Schubert Speaks   175

HECTOR BERLIOZ *(1803–69)*   179
    The Man, *Romain Rolland*   180
    The Composer, *W. H. Hadow*   183
    Berlioz Speaks   192

GIOACCHINO ROSSINI *(1792–1868)*   195
    The Man, *Francis Toye*   196
    The Composer, *Francis Toye*   200
    Rossini Speaks   209

GIACOMO MEYERBEER *(1791–1864)*   211
    The Man, *Heinrich Heine*   212
    The Composer, *R. A. Streatfeild*   214
    Meyerbeer Speaks   217

FELIX MENDELSSOHN *(1809–47)*   219
  The Man, *Eduard Devrient*   220
  The Composer, *Sir George Grove*   223
  Mendelssohn Speaks   230

ROBERT SCHUMANN *(1810–56)*   232
  The Man, *Gustav Jansen*   233
  The Composer, *W. H. Hadow*   235
  Schumann Speaks   253

FRÉDÉRIC CHOPIN *(1810–49)*   255
  The Man, *George Sand, Franz Liszt*   256
  The Composer, *Olin Downes*   259
  Chopin Speaks   267

CÉSAR FRANCK *(1822–90)*   270
  The Man, *Vincent d'Indy*   271
  The Composer, *Leland Hall*   274
  Franck Speaks   279

CHARLES GOUNOD *(1818–93)*   281
  The Man, *Howard Paul*   282
  The Composer, *R. A. Streatfeild*   283
  Gounod Speaks   287

JULES MASSENET *(1842–1912)*   290
  The Man, *Herbert Peyser*   291
  The Composer, *Martin Cooper*   294
  Massenet Speaks   299

FRANZ LISZT *(1811–86)*   303
  The Man, *Amy Fay, Countess Marie d'Agoult*   305
  The Composer, *Cecil Gray*   307
  Liszt Speaks   318

RICHARD WAGNER *(1813–83)*   320
  The Man, *Deems Taylor*   322
  The Composer, *Edward J. Dent*   327
  Wagner Speaks   338

CONTENTS

JOHANNES BRAHMS *(1833–97)*   341
The Man, *Karl Geiringer*   342
The Composer, *Daniel Gregory Mason*   347
Brahms Speaks   354

BEDŘICH SMETANA *(1824–84)*   356
The Man, *Josef Schwarz*   357
The Composer, *Kurt Pahlen*   359
Smetana Speaks   361

ANTONIN DVOŘÁK *(1841–1904)*   363
The Man, *Paul Stefan*   364
The Composer, *Vladimir Helfert*   366
Dvořák Speaks   370

PETER ILITCH TCHAIKOVSKY *(1840–93)*   373
The Man, *Mme. Anatol Tchaikovsky*   375
The Composer, *Richard Anthony Leonard*   377
Tchaikovsky Speaks   387

MODEST MUSSORGSKY *(1839–91)*   391
The Man, *Nicolas Slonimsky*   392
The Composer, *Gerald Abraham*   395
Mussorgsky Speaks   398

NIKOLAI RIMSKY-KORSAKOV *(1844–1908)*   400
The Man, *Nicolas Slonimsky*   401
The Composer, *M. Montagu-Nathan*   403
Rimsky-Korsakov Speaks   410

EDVARD GRIEG *(1843–1907)*   412
The Man, *Gerhard Schjelderup, Percy Grainger*   413
The Composer, *Kristian Lange and Arne Östvedt*   416
Grieg Speaks   420

GIUSEPPE VERDI *(1813–1901)*   422
The Man, *Franz Werfel*   423
The Composer, *F. Bonavia*   426
Verdi Speaks   436

GIACOMO PUCCINI *(1858–1924)*   439
    The Man, *Richard Specht*   440
    The Composer, *Donald Jay Grout*   444
    Puccini Speaks   448

ANTON BRUCKNER *(1824–96)*   450
    The Man, *Gabriel Engel*   451
    The Composer, *H. C. Colles*   453
    Bruckner Speaks   457

GUSTAV MAHLER *(1860–1911)*   459
    The Man, *Alma Mahler Werfel*   460
    The Composer, *Bruno Walter*   463
    Mahler Speaks   471

HUGO WOLF *(1860–1903)*   473
    The Man, *David and Frederic Ewen*   474
    The Composer, *Ernest Newman*   476
    Wolf Speaks   481

CAMILLE SAINT-SAËNS *(1835–1921)*   483
    The Man, *Philip Hale*   484
    The Composer, *Romain Rolland*   485
    Saint-Saëns Speaks   490

CLAUDE DEBUSSY *(1862–1918)*   493
    The Man, *Oscar Thompson*   494
    The Composer, *Paul Rosenfeld*   497
    Debussy Speaks   505

APPENDICES
    I. Principal Works of the Great Composers   511
    II. For Further Reading: A Select Bibliography in English   543
    III. Contributors   555

Acknowledgments   563

Index   571

THE WORLD OF GREAT COMPOSERS

GIOVANNI PIERLUIGI DA PALESTRINA

c. 1 5 2 5 – 1 5 9 4

GIOVANNI PIERLUIGI DA PALESTRINA brought the first important epoch in Western music—the age of polyphony—to its most advanced stage of technical perfection, and to its highest point of artistic fulfillment. He was born Giovanni Pierluigi in or about 1525, but he is known as Palestrina after the town of his birth, twenty miles outside Rome. He attended the choir school of Santa Maria Maggiore in Rome after which, in 1544, he became choirmaster and organist of Sant' Agapit Cathedral in his native town. In 1551 he was appointed director of the Julian Choir in Rome where, three years later, he published his first book of Masses. After that, Palestrina served as a singer in the Pontifical Choir, as musical director of St. John Lateran, and as musical director of Santa Maria Maggiore. In 1563 he published his first volume of motets. His masterwork, the *Missa Papae Marcelli,* came out in 1567, a model for his contemporaries and immediate successors. There is a theory that this work was directly responsible for frustrating the efforts of the Council of Trent in 1562 to reform church music through a return from complex polyphony to the simple plainsong, but it is legend and not fact. In 1567, Palestrina left Santa Maria Maggiore and was employed by Cardinal Ippolito d'Este. He returned to his old post as musical director of the Julian Choir in 1571 and remained there to the end of his life. He died in Rome on February 2, 1594 and was buried in the Cappella Nuovo at the old St. Peter's Church.

1

THE MAN

ZOË KENDRICK PYNE

To Palestrina the practical and material side of his profession was of utmost importance. It need hardly be said that the conditions of life in a small town like Palestrina and in the great city of Rome were absolutely different. In the Sabine Hills, a small settled income, wines, and olives, probably provided as many amenities as the circumstances required, but now the exigencies of an official position and a growing family pressed more heavily upon the composer. It has been made a subject of implied reproach that he was never indifferent to the financial aspect of a question, nor ever neglected an opportunity of attaching himself to a wealthy patron; but he should rather be praised for precisely those qualities which prove him to have been a good husband, careful father, and a prudent man, qualities—all of them—by no means inseparable from genius. Moreover, it is fairly obvious that he could never have enriched the world with the extraordinarily large number of his compositions had he not possessed in a high degree the capacity for managing his affairs, and thereby securing the necessary environment of calm and comparative ease for intellectual labors. The honeyed phrases of his dedications were the usual custom . . . and it has been wittily said that a powerful patron might be considered in the light of a policeman, by means of whom it was possible to redress one's private wrongs, and make headway against one's enemies. . . .

His monthly salary at Santa Maria Maggiore amounted at first to thirteen, later, sixteen scudi on the addition of another chorister to the three already in his charge, in all about one hundred and ninety-two scudi (approximately $750 a year). For this sum, Palestrina was expected to feed the boys and give them musical instruction. That is to say, he received six scudi as salary, and two scudi and a half per head for each chorister. As quarters in the precincts were always assigned to members of the choir, there would be no expenditure necessary for housing. Presents were customary after the

2

great festivals of the Church. . . . To these sources of income must be added Palestrina's pension as ex-member of the Pontifical Choir, amounting to a yearly sum of about $250. Then comes an uncertain sum for dedications to rich patrons—habitual at the time—and the organization of music for occasions festive or mournful. The present was an epoch in which men of wealth and position desired to pose as excellent musicians, so that there were always compositions to be corrected and put into shape, or lessons to give. Professional pupils according to the custom of the times lived in the master's house and became part of his family. Palestrina also had property and turned it to practical account. This was to be added to by the death of his father, and until the close of his own life, documentary evidences of the acquisition of small pieces of property show that this tended to increase. He was certainly not rich, but, all things considered, his income compares not unfavorably with many a church musician of high repute today.

· · · · ·

Through the Register of Deaths belonging to St. Peter's, we learn that Lucrezia, Palestrina's wife, after a married life lasting thirty-three years, died and was buried on July 23, 1580 in the Cappella Nuovo of St. Peter's. The mother did not long survive the death of her two sons. Palestrina, however, does not appear to have been left entirely alone. His youngest son, Igino, married Virginia Guarnacci in 1577, and in the register of St. Peter's occurs an entry referring to the baptism of their son, Tommaso. But it is to be surmised that the domestic situation was no easy one for Palestrina. He had not only lost his beloved wife and two sons but also the head of his household. As Master of the Julian Choir he had boys under his care, and a young daughter-in-law with small children—a baby was born only three days after Lucrezia's death—may quite conceivably have lacked the experience and leisure for the management of so complicated a household. Be this as it may, in 1581, Palestrina married again, choosing a wife suitable for a man of advancing years and failing health. Victoria Dormuli was a rich widow, and beyond this little is known of her.

THE COMPOSER

HUGO LEICHTENTRITT

When the spirit of the Italian Renaissance is discussed, Palestrina cannot be passed over lightly, for his music shows some of the most characteristic aspects of Renaissance art in their purest form. He spent his entire artistic career at Rome in the service of the Catholic Church, most of the time at the famous Papal chapel of St. Peter's, though he was absent from it for about seventeen years. This absence illustrates very forcibly the tendencies of the Roman Counter Reformation. In 1555, Pope Paul IV set up an iron rule. He pursued with the greatest severity everything and everybody likely to injure the Catholic Church in the eyes of the world. Michelangelo's glorious fresco paintings in the Sistine Chapel were offensive to him because of the nude bodies that were represented, and he ordered the painter Daniel da Volterra to supply them with appropriate clothing. This fact alone makes it manifest that the half-pagan Renaissance spirit, with its delight in reminiscences of antiquity, was vanishing, that a severe new bent of mind had become dominant. Another of Paul's reforms was the removal of all married singers from the Papal chapel, in order to enforce celibacy and accentuate the clerical character of all the institutions of the Catholic Church. Palestrina had to quit his post and was called back only years later, when another Pope of less severity occupied the Papal throne. Palestrina's music does not manifest in any way the characteristic traits of the spirit of the Counter Reformation, which becomes evident only a generation later in the music of the Baroque Age. Yet the astonishing fact remains—one might call it an irony of fate—that this music of Palestrina's, so full of the Renaissance spirit, so traditional in its general aspects, so unsensational in a propagandistic sense, was destined to become the most powerful musical ally of the Catholic Church in its combat with Protestantism. To this very day Palestrina's music is justly admired as the most comprehensive, convincing, and suc-

4

cessful interpretation of the true Catholic spirit, not only in music proper but in all the world of art.

In the music of Palestrina a student expert in problems of style can find summed up the entire process of transformation which the Dutch style underwent in Italy. Palestrina had learned his art from the Dutch masters, and he himself finally mastered the Dutch technique of counterpoint and construction to perfection. Yet his music would not have meant much to posterity had it remained only a copy, however skilful, of the Dutch manner. What makes it unique and incomparable is the fact that this master alone knew how to apply to the severe and complex Dutch art of design and construction the Italian melodic bent, sense of color and proportion, the Italian accent, voice and soul. The broad stream of these characteristic traits of the Italian Renaissance carries along with it as smaller tributaries of the traditional Dutch traits. Palestrina is not in the least a revolutionary artist, bent on forcibly overthrowing a former state of things; his music shows us a classical paradigm of evolution, of gradual and legitimate transformation.

It is the general fare of revolutionary art to represent a new start which is bound to be superseded by subsequent progress, where a great evolutionary art means not a beginning but a conclusion, a climax, an arrival at perfection. And Palestrina, like Orlando di Lasso (1532–94), like Bach, Mozart, Beethoven, Verdi, and Wagner belongs among the great names of evolutionary art.

The lasting value of Palestrina's art is based upon two essential qualities: purity of style, and the coupling of ideal contents with ideal form. Though Palestrina's music is narrower in scope than that of other masters of the first magnitude—Bach, Mozart, Beethoven— yet within its limits it must be called one of the sublime achievements of all art. It is the ideal ecclesiastical music, superior even to Bach's church music. The Catholic spirit certainly has never found a more congenial or more convincing artistic expression. As regards its form, attention must be called to the perfect equilibrium that is maintained between the logical construction of its contrapuntal design and its wonderfully rich effects of sound, full of color, light, and shade. Only in Mozart's music do we meet with a similar equilibrium, though on a very different plane. Works like Palestrina's

5

Missa Assumpta Es (1567), *Missa Papae Marcelli* (1567), *Stabat Mater* (1595), and Motets from the *Canticle of Solomon* (1584) show us characteristic aspects of his art in various directions and prove the immense range of his religious music, its peculiar combination of seraphic mildness and exuberant brilliance, of ravishing beauty and passionate outcry, of soaring heights of ecstasy and profound seriousness of meditation.

Palestrina's motets and Masses are the musical counterparts of the paintings of Perugino, Leonardo da Vinci, Raphael, Fra Filippo Lippi, Fra Bartolomeo, and Andrea del Sarto. In certain seraphic sounds in Palestrina's motets and Masses we perceive a spirit akin to that of the touching and adorable Fra Angelico da Fiesole, a century earlier, whose frescoes in the convent of San Marco in Florence are unique in their purity and childlike confidence. Whoever has felt the mysterious power of Raphael's Sistine Madonna in the Dresden Gallery, its inexplicable purity, grace, and simplicity coupled with a sublime religious emotion, will also be touched profoundly by Palestrina's music which is so similar in effect. The art of sculptors like Donatello and Luca della Robbia also has its musical reflection in the clearness, the wonderful precision and beauty of Palestrina's plastic design, and such great Renaissance architects as Palladio, Alberti, and Bramante helped Palestrina to acquire his wonderful sense of harmonious proportion and of rhythmical and graceful construction.

Ruskin, discussing the "division of arts" in his *Aratra Pentelici,* speaks at length, with reference to painting, sculpture, and architecture, of the "musical or harmonic element in every art." According to Ruskin, "the science of color is, in the Greek sense, the more musical, being one of the divisions of the Apolline power." He also explains that " the second musical science, which belongs peculiarly to sculpture (and to painting so far as it represents form) consists in the disposition of beautiful masses. That is to say, beautiful surfaces limited by beautiful lines. Sculpture is defined by Ruskin as "the art which by the musical disposition of masses, imitates anything of which the imitation is justly pleasant to us; and does so in accordance with structural laws having due reference to the materials employed." All these observations of Ruskin's lose nothing

6

of their significance or validity if we change the observer's point of view and look at the problems primarily from the angle of music. With very slight modification those mutual relations can be beautifully exemplified by Palestrina's music.

PALESTRINA SPEAKS

Our wisest mortals have decided that music should give zest to divine worship, so that those whom pious devotion to religious practice has led to the temple might remain there to delight in voices blending in harmony. If men take great pains to compose beautiful music for profane songs, they should devote at least as much thought to sacred song, nay, even more than to mere worldly matters. Therefore, though well aware of my feeble powers, I have held nothing more desirable than that whatever is sung throughout the year, according to the season, should be agreeable to the ear by virtue of its vocal beauty, insofar as it lay in my power to make it so.

. . . . .

There exists a vast mass of love songs of the poets, written in a fashion entirely foreign to the profession and name of Christians. They are the songs of men ruled by passion, and a great number of musicians, corrupters of youth, make them the concern of their art and their industry; in proportion as they flourish through praise of their skill, so do they offend good and serious-minded men by the depraved taste of their work. I blush and grieve to think that once I was of their number. But while I cannot change the past, nor undo what is done, I have mended my ways. Therefore, I have labored on songs which have been written in praise of our Lord, Jesus Christ, and His Most Holy Virgin Mother, Mary; and I have produced a work which treats of the divine love of Christ and his spouse the Soul, the Canticle of Solomon.

. . . . .

Worldly cares of any kind . . . are adverse to the Muses, and particularly those which arise from a lack of private means. For, when

7

the latter afford a sufficiency (and to ask more is the mark of a greedy and intemperate man), the mind can more easily detach itself from other cares; if not, the fault lies within. Those who have known the necessity of laboring to provide this sufficiency, according to their station and way of life, know full well how it distracts the mind from learning and from a study of the liberal arts. Certainly, I have known this experience all my life, and more especially at present (1588). Yet I thank the Divine Goodness, first, that the course is now almost finished, and the goal in sight; secondly, that in the midst of the greatest difficulties I have never interrupted my study of music. Dedicated to the profession since boyhood and engrossed in it to the best of my abilities and energies, indeed, what other interest could I have had? Would that my progress has equalled my labor and my diligence!

I have composed and published much; a great deal more is lying by me, which I am hindered from publishing because of the straitened means of which I have spoken.

CLAUDIO MONTEVERDI

1 5 6 7 – 1 6 4 3

CLAUDIO MONTEVERDI—first significant composer of operas, and personification of the transition between the polyphonic and Baroque eras—was born in Cremona, Italy, in 1567. As a chorister at the Cremona Cathedral he studied with Marc' Antonio Ingegneri, and at fifteen published a volume of three-part motets. In or about his twenty-third year he was employed as a madrigal singer and viola player by the Duke of Mantua, rising to the post of Maestro di Cappella in 1602. Between 1587 and 1605 he published five volumes of madrigals. Soon after opera had come into being in 1594 (through the efforts of the *Camerata,* a group of Florentine intellectuals who hoped to restore classic Greek drama), Monteverdi was attracted to the new medium. His first opera was *Orfeo,* introduced in Mantua on February 22, 1607, the earliest opera in music history still performed. In 1608 he completed a second opera, *Arianna,* of which only the *Lament* has survived. From 1613 until the end of his life he was the Maestro di Cappella of the San Marco Cathedral in Venice where he wrote both religious music and operas. His last opera, *L' Incoronazione di Poppea,* was produced in Venice in the fall of 1642. He died in Venice on November 19, 1643.

THE MAN

DAVID EWEN

Unlike so many other famous musicians of his time, Monteverdi could not shake works out of his sleeve. Others might manufacture one work after another from a convenient matrix. He was, above everything else, the artist-craftsman, fashioning each of his compositions to its own measurements and design. He wrote copiously, but only after long and fastidious preparation.

Temperamentally he was unsuited for the age of patronage that demanded from its hirelings musical works on order—often tailor-made to specifications. He was frequently in despair—sometimes actually made physically ill—by the insistent commissions heaped upon him by patrons who preferred facility and pleasing sounds to careful structures and fastidious art. "I do most heartily pray your Most Serene Highness, for the love of God, no longer to put so much work on me and to give me more time for my great desire to serve you," he was forced to write to his employer. "Otherwise the excess of my fatigue will not fail to shorten my life."

His only existing portrait shows a face both somber and strong. The eyes, under massive brows, are grave, severe, and touched with melancholy. The lips are pressed hard together. He was honest and direct in all his dealings, a man without malice or guile, a man of strong inner resources. He had suffered greatly throughout life. Yet suffering could not weaken his formidable powers of creation. Though he was interested in art and literature, and sometimes dabbled in alchemy, he was first and foremost a composer to whom writing music was as essential as food and drink. Through work he was able to forget not only his personal suffering but fatigue and even the passing of time.

He was the modernist of his day. His unresolved discords created confusion and dismay among the pundits of his time. Artusi, a gifted musician in his own right, sneered at Monteverdi's music as appealing more to the senses than to reason. Monteverdi's restless intellect groped constantly for new ways of expressing itself, just as it continually sought stimulation in classic literature (Plato especially) and in great works of art. Throughout his life he remained sensitively attuned to the new musical forms and styles arising in different parts of Europe; and he always possessed the remarkable resiliency to adopt these new methods when he felt they could serve his artistic purpose.

THE COMPOSER

HENRI PRUNIÈRES

Claudio Monteverdi straddled the 16th and 17th centuries. Having mastered the Renaissance forms, he was the chief molder of those of the 17th century. The musico-dramatic reform might have been a blind alley were it not for his advent. He was truly the man required to bring these rudimentary efforts to a successful issue.

In the service of the Duke of Mantua, Monteverdi had devoted himself to the madrigal, rousing the anger of such upholders of tradition as Artusi who censured his taste for dissonances and his sacrifice of reason to the senses. His impetuous genius was uncontainable in this form, and he approached the madrigal much as Beethoven approached the symphonic form in his Ninth Symphony. The Monteverdian madrigal contains in an embryonic form the modern harmonic language, the musico-dramatic style, and the descriptive symphony. With Monteverdi individual expression took the place of the generalized form of expression which the 15th century had inherited from the Gothic musicians. Hence, among the older masters, his special appeal. The mighty agitation and passion were put into a musical language which, in essentials, has subsisted up to the present time. Monteverdi stands out from his contemporaries, like François Villon from the 15th-century poets: he conceived a new art.

In his first four books of madrigals, published between 1587 and 1603, Monteverdi goes no further than the harmonic processes of Luca Marenzio (1553–99), Marc' Antonio Ingegneri (1545–92) and others; but even here, in his use of these processes there is originality. His dissonances are produced, like theirs, by syncopations, appogiaturas, and passing notes; the false relation is used for expressive purposes, and dissonances for modulations. But whereas others employed the dissonances for a passing accidental, soon left behind for calmer prospects, Monteverdi cherished it as desirable in itself. There is no repose resulting from the use of common chords in his music; it is predominantly dissonant.

11

Again, while earlier madrigals were of an essentially vocal character, Monteverdi, particularly after the fourth book, seems to have instruments rather than voices in mind. . . . So convincing are the proportions of Monteverdi's madrigals, so clearly is the thought expressed, that they may perfectly well be played by instruments, indeed they were originally. Many of the madrigals in the fourth and fifth books were obviously intended to be sung by a solo voice, while the lower parts were played by viols in the form of an accompaniment.

Thus Monteverdi, possibly under the influence of the musico-dramatic reform which was engaging progressive minds at the end of the 16th century, proceeds towards a form of accompanied monody. He is the great craftsman in the evolution of the dramatic cantata from the lyrical madrigal. Certain pieces of the fifth book already disclose, in declamatory passages on repeated notes, their rhythm following the prosody and the dramatic values, the recitative style of the composer of *Orfeo*.

The fifth book not only contains the germ of the future orchestra and the monodic song, but is evidence of an harmonic revolution which dominates the evolution of musical language during the 17th century. For the first time chords of the dominant seventh and ninth are used without preparation to determine the tonal cadences. The major and minor modes had, of course, long been freely employed, but in a doubtful manner. By his use of the dominant seventh in tonal modulations, Monteverdi instinctively created the whole technique or successions of chords and tonalities, codified in Rameau's *Traité d'harmonie,* and practised in the classical masterpieces of the end of the 18th century.

The fact is that he was constructing a new harmonic language and threatened the foundations of polyphony by the introduction of a dramatic and personal sentiment.

.   .   .   .   .

The Duke of Mantua, Vincenzo Gonzaga, and also his sons, had been won over to the cause of the musical drama. They encouraged Monteverdi to set to music the libretto of *Orfeo* by the State secretary, Alessandro Striggio, son of the famous madrigalist and poet.

In the Carnival of 1607, the work was performed before a select party at the Accademia degli Invaghiti and was repeated on February 24 and March 1 at the Court Theater. Its success was decisive.

Orfeo is beyond question the masterpiece of the *riforma melodrammatica*. Monteverdi identified himself with the Florentine aesthetic, but refused to make music a slave of poetry, for he believed that each was equally capable of expressing the innermost feelings.

After several successful attempts in his madrigals, Monteverdi succeeded in *Orfeo* in rousing the passions in the manner of classical antiquity. He enriched the form invented by the *Camerata* in Florence with a host of devices borrowed from the Italian madrigalists and organists and from the French composers of court airs and ballets.

In style, Striggio's tragedy is closely related to the pastorals of Rinuccini and Chiabrera. One might criticize the same kind of rather conventional nobility, but the work contains tragic scenes treated with great restraint.

What is altogether peculiar to Monteverdi is his use of symphonic pieces in the manner of leading motives, thereby assuring a formal unity in the work. The piece entitled *Ritornello* may be considered the *Leitmotiv* of *Orfeo*. It reappears several times, notably in the seven-part symphony which stands out as an urgent supplication at the end of the second act. The "Infernal Symphony," which opens the third act, reappears following Orpheus's despair in Act V, as if to suggest the abode of Eurydice.

The musical drama is dependent on the declamation, but we are now far from the inorganic recitative of the Florentines. Monteverdi's recitative is melodically inflected. In the admirable recitation of the Messenger, so moving in its simplicity, a few chromatic accents and a sudden change from the chord of E major to the one of G minor create an impression of anguish and horror. In the opening scene of Orpheus's despair the care in rendering every shade of meaning is matched only by the dramatic power. . . .

Orfeo contains examples of all the then known forms of the aria. The *arioso*, based on recitative, predominates. A melodic passage followed by a recitation and the first passage repeated appears as the prototype of the *aria da capo*. There are also many strophic airs, but the most curious forms are those in which instruments are associated with the voices. The aria in the third act in which Orpheus attempts to move the power of Hades is one of the oldest examples of the concerted air.

Remarkable throughout the score is the extraordinary variety. In the two *Euridices* of Jacopo Peri (1561–1633) and Giulio Caccini (c. 1546–1618) there is never any gradation. *Orfeo,* on the other hand, abounds in contrasts. The first act is a luminous fresco in pale shades, consisting almost entirely of joyful choruses of shepherds, danced or sung. The opening of the second act sets a mournful tone: the music of Orpheus, who sings of his country, is grave and solemn as if the hero were troubled by a foreboding; and when in the distance the messenger utters her heartrending cries he immediately realizes his fate. An abrupt modulation from C to A major marks Silvia's entry, producing the effect of a cloud obscuring the scene, and the music remains darkly colored until the end of the act. In the third act, Monteverdi substitutes brass instruments for the strings and produces a lugubrious and fitting accompaniment for a view of the infernal regions. The fourth act is in half-tones throughout to suggest the eerie glow of the underground, and the last act progressively proceeds from Orpheus's gloomy despair to the golden light of an apotheosis in sound. In later works Monteverdi obtains these effects of color solely by means of harmony and rhythm; in *Orfeo* he relied on the orchestra. One sees that he realizes the expressive power of each instrument, but it is often forgotten that others realized as much before. Gradually the orchestra was simplified; the balance was shifted, the foundations were made more secure, and as a result it lost some of its variety and glamor.

We find in *Orfeo* a large number of instrumental pieces of various models: *ritornelli* written to a strict metrical plan, homophonic and polyphonic sinfonie, toccate, ricercari, and moresques. Besides the dramatic recitatives are *ariosi*, strophic airs, metrical airs, syllabic and contrapuntal choruses and ballets, mimed, sung, and danced. Monteverdi brought to this new form of the tragedy in recitative all the technical resources at the command of his genius. The aristocratic spectacle of Florence became in his hands the modern musical drama of passions.

. . . . .

On May 28, 1608, *Arianna* was given before an immense audience at the palace of Mantua. From the score only the "Lament of Arianna" survives. Written in recitative style, with the periodical return of the plaint *Lasciate mi morire!* it is still of poignant and even overwhelming effect. This is surely Monteverdi's finest dramatic page—a noble expression of grief recalling the masterpieces of ancient Greece.

Almost nothing remains of the dramatic music which Monteverdi composed between *Orfeo* and *Arianna* and the Venetian opera. *Il Ritorno di Ulisse* (1641) should be considered as an improvisation of genius, a vast sketch in which certain parts have been worked out, and the others scarcely outlined. Ulysses and Penelope are vigorously drawn and certain episodic roles are fashioned with verve: the shepherd Eumeus, the servant Melanto, the beggar Iro. The gods express themselves in a solemn and high-sounding style. The orchestra rarely intervenes, though it does so notably in the scene of the massacre of the suitors and, again, to accompany the beautiful air of Penelope in the third act, which associates all Nature with her happiness.

If *L'Incoronazione di Poppea* dates from the year of its performance (1642), Monteverdi was seventy-four years old. Nothing, however, in this vigorous and sensual score reveals signs of age. All of the personages act with intensity. Monteverdi recreates for us Imperial Rome. The libretto, by Busenello, gave him the opportunity to depict scenes of love, of crime, of orgies, of fêtes, of banquets. Musically, Monteverdi renounces the sumptuous orchestra which he used at the court of Mantua. Beyond the harpsichord and some lutes and bass viols necessary to sustain the voices he scarcely uses anything except a few violins and viols, and, for the descriptive effects, trumpets and trombones, oboes and bassoon, perhaps also some flutes and horns. But we cannot be sure of these details. The scores rediscovered in Venice and in Naples are very schematic.

Monteverdi composed at the same time religious works which

15

were very different from one another, some being in the traditional polyphonic style, others in a very modern concerted style. His sincere mysticism expressed itself in music of profound contemplation, even ascetism. But to proclaim his pious love for God, he used melodic figures which could as well be addressed to an adored mistress.

MONTEVERDI SPEAKS

I consider that the principal passions or emotions of the soul are three: namely, anger, serenity, and humility or supplication. The best philosophers affirm this. The very nature of our voice indicates this by having high, low, and middle ranges. The art of music reaffirms this in these three terms, "agitated," "soft," and "moderate." In the works of the composers of the past I have found examples of the "soft" and "moderate" types, but never of the "agitated" style described by Plato in the third book of *Rhetoric* in these words, "take that harmony that would fittingly imitate the brave man going to war." Aware that contrasts move our soul, and that such is the purpose of all good music as Boethius asserts by saying "music is a part of us, and either ennobles or corrupts our behavior"—for this reason I have applied myself diligently to the rediscovery of this style.

Reflecting that all the best philosophers maintain that the pyrrhic or fast tempo was used for lively, warlike dances, and that the slow spondaic tempo for the opposite, I decided upon the semibreve (whole note) and proposed that each semibreve correspond to a spondee. Reducing this to sixteen semichromes (sixteenth notes), struck one after the other and joined to words expressing anger and scorn, I recognized in this brief example a resemblance to the emotion which I was seeking, although the words did not follow the rapid beats of the instrument.

To obtain better proof, I resorted to the divine Tasso, as a poet who expresses most appropriately and naturally in words the emotions which he wishes to depict, and I chose his description of the

16

combat between Tancredi and Clorinda, as the theme for my music expressing contrary passions aroused by war, prayer, and death.

In the year of 1624, I had this composition performed in the noble house of the most Illustrious and Excellent Signor Girolamo Mocenigo in Venice. It was received by the best citizens of that noble city with much applause and high praise.

Having met success with my first attempt at depicting anger, I proceeded with even greater zeal to make fuller investigations, and composed other works—both ecclesiastical and chamber works. These found such favor with other composers that they not only spoke their praise by word of mouth but, to my great joy and honor, wrote it by imitating my work. For this reason I have thought it best to make known that the investigation and the first efforts in this style—so necessary to the art of music and without which it can rightly be said that music has been imperfect up to now, having had but two styles, soft and moderate—originated with me.

. . . . . .

I put my ideas into practice when I wrote the *Lament of Arianna.* I found no book that could instruct me in the method of imitating the emotions; still less, one that could make it clear to me that I should be an imitator of nature. Plato was the exception, one of whose ideas was, however, so obscure that, with my weak sight and at such great distance, I could hardly apprehend the little he could teach me. I must say that it cost me great effort to complete the laborious work needed to achieve the little I have accomplished in the imitation of nature. For this reason, I hope I shall not cause displeasure. If I should succeed in bringing this work to a conclusion, as I so dearly wish, I should count myself happy to be praised less for modern compositions than for those in the traditional style.

JEAN-PHILIPPE RAMEAU

1 6 8 3 - 1 7 6 4

JEAN-PHILIPPE RAMEAU, who established the traditions of French classic opera as well as the science of harmony, was born in Dijon, France, on September 25, 1683. After studying the organ, harpsichord, and violin, and attending the Jesuit College at Dijon, he visited Italy briefly in 1701. In 1702 he served as assistant organist in Avignon, and as first organist at Clermont-Ferrand. It was during this period that he started writing music for the harpsichord. From 1705 to 1709 he lived in Paris and studied the organ with Louis Marchand, in 1706 publishing the first volume of his *Pièces de clavecin.* In 1709 he succeeded his father as organist of the Dijon Cathedral. He later returned to Clermont-Ferrand where he prepared his first book on musical theory, the *Traité de l'harmonie,* published in Paris in 1722. The modern science of harmony can be said to have originated with this volume. He returned to Paris in 1723 and remained there for the rest of his life. He was engaged by the powerful music patron, Riche de la Pouplinière, as household music master, organist, and conductor of a private orchestra. Rameau's first important opera was *Hippolyte et Aricie,* introduced at the Opéra in 1733. Subsequent operas—the most significant being *Castor et Pollux* (1737)—made him the most illustrious successor to Jean-Baptiste Lully (1632–87) in setting French texts to music, establishing a French style and tradition of dramatic music, and digressing sharply from the pleasing lyricism of the Italians. But Rameau was severely criticized for his complexity of style and emphasis on the dramatic over the lyric. The climax of the attacks against him came in 1752, just after a visiting Italian company had introduced to Paris Pergolesi's little comic opera, *La serva padrona.* A musical war, now known as *"la guerre des bouffons,"* erupted in Paris between those (people like Jean-Jacques Rousseau and other Encyclopedists) who upheld the Italian manner and those (Voltaire among others) who sided with Rameau. But Rameau lived to see the vindication of his ideas and the complete annihilation of his enemies. He received numerous honors during his last years which were passed mostly in seclusion. He died in Paris on September 12, 1764.

THE MAN

MICHEL-PAUL-GUIDE CHABANON

Rameau was very tall, thin, and spare. He looked more like a phantom than a man. . . . He disclosed little of himself, spoke little of himself, either to his friends or in the bosom of his family. This is remarkable in a man so celebrated; it indicates a kind of self-indifference rare among those whom nature has set apart with high endowment. Rameau spent the greater part of the day strolling about alone, seeing no one, and seeking no one. Seeing him thus, I long believed that he was plunged in learned meditation; but one day he assured me that he was not thinking of anything whatsoever, that he was always pleased when I addressed him and drew him out of this empty, idle revery. Thereafter I availed myself of this permission, but I never addressed him without getting the impression, in the first moment, that he was returning from the depths of some profound ecstasy; several times I had to mention my name before he recognized me, although we had talked together only a few days previously.

He loved glory, there is no doubt of that, since he acquired so much of it; (this conclusion does not seem rash to me) but I am convinced that he concerned himself little with his own fame. Sometimes it even seemed to vex him; he would hide himself at the theater, take refuge from the gazing eyes of the public who pointed him out to one another and applauded. This was no display of false modesty; of that he was incapable, and he was a stranger to any sort of affectation.

A year ago, after the first performance of *Castor et Pollux* . . . I

19

caught sight of him walking about in a lonely, very poorly lighted room; when I started running towards him to embrace him he took abruptly to his heels and did not come back until he had heard my name. Excusing the bizarre reception he had given me he said that he was fleeing from compliments because they embarrassed him and he did not know what to answer. On this same occasion, he told me more on the subject of several innovations they had tried to make him add to his opera. "My friend, I have more taste now than I used to have, but I have no more genius left at all."

He never prostituted his art and he could not do so; sufficient unto himself, he lived only with and for his genius and neglected even the society of men. The wise and tranquil independence he enjoyed was in no sense the fruit of reflection; it was part of his nature. He was born philosophical, just as the oak is born sturdy.

If he saw the great of this world it was only when they had need of him, and then he behaved with them as he did with ordinary men. He had his mind only on the business in hand and paid no attention to the high personages with whom he dealt. One day he was rehearsing an opera to be performed at court. The *maître de ballet* had for a long time been vainly remonstrating with Rameau that two minuets were too long. The composer seemed not to hear. The dancer finally hit upon what he regarded as a sure means of lending authority to his advice and censure, attributing them to a personage of high place. "So-and-so finds your minuets too long, Monsieur Rameau!" "Monsieur," retorted Rameau, "if he hadn't been told to find them too long, he would have found them too short."

THE COMPOSER

BERNARD CHAMPIGNEULLE

In the early part of the 18th century—when there flourished so many composers admirable for their fertility and creativity—Johann Sebastian Bach appeared as a summit, majestically crowning the musical world of his times. Pursuing his calling with simplicity and dignity, the old cantor of the Thomasschule died without having exerted much of an influence on his contemporaries. During this same time, Rameau established the basic rules of harmony, and in doing this inaugurated a new era for music.

Jean-Philippe Rameau was eighteen when his father, the organist of the Dijon Cathedral, sent him to Italy to complete his musical education. It seems that the young man acquired from this trip a certain contempt for Italian music. He then became an organist at Avignon, then at Clermont-Ferrand, and finally succeeded his own father at Dijon. He was a recluse; he seemed to hate the world. Loyal and upright by nature he was regarded by many of his contemporaries as a formidable character. Until his fortieth year he consecrated himself in isolation to the study of the abstract science of harmony. He was thunderstruck to remark how, in spite of the documents of many masters, the theory of music lay in a state of complete confusion. Since Lully, harmony had become the primordial element in composition, giving direction to the writing of music. Rameau now became active in trying to give a precise clarification to its dominant role. Since the age of polyphony and the emergence of monody, had not music, after all, become above all else an ordered succession of chords, containing within themselves the material for expressive discourse? Rameau now tried to bind up the scattered elements of harmony by setting basic rules, thus arriving at an ultimate truth which could assure a definitive set of rules for the creation of beauty in sound. The *Traité de l'harmonie* (1722) caused a sensation in the musical world. Here its author presented himself as one of the world's most illustrious musicians. The theoretical works he subsequently published—and most notably the *Nouveau système de musique théorique* (1726)—only served further to confirm his authority.

Except for his charming set of little pieces for the harpsichord gathered in the first book of *Pièces de clavecin* in 1706, Rameau had produced no genuine music of importance at the time he first became famous as a theoretician. But then he became music master to La Pouplinière, the generous patron, and was made director of the concerts at his establishment. Thanks to the influence and generosity of his patron, Rameau was able to present, at the Opéra, *Hippolyte et Aricie* in 1733. His work aroused considerable and heated controversy. There were those who accused Rameau of utilizing bizarre harmonies, of assigning too much importance to the orchestra, and all in all of being too complicated a composer. To many, Rameau appeared as a pedant, a revolutionary who sought audaciously to impose upon his musical writing theories and techniques of music that belonged solely to the abstract world. Nevertheless his work made a strong impression and exerted a profound influence. *Les Indes galantes* (1735), his masterwork *Castor et Pollux* (1737), and *Les Fêtes d'Hébé* (1739) were acclaimed in Paris. Rameau emerged triumphant. He became composer of the king's chamber music, enlivening the proceedings at the court of Versailles with performances of many comedy-ballets, opera-ballets, including *La Princesse de Navarre* (1745), *Platée* (1749) and *Les Surprises de l'amour* (1757).

But Rameau later met with considerable opposition. . . . There erupted in Paris in 1752 a war known as *"la guerre des bouffons,"* in which the author of *Dardanus* (1739) became a prey to the attacks of such philosophers as Diderot, Rousseau, and Grimm. The "new spirit" which glorified the Italian art as opposed to the French leveled severe blows against him, and he was severely attacked. Always an irritable, even cantankerous, man, he became in his last years enveloped in gloom. Fifteen years after his death none of his operas survived in the repertory. Styles had changed. Gluck now reigned supreme. The taste of the times was partial to the opéra-comique, to a simple, easy, sentimental style. But there was another reason beyond the quality of Rameau's music itself, mitigating against him. Rameau's operas—like the others which belonged to what we may well describe as the "old regime"—represented ancient characters dressed in highly stylized costumes. They were anachronisms who could make no impression whatsoever on the senses. The new spectacles favored in France rid themselves of these ridiculous conventions, replacing them with others perhaps more readily understandable to audiences. The applause went out to sentimental rhetoric speaking for Romanticism and the Revolution. After that came the Italian invasion, and then Wagner. The Wagnerian legends —more violent, more rugged—made a stronger appeal to the public at the end of the 19th century than the myths sprung from Hellenic culture and sources which Rameau had handled for the delight of a more genteel society.

However, his work as a theoretician continued to be studied, and it became universally recognized that his principles of harmony served as the foundation upon which rested all modern musical education. But a return to Rameau, the composer, is in sight. In 1885 there was undertaken a monumental edition of all of Rameau's works under the editorial supervision of Camille Saint-Saëns and Charles Malherbe. Debussy spoke of his unqualified admiration for this master. If the characters of Rameau's operas did not express themselves through recitatives and arias in a direct manner—and in a more flowing style to touch the heart directly—this was not the fault of the composer, but of a style and of conventions which he practised and followed. What appears remarkable to us today is that Rameau, this theoretician, this mathematician of music, was endowed at the same time with such poetic genius. Voltaire called him "our Euclid-Orpheus." Rameau moved with equal ease through many different levels—from serenity to passion, from intense declamation to graceful badinage. He brought to music a remarkable clarity of writing, a marvelous equilibrium of temperament, and a nobility of style not often encountered in the music for the theater of his age.

RAMEAU SPEAKS

Music is a science which ought to have certain rules. These rules should be derived from a self-evident principle which cannot become known to us without the help of mathematics. I must concede that, despite all the experience I acquired in music through its practice over a considerable period of time, it was only with the help of mathematics that I was able to unravel my ideas, that light replaced an obscurity I had previously not recognized as such. If I had been unable to distinguish principle from rule, the principle soon presented itself to me in a simple and convincing manner. As a result, it then led me to recognize the consequences as many rules related through them to the principle itself. The true sense of these rules, their correct application, their relation to one another, and the order they should observe among themselves (the simplest serving as an introduction to the less simple, and so on by degrees) and finally the choice of terms—all this of which I had previously been ignorant, developed with so much clarity and precision in my mind that I could not avoid concluding that it would be most desirable to have the musical knowledge of this century's composers equal their capacity to create beauty.

.   .   .   .   .

To enjoy the effects of music fully we must lose ourselves in it completely. To judge it, we must relate it to the source through which we are affected by it. This source is nature. Nature endows us with those feelings that move us in all our musical experiences; we might call this gift, instinct. Let us permit instinct to inform our judgments! Let us penetrate the mysteries it unfolds to us before we pronounce our verdicts! . . .

A mind preoccupied while listening to music is never free to judge it. If, for example, we think of attributing the essential beauty of this art to changes from high to low, fast to slow, soft to loud— means at arriving at a variety of sounds—we will then judge everything according to this prejudice without a consideration of how weak these means are, how scant merit there is in our use of them. We will fail to perceive that they are foreign to harmony which is the sole basis of music, the true source of its most glorious effects.

A truly sensitive spirit must judge in quite a different way. If the spirit is not moved by the power of expression, by the vivid colors of which the harmonist alone is capable, then it is not absolutely satisfied. The spirit may, of course, lend itself to whatever may entertain it, but it must evaluate things in proportion to the impact the given experience exerts.

Harmony alone has the capacity to stir emotions. This is the one source from which melody emanates and derives its power. Contrasts between high and low, fast and slow, soft and loud make only superficial modifications in a melody, and they add almost nothing.

24

ANTONIO VIVALDI

1 6 6 9 – 1 7 4 1

ANTONIO VIVALDI—who brought instrumental music of the Baroque Era to its most advanced stage of technical and artistic development before Johann Sebastian Bach—was born in Venice, Italy, probably on June 11, 1669. Although his father was a violinist in the orchestra of the San Marco Cathedral and he himself was early given instruction in music (notably with Giovanni Legrenzi), Vivaldi was directed not to a professional career in music, but to the Church. In 1693 he began his studies for the priesthood and received holy orders about a decade later. But he did not abandon music; all the while he developed himself as a violin virtuoso, and composed a considerable number of pieces. In 1703 he became a teacher of the violin at the Ospitale della Pietà in Venice, subsequently serving as its musical director for many years. Meanwhile, he traveled about Europe a good deal, achieving considerable renown as a violinist; and for a four year period, probably between 1718 and 1722, he was Maestro di Cappella to Prince Philip, Landgrave of Hesse-Darmstadt in Mantua. In 1735, he was back at his post at the Ospitale in Venice, one of its leading musical figures. In 1740, he went to Vienna with the hope of finding a lucrative post at the court of Charles VI. He failed to receive royal favor, and the last months of his life were spent in that city in abject poverty and complete obscurity. He died in Vienna in July 1741, and, like Mozart, was consigned to a pauper's grave.

Vivaldi was an extraordinarily prolific composer. The catalogue of his compositions include about fifty operas, besides two oratorios, twenty-four secular cantatas, twenty-three sinfonias, seventy-three solo or trio sonatas, and about four hundred and fifty concertos. It was in the concerto—a form he inherited from Giuseppe Torelli

25

(1658–1709) and Arcangelo Corelli (1653–1713) and passed on to Johann Sebastian Bach—that he achieved his greatest triumphs.

THE MAN

MARC PINCHERLE

Let us try to discover the man. As to outward appearance, we can summon up a rather exact image of Vivaldi without too much difficulty. Five portraits are extant, two of which are worth describing in detail. There is the very lively sketch made by P. L. Ghezzi in 1723. Vivaldi appears in profile, half-length. He is portrayed as having long and curly hair, a somewhat receding forehead, a prominent arched nose, widely dilated nostrils, a large mouth, half open, and a pointed chin. His glance is lively, his expression interested and wilful. The engraving by François Morellon de La Cave, a Dutch artist of French origin, done two years later than the Ghezzi sketch, is much more formally worked out but also much less expressive. The composer is seen firmly planted before his writing desk; he holds in his right hand, which is brought up against his chest, a notebook of music paper where some measures typical of Vivaldi may be read. The features of the face are vague and a little sheeplike, the hair so well groomed that it may be taken for a wig. The full, round cheeks give Vivaldi the look of a nice young man, well fed and happy to be alive. Nevertheless, to express the turbulence of inspiration the portraitist has opened wide the collar of his shirt and put in a ribbon that floats from it untied. . . .

Ghezzi's drawing has our confidence more than La Cave's or his plagiarists. All save Ghezzi were working on behalf of the general public, if not for posterity; they try above all to be decorative. Ghezzi had no ulterior motive in dashing off a likeness of his prominent contemporary on a loose piece of paper. Besides, that determined and headstrong look is much more in line with Vivaldi's character than the unctuous smile of the academic portraits.

It is known that he could at times express himself sharply. On the manuscript of the *Concerto in A* dedicated to Pisendel he believed

26

that in measures 61–66 of the finale he had to indicate by figures some simple harmonies that should have been self-evident. And to show clearly to the recipient that this precaution was not directed to him and was aimed only at blockheads, he added in large letters, *"per li coglioni."*

He also knew how to be playful. Caffi . . . mentions a certain number of humorous compositions—*Concerto de' Cucchi* (*Concerto of the Cuckoos*), *Coro delle Monache* (*Choir of the Nuns*), and others—designed to serve as entertainment to the aristocrats.

If we cannot safely accept as accurate the kindly facial expression given to Vivaldi by La Cave and those who copied him, we can place no more confidence in the air of robust health that they bestowed on the composer. . . . He was weakly, having been afflicted from birth with a serious illness. Indeed, this prohibited all physical effort to such a degree that he could not travel without a retinue of four or five persons.

He was not, however, prevented from being uncommonly hard working and from combining the manifold activities of virtuoso, teacher, composer, and impresario. Those of his letters that have been preserved give an exact and picturesque idea of this last aspect of his personality. They deal with a single opera season at Ferrara. Vivaldi recruited the virtuosos and the dancers, discussed the tickets, adjusted the length of the show to the nature of its expected public, had the copies made, and resisted the whims of the dancers who held it their right to do as they pleased. In all this correspondence there is evidence of a good dose of practical common sense.

Also recorded in Vivaldi's letters is much docility and humbleness before the great. In this the composer conformed to established practice. The few dedications of his that have lasted down to our time do not hesitate to push eulogy to the point of patent flattery. This, it is true, was apparently still the absolute rule at the close of the 18th century as it had been ever since the 16th. . . .

So it is that Vivaldi appears to us, when we have collected all the scattered testimony, as a man composed of contrasts—weak and sickly, yet of a fiery temperament; quick to become irritated, quick to become calm; quick to pass from worldly thoughts to a superstitious piety; tractable when necessary, but persevering; mystical, yet ready to come down to earth again when a specific concern was at issue, and by no means unskilful in handling his affairs. But above all, he was possessed by music and moved, in the words of De Brosses, "to compose furiously and prodigiously."

THE COMPOSER

DONALD JAY GROUT

A feature of the 18th century which is hard for us nowadays to appreciate, yet which was incalculably important, was the constant public demand for new music. There were no "classics," and few works of any kind survived more than two or three seasons. Bach had to provide new cantatas every year for Leipzig and Handel a new opera for London; and Vivaldi was expected to furnish new oratorios and concertos for every recurring festival at the Ospitale della Pietà in Venice. Such unceasing pressure accounts both for the prodigious output of many 18th-century composers and for the phenomenal speed at which they worked: Vivaldi perhaps holds the record with his opera *Tito Manlio,* said to have been completed in five days; and he prided himself on being able to compose a concerto faster than a copyist could copy it.

Like his contemporaries, Vivaldi composed every work for a definite occasion and for a particular company of performers. He was commissioned to write forty-nine operas, most of them for Venice, but a few also for Florence, Verona, Rome, and other Italian cities. His duties at the Pietà required him to write oratorios and church music, of which a large quantity survives in manuscript. Chiefly for the Pietà, also, he wrote concertos, the form of instrumental music commonly used at church festival services. About 440 concertos of his are extant, in addition to twenty-three sinfonias and seventy-three solo or trio sonatas.

Vivaldi is known today only as a composer of orchestral music; the only works printed during his lifetime (mostly at Amsterdam) were about forty sonatas and a hundred concertos. It is a mistake, however, to ignore Vivaldi's achievements in opera, cantata, motet,

28

and oratorio. So very little is known about the Italian opera of the early 18th century that it is impossible to estimate Vivaldi's merits in comparison with Alessandro Scarlatti (1660–1725), Antonio Lotti (c. 1667–1740), Francesco Gasparini (1668–1727), Tomaso Albinoni (1671–1750), C. F. Pollaroli (1653–1722), Antonio Caldara (1670–1736), Handel, or others whose operas were produced at Venice during the first third of the century. But Vivaldi was certainly successful in his day; during the years in which he was writing operas (1713–39) the theaters of Venice staged more works of his than of any other composer, and his fame was by no means limited to his own city and country. The few accessible specimens of his church music show that in this realm also Vivaldi was a composer of real stature. The fact that many solo and choral passages in his works sound as though they might have been written by Handel proves merely that both composers used the international musical language of the early 18th century.

Vivaldi is remembered now chiefly for his purely instrumental music, partly because compositions like motets and concertos are less attached than operas or oratorios to external conditions of performance and hence are less liable to fall out of circulation when performance conditions change. But it is also true that Vivaldi's instrumental works, and especially the concertos, are perennially attractive because of the freshness of their melodies, their rhythmic verve, their skilful treatment of solo and orchestral string color, and the balanced clarity of their form. Many of the sonatas, as well as some of the early concertos, are in the 17th-century contrapuntal style of Arcangelo Corelli (1653–1713). However, in his first published collection of concertos (op. 3, c. 1712) Vivaldi already showed that he was fully aware of the modern trends towards distinct musical form, vigorous rhythm, and idiomatic solo writing exemplified by Giuseppe Torelli (1658–1709) and Albinoni.

About two-thirds of Vivaldi's concertos are for one solo instrument with orchestra—usually, of course, a violin, but with a considerable number also for the violoncello, flute, or bassoon. In the concertos for two violins the soloists are usually given equal prominence, producing the texture of a duet for two high voices typical of the Late Baroque; but many works that call for several solo instruments are in effect solo or duet concertos rather than genuine *concerti grossi* in that the first violin or the first and second violins, and not infrequently the wind instruments as well, are treated in a virtuoso manner that sets them markedly apart from the rest of the concertino. There are also a few important concertos for solo instruments with continuo, without the usual ripieno strings.

Vivaldi's usual orchestra at the Pietà probably consisted of twenty to twenty-five stringed instruments, with harpsichord or organ for the continuo; this is always the basic group, though in many of his concertos he also calls for flutes, oboes, bassoons, or horns, any of which may be used either as solo instruments or in ensemble combinations. The exact size and makeup of Vivaldi's orchestra varied, of course, depending on the players that might be available on a particular occasion. Vivaldi's writing is always remarkable for the variety of color he achieves with different groupings of the solo and orchestral strings; the familiar *La Primavera (Spring)* concerto —first of a group of four concertos, *Le Quattro stagione (The Four Seasons)*, in op. 8 (1725) representing programmatically the four seasons—is but one of many examples of his extraordinary instinct for effective sonorities in this medium.

Most of Vivaldi's concertos are in the usual eighteenth-century pattern of three movements: an Allegro; a slow movement in the same key or a closely related one (relative minor, dominant, or subdominant); and a final Allegro somewhat shorter and sprightlier than the first. Though a few movements are found in the older fugal style, the texture is typically more homophonic than contrapuntal— but homophonic in the Late Baroque sense, with much incidental use of counterpoint and with particular emphasis on the two outer voices. Typical of the Late Baroque, also, is Vivaldi's constant use of sequential patterns.

The formal scheme of the individual movements of Vivaldi's concertos is the same as in Torelli's works: *ritornellos* for the full orchestra, alternating with episodes for the soloist (or soloists). Vivaldi differs from Torelli and all earlier composers not by virtue of any innovation in the general plan of the concerto but because his musical ideas are more spontaneous, his formal structures more clearly delineated, his harmonies more assured, his textures more varied, and

30

his rhythms more impelling. Moreover, he establishes between solo and *tutti* a certain dramatic tension; he does not merely give the soloist contrasting idiomatic figuration (which Torelli had already done) but makes him stand out as a dominating musical personality against the ensemble as the solo singer does against the orchestra in opera—a relationship inherent in the ritornello aria (the precursor and model of the concerto form), but one which Vivaldi first brought to full realization in a purely instrumental medium. "The tutti announces the propositions that are to be debated in the course of the movement; and the arguments which these provoke give rise to the musical contest between soloist and orchestra, ending in a reconciliation or synthesis of emotions and ideas" (Brijon).

As a rule, all the thematic motives appear in the tutti, though occasionally an important new theme may be announced in the opening solo, as in the first movement of the concerto for three violins in A minor, op. 3, no. 8. Vivaldi's tutti may be analyzed as a rather loose series of related but separable musical ideas any of which can be selected for development in the course of the movement; this treatment represents a stage midway between the older Baroque practice of spinning out a single theme and the later Classical practice of developing contrasted themes.

All of Vivaldi's opening themes are so constructed as to define the tonality of the movement with the utmost precision: they consist of emphatically reiterated primary triads, triadic melodies, scales, or combinations of these elements. So stark a harmonic vocabulary could result in monotony; but this danger is avoided, thanks to an unflagging vitality that drives the music onward in an ever varied but never ceasing rhythmic torrent from the beginning of a movement to its very last measure. Moreover, once the main tonality is firmly established, the harmony is varied not only by the usual cycle of modulations but also by devices such as the use of minor thirds and sixths in a major key, or of chromatic chords to signal the approach of a cadence. Triplet division of the beat is common. The phraseology of themes and sections is often irregular and sometimes quite subtle.

Vivaldi was the first composer to give the slow movement of a concerto equal importance with the two Allegros. His slow movement is usually a long-breathed expressive cantabile melody, like an Adagio operatic aria or arioso, to which the performer was of course expected to add his own embellishments. The slow movements show a predilection for minor keys, especially E minor. There is no standard formal scheme for these middle movements; many of them have particularly interesting sonorities in the accompaniments, which usually are lightly scored in contrast to the two Allegros.

In his program music, such as the widely admired *Seasons* concertos and a dozen or so others of similar cast, Vivaldi shared the half-serious, half-playful attitude of the 18th century toward the naive realism implied in such musical depictions. Although the pictorial intentions doubtless often suggested particular effects of color or modification of the normal order of movements, the external program is completely absorbed into the standard musical structure of the concerto. The *Seasons* were among the first of many descriptive symphonic works in the 18th century which are the predecessors of Beethoven's *Pastoral Symphony*.

In Vivaldi's music one can find traces of all the different changes occurring in the first half of the 18th century. At the conservative extreme are some of the sonatas and concertos in the style of Corelli; at the progressive extreme are the solo concerto finales, the orchestral concertos (that is, those without solo instruments), and most of the twenty-three works which Vivaldi called sinfonias. As usual in this period, the terminology is imprecise, but the music, especially that of the sinfonias, clearly demonstrates that its composer is entitled to be reckoned among the earliest forerunners of the pre-Classic symphony: the conciseness of form, the markedly homophonic texture, the melodically neutral themes, the minuet finale, even many of the little mannerisms of style that were formerly thought to have been invented by the German composers of the Mannheim school—all are found in Vivaldi.

Vivaldi's influence on instrumental music in the middle and later 18th century was equal to that of Corelli a generation earlier. Vivaldi was one of the most important figures in the transition from Late Baroque to early Classical style; the assured economy of his writing for string orchestra was a revelation; his dramatic conception of the role of the soloist was accepted and developed in the Classi-

32

cal concerto; above all, the concise themes, the clarity of form, the rhythmic vitality, the impelling logical continuity in the flow of musical ideas, all qualities so characteristic of Vivaldi, were transmitted to many other composers and especially directly to Johann Sebastian Bach. Bach copied at least nine of Vivaldi's concertos, arranging six of them for harpsichord, two for organ, and one (originally for four violins) for four harpsichords and string orchestra. Vivaldi's influence is apparent both in the general scheme and in the details of many of Bach's original concertos, as well as in those of his German contemporaries. Finally, Vivaldi, more than any other single composer, through his concertos impressed on the 18th century the idea of an instrumental sound in which the effect of solo-tutti contrast was important, an idea that prevails not only in concertos of the period but in much of the other orchestral music and keyboard music as well.

VIVALDI SPEAKS

It was twenty-five years ago (1712) that I said Mass for what will be the last time, not due to interdiction or at anyone's behest, as His Eminence can appraise himself, but by my own decision on account of an ailment that has burdened me since birth. When I had barely been ordained a priest I said Mass for a year or a little more. Then I discontinued saying it, having on three occasions had to leave the altar without completing it because of this ailment. For this same reason I nearly always live at home, and I only go out in a gondola or coach, because I can no longer walk on account of this chest ailment, or, rather, this tightness in the chest. No nobleman invites me to his house, not even our prince, because all are informed of my ailment. Immediately after a meal I can usually go out, but not ever on foot. Such is the reason I never say Mass. I have spent three carnival seasons at Rome for the opera and . . . I never said Mass. . . . I have been called to Vienna and I never said Mass. I was at Mantua . . . in the service of the exceedingly devout prince of Darmstadt with those same women who have always been treated by His Serene Highness with great benevolence, and I never said Mass.

JOHANN SEBASTIAN BACH

1 6 8 5 - 1 7 5 0

JOHANN SEBASTIAN BACH, the most distinguished member of a family that had produced professional musicians for several generations, was born in Eisenach, Germany, on March 21, 1685. His early music study took place with his brother, Johann Christoph, after which he became a choirboy in Lüneburg. In 1703 he was engaged as organist at Arnstadt where he wrote his first church cantatas and music for the clavier. As an organist in Mühlhausen, he married Maria Barbara in 1707. His first important appointment came in Weimar in 1708 as court organist and chamber musician to Duke Wilhelm Ernst. He held this post nine years, during which time he became one of the most brilliant organ virtuosos of his time and wrote numerous masterworks for this instrument. From 1717 to 1723 Bach was Kapellmeister and director of chamber music for Prince Leopold of Anhalt at Cöthen, an office that directed his creative energies toward the writing of orchestral and chamber music. During this period he completed his famous Brandenburg Concertos and suites for orchestra, concertos for various solo instruments and orchestra, and solo sonatas and suites for single instruments. His first wife died in Cöthen in 1720, and one year later Bach married Anna Magdalena. Between 1723 and his death, Bach was the Cantor of the Thomasschule in Leipzig. His duties in that city included teaching, playing the organ, and writing the music for and directing church services. Some of his most monumental choral works were completed in Leipzig, including the Mass in B minor and the *Passion According to St. Matthew*. Towards the end of his life Bach suffered from blindness. He died in Leipzig on July 28, 1750.

At the time of his death few recognized his real stature. He remained a comparatively obscure and rarely performed composer until, seventy-five years later, the revival of some of his crowning choral works set into motion a worldwide reevaluation of his music. Until such a reevaluation was crystallized, several of Bach's sons were considered far greater composers than he, notably Wilhelm Friedemann (1710–84), Carl Philipp Emanuel (1714–88), and John Christian (1735–82).

THE MAN

JOHANN NIKOLAUS FORKEL

ALBERT SCHWEITZER

Besides Bach's great merit as an accomplished performer, composer, and teacher, he had the merit of being an excellent father, friend, and citizen. His virtues as a father he showed by the care for the education of his children; and the others, by his conscientious performance of his social and civil duties. His acquaintance was agreeable to everybody. Whoever was in any respect a lover of the arts, whether a foreigner or a native, could visit his house and be sure of meeting with a friendly reception. These social virtues united with the great reputation of his art, caused his house to be very seldom without visitors.

As an artist he was uncommonly modest. Notwithstanding the great superiority which he had over the rest of his profession, and which he could not but feel; notwithstanding the admiration and reverence which were daily shown him as so outstanding an artist, there is no instance of his having ever assumed upon it. When he was sometimes asked how he had contrived to master the art to such a high degree, he generally answered: "I was obliged to be industrious; whoever is equally industrious will succeed equally well." He seemed not to lay any stress on his greater natural talents.

All the opinions he expressed of other artists and their works were friendly and equitable. Many works necessarily appeared to him trifling . . . yet he never allowed himself to express a harsh opinion, unless it were to one of his scholars, to whom he thought himself obliged to speak pure and strict truth. Still less did he ever suffer himself to be seduced by the consciousness of his strength and superiority to display a musical bravado. . . . The many, sometimes adventurous, pranks that are related of him—as for example that occasionally dressed like a poor village schoolmaster he went into church and begged the organist to let him play a chorale in order to enjoy the general astonishment excited in the persons present by his performance, or to hear the organist say he must be either Bach or the devil, and so forth—are mere fables. He himself would never hear of anything of the sort. Besides, he had too much respect for the art thus to make a plaything of it. An artist like Bach does not throw himself away.

In musical parties where quartets or fuller pieces of instrumental music were performed and he was not otherwise employed, he took pleasure in playing the viola. . . . When an opportunity offered, in such parties, he sometimes also accompanied a trio or other pieces on the harpsichord. If he was in a cheerful mood, and knew that the composer of the piece, if he happened to be present, would not take it amiss, he used to make extempore, either out of the figured bass or a new trio, or of three single parts of a quartet. . . .

He was fond of hearing the music of other composers. If he heard in a church a fugue for a large body of musicians, and one of his two eldest sons happened to stand near him, he always, as soon as he had heard the first entries of the theme, said beforehand what the composer ought to introduce, and what possibly might be introduced. Now, if the composer had performed his work well, what Bach had predicted happened; then he was delighted, and jogged his son to make him observe it. This is a proof that he valued, too, the skill of others. . . .

Bach did not make what is called a brilliant success in this world. He had, on the one hand, a lucrative office, but he had, on the other, a great number of children to maintain and to educate from its income. He neither had nor sought other resources. He was too much occupied with his business and his art to think of pursuing those ways which, perhaps, for a man like himself, especially in his times, would have led to a gold mine. If he had thought fit to travel, he would (as even one of his enemies had said) have drawn upon himself the admiration of the world. But he loved a quiet domestic life, constant and uninterrupted occupation with his art, and was . . . a man of few wants.*

In the conflicts that agitated his life and embittered his soul, Bach does not always appear in a sympathetic light. His irritability and his stubborn belief that he was always in the right can neither be excused nor glossed over. Least of all can we find excuse for the fact that at first he would be too easy-going, would always remember too late what he called his rights, and then, in his blind rage, would make a great affair out of what was merely a trifle.

Such was Bach in his relations with people whom he suspected of a desire to encroach upon his freedom. The real Bach, however, was quite another being; all testimonies agree that in ordinary intercourse he was the most amiable and modest of men. He was, above all, upright and incapable of any injustice. His impartiality was well known. . . .

In the portraits in which Bach's physiognomy has been preserved for us we can read a good deal about the nature and bearing of the man. Until recently virtually only two original portraits of the master were known. . . . But . . . Professor Fritz Volbach of Mayence has since discovered yet another portrait of Bach. It is a realistic piece of work, showing the face of a man who has tasted of the bitterness of life. There is something fascinating in the harsh expression of these features, which are painted full face. Round the tightly compressed lips run the hard lines of an inflexible obstinacy. It is thus that the Cantor of St. Thomas's may have looked in his last years as he entered the school where some new vexation or another was awaiting him.

In the two other portraits, the severity is softened by a touch of easy good nature. Even the short-sighted eyes look out upon the world from their half-closed lids with a certain friendliness that is not even negated by the heavy eyebrows arched above them. The face cannot be called beautiful. The nose is too massive for that, and the underjaw too prominent. How sharply this projected may be estimated from the fact that the front teeth of the lower jaw are

---

* The above paragraphs are by Forkel; what follows below is by Schweitzer.

level with those of the upper, instead of closing within these. . . .

The longer we contemplate it, the more enigmatic becomes the expression of the master's face. How did this ordinary visage become transformed into that of the artist? What was it like when Bach was absorbed in the world of music? Was there reflected in it then the wonderful serenity that shines through his art?

In the last resort, the whole man is for the most part an enigma, for to our eyes the outer man differs so much from the inner that neither seems to have any part in the other. In the case of Bach, more than in that of any other genius, the man as he looked and behaved was only the opaque envelope destined to lodge the artistic soul within. . . . His is a case of dualism; his artistic vicissitudes and creations go on side by side with the normal and almost commonplace tenor of his work-a-day existence, without mixing with or making any impression on this.

THE COMPOSER

C. SANFORD TERRY

Chronological exactitudes are generally misleading in measure as they are precise. Still, it is a tenable thesis that modern music begins with Bach and Handel. For of the masters before the Vienna dispensation they alone speak a language we entirely comprehend. That they were born in the same year is one of history's happy coincidences; that they never met, one of chance's most quippish pranks. Emerging together, they dominated a musical sphere not otherwise impressive. Gluck was under forty when Bach died, his highest achievement unfulfilled; Haydn was eighteen. When Handel followed his contemporary to the grave, Mozart was a child of three and Beethoven's birth was eleven years distant. So, the earlier half of the 18th century belongs to Bach and Handel. They shine with uncontested brilliance from a sky that holds no other suns.

It is a commonplace that to comprehend a genius we must approach him through the circumstances that surrounded his birth.

For, as Emerson remarked, the truest genius is "the most indebted man" or colloquially, "genius is one part inspiration, and three parts perspiration." Bach himself when asked the secret of his mastership replied simply, "I worked hard." . . . Compared with Handel's, his career was monastic in its seclusion, experimental in its habit. Before he was ten he was furtively copying compositions of the masters of the keyboard for his own instruction. Later, he transcribed the accessible scores of Palestrina, Antonio Caldara (1670–1736), Antonio Lotti (c. 1667–1740), Antonio Vivaldi and Giovanni Legrenzi (1626–90); and of the French school, studied those of François Couperin-le-Grand (1668–1733), Nicolas de Grigny (1671–1703), André Raison (c. 1687–1714), and Gaspard Le Roux (c. 1660–c. 1707). England, too, came within the orbit of his curiosity. Indeed, there is little music from Palestrina onwards of which there are not copies in his industrious script. Handel, too, quarried, but with how different a purpose, appropriating themes his indolent Muse found it inconvenient to provide! But Bach . . . confronts us as a student, almost demoniacally urged to unravel and discover the principles of his art. In no other of the great masters was this call so insistent, none who faced such obstacles to answer it. He paid his adventurous visits to those giants of the North, Georg Böhm (1661–1733) and Johann Reinken (1623–1722), while he was still in his teens. He was hardly settled in his first employment at Arnstadt before he took French leave, and risked dismissal, in order to receive lessons from Dietrich Buxtehude (c. 1637–1707) at Lübeck. Even in the maturity of his genius the neighborhood of a fellow craftsman drew him always to seek his acquaintance, and haply his instruction. Twice, and vainly, he sought Handel's conversation. His famous Dresden encounter with Marchand is but an example of his eagerness to learn from any who had knowledge to impart. Unremitting study and self-criticism fashioned his individual style. Indeed, if the early neglect that obscured his memory was due in part to his failure to explore the art forms then coming to birth, it was no less the result of meticulous self-discipline that refined his work beyond the comprehension of the generations that knew and followed him.

What, then, were the conditions out of which his genius emerged? Why did he express himself in the forms in which he is familiar to us? How comes it that, while Handel was fluent in opera, Bach was careless, even contemptuous, of the stage? How is it that, unlike the other masters of his period, we associate with him no new musical form? And why do we group him as the last portent of the old dispensation no less than the first of the new? These are questions which invite a historical retrospect.

In the middle age of European civilization music was the handmaid, one might say the slave, of religion. Hence its earliest expression was ecclesiastical plain-song, monodic, unisonal. But, at an early period, it achieved a complex technique distinguished as polyphonic or contrapuntal, in which several melodies impose themselves on a fixed theme or *cantus,* in such a way that each voice—for the original art was vocal—adds a strand of accompanying melody to the main theme, parallel to it, consonant with it, and yet in itself complete and melodic. That it was practicable, and also agreeable, to sing two melodies together at a fixed interval, instead of one in unison or at the octave, was a discovery which sprang, we must believe, from circumstances rather than deliberate design. For men's voices, of which the medieval choir was composed, fall naturally into two categories, tenor and bass, pitched roughly a fourth or fifth apart. Consequently a plainsong *cantus* low enough to suit the basses might be inconvenient for the tenors, while a melody fitted to the tenors might soar too high for the basses. Hence, perhaps in the 9th century, an "inspired precentor," a recent pen has called him, had the happy thought to invite his singers to recite the *cantus* at the convenient pitch of their individual voices: a cacophony in consecutives we probably should find it, but not disagreeable to the innovator, who, unknowingly, made the first approach towards the art of weaving simultaneous melodies into a coherent whole.

So, here was a primitive descant, the chief of the strands of complex polyphony. And, since dissonance resulted where before there was consonance, the new art was named *diaphonia* (dissonance), or *organum,* after the organized voice (*vox organalis*), which sang at the fourth or fifth, while the principal voice (*vox principalis*) declaimed the foundation melody or *cantus.* Thus was brought to birth the scheme of woven melody, of vocal polyphony, of which Bach's scores afford the supreme example. It is not convenient here to trace its

40

development in the interval, from the tiny seed to the spacious tree. But its general course is clear. In time, by experiment or accident, other intervals, the third and sixth, were found as agreeable as the fourth and fifth on which to pitch the organized voice. Or, the organized and principal voices were duplicated at the octave, thereby producing *four* moving themes. But always their motions were parallel to the *cantus;* if the *cantus* rose or fell, the *vox organalis* did so sympathetically by a precisely similar interval. But eventually, after a further interval of experiment, the *cantus* ceased to put chains on the organized voices. Strict parallelism was abandoned, free motion was attempted, the *vox organalis* moving up when the *vox principalis* moved down, and vice versa, till at length composers were able to treat the *organum* as the vehicle of independent and agreeable melody.

But, even at this stage of its development, music was separated from Bach by a chasm we might suppose unbridgeable. For to him, as to us, it predicated the correlation of three complementary factors —melody, rhythm, harmony. In elementary form the first two are as ancient as man's earliest vocal sounds. But harmony is an almost recent ingredient. For the early polyphonists did not analyze music vertically, as we do. Their preference was to build horizontal or parallel melodies, capable of simultaneous utterance, linked rhythmically, exhibiting acoustic smoothness (*i.e.,* harmony) at certain points or cadences of repose, but elsewhere displaying a lack of harmonic relevance which, to us, is disagreeable. Still, in the 16th century a closer approximation to our modern harmonic system was gradually achieved, until the polyphony of the Middle Ages found its highest expression in Palestrina, a master unsurpassed by Bach himself in the noble sincerity of his art.

With Palestrina we enter a golden age, when musical culture was never so widespread, nor its votaries lit by a holier flame. Vocal polyphony began to move in melodious obedience to rules; and harmony, though still immature, became ordered and expressive. And yet, in their artistry, how immense an interval separates Palestrina's *Stabat Mater* from Bach's *Magnificat* (1723)! It could not astonish us if the space between them was measured in centuries. In fact, only ninety years, three generations, divide Palestrina's death in 1594 from

Bach's birth in 1685. Thus, in the equipment Bach was familiar with, music reached him after a surprisingly short period of incubation. For Palestrina was barely in sight of the forms Bach employed. Music was still obedient to the limitations of religious usage and tradition, though no longer exclusively ecclesiastical in its uses. It was sung *a cappella* and was exclusively vocal; it lacked instrumental accompaniment; it demanded a choir of singers, it ignored a solo voice; the vocal aria was not invented; neither organ nor clavier had developed their technique, and the orchestra was not yet constituted. Moreover, key-consciousness had not been attained, nor was the principle of measured time comprehended. These developments were revolutionary, and they were the achievement of the bustling ninety years that separate Palestrina from Bach, in broad terms, the 17th century, that age of turmoil and yet of swift progress. It invented new forms of musical expression. It set instrumental music on an independent course. Beginning in bondage to the old modes, it ended by preferring the Ionian and the Aeolian—the keys of C major and A minor—and transposed them to various pitches to build our major and minor scales. A pulsing century of rapid, organized growth, perfected and crowned by the absorptive genius of Bach.

The first and crucial advance along this path of high adventure was the so-called monodic revolution, conveniently synchronous with Palestrina's death. Its impulse was the intellectual stirring we call the Renaissance, that overpowering inclination of the individual to express himself, to look out on the universe from his own windows, and no longer through the spectacles tradition and authority had fixed on his nose. Thus impelled, and seeking to become the vehicle of individual emotion, music demanded fresh modes of utterance, new forms in which to interpret the aspirations and accomplishments of the human mind. Concretely, the pioneers of the "New Music," as these 16th century rebels against tradition styled it, asked that music should no longer decorate only the unemotional corporate worship of the Church Catholic, but should equip itself to interpret secular themes, no longer in the staid formulas of the ecclesiastical *cantus,* but in dramatic periods as naturally inflected as the tones of an actor. In a word, the individual, who so far had been submerged in the collective voice, now claimed a medium appropriate to his self-expression.

But the distinction of Giovanni Bardi and his fellow innovators is not so much that they introduced unisonous dramatic forms—the recitative and aria—as that they sponsored them in the Academies, in which till now polyphony alone was admitted and taught. So here is the convenient starting point of modern music. Only six years after Palestrina's death, Jacopo Peri (1561–1633) produced (1600) his *Eurydice* at Florence, the first notable work of an operatic school which maintained its continuity, though not its monopoly, thenceforward till the era of Verdi and Puccini. And, with suggestive coincidence—for the two forms are scarcely distinguishable—the same year witnessed the Roman production of *Rappresentazione di anima e di corpo* by Emilio del Cavalieri (c. 1550–1602), with scenery, dresses, action, and recitative, closely similar to Peri's work in form and style. Thus in Italy modern opera and modern oratorio came to birth simultaneously. And in Italy opera survived. But oratorio, deserting the land of its origin, fared northward, and eventually mated with the genius of Bach.

Meanwhile the potentialities of instrumental music were not overlooked by the revolutionary Florentines—indeed the word *sonata*, signifying music mechanically sounded, came into simultaneous vogue with *cantata*, the new music sung by the human voice. Monteverdi boldly employed every instrumental resource at his disposal to elaborate his operatic scheme, and for purely instrumental effects. So, the orchestra discovered an independent role. And conveniently and coincidentally, superseding the antique viols, the violin family presented it with its most cherished and effective member.

Probably few of us realize how recent was the vogue of the violin in Bach's lifetime. It is not found in a music score before 1587. Andrea Amati, who first gave it a form distinguished from a treble viol, died (c. 1611) less than a century before Bach's birth. But Antonio Stradivari, the greatest of the Cremona makers, was his contemporary and predeceased him (d. 1737) by only thirteen years. Giovanni Battista Vitali (c. 1644–92), the earliest master of the violin sonata-form, died when Bach was a schoolboy at Eisenach. Giuseppe Torelli (1685–1709) whose concerti grossi established the features

43

Bach himself accepted, published (1709) them actually after Bach had reached manhood. Arcangelo Corelli (1653–1713) died while Bach was in service at Weimar, and his favorite Antonio Vivaldi preceded him to the grave by only seven years. With his contemporary, the brilliant Giuseppe Tartini (1692–1770), Bach, perhaps, was not familiar. But the Italian school of violin-playing culminated in him, and greatly surpassed the prevalent standards; to what an extent is revealed by the fact that, when Corelli's sonatas reached Paris in 1753, three years after Bach's death, not a violinist is said to have been found there with ability to play them! The statement, if correct, permits us to relate Bach's technique to that of his period.

If Bach's instrumental music largely declares an Italian parentage, his clavier works associate him with another national school. For their models he looked principally to France, and his introduction to them at Celle was an early experience of his career. France's musical renaissance expressed itself in the clavier suite. The word is French, but the music it denotes was not localized. It everywhere comprehended a string of dance measures whose characteristics were their profusion and diversity. Their contrasts, no doubt, originated the idea of bringing a number of them together in what became the earliest cyclic art form. At the outset, no rigid principle selected the movements admitted to the suite. But, by the middle of the 17th century, four had established a universal claim for inclusion—the German Allemande, the French-Italian Courante, the Spanish Saraband, and the Italian Gigue. You find them, and in that order, in Bach's Suites and Partitas, in the whole eighteen of which the Gigue is only once missing as the final movement. Arrangements of this kind bore no general title. In England they were called "Lessons" (as by Handel and John Christian Bach); in Germany "Partitas" or "Partien" (as by Bach); in France "Suites" and "Ordres"; in Italy "Sonatas." But the French composers, especially François Couperin and Jean-Baptiste Lully (1632–87), so identified the form with their own country that Bach not only took them as his models, but distinguished his own compositions with a French label.

On other grounds Bach was attracted to Couperin, though hardly indebted to him. As he demonstrated in the famous "Forty-Eight," (1722–44) his adoption of equal temperament for the clavier enabled

44

him to play in every key, minor and major, and so brought the neglected black notes into use. But this innovation, along with the complexity of his music, necessarily jettisoned the old system of fingering, which kept the thumb and every finger but the second and third on each hand normally out of action. Bach, on the contrary, gave the thumb its regular function in the scale and made the neglected fourth finger pull its weight. Couperin also devised a system which brought the thumb into use, though in a less methodical way. But his treatise was not published till 1717, and Bach cannot have been indebted to it. Yet, there are clear proofs that his French contemporary—Couperin died in 1733—interested him deeply and had his admiration.

France's influence on Bach is otherwise revealed. His Suite or Overture in B minor, published in 1735, consists, like his French Suites (c. 1722), of dance movements. But it differs in that it opens with a slow introduction followed by a fugal Allegro, as do his orchestral overtures and those Handel wrote for the stage. The form is that of the classic opera overture as Lully wrote it, and as it continued till Gluck reformed it after Bach's death.

Bach's intellectual curiosity was insatiable, and, excepting Beethoven, unique among the masters. The compulsion of curiosity which dragged him as a youth to Hamburg and Lübeck, invited him to his contest with Marchand, and twice set him on the road in pursuit of Handel, moved him as urgently to investigate the music of other countries. And his larger suites for the clavier appear to indicate that the English school was not unfamiliar to him. They were known to his sons as the "English Suites," (c. 1725) Forkel gathered, because they were written for an Englishman of rank, an obvious conjecture but improbable solution. Another explanation has been found in the fact that the first Suite opens on the theme of a Gigue by Charles Dieupart, a popular French harpsichordist in London during Bach's early manhood. But I think a more satisfactory explanation can be deduced from the fact that, unlike their French fellows, each English Suite begins with a prelude, as do those of Henry Purcell (c. 1659–95) and his precursors. Since Bach was acquainted with Dieupart, Purcell would hardly be unknown to him— indeed attributed to him in the Bachgesellschaft Edition is a Toccata and Fugue by Purcell, the only Englishman whose place among the great masters is universally conceded. It is agreeable to reflect that Bach knew English music at a period of distinction it has never excelled, but to-day boldly and confidently soars to approach.

So, with one reservation, the ancestry of Bach's keyboard and instrumental music is French and Italian. But that of his vocal works is uncompromisingly German. They reveal him, indeed, as the very flower of the German Renaissance, the greatest voice out of Germany after Luther, and, in his most serious aspect, Luther's corollary. That he should have emerged at this period is the more remarkable when we reflect on Germany's musical insignificance to this point. Herself an unwieldy system of noncohering states, lacking a common pivot, political or artistic, and controlled by no national instinct, she had so far reacted feebly to those impulses shaping musical culture elsewhere. Moreover, early in the century of Bach's birth she plunged into the vortex of the Thirty Years' War, and emerged from it less than forty years before he saw the light. Yet, so soon as the Treaty of Westphalia gave peace, even a nebulous unity, to her disjointed system, at a bound she achieved sovereignty in the realm of music. It was, however, not in Handel's operas and operatic oratorios that her new voice was heard, but in utterances of noble elevation in which Bach's genius displayed itself—the Passion, cantata, chorale. Let me indicate concisely the paths by which they reached him.

Sir Hubert Parry once deduced, from her late submission to it, that Germany was less apt for music than her neighbors. Charles Burney came to that conclusion twenty-five years after Bach's death. In truth, music tardily fired Germany's soul, not as an aesthetic experience, but as the vehicle of religious emotion. It has been said that the German Renaissance is only another name for the German Reformation. Certainly it is so in the sphere of music, where the chorale and cantata as clearly express Germany's Renaissance culture as the galleries of Italy or the drama of England reveal the peculiar genius of their peoples.

The Reformation stemmed the tide of church music in Germany along the channels it so far had followed. For the Evangelical Church rejected the musical apparatus of the ancient creed along with its dogma and ritual, preferring its music, like its liturgy, to be congregational in form and utterance. Luther set the new course in his *Achtliederbuch,* the first Lutheran hymn-book, published in 1524, the source of an expanding stream of dignified hymnody which is Lutheran Germany's proudest heritage—"the *Feste Burg* of German music," Sir Charles Stanford appropriately called it. Thus, reaching out on one side to the severe plain-song of the Latin Church, and, on the other, to popular folksong from which it did not disdain to borrow, the chorale was deep rooted in the affection of the German people within a century of Luther's death, and fed the genius of her composers. Set in four-part harmony, it assisted the development of a new harmonic structure. And, since it was essentially the apparatus of religion, it aided and inspired the organist to develop and perfect his technique.

So in the critical ninety years between Palestrina's death and the birth of Bach the chorale became the most vital factor in Germany's musical experience. Of the cantata, Passion, oratorio, motet, organ prelude, fugue, and variation, it controlled the form and supplied the material. Bach's art is inextricably associated with it. His earliest and his last work as a composer was based on it. All the chorales in common use he harmonized with matchless skill. They are rarely absent from his cantatas and oratorios. They provide the core of his Passions, the most intimate part of his motets. His organ technique was developed on them, and they are the theme of the bulk of his music for that instrument. In brief, he associated them with all he did in the service of God, embellishing them like precious jewels in a holy shrine.

Historically, as its name declares, the cantata was Italian. But for the composition the word came to denote Bach preferred the term *concerto,* invented early in the 17th century to distinguish new style concerted music from plain-song monotone. To Giacomo Carissimi (1605–74), who died only eleven years before Bach's birth, are referred its distinctive features—the association of declamatory recitatives, solo arias, and orchestral interludes in a short work suitable for the Church or concert room. In this shape it passed from Italy to Germany, where it was forthwith admitted to the Lutheran Liturgy, in which, at first, its use seems to have been restricted to festival occasions. But it soon established itself as the *Hauptmusik* of the Sunday morning service. The earlier German cantatas, however, those of Heinrich Albert (1604–51), Heinrich Schütz (1585–1672), or Andreas Hammerschmidt (1612–75), for instance, were modeled rather on the chamber cantata and had little affinity with Bach's massive compositions, except in their use of the chorale. For he brought to their creation the elaborate technique he had acquired already on the organ. Yet, their virtuosity is not their most distinctive characteristic. For, they were heard in a form of public prayer closely coordinated. It pivoted on the Gospel for the day; the opening motet anticipated it, the hymns were based on it, so was the sermon, whose text was taken from it, and so was the cantata that preceded it. Thus, Bach's cantatas are not wholly intelligible to us unless we realize that, when writing them, he placed himself in the pulpit, as it were, to expound the Gospel text in terms of music. To the task he brought a mind well versed in theological dialectics, and, with it, a devout spirit as profound as it was sincere, resolved to give his exposition the most persuasive force of which his art was capable. His cantatas might aptly be termed sermons; for, in intention, they are no less.

The Masses have the design and derivation of the cantatas—they apply the new style to portions of the liturgy formerly polyphonic. Bach's Mass in B minor (1733–38), in effect, consists of three cantatas, the *Kyrie, Gloria,* and *Credo,* with an epilogue. The Magnificat, also, is an elaborate cantata, and in its first state actually was punctuated with chorales. But the motets and Passions are in another category. Their ancestry, in the one case, is patently German, and, in the other, that strain predominates. Bach's motets are distinguished from his cantatas in form and in purpose. They are *a cappella* music, exclude the solo aria, dramatic recitative, operatic orchestra, and are the finest flower of his polyphonic technique. But their austerity was the consequence of their usage. For, with one possible exception, they are funeral music, *Trauermusik.* Bach's talented relatives, Johann Christoph and Johann Michael, wrote similar motets, and so did his predecessors in the Leipzig Cantorate. As we have it in Bach's authorship, therefore, the motet is patently of German ancestry, an interesting association of the polyphonic tradition with the Lutheran ritual.

The Passion music also sprang from a German source. For the custom of chanting the Passion story in Holy Week was ancient, and Luther's conservatism retained it. At Leipzig its performance took place at the Vespers on Good Friday afternoon, either in St. Thomas's or in the sister church of St. Nicholas. But the elaborate compositions Bach wrote were only in Leipzig's very recent experience. Until 1721 the setting used was contemporary with Luther! Leipzig heard the first *musicirt Passion* (a composition which, like Bach's, employed the resources of the new style) only two years before Bach came to St. Thomas's. His *St. John Passion,* performed in 1723, was but the second of its kind performed at Leipzig, where conservative feeling was scandalized by the trespass of opera upon a domain so sacred.

Assuredly Bach did not merit this resentment; it is his distinction to have rescued the Passion from the trappings of the theater, and to have placed it, in its noblest form, at the service of religion. For the spirit that animated Palestrina passed from Italy when opera was born, and the modern oratorio, of which Bach's are the perfect example, was begotten of the exiled Italian tradition by its union with the Passion music of Germany. They first met in Heinrich Schütz, the earliest German composer to free himself from Italian conventions and so to evolve a national style. Born exactly one hundred years before Bach, he exhibits in his Passions a reverent emotionalism which makes him Bach's direct ancestor. He admits no arias, uses no reflective chorales. But his recitative is flexible, his choruses are terse and dramatic, and, like Bach, he sets forth his text with reverent restraint. In a word, we first detect in him the serious purpose which is the characteristic of German music. But a generation later the influence of opera, established and vigorous at Hamburg, threatened to deflect the Passion from its dignified and appropriate course. In 1704 Reinhard Keiser (1674–1739), a man eleven years Bach's senior, produced there a dramatic Passion which contemptuously discarded the Bible text, ejected the chorale, and unfolded the narrative in conventional rhymed stanzas. Some of his imitators even inserted stage directions in the text! Thus, when

49

Bach took office in Leipzig in 1723 the German Passion was in critical peril. It is not the least of his achievements to have rescued it from Hamburg's contaminating secularism and completely to have vindicated the German tradition. He reinstated the Bible text, infused a religious intention into the secular forms oratorio borrowed from opera, elevated the chorale to a height of emotional appeal it had not yet attained, and produced a masterpiece, dramatic, but essentially devotional. Its technical majesty excites our homage. But chiefly we bow before the fact that it affords a presentation of the Bible story deeply pondered, supremely reverent, fundamentally devotional.

Of all the forms in which Bach expressed himself oratorio and fugue were the modes of utterance most attuned to his nature. His fugues are unique because, among his predecessors and contemporaries, he alone fully realized the romantic and artistic possibilities of the fugal form. His personality is behind every bar of them. They are the poetry of a master who found it natural and congenial to express himself in that form. His relation to the fugue, in fact, is that of Beethoven to the sonata, and Haydn to the quartet.

A natural adaptation of the vocal canonic form, the fugue reached Bach through German models, though Forkel names the Italian Girolamo Frescobaldi (1583–1643) among those he studied. In an earlier generation the contrapuntist Andrea Gabrieli (c. 1520–86) had been remarkable. Through his pupil Jan Pieterzoon Sweelinck (1562–1621) his technique passed directly to Georg Böhm and Johann Reinken, and so to Bach, who sat at the feet of both of them. Bach was also in intimate contact with the two masters of his early years, Johann Pachelbel (1653–1706) and Dietrich Buxtehude. Of the former his eldest brother and teacher was the pupil, and to hear the second he journeyed to Lübeck in his teens, might indeed have succeeded him there if the charms of Fräulein Buxtehude had sufficiently assisted her father's design! From these mentors he received the principles of his own more brilliant art. But, till he expounded it by rule and example, the fugue was a contrapuntal, soulless exercise. Among its masters Bach had high regard for Johann Josef Fux (1660–1741) of Vienna, whose *Gradus ad Parnassum*, published in 1725, was a standard manual. But in Fux's hands the fugue was a mechanical and lifeless exercise. "First choose a subject suitable to the key you intend to compose in," he directs, "and write it down in that part in which you propose to begin. Then repeat the subject in the second part, either at the interval of a fourth or fifth, adding such notes in the first part as will agree with it." And so on, with the prosaic precision of a cookery-book! Still, sanctioned in the generation that preceded Bach's birth, these elementary prescriptions afforded the foundation on which he reared his more splendid art. Applying the expanded key-system of his *Well-Tempered Clavier*, and enriching his themes with a wealth of melody and contrapuntal resource the fugue had never experienced, Bach evolved a nervous organism out of Fux's skeleton and fashioned a poem from an exercise.

We have reviewed, very inadequately, the language in which Bach worked. And what is our conclusion? He spoke in forms that are now archaic. He invented no new one. None was more firmly linked with the past than he, none more obedient to its conventions. No other of the great composers was so medieval in the circumstances of his life. He spent it in one corner of Germany, and for the last twenty-five years of it never, save once, travelled above a hundred miles from his center. Indeed, he worked in such artistic isolation, was so shut in upon himself, had such little opportunity to test his genius by experiment, that we must suppose him driven to compose by sheer compulsion from within.

But, medieval though he was in the forms in which he expressed himself, his technical skill in them remains unique and unsurpassed. No one has approached him in the miraculous complexity of his part-writing, or in his ingenuity in weaving melodic strands into a single fabric. No one equally displays his gift of melody, his sense of form, the virile quality of his themes, the boldness of his technique, even the daring of his harmonic coloring. Thus, even within the forms he used, Bach is dateless, his art perennial, immortalized by the intense individualism that informed it. Directed by a faith childlike in its simplicity, he used it to interpret the infinite, saw the heavens opened, and was prophetically oracular. Only Beethoven approaches him in this quality, and both stand upon a peak of wonder. From Mozart onwards his peers have done homage to his example, even

51

in forms he never knew. So, he belongs to no age, at once remote from us and yet intimately close. Schumann summed him up in a sentence: "Music owes as much to Bach as a religion to its founder."

BACH SPEAKS

[From a letter to I. Erdmann, October 28, 1730, when Bach considered leaving his post in Leipzig.]

At first it was not wholly agreeable to me to become a Cantor [at the Thomasschule in Leipzig] after having been a Kapellmeister, on which account I delayed making a decision for a quarter of a year. However, this post was described to me in such favorable terms that finally—especially as my sons seemed inclined towards study— I ventured upon it in the name of the Most High, and betook myself to Leipzig, passed my examinations, and then made the move. Here, by God's will, I am to this day. But now, since I find (1) that the appointment here is not nearly so considerable as I was led to understand, (2) that it has been deprived of many prerequisites, (3) that the town is very dear to live in, and (4) that the authorities are strange people, with little devotion to music, so that I have to endure almost constant vexation, envy, and persecution, I feel compelled to seek, with the Almighty's aid, my fortune elsewhere. Should your Excellency know of, or be able to find, a suitable appointment in your town for an old and faithful servant, I humbly beg you to give me your gracious recommendation thereto; on my part I will not fail, by using my best diligence, to give satisfaction and justify your kind recommendation and intercession.

My position here is worth about seven hundred thalers, and when there are rather more funerals than usual the perquisites increase proportionately; but if the air is healthy the fees decrease, last year, for example, being more than one hundred thalers below the average from funerals. In Thuringia I can make four hundred thalers go further than twice as many here, on account of the excessive cost of living.

And now I must tell you a little about my domestic circumstances. I am married for the second time, my first wife having died in

Cöthen. Of the first marriage, three sons and a daughter are still living, whom your Excellency saw in Weimar, as you may be graciously pleased to remember. My oldest son is *Studiosus Juris*, the other two are one in the first and the other in the second class, and the eldest daughter is still unmarried. The children of the other marriage are still little, the eldest boy, being six years old. They are one and all born musicians, and I can assure you that I can already form a concert, vocal and instrumental, with my family, especially as my wife sings a good soprano, and my eldest daughter joins in quite well.

GEORGE FRIDERIC HANDEL

1 6 8 5 – 1 7 5 9

GEORGE FRIDERIC HANDEL, genius of the oratorio, was born in Halle, Saxony, on February 23, 1685. He studied music in his native city with Friedrich Zachau. In 1703 Handel played the violin in the opera orchestra in Hamburg where his first operas—*Almira* and *Nero*—were produced early in 1705. A year later he embarked on an extended trip to Italy where he wrote two oratorios and some more operas. In 1710 Handel became Kapellmeister at the court of the Elector of Hanover. In 1711, he paid his first visit to London, where his opera *Rinaldo* was successfully produced at the Haymarket Theater on February 24. He returned to England in 1712 with the intention of paying only another brief visit, but this time he stayed on for the rest of his life. He became a British subject in 1727. From 1717 to 1720 he was Kapellmeister for the Duke of Chandos. When the Royal Academy of Music was founded in London for the production of Italian operas, Handel was made its director. For this theater he wrote numerous operas beginning with *Radamisto,* given on April 27, 1720. In short order Handel became one of the most famous composers in England. But he also made powerful enemies among those who resented him because he was a foreigner, because he was so successful, and because he had such boorish manners. To dim the luster of his popularity, these enemies brought to London one of Italy's most eminent opera composers, Giovanni Bononcini (1670–1747). At first Bononcini proved extremely popular, but with *Ottone* in 1723 Handel completely and permanently established his ascendency over his rival. His triumph, however, proved short-lived: English audiences were beginning to turn away from Italian grand opera, particularly after the success of John Gay's *The Beggar's Opera* in 1728 which provided them with a more popular and

54

contemporary form of stage entertainment. The Royal Academy went into bankruptcy. Undaunted, Handel started other opera companies, but each carried him ever nearer to the brink of financial and physical ruin.

After 1741 he abandoned opera to concentrate his formidable energies and powers on the oratorio. Beginning with the *Messiah,* introduced in Dublin on April 13, 1742, Handel completed a rich library of oratorio music without parallel, including *Semele, Judas Maccabaeus, Solomon, Theodora,* and *Jephtha.* It was in this medium that he realized his fullest potentialities as a composer. Like Bach, Handel suffered blindness in his last years. He died in London on April 14, 1759, and was buried in Westminster Abbey where a monument by Roubliliac was erected showing the composer in front of his desk on which rests the open score of the *Messiah* with the words "I know that my Redeemer liveth."

THE MAN

CHARLES BURNEY

NEWMAN FLOWER

The figure of Handel was large, and he was somewhat corpulent and unwieldy in his motions; but his countenance . . . was full of fire and dignity such as impressed ideas of superiority and genius. He was impetuous, rough, and peremptory in his manners and conversation, but totally devoid of ill-nature or malevolence; indeed, there was an original humor and pleasantry in his most lively sallies of anger or impatience which, with his broken English, were extremely risible. His natural propensity to wit and humor and happy manner of relating common occurrences in an uncommon way enabled him to throw persons and things into very ridiculous attitudes. Had he been as great a master of the English language as Swift, his *bon mots* would have been as frequent and somewhat of the same kind.

Handel wore an enormous white wig, and when things went well at the oratorio, it had a certain nod or vibration which manifested

55

his pleasure and satisfaction. Without it, nice observers were certain that he was out of humor.

Handel was in the habit of talking to himself so loud that it was easy for persons not very near to him to hear the subject of his soliloquies.

Handel's general look was somewhat heavy and sour, but when he did smile it was like the sun bursting out of a black cloud. There was a sudden flash of intelligence, wit, and good humor beaming in his countenance which I hardly ever saw in any other.*

. . . . .

When the curtain came down on *Radamisto* on that June night of 1720, Handel had completed a phase of his life—probably the happiest phase of his life. All these works (*Radamisto* among them) had been the achievements of youth, for, although he was now thirty-five, both mind and body had all the strength of early youth. That mind which knew no dullness, nor lost its brilliance, was to mature; his body, as youth passed, to halt in its freshness. He never studied his health. Only when illness pulled him away from his work did he realize that "this infernal flesh," as he once called it, was the master of him. He took no exercise save to go from one place to another for business purposes, and he ate far heavier dinners than he should have. He drank a great deal too much beer and coffee, and he was a slave to tobacco. He rode when he could do so, to save himself the trouble of walking. When composing, he sat at work all day, on through the night and through the day following. Food was put on his table and he ignored it. Sleep twitched at his eyelids, and he forced it away. The claims of his body for rest were always subservient to the demands of a mentality that could neither rest nor be still.

The wonder is that he did not die before he was forty, for he treated his body as some brute would treat a wretched mongrel that followed at his heels. . . . Failures were to come, but out of every failure he drew new strength. When the treasury was empty and creditors were pressing, when enemies herded about him and brought

---

* The paragraphs above are by Burney; those below, by Flower.

56

the flail of hatred upon his back, he discovered a new vitality in the silence of his room.

His music had brought to his feet women in plenty. The women in London society crowded about him to get him to their salons. Old women; young women. He had a peculiar way with them. He loved a battle with a bright conversationalist of the other sex. But he had no interest in the sex as such. Only on two occasions in his life did the question of marriage ever seriously occur to him. Once he even went so far as to become engaged. . . . The *affaire* ended abruptly, for the mother of the girl in question objected to her daughter's marrying a musician. He must give up music or her daughter. Handel decided quickly. His art was his wife and his mistress, and he said so, and went his way.

A second woman intrigued him. Again music was the difficulty. A musician was only a roving mountebank, was the remark thrown at him. Again he decided as before.

So youth crept forward and ripened. He matured. He liked the society of women—those women who loved art. His courtesies, his gentleness to them were extreme. The years passed. He became, by easy stages, the accepted bachelor, sexless, safe. . . .

Handel, just past fifty years of age, was full of fight, just as his body was becoming full of rheumatism. At times he could scarcely move for the pain that racked his right side. The act of playing an instrument gave him intense agony. Sleeplessness was beginning to worry him. Heavy moods of depression assaulted him like grim overhanging clouds, and endured for days. His temper became violent; some of his actions were almost brutish. As suddenly the rheumatic pains would depart, he would sleep for a couple of days like a dog, then, waking, eat heavily and enjoy again his wine, his beer. The scowls on his face, that kept those about him from approaching unless driven to do so by actual necessity, departed with the other ills, and the kindly smile would reappear like sunshine after the rain. Then would he crack his jokes, fling his repartee across the table at his colleagues like darts of fire, and go on working more furiously than ever, careless of what his body would have to pay for it. For the enemy of which he had the smallest fear was pain.

57

THE COMPOSER

ROMAIN ROLLAND

No great musician is more impossible to include in the limits of one definition, or even of several, than Handel. It is a fact that he reached the complete mastery of his style very early (much earlier than Bach), although it was never really fixed, and he never devoted himself to any one form of art. It is even difficult to see a conscious and a logical evolution in him. His genius is not of the kind which follows a single path and forges right ahead until it reaches its object. For his aim was no other than to do well whatever he undertook. All ways were good to him—from his early steps at the crossing of the ways, he dominated the country and shed his light on all sides, without laying siege to any particular part. He is not one of those who impose on life and art a voluntary idealism, either violent or patient; nor is he one of those who inscribe in the book of life the formula of their campaign. He is of the kind who drink in the life universal, assimilating it to themselves. His artistic will is mainly objective. His genius adapts itself to a thousand images of passing events, to the nation, to the times in which he lived, even to the fashions of his day. It accommodates itself to the various influences, ignoring all obstacles. It weighs other styles and other thoughts, but such is the power of assimilation and the prevailing equilibrium of his nature that he never feels submerged and overweighted by the mass of these strange elements. Everything is duly absorbed, controlled, and classified. This immense soul is like the sea itself, into which all the rivers of the world pour themselves without troubling its serenity.

The German geniuses have often had this power of absorbing thoughts and strange forms, but it is excessively rare to find amongst them the grand objectivism and this superior impersonality which is, so to speak, the hallmark of Handel. Their sentimental lyricism is better fitted to sing songs, to voice the thoughts of the universe in song, than to paint the universe in living forms and vital rhythms.

Handel is very different and approaches much more nearly than any other in Germany the genius of the South, the Homeric genius of which Goethe received the sudden revelation on his arrival at Naples. This capacious mind looks out on the whole universe and on the way the universe depicts itself, as a picture is reflected in calm and clear water. He owes much of this objectivism to Italy, where he spent many years and the fascination of which never effaced itself from his mind, and he owes even more to that sturdy England which guards its emotions with so tight a rein, and which eschews those sentimental and effervescing effusions so often displayed in the pious German art; but that he had all the germs of his art in himself is already shown in his early works at Hamburg.

From his infancy at Halle, Zachau had trained him not in one style but in all the styles of the different nations, leading him to understand not only the spirit of each great composer but to assimilate the styles by writing in various manners. This education, essentially cosmopolitan, was completed by his three tours in Italy and his sojourn of half a century in England. Above all he never ceased to follow up the lessons learned at Halle, always appropriating to himself the best from all artists and their works. If he was never in France (it is not absolutely proved), he knew her nevertheless. He was anxious to master the French language and musical style. We have proofs of that in his manuscripts and in the accusations made against him by certain French critics. Wherever he passed, he gathered some musical souvenir, buying and collecting foreign works, copying them, or rather (for he had not the careful patience of J. S. Bach, who scrupulously wrote out in his own hand the entire scores of French organists and the Italian violinists) copying down in hasty and often inexact expressions any idea which struck him in the course of reading. This vast collection of European thoughts, which remains only in remnants at the Fitzwilliam Museum at Cambridge, was the reservoir, so to speak, from which his creative genius continually fed itself. Profoundly German in race and character, he had become a world citizen like his compatriot Leibnitz, whom he had known at Hanover, a European with a tendency for the Latin culture. The great Germans at the end of that century, Goethe and Herder, were never more free or more universal than this great

59

Saxon in music, saturated as he was with all the artistic thoughts of the West.

He drew not only from the sources of learned and refined music —the music of musicians; but also drank deeply from the founts of popular music—that of the most simple and rustic folk. He loved the latter. One finds noted down in his manuscripts the street cries of London, and he once told a friend that he received many inspirations for his best airs from them. Certain of his oratorios, like *L'Allegro ed Il Pensoroso* (1740), are threaded with remembrances of his walks in the English country, and who can ignore the *Pifferari* (Italian peasant's pipe) in the *Messiah* (1742), the Flemish carillon in *Saul* (1739), the joyous popular Italian songs in *Hercules* (1745), and in *Alexander Balus* (1748)? Handel was not an artist lost in introspection. He watched all around him, he listened, and observed. Sight was for him a source of inspiration, hardly of less importance than hearing. I do not know any great German musician who has been as much a visual as Handel. Like Johann Adolph Hasse (1699–1783) and Arcangelo Corelli (1653–1713), he had a veritable passion for beautiful pictures. He hardly ever went out without going to a theater or a picture sale. He was a connoisseur, and he made a collection in which some Rembrandts were found after his death. It has been remarked that his blindness (which should have rendered his hearing still more sensitive, his creative powers translating everything into sonorous dreams) soon paralyzed his hearing when its principal source of renewal was withdrawn.

Thus saturated in all the European music of his time, impregnated with the music of musicians and the still richer music which flows in all Nature herself, which is specially diffused in the vibrations of light and shade, that song of the rivers, of the forest, of the birds, in which all his work abounds and which have inspired some of his most picturesque pages with a semi-romantic color, he wrote as one speaks, he composed as one breathes. He never sketched out on paper in order to prepare his definite work. He wrote straight off as he improvised, and in truth he seems to have been the greatest improviser that ever was. He wrote his music with such an impetuosity of feeling and such a wealth of ideas that his hand was constantly lagging behind his thoughts, and in order to keep apace

with them at all he had to note them down in an abbreviated manner. But (and this seems contradictory) he had at the same time an
exquisite sense of form. No German surpassed him in the art of writing beautiful, melodic lines. Mozart and Hasse alone were his equals
in this. It was to this love of perfection that we attribute that habit
which, despite his fertility of invention, causes him to use time after
time the same phrases (those most important and dearest to him),
each time introducing an imperceptible change, a light stroke of the
pencil, which renders them more perfect. The examination of these
kinds of musical *eaux-fortes* in their successive states is very instructive for the musician who is interested in plastic beauty. It shows
also how certain melodies, once written down, continued to slumber
in Handel's mind for many years until they had penetrated his subconscious nature and until they were applied at first, by following
the chances of inspiration, to a certain situation which suited them
moderately well. They are, so to speak, in search of a body where
they can reincarnate themselves, seeking the true situation, the real
sentiment of which they are but the latent expression; and once having found it, they expand themselves with ease.

Handel worked no less with the music of other composers than
with his own. If one had the time to study here what superficial
readers have called his plagarisms, particularly taking, for example,
Israel in Egypt (1739), where the most barefaced of these cases
occur, one would see with what genius and insight Handel has
evoked from the depths of these musical phrases their secret soul,
of which the first creators had not even a presentiment. It needed his
eye, or his ear, to discover in the serenade of Alessandro Stradella
(1642–82) its Biblical cataclysms. Each read and heard a work of
art as it is, and yet not as it is; and one may conclude that it is not
always the creator himself who has the most fertile idea of it. The
example of Handel well proves this. Not only did he create music,
but very often he created that of others for them. Stradella and
Dionigi Erba (17th and 18th centuries) were only for him (however
humiliating the comparison) the flames of fire and the cracks in the
wall through which Leonardo saw the living figures. Handel heard
great storms passing through the gentle quivering of Stradella's
guitar.

61

This evocatory character of Handel's genius should never be forgotten. He who is satisfied with listening to this music without *seeing* what it expresses—who judges this art as a purely formal art and who does not feel his expressive and suggestive power, occasionally so far as hallucination, will never understand it. It is a music which paints emotions, souls, and situations, seeing the epochs and the places which are the framework of the emotions, and which tint them with their own peculiar moral tone. In a word, his is an art essentially picturesque and dramatic. . . . The intimate sense of his works was falsified in the century which followed his death by the English interpretations, strengthened further still in Germany by those of Mendelssohn and his numerous following. By the exclusion of and systematic contempt for all the operas of Handel, by an elimination of nearly all the dramatic oratorios, the most powerful and the freshest, by a narrow choice more and more restrained to the four or five oratorios, and even here, by giving an exaggerated supremacy to the *Messiah,* by the interpretation finally of these works, and notably of the *Messiah,* in a pompous, rigid, and stolid manner with an orchestra and choir far too numerous and badly balanced, with singers frightfully correct and pious, without any feeling or intimacy, there has been established the tradition which makes Handel a church musician after the style of Louis XIV, all decoration—pompous columns, noble and cold statues, and pictures by Le Brun. It is not surprising that this has reduced works executed on such principles and degraded them to a monumental tiresomeness similar to that which emanates from the bewigged Alexanders and the very conventional Christs of Le Brun.

It is necessary to turn back. Handel was never a church musician, and he hardly ever wrote for the church. Apart from his psalms and his Te Deum, composed for the private chapels and for exceptional events, he wrote instrumental music only for concerts and for open-air fêtes, for operas, and for those so-called oratorios which were really written for the theater. The first oratorios he composed were acted. And if Handel resolutely abstained from theatrical representation—which alone gives the full value to certain scenes, such as the orgy and the dream of Belshazzar, expressly conceived for acting —on the other hand he stood out firmly for having his oratorios at the theater and not in the church. There were not wanting churches any less than dissenting chapels in which he could give his works, and by not doing so he turned against him the opinion of religious people who considered it sacrilegious to carry pious subjects on the stage, but he continued to affirm that he did not write compositions for the church, but worked for the theater—a free theater.

. . . . .

It remains for us, after having attempted to indicate the general characteristics of Handel's art, to sketch the technique of the different styles in which he worked.

It is difficult to speak of the opera or of the oratorio of Handel. It is necessary to say: *of the operas* or *of the oratorios,* for we do not find that they point back to any single type. We can verify here what we said at the commencement of this chapter about the magnificent vitality of Handel in choosing amongst his art forms the different directions of the music of his times.

All the European tendencies at that time are reflected in his operas: the model of Reinhard Keiser (1674–1739) in his early works, the Venetian model in his *Agrippina* (1709), the model of Alessandro Scarlatti (1660–1725) and Agostino Steffani (1654–1728) in his first early operas; in the London works he soon introduces English influences, particularly in his rhythms. Then it was Bononcini whom he rivaled. Again, those great attempts of genius to create a new musical drama, *Giulio Cesare* (1724), *Tamerlano* (1724), *Orlando* (1733); later on those charming ballet-operas inspired by France, *Ariodante* (1735), *Alcina* (1735); later still, those operas which point toward the opéra-comique and the light style of the second half of the century, *Serse* (1738), *Deidamia* (1741). . . . Handel continued to try every other style without making any permanent choice as did Gluck, with whom alone he can be compared.

One sees what a variety of forms and styles he used. Handel was too universal and too objective to believe that one kind of art only was the true one. He believed in two kinds of music only, the good and the bad. Apart from that he appreciated all styles. Thus he has left masterpieces in every style, but he did not open any new way in opera for the simple reason that he went a long way in nearly all paths already opened up. Constantly he experimented, invented, and always with his singularly sure touch. He seemed to have an extraordinarily penetrating knowledge in invention, and consequently few artistic regions remained for him to conquer. He made as masterly a use of the recitative as Gluck, or of the arioso as Mozart, writing the acts of *Tamerlano,* which are the most touching and heartrending dramas, in the manner of *Iphigénie en Tauride,* the most moving and passionate scenes in music such as certain pages of *Admeto* (1727) and *Orlando,* where the humorous and the tragic are intermingled in the manner of *Don Giovanni.* He has experimented happily here in new rhythms. There were new forms, the dramatic duet or quartet, the descriptive symphony opening the opera, refined orchestration, choruses, and dances. Nothing seems to have obsessed him. In the following opera we find him returning to the ordinary forms of the Italian or German opera of his time.

. . . . .

Still less can we say that he held to a rigid form with his operas, which were continually adapted to the changing tastes of the theater public of his age and of the singers whom he had at his disposal; but when he left the opera for the oratorio he varied no less. It was a perpetual experiment of new forms in the vast framework of the free theater (*théâtre en liberté*) of the concert drama; and the sort of instinctive ebb and flow in creation seems to have caused his works to succeed one another in groups of analogous or related compositions, each work in a nearly opposite style of feeling and form. In each one Handel indulged momentarily in a certain side of his feelings, and when that was finished he found himself in the possession of other feelings which had been accumulating whilst he was drawing on the first. He thus kept up a perpetual balance, which is like the pulsation of life itself. After the realistic *Saul* comes the impersonal epic of *Israel in Egypt.* After this colossal monument appear the two genre pictures, *The Ode for St. Cecilia's Day* (1739) and *L'Allegro ed Il Penseroso.* After the Herculean *Samson* (1743), a heroic and popular tragic comedy sprang forth, the charming flower of *Semele* (1744), an opera of romanticism and gallantry.

But if the oratorios are so wonderfully varied, they have one

characteristic in common even more than the operas; they are musical dramas. It was not that religious thought turned Handel to this
choice of Biblical subjects, but as Kretzschmar has well shown, it was
on account of the stories of the Bible heroes being a part of the very
life-blood of the people whom he addressed. They were known to all
whilst the ancient romantic stories could only interest a society of
refined and spoiled dilettanti. Without doubt, these oratorios were
not made for representation, did not seek scenic effects, with rare
exceptions, as for instance the scene of the orgy of *Belshazzar* (1745),
where one feels that Handel had drawn on the direct vision of theatrical representation, but passions, spirits and personalities were
represented always in a dramatic fashion. Handel is a great painter
of characters, and the Delilah in *Samson,* the Nitocris in *Belshazzar,*
the Cleopatra in *Alexander Balus,* the mother in *Solomon* (1749), the
Dejanira in *Hercules,* the beautiful Theodora, all bear witness to the
suppleness and the profundity of his psychological genius. If in the
course of the action and the depicting of the ordinary sentiments he
abandoned himself freely to the flow of pure music, in the moments
of passionate crises he is the equal of the greatest masters in musical
drama. Is it necessary to mention the terrible scenes in the third act
of *Hercules,* the beautiful scenes of *Alexander Balus,* the Dream of
Belshazzar, the prison scenes in *Theodora* (1750), or in the first act
of *Saul,* and dominating all, like great pictures, certain of the choruses of *Israel in Egypt,* in *Esther* (1732) and in *Joshua* (1748), and in
Chandos Anthems (1717–20), which seem veritable tempests of passion, great upheavals of overpowering effect? It is by these choruses
that the oratorio is essentially distinguished from the opera. It is in
the first place a choral tragedy. These choruses, which were nearly
eliminated in Italian opera during the time of the Barberini, held a
very important place in French opera, but their role was limited to
that of commentator or else merely decorative. In the oratorio of
Handel they became the very life and soul of the work. Sometimes
they took the part of the ancient classical chorus, which exposed the
thought of the drama when the hidden fates led on the heroes to
their destinies—as in *Saul, Hercules, Alexander Balus, Susanna* (1749).
Sometimes they added to the shock of human passions the powerful

65

appeal of religion and crowned the human drama with a supernatural aureole, as in *Theodora* and *Jephtha* (1752). Or finally they became the actual actors themselves, or the enemy-people and the God who guided them. It is remarkable that in his very first oratorio, *Esther,* Handel had this stroke of genius. In the choruses there we see the drama of an oppressed people and their God who led them by his voice superbly depicted. In *Deborah* (1733) and *Athalia* (1733) also, two nations are in evidence. In *Belshazzar* there are three, but his chief work of this kind, *Israel in Egypt,* the greatest choral epic which exists, is entirely occupied by Jehovah and His people.

The oratorio being a "free theater," it becomes necessary for the music to supply the place of the scenery. Thus its picturesque and descriptive role is strongly developed, and it is by this above all that Handel's genius so struck the English public. Camille Saint-Saëns wrote in an interesting letter to C. Bellaigue, "I have come to the conclusion that it is the picturesque and descriptive side, until then novel and unreached, whereby Handel achieved the astonishing favor which he enjoyed. This masterly way of writing choruses, of treating the fugue, had been done by others. What really counts with him is the color—that modern element which we no longer hear in him. . . . He knew nothing of exoticism. But look at *Alexander's Feast* (1736), *Israel in Egypt,* and especially *L'Allegro ed Il Penseroso,* and try to forget all that has been done since. You find at every turn a striving for the picturesque, for an effect of imitation. It is real and intense for the medium in which it is produced, and it seems to have been unknown hitherto."

Perhaps Saint-Saëns lays too much weight on the "masterly way of writing his choruses," which was not so common in England, even with Henry Purcell (c. 1659–95). Perhaps he accentuates too much also the real influence of the French in matters of picturesque and descriptive music and the influence which it exerted on Handel. Finally, it is not necessary to represent these descriptive tendencies of Handel as exceptional in his time. A great breath of nature passed over German music and pushed it toward tone-painting. Georg Philipp Telemann (1681–1767) was even more than Handel a painter in music and was more celebrated than Handel for his realistic effects. But the England of the 18th century had remained very conservative in music and had devoted itself to cultivating the masters of the past. Handel's art was then more striking to them on account of "its color" and "its imitative effects." I will not say with Saint-Saëns that "there was no question of exoticism with him," for Handel seems to have sought this very thing more than once; notably in the orchestration of certain scenes for the two Cleopatras, of *Giulio Cesare*, and of *Alexander Balus*. But that which was constantly with him was tone-painting, the reproduction through passages of music of natural impressions, a painting very characteristic and, as Beethoven put it, "more an expression of feelings than painting," a poetic evocation of the raging tempests, of the tranquility of the sea, of the dark shades of night, of the twilight which envelops the English country, of the parks by moonlight, of the sunrise in springtime, and of the awakening of birds. *Acis and Galatea* (1708), *Israel in Egypt, L'Allegro*, the *Messiah, Solomon*, all offer a wondrous picture gallery of Nature, carefully noted by Handel with the sure stroke of a Flemish painter and of a romantic poet at the same time. This romanticism struck powerfully on his time with a strength which would not be denied. It drew upon him both admiration and violent criticism. A letter of 1751 depicts him as a Berlioz or Wagner, raising storms by his orchestra and chorus.

"He cannot give people pleasure after the proper fashion," writes this anonymous author in his letter, "for his evil genius will not allow him to do this. He imagines a new *grandioso* kind of music, and in order to make more noise he has it executed by the greatest number of voices and instruments which one has ever heard before in a theater. He thinks thus to rival not only the god of musicians, but even all the other gods, like Iole, Neptune, and Jupiter: for either I expected that the house would be brought down by his tempest or that the sea would engulf the whole. But more unbearable still was his thunder. Never have such terrible rumblings fallen on my head."

Similarly Goethe, irritated and upset, said after having heard the first movement of the Beethoven C minor Symphony, "It is meaningless. One expected the house to fall about one's ears."

It is not by chance that I couple the names of Handel and Beethoven. Handel is a kind of Beethoven in chains. He had the unapproachable manner like the great Italian artists who surrounded him: the Porporas, the Hasses; and between him and them there was a whole world. Under the classic ideal with which he covered himself burned a romantic genius, precursor of the *Sturm und Drang* period; and sometimes this hidden demon broke out in brusque fits of passion—perhaps despite itself.

. . . . .

The orchestral music of Handel comprises twelve Concerti Grossi, op. 6 (1739), the Oboe Concertos (1740), the symphonies from his operas, oratorios, and his open-air music—*Water Music* (1717), *Fireworks Music* (1749)—and Concertos for two horns.

Although Handel was in art a visualist and though his music had a highly descriptive and evocatory power, he made only a very restrained use of instrumental tone color. However, he showed on occasion a refined intelligence in its use. The two oratorios written at Rome when he found himself in the society of the Cardinal Ottoboni, and his great virtuoso works, the *Triumph of Time* and *The Resurrection* of 1708, have a fine and well-varied orchestration. In London he was one of the first to introduce the use of the horn into the orchestra of the opera. "He was the first," says Volbach, "to assert the expressive personality of the violoncello." From the viola he knew how to secure many curious effects of indefinite and disquieting half-tones, he gave to the bassoons a lugubrious and fantastic character, he experimented with new instruments, small and great, he used the drum (*tambour*) solo in a dramatic fashion for Jupiter's oath in *Semele*. For special situations, by instrumental tone colors he secures effects not only of dramatic expression but also of exoticism and local color. It is so in the two scenes from the two Cleopatras, *Giulio Cesare* and *Alexander Balus*.

But great painter as Handel was, he did not work so much through the brilliancy, variety, and novelty of his tone colors as by the beauty of his designs and his effects of light and shade. With a voluntarily restrained palette and by satisfying himself with the sober colors of the strings, he yet was able to produce surprising and thrilling effects. Volbach has shown that he had less recourse to the contrast and mixing of instruments than to the division of the same family of instruments into different groups. On the other hand, Handel, when he considered it advisable, reduced his instrumental forces by suppressing the viola and the second violin, whose places were taken by the harpsichord. All his orchestral art is in the true instinct of balance and economy, which, with the most restricted means in managing a few colors, yet knows how to obtain as powerful impressions as our musicians of today, with their crowded palette. Nothing, then, is more important if we wish to render this music truly than the avoidance of upsetting the equilibrium of the various sections of the orchestra under the pretext of enriching it and bringing it up to date. The worse fault is to deprive it, by a useless surplus of tone colors, of that suppleness and subtlety of nuance which is its principal charm.

Let us consider his concerti grossi. None of his works are more celebrated and less understood. Handel attached to them a particular value, for he published them by subscription, a means which was usual in his day, but which he himself never adopted except under exceptional circumstances.

One knows that the kind of concerti grossi, which consists chiefly in a dialogue between a group of solo instrumentalists (the concertino) and the full body of instruments (concerto grosso), to which is added the cembalo, was, if not invented, at least carried to its perfection and rendered classical by Corelli. The works of Corelli, aided by the efforts of his followers, had become widely known in Europe. Francesco Geminiani (1687–1762) introduced them into England, and without doubt Handel did not hesitate to profit by the example of Geminiani, who was his friend; but it is much more natural to think that he learned the concerto grosso at its source at Rome from Corelli himself during his sojourn there in 1708. Several of the concertos in his Opus 3 date from 1710, 1716, 1722. The same feature shows itself right up to the time of his apprenticeship at Hamburg; in any case he might have already known the Corellian style, thanks to the propaganda of Georg Muffat (1653–1704), who spread this style very early in Germany. After Corelli came Pietro Locatelli (1695–1764), and especially Vivaldi, who singularly transformed the concerto grosso by giving it the free character of program music and by turning it resolutely toward the form of the sonata in three parts. But when the works of Vivaldi were played in

London in 1723, and the works which aroused such a general enthusiasm became thoroughly known to Handel, it was always to Corelli that he gave the preference; and he was very conservative in certain ways even about him. The form of his concerto, of which the principal movements varied from four to six, oscillated between the suite and the sonata and even glanced toward the symphonic overture. It is this for which the theorists blame him, and it is this for which I praise him. For he does not seek to impose a uniform cast on his thoughts but leaves it open to himself to fashion the form as he requires, so that the framework varies accordingly, following his inclinations from day to day.

The spontaneity of his thought, which has already been shown by the extreme rapidity with which the concerti were composed—each in a single day at a single sitting, and many each week—constitutes the great charm of these works. They are, in the words of Kretzschmar, grand impression pictures, translated into a form at the same time precise and supple, in which the least change of emotion can make itself easily felt. Truly they are not all of equal value. Their conception itself, which depended in a way on mere momentary inspiration, is the explanation of this extreme inequality. One ought to acknowledge here that the Seventh Concerto, for example (the one in B-flat major), and the last three have but a moderate interest. They are amongst those least played, but to be quite just we must pay homage to these masterpieces, and especially to the Second Concerto in F major, which is like a Beethoven concerto: for we find there some of the spirit of the Bonn master.

Let us now come to that class of Handel's instrumental music to which historians have given far too little attention, and in which Handel shows himself a precursor, and at the same time a model. I refer to his open-air music.

This took a prominent place in the English life. The environs of London were full of gardens where, Pepys tells us, "vocal and instrumental concerts vied with the voices of the birds." Handel wrote pieces especially intended for these garden concerts. Generally speaking, he attached very little importance to them. They were little symphonies or unpretentious dances like the *Hornpipe*, composed for the concert at Vauxhall in 1740.

But he composed on these lines some works tending toward a much vaster scale: in 1717 the famous *Water Music,* written for the royal procession of barges on the Thames, and the *Fireworks Music* made to illustrate the fireworks display given in Green Park on April 27, 1749, in celebration of the peace of Aix-la-Chapelle.

The *Water Music* has a grand serenade in the form of a suite comprising more than twenty movements. It opens with a pompous opera overture; then come dialogues, with echoes of horns and drums, where the brass and the rest of the orchestra, which are arranged in two sections, respond. Then follow happy and soothing songs, dances, a bourrée, a hornpipe, minuets, popular songs which alternate and contrast with the joyful and powerful fanfares. The orchestra is nearly the same as in his usual symphonies except that considerable importance is given to the brass. One even finds in this works certain pieces written in the chamber-music style, or in the theatrical manner.

With the *Fireworks Music* the character of open-air music is even more definitely asserted, quite as much by the broad style of the piece as by the orchestration, which is confined entirely to the wind instruments. The composition is divided into two parts: an overture which was to be played before the grand fireworks display, and a number of little pieces to be played during the display, which corresponded to certain allegorical set pieces. The overture is a sort of stately march in D major, and has some resemblance to the overture of the *Ritterballet* (Huntsman's Dance) of Beethoven, and which is, like it, joyful, equestrian, and sonorous. The shorter movements comprise a bourrée, a *Largo a la Siciliana,* entitled *Peace,* of a beautiful, heroic grace, which lulls itself to sleep; a sprightly Allegro entitled *The Rejoicing,* and two minuets for conclusion. It is an interesting work for the organizers of our popular fêtes and open-air spectacles to study. If we have said that after 1740 Handel wrote hardly any other instrumental music than the *Fireworks Music* and the two monumental concertos, *a due cori* (for two horns), we have the feeling that the last evolution of his thought and instrumental style led him in the direction of music conceived for the great masses, wide spaces, and huge audiences. He had always in him a popular vein of thought. I immediately call to mind the many popu-

71

lar inspirations with which his memory was stored and which vivify the pages of his oratorios. His art, which renewed itself perpetually at this rustic source, had in his time an astonishing popularity. Certain airs from *Ottone* (1723), *Scipione* (1726), *Arianna* (1734), *Berenice* (1737), and such other of his operas, were circulated and vulgarized not only in England but abroad, and even in France (generally so unyielding to outside influences).

It is not only of this popularity, a little banal, of which I wish to speak, which one could not ignore—for it is only a stupid pride and a small heart which denies great value to the art which pleases humble people; what I wish to notice chiefly in the popular character of Handel's music is that it is always truly conceived for the people, and not for an elite dilettanti, as was the French opera between Jean-Baptiste Lully (1632–87) and Gluck. Without ever departing from his sovereign ideas of beautiful form, in which he gave no concession to the crowd, he reproduced in a language immediately "understanded of the people" those feelings in which all could share. This genial improviser, compelled during the whole of his life (a half-century of creative power) to address from the stage a mixed public, was like the orators of old who had the cult of style and instinct for immediate and vital effect. Our epoch has lost the feeling of this type of art and men: pure artists who speak *to* the people and *for* the people, not for themselves or for their confrères. Today the pure artists lock themselves within themselves, and those who speak to the people are most often mountebanks. The free England of the 18th century was in a certain measure related to the Roman Republic, and indeed Handel's eloquence was not without relation to that of the epic orators, who sustained in the form their highly finished and passionate discourses, who left their mark on the shuddering crowd of loiterers. This eloquence did on occasion actually thrust itself into the soul of the nation as in the days of the Jacobite invasion, where *Judas Maccabaeus* (1747) incarnated the public feeling. In the first performances of *Israel in Egypt* some of the auditors praised the heroic virtues of this music, which could raise up the populace and lead armies to victory.

By this power of popular appeal, as by all the other aspects of his genius, Handel was in the robust line of Pier Francesco Cavalli

(1602–76) and of Gluck, but he surpassed them. Alone, Beethoven has walked in these broader paths and followed along the road which Handel had opened.

HANDEL SPEAKS

I believe the question can be reduced to this: whether one should prefer an easy and more perfect method to another which is accompanied by great difficulties capable not only of disgusting pupils with music, but also of wasting precious time that could be better utilized in probing more deeply into this art and in developing one's talent. It is not that I should like to declare that one can draw no benefit from solmization, but since one can acquire the same knowledge in much less time by the method used so successfully at present, I do not see why one should not take the road that leads more rapidly and easily to the desired end. As regards the Greek modes . . . no doubt knowledge of them is necessary to those who would study and play ancient music, which was composed according to those modes, but since we have freed ourselves from the narrow limits of ancient music, I do not see what use can be made of Greek modes in modern music.

.   .   .   .   .

[On writing the "Hallelujah Chorus" from the *Messiah*.] I did think I did see all Heaven before me—and the great God himself. . . . Where I was in my body or out of my body as I wrote it I know not. God knows.

[To a nobleman after the first London performance of the *Messiah*.] I should be sorry, My Lord, if I gave pleasure to men; my aim is to make them better.

73

CHRISTOPH WILLIBALD GLUCK

1 7 1 4 – 1 7 8 7

CHRISTOPH WILLIBALD RITTER VON GLUCK followed Rameau in the revolt against the Italian opera school, thus paving the way to music drama. Born in Erasbach, Upper Palatinate, on July 2, 1714, he received music instruction in various village schools. At eighteen he was earning his living playing dance music and singing in church choirs in Prague. In 1736 he found employment as chamber musician in Prince Lobkowitz's palace in Vienna. The year after he traveled to Italy, where he studied with the eminent Italian opera composer, Giovanni Battista Sammartini (1701–75). On December 26, 1741, Gluck's first opera, *Artaserse*, was successfully introduced in Milan. After completing several more Italian operas, produced both in Italy and London, he returned to Vienna in 1748 where his *Semiramide riconosciuta* successfully reopened the Burgtheater on May 14. In 1750 he married Marianna Pergin, and in 1754 he was appointed Kapellmeister of the Vienna Court Theater. In this office he wrote numerous operas, and a considerable amount of music for ballet and various entertainments. Now increasingly impatient with the formal and stilted procedures of Italian opera (particularly those whose flowery, historical librettos were provided by Pietro Metastasio, the Viennese court poet) and strongly influenced by Rameau, Gluck sought to write operas with greater simplicity and dramatic truth, sincerer emotion and sounder musical values. Encouraged by Count Giacomo Durazzo, director of the Viennese court theaters, and with Raniere de Calzabigi as his librettist, Gluck wrote *Orfeo ed Euridice*, produced at the Burgtheater on October 5, 1762. Also in this new style were *Alceste*, produced on December 16, 1767, and *Paride e Elena*, produced on November 30, 1770.

In 1773, Gluck came to Paris where his new opera, *Iphigénie en*

74

Aulide, proved a major success when it was presented at the Opéra on April 19, 1774–this despite the many obstacles placed in the way of its production by many Frenchmen who esteemed Italian opera highly. After the success of the French première of *Orfeo ed Euridice,* Gluck's enemies hoped to counteract his victories by bringing to Paris one of Italy's most renowned opera composers, Niccolò Piccini (1728–1800). The climax of the rivalry between the two composers came when both were commissioned by the Opéra to write music for the same subject, *Iphigénie en Tauride.* Gluck's opera was given first (May 18, 1779) and was a triumph. Piccini's opera was received coldly. Gluck's victory was now complete. His last years were spent in Vienna as an invalid, due to partial paralysis. He died in Vienna of an apoplectic stroke on November 15, 1787.

THE MAN

ROMAIN ROLLAND

Gluck's appearance is known to us through the fine portraits of the period: through Houdon's bust, Duplessis' painting, and several written descriptions—notes made by Burney in 1772 in Vienna, by Christian von Mannlich in 1773 in Paris, by Reichardt in 1782 and 1783 in Vienna.

He was tall, broad-shouldered, strong, moderately stout, and of compact and muscular frame. His head was round, and he had a large red face strongly pitted with the marks of smallpox. His hair was brown, and powdered. His eyes were gray, small and deep-set but very bright; and his expression was intelligent but hard. He had raised eyebrows, a large nose, full cheeks and chin, and a thick neck. Some of his features rather recall those of Beethoven and Handel. He had little singing voice, and what there was sounded hoarse though expressive. He played the harpsichord in a rough and boisterous way, thumping it but getting orchestral effects out of it.

In society he often wore a stiff and solemn air, but he was quickly roused to anger. Burney, who saw Handel and Gluck, compared their characters. "Gluck's temper," he said, "was as fierce as Handel's, and Handel's was a terror to everybody." Gluck lacked self-control, was irritable, and could not get used to the customs of society. He was plain-spoken to the verge of coarseness, and, according to Christian von Mannlich, on the occasion of his first visit to Paris, he scandalized twenty times a day those who spoke to him. He was insensible to flattery but was enthusiastic about his own works. That did not prevent him, however, from judging them fairly. He liked few people—his wife, his niece, and some friends; but he was undemonstrative and without any of the sentimentality of the period; he also held all exaggeration in horror and never made much of his own people. He was a jolly fellow, nevertheless, especially after drinking—for he drank and ate heartily until apoplexy killed him. There was no idealism about him, and he had no illusions about either men or things. He loved money and did not conceal the fact. He was also very selfish, "especially at the table," von Mannlich says, "where he seemed to think he had a natural right to the best morsels."

On the whole he was a rough sort and in no way a man of the world, for he was without sentiment, seeing life as it was and born to fight and break down obstacles like a wild boar with blows of its snout. He had unusual intelligence in matters outside his art and would have made a writer of no small ability if he had wished, for his pen was full of sharp and acrid humor and crushed the Parisian critics and pulverized La Harpe. Truly he had so much revolutionary and republican spirit in him that there was no one to equal him in that direction. No sooner had he arrived in Paris than he treated the court and society in a way no other artist had ever had the courage to do. On the first night of *Iphigénie en Aulide,* and at the last moment, after the king, the queen, and all the court had been invited, he declared that the performance could not be given because the singers were not ready; and in spite of accepted custom and people's remarks, the piece was put off until another time. He had a quarrel with Prince Hénin because he did not greet the prince properly when they met at a party, and all Gluck said was, "The custom in Germany is to rise only for people one respects." And—sign of the times—nothing would induce him to apologize; more than that, Prince Hénin had to go to Gluck when he wished to see him.

Gluck allowed the courtiers to pay him attentions. At rehearsals he appeared in a nightcap and without his wig and would get the noble lords present to help him with his toilet, so that it became an honor to be able to hand him his coat or his wig. He held the duchess of Kingston in esteem because she once said that "genius generally signified a sturdy spirit and a love of liberty."

In all these traits one sees the Encyclopedists' man—the mistrustful artist jealous for his freedom, the plebeian genius, and Rousseau's revolutionary.

THE COMPOSER

WILLIAM FOSTER APTHORP

In the year 1741, when Handel's last opera, *Deidamia,* was given in London, Gluck's first, *Artaserse,* was brought out in Milan, a coincidence to be deemed significant by superstition. The grand autocrat of the old regime makes his parting bow just as the herald of the new comes upon the scene: *"le roi est mort! vive le roi!"* . . .

Even in this, his first opera, he determined to cut loose from many of the traditions of the "oratorio" school, and write music that should be at once dramatic and more scenic. But he told no one of his intention, and finished his score—all but one aria—to suit himself. With this one aria lacking, the opera was put into rehearsal, and every musical dabster present pooh-poohed the "new style" most contemptuously. This Gluck had counted on; before the final rehearsal he wrote the missing aria wholly in the conventional style, and a still larger gathering of *cognoscenti* than had been at the first rehearsal praised it highly, even suspecting it of coming from the pen of Giovanni Battista Sammartini. The audience on the opening night straightway quashed this verdict, though, crying out that that particular aria was simply insipid and quite unworthy of the rest of the score. Thus did our young *Oberpfälzer* slyboots score one off his first judges!

So Gluck had from the first this ambition to make the opera more dramatic than his predecessors and contemporaries had done. But he had as yet no definite formula; his innovations were still evolutionary rather than revolutionary; he did nothing that could be called radical. Yet what he did was new enough to scare the critics who, as academic policemen, guarded nothing more carefully than the inviolable sacredness of the traditional form. But, if severely handled at times by the critics, Gluck would now and then get compensating sympathy from others. When a certain passage in the aria *"Se mai senti spirarti sul volto"* in his *Clemenza di Tito* (1751) was scathingly criticized, it was shown to old Francesco Durante (1684–1755) who said: "I do not feel like deciding whether this passage is entirely in accordance with the rules of composition; but this I can tell you, that all of us, myself to begin with, would be very proud of having thought of and written such a passage."

From 1741 on, Gluck continued writing Italian operas; with enormous success in Italy and Vienna, in spite of the critics. He traveled a good deal, and the hearing of some Rameau operas in Paris must have given him wholesome food for meditation. From about 1755 to 1761 he showed signs of lapsing into mere conventionalism and seemed to treat opera-writing as sheer practice work, to gain technical facility. He had plainly become dissatisfied with the scope and efficacy of his dramatic innovations in opera, and was meditating a more thorough and logically formulated reform.

At last, in or about 1760, he met the right man to help him: the Italian poet, Raniere de Calzabigi. With him he talked the problem over: the defects of the Italian *opera seria* and how these defects were best to be cured. The two pitched upon the following items as lying at the root of the reigning evil: the irresponsible vanity of the virtuoso singer, and the flaccid conventionality of the Metastasio libretto—full of poetic beauty (of a sort) but almost totally lacking dramatic quality, especially such as could be intensified by music.

The practical upshot was that Calzabigi wrote the text of *Orfeo ed Euridice* and Gluck set it to music. One cannot help smiling at the work's having first to be submitted to Metastasio, to avoid the foregone conclusion of a fiasco; the court poet's influence was not to be trifled with! Still more one must smile at Metastasio's carry-

78

ing his friendship for Gluck and Calzabigi to the point of "agreeing to offer no active opposition to the new work," sure in his good heart that the public would take the trouble of damning it off his hands; he little dreamt that he was digging his own grave!

Orfeo, brought out at the Vienna Burgtheater on October 5, 1762, was the first cannon-shot of the new revolution. It was no "*Veni, vidi, vici,*" being considerably discussed at first; but the public came to it gradually. Much the same was true of *Alceste*—libretto by Calzabigi after Euripides—given on December 16, 1767. This work fairly separated the sheep from the goats in the Viennese public; the more seriously inclined saw that it was on a still higher plane of tragic grandeur than *Orfeo,* but a large mass of opera goers found it rather too much of a good thing. "If this is the sort of evening's entertainment the Court Opera is to provide, goodbye; we can go to church without paying two gulden!" Gluck had to find out that fighting long-established convention is no bed of roses, and that impeccably attired patrons of aristocratic opera are much inclined to resent seriousness that has not been cured of its deformity by sweetly-warbling divinities of the virtuoso species. But unquestionable success came with time, and *Alceste* established Gluck's position even more firmly than *Orfeo* had done.

Passing over *Paride e Elena* (1770)—a strong work, but ill received by the public—we come to Gluck's meeting with the second poet who was to have a determining influence on his destiny: Du Rollet, attaché to the French legation in Vienna. Du Rollet encouraged Gluck's already-formed wish to go to Paris. . . . [Gluck] had become dissatisfied with the executive means he found in Vienna and longed for the Académie de Musique where there were "well-skilled and intelligent actors, who combined a noble and soulful play of gesture with the art of song." Du Rollet took Racine's *Iphigénie en Aulide* and turned it into a libretto, Gluck set to work forthwith upon the score; even before it was completed it was pronounced to be just the thing for Paris.

To wish to go to Paris was one thing; to get officially invited there, another. It seemed to French chauvinism that Paris already had quite enough foreigners to put up with in resident Italian musicians, and that the prospect of having to do with an admittedly strong

German, and an aesthetic revolutionary to boot, was rather appalling. There was plotting and counterplotting galore, letter-writing without end. At last Marie Antoinette's influence carried the day—she had been Gluck's pupil in Vienna before her marriage.

When Gluck came to Paris in 1773 with *Iphigénie* all ready for the boards, his expectations of the personnel of the Académie de Musique were not wholly fulfilled. He found the acting as good as he had expected, but the principals, chorus, and orchestra had fallen into the most deplorable musical habits; it took all his personal force, indomitable Teutonic pertinacity, and skill as a conductor to whip them up to the mark. He succeeded though, and *Iphigénie en Aulide* was brought to a satisfactory performance on April 19, 1774. Then the storm broke loose!

The chief contestants in this famous Gluck controversy were, on Gluck's side, the Abbé Arnaud and the *Anonyme de Vaugirard* (really Suard by name); on the opposing side, Marmontel, La Harpe, Guinguené, d'Alembert, the Chevalier de Chastilleux, Framéry, and Coqueau. Grimm held a dignifiedly neutral position, or tried to make believe he did; two of the most important of Gluck's favorers were Jean-Jacques Rousseau and Voltaire, but neither of the two took any active part in the fight. La Harpe—whose sharp wit fairly took the bit in its teeth and got beyond his own or any one's control —was the *enfant terrible* of the whole business, and did his own side as much harm as good; the *Anonyme de Vaugirard* took an especial delight in getting a rise out of him and prodding him to desperation.

Upon the whole, with all the wit, acute thought, and literary ability brought to bear upon the matter, first and last, this once-great controversy is not very edifying reading now. It is always the same old story. . . . Read the discussion between Monteverdi and Artusi . . ., the pen-and-ink tiffs between Wagnerians and anti-Wagnerians . . ., and you will have read practically all that was urged for and against Gluck. . . . The anti-Gluck side of the controversy is well summarized by Schmid: "These criticisms had two different purposes: first they tried to prove that the Ritter von Gluck lacked all power of song, and next, that he set things to music that were not appropriate to song."

The impression produced by *Iphigénie en Aulide* as the performances wore on was still strengthened by *Orfeo ed Euridice* given in August 1774. Gluck returned to Vienna for a while, taking with him a remodelled version of the text of his *Alceste* by du Rollet and Quinault's libretto of *Armide,* meaning to retouch the former score and reset the latter text for Paris. He was at work on both scores in Vienna when he got the news of the latest trick of his opponents in Paris: the Italian, Niccolò Piccini had been invited and was to set Quinault's *Roland* for the Académie de Musique. Gluck's pride was bitten to the quick; a flaming letter of his to du Rollet found its way (without his leave) into the *Année littéraire,* and only served still further to exasperate the opposition. The Italophiles now had a champion of their own, and the Gluck controversy became the Gluck-Piccini war, compared to which the old Handel-Bononcini business in London was a mere squabble.

In 1776, Gluck came back to Paris, and *Alceste* was given at the Académie de Musique on April 23. It was a bad night for the Gluckists; the opera was roundly hissed, the disappointed composer whimpering out *"Alceste est tombée!"* upon a friend's shoulder. *"Oui, tombée du ciel"* replied the latter, fain to seek consolation in an epigram. But the fiasco was only for a while; the gradual success of *Alceste* in Vienna was repeated in Paris, and Gluck once more ended by carrying the day.

On September 23, 1777, *Armide* was brought out; the immediate result was about the same as usual, only that indifference took the place of hissing. For one thing, the anti-Gluckists could not howl at Gluck's "impudence" in daring to reset a text already set by the great Lully, as it had been feared they would; for their own Piccini had put them in a glass house by setting Quinault's *Roland* of which Lully was also the original composer. Moreover, Gluck had paid French taste no mean compliment in taking Quinault's *Armide* exactly as it stood, without subjecting it to those modifications which he had had in all his previous classical libretti. But the indifference with which *Armide* was greeted at first soon wore off, and by the time Piccini was ready with his *Roland* Gluck's position was again very strong, indeed. Piccini, to say the truth, was a rather laggardly champion, taking an infinite time in coming up to scratch, which is partly to be accounted for by the poor man's not knowing a word

81

of French when he first set out to work on his score. But on January 27, 1778, *Roland* was at last brought out, after endless trouble and squabbling at rehearsals; as a first cannon-shot into the Gluckist camp, it did a certain amount of execution, at least the controversy became doubly acrid after it. It remained at white heat until the final "duel" settled matters.

It was agreed that both Gluck and Piccini should write an opera, *Iphigénie en Tauride;* they could thus fight it out between them on the same ground. Gluck took a libretto by Guillard; Piccini, one by Dubreuil. This "duel," as usual, was rather a long one, Gluck's opera being given on May 18, 1779, Piccini's not until January 23, 1781, some time after Gluck had left Paris for good. The result, however, was decisive; Gluck's *Iphigénie* capped the climax of his Paris success, and was indeed the first of his Paris operas that won unquestionable public favor on the opening night, whereas Piccini's had a mere *succès d'estime* even with its own party, the more eager of whom tried to explain its quasi-failure with the general public by the undeniable fact that, on the second night, the beauteous Laguerre (who sang Iphigénie) was hopelessly the worse for strong liquor—*"Iphigénie en champagne!"* said pert Sophie Arnould, who had sung Gluck's first Iphigénie.

It is quite plain that the success of Gluck's *Iphigénie en Tauride* was thoroughly genuine, based on the quality of the work itself. No less strong an opera could have so utterly routed Piccini's as it did; especially as Gluck, after his *Iphigénie*, had had a palpable failure with his *Écho et Narcisse* on September 24, 1779, thus leaving Paris with his latest opera on record as a fiasco. Piccini was, in truth, no weakling at all; he was even something of a dramatic reformer in opera himself, quite as much as Gluck in his earlier Italian and Viennese days. But Gluck had far outstripped him since then, and . . . Piccini was swept from the stage into oblivion, not because he was weak, but because Gluck was stronger. . . . Had he not been inadvisedly brought to Paris to take part in that unequal contest with the doughty Austrian, he might have gone comfortably down in history as a worthy forerunner of the Gluck reform; but, being brought face to face with and in opposition to it, he was crushed.

Écho et Narcisse was Gluck's last work for the stage; with it he leaves the history of opera.

As a reformer, Gluck was but little of a radical, hardly anything of a theorist. The best confession of artistic faith we have from his pen, his preface to *Alceste*, stands in history with *Euridice* of Jacopo Peri (1561–1633) and Victor Hugo's to *Cromwell* as one of the most famous of its kind. But there is very little theorizing in it; it is, for the most part, negative in character, pointing out what is most to be avoided in opera writing. It is a document of sheer sound artistic common sense, not a philosophico-scientific marshalling of principles to a firmly based theory; admirable as far as it goes, but not going far. Had Gluck's reform rested with this document alone, there would have been little life in it.

The real essence and mainspring of this much talked-of reform was Gluck's own intrinsic dramatic genius; his true strength as a reformer lay in his work, not in his doctrine. In him the old dramatic spirit of Peri, Monteverdi, and Pier Francesco Cavalli (1602–76) breathed forth fresh and strong again; and it was the vigorous expression he gave to this spirit in his music that won him adherents, while his ruthless sacrifice of the time-honored conventional operatic frippery to this expression made him enemies among those to whom old habits were dear.

What was new in Gluck was his musico-dramatic individuality, his style, for there was little really new in his principles. Not only did these date back, as far as they went, to the earliest days of opera, but the artistic sins and abuses he stigmatized—the slavish subserviency of composers to the whims of the virtuoso singer, the sacrifice of dramatic interest to irrelevant musical developments—had been pointed out and deplored by more than one musician before him.

Gluck's reform did not lack precursory heralds; the evils he set himself to cure had long been recognized as such, and he was not the first to attempt to cure them. But he was the first to strike the decisive blow, to go, if not quite to the root of the matter, at least as near to the root as was necessary for his purpose. And, as for his lack of radicalism, note how, in his preface, all of his negative theses have their conditioning *if* and *when*. He does not oppose vocal ornamentation, for instance, absolutely and along the whole line, but only when it becomes damaging to dramatic common sense. He showed the same lack of uncompromising radicalism in his practice: there is many a vocal show-piece in his operas, but brought in the right place, not into the midst of an ardent dramatic action.

Gluck is fairly to be regarded as the father of modern opera; a sufficient commentary on this is the very fact that his are the earliest operas that hold the stage to this day. He followed Karl Philipp Emanuel Bach (1714–88) and Haydn in employing a standard composition of the orchestra, and banished the time-honored harpsichord from it; he was thus the first opera composer to write out his scores completely, leaving nothing to be added by the harpsichordist. He was equally great in impassioned or pathetic melody and in every form of recitative; his dramatic use of the chorus can hardly be surpassed in mastery. The opening scenes of the first and second acts of *Orfeo*—Euridice's funeral rites and Orfeo's entrance into Hades—are still unsurpassed masterpieces in this last particular.

Like most "new" men, Gluck was terribly fastidious about the style in which his works were to be given. Concerning Orfeo's aria, *"Che farò senza Euridice?"* he writes to the Duke of Braganza: "Were one to make the slightest change in it, in the tempo or the mode of expression, it would become an air for the marionette stage. In a piece of this order, a more or less sustained note, a forcing of the tone, a neglect of the proper tempo, a trill, roulade, etc., can entirely destroy the effect of a scene." He was an inexorable rehearser, infinitely hard to satisfy.

In a specific sense, Gluck's great achievement was to fix the form of French grand opera for nearly a century, taking the form as already established by Lully and Rameau for a basis. What may be called the Gluck formula subsisted with but slight modification in France until Meyerbeer came above the horizon. From *Orfeo ed Euridice* to *Iphigénie en Tauride,* his operas are distinctly *grand* operas; to produce their proper effect, they need not only fine acting and singing and a competent orchestra, but a vast, well-equipped stage and the most copious spectacular paraphernalia, especially a superb ballet. They are essentially spectacular operas.

Gluck united in an unparalleled degree warmth of temperament with a certain classic reserve in expression; he was at home

84

in classical and mythological subjects, in the stately classic manner. The true "romantic" strenuousness he had not; he would have made but a poor hand at it with a Shakespearian libretto. But it would be a dull ear that could not catch the poignancy that lurks behind his measured dignity of expression, a dull heart that did not beat responsively to the expansive force of his emotional heat. Perhaps he is at his most poignant in his musical pictures of perfect happiness; in grief and pathos he is great; but in serene, unalloyed bliss, greater still. There is a deeper well of tears in the chorus of the beatified spirits in his *Orfeo* than in *"Che farò senza Euridice?"* or *"Malheureuse Iphigénie!"* Few men have produced such overwhelming effects on the lyric stage with so beautiful a simplicity of means; let us part from him with his pet maxim (whether wholly true or not matters little) on his lips: "Simplicity and truth are the sole right principles of the beautiful in works of art."

GLUCK SPEAKS

When I undertook to set the opera *Alceste* to music, I resolved to avoid all those abuses which had crept into Italian opera through the mistaken vanity of singers and the unwise compliance of composers, and which had rendered it wearisome and ridiculous, instead of being, as it once was, the grandest and most imposing stage work of modern times. I endeavored to reduce music to its proper function, that of seconding poetry by enforcing the expression of the sentiment, and the interest of the situations, without interrupting the action, or weakening it by superfluous ornament. My idea was that the relation of music to poetry was much the same as that of harmonious coloring and well-disposed light and shade to an accurate drawing, which animates the figures without altering their outlines. I have therefore been very careful never to interrupt a singer in the heat of a dialogue in order to introduce a tedious ritornelle, nor to stop him in the middle of a piece either for the purpose of displaying the flexibility of his voice on some favorable vowel, or that the orchestra might give him time to take breath before a long sustained note. Furthermore, I have not thought it right to hurry through the second part of a song if the words happened to be the most important of the whole, in order to repeat the first part regularly four times over; or to finish the air where the sense does not end in order to allow the singer to exhibit his power of varying the passage at pleasure. In fact, my object was to put an end to abuses against which good taste and good sense have long protested in vain.

My idea was that the overture ought to indicate the subject and prepare the spectators for the character of the piece they are about to see; that the instruments ought to be introduced in proportion to the degree of interest and passion in the words; and that it was necessary above all to avoid making too great a disparity between the recitative and the air of a dialogue, so as not to break the sense of a period or awkwardly interrupt the movement and animation of a scene.

I also thought that my chief endeavor should be to attain a grand simplicity, and consequently I have avoided making a parade of difficulties at the cost of clearness; I have set no value on novelty as such, unless it was naturally suggested by the situation and suited to the expression. In short, there was no rule which I did not consider myself bound to sacrifice for the sake of effect.

JOSEPH HAYDN

1 7 3 2 – 1 8 0 9

FRANZ JOSEPH HAYDN was born in Rohrau, lower Austria, on March 31, 1732. As a child he went to live in the house of a relative, Johann Matthias Frankh, who gave him a thorough musical training. Between 1740 and 1748 Haydn was a chorister at St. Stephen's Cathedral in Vienna. During that period he earned his living by teaching, playing the harpsichord, and doing hack work, but all the while immersing himself deeply into serious music study. In 1755 he was engaged by Karl Joseph von Fürnberg as conductor of his orchestra, for which he wrote various nocturnes and divertimentos. It was during this period that he also created his first string quartets. While employed at the palace of Count Morzin, between 1758 and 1760, he wrote his first symphonies. In 1760 he married Maria Anna Keller, a marriage that proved unhappy from the beginning and soon gave way to a permanent separation. In 1761, Haydn became second Kapellmeister for Prince Paul Anton Esterházy at his estate in Eisenstadt. When the Esterházys built a new palace at Esterház, Haydn assumed the status of full Kapellmeister (1766) and held this post for almost a quarter of a century. For the many concert and opera performances at Esterház, Haydn produced a vast repertory of compositions in virtually every field and form, arriving at full maturity as creative artist. He rarely left Esterház, except for occasional visits to Vienna where he met Mozart and became one of his most devoted friends and admirers.

In 1790, Haydn withdrew from his Esterház post and went to live in Vienna. In 1791 and 1794, Johann Peter Salomon, impresario and violinist, invited him to London to lead orchestral concerts. For these performances Haydn wrote twelve celebrated symphonies now identified as the *London* or *Salomon* Symphonies. Back in

Vienna after the second visit, Haydn wrote in 1797 a patriotic hymn which became the Austrian national anthem. Between 1798 and 1801 he completed two choral masterworks, *The Creation* and *The Seasons*, his first attempts at writing oratorios. He died in Vienna on May 31, 1809, and was buried in the Hundsthurm churchyard; in 1820 his remains were reinterred in the upper parish church of Eisenstadt.

THE MAN

ALBERT CHRISTOPH DIES

Haydn was something under middle height. The lower half of his figure was too short for the upper. This is frequently to be observed with small people of both sexes, but in Haydn it was very noticeable because he kept to the antiquated style of trousers reaching only to the hips. . . . His features were rather regular, his glance speaking, fiery and yet temperate, kindly and inviting. When he was in a serious mood his features, along with his glance, expressed dignity; otherwise he readily assumed a smiling mien in conversation. I never heard him laugh out loud. Haydn had a moderately strong build; his muscles were spare. His hawk nose (he suffered much from a nasal polyp which doubtless actually enlarged this organ) as well as the rest of his face was deeply marked with smallpox. The nose itself was pockmarked, so that the nostrils each had a different shape.

Haydn considered himself ugly and mentioned to me a prince and his wife who could not stand his appearance "because," he said, "I was too ugly for them." But this supposed ugliness lay not at all in the cut of his features but solely in the skin, eaten away with pockmarks and of a brown tint.

For the sake of cleanliness, Haydn wore, even in his youth, a wig with a braid and a few side curls. Fashion had no influence on the shape of his wig; until his death he remained faithful to the same style and wore the wig only two inches above his eyebrows, so that his forehead looked disproportionately low.

Orderliness seemed as native to him as industry. Tidiness and cleanliness were conspicuous in his person and in his whole household. He never, for instance, received visits before he was fully dressed. If surprised by a friend, he sought to gain at least enough time to put on his wig again.

His love of order prompted Haydn to arrange a careful schedule of work and business hours; he was displeased when necessity forced him to a deviation. It would be far from true, however, to say he was a man who lived by the clock. At the end I will set forth his daily schedule; from this the reader will be able to observe how the hours were divided and assigned. He was a sensible manager of money. I several times heard him accused of avarice by people who did not know him very well. I had opportunity enough to inquire into this charge and found it false. The miser has no feeling for the want of others and does not help even his nearest relatives. When Haydn needed money he was most energetic about earning it; but as soon as it had been acquired and was in his hands, he felt the disposition to share it. He could often call his household together with the words, "Children, here is money!" and give to each, according to his service, five, ten, fifteen or twenty florins.

There was in his character much cheerfulness, sport and mischief, the more popular and also the more subtle, but always the most highly original musical wit. People have often called it humor and have traced back to it, with justice, his predilection for musical teasing.

He was a man of gratitude. As soon as he could, he secretly repaid kindnesses done him in his youthful years—but did not forget, meanwhile, his numerous relatives. Honor and fame were the two driving forces that dominated him; yet no instance is known to me when they degenerated to a greed for renown. His natural modesty prevented this. He never disparaged other musicians.

In younger years he was said to have been highly susceptible to love. Of this I would have said nothing, but I noticed that into old age he remained most courteous to women and even kissed their hands.

His division of the hours and the order that resulted may strike some of my readers as machine-like. But if you consider the many works that flowed from Haydn's pen you will admit that he simply used his time wisely. He had observed his body and knew what he could expect of it; idle he could not be; change gratified him; order had come to be second nature to him; and so his daily schedule took shape.

In the warmer season Haydn got up at half-past six and shaved himself at once. This task he left to no other hand until he was in his seventy-third year. Then he dressed completely. If a pupil was present while he was dressing, he had to play the lesson assigned on the piano. The mistakes were noted, principles thereon expounded, and a new assignment then given for the next lesson.

At eight o'clock Haydn took his breakfast. Right after that he sat down at the piano and improvised until he found ideas that served his intent. These he immediately committed to paper. Thus were born the first draft of his compositions.

At half-past eleven he received visitors or took a walk and paid visits himself. The hour from two to three was set aside for dinner. After dinner he always undertook some little domestic chore or else he went into his library and took a book to read.

At four o'clock he went back to his musical labors. He took the drafts sketched out in the morning and orchestrated them. To this work he devoted three or four hours. At eight o'clock in the evening he usually went out but came home at nine and either set to work on his scores again or took a book and read until ten o'clock. The time around ten was reserved for the evening meal. Haydn had made it a rule to consume nothing in the evening but bread and wine; this rule he violated only now and then when he was invited somewhere for supper. He loved gay talk at the table; in general he liked cheerful conversation. At half-past eleven he went to bed; in his old age, even later.

Winter time, as a rule, made no difference to his daily schedule except that he rose half an hour later in the morning; everything else remained as in the summer.

In advanced age, especially in the last five or six years of his life, bodily weakness and illness ruined the schedule described above. The active man could at last no longer work.

THE COMPOSER

W. OLIVER STRUNK

In Haydn's London diary, among the entries for 1791, there is this note: "On December 5 there was a fog so thick that one might have spread it on bread. In order to write I had to light a candle as early as eleven o'clock." Could Haydn have known what had happened in Vienna on that critical morning, he would not have cared to write at all. As it was, he wrote on; two weeks later he received news of Mozart's death. "I am as pleased as a child at the thought of coming home and embracing my good friends," he writes to Marianne von Genzinger on the 20th. "My one regret is that the great Mozart will not be among them, if it be true, as I trust it is not, that he is dead. Not in a hundred years will posterity see such a talent again."

Though the Haydn who penned these lines was no longer a young man, his vitality was unimpaired, his productivity unabated. "I am still sprightly and in the full possession of my strength," he had assured Mozart before leaving Vienna; early in 1792 he reports with evident satisfaction to Frau von Genzinger that he has never written so much in one year as in that just passed. His reputation, already distinguished, now assumed such proportions that, in later life, he often insisted that he had become famous in Germany only by way of England. Strangers stopped to stare at him, exclaiming: "You are a great man!" Within less than a year three fashionable artists had painted his portrait. Honored with a Doctor's degree conferred by Oxford University, fêted by professional and amateur musicians, sought after by peer and commoner alike, Haydn took most satisfaction, perhaps, in his new-found independence. "How sweet a little liberty tastes!" he writes. "I used often to sigh for freedom—now I have it, in a measure. I appreciate it, too, though my mind is burdened with a multitude of tasks. The knowledge that I am no longer a hired servant repays me for all my trouble." For thirty years Haydn had written for select group of connoisseurs;

91

now, at fifty-nine, the opportunity to address a wider audience had come to him at last. The change brought with it a new sense of responsibility—to art and to society—a sense of responsibility that found ultimate expression in his great oratorios, *The Creation* (1798) and *The Seasons* (1801).

As Mozart's biographer, Otto Jahn, once observed, the difficult task is to portray the Haydn of the 50's, 60's, and 70's. "Thus far we know little, if anything, about him and about the conditions and influences to which he was subject. The Haydn everyone knows is not Mozart's forerunner, but his contemporary and successor." Our knowledge of the musical environment from which Haydn sprang goes further than Jahn's, but for most of us the works of his earlier years still remain uncharted territory. Let us begin, then, on familiar ground—with the music of the post-Mozartian Haydn. We will follow him the more easily through the vicissitudes and complexities of his upward climb if we have first seen the goal at which he aimed. And we will recognize the more readily that his music is something more than an introduction to Mozart and Beethoven, that his role in musical history is something more than a pioneer, if we take as our starting point the works of his last period.

During the London years Haydn is preoccupied with instrumental composition; after his return to Vienna, "the father of the symphony" tends more and more to write for voices. Up until the time of the composition of *The Seasons* there is no slackening of his pace. The piano variations in F minor (1793), the three last piano sonatas (c. 1794), a set of three piano trios dedicated to Mrs. Schroeter, his "invariable and truly affectionate" correspondent (c. 1795), another for Mrs. Bartolozzi, the wife of the London engraver (1795–96), the six "Apponyi" string quartets (1793), and the twelve "London" symphonies (1791–95)—these major instrumental works are surely no mean achievement for a man in his sixties. To the next five years belong the eight string quartets dedicated to Count Erdödy and to Prince Lobkowitz (c. 1799), four of the last six Masses (1796–99), the Te Deum in C (c. 1798), and the two oratorios. With the composition of *The Seasons*, Haydn's creative activity is practically ended. In 1801 he writes the *Schöpfungsmesse* and in 1802 the *Harmonie-messe*. Then, in 1803, he completes two movements of his last string quartet (1803), dedicated to Count Fries. It was never finished. "I am no longer able to work at anything big," he writes to Thomson in the following year. "My age weakens me more and more." Yet for a time his imagination remains as keen as ever: in 1806, on his seventy-fourth birthday, he expresses the conviction that there are no limits to music's possibilities, that what may still be accomplished in music is far greater than what has been accomplished in the past. Often, he says, there come to him ideas through which the art might be advanced much further; his physical limitations, however, no longer permit him to undertake their expression.

"The secret of music's effect lies essentially in this: that in composition everything comes as it must come, yet otherwise than we expect." However one-sided his view of the romantic scene may have been, Eduard Hanslick was a shrewd judge of classical values; in its application to the music of the last quarter of the 18th century this brilliant aphorism of his comes very near the mark. The kind of effect he has in mind is not possible in every stage of the development of a style. In the experimental stage its presence is inconceivable; in the conventional stage, which follows, we seldom meet with it. Only when the rules of the game are well established is it feasible for the composer to play on the expectation of his listener. And even then, to play on expectation he must first arouse it. To secure emphasis he must first exercise self-control. He cannot afford to be continually surprising his listener. He must be simple before he is complex, regular before he is irregular, straightforward before he is startling. The composer of the *Surprise Symphony* understood the working of these first principles. He could be simple, regular, and straightforward; this is a point that need not be brought home to the modern reader, who is only too apt to exaggerate the extent—or misunderstand the purpose—of this side of Haydn's writing. He could also be original without being eccentric; this the more generous among his contemporaries were always ready to concede. "That sounds queer," Kozeluch once remarked to Mozart, startled by a bold transition in a Haydn quartet, "would you have written it that way?" "Scarcely," Mozart replied, "but do you know why? Because neither you nor I would have hit on the idea."

Eminently suited to the display of the particular sort of originality that consists in playing on the expectation of the listener is the sonata form, as Haydn saw it toward the end of his career. In this type of movement the climax of interest regularly coincides with the beginning of the third part—the return of the principal tonality and the principal idea; artistic success or failure depends largely on the way this climax is hastened or delayed and on the angle from which it is approached. Once the third part has begun the listener's recollection of what has gone before leads him to anticipate the composer's every step; in this part of the design each deviation from the familiar path is a potential source of aesthetic pleasure or disappointment.

The compositions Haydn wrote for London are so full of this kind of originality that it is difficult to single out any one work to illustrate it. Let us choose one of the most familiar—the last of the three symphonies of 1795, the last of all Haydn's symphonies, the so-called "London" Symphony in D. Turn to the finale and observe how skillfully Haydn prepares the "return," growing more and more deliberate as he approaches the critical point, wandering further and further from the key at which he intends to arrive, then thinking better of it and making an unlooked-for close that is at once the end of the second part and the beginning of the third; before we have realized it, the "return" has been accomplished. Or turn to the first movement, compare the third part with the first, and observe how artfully Haydn delays restatement of the "second subject"—as is quite usual with him, it is the "first subject" all over again;—only when we have almost given up hope of hearing it does he bring it in at last. It is in the original treatment of just such details as these that the superiority of the London Haydn over the rank and file is most evident. In the compelling audacity of their design, the compositions Haydn wrote for London represent the final development of form in classical music. While he was writing these compositions, plans were already taking shape in his mind for a work that was to make his name last in the world.

"Since time immemorial the Creation has been regarded as the most exalted, most awe-inspiring picture that mankind can contemplate. To accompany this great drama with suitable music can surely have no other result than that of intensifying these sacred emotions in men's hearts and of making them more submissive to the benevolent omnipotence of their Creator." These lines from a letter Haydn wrote in 1801—three years after he had completed *The Creation*—throw a revealing light on the frame of mind in which the aging master approached this most exacting of all the tasks he set himself. For the devout Catholic who habitually began and ended his manuscripts with the words, "In nomine Domini" and "Laus Deo," the subject was made to order. The work of composition occupied him for two full years. "I spend much time on it," he said, "because I intend it to last a long time." For once, the composer who "never wrote until he was sure of himself" made systematic sketches. To Griesinger, his first biographer, he confessed that he had half finished his score before its success was apparent to him. "I was never so devout as during the time I was working on *The Creation*," Griesinger quotes Haydn as saying. "Every day I fell on my knees and prayed God that he might give me strength to bring this work to a satisfactory conclusion." Early in 1798, shortly after the composer's sixty-sixth birthday, that satisfactory conclusion was announced. Before the oratorio had been publicly performed, Haydn was at work on *The Seasons*.

"With the decrease of my mental powers, my inclination and the urge to work seem almost to increase," Haydn wrote in June, 1799, to the publishers Breitkopf & Härtel. "Every day I receive many compliments—even on the fire of my last works; no one will believe what trouble and strain I endure to produce them." Goethe's friend Zelter called *The Seasons* "a work of youthful vigor and mature mastery." Schiller's friend Streicher came nearer the truth in 1809 when he called it "a musical debauch." "Without it," he added, "Haydn would assuredly have enjoyed ten more years of activity." Haydn himself said that *The Seasons* had "finished" him.

Haydn often regretted that he was never able to visit Italy. But it is a question whether he would have profited half as much from such a visit as he did from his two visits to England. Without them neither *The Creation* nor *The Seasons* would have been written. The two oratorios owe something to English poetry—one is based on an adaptation from Milton's *Paradise Lost,* the other on Thomson's *Seasons.* They owe more to the English audience and to the Anglicized Handel, whose music was virtually new to Haydn when he arrived in

95

London. The Handel Commemoration in 1791 and the "Concerts of Ancient Music" were revelations. To the English composer, Shield, who asked his opinion of *The Nations Tremble* in Handel's *Joshua*, Haydn replied that he had long been acquainted with music, but never knew half its powers before he heard it; when Shield praised the recitatives in Haydn's early oratorio *Il Ritorno di Tobia* (1775), Haydn declared that the recitative *Deeper and Deeper Still* in Handel's *Jephtha* surpassed them in pathos and contrast. Power, pathos, and contrast—these are the secrets of Handel's greatness, and when Haydn returned to Vienna he took them with him. Written for the concerts of the "Society of Noble Amateurs," *The Creation* and *The Seasons* speak to the plain man.

One type of artist is concerned with design, another with expression. Haydn is concerned with both. The classic perfection of the "London" symphonies and the "Apponyi" quartets has its counterpart in the romantic intensity of the works of his last years in Vienna. In the light of later development Haydn's romanticism may appear somewhat restrained to us; to his contemporaries it was bold and even startling. The rich sonorities of his last quartets and orchestral accompaniments point to Beethoven and to Weber. The simple piety of his *Creation* is no less affecting than the artless realism of his *Seasons*. The ordered lawlessness of his *Representation of Chaos* breaks down old barriers. "It is impossible and contrary to rule that so excellent a piece should be accepted, universally and at once, for what it is and alone can be," Zelter wrote in Breitkopf's journal. "Certain deep-rooted theories, derived from the works of an earlier period, remain eternally at odds with the spirit of progress, leading inevitably to the kind of criticism that is always demanding, but does not know how to accept." Haydn thanked Zelter for praising the *Chaos* by saying: "You could and would have written it just as I did." To which Zelter replied, modestly and with perfect truth: "I could never have written it as you did, great master, nor shall I ever be capable of doing so."

As he approached the end of his career, Haydn became increasingly sensible of the social responsibility of the artist, and of all the testimonials showered on him during his declining years he prized those most that bore witness to his honorable discharge of this obligation. He took particular pride, Griesinger tells us, in the honorary citizenship conferred on him by the municipal authorities of Vienna, seeing in this an illustration of the old saying, "Vox populi, vox Dei." Another tribute of the same kind, simpler, perhaps, but no less sincere, moved him to write what is at once the most revealing and the most touching of all his letters. From the little town of Bergen, capital of the island of Rügen in the Baltic, a society of amateurs wrote to thank him for the pleasure that performing his *Creation* had given its membership.

"Gentlemen: (Haydn replied) It was a truly agreeable surprise to me to receive so flattering a letter from a quarter to which I could never have presumed that the productions of my feeble talent would penetrate. Not only do you know my name, I perceive, but you perform my works, fulfilling in this way the wish nearest my heart: that every nation familiar with my music should adjudge me a not wholly unworthy priest of that sacred art. On this score you appear to quiet me, so far as your country is concerned; what is more, you give me the welcome assurance—and this is the greatest comfort of my declining years—that I am often the source from which you, and many other families receptive to heartfelt emotion, derive pleasure and satisfaction in the quiet of your homes. How soothing this reflection is to me!

"Often, as I struggled with obstacles of all kinds opposed to my works—often, as my physical and mental powers sank, and I had difficulty in keeping to my chosen course—an inner voice whispered to me: 'There are so few happy and contented men here below— on every hand care and sorrow pursue them—perhaps your work may some day be a source from which men laden with anxieties and burdened with affairs may derive a few moments of rest and refreshment.' This, then, was a powerful motive to persevere, this the reason why I can even now look back with profound satisfaction on what I have accomplished in my art through uninterrupted effort and application over a long succession of years."

The fifty most active years of his life—the fifty years between the first compositions and his *Seasons*—coincide with one of the most restless and fruitful half-centuries in all musical history—the half-century between Bach's death in 1750 and Beethoven's first sym-

97

phony in 1800. Old forms and old methods had gone the way of old ideals; pathos had yielded to sentiment, severity to informality; music had become less comprehensive, more individual, less uniform, more many-sided, less intellectual, more spontaneous. Tastes had changed, and a combination of forces—social, cultural, and artistic— had brought about a complete reversal of musical values. Before the pre-classical movement had reached its height in the music of Bach and Handel, these forces were already working toward its dissolution; by the middle of the century they had undermined the old structure and laid out in bold outline the ground plan of the new.

"We have gradually rid ourselves of the preconceived idea that great music is at home only in Italy. Respect for those illustrious names in *ini* and *elli* is disappearing, and Germans, formerly occupied with the modest business of accompaniment, have raised themselves to the first place in the orchestra of the powers. We no longer listen to the swaggering foreigners, and our scribes, who only yesterday were so bent on propagating fair copies of the empty eccentricities of Italians devoid of ideas, now vie with one another for the honor of making the works of their countrymen known."

So Marpurg wrote in 1749, and it is noteworthy that this somewhat rhetorical declaration of his, far from being a random observation, stands at the very beginning of his *Critical Musician*. That just at this time there should have been a belated reawakening of national feeling among German musicians is highly significant. Having assimilated all that Italy could give, Germany was ready to strike out for herself, and in her leading musical centers—Berlin, Mannheim, and Vienna—native musicians were even now contending for the supremacy.

It was at this moment that Haydn, dismissed at seventeen from the cathedral choir-school in Vienna, faced the problem of shifting for himself. His immediate musical environment, while not precisely dominated by the Italian tradition, was less aggressively German than that of Berlin or Mannheim; what is perhaps more important, it was an eminently popular environment, related in a variety of ways to the everyday life of the community. The popular theater was in a flourishing condition. Georg Christoph Wagenseil (1715–77), Josef Starzer (1726–87), and Johann Adam Karl Georg von

Reutter (1708–72) were putting the music of the street and the dance-hall to artistic uses in their serenades and divertimenti; Georg Matthias Monn (1717–50), another Viennese musician of the older generation, is thought to have been the first to introduce the minuet in a symphony. Haydn, true to his surroundings, began by composing music of just this kind. One of his earliest experiments was a serenade, and, according to one account, it was an improvised performance of this piece that brought him his first commission and led to the composition of his first "opera," *Der krumme Teufel* (1752). To the same category belong his earliest quartets, written for his first patron, Baron Fürnberg in Weinzierl, and the numerous divertimenti for various combinations that he wrote before and during his brief service as musical director to Count Morzin in Lukavec. *Le Midi* (1761), one of his first symphonies, already contains a minuet. To recognize the Haydn we know in the compositions of this early period is no easy matter; at no other time in his life is the Italian influence more marked. While contemptuously repudiating the "scribbler" Giovanni Battista Sammartini (1701–75), whom Mysliweczek had called the father of his style, Haydn was always ready to acknowledge his debt to Niccolò Porpora (1686–1768). Berlin and Mannheim are negligible factors, so far, though by 1760 Haydn was not only a fervent admirer of Bach's son Carl Philipp Emanuel (1732–95), but had already gone so far as to dedicate one of his compositions to Stamitz's patron, the Elector Karl Theodor. "I wrote industriously, but not quite correctly," Haydn said himself, and when in 1805 a score of his first mass was discovered and brought to him after fifty-three years, his comment was: "What pleases me most in this work is a certain youthful fire."

The next few years brought important changes in Haydn's outward circumstances and in the kind of music he was called upon to supply. In 1761, on his appointment as second Kapellmeister to Prince Paul Anton Esterházy at Eisenstadt, he found himself in a responsible and highly desirable position exceedingly favorable to the development of his gifts and reputation; in 1762, on Paul Anton's death and the arrival of his brother and successor, Prince Nicholas, his responsibilities were materially increased, for the new employer was not only an ardent music-lover, but an amateur performer as well, and the demand for new compositions was relentless and almost unlimited. Then, in March, 1766, Haydn was made first Kapell-meister, and a few months later the opening of the magnificent residence Prince Nicholas had built at Esterház—with its opera house seating four hundred and its marionette theater—again increased his responsibilities, obliging him to devote serious attention to operatic composition, a branch of music in which he had thus far had little experience.

Haydn's first fifteen years at Eisenstadt and Esterház constitute a period that is surely one of the most interesting of his long career: it is the period during which the foundation of his later reputation was laid; during which the works of his first maturity were written; during which he ceased to feel the influence of his lesser contemporaries and, abandoning their conventions, became himself a determining influence in the career of the younger Mozart. Entering the Ester-házy service an almost unknown musician, Haydn began at once to attract attention, not only in Vienna, but in other musical centers. In 1763, Breitkopf's catalogues announce eight "quadros" and six trios for strings, with two concertos and a divertimento for the harp-sichord, as available in manuscript; from the same year dates one of the earliest notices of Haydn on record, a manuscript note in an interleaved copy of Walther's *Lexikon* now in the Library of Congress: "Haydn, an incomparable musician and composer, lives in Vienna and distinguishes himself in the writing of fine quartets, trios, and symphonies." The first recorded publication of a work of Haydn's occurred in March of the following year, when the Paris publisher Venier advertised an edition of one of the early quartets in his series *Sinfonie a più Stromenti Composte da Vari Autori (Opera Decima Quarta)* under the title *Les noms inconnus bons à connoitre* (Unknown names worth knowing) in company with com-positions by Van Maldere, Beck, Pfeiffer, Schetky, and Fränzl. By 1775 a formidable array of Haydn's sonatas, duos, trios, quartets, and symphonies had been engraved (apparently without the composer's authorization!) in Paris, Amsterdam, and London; the Vienna edi-tions began in 1774 with Kurtzböck's printing of six sonatas. As early as 1766 Haydn is mentioned in magazines published in Leipzig and Hamburg, while in Vienna he was already being called "the darling of our nation." So universal, in fact, was the recognition accorded Haydn by the end of this period that in responding in 1776 to a request for an autobiographical sketch he could write: "In my chamber music I have had the good fortune to please almost everywhere, save in Berlin!"

Successively considered, the compositions of the decade 1765 to 1775 reveal Haydn's steadily increasing mastery of form and content. Not satisfied with the facile polish of his fourth series of string quartets (op. 9, 1769), he strove in those that followed toward greater refinement of workmanship, toward more intense formal concentration, toward the suppression of the episodic and conventional (op. 17, 1771), resorting in the last series written during this period (op. 20, 1772) to time-honored contrapuntal devices to enhance the interest and insure the balance of his texture. At the same time Haydn contrived to give his music a more individual note. In their book on Mozart, Wyzewa and Saint-Foix draw attention to certain particularly striking examples of this tendency in the works of the early 1770's—the C minor Piano Sonata (1771), the quartets op. 20, "à la fois pathétiques et savants" (1772), the Trauersymphonie (c. 1772) the Farewell Symphony (1772)—and speak of the year 1772 as the "romantic crisis" of Haydn's artistic career. A year or two later, the same writers tell us, still another change took place in Haydn's manner. Now he surrenders to the "galant" style, and henceforward his principal aim is to impress us agreeably or to amuse us with ingenious turns of musical rhetoric.

Then, in 1781, came the publication of the "Russian" quartets, op. 33, the series that ushered in the style Haydn himself described as "entirely new." Here is the turning point in his career. Until now Carl Philipp Emanuel Bach had been Haydn's principal model; with the appearance of the "Russian" quartets Mozart began to take Bach's place. In the "Paris" symphonies (1786), the Oxford Symphony (1788), and the two sets of quartets written in 1789 and 1790 for the Viennese wholesale merchant Johann Tost, Haydn attained full maturity, and the transition to the works of the last decade was only a step.

While Haydn had been at work, a new kind of music had grown from tentative beginnings to conscious maturity; his own music had itself passed through every stage in that growth, now following in a path cleared by others, now leading the way. With the possible exception of Handel, no great composer was ever more prolific; with the possible exception of Beethoven, no great composer ever maintained so fresh an outlook. Keeping pace with contemporary developments and more often anticipating them, Haydn ended even more progressively than he had begun.

HAYDN SPEAKS

As soon as I caught an idea, all my efforts were bent to make it conform to the rules of art and be supported by them. In this way I tried to help myself. It is in this that our new composers are most lacking: they line up one small passage after another and break off when they have hardly begun. Nothing remains in the memory of the hearer after he has listened to such works.

. . . . .

When I judged a thing to be beautiful, that is to say, when my ear and mind were satisfied with it, I preferred to let a little solecism creep in rather than to sacrifice it to a dry academic rhetoric.

. . . . .

I never was a quick writer, and always composed with care and deliberation. That alone is the way to compose works that will last, and a real connoisseur can see at a glance whether a score has been written in undue haste or not.

. . . . .

It is the air which is the charm of music, and it is that which is most difficult to produce. The invention of a fine melody is the work of genius. . . . In vocal composition the art of producing beautiful melody may now almost be considered as lost; and when a composer is so fortunate as to throw off a passage that is really melodious, he is sure, if he be not sensible of its excellence, to overwhelm and destroy it by the fullness and superfluity of his instrumental parts.

102

. . . . .

Art is free and must not be enslaved by mechanical regulations. The cultivated ear must decide, and I believe myself as capable as anyone of making laws in this respect. . . . Supposing an idea struck me as good and thoroughly satisfactory both to the ear and the heart. I would far rather pass over some slight grammatical error than sacrifice what seemed to me beautiful to any mere pedantic trifling.

. . . . .

I have had converse with emperors, kings, and great princes and have heard many flattering praises from them; but I do not wish to live on a familiar footing with such persons, and I prefer people of my own class.

. . . . .

Since God has given me a cheerful heart, He will forgive me for serving Him cheerfully. Whenever I think of the dear Lord, I have to laugh. My heart jumps for joy in my breast.

WOLFGANG AMADEUS MOZART

1756 – 1791

WOLFGANG AMADEUS MOZART was born in Salzburg, Austria, on January 27, 1756. He began to study the harpsichord when he was four, and wrote his first compositions at five. His childhood exploits in music have become legends, the yardstick by which all prodigies were henceforth measured. In his boyhood he made sensational appearances in European courts. Before he reached his fourteenth birthday he had four violin sonatas published in Paris, his first symphonies performed in London, and an opera buffa commissioned from the Austrian Emperor.

Strange to say, he was appreciated least of all in his native city. Despite his triumphs elsewhere in Europe, he was treated by his employer—the Salzburg Archbishop—like a menial servant, subjected to considerable abuse. In 1777 he sought escape from his ignominious existence by seeking a lucrative post elsewhere. He traveled throughout Germany, and in 1778 came to Paris. But the mature musician—even though a musician of formidable endowments and achievements—was much less electrifying than a child prodigy. Only insignificant offers came his way. Mozart had to return to Salzburg, to his humble post in the Archbishop's court.

The successful première of his opera, *Idomeneo*, in Munich on January 29, 1781, once again made him impatient with Salzburg. In 1782, he broke permanently with the city of his birth, and with his employer, and went to live in Vienna, from then on his permanent home. A commission from the Emperor to write an opera— *Die Entführung aus dem Serail (The Abduction from the Seraglio)*, introduced on July 16, 1782—encouraged him to believe that a turn of fortune had finally come. Optimistic about his future, Mozart married Constance Weber on August 4, 1782. But in Vienna, as in

104

Salzburg, he encountered only frustrations and disappointments. He made powerful enemies, most notably the influential court composer, Antonio Salieri (1750–1825), who did everything he could to impede Mozart's progress. Besides this, the frugal Emperor made no attempt to employ him. Compelled to earn a living by teaching and performing, Mozart lived in abject poverty. But nothing was able to stem the tide of his production. He wrote masterwork after masterwork in every conceivable form, of a quantity and a quality to stagger the imagination. Some in Vienna recognized Mozart's genius; one of these was Joseph Haydn who described the younger man as "the greatest composer I know either personally or by name."

There were some major successes, to be sure: that of *Le Nozze di Figaro* (*The Marriage of Figaro*), introduced at the Burgtheater on May 1, 1786; that of *Don Giovanni*, at Prague on October 29, 1787. There was even a post at the Viennese court: When Gluck died late in 1787, Mozart succeeded him as court composer and chamber musician, but at a sharply reduced salary.

Mozart's personal fortunes remained at a low ebb for the rest of his life. He was often compelled to turn to friends for sadly-needed loans to keep body and soul together. Impoverished, his spirit crushed, his body now wracked with pain through illness, he nevertheless continued to create crowning works of music. In the last year of his life—with his spiritual and physical resources at their lowest—he completed the opera *Die Zauberflöte* (*The Magic Flute*), introduced in Vienna on September 30, 1791; the Requiem, which was left unfinished by his death and was completed by his pupil, Süssmayr; the *Ave Verum*, for chorus; the B-flat major Piano Concerto; and the E-flat major String Quintet. He died in Vienna on December 5, 1791. After a pitiful ceremony, attended only by a handful of friends, Mozart was buried in a pauper's section of St. Marx Cathedral, with no tombstone or cross to identify the place.

THE MAN

MICHAEL KELLY

ADOLPH HEINRICH VON SCHLICHTEGROLL

He was a remarkably small man, very thin and pale, with a profusion of fine hair, of which he was rather vain. He gave me a cordial invitation to his house, of which I availed myself, and passed a great part of my time there. He always received me with kindness and hospitality. He was remarkably fond of punch, of which beverage I have seen him take copious draughts. He was also fond of billiards, and had an excellent billiard table in his home. Many and many a game have I played with him, but always came off second best. He gave Sunday concerts, which I always attended. He was kindhearted, and always ready to oblige, but so very particular when he played that, if the slightest noise were made, he instantly left off. . . . He conferred on me what I considered a high compliment. I had composed a little melody to a canzonetta of Metastasio which was a great favorite wherever I sang it. It was very simple, but had the good fortune to please Mozart. He took it and composed variations upon it, which were truly beautiful; and he had the further kindness and condescension to play them whenever he had an opportunity.*

. . . . .

Mozart never reached his natural growth. During his whole life his health was delicate. He was thin and pale, and though the form of his face was unusual, there was nothing striking in his physiognomy but its extreme variableness. The expression of his countenance changed every moment, but indicated nothing more than the pleasure or pain which he experienced at the instant. He was remarkable for a habit which is usually the attendant of stupidity. His body was perpetually in motion; he was either playing with his

---

* The above paragraph is by Kelly; those below are by von Schlichtegroll.

106

hands or beating the ground with his foot. There was nothing extraordinary in his other habits, except his extreme fondness for the game of billiards. He had a table in his house on which he played every day by himself when he had no one to play with. His hands were so habituated to the piano that he was rather clumsy in everything else. At table he never carved, or if he attempted to do so, it was with much awkwardness and difficulty. His wife usually undertook the office.

The same man who, from his earliest age, had shown the greatest expansion of mind in what related to his art, in other respects remained a child. He never knew how properly to conduct himself. The management of domestic affairs, the proper use of money, the judicious selection of his pleasures, and temperance in the enjoyment of them, were never virtues to his taste. The gratification of the moment was always uppermost with him. His mind was so absorbed by a crowd of ideas, which rendered him incapable of all serious reflection, that, during his whole life, he stood in need of a guardian to take care of his temporal affairs. His father was well aware of his weakness in this respect and it was on this account that he persuaded his wife to follow him to Paris in 1777, his engagements not allowing him to leave Salzburg himself.

But this man, so absent, so devoted to trifling amusements, appeared a being of a superior order as soon as he sat down to a piano. His mind then took wing, and his whole attention was directed to the sole object for which nature designed him, the harmony of sounds. The most numerous orchestra did not prevent him from observing the slightest false note, and he immediately pointed out, with surprising precision, by what instrument the fault was committed, and the note which should have been played.

Music was his constant employment and his most gratifying recreation. Never, even in his earliest childhood, was persuasion required to get him to go to the piano. On the contrary, it was necessary to take care that he did not injure his health by application. He was particularly fond of playing in the night. If he sat down to the instrument at nine o'clock in the evening, he never left it before midnight, and even then it was necessary to force him away from it, for he would have continued to modulate, to play voluntaries, the whole night. In his general habits he was the gentlest of men, but the least noise during the performance of music offended him violently. He was far above that affected or misplaced modesty which prevents many performers from playing till they have been repeatedly entreated. The nobility of Vienna often reproached him for playing with equal interest before any person that took pleasure in hearing him.

Of his operas, Mozart esteemed most highly *Idomeneo* and *Don Giovanni.* He was not fond of talking of his own works; or, if he mentioned them, it was in a few words. Of *Don Giovanni* he said one day: "This opera was not composed for the public of Vienna, it is better suited to Prague; but to say the truth, I wrote it only for myself and my friends."

The time which he most willingly employed in composition was the morning, from six to seven o'clock when he got up. After that, he did no more for the rest of the day unless he had to finish a piece that was wanted. He always worked very irregularly. When an idea struck him, he was not to be drawn from it. If he was taken from the piano, he continued to compose in the midst of his friends, and passed whole nights with his pen in his hand. At other times he had such a disinclination to work that he could not complete a piece till the moment of its performance.

THE COMPOSER

W. J. TURNER

Bernard Shaw once remarked that nothing could be more uncharacteristic of Mozart than the portraits of the beautiful young man exhibited above his name in all the music shops of the world today. These portraits show Mozart as the most handsome, the most regular-featured of all great composers. These "classic" proportions seem at first sight to be peculiarly appropriate to a composer who is today universally admired as the classic of classics. Where else in music shall we find those qualities of serenity, limpidity, simplicity, lucidity, which we concentrate in one adjective: Mozartian?

It is impossible to find a parallel to that flawless perfection. Whether we take a whole opera—such as *The Marriage of Figaro* (1786)—or a mere scrap scribbled impromptu on the page of a visitors' book—such as the Gigue written in 1789 for the Leipzig organist, Engel—we are confronted with a completely finished musical composition in which there is not a superfluous bar, not a redundant or meaningless note. There is no waste in Mozart—no overlapping, no exaggeration, no strain, no vagueness, no distortion, no suggestion. He is so simple that he is meaningless. His music *disappears*, like the air we breathe on a transparent day. Everybody who has really appreciated Mozart will admit that at one time or another they have felt a Mozart masterpiece as one would feel a still, bright, perfect, cloudless day. Such a day has no meaning, none of the suggestiveness, the "atmosphere," the character of a day of cloud or storm, or of any day in which there is a mixture of warring elements whose significance has yet to appear. Such a day does not provoke or in the faintest degree suggest one mood rather than another. It is infinitely protean. It means just what you mean. It is intangible, immaterial—fitting your spirit like a glove.

Thus, as Sir Charles Stanford has said, when you are a child Mozart speaks to you as a child—no music could be more simple, more childlike—but when you are a man you find to your astonishment that this music which seemed childlike is completely adult and masculine. At every age this pure pellucid day, this intangible transparency, awaits you and envelops you in its unruffled light. *Then* suddenly there will pass through you a tremor of terror. A moment comes when that tranquility, that perfection will take on a ghastly ambiguity. That music still suggests nothing, nothing at all; it is just infinitely ambiguous. Then you remember the phrase of a German critic who wrote of the "demoniacal clang" of Mozart. Then you look at a genuine portrait of Mozart, and instead of that smooth Praxitelean young beauty, you see a straight jutting profile with a too-prominent nose and an extraordinary salience of the upper lip, and for an instant you feel as if you have had a revelation. But that revelation escapes you as suddenly as it came, and you are left face to face with a mask whose directness and clarity is completely baffling.

In endeavoring to explain Mozart to oneself, it is well to remember first of all that he was the most remarkable example of a child prodigy that has ever been known. He played the harpsichord in public at five years old. At seven he composed, and played on the harpsichord, the organ, and the violin. In 1764, at the age of eight, after touring Europe, he came to London and played before the Royal Family; in London he published his third set of sonatas and wrote an anthem for four voices entitled *God is Our Refuge,* which was presented to the British Museum. At the age of ten he wrote an oratorio which had a great success in Holland, and a year later, in Vienna, he wrote an *opera buffa, La Finta Semplice,* for the Emperor Joseph II. At fourteen he was taken to Italy by his father, and in Rome during Holy Week he went to the Sistine Chapel to hear the famous *Miserere* of Gregorio Allegri (1582–1652). Immediately on returning to his lodging he wrote down the *Miserere* from memory, note for note. The same year he was subjected to the severest possible examination by the Bologna Accademia Filarmonica, passed it successfully, and was awarded the degree of *compositore,* although the regulations did not admit of any candidates under twenty years of age. This exercise is Number 86 in Köchel's catalogue, and, in Professor Donald Tovey's words, is "written in the severe ecclesiastical style of the sixteenth century," and abounds in "points of ingenious imitation and device." In 1770, at the age of fourteen, he wrote an opera entitled *Mitridate Rè di Ponto* for La Scala, of Milan. The orchestra of La Scala was at that time the largest in Europe; Mozart directed it seated at the harpsichord as the fashion then was. The opera was received with enthusiasm and ran for twenty nights.

From the age of fourteen onwards Mozart poured forth a constant stream of compositions of all kinds. What is astonishing is that this immense early productivity seems in no way to have harmed the natural growth of his mind, for although there are pieces of church music written before the age of fifteen which the best critics claim as masterpieces, yet there is perceptible in his music a real development of his natural powers which ends only with his death.

It is suggested by some writers that the fact that Mozart acquired at the age of fourteen a technique equal to, if not surpassing, that of any living composer explains why he was able to pass through the critical years of adolescence from fourteen to twenty in ceaseless musical composition without straining his mind. For Mozart had to acquire the usual education, and his letters suggest—as later his invention in the *Seraglio* of the character of Osmin, words and all, proves—that he had great literary ability and possibly the same inexhaustible fertility in language that he had in music. But Mozart's intellectual force was a quality inherent in the structure of his mind. One day the physiologists will be able to show us in a physiological generalization Mozart's peculiar gift for form. Many writers on aesthetics think music is the most abstract of the arts, but it is certainly true that Mozart's are the purest works in music. One may speak of a movement of Mozart just as a mathematician might speak of a beautiful proposition of Euclid. Whereas in the music of most composers it is a case of content *and* structure, it is with Mozart a case of structure only, for there is no perceptible content—*ubi materia ibi geometria.* Nowhere, perhaps, is this more strikingly shown than in the overture to *The Marriage of Figaro.* I would suggest to the reader that he should buy the phonograph records of this overture and of Rossini's overture to *The Barber of Seville,* and compare them. The difference is astonishing. Rossini was born the year after Mozart's death; he also had the advantage of following instead of preceding Beethoven, and he was a composer of striking natural genius. But, after *Figaro,* listen to the *Barber of Seville* overture, with its alluring tunefulness over its easy *tum-ti, tum-ti, tum-ti, tum-ti* bass, and you will be struck with its straggling formlessness. Its tunes are very engaging, but you can carry them away with you and hear them mentally on a penny whistle, a cornet, or any instrument you like. They are like bright threads in a commonplace piece of stuff, which you can pull out without compunction as there is no design to spoil. But you can do nothing of the sort with the *Figaro* overture. There are no bright threads to pull out. There is no melodic content as such. You cannot even hear the music in your memory apart from the rush of the strings and the accents of the wood wind. It cannot be played upon the piano. Take away a note of it and the whole is completely disintegrated. Nor can anyone put his hand upon his heart and say what feeling that music arouses in his breast. It

111

is completely without expression, as expression is vulgarly understood; but the oftener you hear it the more excited you become, the more passionate grow your asseverations that there was never music like this before or since. Its effect upon the mind is out of all proportion to its impingement on the senses. To hear it is as though one had been present at a miracle and had seen a mountain of matter blown into a transparent bubble and float vanishing into the sky. Your desire to hear that overture again and again and again is the simple but intense desire to see the miracle repeated. It is an astonishing experience, and it is an experience which only Mozart can give us.

It would be useless to attempt to explain this peculiar intellectual gift which was Mozart's in a degree that separates him from all other composers. It must just be stated and left. But there are certain facts known about Mozart which are so relevant to this point that they should be mentioned now. He was exceptionally good at dancing and playing billiards, which were his two chief pleasures. He was small, but his limbs, feet, and hands were beautifully proportioned. He composed away from any musical instrument, entirely in his head, and could complete the whole of a work, from the first note to the last and then write it down—often some weeks or more later —from memory. Thus the overture to *Don Giovanni*, written on the night of October 28th, 1787, for the first performance of the opera in Prague on the next day, while his wife kept him awake by telling him fairy stories, was not composed on that night but merely copied out from memory. He would often compose at meals, and while composing would take his napkin by two corners and continually fold and refold it very neatly and exactly. To me this is all extraordinarily illuminating. Conciseness—even conciseness so unparalleled and amazing as Mozart's—is not surprising in a composer who could work in this way. One also cannot but think that his invariable serenity and good temper—upon which all who knew him have left comment—was yet another sign of perfect physical and mental poise. It is on record that Mozart never used glasses and that his eyesight was perfect at his death in spite of the strain which manuscript music imposes. This, also, is not without significance. Mozart may be bracketed with Schubert as one of the two composers whose fertility in melodic invention exceeds all others, but the listener never feels that Mozart is being swept along the current of his own emotions as he feels Schubert is. In listening to such works as Schubert's Octet or his *Unfinished Symphony,* one is conscious sometimes of a dissolution, almost a liquefaction, of the composer's sensibility, which streams into the music like treacle. It is this that makes Schubert's music often so formless. The composer is simply melting helplessly away, and it seems as if only death can conclude the process. Yet melting, tender, exquisitely sweet as Schubert's melodies can be, they are never in themselves intrinsically sweeter or tenderer than Mozart's, but only in their effect. They seem sweeter because of the absence of that intellectuality, that lucid precision which was so integral a part of Mozart's mind. There are passages in Mozart's piano concertos which are so piercing in their intense sweetness that I have often stopped playing and laughed aloud with excess of pleasure; but Mozart's mental grip never loosens; he never abandons himself to any one sense; even at his most ecstatic moments his mind is vigorous, alert, and on the wing. It is from this astounding elasticity that his conciseness largely derives. Most artists are unable to tear themselves away from their most delightful discoveries; they linger on them and handle them fondly, but not Mozart. He dives unerringly on to his finest ideas like a bird of prey, and once an idea is seized he soars off again with undiminished power.

Yet impossible as it is in Mozart's music to separate form from content—which is his great, his unique intellectual distinction, the quality in which he surpasses all other composers—we can range his forms in a hierarchy of value. The overture to *Figaro* is perfect. There is nothing to be altered, there is not a note we could wish different, and nobody but Mozart could have written it; but, nevertheless, the overture to *The Magic Flute* (1791) is a finer work. It also is perfect, but it is artistically greater than *Figaro.* Wherein is it greater? Well, I believe we shall go least astray if we make the comparison in purely quantitative terms. The overture to *The Magic Flute* is a greater composition than the overture to *Figaro* because while form and content are equally one, while "matter" has once again been turned to "form," more matter has been involved in the operation. It was a bigger and more difficult bubble to blow.

I am conscious that some readers will dislike the manner in which

113

I have put this comparison of *Figaro* with *The Magic Flute*. They will wonder why I do not use the familiar terms: *Figaro* is a comic opera, *The Magic Flute* is a more serious work. It expresses Mozart's religious feeling, his idealism; that is why, they will say, *The Magic Flute* overture is superior. Such expressions, I admit, are not without meaning, but they are misleading. The world is full of music which is none the less worthless because it is "serious" or "religious." What we can say is that there is present in the music of *The Magic Flute* a quality which is not present in *Figaro*, and a quality which we instinctively feel to be infinitely more precious. That "infinitely" is a concession to my own feeling. I hope it will appease the fanatical admirers of Beethoven, but my reason urges me to take it out. However, it must be recognized that Beethoven almost consistently attempted to blow bigger bubbles than Mozart. That he so frequently failed, that his bubbles so often burst instead of sailing off beautifully, as Mozart's do, into the upper regions of the mind, will not prevent his admirers ranking him instead of Mozart as the greatest of all musicians. I do not really object to this very seriously, because one or two of Beethoven's biggest bubbles do float off successfully, although I confess I always watch them with anxiety, never with that utter confidence which Mozart inspires. But when we remember that Mozart died at the age of thirty-five, and reflect upon such works as *Don Giovanni* (1787), the *Requiem* (1791), *The Magic Flute,* and much of his earlier church music, it is permissible to believe that he would have successfully achieved even bigger things.

Personally, I would go farther. I very much doubt if Beethoven or any other composer has exceeded Mozart in vital energy. The last movement of Beethoven's Seventh Symphony has been called the "apotheosis of the dance," and in actual "sound and fury" it far exceeds anything Mozart ever wrote; but I do not feel there is as quick, as tense a "rush" in it as there is in the *Figaro* overture; there is only a bigger volume of noise. It is the rumble of thunder compared with the flash of lightning. Nor is there in all Beethoven's great and intensely dramatic overtures anything more impressive, more dramatically effective than the use made of the opening chords in *The Magic Flute* overture; but Mozart secures this dramatic intensity with a far greater economy of sound. He never bludgeons the senses into recognition of his powers, as so many inferior composers do; he appeals directly to the imagination.

It is not astonishing that a mind so well-balanced as Mozart's should show so great a sense of humor. In this he surpasses all other composers, and as the sense of humor is essentially intellectual, it is natural that Mozart, the most intellectual of composers, should be the greatest master of comic opera. But what is altogether unexpected is his power to make one's flesh creep. Nothing has ever been written of such truly diabolical verve as the aria for the Queen of the Night in *The Magic Flute.* It is the rarest event to find a light soprano who can sing this at all; it is certain that we shall never have it sung so as to do full justice to its startlingly coldblooded ferocity. And yet that aria has the smooth, glassy surface of a mere bit of coloratura virtuosity; but it is the surface of ice beneath which is a fathomless black water. This sinister ambiguity is a quality quite apart from the more familiar power of striking the imagination which he shows in the music which announces and accompanies the entrance of the statue at the supper-party in the last act of *Don Giovanni.* This is the most famous of Mozart's dramatic touches, and nobody can deny that there is not a more thrilling moment than this in the whole of Wagner's *Ring,* or, indeed, in any opera that has ever been written.

Yet I would like to insist that there is another and even more troubling quality in Mozart's music. Linked with the "demoniacal clang" which is probably the result of that bareness which makes Mozart's music appear a mere rhythmical skeleton beside the work of more sensuous composers such as Brahms and Wagner (but a skeleton of electric vitality!), there is a profoundly disturbing melancholy. It is never active in Mozart's work as it is frequently in the work of Tchaikovsky, in Brahms, in Chopin, and even in Beethoven. It is a still, unplumbed melancholy underlying even his brightest and most vivacious movements. It is this which gives his music that ambiguity to which I drew attention at the beginning of this essay. It would be an interesting psychological study to try to discover its meaning. It may be that Mozart's life was a profoundly unhappy one —he was certainly unfortunate in his environment, far more unfortunate than Beethoven, for he never had Beethoven's comparative

115

financial security, nor did he ever enjoy such appreciative and discriminating friends. It is probable that his extreme sensitiveness in unfavorable surroundings caused him great suffering, and that he was unfortunate in his relations with women; but such in varying degree are the trials of all artists of genius, and I do not think they will account for the peculiar, all-pervading, transparent gloom of Mozart's music. I am not even sure that "gloom" and "melancholy" are the right words to use. Mozart is very mysterious—far more mysterious than Beethoven, because his music seems to express much less of his human character. I believe that Mozart's personal life was a failure. In his last years he abandoned himself to frivolous gaiety. Without being dissipated, he wasted his time and strength upon masked balls, dancing, feasting, and idle gallantry. It is impossible to believe that he found such a life satisfactory. Why, then, did he pursue it?

Mozart was not without that sense of spiritual life which we call religious. On the contrary, he had this sense as highly developed as his sense of humor—he was no La Rochefoucauld. The *Requiem, The Magic Flute, Don Giovanni,* the *Twelfth Mass* in C major (1776), and a great deal of purely instrumental music exist to prove it. If it were not so, Mozart would be enormously less important. But Mozart obviously lacked that quiet, steady, flaming faith which burns so intensely in Bach and Beethoven. This is the secret of that all-pervading gloom, that quiet hopelessness. I do not mean, merely, that Mozart was a child of the 18th century and consequently a realist and a skeptic. The true 18th-century man of the world is not troubled by any religious feelings at all; he entirely lacks spiritual sensibility. All men are materialists, because all life is "matter," even if that "matter" resolve itself into positive and negative electricity—though God alone knows what that means! But "matter" varies in its sentient power. One piece of matter "Mr. A" can see but cannot hear: he is deaf, for him sounds do not exist; another piece of matter "Mr. B" hears but cannot see; another, "Mr. C" hears *and* sees, but he is color-blind: for him colors do not exist, yet he, living among the blind and deaf, may easily convince himself that he misses nothing, and that these "colors" of which a few odd people talk, are fantastic or sentimental illusions. This is the position of the true 18th-century

116

"materialist." Mozart was not one of these; he was vividly aware of the spiritual colors of life, they were to him as concrete as heat and cold.

But something else was lacking. I am conscious of it, but I do not quite know how to describe it. I can only point to Beethoven's Ninth Symphony and declare that I find it unmistakably present there. Mozart could not have written the last movement of that symphony. He was not capable of it. It expresses an emotion he had never felt. To describe this emotion as "joy" is utterly inadequate and ridiculous. It is a spiritual sublimity which surpasses in value all other human emotions, and which only the few supreme spirits of this earth have ever expressed. In many millions of years from now, men—if there are still men or descendants of men living on this planet—may be able to explain in biological terms the value of this emotion; or, rather, it will have become intelligible to them—as the value of the abstract feeling for justice is today becoming intelligible. At present it is the rare emotional possession of the few, but nothing can prevent its slowly dominating mankind. Its power is irresistible because it is latent in us all. Bach and Beethoven knew this, and therefore—to use the extraordinarily apt and suggestive words of the Jacobean translators of the old Hebrew folk-tales—they "walked with God." Mozart did not. Mozart danced with the masked daughters of Vienna and wasted his spirit, not in passion or in sudden excesses of lust—which might not have harmed him, which might even have been beneficial to him—but in the aimless dissipation of the man without faith. This spiritual "faith" in which Beethoven and Bach lived is altogether different from that romantic faith in themselves which came into fashion for artists and men of genius in Europe at the beginning of the 19th century, when Napoleon began to talk about his "star" and Byron set the fashion of extravagant, egoistic gestures. Bach had none of this, and in so far as Beethoven indulged in it it did him harm. Mozart was not handicapped through having lived before the invention of that comfortable padded cell of the soul, that lotus-island, the Nietzschean vanity of the superman-artist; and of all artists who have ever lived Mozart was least likely to fall a victim to such a snare. He had too penetrating an intelligence, too keen a sense of humor. No, he was deficient

117

in an active power which Beethoven and Bach possessed, and I think he was deficient in nothing else. In all else he was indeed superior to Beethoven and Bach, and, consequently, to all others.

But now that I have put my finger on what I believe to be the radical weakness of Mozart, and have given my explanation of the melancholy of his music—namely, that Mozart had extreme spiritual sensitiveness but no spiritual faith in life (and by that I do not mean acceptance of any theological dogma)—I think I can give a different interpretation of one of Mozart's apparent failures. In Donald Tovey's brilliant article on "sonata form" in the *Encyclopædia Britannica,* he says: "The sonata style never lost with him (Mozart) its dramatic character, but while it was capable of pathos, excitement and even vehemence, it could not concern itself with catastrophes and tragic climaxes." He then goes on to say that the G minor Symphony (1788) shows poignant feeling, but that it is not an embodiment of sad experiences. So far Professor Tovey, although writing about the "sonata form," is accusing Mozart of a lack of emotional content, but then he continues: "In the still more profound and pathetic G minor Quintet (1787) we see Mozart for once transcending his limits. The slow movement rises to a height not surpassed by Beethoven himself until his second period; *an adequate finale is unattainable with Mozart's resources, and he knows it.*" But in what way, may one ask, has Mozart transcended his limits in this work if the slow movement only rises to a height surpassed by Beethoven in his *second* period and his resources do not admit of his writing an adequate finale?

That the slow movement of the G minor Quintet is surpassed by Beethoven in his second period I should be inclined to deny. That the technical resources of the man who wrote that wonderful Allegro, that astonishing minuet, that rich and tragic slow movement, and those poignant introductory bars, were inadequate to a satisfactory finale is to me unbelievable. That Mozart—whose technical mastery at every point surpasses Beethoven's in the opinion of, I should imagine, ninety-nine per cent of scholars—should have been incapable of satisfactorily *concluding* an admitted masterpiece through lack of technical resource is completely unconvincing. What, then, does Professor Tovey mean? Let us examine that last movement of the G minor Quintet. What is wrong with it? In my opinion, this:

118

Mozart has written a really great work, he has taken plenty of room, the design of the Quintet is magnificently spacious, and he can fill it. Not only has he all the technical resources necessary—to talk of Mozart ever lacking technical resources seems to me ludicrous—but he is in the rich, abundant, creative mood to fill it, and so to fill it that it strikes Professor Tovey as "profound and pathetic"—words which he does not use lightly. The third movement, *Adagio,* is tragic in its intensity. But what, then, happens? Mozart concludes with a finale, light, sparkling, and gay, but once more masking an abyss of black melancholy. A finale that is utterly inadequate—admitted! But why inadequate? It is not technically inadequate. To spin that light-hearted gossamer *Allegro* so that, after what we had heard, it should captivate and delude, not shock and disgust, the listener, called for that technical skill which Mozart alone possessed. But, still, inadequate! That finale is beyond all denial inadequate. Why? Because after the poignant, heart-breaking intensity of the slow movement some affirmation of the soul is inexorably demanded. *Mozart could not make that affirmation.* He could not even attempt to make it. If he had attempted but had failed, *then* we could speak of inadequate resources. But he had no faith, he could not lift up his heart and sing from the bottom of that abyss, he could not stretch his wings and rise up out of it, he could only shrug his shoulders and blow us another bubble. Therefore, and therefore only, he is not the world's greatest composer.

MOZART SPEAKS

If one has talent it pushes for utterance and torments one; it will out. And then one is out with it without questioning. And, look you, there is nothing in this thing of learning out of books. Here, here, and here [the ear, the head, the heart] is your school. If everything is right there, then take your pen and down with it; afterwards ask the opinion of a man who knows his business.

· · · ·

Melody is the essence of music. I compare a good melodist to a fine racer, and contrapuntists to hackpost horses. Therefore be advised, let well alone, and remember the old Italian proverb, "Who knows most, knows least."

. . . . .

I cannot write poetically. I am no poet. I cannot divide and subdivide my phrases so as to produce light and shade. I am no painter. I cannot even give expression to my sentiments and thoughts by gestures and pantomime. I am no dancer. But I can do it with tones. I am a musician.

. . . . .

It is a mistake to think that the practice of my art has become easy to me. I assure you no one has given so much care to the study of composition as I. There is scarcely a famous master in music whose works I have not frequently and diligently studied.

. . . . .

In opera, willy nilly, poetry must be the obedient daughter of music. Why do Italian operas please everywhere, even in Paris, as I have been a witness, despite the wretchedness of their librettos? Because in them music rules and compels us to forget everything else. All the more must an opera please in which the plot is well carried out, and the words are written simply for the sake of the music and not here and there to please some miserable rhyme which, God knows, adds nothing to a theatrical representation, but more often harms it. Verses are the most indispensable things in music, but rhymes, for the sake of rhymes, the most injurious. Those who go to work so pedantically will assuredly come to grief along with the music. It were best if a good composer who understands the stage, and is himself able to suggest something, and a clever poet could be united in one, like a phoenix.

. . . . .

When I am at peace with myself, and in good spirits—for instance, on a journey, in a carriage, or after a good meal, or while taking a walk, or at night when I can't sleep—then thoughts flow into me most easily and at their best. Where they come from and how—that I cannot say; nor can I do anything about it. I retain the ideas that please in my mind, and hum them—at least so I am told. If I hold fast to one, that I think is suitable, others, more and more, come to me, like the ingredients for a *paté*, from counterpoint, from the sound of the various instruments, and so forth. That warms my soul, that is if I am not disturbed, and keep on broadening those ideas and making them clearer and brighter until the whole thing is fully completed in my mind.

. . . . .

I'd be willing to work forever and forever if I were permitted to write only such music as I want to write and can write—which I myself think good.

LUDWIG VAN BEETHOVEN

1 7 7 0 - 1 8 2 7

LUDWIG VAN BEETHOVEN was born in Bonn, Germany, on December 16, 1770. Taught first by his father (a singer in the Electoral Choir) and later by some local teachers—of whom Christian Gottlieb Neefe was the most influential—Beethoven made outstanding progress in his music studies. His first public appearance took place when he was eight; at eleven he wrote several piano sonatas; and at twelve he served as court organist. In 1787 he paid a brief visit to Vienna where he improvised for Mozart who declared "You will some day leave a mark on the world." Back in Bonn he was employed at court, gave private lessons, and wrote a good deal of music. His talent made a deep impression on some of Bonn's most influential citizens, including Frau von Breuning and Count Waldstein who remained among his most ardent friends and admirers.

A few months after his father's death in 1792 Beethoven left Bonn for good and set up permanent abode in Vienna. For a while he studied with Haydn, Albrechtsberger, and Salieri. Despite his uncouth manners and the fiery independence of his spirit, he soon made rapid headway as a performer in leading Viennese palaces and salons, as a teacher in the households of the rich, and as a composer. On his first public appearance in Vienna (March 29, 1795), when he introduced his Piano Concerto in B-flat major, he was described by one Viennese critic as a "giant among pianoforte players." On April 20, 1800 he made his bow as a composer of symphonic music when he directed the première of his first symphony in Vienna.

If the convenient demarcation of Beethoven's creative evolution into three periods is acceptable, then the first ended in or about 1800. By then he had completed, among other works, his first six string quartets, his first ten piano sonatas, his first four piano trios, his septet, and his first symphony. In 1802, between the end of this first period, and the flowering of the second, tragedy struck: Beethoven realized he was going deaf. His abject despair is voiced in a remarkable document now known as the "Heiligenstadt Testament." Under the pressure of his nearing isolation from the world of sound, Beethoven became increasingly eccentric, suspicious, and insulting. But he also uncovered such new depths of musical expression, and such new areas for musical cultivation, that many of his friends, including members of nobility, continued to shower on him their admiration and financial rewards. In this period, about which he himself said he was "making a fresh start," he produced the *Eroica*, Fourth, Fifth, *Pastoral*, and Seventh symphonies; the *Moonlight*, *Waldstein*, and *Appassionata* piano sonatas; the Fourth and Fifth piano concertos; the opera, *Fidelio;* the violin concerto; the three *Rasoumovsky* string quartets; and many other masterworks.

A pause from this Titanic achievement occurred between 1812 and 1818. After that there emerged the third of Beethoven's creative periods, during which he completed the Ninth Symphony, the *Missa Solemnis*, the last piano sonatas and the last string quartets.

Beethoven never married. Throughout his life he was strongly attracted to women, but usually the object of his love was someone out of his reach, either because of her youth or social position. An extraordinary document was found after Beethoven's death—a letter to his "immortal beloved"—in which he speaks of his suffering in being unable to find a woman to share his life. But whether this "immortal beloved" was any single woman or womankind in general has never been discovered.

Though totally deaf, Beethoven directed the première of his Ninth Symphony in Vienna on May 7, 1824. This was his last public appearance. He died in Vienna on March 26, 1827.

THE MAN

ANTON SCHINDLER

FRANZ GRILLPARZER

Beethoven's height was about five feet four inches. His body was stodgy, of firm bone structure and strong muscles. His head was unusually large, with long bristly hair, almost entirely gray, and usually neglected and hanging around his head, giving him a somewhat savage appearance, particularly when his beard had reached abnormal length, which was often the case. His forehead was high and broad; his brown eyes were small and—when he laughed—almost entirely hidden in his head; on the other hand, they would, at times, appear excessively large, rolling and flashing, with pupils turned upwards. Sometimes, when an idea took possession of him, they would become immovable and he would stare before him. Beethoven's entire appearance would then undergo a striking change, take on an inspired and imposing aspect, and the small figure—corresponding to the stature of his soul—would seem to rise to gigantic heights. These moments of inspiration occasionally came to him in the gayest company and in the street, when he excited the attention of all passerbys. What was going on within him was expressed only by his glowing eyes and face; he never gesticulated either with his hands or head. . . . His nose was broad. His smile illumined his countenance, and gave it a surpassingly kind and sweet expression which was particularly encouraging to strangers. His laughter was loud and ringing, and distorted somewhat the spiritualized and strongly marked face: the big head began to swell, the face grew still broader, and very often resembled a grinning mask. It was a good thing that this effect passed quickly. His chin had a dimple, and two longish dents on either end, lending a rather peculiar appearance on the whole. His skin was of a yellowish coloring which, however, disappeared in the summer when on his long wanderings

124

in the open air it would take on a brownish-reddish tint, covering his full red cheeks like varnish.

A dress coat of fine blue cloth (the favored color in those days) with metal buttons, became him excellently. Such a one, and another of green cloth, were never missing from his wardrobe. In summer, he was always seen wearing white pantaloons, shoes, and white stockings (the fashion at the time). Vest and tie were always white and immaculate, no matter what the season. In addition to this attire imagine a light gait and an upright carriage—these ever characterizing the master—and you have before you Beethoven's personality.*

I was a boy when I saw Beethoven for the first time. It may have been 1804 or 1805, at a musical soirée in the house of my uncle Joseph Sonnleithner, at that time head of an art and music firm in Vienna. Together with Beethoven were present Cherubini and Abbé Vogler. Beethoven was, at that time, slender, and dressed in black and with great elegance. He wore spectacles which I so well remember, because in later years he never used this aid to sight. . . . A few years later I resided with my parents in the village of Heiligenstadt, near Vienna. Our apartment faced the garden, while Beethoven rented the rooms facing the street. Both apartments were connected by a common corridor, which led to the stairway. My brother and I paid little attention to the queer man (he had in the meantime grown stouter and was carelessly, even untidily dressed), when he shot by grumbling. . . .

In one of the following summers, I visited my grandmother who had her summer residence in Döbling. Beethoven, too, lived there at the time. Opposite the windows of my grandmother there stood a decrepit house owned by a man named Flehberger, notorious for his debauchery. This Flehberger had a daughter, Lise, who was pretty, but had not the best reputation. Beethoven seemed to take great interest in the girl. I still see him, coming down the Hirschengasse, his white handkerchief, in his right hand, trailing on the ground. He stopped at the portal of the Flehberger court, where the giddy beauty, standing on a hay wagon or a manure cart, was tossing her pitchfork vigorously and laughing all the time. I never noticed that Beethoven addressed her; he simply stood and gazed at her

---

* The paragraphs above are by Schindler; those below, by Grillparzer.

until the girl (whose taste ran more in the direction of peasant lads) provoked his anger by a derisive word, or by persistently ignoring him. Then with a sudden turn he ran away, but never failed to return and to stop at the Flehberger portal the next time. Yes, his interest in her went so far, that, when her father, because of a drunken brawl, was sent to the village jail, he personally intervened with the village community, and pleaded for his release, whereby, however, he so stormily handled the councillors, that he was almost forced unwillingly to share his imprisoned protegé's society. . . .

I received word from the director of the two theaters, Graf Moritz Dietrichstein, that Beethoven had prevailed upon him to induce me to write an opera for him. . . . Schindler, at that time Beethoven's business manager, and the author of a biography of Beethoven, came to see me. He begged me in the name of his lord and master, who was unwell, to come to see him. I got dressed, and we at once started to Beethoven's home which was somewhere in the suburbs. I found him in a dirty night dress lying on an untidy bed, a book in hand. . . . When we entered, Beethoven arose from his bed, shook hands with me, overflowing with friendliness and began to speak of the opera. "Your work is living here," he said, pointing to his breast. "I am leaving for the country in a few days, and I shall then begin to compose it". . . .

In the course of the summer, Schindler and I accepted an invitation from Beethoven to visit him in Hetzendorf. I do not remember whether Schindler told me on the way there, or whether I had heard it previously, that Beethoven had been prevented from starting to work on the opera because of urgent orders. I, therefore, avoided mentioning the subject. We went out walking and conversed as well as it was possible, half speaking and half writing. I am still deeply moved when I think of Beethoven himself bringing in five bottles of wine when we were seated at the table. He set one before Schindler's plate, one before his own, and three before mine, probably in his good-natured, wild-naïve manner, to give me to understand that I was welcome to drink as much as I pleased.

When I left without Schindler, who was staying on, Beethoven insisted on accompanying me. He sat next to me in the open carriage, but instead of getting out at the country limits, he went all the way to the city with me, got out at the city limits, shook hands with me most cordially, and started off on his long way back home. After he had descended, I saw a piece of paper lying where he had sat. I thought he had forgotten it, and hailed to him to come back for it. But he shook his head, and laughing out aloud as though at a good joke, ran all the faster in the opposite direction. I unwrapped the paper and found that it contained the exact amount for the fare that I had bargained for with the driver. So estranged was he from the customs and manners of the world that he did not realize what an insult might lie in such an act, under different circumstances. I took it as it was meant, and laughingly gave the driver the money thus presented.

Later I saw him again only once. I do not remember where. He told me: "Your opera is finished." Whether he meant just in his head, or whether he was alluding to the innumerable notations which he was in the habit of making . . . I cannot say. It is certain, however, that after his death, not a single note was found referring to the work planned by us.

THE COMPOSER

PAUL BEKKER

Beethoven was not a revolutionary musician. He was born in the *Sturm und Drang* period, but was not of it. He felt indeed no need for rebellion; the work of his predecessors did not restrict him, it saved him from wasting time and energy on experiment. . . . Beethoven . . . avoided anything speculative wherever possible. When he varied from tradition he did so in no spirit of wilfulness, but in obedience to the demands of the poetic idea which inspired him and upon which his whole work was based. Music was to him an exquisitely and delicately adapted vehicle for the expression of a spiritual and intellectual creed, a faithful mirror of his inner life and experience. Words and their attendant images, the limitations inseparable from exact definition, are not evaded but are spiritualized and transcended and expressed upon a higher plane of abstraction

127

through the power of music. Instrumental tone is used to reflect and interpret the occurrences of a world far removed from actuality, a world, however, which is an abstract representation of an actual region of the intellectual and emotional life, and is consequently subject to the motions and laws of its prototype.

Beethoven entertained no doubts as to the psychological bases of his art. As Neefe's pupil he had early received and accepted the doctrine of a necessary correspondence between things musical and things spiritual in the mind of the musician. This was a point of view to which he clung throughout his life. Neefe was both by nature and by training a musician of the type which is distinguished rather for philosophic and aesthetic interest in the art of music than for exact knowledge of musical science. There is no doubt that Beethoven was strongly influenced by Neefe's teaching, for in later years his interest developed and expanded upon the lines suggested by Neefe; he studied aesthetics, was ready to argue upon the subject and to defend certain clear convictions. There is a widespread but erroneous idea that Beethoven approached his art only from the practical side, that he set aside or even despised theoretical discussions as to essence and content. On the contrary, he constantly sought an aesthetic basis for artistic expression. He endeavored to think clearly, to get at the meaning of things, to develop the artistic instinct on logical and regular lines. His work is sprinkled with question marks; letters, diaries, and conversations testify alike to his keen critical intellect and grasp of aesthetics. Unfortunately, the majority of Beethoven's associates were intellectually insignificant, so that the recorded results of his thinking have come down to us for the most part only in some comment preserved by chance, some brilliantly illuminating remark, but when he came in contact with more independent and stimulating minds, he quickly took fire and became communicative. With the poet, Hofrat Kuffner, he discussed oratorio; with Grillparzer, opera; and those parts of the notebooks which touch on these conversations show that Beethoven's mental activity was keen and his judgment acute upon various aesthetic problems.

It did not occur to him to regard his work as "absolute" music, in the false sense of that term, meaning music for its own sake, devoid of content. In later years he complained to Schindler that the times were imaginatively bankrupt. "When I wrote my sonatas," he said, "people were more poetic and such indications [of the music's meaning] were superfluous. At that time everyone recognized that the Largo of the Sonata in D, op. 10, no. 3 (1796–98) expressed a melancholic state of mind, that it portrayed every subtle shade, every phase of melancholy, without the need of a title to give a clue to the meaning, and similarly, everyone saw that the two sonatas, op. 14 (1795–99), represented a struggle between two opposing principles, an argument between two persons; its interpretation is as obvious as that of the other work." About the same date, Beethoven, presumably in connection with his complaint about the decay of imagination in music lovers, declared his intention of giving poetic titles to his earlier works. One can scarcely regret that he did not carry out his plan. Such titles would have helped intelligent listeners very little, while the addition of a written "program" would not make up for the lack of imagination in the unintelligent. For a proper understanding of Beethoven's work prolonged and sympathetic experience and intense mental application are essential; hints in the form of a program and tags of verse will carry no one very far.

A short-sighted view of aesthetics has wrongly deduced that definite content in music is unnecessary and that a clear intellectual grasp of pure musical creations is impossible. Feeble and unclear thinking of this kind was entirely foreign to Beethoven. He demanded intellectual cooperation. He regarded listening to music as a living experience, and with him the terms "to compose" and "to write poetry" were interchangeable. "Read Shakespeare's *Tempest,*" he replied when questioned as to the meaning of the D minor Sonata, op. 31, no. 2 (1802), and the F minor Sonata, *Appassionata,* op. 57 (1804). When composing he kept a definite mental image before him and worked to it. His works were "inspired by moods which the poet translates into words and I into music; they rage and storm in my soul till they stand before me in the form of notes of music." On the title pages of his *Consecration of the House Overture,* op. 124 (1822), he writes with naïve self-confidence not "composed" but "made into poetry by Ludwig van Beethoven."

It is but a short step from such a viewpoint to program music.

129

Beethoven is, indeed, more of a program-music writer than is generally supposed. The gap which exists today between program and other music was unknown to him. He knew and valued the possibilities of a program and accepted it as a part of his musical heritage. Where it suited his purpose he used it; where it did not, he dispensed with it. He brought free artistic judgment to bear on each problem of musical expression as it arose.

The heights which he could attain in program music when he spent time and effort upon it are revealed in the *Pastoral Symphony*, the Sixth, op. 68 (1807–8). Here we have a conventional program, not differing in form from the work of former generations. Scenes of country life which afforded opportunity for tone painting are strung loosely together without any particular grace of thought. The subject delighted him, reminding him of his own experiences of the secret charms of Nature which he savored with the sentiment proper to a true disciple of Rousseau. His program was a foundation upon which his own imagination could build, the tangible course of an intangible train of imaginative thought. This program within a program is designated by Beethoven as "an expression of feeling." He tells us expressly that "anyone who has the least understanding of the countryside will know at once what the author wishes to express." Emphasis upon the author's "wish to express" and upon the necessity of responsive thought in the hearer proves that the composer's poetic intention oversteps the limits of a conventional title. Beethoven is silent about his program, not because he has none, but because he takes it for granted that his hearer will understand his meaning and that descriptive words are superfluous.

There is, nevertheless, something aesthetically hybrid about the *Pastoral Symphony*. The composer's imagination was hampered and limited to some extent by the necessity of suiting his emotional expression to the different sections which he had previously marked out. He realized this difficulty himself and, as a rule, subsequently avoided a program divided into scenes or sections. He substituted short characteristic titles, sufficient to give his fancy an objective without confining it strictly to a certain course with fixed halting places. Napoleon, Egmont, Coriolanus, Leonora thus provided themes upon which Beethoven's mighty imagination could exercise its full powers untrammeled. A spark was sufficient to kindle his poetic fire. The impression is none the less vivid because he painted with a bold sweep of the brush and did not tie himself to detail. He had transcended words and no longer needed their support. Why should he seek to fold the full-blown rose in the bud once more? He had substituted bold emotional painting for the detailed picture series of the older program music, and the superiority of his method was self-evident. Beethoven discovered a new aesthetic basis for his program music which in his hands became emotional revelation instead of superficial description.

He produced a considerable number of works of this type. Each enshrines a particular poetic concept and each bears witness to Beethoven's view of a particular problem. They form a connecting link between the lower type of program music—from which they differ by their greater imaginative freedom, and the music without a program—the meaning of which they help to make clear. They mirror certain ideas, certain habits of thought which provide a clue to Beethoven's inner life.

The whole world revealed to us is one of tremendous events and visions. It is manifested in many forms, but a single principle vitalizes the whole. The principle is the heroic struggle for absolute freedom of personality, and it persists throughout Beethoven's program music, diversely clothed by the imagination, like manifold variations upon a single *Leitmotiv*. Handel had worked before him upon not dissimilar lines. His personality also was strong, straightforward, sympathetic, capable of appreciating greatness, and on this account he had Beethoven's wholehearted admiration. Handel took his material without exception from the remote past. Heroes of the Old Testament or of classical antiquity fired his imagination. His ideal man was a powerful spectacular figure, imposing his will upon the world of lesser men surrounding him, and he represented such heroes with scrupulous effect. Beethoven's idea of a hero was essentially different. . . . He was more interested in the inward workings of the hero's soul than in his startling effect upon his fellows. He sought special characteristics, probed into motives, compared and assimilated them to his own thoughts and opinions, so

131

that his portrait became a critical study. He took account of his hero's circumstances and surroundings and attempted to reconstruct mentally the world in which he had lived and worked. Living as he did in a time of upheaval and revolution, political events held first place in his interest.

Beethoven is frequently described as a republican, without reference to the fact that he was by nature uncompromisingly, almost arrogantly, aristocratic. He was, indeed, a curious mixture of the aristocrat and the democrat. Like every true artist, conscious of his high calling, he believed in the principle of authority. He went as a freedom-loving Rhinelander to Vienna and there saw the full disadvantages of the old, aristocratic, political order. While there he heard news of an oppressed people's violent bid for freedom, of their abolition of abuses such as were perpetrated daily before his eyes. He heard of the rapid progress of liberated France and saw that a Republic, such as had long been considered an impracticable Utopia, was possible for a modern state. Looking back he compared it to Greece at the height of her glory—to the artist's golden age of human culture. He thus became a theoretical republican, partly from hatred of the abuses of the monarchical system, partly from sympathetic enthusiasm for a political ideal of the future, but his democratic opinions could hardly have stood this practical test. His pride as an artist knew no compromise, and he would have set his face like flint against any notions of equality or fraternity which would allow others to approach his throne without due respect. He was, moreover, creatively inspired, not by the movement of an entire people towards freedom, but by the nobility of certain outstanding leaders. In his works he celebrates the political hero who leads his people through battle to freedom and happiness. At that time Beethoven believed in the coming of such a hero. He believed, too, that freedom thus achieved was the end to which human development tended, and that the deeds of the expected leader would represent the most exalted plane of practical human endeavor.

Beethoven turned his gaze from the affairs of nations and peoples to the affairs of the sexes and of the family. Here again, even in the tenderest idyll, he dealt with human idiosyncrasies upon the heroic plane. He was interested in love as a plighting of eternal troth between a man and a woman, as a self-sacrificing devotion able to withstand the hardest test. Unselfish love between husband and wife, as distinct from mere sensuous attraction or desire for possession, was his theme and gave him a fresh source of spiritual inspiration. The idea behind the *Leonore Overture No. 3*, op. 72b (1806), is that of freedom of the individual achieved through loving sacrifice; it is the "heroic theme" once more in a new form, in relation to the lives of two people instead of to the common weal. Glorification of personal freedom follows glorification of political freedom; the *Leonore Overture* follows the *Eroica* Symphony, the Third, op. 55 (1803). The next development was a philosophical contemplation of the self. Victory is no longer won by a hero as representative and savior of his fellows, as in the *Eroica,* nor by the love of a man and woman as in the *Leonore Overture* and in the opera *Fidelio* (1803–5), but by a hero who stands alone in a hostile world. The *Egmont Overture,* op. 84 (1810), and the *Coriolon Overture,* op. 62 (1807), are Beethoven's great tragic creations. They stand out not for outward freedom but for freedom of will, and, though victorious, their victory proves their ruin. They indicate a period of transition in Beethoven's inner life, a period when he believed deliberately chosen annihilation of self to be the desirable consummation of effort. Yet he drew fresh power from the depths of pessimism which threatened to overwhelm him. He gained a new assurance and proceeded to greater heights than had hitherto been within his reach.

Despair over the world's travail and over his own fate now lay behind him; he had pierced the veil of life and had looked fearless upon the naked truths of existence. It did not break him; he did not become either a perpetual penitent or a prophet of the transitoriness and nothingness of earthly things. He had done with life's hard problems and he lifted his eyes to free and sunny heights. He still loved this present life for the very struggles and sorrows which it brings, for through pain he had found joy. A new heroic ideal began to dawn in him. He seems to have felt himself lifted above earth's confusion, to have received a promise and a foretaste of eternal bliss. In his own person he became an incarnation of his own ripened conception of the heroic character, raised above the many griefs and scanty joys

133

of this troublous life, yet not out of love with it. The love of life which no sorrow could stifle rings through his last works, bringing to those who are able to hear news of the salvation of joy which he had found, whose praises he sounds in a paean of ecstasy, as in the *Ode to Joy*, in the Ninth Symphony, op. 125 (1825).

Beethoven's program music affords a comprehensive view of his work as a whole, but it is not the only window to the world of his thought. His opera and his songs are a valuable supplement to his instrumental program music. They are not numerous but they are grandly conceived and are artistically perfect.

His greatest lyrical vocal work, on the contrary, the famous *Missa Solemnis*, op. 123 (1818–23), far surpasses his instrumental program music with its inherent limitations. In intention it is the most powerful and ambitious of his works. It is based on a formula originally intended to be a confession of faith of an ideal, universal human society, but he makes it the perfect expression of one man's faith—his own.

Beethoven's relations with the organized religion of his day were always cool. Neither as man nor as artist could he blindly accept dogma as true and indefeasible. He was brought up in a formalized Catholic doctrine whose narrowness left him coldly indifferent. Protestantism was too prosaic to appeal to his hot artist's imagination. As a result he kept aloof from church matters, and he satisfied his religious needs in contemplating Nature, which revealed to him more than the words of any priest had been able to do. The more he penetrated the metaphysical sources of life the deeper became his philosophic understanding of the relationship of the individual to the universe; the higher his spirit climbed to transcendental regions, where he discovered that the true Godhead dwelled in man, the more he longed to express his new vision of things in terms of the old creed of Christendom. He found that what was narrow and limited in the Christian doctrine was not of its essence, but had been artificially grafted upon it by short-sighted and illiberal interpreters. As a free-thinking artist who had thrown off petty superstition, he now attempted to give artistic expression to his own religious perceptions of creed, he dared to make use of the lofty words which had served for centuries as the symbol of faith in God. Nature was

134

Beethoven's divinity; from her he had learned to accept all phenomena as reflections of the Godhead. He felt himself to be a chosen vessel of supernatural revelation, a hero, a savior, who had suffered, and rising, had felt the divine life within him. In Beethoven's faith, in his sense of the God in man, was something more than the pantheism of Spinoza and Goethe. It was closely bound up with the idea of personality. To the doctrine of Nature in God and God in Nature, he added a mystical apprehension of God as dwelling in one single artistically creative individual.

The sum of his message was freedom, artistic freedom, political freedom, personal freedom of will, of art, of faith, freedom of the individual in all the aspects of life, and he gives it symbolic expression through the heroic idea in drama and in poetry. . . . He preserved a jealous, personal independence, taking what the world offered as due tribute and giving what he had to give as an act of grace. He was never more obstinate and autocratic than any previous musician, with the possible exception of Handel; and he proclaimed the individual's unalienable right to act freely within the body politic. He strove for the ideal conscious freedom in faith and knowledge, echoing the battle cries of his epoch, "the Rights of Man," and "all men are born free and equal." Freedom, as he understood it, however, did not mean libertinism and caprice. . . . Thus, Coriolanus perishes through inordinate pride of power, and Napoleon's name is erased from the score of the *Eroica* because he made himself a tyrant. Beethoven's idea of freedom rests upon a firm ethical basis. It is a happiness to be achieved only through a stern conflict with fate, the very opposite of effeminate self-indulgence; for only by self-discipline and steady devotion to duty can the depths of the true self be revealed and qualities be developed which make hard-won freedom worth having.

Thus Beethoven developed the poetic idea and expressed it in his program music and songs in a manner comprehensible to the senses, but he was not confined to music of this type. His characteristic handling of material made a further development in the direction of abstraction logically inevitable. The whole body of his thought could not be contained in the program themes which chance suggested and which he used so frugally, nor in his vocal

135

music. Many of his spiritual experiences, expressed in music—and particularly in his last quartets—were inexpressible in words. For these it was useless to seek suitable texts or titles. They are, nevertheless, conveyed immediately to the mind through the ear. Objectivity, hard and fast intellectual concepts, everything material is set aside. Beethoven no longer speaks in parables, but proclaims the faith attained through parables. He has found the realities behind appearances and now recalls them, stripped of material disguises, through the musician's world of sound. Only one sensible symbol remains, the form of the tone phenomena—form not in its narrowest, pedagogic, but in its widest sense, as a deliberate, artistic organization of all the elements available to music at that time: melody, harmony, tone color, dynamic phrasing. Analysis of the forms thus constructed and close study of their inherent emotional and spiritual effects will bring aesthetic understanding of this last section of Beethoven's creative work.

In his non-programmatic, instrumental music, which forms the greater part of his work, Beethoven uses the most mysterious and yet the most direct means of human communication. He has himself provided a few sign posts such as *"Marcia funebre sulla morte d'un eroe"* in the *Eroica; "La malinconia"* in the B-flat Major String Quartet, op. 18, no. 6 (1798–1800); *"Das Lebewohl"* in the E-flat Major Piano Sonata, op. 81a (1809), which are very nearly "programs." comments such as "lamentation sinking to exhaustion," "reviving little by little" in the A-flat Major Piano Sonata, op. 110 (1821), "devout Thanksgiving to God on recovery from sickness" in the A minor quartet, op. 132 (1825), "straightened" in the Biblical sense in the Cavatina of the B-flat Major Quartet, op. 130 (1825), and "resolution in the face of difficulty" in the String Quartet in F major, op. 135 (1826) exceed the limits of customary musical directions. How revealing are the remarks inserted in the great A-flat Major Piano Sonata: "rather lively and with the most intense feeling," "lively with a marching swing," "slowly and with yearning," and "quickly, but not too quickly and with decision." They are a strange development from the generalized tempo suggestions of tradition. They are almost programmatic in their clearness and definition, and form a kind of summary of the contents of a poem which is sketched out only on broad emotional lines.

Beethoven's use of the stereotyped Italian terms is also significant. He uses *moto legato, espressive marcato, ritardando, a tempo, dolce,* and *cantabile* with the utmost prodigality, using them to express the poet's meaning rather than as mechanical indications to the performer. Calculated "effects" are indeed steadily rejected, and in the last piano concerto, the *Emperor*, op. 73 (1809), the one opportunity for virtuosity which he had hitherto preserved—the cadenza— is omitted. The work is a delicately and intricately conceived organism in which the personality of the exponent finds no opportunity to spread itself. Hitherto the composer's directions had been used and regarded as hints from which the performer could proceed to his own individual interpretation; they now become ineluctible commands. They have ceased to serve as the scaffolding of a program, but they give the emotional meaning of the composition in crystallized form. They may be compared to the projecting towers and spires of a submerged city, rising above the surface of the waters and inciting imagination to seek for its hidden glories through depths of ocean. Beethoven soon found the traditional Italian terms inadequate. He sometimes strung them together into whole sentences, dealing with the intricate score part by part. He indicated the rhythm of groups of bars, and for a time expected miracles from the use of the metronome. He hunted out complicated Italian phrases and, where these were insufficient, he employed German comments. In the end he came to use all these methods simultaneously, the metronome, Italian and German marks of expression.

This careful attention to detail implies more than the fear that his work might be misinterpreted or inexactly rendered. He believed indications of tempo and style of performance to be just as much an organic part of his work, an expression of his poetic meaning, as signs of pitch and phrasing. The complete artist, he took nothing for granted; he would allow no vagueness, knowing exactly what he wished to express and how to make every detail contribute to his meaning.

Just as Beethoven made poetry out of the old mechanical "marks," so he increased the expressiveness of musical dynamics. Dynamic as a means of suggesting emotional grades was, of course, known to former generations of musicians. The earliest instrumental music borrowed the method of contrasting tones of various strengths from choral music. . . . [But] shades of emotion too delicate to find expression in terms of melody, rhythm, or harmony are perfectly mirrored in Beethoven's dynamics. Abrupt transitions of mood, which one would believe it impossible to link up, are made convincing by dynamic changes: for example, in the third and fourth movements of the Fifth Symphony in C minor, op. 67 (1805–7), and in the last part of the *Egmont Overture*. His dynamic methods are as serviceable and delightful for the expression of lesser, more delicate, emotional impulses—for the sudden turning of a rising tone mass, for the stifled pangs of restrained passion, the unexpected damping and extinction of hot emotion, alternations of vacillation and decision—as for bolder contrasts. He estimates the value of these things with absolute exactitude and presses them into the service of his central idea, the poetic idea, which gives unheard-of persuasiveness to the language of dynamics and musical marks of expression. Through these means, it also controls form in the narrower sense of the word, careful juxtaposition and sequence of rhythm, melody, harmony, and coloring. Here, again, Beethoven built upon the work of his predecessors, transfiguring it in the light of creative genius. In his hands these media attained fresh significance; one feels, indeed, that their origin, construction, and *raison d'être* are revealed for the first time. Beethoven's characteristic forms owe their originality not so much to their outward scheme of construction as to the superiority with which they adapt themselves to, and reflect, ideas which they were built to enshrine.

Thought associations and emotional associations alternate in Beethoven's work. They even cross, unite, separate, contrast with each other and supplement each other; but they remain essentially and recognizably distinct. On the one hand is pure lyricism, confined to the exposition of purely emotional impulses; on the other, a more explicit, more descriptive, more argumentative side of musical art. The latter arises in intermingled train of thought, the former is direct and simple in origin; the former makes for breadth, the latter

138

for the heights and depths. They find expression in Beethoven's two most important musical forms, the sonata and variations.

The sonata form represents "drama" in instrumental music. Its construction is determined by a multiplicity of intellectual activities, by spiritual conflicts, by spiritual events, peaceful or tragic. It arises in the interaction of contradictions, in the energy of conflicting claims and assertions. Within the framework of the sonata, an organically developed action, a logical sequence of scenes, an exact opposition of character take place. It is unnecessary to conceive this dramatic action in absolutely material terms, yet its existence as the constructive principle of the sonata cannot be disregarded without misrepresentation of its aesthetic character.

Variation is the sonata's artistic antithesis. It does not bring a number of melodic entities into relation, but takes a single melody and analyzes it. It grows, not by addition of matter from without, but by inward subdivision; its changes all spring from the same root. The essential quality of a single underlying concept is displayed in a series of metamorphoses. It consists, not in the mingling of many elements, as in the sonata, but in the analysis of a single element. It thus exploits one selected mood to the limits of thought, but it lacks the fructifying effect of contradiction. The aesthetic character of variation is passive, that of the sonata active; but the former, perfected by Beethoven and blended with fugal elements of pure emotional expansiveness, is the highest form of lyrical music. It springs from the original lyrical form, the song; and may be resolved into its elements, mood-atoms, which revolve for a time about a center, like planets round the sun, to be presently reabsorbed into the mass from which they were detached. Sometimes this activity presents the vitality, richness, and variety of phenomena of a great planetary universe; at other times it appears the product of a whim, a merely superficial, kaleidoscopic play. The latter is the variation form more frequently to be met, but Beethoven contributed to deepen it, to free it from mere virtuosity, to make it a great medium of emotional expression. He bent the thought-architecture of the sonata to his will and ennobled the emotional range of the variation, thereby giving eternal value to the two greatest musical forms, other than program music.

139

The active and comprehensive tendencies of the sonata determine the relationship of its several parts. It remains for the musician's skill to construct a higher synthesis out of the contradiction of these parts, and the sharper the contrasts offered, the more strikingly will the idea of the whole be reflected from the several angles. The consequent need of change in the form of the movements explains why Beethoven gradually made the variations (as the greatest possible contrast to the sonata phase) the most important member after the leading development movement, of the cyclic sonata form.

Between the two extremes stands, as a connecting link, the rondo, a hybrid of variation and sonata. It differs from the variation form in being based on not one but several concepts; yet it strings them together but loosely, avoiding the strict logic of the sonata. The rondo consists in an almost rhapsodic multiplicity of moods; it may occasionally be used to express spiritual depths, but is usually confined to a stimulating play of pleasant, trifling thoughts or feelings. It had a long history behind it when Beethoven took it over, probed, as usual, to the root of its value and achieved wonder with it. His creative capacities were various and inexhaustible. He was not always upon the heights or in the depths, but he knew and prized the norm of life and thought. He found the rondo useful, for not every thought can support the merciless logic of the sonata-form proper, nor every emotion endure the keen analysis of the variation form.

Beethoven's genius rescued him from the degrading power of the commonplace in everyday life, even when it pressed upon him most heavily. It is customary to overlook this aspect of his life; yet the picture of Beethoven, as man and musician, is incomplete without it. Reaction from the high tragedy of his dreams, from high intellectual tension, from ecstatic visions, took the form, not of pleasant, ordinary light-heartedness, but of resounding, almost hysterical outbursts of laughter; moods of super-sensitiveness gave place suddenly to explosive demoniac humors. As a pianist, Beethoven had a knack of breaking in upon the hush which followed his imaginative interpretations with peals of harsh laughter, bringing his hearers back from supernal regions to earth with brutal suddenness, and he did the same thing as a composer. He abolished the quiet elegance, the cheerfulness, and grace of the old minuet, substituting terrific natural force, freed from narrow rhythmic conventions, restless, sometimes darkly passionate, sometimes full of wild joy, sometimes showing the reverse side of things with quiet humor, sometimes resolving deep pathos in lightly swinging dance rhythms. It ceases to be a dance of polite society, formal and conventional, and becomes a dance of elemental spirits. From the old minuet, with its drawing-room associations, is derived the humorous musical poem—the characteristic scherzo of Beethoven.

We have now touched on all the principal forms used by Beethoven. They were based on the nature of things; they were no mere devices, but characteristic embodiments of certain poetic ideas through the symbols of music. They provided the aesthetic foundations of a highly abstract art. In Beethoven a composer arose who completely understood the possibilities of that art and ruled its form with the absolute confidence of an infallible despot. He knew the secret forces of his spiritual kingdom. He worked with unremitting critical consideration, tireless experiment, a constantly increasing consciousness of his own enormous power. He was artist enough to enforce his will without breaking with tradition, and was able to improve upon forms which came down to him in an apparently complete and unadaptable state. He breathed his own spirit into them, till it filled them almost to the bursting point. The might of his inspiration made light of the rules of etiquette. The last secrets of a soul, of an elemental stormy personality, are revealed without reserve. The impulse to self-revelation came from within, not from without. He made himself the subject of artistic exposition, choosing as his medium an art magically expressive of all thoughts and feelings of mankind—wordless instrumental music.

BEETHOVEN SPEAKS

From where do I get my ideas? I cannot say with certainty. They come uncalled, directly, indirectly. I could grasp them with my hands: in the open, from Nature, in the forest, in the quiet of the night, in the early morning. Sometimes moods which the poet expresses in words come to me in tones. They ring, storm, and roar until they finally stand before me in notes.

.   .   .   .   .

I *must* write—for what weighs on my heart, I *must* express. . . . I live only in my music, and I have scarcely begun one thing when I start another. . . . With whom need I fear to measure my strength?

.   .   .   .   .

Music is a higher revelation than any wisdom or philosophy. It is the wine that inspires new creations, and I am the Bacchus, who presses out this wine for men, and make them spiritually drunk. . . . I have no friend, and must live alone, but I know that in my art God is nearer to me than to others. I approach Him without fear. I have always known Him. Neither am I anxious about my music, which no adverse fate can overtake, and which will free him who understands it from the misery that afflicts others.

.   .   .   .   .

The Heiligenstadt Testament (1802)

O ye men who regard or declare me to be malignant, stubborn, or cynical, how unjust ye are toward me. You do not know the secret cause of my seeming so. From childhood onward my heart and mind prompted me to be kind and tender, and I was ever inclined to accomplish great deeds. But only think that during the last six years, I have been in a wretched condition rendered worse by unintelligent physicians. Deceived from year to year with hopes of improvement, and then finally forced to the prospect of lasting infirmity (which may last for years or be totally uncurable).

Born with a fiery, active temperament, even susceptive of the diversion of society, I had soon to retire from the world, to live a solitary life. At times, even, I endeavored to forget all this, but how harshly was I driven back by the redoubled experience of my bad hearing! Yet it was not possible for me to say to men: "Speak louder, shout, for I am deaf." Alas! How could I declare the weakness of a sense which in me ought to be more acute than in others—a sense which formerly I possessed in highest perfection, a perfection such as few in my profession enjoy, or even have enjoyed. No, I cannot do it.

Forgive, therefore, if you see me withdraw, when I would willingly mix with you. My misfortune pains me doubly, in that I am certain to be misunderstood. For me there can be no recreation in the society of my good fellow creatures, no refined conversations, no interchange of thought. Almost alone, and only mixing in society when absolutely necessary, I am compelled to live as an exile. If I approach near to people, a feeling of hot anxiety comes over me lest my condition be noticed—for so it was during these past six months which I spent in the country. . . . But how humiliating it was when one standing close to me heard a distant flute, and I heard nothing, or a shepherd's singing, and again I heard nothing. Such incidents almost drove me to despair; at times I was on the point of putting an end to my life. Art alone restrained my hand. Oh! it seemed as if I could not quit this earth until I had produced all I felt within me, and so I continued this wretched life—wretched, indeed, with so sensitive a body that a somewhat sudden change can throw me from the best into the worst state . . .

Patience, I am told, I must choose as my guide. . . . Oh, my fellow men, when one day you read this, remember that you were unjust to me, and let the unfortunate console himself if he can find one like himself, who in spite of all obstacles which nature has thrown in his way has still done everything in his power to be received into the ranks of worthy artists and men. . . .

So let it be. I joyfully hasten to meet death. If it comes before I have had opportunity to develop all my artistic faculties, it will come, my hard fate notwithstanding, too soon, and I should probably wish it later—yet even then I shall be happy, for will it not deliver me from a state of endless suffering? Come when thou wilt, I shall face thee courageously. Farewell, and when I am dead, do not entirely forget me. This I deserve from you, for during my lifetime, I often thought of you and how to make you happy. Be ye so. . . .

Thus I take my farewell of you—and indeed sadly—yes, that fond hope which I entertained when I came here, of being at any rate healed up to a certain point, must be entirely abandoned. As the leaves of autumn fall and fade, so it has withered away for me; almost the same as when I came here do I go away—even the high courage which often in the beautiful summer days quickened me, that has vanished. O Providence, let me have just one more day of joy; so long is it since true joy filled my heart. Oh when, oh when, oh Divine Being, shall I be able once again to feel it in the temple of nature and men. Never—no—that would be too hard.

. . . . .

To the Immortal Beloved (1812)

My angel, my all, my very self. A few words today, only, and in pencil (your pencil). . . . Why this profound sadness where necessity speaks? Can our love exist otherwise than through sacrifice—through demanding less than all—can you help it that you are not wholly mine, and that I am not wholly yours?—Oh, God! gaze into the loveliness of nature and solace your heart with a sense of the inevitable. Love demands everything and love is wholly right, *thus it is for me with you, and for you with me*—only, you are so prone to forget that I must live for myself and for you as well; were we wholly united you would feel the pain of it as little as I. . . . We shall, I fancy, see one another soon, besides, I cannot this morning share with you all that has passed through my mind during the last few days about my life. Were our hearts always close to one another I would have no thoughts of this kind. My heart is full—to tell you so much; ah—there are moments when I feel that speech in itself is nothing after all—be of good cheer—remain my true, my only treasure, my all, as I am yours; the gods must send us the rest, that which must be for us and shall be.

You are suffering, you my dearest creature. Only now have I learned that letters must be posted very early in the morning. Mondays—Thursdays—the only days when the post goes from here to K.— You are suffering. Ah, wherever I am, you are there with me. . . . I hold converse with myself, and you, I arrange things so that I may live with you, what a life!!!! thus!!! without you—pursued hither and yon by the kindness of humanity, which in my opinion—I little deserve and as little care to deserve. The humility

144

of men to men—it pains me—and when I consider myself in connection with the universe, what am I and what is he—whom one calls the greatest (?)—and yet—herein again the divine is immanent in the human—

I weep when I think that you probably will not have the first news from me until Saturday evening—much as you love me—my love for you is stronger—but do not ever hide your real self from me—Good night—as I am taking the baths I must go to sleep. . . . Oh God—so near! so far! is not our love a truly celestial abode—but also immovable as the firmament!

Even from my bed my thoughts press out to you, my immortal beloved, from time to time joyfully, then again sadly, waiting to learn whether fate will lend ear to us—Life is possible for me either wholly with you or not at all—yes, yes I have resolved to wander far from you until I can fly to your arms and say that there I am truly at home, can send my soul enfolded by you into the realm of spirits.—Yes, unhappily it must be so.—You will be courageous, the more so because you know my fidelity to you, never can another possess my heart, never—never!—O God, why must one part from what one loves; and yet my present life in Vienna is a grievous life—your love makes me at once the happiest and unhappiest of men—at my age I now need a certain uniformity and regularity of life—are these compatible with our relations?

Angel, I have just learned that the post goes every day, and so I must close, that you may receive the L. at once. Be calm, only by a calm consideration of our existence can we attain our purpose of living together—be calm—love me—today—yesterday—what tearful yearnings for you—you—you—my life—my all—farewell Oh, keep on loving me—never misjudge the faithful heart of your beloved L. Ever yours—ever mine—ever for one another.

KARL MARIA VON WEBER

1 7 8 6 – 1 8 2 6

KARL MARIA VON WEBER, first significant composer of German Romantic operas, was born in Eutin, Oldenburg, on November 18, 1786. At ten he started taking lessons in piano with J. P. Heuschkel, and in his eleventh year he spent a few months in Salzburg studying counterpoint with Michael Haydn. After additional study with various teachers, including Abbé Vogler, Weber became conductor of the Breslau Theater in 1804. Meanwhile he had completed several operas, two of which were performed unsuccessfully. In 1806 he assumed the post of Musik-Intendant to Duke Eugen of Württemberg, and in 1807 he was employed as secretary and music master to Duke Ludwig of Stuttgart. A period followed in which Weber made successful concert appearances throughout Germany as pianist. In 1810, the première of his opera, *Silvana,* in Frankfort brought him his first success as a composer, and was followed a year later by the equally impressive first performance of his comic opera, *Abu Hassan,* in Munich. In 1813 Weber assumed his first significant post, conductor of German operas in Prague. Three years later he became musical director of German opera in Dresden. There he instituted numerous reforms in performances which made his company one of the most distinguished in Europe. His position in Dresden made secure by an appointment confirmed for life, Weber married Caroline Brandt, a singer, on November 4, 1817.

Weber's high-minded efforts in behalf of German opera, in performances of the highest order, awakened in him the ambition to create a national German opera based on a German text and emphasizing German traditions, backgrounds and culture. This task took him three years, but with the completion of his masterwork, *Der*

146

Freischütz, introduced with phenomenal success in Berlin on June 18, 1821, the German romantic movement in opera was launched and established.

Weber wrote two more significant German operas after that. *Euryanthe* was commissioned for Vienna by the impresario, Domenico Barbaja, and introduced in that city on October 25, 1823. Weber wrote his last opera, *Oberon,* for Covent Garden, in London. Though his health was poor at the time, he went to London to help prepare rehearsals and to direct the opera's première on April 12, 1826. The task proved fatal. He died in his sleep in London on June 5, 1826, and was buried in that city. Eighteen years later his remains were removed to a new burial place in Dresden, when Richard Wagner delivered an oration and directed the performance of a piece he had written expressly for this occasion.

THE MAN

ANDRÉ COEUROY

Heinrich Heine, who met Weber in Berlin in 1822, describes him in one of his letters as follows: "Weber's appearance does not make a very favorable impression. Short, with ugly legs and a long face, he has not a single attractive feature. But what a stern expression in that face! What a pensive look! It bears the same calm strength of will, the same serene resolution, which attract us with magnetic force in the portraits of the Old German School." This description evidently comes near to the truth. But Heine omitted an essential characteristic: sound humor, which in Weber was always associated with his calmness and seriousness. He possessed a natural gaiety, often *gaminerie,* which even his sufferings could not obliterate.

In Stuttgart (1808) he was a member of the club, *Faust's Höllenfahrt,* where everyone was known by a nickname: Hiemer was called "Good Rhymer," Danzi, "Lamb's Lettuce," and Weber, "Cabbage Salad." Weber was fond of giving everybody nicknames: Gretchen Lange was called by him "Puzzicaca"; Caroline Brandt, "Muckerl," "Mucks," "Mucki," "Schneefuss" (Snow Foot) or "Krokodil."

147

In one of his letters to Gänsbacher, he gives his sweethearts the names of musical keys "on which he would still like to modulate." In Darmstadt he had a dog whom he named "Miss," so that when he called it in the street all the girls would turn around. Later, in Hamburg (1820), he bought a monkey, and gave him the name of his enemy, Spontini. Sometimes he went too far in his humor. Once, after having been severely reprimanded by the King of Württemberg, he met in the castle an old woman who asked him where she could find the washerwoman of the Court. "There," said Weber, pointing to the King's private apartment. The King, furious at this jest, had Weber immediately arrested and put into prison. There, on October 24, 1808, he composed his song, *Ein steter Kampf ist unser Leben.*

These and other similar adventures which we have not the space to recount here, do not fit in with the ethereal portrait which Berlioz or Musset made of him. His love adventures show that he was not inclined to platonic views. It is true that he was less licentious than many romantics of his time, but, nevertheless, up to the time of his marriage he passed from one love to another. He is continuously in search of "a heart whom he can trust," but fails to find it. In 1813 he writes from Prague to his friend Gänsbacher: "With slight variations it is always the same theme, and you know what I think of this melody." At about that time he began to despise women, though he admitted that they were "born artists." They had played with his feelings, and none had come near his ideal woman. He wrote: "I feel that I must love. I adore women, and at the same time I hate and despise them." Even when, in 1814, his lasting love for Caroline Brandt began, he hesitated between his love for the woman and his love of music. "It is indeed a hard necessity to have to sacrifice the man to the artist." He finally decided to marry her (and wisely persuaded her to abandon her career as an artist), and never had to regret his choice. She became his perfect companion, and her intelligent advice was most useful to him; she was his *"servante de Molière,"* and jokingly he called her his "popular gallery." It was she, for instance, who persuaded him to cut out the allegoric scene which Kind had written as a prologue to the *Freischütz.* There are many allusions to his domestic happiness in his letters to Gänsbacher: "How happy I am in my house, how my dear Lina beautifies my life! Indeed I am a happy man, and wish you the same" (1818). It was a calm and modest life. His wife acted also as cook, and we read in his diary: "Today I have eaten for the first time our personally cooked food" (*unser persönliche Küche*).

Weber had found his balance of mind. If a sense of humor cannot always fight against suffering, a solid and sincere faith brings comfort. In his illness he often said, "God's will be done," and after every success he thanked his Master. After composing the first act of *Oberon*, he asked for God's protection; and though he was commissioned to write his two Masses, he wrote them as a work of love and faith. On the last page of the second Mass we read: *Soli Deo Gloria*.

His filial devotion was equally great. Although he had no reason to be grateful to his father, who exploited him as a child prodigy, he paid his debts and supported him to the end. Of his mother he always spoke in affectionate terms, praising her sweetness and the good influence which she had on him. Weber resembled her very much. To her he owed that great sensitiveness which caused the least adverse criticism, even in insignificant papers, to be a torture to him, and made the coldness with which Goethe received him upset him deeply. This trait of his character was very marked in his youth, during which he had no playmates, and was given to reading sensational novels. But his strong manly ideal, "proud humility and humble pride," saved him; it was the humility of the man and the sinner, the pride of the creative artist. He was ambitious, but aimed rather at honest artistic success than at money and honor. After a performance of *Silvana* at Berlin (1812), Dieberg, a composer and a friend of his, reproached him with monotony. Weber at once wrote in his diary: "If there is no variety in my ideas, I lack genius. Must I then give my life, my work, my love, to an art for which God has not given me the true vocation? This doubt makes me most unhappy, for on no account do I wish to be one of the many thousand mediocre composers. If I cannot reach a high position, it would be better to beg for my bread by giving piano lessons. But I will uphold my motto: 'Tenacious to the last,' and time will show if I have lived up to it."

Weber's greatest endeavor was to "have a clear insight into his own self," and this maxim governed his entire work. A long period of incubation preceded the creation of each composition.

After the success of his *Silvana* he took heart again. "Even my enemies say that I have genius," he wrote; "thus, while fully aware of my shortcomings, I shall not lose my self-confidence, and while watching myself carefully proceed on the path which art has traced for me."

Straightforwardness, honesty in art, a keen sense of duty, devotion to work, and greater orderliness; these were the true characteristics of Weber.

THE COMPOSER

ALFRED EINSTEIN

The material of Romantic opera had long been available. In French opéra-comique, in opera buffa, in the German Singspiel, and notably in the Singspiel's coarse base-born brother, the fairy pantomime (*Zauberposse*), all its elements were latent. There had been a number of attempts in the 18th century to create a German national opera, for instance by Ignaz Holzbauer (1711–83) on a German historical subject, and by Anton Schweitzer (1735–87) on affecting texts by Wieland, dealing with classical antiquity and medieval England. The result, however, was little more than Italian opera performed in German. The movement received its vital impetus from the German romantic spirit, which had owed nothing to these experiments, but much to Gluck, to the Mozart of *Don Giovanni* and *Die Zauberflöte*, and to the whole Beethoven.

What do we mean by the Romantic spirit of opera? In the first place it was a question of subject matter. In spite of the respect felt for Gluck, there set in a revulsion from classical antiquity and with it a growing taste for folklore. Quite a new idea of "wonder" was conceived. In the older opera it had merely meant fantasy and surprise, an opportunity for stage engineers; in Romantic opera it became the moving spirit in everything that happened. Legend and

150

superstition provided a world of marvels, filling the air and exerting horrifying or beneficent influences upon human destinies. All Nature's secret forces took on an individual life and were more or less personified. E. T. A. Hoffmann (1776–1822) was the first in the field with his opera *Undine,* based on Fouqué's ingenuous, pathetic, fairy tale, and in the demoniacal spirit Kühleborn created its typical character. Almost simultaneously Ludwig Spohr (1784–1859) tackled the subject of Faust and arrested the attention of his contemporaries, particularly with the note he struck in the *Witches' Dance.* The actual birth of Romantic opera, however, must be held to date from the creation of a master musician who by force of a peculiarly sensuous quality in his melodic style was from the outset something more than a mere follower of Mozart. I refer to Karl Maria von Weber and his *Freischütz.*

Hoffmann was right in saying, after the first indescribably exciting performance of this work in Berlin in 1821, that since Mozart's time there had been two outstanding achievements in German opera, Beethoven's *Fidelio* and this *Freischütz.* Here, in *Der Freischütz,* the musician's art is no longer merely draughtsmanship; it is also coloring. Here the German woodland comes to life with all its magic in the horn music of the huntsmen's choruses and all its eeriness in the evocation of the haunted glen; here a born dramatist breathed abounding life into the girlish figures of Agathe and Ännchen (the latter a portrait of the composer's wife), into the weak-willed young huntsman—a truly tragic figure, this—and, above all, created with a couple of strokes of genius the character of Caspar, "the monster," in Beethoven's words, "that stands there like a house." But *Der Freischütz* was in point of form only a *Singspiel.* Weber had higher ambitions. *Euryanthe* (1823) represents his endeavor to establish "grand Romantic opera," the German equivalent of opera seria. The worthy Spohr, an ever enterprising if not always successful innovator, had anticipated him in this with his noble *Jessonda;* nevertheless the historic point of departure is the "programmatic" purpose of *Euryanthe.* That purpose Weber himself put into words in answer to a proposal from Breslau for a concert performance of the work. "*Euryanthe,*" he said, "is a dramatic essay, counting upon the collaboration of all the sister arts for its effect, and assuredly ineffectual

151

if deprived of their assistance." And again on an occasion when it was suggested that the opera might be improved by cuts: "With so organic a whole as a grand opera must be, to make excisions is excessively difficult when the composer has thoroughly thought out his work."

The problem of the unity of opera was Weber's preoccupation, and the efforts it cost him are obvious when we compare *Euryanthe* with *Der Freischütz;* but the result of those efforts was to make plain the way for the greatest of his successors. Weber employed various means of unification. Recitatives, linking the formal numbers of the opera, were in Weber so much enriched in melodiousness, in expressive power, and in the accompanying orchestral commentary as to undermine the prevailing system of set pieces. Yet more effective and radical as a means towards melodic consistency was the use of recurring musical ideas at dramatically significant points, in both the vocal and orchestral parts. Gluck and Mozart had already employed unifying basic motifs, in the finer sense of the word, to characterize their personages; Luigi Cherubini (1760–1842) in *Les Deux journées* had made important use of a motif for associative and evocative effect, and Weber had done the same thing several times with great subtlety in *Der Freischütz,* the finest example occurring in the Wolf's Glen music, when the hapless marksman shakes off his last misgivings before committing his mad act, to the strains from the orchestra of the peasants' mocking chorus. But in *Euryanthe* this principle was much more deliberately employed, and with the psychological penetration of genius. When Emma's grim funeral music—already familiar to the audience from the magnificent overture to the work—announced in its transformation at the end of the opera that the sinner is redeemed, the seed was planted from which, at Wagner's hands, the whole form of music drama was to grow. Wagner did more than perform an act of piety when he began his career at Dresden with a performance of *Euryanthe.*

The most admirable aspect of the consistency of Weber's opera, however, lies in its characteristic coloring. This was a quality with which he endowed each one of his operas. It was derived from his singular power, typical of the true romantic, of so handling the orchestra that the individual instruments yielded peculiar and hitherto unknown effects, while colors were mingled in the most varied ways. As in *Der Freischütz* the homeliness of the German woodland and its dark mystery turn into music, so in *Euryanthe* does the chivalry of medieval France, in *Preciosa* (1821) the racial traits of the Spanish gypsy, in *Oberon* (1826) the gorgeous fantasy of the Orient and the fairyland of the West. All turn to music, which clothes each of these works in a veil of magical radiancy.

WEBER SPEAKS

To appraise a contemporary work of art properly, there is needed that calm, dispassionate mood which, while sensitive to all kinds of impressions, is protected against preconceived judgments and feelings. There is needed a mind completely open to the material under consideration. Only then is the artist given the power to go forth in the world with those feelings and images which he has created, which he, the master of each passionate emotion, allows us to experience with him and through him: pain, pleasure, horror, joy, hope, and love. We can ascertain almost immediately whether he is capable of creating a mighty and enduring structure, or whether he has captured our interest with details rather than the work as a whole.

In no type of art work is this more difficult to avoid (and consequently more often present) than in opera. By opera I mean, of course, that which satisfies Germans: an art work complete in itself, in which the partial contributions of related arts are fused into each other, disappear, and finally emerge again to create a new world.

Generally, a few striking numbers decide the success of the whole. Seldom do these excerpts—pleasant at first hearing—fuse into the over-all effect at the close, as they should, since it is a complete work that should first win over the listener, who, only after greater familiarity, finds delight in the separate parts.

The nature and inner essence of opera, a whole made up of wholes, presents this immense difficulty which only the outstanding giants of music succeed in overcoming. Each musical composition within it gives the impression of an independent, organic, self-contained unit.

153

Yet it should become a part of the over-all structure when the latter is viewed in its entirety.

Here lies the great, the mysterious secret of music, felt yet not expressed. The opposing natures of anger and love, the torment of ecstatic suffering in which salamander and sylph embrace, are here united. In a word, what love is to man, music is to the arts and to mankind. For music is truly love itself, the purest, most ethereal language of the emotions, embodying all their changing colors in every variety of shading and nuance. While it is understood at once by a thousand different people it contains only a single basic truth. This truth is musical speech, however unusual the form in which it may appear, and this truth asserts its rights in the end. Creative and important works of art of all eras prove this contention again and again. What, for example, could have sounded stranger and more alien than the works of Gluck when everyone was overwhelmed by the sensual floods of Italian music?

FRANZ SCHUBERT

1 7 9 7 — 1 8 2 8

FRANZ PETER SCHUBERT was born in Vienna, Austria, on January 31, 1797. In early boyhood he received instruction on the violin, piano, organ, in singing and thorough bass from his father and Michael Holzer. Between 1808 and 1813, as a member of the Vienna Court Choir, he attended the "Konvict" School for choristers. There he wrote his first compositions, including his first song *Hagars Klage* in 1811, and his first symphony in 1813. In the latter year his voice broke and he had to leave the Konvict. From 1814 to 1816 he was a teacher in his father's school. In 1814 he completed a Mass, an opera, two string quartets, piano pieces and songs, among the last being a masterpiece, *Gretchen am Spinnrade*. In 1815 he produced almost 150 songs (including the *Erlkönig*), two symphonies, two Masses, an opera, four operettas, and four piano sonatas.

In 1816 he gave up the teaching profession, went to live with his friend Franz von Schober, and devoted himself henceforth exclusively to composition. He lived on the generosity of several friends who recognized his genius and loved him—the prominent opera singer Johann Michael Vogl, the poet Johann Mayrhofer, Schober, and Joseph von Spaun among others. On two occasions—in the summers of 1818 and 1824—Schubert worked as a music teacher at the family estate of Count Esterházy in Zélész, Hungary. Otherwise he never held a job, though he applied for several, and earned only a pittance for his music. The rare occasions when his compositions were publicly performed proved disastrous: the operettas *Die Zwillingsbrüder* and *Die Zauberharfe*, produced in 1820, and *Rosamunde*, a play with his incidental music, in 1823. His first publication, a volume of songs that included the *Erlkönig*, issued in 1821, was made possible only through the bounty of his friends.

The disintegration of his health after 1823 contributed to deepen the depressions caused by his failure to gain recognition. Yet neither sickness nor pain, poverty nor frustration could keep him from creative work. He completed hundreds of compositions, producing one masterpiece after another. At long last, on March 26, 1828, a concert of his music aroused considerable enthusiasm. Convinced that the tide had now turned in his favor, Schubert planned not only many new ambitious works but also some additional study of counterpoint with Simeon Sechter. But none of these plans materialized. He died in Vienna on November 19, 1828, and by his own request was buried in a grave near Beethoven's. Only many years after his death was his true greatness appreciated by the music world at large. Patient research by several notable musicians—including Robert Schumann, George Grove, and Arthur Sullivan—helped locate many of Schubert's manuscripts which had long been reposing, forgotten and dishevelled, on dusty shelves.

THE MAN

ANSELM HÜTTENBRENNER

Schubert's outward appearance was anything but striking and prepossessing. He was of short stature, rather stout, with a full round face. His brow had an agreeable curve. Because of his near-sightedness, he always wore eyeglasses. He never concerned himself with dress, and he detested going into high society because it meant careful dressing. He could not bring himself to discard his spoiled frock coat for a black suit. To bow or scrape or cringe in society was odious to him, and to hear words of flattery about himself disgusted him.

When Schubert and Mayrhofer were living together in the Wipplingerstrasse, the former would sit at his writing desk every day at six o'clock and compose without a break until one o'clock in the afternoon, smoking a few small pipes. If I came to see him in the morning, he would play to me what he had ready and waited to hear my opinion. If I praised any song especially he would say: "Yes, that was a good poem, and when one has something good the music comes easily, melodies just stream into one, so that it is a real joy. With a bad poem, everything sticks. One may make a martyrdom of it, but nothing but dry stuff comes out."

Schubert never composed in the afternoon. After the noonday meal he would go to a café-house, drink a small portion of black coffee, smoke for an hour or two, and read newspapers at the same time. Ordinarily, Schubert drank beer at the *Schwarze Katze* in Annasstrasse or the *Schnecke* near St. Peter's. . . . But when we were more affluent we would drink wine. Before a glass of wine, Schubert became most loquacious. His opinions on musical matters were acute, succinct, penetrating and to the point. When, at social gatherings, there was serious conversation about music, Schubert enjoyed listening and rarely joined in. But if a presumptuous amateur would show complete ignorance, Schubert's patience would snap and he would bark: "Better say nothing about things you do not understand at all, and never will!" Schubert rarely spoke about his works or himself, and when he did it was usually in a few well chosen words. His favorite subjects were Handel, Haydn, Mozart, and Beethoven. He had the highest esteem of all for Beethoven. Schubert was enchanted by the operas of Mozart. His favorite works were: the *Messiah* of Handel, *Don Giovanni* and the *Requiem* of Mozart, and the Fifth Symphony and the Mass in C major of Beethoven.

He was not an elegant pianist but was always sure of himself and played with facility. He played the violin and viola, and he also sang. His voice was weak but very agreeable. When Schubert would sing his own Lieder in the company of musicians he generally accompanied himself. When others sang them, he would sit in a remote corner of the room, or even in another room, and listen quietly.

Schubert was very religious and believed implicitly in God and the immortality of the soul. His religious ardor was reflected in many of his songs. At times when he was in dire need he never lost courage and if, at times, he had more than he needed, he willingly shared it with others who appealed to him.

Once, while taking a walk with Schubert in the country in 1821, I asked him if he had ever been in love. As he was generally cold and

157

uncommunicative to women at parties, I was inclined to believe he disliked them. "Oh, no!" he said. "I loved someone very dearly, and she loved me, too. She was the schoolmaster's daughter [Theresa Grob], somewhat younger than I was. She sang the soprano part in a Mass I had composed—most beautifully and with great feeling. She was not exactly pretty, and her face had pockmarks. But she had a heart of gold. For three years she hoped I would marry her. But I was unable to find a position which would have provided for us. She then acceded to the wishes of her parents by marrying somebody else. I still love her and there has been no one who has appealed to me so much."

THE COMPOSER

DONALD FRANCIS TOVEY

Schubert's masters at the "Konvict," or court chapel choir school, have been severely blamed for neglecting his education and allowing him to compose without restraint. One of these masters left on record the honest remark that when he tried to teach Schubert anything, he found the boy knew it already. . . . But we are not yet justified in inferring that the master really taught Schubert nothing. And there is abundant evidence that the child taught himself with remarkable concentration, if not with severity. One of the most trying tasks ever imposed on a young musician is that . . . which consists of composing an instrumental movement that follows, phrase by phrase, the proportions and modulations of a selected classical model. . . . Now the earliest song of Schubert that we possess is *Hagars Klage* (1811), an enormous rigmarole with at least twelve movements and innumerable changes of key; evidently (one would guess) a typical example of childish diffuseness. It turns out, however, to be accurately modelled, modulations and all, on a setting of the same poem by Johann Rudolf Zumsteeg (1760–1802), a composer of some historical importance as a pioneer in the art of setting dramatic narrative for voice with piano accompaniment. . . . Yet within the limits of *Hagars Klage* Schubert makes decisive progress, beginning by following his model closely until about the middle of the work. At this point, Zumsteeg's energy begins to flag, and the child's energy begins to rise. Schubert's declamation improves, and before he has finished his long task he has achieved a sense of climax and a rounding-off which Zumsteeg hardly seems to have imagined possible. Songwriting, whether on a large or a small scale, was still in its infancy. A few masterpieces appear sporadically among the experiments, themselves few and heterogeneous, of Haydn, Mozart, and Beethoven. The real development of the art-forms of song was worked out by the child Schubert with the same fierce concentration as that with which the child Mozart laid the foundations of his sonata forms.

Within the four years from this first attempt to "play the sedulous ape," Schubert had written three stout volumes of songs of all shapes and sizes, besides a still larger quantity of instrumental music. A professional copyist might wonder how the bulk was achieved by one penman within the time. And as the songs lead up to and include *Gretchen am Spinnrade* (1814) and *Erlkönig* (1815), it seems futile to blame Schubert's teachers for not teaching him more before he was seventeen. The maturity of this famous couple of masterpieces remains as miraculous when we know the mass of work by which the boy trained himself for them as when we know them only in isolation. *Gretchen am Spinnrade,* the earlier of the two, is an even more astonishing achievement than *Erlkönig.* There is no difficulty in understanding how the possibilities of *Erlkönig* would fire the imagination of any boy, though only a genius could control to artistic form the imagination thus fired. Schubert's *Erlkönig* is as eminently a masterpiece in musical form as in powerful illustration of the poem. It has the singular luck to be rivalled, and to some tastes surpassed by the setting of Karl Loewe (1796–1869), a work not much later in date but much more in touch with modern methods. Loewe brings out the rationalistic vein of Goethe's ballad by setting the Erlking's words to a mere ghostly bugle call which never leaves the notes of its one chord. Schubert uses melodies as pretty as the Erlking's promises. In other words, Loewe's point of view is that of the father assuring the fever-stricken child that the Erlking, with his daughter and his whisperings, are nothing but the marsh-mists

159

and the wind in the trees; while Schubert, like the child, remains unconvinced by the explanation. His terror is the child's; Loewe's terror is the father's. Schubert has already at the age of seventeen mastered one of his cardinal principles of song-writing, which is that wherever some permanent feature can be found in the background of the poem, that feature shall dominate the background of the music. The result is that, after all, he naïvely achieves a more complete setting of the poem with his purely musical apparatus than Loewe with his rational adroitness. Loewe has almost forgotten that the father, with his child in his arms, is riding at full gallop in the hope of reaching shelter before the marsh-fever takes its toll. Schubert, composing, like Homer, "with his eye on the object," represents the outward and visible situation by means of an "accompaniment" the adequate performance of which is one of the rarest *tours de force* in piano playing. . . . But Schubert's accompaniment also realizes the inward and spiritual situation. With the Erlking's speeches, the accompaniment, while still maintaining its pace, takes forms which instantly transfer the sense of movement from that of a thing seen by the spectator to that of the dazed and frightened child in the rider's arms. To some critics this may seem a small point; but it is decisive, not of the superiority of one version over the other, but of the completeness of Schubert's view. Against it all cavil at the "prettiness" of the Erlking's melodies is as futile as a cavil against the prettiness of the Erlking's words. Schubert at seventeen is a mature master of the ironies and tragedy of nature. He is also a better realist than Loewe. . . .

Gretchen am Spinnrade is a far more astonishing achievement for a boy of seventeen than *Erlkönig*. If, for the sake of argument, we summon up the naïve impertinence to ask where this shy choirboy, absorbed incessantly in writing and only just out of school, could have obtained the experience, not of Faust, but of the victim of Faust and Mephistopholes, the answer is not easily guessed; for *Faust*, though published, had not yet been presented on the stage. But plenty of good drama was cultivated in Viennese theaters, and we need not suppose that Schubert avoided it. He then kept his eye on the object, in this case the spinning wheel. And he knew, as Parry has admirably pointed out in *The Art of Music*, not only that the climax comes at the words *"Und ach! sein Kuss!"* but that with that climax the spinning is interrupted, and resumed only with difficulty. With these points settled, all that remains to be postulated is the possession of a noble and totally unsophisticated style, together with some individual power of modulation to secure variety in simplicity throughout a song which is too dramatic to be set to repetitions of a single strophic melody. The style Schubert already had; the individual power of modulation shows itself at the third line of the poem. Before Schubert, only Beethoven would have thought of moving from D minor to C major and straight back again without repeating C as the dominant of F. This modulation is here entirely Schubert's own, for the influence of Beethoven on Schubert had not yet at this time produced in him any directed result beyond a decided opinion that Beethoven was responsible for the *bizarrerie* of most contemporary music. Beethoven and Schubert were, in fact, developing the resources of key-relationship on identical principles; but this fact is not one that ever appears in the guise of any external points of their styles. Schubert's idolatry at this time was devoted to Mozart; and in the art-forms of song there was even less room for Mozart's style than for Beethoven's. With the forms of opera and of instrumental music the position was very different; and, now that we have illustrated Schubert's amazing early maturity in the pioneer work of the song with piano accompaniment, it is time to direct our attention to his work in other and older art forms. . . .

Just as Schubert's juvenile work in song writing culminates at seventeen in *Gretchen am Spinnrade* and *Erlkönig,* so does the equally huge pile of work in larger forms culminates at the same age in the Mass in F (1814). . . . Schubert's first Mass, is, in its way, a not less astonishing phenomenon than *Erlkönig;* and it is far more perfect in form, and even in style, than the ambitious efforts of his later years, the Masses in A-flat (1819–22) and E-flat (1828). . . . I am not acquainted with any models Schubert can have had for the very definite style of church music he here achieves. Possibly he heard a Mass or two by Cherubini, whom Beethoven considered the greatest composer of the age. . . . There is nothing remotely like it in the church music of either Mozart or Haydn. The triumphant performance of this important choral and orchestral work by the choir of Schubert's school was an experience such as very few modern Conservatory students can obtain at the age of seventeen. . . .

Schubert's boyhood, then, culminated in two of his most powerful songs, and a uniquely charming piece of church music. . . . In his early instrumental music there is nothing so important, though the quantity is not less enormous. The earliest pieces, including the earliest string quartets, are fantasies of such ubiquitous rambling that the catalogue-maker cannot specify their keys. . . . Apart from the earliest child's play, the quartets and symphonies of his adolescence [are] . . . for the most part stiff exercises in the outward forms of Mozart with a certain boyish charm of hero-worship in their melodies. The stiffness is anything but Mozartean; it is, in fact, the typical angularity of a conscientious student. Six symphonies, about a dozen string quartets, another dozen of piano sonatas, and a vast number of fragments, show him pursuing a consistent line of work, of observation and experiment; if with ideas in his head, then so much the better for the result; if without, then so much better for the practice. . . .

The first instrumental work which shows his peculiar power beginning to rise up against his greatest weakness of form is the ambitious Quintet in A major (1819) for the unusual combination of piano, violin, viola, cello and double bass. It is known as the *Forellen Quintet* because the fourth of its five movements (the most perfect, though not the most important) is a set of variations on his pretty song *Die Forelle* (*The Trout*). The Scherzo is another successful movement in one of those small melodic and sectional forms which nobody denies to be thoroughly within Schubert's grasp. But the important things are the first movement, the slow movement in F, and the finale. In all three cases the first half of the movement is the boldly drawn exposition of a design on the grandest scale, while the rest, with the exception of a well-managed modicum of development in the first movement, is a mere exact recapitulation of this exposition starting in such a key as to end in the tonic. In the first movement and in the finale Schubert adds insult to the crudity of this procedure by giving the usual direction that the exposition shall be repeated!

Now, the sonata forms, which are here in question, depend largely

162

on the balance and distinction between three typical organic members: an exposition, a development, and a recapitulation. Of these the most delicate is the recapitulation, on which the symmetry of the whole depends. In works like the *Forellen Quintet* Schubert was exhausted by the effort of his grand expositions and fell back with relief upon a mere copyist's task by way of recapituation. This was wrong; but the *a priori* theorist is not less wrong who regards extensive recapitulation as a weakness in the classical schemes. There is no surer touchstone of Schubert's, as of Mozart's, Beethoven's, and Brahms's, treatment of form, than the precise way in which their recapitulations differ from their expositions; and where Schubert is at the height of his power this difference is of classical accuracy and subtlety. . . . Two great movements notorious for their redundancies and diffuseness are the first movement of the String Quartet in G major (1826) and the first movement of the Piano Sonata in B-flat (1828), Schubert's last composition. In both of them the whole interest converges upon the return to what is called the "first subject," involving the return to the main key after the wanderings of a long and dramatic development. The method of that return is entirely different in the two cases; both passages may rank with the most sublime inspirations of Beethoven. In the G major Quartet the return has an overpowering pathos, which is the more surprising since the tone of the whole movement, though at the acme of romance and picturesqueness, is by no means tragic. Yet this passage is the most "inevitable," as well as the most unexpected part of the whole design. The original first subject began with a soft major chord which swelled out and exploded in an energetic phrase in the minor key. The next phrase repeated this event on the dominant. In the return, which is long expected, the soft tonic chord is minor, and the energetic phrase is calm and in the major key. The subsequent theme is not less wonderfully transferred in another way. In the B-flat Sonata the return is more subtle. The whole movement, as in the case of the G major Quartet, runs a course not unusual in Schubert's large designs; opening with a sublime theme of the utmost calmness and breadth; descending, by means of a good though abrupt dramatic stroke, from the sublime to the picturesque, and then drifting from the picturesque through prettiness to a gar-

163

rulous frivolity. But then comes meditation. The frivolous theme it-self begins to gather energy in the course of the development. It originates a dramatic passage which begins picturesquely, and rises from the picturesque to the sublime. When the calm has become ethereal a distant thunder is heard. That thunder has been twice heard during the opening of the movement. At present the key (D minor) is not far from the tonic. The main theme appears softly at a high pitch, harmonized in this neighboring key. The distant thunder rolls again, and the harmony glides into the tonic. The theme now appears, still higher, in the tonic. An ordinary artist would use this as the real return and think himself clever. But Schubert's distant thunder rolls yet again, and the harmony relapses into D minor. The tonic will have no real weight at such a juncture until it has been adequately prepared by its dominant. The theme is resumed in D minor; the harmony takes the necessary direction, and expectancy is now aroused and kept duly excited, for a return of the first subject in full. Accordingly, this return is one in which transformations would be out of place; and so Schubert's recapitulations of his first subject is unvaried until the peculiarities of his transition themes compel the modulations to take a new course.

At the risk of entering into further technicalities, we must now consider Schubert's dealings with what the idiotic terminology of sonata form calls the "second subject." The grounds for this term appear to be that there are no rules whatever to determine how many themes a sonata-exposition shall contain, nor how its themes shall be distributed; but that whatever is contained in or about the tonic key, from the outset to the first decisive change of key shall be called *the first subject,* and that whatever is contained from that decisive change of key to the end of the exposition shall be called *the second subject.* The material that effects the decisive change of key will obviously be called *the transition.* But as for what and where the different themes are, Haydn may run a whole exposition on one theme, Mozart may reserve one of his best themes for the development, and Beethoven may have one-and-a-half themes in his first subject, a very definite new theme for his transition, five-and-a-half themes in his second subject, and still a new one in the course of his development. And in all three composers you will have no reason

164

to expect any two works to be alike; and all three composers may adopt each other's procedures.

The real fixed points in the matter are that there is at the outset a mass of material clearly establishing the tonic key; that there then follows a decisive transition to another key; and that in that other key another mass of material completes the exposition. In any case, the exposition asserts its key in order to maintain them.

Schubert's first subjects are generally of magnificent breadth, and the length of his big movements is not actually greater than their openings imply. If Beethoven had to set to work from any one of Schubert's finest openings two things are certain: that he would have produced quite as long a movement, and that its materials would have been very differently distributed, especially as regards the continuation of the second subject. Up to that point all is well with Schubert. . . . His transition is usually an abrupt and some-times primitive dramatic stroke; whereas with Mozart it is, when not merely formal, an occasion of magnificent musical draughtsmanship such as Schubert achieved for another purpose in the passage in the B-flat Sonata which we have just discussed. Schubert, in avoiding the problems of such draughtsmanship, is only doing as Beethoven often did in his best early works; for Beethoven, too, found it easier to be either clever or abrupt at this juncture than to achieve Mozart's calm breadth of transition until his own style and scale of form had passed altogether beyond Mozart's horizon. Meanwhile, why should he or Schubert reject more startling methods which perfectly suit the circumstances of their early works (for Schubert did not know that his early works were going to last)? An author is perfectly justi-fied in simply saying, "Then a strange thing happened" on two con-ditions: first, that what happens is really strange; secondly, that the strange event is not a mere device of the author to get out of a diffi-culty.

Schubert's strange event is usually the beginning of his second subject in a quite unexpected key, remote from that in which it is going to continue. The masterly examples are to be found in the following first movements: in the great String Quartet in C (1813); in the Symphony in C (1828); the E-flat Piano Trio (1827); the Grand Duo for piano four hands (1824); and, once more, the Sonata in

B Flat. This last case is on the borderline; but the device is a true art form, widely different from the things in Beethoven which may have suggested it (see Beethoven's Sonatas, op. 10, no. 3, and op. 28); and Schubert's ways of bringing the unexpected key round to the orthodox one are thoroughly masterly. The trouble begins after this problem is solved. Then Schubert, feeling that the rest of his exposition must not be less spacious than its enormous opening, fills up most of what he guesses to be the required interval with a vigorous discussion of the matter already in hand. Even if the discussion does not lead him too far afield, it inevitably tends to obliterate the vital distinction between the exposition and the development, a distinction universal in the arts . . . quite irrespective of their names and shapes. The cruellest irony in this situation is that Schubert, whether he knows it or not, is only following or anticipating the advice so constantly given nowadays to orthodox young composers "to stick to the main themes and not dissipate energy on a multitude of new ones." Schubert is commonly cited as the awful example of such dissipation, which is supposed to lead to the bottomless pit of Liszt's symphonic poems. But these nefarious works are, in point of fact, fanatical efforts to evolve a new kind of music out of transformations of a single musical germ. And the first and greatest of the symphonic poems on Liszt's principles happens to be Schubert's *Wanderer Fantasy* (1822), a masterpiece of independent form which the *Lisztianer* were desperately anxious to explain away.

The real classical procedure with the continuation of a big second subject, the procedure of Mozart and Beethoven, is to produce a series of new sentences, all conspicuously shorter than the main themes, but not less sharply contrasted in length and shape among themselves. If the key of the second subject is not remote, one of these themes will probably have a strong admixture of a remote key within its own single phrase. This instantly serves all the purpose of Schubert's widest digressions. I have here sometimes called these items "themes," and sometimes "sentences." It does not matter a pin whether they are new themes or old; what matters is that they have the manner of exposition and not of development. They are epigrams, not discussions. That is why they make paragraphs that will bear recapitulation in the later stages of the movement, while Schu-

166

bert's expositions will not, though there is no other means of dealing with them. Schubert himself achieves the right kind of paragraph to perfection in the unique case of the *Unfinished Symphony* (1817); the very case which is most often quoted against him as illustrating his besetting sin of "vain repetitions," because its admirably terse and rhythmically uneven phrases persistently recur to the same theme. But Haydn, Mozart, and Beethoven would have recognized that Schubert had in this case grasped the secret of their own technique.

So far, then, we already see that it is no technical matter to sift "right" and "wrong" from Schubert's instrumental form, even with the earlier great masters to guide us. But when we find (as, for instance, in the first movement of the great C major Symphony) that some of the most obviously wrong digressions contain the profoundest, most beautiful, and most inevitable passages, then it is time to suspect that Schubert, like other great classics, is pressing his way towards new forms. In any case, where a work of art, or a human being, has ubiquitous great quantities together with a manifest lack of unity, there may be great difficulty (and, perhaps, small profit) in determining which of its conflicting personalities is the more real. If the progress is (as we have seen in the Sonata in B-flat) from the sublime to the garrulous, we shall naturally appeal from Schubert garrulous to Schubert sublime; but in the C major Symphony the whole tone is sublime, and nowhere more so than in the grotesque finale which fell on a blind spot in Hans von Bülow's sense of values. It is impossible in a summary non-technical statement to demonstrate what were the new forms towards which Schubert was tending; and the mechanical triviality of the accepted doctrines of sonata-form makes even a detailed technical demonstration more difficult than work on an unexplored subject. I must therefore beg permission to leave this matter with the dogmatic statement that the fruition of Schubert's new instrumental forms is to be found in Brahms, especially in the group of works culminating in the Piano Quintet, op. 34. . . .

Schubert's larger works belong to the main stream of our musical history; their weaknesses are relaxations of their powers, and Schubert has no devices (unless we count the absurdities of the *Forellen Quintet*) for turning them into an artificial method with a point of its own. Hence it is as easy for a later master in the main stream of musical thought to absorb and develop the essentials of Schubert's ideas as it is for a poet similarly situated to absorb the essentials of Shakespeare's. Neither Shakespeare nor Schubert will ever be understood by any critic or artist who regards their weaknesses and inequalities as proof that they are artists of less than the highest rank. . . .

Other elements in Schubert's sonata form are in much the same condition as his expositions; a condition in which weakness in the actual context is often indistinguishable from new power in some future art. The part of a sonata movement known specially as the development is, of course, already at an almost hopeless disadvantage in Schubert because his exposition will have already digressed into developments of its own. But nothing could be wider of the mark than the orthodox statement that Schubert is weak in this part of his form. His best developments are in themselves magnificent; but he has in some four or five cases committed an indiscretion which is a characteristically youthful result of the impression made upon him by the first movement of Beethoven's *Eroica Symphony,* the development of which produces a brilliant cumulative effect in its earlier stages by reproducing its first topic in another key after an energetic different line of argument has been worked out. This procedure Beethoven handles so tersely as to give a feeling of enormous breadth to a development elsewhere crowded with other matters; but when Schubert decides to resume his first topic in this manner he has no room for much beyond a plain transposed reproduction of the two pages of argument it has already cost him. After thus repeating his argument he generally has in store some stroke of genius by which its end shall bring about a beautiful return to the tonic; and the most primitive of Schubert's developments is more highly organized than that of the first movement of Schumann's Piano Quintet, in which Schubert's simplest plan is very successfully carried out in terms not so much of a mosaic as of a Dutch-tile fireplace. . . .

The most notorious of Schubert's developments is that in the first movement of the E-flat Piano Trio; where he goes over his argument, itself a cumulative slow crescendo, three times. When the third statement begins, its effect is, at the moment, disastrous, but it leads grandly enough to the return of the main theme in the tonic; and thus even here what is wrong is not the scheme in itself, but the impossible scale on which it is worked. In the first movement of the String Quintet in C major (1828), where the process consists of twice two stages, the one lyric and the other (on the same theme) energetic, the total impression is by no means unsuccessful, though processional rather than dramatic. There is no reason why it should not indicate a new type of form, such as Schumann actually produced, with less than his usual hardness of outline, in his D minor Symphony.

In both the E-flat Piano Trio and the String Quintet there can be no doubt as to the magnificence of the harmonies and changes of key, not only from one moment to the next, but as an entire scheme. This is still more eminently the case with the considerable number of Schubert's developments, some of them long and some short, that have no redundancy in their plan. I have already described the wonderful end of the development in Schubert's last composition, the Piano Sonata in B-flat; the whole development is a masterpiece, the more remarkable in that it all arises from the weakest part of the exposition. It would be a mistake to ascribe any part of its effect to its origin in that weakness; Schubert, in the year of his death, had not yet attained the power of Shakespeare and Beethoven in blending tragedy and comedy; though he had long overcome his early resentment against Beethoven's use of that power. It is impossible to set limits to what he might have achieved in a longer life; both Beethoven and Shakespeare were older than Schubert before they could be sure of finding the right continuation and the right contrast to any note as sublime as that of Schubert's greatest openings.

At least two of Schubert's first movements may be considered flawless; at all events, that is by far the best assumption on which to interpret them. The first movement of the *Unfinished Symphony* has already been cited; its development is in superb dramatic contrast to the exposition, and nothing can be more characteristic of the greatest composers than the subtlety, pointed out by Sir George Grove, of alluding to the syncopated accompaniment of the second subject without the theme itself. The other masterpiece among Schu-

169

bert's first movements is little known, and not easily accessible. It is the first movement of an unfinished piano sonata in C (1815), not included in the usual collections of his piano works. Perhaps it is the most subtle thing he ever wrote. To describe it would involve a full account of Schubert's whole range of harmonic ideas, which are here sounded to their utmost depths. And these depths are not such that later artistic developments can make them seem shallow. Schubert's harmonic range is the same as Beethoven's; but his great modulations would sound as bold in a Wagner opera as in a Beethoven symphony. We have now seen in what ways the weaknesses of Schubert's expositions and developments are intimately involved in tendencies towards new kinds of form; and it remains to consider his recapitulations and codas. When Schubert's instrumental works are at their best his handling of the recapitulation (that is to say, of what follows after his development has returned to the tonic) is of the highest order of mastery where the original material permits. He shows an acumen not less than Beethoven's in working out inevitable but unexpected results from the fact that his second subject (or his transition to it) did not begin in the key in which it was destined to settle. To describe these results would be too technical a procedure; but the reader may go far to convince himself of their importance by taking the cases of the *Unfinished Symphony* and the C major Symphony and comparing what actually happens in the recapitulation with what would have been the course of modulations with a plain transposition to the second subject into such a key as would lead to the tonic automatically. . . .

Since the indiscretions of Schubert's expositions, though they may spoil the effect of his developments, do not prevent him from almost always developing magnificently and sometimes faultlessly, we may say that up to the end of the recapitulation, Schubert's energy stands the strain of his most impracticable designs. Further it seldom goes, and the codas of his first movements, with the solitary exception of the C major Symphony, are all in the manner of an expiring flame, often supremely beautiful, sometimes abruptly dramatic, but never revealing new energies like the great codas of Beethoven. In the codas of finales Schubert's energy is capable of expansion, for the enormous sprawling forms of the typical Schubert finales are the outcome of a sheer irresponsibility that has involved him in little or no strain, though he often shows invention of the highest order in their main themes. Here, again, there are two exceptional masterpieces of form, in both of which the grotesque is the veil of the sublime: the finales of the String Quintet and the C major Symphony.

But the mention of Schubert's finales opens up the whole question of his range of style. In the present discussion I have been compelled to make frequent use of the word "sublime," not by way of mere reaction against the current impression that Schubert is a composer of secondary importance in his larger works, but by way of accurate definition. The only qualification the term needs is that in Schubert it is still associated with the picturesque and the unexpected; it is, in fact, as sublime as any artist's earlier works can be. No one calls the clear night sky picturesque; and when Beethoven was inspired by it to write the slow movement of his String Quartet in E minor he was older than Schubert lived to be. It is, however, one thing to write under the direct inspiration of the night sky, and another thing to set a description of it to music; and there is a wonderful song for tenor solo with male voice chorus and piano, in which the piano part, representing the innumerable multitude of stars, achieves the sublime by Schubert's characteristic picturesqueness (*Die Nacht*). In the voice parts Schubert is, of course, already an older and more experienced artist; more experienced, in fact, than Beethoven, and so in this way, as in many others from *Erlkönig* onwards, the spacing of the words and the turns of melody are as severe and indistinguishable from familiar forms or formulas as the lines of a Greek temple. Now, it is in this matter of the sublime use of formulas that we can trace gradations of Schubert's style. When he begins a big instrumental piece with a formal gesture (as in the big A major Piano Sonata, 1828, and the *Forellen Quintet*), his intention and achievement are usually grandiose; and this applies to most of his argumentative sequences and processes of development. He can seldom rise above the grandiose when either his musical forms or his verbal subjects give him a sense of responsibility. On official occasions he is rustic, if not awkward; and though the beautiful figures of his last two Masses (in A-flat and E-flat) out-

171

weigh the clumsiness of their officially necessary fugues, it is perhaps only in the *Incarnatus* of the A-flat Mass that his church music reveals the depths of the Schubert vein of imagination. In a *Kyrie* or a *Benedictus* there is a vein of beauty which rises far above, but which is not incompatible with, a vein of rather too comfortable piety prevalent in the religious poetry of the period; and we have an excellent opportunity for measuring the difference between the wrong and the right stimulus to the imagination of a rustic tone poet by comparing Schubert's grandiose song, *Die Allmacht* (1825), . . . with its origin, as to modulations and general aspirations, in the aria known in English as "In Native Worth" in Haydn's *Creation*. Here it is Haydn, another rustic composer, who quietly reaches the sublime in describing man made in God's image; while Schubert, dealing with verses that begin with the Almighty speaking through thunderstorms and end with the heart of man, achieves Haydn's finest modulation twice in a plainly repeated passage instead of once as a divinely unexpected variation.

It is tempting, but dangerous, to draw inferences unsupported by musical facts, from the statistics of Schubert's song-text, . . . from the merits of the poems he set to music. His friend, Mayrhofer, who was said to toss him song after song across a table to be set as fast as the next poem could be written, was no Goethe, nor does he compare with the unpretentious Wilhelm Müller; yet most of the Mayrhofer songs rank with the Goethe and Wilhelm Müller songs among the greatest of Schubert's or any musician's achievements in lyric music. At his own best Mayrhofer will "do." . . . Yet *Viola, eine Blumenballade* inspired Schubert at the height of his power to one of the last of his very long songs, a masterpiece of form, using every suggestion of the words to purposes of an imagination as true as Wordsworth's.

Müller, the poet of Schubert's two great song cycles, we are in some danger of underrating; he deserves at all events full credit for the quality ascribed by Pope to Homer and by Johnson to Thomson, of always writing "with his eye on the object"; and his style is absolutely free from affectation. It is, like all German poetry of its class, untranslatable without disastrous injustice. . . .

The cumulative pathos of *Die schöne Müllerin* (1823) owes its

172

force to the radiant happiness which culminates in the middle of the song cycle when the younger miller in his *Wanderjahr* is accepted by his beloved miller's daughter, who afterwards deserts him. The story of the *Winterreise* (1827) is as simple, but is not directly told; all we know is that the wanderer sets forth in mid-winter to leave the town where his beloved has jilted him, and that everything he sees reflects back upon lost happiness and forward to death that will not come. The text of each song is a straightforward verse description of some common scene of country life. . . . These two song cycles, *Die schöne Müllerin* and *Die Winterreise,* must be taken as two single works. To regard them as forty-four songs will only lead us to the endless shallows of a criticism occupied with questions of which is the prettiest, the most important, or the most distinguished. The prettiness and perfection of any single member does, no doubt, seem sufficient to itself, . . . but the cumulative effect of the whole cycle is overwhelmingly greater than the sum of its parts. Even taken by itself, *Trockne Blumen* has a pathos that makes us grudge Schubert forgiveness for subsequently writing on it a set of variations, which was a bad thing to do; and writing them for flute, which was worse; and making some of them brilliant, which was blasphemous. But in its context *Trockne Blumen* is a song which many a singer has found difficult to learn because its pathos destroys all control of the voice.

The final song, *Des Baches Wiegenlied,* is not less difficult, and its supreme art lies in its being merely strophic, with melody and accompaniment unaltered throughout all its stanzas. The criticism of vocal music will never attain what should be regarded as its ordinary professional competence until it recognizes that the merely strophic song with a single melody for all stanzas is no mere labor-saving device, but, as Brahms always maintained, the highest accomplishment of the song-composer's invention, compared to which the declamatory song is child's play. Schubert himself has produced too many masterpieces of declamatory song, such as *Der Wanderer* (1816), *Der Doppelgänger* from the *Schwanengesang* (1828), and *Der Tod und das Mädchen* (1817), not to stultify any theory of song-writing that does not accept Wagner and Hugo Wolf as masters of the theory of musical declamation; but a criticism that regards that

173

theory as constituting the whole, or even the highest art of vocal music, is fundamentally incapable of understanding verse. . . .

One technical principle, not difficult to understand, suffices to dispose of any *a priori* objections to what has been called the "lazy" method of the strophic song with the same tunes to all stanzas. The objection rests on an ignorant belief in the bar-stroke as a genuine and rigid musical unit, together with the idea that no other basis of accent counts. Composers with poor rhythmic invention produce melodies in accordance with these limitations; and they are rightly afraid of deviating from them; since they cannot do so with conviction. But great masters like Schubert play with all possible occasions of musical accent as great poets play with verse accents; and the various occasions of accent coincide only in order to make special points. The first notes of the first song in the *Winterreise* show the method at once. The first note is off the beat (in anacrusis); but is higher than the second. The beat comes on the second, which is an expressive discord. The height of the first note provides enough accent to fit any prosodic inversion without interrupting by declamatory pedantries the dogged march of the jilted lover as he leaves the town of his joy and sorrow. But the note is not so high as to make an accent where the iambic feet of the verse are normal. Then the sensitive discord on the first note of the bar asserts itself.

Schubert is not less masterly in the handling of paragraphs as wholes. He never over-punctuates, as is the inveterate tendency of the conscientiously declamatory composers. *Dass sie hier gewesen,* a series of statements that the air, the flowers, and so forth, prove that the beloved has been there, is set by Schubert, strophically, to a musical paragraph beginning outside the key and corresponding in every point of musical analysis to the grammatic structure of the poem, so that it is as impossible to lose the thread of its series of dependent clauses as to misunderstand its sentiment. In the first of the *Schwanengesang* (a publisher's title for a selection of Schubert's last songs) *Rauschendes Bachlein,* the *Bachlein* continues its movement while the thought of the beloved hanging her head in a pensive mood is expressed at a tempo twice as slow as that of the rest of the setting. In short, Schubert the songwriter is as great a master of movement (which is form) as Mozart or Beethoven. All his structural devices seem so absurdly simple, when pointed out, that only the cumulative effect of their number, variety, and efficiency will suffice to undo the injuries that our understanding of Schubert's art has suffered from overemphasis on his incapacity to theorize in words, and from academic ignorance of the nature of musical art forms on a large scale. Vogl, the singer, who, in Schubert's own lifetime, recognized and produced his songs, spoke of his insight into poetry as "clairvoyant"; and that praise was useful in his day. At present we cannot too strongly emphasize the fact that, clairvoyance or common sense, Schubert's mastery in his songs includes an immense technique consciously developed and polished from childhood in over six hundred extant examples, many of them several times rewritten. His inability to explain himself in verbal or analytic theory is the inability of a master to explain an art to people who, thinking they know all about it, do not, in fact, know that it exists. . . .

When all the pretty and picturesque things, and even all the dramatic things in Schubert's songs, have had their due; even after *Der Doppelgänger*, which many consider the greatest of his songs, has been revered for its awful transcendence of Heine's grim pathos; still the full measure of Schubert is revealed when, unoppressed by ceremonies and official responsibilities, he joins Beethoven and Wordsworth in Nature-worship. The classical interests of Goethe and Schiller contribute largely to this strain, and Schubert is magnificently himself when dealing with Greek subjects, and with "cosmic emotion," as in Mayrhofer's *Auflösung* (1824) . . . or, in a less remote vein, the great long *Waldesnacht*.

It is in this mighty framework that the sorrows of the Miller and the banished Winter Traveler become universal; and the calm of *Du bist die Ruh* (1823) is as mystic as the glory of Beatrice's eyes which drew Dante from heaven to higher heaven.

SCHUBERT SPEAKS

Everybody was astounded at the piety I expressed in a hymn to the Holy Virgin (the *Ave Maria*), and which, it would seem, moves everyone's soul and puts people in a devout frame of mind. I believe that arises from the fact that I never force myself into a devout mood, and never compose such hymns or prayers except when I am unconsciously inspired by Her. Then, however, it is generally real, true devotion.

. . . . .

All I have created is born of my understanding of music, and by my own sorrow. It is the latter that seems to interest the world least of all.

. . . . .

O imagination! Man's greatest treasure, inexhaustible source at which both Art and Learning come to drink! O remain with us, though recognized and venerated only by the few, so that we may be safeguarded from the so-called enlightenment, that hideous skeleton without blood or flesh.

. . . . .

Sorrow strengthens the understanding and strengthens the character, whereas happiness seldom troubles about the former, and only makes for weakness or frivolity in the latter.

. . . . .

Picture to yourself someone whose health is permanently injured and who, in sheer despair, does everything to make it worse instead of better. Picture to yourself, I say, someone whose brilliant hopes have come to nothing, someone to whom love and friendship are at most a source of bitterness, someone whose inspiration (whose creative inspiration, at least) for all that is beautiful threatens to fail, and then ask yourself if that is not a wretched and unhappy being. "*Meine Ruh is hin, mein Herz ist schwer, ich finde sie nimmer und nimmer mehr.*" That could be my daily song now, for every night when I go to sleep I hope never to wake again, and each morning I am only recalled to the griefs of yesterday. So I pass my days, joyless and friendless (1824).

176

. . . . .

My Dream*

I was a brother among many brothers. Our parents were good
folk. I was devoted to them with a deep love.—Father once took us
to a banquet. There my brothers grew exceedingly merry. But I
was sad. Then Father came and ordered me to enjoy the delicious
food. But I could not. So he grew angry and banished me from his
sight. I turned away and, with a heart full of boundless love for
those who scorned it, I wandered far from there. For years I felt
divided between the utmost grief and the greatest love. Then came
tidings of my Mother's death. I hastened to see her; and Father,
whose heart was softened by sorrow, did not prevent me. Then I
beheld her corpse. Tears flowed from my eyes. I saw her lying there
like the happy old past, in the spirit of which, according to the
desire of the departed one, we were to live, as she herself had lived.

And in sorrow we followed her corpse, and the coffin sank into the
earth.—From that day on I lived again at home. Then once more
Father led me to his favorite garden. He asked me if I liked it. But
I hated the garden and dared not say so. Then, flushing, he asked
me for the second time if I liked the garden. Trembling I said no.
Then Father struck me and I fled. And for the second time I turned
my steps and, with a heart full of boundless love for those who
scorned it, again I wandered far away. For long, long years I sang
songs. When I would sing of love, it turned to pain. And again, when
I would sing of pain, it turned to love.

Thus love and pain divided me.

And once I had word of a saintly maiden who had just died. And
a circle was formed about her grave wherein many youths and old
men forever paced as though in bliss. Softly they murmured, so as
not to arouse the maiden.

From her tombstone heavenly thoughts, like delicate sparks whose
sound was scarcely audible, seemed forever to be showered upon
the youths. Sorely I longed to walk there too. But they said: nothing

---

* This prose-poem allegory was written by Schubert on July 3, 1822. The
Freudian psychoanalyst, Dr. Edward Hitschmann, wrote that "this serious
visionary narrative may be rightly regarded as an allegorical mirroring of his
inner development."

177

short of a miracle can bring you into this circle. However, with slow steps and lowered gaze I approached the tombstone and, before I was aware, I found myself in the circle, which gave forth a sound of wondrous loveliness; and I felt as though eternal bliss were being pressed into a single moment. Father too I beheld, reconciled and loving. He folded me in his arms and wept. But not as much as I.

HECTOR BERLIOZ

1 8 0 3 – 1 8 6 9

HECTOR-LOUIS BERLIOZ, son of a physician, was born in Côte-Saint-André, France, on December 11, 1803. In 1821 he was sent to Paris to study medicine, but three years later he deserted the sciences to concentrate on music. In 1825, while attending the Paris Conservatory, his Mass was successfully introduced at the St. Roch Church. Two concert overtures were heard in 1828, and on December 5, 1830 there took place the première of his first masterwork, the *Symphonie fantastique*, inspired by his unrequited love for the Shakespearean actress, Harriet Smithson, whom he had not even met personally. Meanwhile, in October of 1830, Berlioz had won the Prix de Rome. But, hating Italy, he did not complete the required three-year stay in Rome. Returning to Paris in 1832, he arranged a performance of his *Symphonie fantastique* to make an impression on Harriet Smithson, and they met for the first time. A stormy courtship followed, culminating in marriage on October 3, 1833. But theirs was a violent clash of temperaments from the beginning. After the birth of a son, they separated permanently.

That second performance of the *Symphonie fantastique* proved a sensation. Paganini, who was present, commissioned Berlioz to write a major work, which turned out to be *Harold in Italy*, introduced on November 23, 1834. The opera *Benvenuto Cellini*, introduced at the Opéra on September 10, 1838, the dramatic symphony, *Romeo and Juliet*, heard in 1839, the concert overture *Le Carnaval romain* in 1844, and the dramatic legend *The Damnation of Faust* in 1846 placed Berlioz among the most provocative, exciting and iconoclastic composers in France at that time—even though neither *Benvenuto Cellini* nor *The Damnation of Faust* were successful when introduced. In 1842, Berlioz began the first of several extensive tours conducting programs of his music in Europe and Russia; in 1852, and again in 1855, he was a guest of Liszt in Weimar for the celebration on each occasion of a "Berlioz Week." In 1856 he was elected a member of the Institut de France.

From 1852 until his death Berlioz was the librarian of the Paris Conservatory. He did not remarry until 1854, when his estranged wife died. His second wife, Maria Recio, brought him no greater happiness than the first. The death of Berlioz's son in 1867, and the shattering effects of a nervous ailment, combined to embitter Berlioz's last years. He died in Paris on March 8, 1869.

Berlioz had distinguished himself not only as a composer and conductor, but also as a trenchant music critic for several Paris journals and as the author of one of the most celebrated musical autobiographies and an epoch-making treatise on orchestration, *Traité d'instrumentation et d'orchestration modernes.*

THE MAN

ROMAIN ROLLAND

Everything about Berlioz was misleading, even his appearance. In legendary portraits he appears as a dark southerner with black hair and sparkling eyes. But he was really very fair and had blue eyes, and Joseph d'Ortigue tells us they were deep-set and piercing, though sometimes clouded by melancholy or langor. He had a broad forehead furrowed with wrinkles by the time he was thirty, and a thick mane of hair, or, as E. Legouvé puts it, "a large umbrella of hair, projecting like a movable awning over the beak of a bird of prey." His mouth was well cut, with lips compressed and puckered at the corners in a severe fold, and his chin was prominent. He had a deep voice, but his speech was halting and often tremulous with emotion; he would speak passionately of what interested him, and at times be effusive in manner, but more often he was ungracious and reserved. He was of medium height, rather thin and angular in figure, and when seated he seemed much taller than he really was. He was very restless and inherited from his native land, Dauphiné, the mountaineer's passion for walking and climbing and the love of a vagabond life which remained with him nearly to his death. He had an iron constitution, but he wrecked it by privation and excess, by his walks in the rain and by sleeping out-of-doors in all weathers, even when there was snow on the ground.

But in this strong and athletic frame lived a feverish and sickly soul that was dominated and tormented by a morbid craving for love and sympathy, "that imperative need of love which is killing me. . . ." To love, to be loved—he would give up all for that. But his love was that of a youth who lives in dreams; it was never the strong, clear-eyed passion of a man who has faced the realities of life and who sees the defects as well as the charms of the woman he loves. Berlioz was in love with love and lost himself among visions and sentimental shadows. To the end of his life he remained "a poor little child worn out by a love that was beyond him." But this man who lived so wild and adventurous a life expressed his passions with delicacy; and one finds an almost girlish purity in the immortal love passages of *Les Troyens* or the *"nuit sereine"* of *Roméo et Juliette*. And compare this Virgilian affection with Wagner's sensual raptures. Does it mean that Berlioz could not love as well as Wagner? We only know that Berlioz' life was made up of love and its torments. The theme of a touching passage in the introduction of the *Symphonie fantastique* has been identified by Julien Tiersot, in his interesting book, with a romance composed by Berlioz at the age of twelve when he loved a girl of eighteen "with large eyes and pink shoes"—Estelle, *Stella montis, Stella matutina*. These words—perhaps the saddest he ever wrote—might serve as an emblem of his life, a life that was a prey to love and melancholy, doomed to wringing of the heart and awful loneliness; a life lived in a hollow world among worries that chilled the blood; a life that was distasteful and had no solace to offer him in its end. He has himself described this terrible *"mal de l'isolement"* which pursued him all his life, vividly and minutely. He was doomed to suffering, or, what was worse, to make others suffer.

Who does not know his passion for Harriet Smithson? It was a sad story. He fell in love with an English actress who played Juliet.

(Was it she or Juliet whom he loved?) He caught but a glance of her, and it was all over with him. He cried out, "Ah, I am lost!" He desired her; she repulsed him. He lived in a delirium of suffering and passion; he wandered about for days and nights like a madman, up and down Paris and its neighborhood without purpose or rest or relief until sleep overcame him wherever it found him—among the sheaves in a field near Villejuif, in a meadow near Sceaux, on the bank of the frozen Seine near Neuilly, in the snow, and once on a table in the Café Cardinal, where he slept for five hours, to the great alarm of the waiters, who thought he was dead. Meanwhile, he was told slanderous gossip about Harriet, which he readily believed. Then he despised her and dishonored her publicly in his *Symphonie fantastique*, paying homage in his bitter resentment to Camille Moke, a pianist, to whom he lost his heart without delay.

After a time Harriet reappeared. She had now lost her youth and her power; her beauty was waning, and she was in debt. Berlioz' passion was at once rekindled. This time Harriet accepted his advances. He made alterations in his symphony and offered it to her in homage of his love. He won her and married her, with fourteen thousand francs' debt. He had captured his dream—Juliet! Ophelia! What was she really? A charming Englishwoman, cold, loyal, and sober-minded, who understood nothing of his passion; and who, from the time she became his wife, loved him jealously and sincerely and thought to confine him within the narrow world of domestic life. But his affections became restive, and he lost his heart to a Spanish actress (it was always an actress, a virtuoso, or a part) and left poor Ophelia and went off with Maria Recio, the Inès of *Favorite*, the page of *Comte Ory*—a practical, hardheaded woman, an indifferent singer with a mania for singing. The haughty Berlioz was forced to fawn upon the directors of the theater in order to get her parts, to write flattering notices in praise of her talents, and even to let her make his own melodies discordant at the concerts he arranged. It would all be dreadfully ridiculous if this weakness of character had not brought tragedy in its train.

So the one he really loved and who always loved him remained alone without friends in Paris, where she was a stranger. She drooped in silence and pined slowly away, bedridden, paralyzed, and unable to speak during eight years of suffering. Berlioz suffered too, for he loved her still and was torn with pity—"pity, the most painful of all emotions." But of what use was this pity? He left Harriet to suffer alone and to die just the same. And what was worse, as we learn from Legouvé, he let his mistress, the odious Recio, make a scene before poor Harriet. Recio told him of it and boasted about what she had done. And Berlioz did nothing—"How could I? I love her."

THE COMPOSER

W. H. HADOW

In criticizing the works of a great composer there are only two questions which it is of any moment to consider. We may ask what was his power of imagination, we may ask what was his command of technical resource, and there inquiry must stop. . . .

There can be no two opinions as to the existence of great imaginative power in Berlioz's work. The very pace at which he often composed is in itself sufficient evidence. The "March to the Gallows" from the *Symphonie fantastique* (1830–31) was written in one night; the "Pilgrim's March" in *Harold in Italy* (1834), improvised in a couple of hours; the *Élégie* (1831), one of the wildest and most complicated songs in existence, was created in a single flash, while for the *Lachrymosa* in his Requiem (1837) he had to invent a system of shorthand in order to embody the ideas that came too fast for ordinary notation. And it must be remembered that this rapid production is not like the facility of a Johann Adolph Hasse (1699–1783) or an Adalbert Gyrowetz (1763–1850), flowing with a diluted repetition of a current commonplace. The thought here is absolutely new, and is presented with a fullness of detail which none but a master could have conceived. There may be in the earlier compositions some traces of Beethoven's influence, and even some echoes of Gluck, and perhaps Gasparo Spontini (1774–1851); but every artist must be the child of his circumstances in the initial stages of his work. Beethoven himself begins under the shadow of

183

Mozart, and nevertheless he emerged later into the free light and air of an artistic personality. Indeed we may assert roundly that there is not one composer in the history of music who has more claim to originality than Berlioz.

On the other hand we must confess, unwillingly enough, that the purity of his imagination was not on a level with its force, and that he wholly lacked that sense of reticence and repression that should be its necessary complement. His thought is sometimes impaired and degraded by that touch of defilement which pathologists note as a possible symptom of insanity; and he never seems to have reflected that, even in the spiritual language of music, there are some things which it is better not to say. Two stories will make this clear. During his stay at Rome he conceived the plan of a grand opera (fortunately never carried out) in which an impious and licentious potentate should organize a burlesque Last Judgment as a mockery to the prophets who denounced him, and find, as the curtain fell, that his pygmy trumpets were silenced by the four angels who announced the real coming of Christ. Again, during his second visit to London he attended the children's service at St. Paul's, and was immensely impressed by its beauty, as Haydn had been before him, and on leaving the cathedral fancied that he saw the whole scene travestied in Pandemonium. It is to this unwholesome morbid element in his nature that we owe the orgies in *Harold*, the "Chorus of the Devils" in *The Damnation of Faust* (1846), and worse than either, the horrible "Witches' Sabbath" in the *Symphonie fantastique*. And as an inevitable consequence, he is almost entirely wanting in the real epic touch, the white Alpine sublimity of Beethoven's Mass in D or Brahms's *Song of Fate*. He can inspire wonder but not awe, terror but not reverence, and much of the work which he intended to be most impressive resolves itself into a series of scenes which sometimes rise to the level of the Inferno, and oftener sink to that of the *Musée Wiertz*.

One region, then, and that of the highest, must be regarded as closed to him. He has left no work which breathes the same serene ether as the *Missa Papae Marcelli* or the *Messiah*. He comes near the line in the *Sanctus* of his *Requiem* and perhaps the final chorus of the *Enfance du Christ* (1850–54). But as a general rule his attempts to express pure religious emotion are either dull, like the "Easter Hymn" in *Faust,* or preoccupied, like the "Pilgrim's Chorus" in *Harold.* Still there is much opportunity for noble achievement in lower fields of poetry, and of this he has made abundant use. Like Ben Jonson in Swinburne's estimate, if he does not belong to the Gods of melody, at any rate he may be numbered among the Titans.

In the first place he has a complete mastery over the whole gamut of fear and pain. The stupendous crashing force of the *Tuba mirum,* the *Lacrymosa* echoing with the agony of a panic-stricken world, the *Judex Crederis* from the *Te Deum* (1849), which reiterates higher and higher the expectation of the Great Judge and the appeal to His mercy, are conceived with a vastness of scale, and carried out with an unerring certainty of effect to which we shall hardly find a parallel. . . . On a lower level, but no less remarkable in execution, is the ride to the Abyss, where Faust and Mephistopheles gallop through a pestilential air, filled with "horrid shapes and shrieks and sights unholy," till the end comes, and the most tragic figure in all dramatic poetry sinks with a despairing cry to meet his doom. To say that these things are not worth portraying is simply to remove the landmarks of artistic expression. Everything is worth portraying which is not essentially foul or obscene, and even a degraded subject may sometimes be ennobled by a dignity of treatment. No doubt the story of Faust is intrinsically horrible, and Berlioz had fixed upon its least sympathetic aspect. But it is not until we come to the hideous chorus of gibbering fiends that we feel that the legitimate bound is exceeded and that horror passes into loathing.

A second noticeable point is his treatment of the passion of love. . . . Apart from the *Symphonie fantastique* to which further allusion will later be made, we have the trio in *Faust,* and the exquisite Adagio in the *Romeo and Juliet* symphony (1839) to sound the note of an emotion which knows that it is true and tries to cheat itself into the belief that it is happy. For there is always an undercurrent of melancholy in his love-making, a sense of present pain, or an apprehension of coming trouble, till tragedy reaches its limit in the heart-broken *Élégie* and the vindictive despair of *Les Troyens* (1856–59).

185

Pathos and humor are proverbially akin, and we need feel no surprise that the composer of *La Captive* (1832) should also have written the fencing scene in *Benvenuto Cellini* (1834–38) and Somarone's delightful "Wedding Cantata" in *Béatrice et Bénédict* (1860–62). There is plenty of rough fun, too, in the Auerbach's *Keller* episode of *Faust*, and above all in the rollicking *Carnaval romain* Overture (1844). But as a rule Berlioz wrote his music seriously and kept his jokes for his *feuilletons*. He did not, perhaps, altogether realize the opportunities for comedy which can be turned to account in a quaint phrase or an unexpected tone. . . . Indeed, if there is any matter for astonishment at all it is that a man who possessed so keen a sense of the ludicrous should not have given it fuller expression in the art which draws as readily from the springs of laughter as it does from the fount of tears.

There remains to be considered one class of poetical ideas which may be called "spectacular": those in which the music is intended to call up some scenic display, religious, chivalrous, martial, or what not, which it presents to us in repose, with no direct appeal to emotion and little exhibition of present activity. Such, for instance, is the intermezzo in *Les Troyens*, which represents a forest during a hunting scene; such is the *Hymne à la France* (1844), with its stately chorus, such the strong movement of the *Menace des Francs* (1851), and the sturdy industrialism of the *Chant des Ouvriers*, and such undoubtedly is the *Kyrie* in the *Requiem*, which suggests some vague remote picture of a cathedral interior, with dim lights and white-robed priests and a hanging cloud of incense. Under this category may come the concert overtures, where Berlioz for once abandons his program, and is content to indicate rather than prescribe; and at its extreme verge may be placed the *Symphonie funèbre et triomphale* (1840) which brings us back again to the world of actual drama.

So far we have examined Berlioz's imaginative power in the light of his own principle: that music is a definite language capable of communicating definite ideas. It is in defense of this principle that he prefaces so many of his instrumental works with a scheme or program describing in set words the emotion which his melodies are

186

expected to arouse, or the scene which they are intended to portray. . . .

Berlioz's most uncompromising piece of program music is the *Symphonie fantastique.* In his letter to Ferrand (April 16, 1830) the composer tells the story which the work is intended to express with a fullness of detail which at least shows that he has the courage of his opinions. The opening Adagio presents a young artist with a lively imagination and a sensitive temperament, plunged in that half-morbid revery which French writers explain as the *"besoin d'aimer."* In the Allegro which follows he meets his fate, "the woman who realizes the ideal of beauty and charm for which his heart has yearned" and gives himself up to the passion which she inspires. His love is typified by a rather sentimental melody, given in full at the opening of the movement, and repeated in various thematic forms throughout the whole work. The second movement proper is an Adagio, in which the artist wanders alone through the fields, listening to the shepherd's pipe and the mutterings of a distant storm, and dreaming of the newborn hope that has come to sweeten his solitude. Next comes a ballroom scene, in which he stands apart, silent and preoccupied, watching the dancers with a listless, careless gaze, and cherishing in his heart the persistent melody. In a fit of despair he poisons himself with opium, but the narcotic instead of killing him produces a horrible vision in which he imagines that he has killed his mistress and that he is condemned to die. The fourth movement is the march to the scene of execution, a long, grim procession, winding up with the *idée fixe* and the sharp flash of the guillotine. Last comes the *pensée d'une tête coupée:* a hideous orgy of witches and demons who dance around the coffin, perform a burlesque *Dies Irae* for its funeral rite, and welcome with diabolic glee a brutalized and degraded version of the original subject. And so the symphony ends with an indescribable scene of chaos and fury, of fiendish mockery and insult, a delirium of passion, mad, riotous, and unrestrained.

Not a very noble or exalted romance it may be, but this is not the point at issue. The only question is how far Berlioz has succeeded in expressing it through the medium employed, and, with all recognition of his marvelous ingenuity of workmanship, we must admit

187

that he has failed. It is inconceivable that any hearer should write down the story from the music unless he had already some knowledge of its outline, and even with the program before us we only feel that a set of vague indeterminate forms are being unduly specialized. The recurrent melody may no doubt symbolize "a white woman's robe," as Heine said, but it could equally well symbolize a hundred other things. The vigor and rush of the opening Allegro no doubt suggests agitation, but it may be one of its various forms. The ball scene, with its exceedingly beautiful waltz melody, contains no necessary thought of despair—much less such despair as would lead to suicide. The "March to the Gallows" is fierce and gloomy enough, but it might be a battle hymn or the funeral march of a warrior, and so with the other movements. They all suggest some generic form under which the particular idea may be classified, but they do not indicate the particular idea itself. And this is not through any inadequacy on the part of the composer, for Berlioz had employed all the resources of a vivid imagination to give shape and color to his idea; it is simply because he has tried to make music perform a task, of which from its very nature it will always be incapable. There is a great deal of fine and noble work in the *Symphonie fantastique*, notably in the three middle movements, but it pleases in spite of the program, not in consequence of it.

The same is the case with the *Harold in Italy* symphony where the scenes are loosely strung together . . . and still more with the *Rêverie et caprice* (1839), for violin.

But it is a pleasanter task to turn and consider the second of the two points of discussion—the estimate of Berlioz as a musician pure and simple. After all, his belief in programs is nothing worse than an aberration of genius, which does not really impair the intrinsic value of the work that it interprets; and the contention has been, not that he is lacking in dramatic power, for he possesses it in a very high degree, but that its action is restricted by the necessary limits of the art to which it belongs. So far as inspiration is concerned his claim to immortality is incontestable; and it only remains to examine the ability that he displayed in dealing with the various modes of expression.

188

Now there can be no question but that Berlioz has left us some melodies of very great worth. *La Captive* is a complete and final answer to the critics who have regarded its composer as unmelodious. The love scene in *Romeo and Juliet* is as beautiful as an Adagio of Schubert; the great septet in *Les Troyens*, the *Choeur des bergers* in the *Enfance du Christ*, Hero's song *Je vais le voir* in *Béatrice et Bénédict*, the *Sanctus* in the *Requiem* are only random instances of work which places him incontrovertibly in the first rank of musicians. Equally successful, though expressive of a more easily attainable ideal, are Mephistopheles' Serenade in Faust, the ball scene in *Symphonie fantastique*, and *Aubade* from *Feuillets d'album* (1845–55). The Harold motif, too, with its curious reminiscence of the opening Allegro in Beethoven's Seventh Symphony, is full of a noble melancholy, while the famous *idée fixe*, though certainly of less value, has nevertheless a marked expression and character of its own.

But every man, as George Sand said, has the defects of his qualities. Berlioz was one of the greatest masters of rhythm and modulation that the world has ever seen, and he frequently ruins his effects in consequence. He varies his meters till he destroys the homogeneity of his stanza, he changes his key with a forcible wrench that surprises without pleasing, in one word, he is so suspicious of monotony that he often falls into restlessness.

And yet how fine his rhythms are! Look at the opening phrase in the *King Lear* Overture (1831), at the accompaniment figure in the *Lacrymosa*, at the fascinating tune of the "Dance of the Sylphs" in *Faust*, and the whole carnival scene in *Benvenuto Cellini*, and a hundred others. Modulation is a lesser gift . . . but only a genius of the highest order could have devised a metrical system of such variety and extent. And it must be remembered that devices which seem to us familiar, like the persistent figure of the *Choeur des ombres* in *Lélio* (1831), or the alternation of tempo in the various presentations of the *idée fixe*, were comparatively or entirely new in Berlioz's day. Rhythm was then, as he says in *À travers chants*, the least developed of all modes of musical expression, and we may well forgive him if he sometimes lost control of a pioneer's enthusiasm and treated as an end in itself the power which his predecessors had underestimated even as a means.

Melody and harmony are so closely interconnected that it may perhaps seem unnecessary to give the latter any detailed criticism. But, as a matter of fact, every great composer has his own special manner of harmonization, by which he can be distinguished almost as readily as by his mastery of form or his power of melodic invention. In this respect Berlioz does not have such an advantage as in some other of the details of his art. His harmony is rarely rich, except where it is used as a vehicle of remote or recondite modulation, and it does not often atone for its commonplace character by any real strength or solidity. Like Gluck he is fond of massing the tenor and bass at the bottom of the chord and separating them from the treble and alto by a wide interval, witness the "Pilgrim's Chorus" in *Harold* and the "Shepherd's Chorus" in the *Enfance du Christ*, but this device though often successful in the strings, produces an unequal "knotty" effect when used for voices. No doubt he writes his parts with extreme rhythmic independence. Many of his choral works read like operatic ensembles, in which each voice has a character and personality of itself, but even this result can sometimes be compatible with a small minimum of variety in the harmonic progression. A similar weakness is observable in his counterpoint, except of course when he used it for purposes of burlesque. When he attempted it seriously, as in the first chorus of *Te Deum,* he usually betrayed a want of mastery, which is intelligible enough, if we realize the immense labor and concentration which the method demands, and the antagonism which he felt for it throughout. On the other hand, the "Amen Chorus" in *Faust* is an admirable travesty and better still is the "Wedding Cantata" in *Béatrice et Bénédict,* with the unanswerable logic of its text and the angular trills and flourishes of its oboe obbligato.

The last point of consideration is his power of orchestral effect in which, perhaps, may be found his most indisputable claim to the admiration of posterity. . . . He possessed in a high degree every quality which successful scoring implies, a complete knowledge of the strength and weakness of each instrument, great skill in the treatment and combination, ready invention, and boundless

190

audacity. Further he displays in this department of his art that sense of economy and reticence which has been noticed as absent elsewhere. He can be as light-handed as Mozart, witness the *Invitation to the Dance,* the opening of the *Rakóczy March,* the first number of the *Tempest Fantaisie,* and yet when the moment comes to be vigorous or impressive there is no one more strong to wield the thunderbolt and direct the whirlwind. Even the crude violence of his "Brigands' Orgy" or his "Witches' Sabbath" becomes almost humanized when we observe, the marvelous, matchless skill with which its horrors are presented.

Even in his smaller works he usually writes for an orchestra of more than normal size, using by preference four bassoons instead of two, and often reinforcing his trumpets with cornets-à-piston, the one piece of doubtful policy in his whole scheme. In the *Requiem* and the *Te Deum* his forces are enormous, the winds doubled, an immense mass of strings (of which he is careful to specify the exact number), and for the *Tuba Mirum* and *Lacrymosa* four small bands of brass instruments at the four cornets, and eight pairs of kettledrums, in addition to big drums, gongs, and cymbals. The rest of his distinctively orchestral works lie between these two extremes, though it may be noted that in the *Tempest Fantaisie* he tries as an experiment his cherished idea of employing the piano, not as a solo instrument, but as a coordinate with strings or woodwind. It would be an endless task to enumerate his triumphs, but we may specify the wonderful viola chords in the *Agnus Dei,* the use of strings and flutes in the *Sanctus*—forerunner of a similar effect in the Prelude to *Lohengrin*—the trombone in the *Francs juges* (c. 1827) and in the magnificent final chorus of the *Te Deum,* and the exquisite woodwind figures, like vanishing soap bubbles, at the end of the "Dance of the Sylphs" as conspicuous examples of poetic conception and unerring certainty of touch. His work, in short, marks a new era in instrumentation, and has been directly or indirectly the guide of every composer since his day.

The final verdict, then, would seen to be that Berlioz possessed undoubted genius, in the highest sense of the term, but that he was confined within limits from which he never succeeded in extricating himself. No composer of equal gifts has made so many mistakes: no musician of such little learning has ever attained to similar heights.

BERLIOZ SPEAKS

When I hear a piece of music . . . I feel a delicious pleasure in which reason has no part. The habit of analysis comes afterwards to give birth to admiration. The emotion increasing in proportion to the energy or the grandeur of the ideas of the composer soon produces a strange agitation in the circulation of the blood; tears, which generally indicate the end of the paroxysm, often indicates only a progressive state of it, leading to something still more intense. In this case I have spasmodic contraction of the muscles, a trembling in all my limbs, a complete torpor of the feet and hands, a partial paralysis of the nerves of sight and hearing. I no longer hear, I scarcely hear—vertigo . . . a semi-swoon.

. . . . .

Music is the most poetic, the most powerful, the most living of all the arts. She ought to be the freest, but she is not yet. . . . Modern music is like the classic Andromeda, naked and divinely beautiful. She is chained to a rock on the shores of a vast sea and awaits the victorious Perseus who shall loose her bonds and break in pieces the chimera called Routine.

I am for free music. Yes, I want music to be proudly free, to be victorious, to be supreme. I want her to take all she can, so that there may be no more Alps or Pyrenees for her. But she must achieve her victories by fighting in person and not rely upon her lieutenants. I should like to have, if possible, good verse draw up in order of battle; but, like Napoleon, she must face the fire herself and, like Alexander, march in the front ranks of the phalanx. She is so powerful that in some cases she would conquer unaided; for she has the right to say with Medea, "I, myself, am enough."

. . . . .

192

The musical problems I have tried to solve are unusual, and called for unusual methods. In the *Requiem*, for example, I use four distinct brass orchestras, answering each other at certain distances around the principal orchestra and chorus. In the *Te Deum*, the organ at one end of the church answers the orchestra and the two choirs that are placed at the other end, while a third large choir represents the people participating from time to time in the sacred performance. But it is the form of these compositions, their breadth of style, their deliberate progressions that provide these compositions with their strangely immense physiognomy and appearance. The result of this gigantic form is that one either misses the direction of the whole or is overwhelmed by an overpowering emotion. At a performance of the *Requiem* I have seen one man listening in terror, stirred to the roots of his being, while another could not comprehend a single idea, however much he might try to do so.

My large scale works include the *Symphonie funèbre et triomphale* for two orchestras and chorus; the *Te Deum*; the *Judex crederis*, which is undoubtedly my most grandiose creation; the cantata *L'Imperiale*, for two choirs; and above all, the *Requiem*. As for those of my compositions conceived along more ordinary designs and formats, and requiring no exceptional methods of performance, it is their inner fire, their expression, the originality of rhythm that have been most injurious to them because of the kind of performance they demand. To perform them properly, performers—and the conductor particularly—must feel as I do. These compositions call for a combination of precision and verve, controlled passion, dreamy tenderness, and an almost morbid melancholy without which the main characters of my figures are either changed or entirely effaced. For this reason, as a rule, it is extremely painful for me to hear my compositions conducted by anybody but myself. . . .

If you were to inquire to which of my compositions I show the greatest preference, my answer would be the same as that of most artists: the love scene in *Romeo and Juliet*.

·   ·   ·   ·   ·

The prevailing characteristics of my music are passionate expression, intense ardor, rhythmical animation, and unexpected effects. When I say passionate expression I mean an expression determined on enforcing the inner meaning of its subject, even when the feeling to be expressed is gentle or tender or even profoundly calm. This is the sort of expression that has been found in the *Enfance du Christ,* in the *Ciel* scene of *The Damnation of Faust,* and in the *Sanctus* of the *Requiem.*

GIOACCHINO ROSSINI

1 7 9 2 – 1 8 6 8

GIOACCHINO ANTONIO ROSSINI was born in Pesaro, Italy, on February 29, 1792. He received some training at the harpsichord and in singing before entering the Bologna Conservatory at fifteen. Financial difficulties in his family compelled him to leave the Conservatory before completing the course of study. In 1810, his first work for the stage—an opera buffa, *La Cambiale di matrimonio*—was produced in Venice. Several more of his operas were given before he achieved resounding success. This came in Venice in 1813 with a serious opera, *Tancredi,* and an opera buffa, *L'Italiana in Algeri.*

Now one of Italy's best-loved opera composers, Rossini was engaged in 1815 by Domenico Barbaja to write two operas a year for performances in Naples, Milan, and Vienna. Since this contract allowed Rossini to accept other commissions, he wrote his masterwork—and one of the most popular opera buffas ever created—for the Argentina Theater in Rome: *The Barber of Seville,* a text previously set with outstanding success by Giovanni Paisiello (1740–1816). The première of Rossini's opera on February 20, 1816, was a pronounced failure—due partly to the organized efforts of Paisiello's admirers to discredit Rossini and create a scandal, and partly to a series of unhappy accidents that marred the performance. The second presentation went much better; and in short order Rossini's version swept Paisiello's opera into complete obscurity.

On March 16, 1822, Rossini married the Spanish opera singer, Isabella Colbran. Soon after that, Rossini left Italy for the first time, and was triumphantly acclaimed in Vienna and London. In 1824, he became the musical director of the Théâtre Italien in Paris. Under the terms of this agreement he wrote his last opera, *William Tell,* introduced on August 3, 1829.

Rossini was now thirty-six years old, at the height of his fame and creative powers yet, though he lived another thirty-nine years he never wrote another opera. The reasons for what has since been described as "the great renunciation" have never been adequately explained, though many have tried to provide logical possibilities. In any event, after 1829, Rossini devoted himself mainly to the writing of piano pieces, choral music, and some insignificant instrumental compositions.

In 1837, Rossini was separated from his wife. After her death in 1845, he married Olympe Pélissier. Between 1836 and 1848 he was the honorary president of the Bologna Conservatory, and from 1855 on he lived in Paris. Most of the time after 1840 Rossini suffered severely from neurasthenia and physical deterioration. He died of a heart attack in Passy, France, on November 13, 1868. His remains, buried at Père Lachaise in Paris, were subsequently removed to the Santa Croce Church in Florence.

THE MAN

FRANCIS TOYE

In considering the reasons that induced Rossini to retire from active musical life, it is perhaps unnecessary to stress the fact that the phenomenon is unique in the history of music and difficult to parallel in the whole history of art. When Rossini wrote *William Tell* he was thirty-six years old; even at the time he settled down in Bologna, when his mind seems to have been definitely made up, he was only forty-four. Is there any other artist who thus, deliberately, in the very prime of life, renounced that form of artistic production which had made him famous throughout the civilized world?

Though countless people endeavored at one time or another to extract an explanation from Rossini himself, few ever succeeded in getting an answer at all. It was the subject above all others that he desired to avoid. For instance, when Aguado once wrote begging him to compose another opera for Paris, he merely replied that he had just sent off the two finest sausages to be found in Bologna, accompanied by precise instructions to Aguado's cook how to prepare them! If this was all Aguado, to whom he owed so much, could get out of him, it may be imagined that there was little chance for the ordinary person. Most of the answers he did give were in fact given many years later, when time had cast a veil over some of the pain and bitterness.

By 1848 he was incapable of serious effort and so remained for many years. The political troubles of the times came to aggravate his already aggravated maladies. He was a nervous and physical wreck. Had the dangerous benefits of psychoanalysis been revealed to the world in the 30's, they might have saved Rossini for music; in the 40's, it would have been too late. Possibly they would have availed nothing, however, unless the discoveries of Wasserman and Ehrlich had already been anticipated by a century. It is difficult not to think that some of Rossini's troubles were of a venereal origin; his later symptoms, disease of the bladder and urinary tract, his premature baldness and toothlessness, seem revelatory. His acute neurasthenia, too, though inherent in his constitution may well have been intensified by the same cause.

Needless to say, these troubles were not so acute in the 30's and early 40's as they became later, but the seeds of them were present and explain much. Nobody except Radiciotti has sufficiently emphasized Rossini's poor health almost immediately after *William Tell*. His nerves in particular were a torture to him. Even granted that the first experience of a railway train may have been terrifying and unpleasant, it is impossible to imagine the journey from Antwerp to Brussels causing anybody to faint! Which is what happened to Rossini in 1836. . . .

It is a fact, no doubt, that Rossini felt mortified by the cavalier treatment meted out to *William Tell* by the Opéra authorities after the revolution, especially when contrasted with the lavishness shown in respect to Meyerbeer's operas. This, however, by no means justifies the assumption that the failure of *William Tell* and a dislike of Meyerbeer were responsible for his retirement. To begin with, it must be emphasized, it was not a failure. So to describe a work that earned for its composer the highest regard of the whole musical world, and achieved in his own lifetime five hundred performances at the Opéra alone, is a sheer misuse of words.

As regards Meyerbeer, the question is a little more complex. Radiciotti has tried to prove that the relations of the two men, far from being antagonistic, were something more than cordial. In my opinion he has failed to establish his case. No doubt Meyerbeer was at great pains to show Rossini every sign of affection and veneration on every possible occasion; but that was Meyerbeer's way. There is some reason, indeed, to think that Rossini saw through the maneuver. There is a well-authenticated story that Rossini, when out walking one day with a friend, happened to meet Meyerbeer, who asked anxiously after his health. Rossini replied with a recital of various distressing symptoms, so, when Meyerbeer had gone, the friend suggested an immediate return home. "Not at all," said Rossini, "I feel perfectly well, but dear Meyerbeer would be so delighted to hear of my death tomorrow that I hadn't the heart to deny him a little pleasure today." . . .

Possibly this aspect of the case is best summed up by saying that it was the exclusiveness of the fashionable craze for Meyerbeer's music rather than the success of the music as such that discouraged Rossini.

There is no reason to doubt that the modesty he showed in his conversations with Weber and Wagner was wholly genuine, and that, when he reproached his friend Pacini for having, in his *Memoirs*, "turned me into an exclamation mark in the history of music instead of a wretched comma," he meant what he wrote. It is generally advisable to take everything said by Rossini about himself with a pinch of salt, but nothing in his career encourages us to think that he had an unduly exalted opinion of his gifts. "Which of all your operas do you like best?" once asked an admirer. *"Don Giovanni!"* came the rapier-like reply. His excellent common sense saved him from being deceived by the flattery so freely lavished on him by his worshipers. He never pretended that he did not write music to make money, so when he had accumulated enough to live on, he felt at perfect liberty to retire, free from the illusion, entertained by so many lesser composers, that the world could not go on without him.

Nor did Rossini retire from sheer laziness. Yet this explanation is often taken for granted. Indeed, an English critic once summed up Rossini as a composer who was so lazy that he wrote his music in bed and retired in early middle age to enjoy social life and the pleasures of the table. Since nearly all the fallacies current about Rossini are contained in this diverting piece of impertinence it may be as well to dispose of them severally.

Scarcely anything about Rossini has been more maligned than the pleasures he took in food and drink. Except in his early years when, like most Italians, he ate and drank with a copiousness unknown to the modern, but not the contemporary, Englishman, he was essentially fastidious in these matters. He took trouble to secure good wines from all over the world, including those from Peru, of all unlikely countries; and in later days he was unashamedly proud of his cellar. He delighted in certain Bolognese products. Nothing, for instance, gave him greater pleasure than the various cheeses, sausages, and hams that friends sent to him in Paris from time to time. He valued these more highly, he wrote to one of them, than all the decorations, orders, and crosses in the world. He took considerable interest in recipes, and his weakness for paté de foie gras is enshrined in the still famous *tournedos Rossini.* Generally speaking, however, rich food does not seem to have appealed to him; which in view of the nature of his maladies is not surprising. What he mainly cared about was that the simple products, like those mentioned above, should be genuine. In short, Rossini, like Debussy, was an epicure; not a glutton like Brahms. . . .

With regard to society, he frequented it not more, but less, after his retirement . . . and in any case it was the illustrious people who came to see him rather than he who sought them out. As a matter of fact, Rossini's social activities throughout his working life were, in general, eminently practical. . . . With regard to the writing in bed it is based presumably on the well-known story of the occasion when Rossini preferred to write a new number rather than get out of bed to pick up one already half completed. As a generality it is not even worth discussing.

Remains the laziness. Rossini himself took great pleasure in emphasizing it on every possible occasion, but that means precisely nothing. The world had decided to call him lazy; he would be the first to say how right the world was. Thus, attention would be diverted from his hidden inner secrets which he guarded so jealously. Such was the procedure adopted by Rossini in many matters, and it worked out surprisingly well. No man has ever taken more pleasure in maligning himself. What did a reputation for idleness, cynicism, and greed matter so long as the reality of suffering and decay remained unsuspected? . . .

The only real justification of the charge of laziness against Rossini lies in his excessive self-borrowings. He did undoubtedly make too frequent use of old material in his various operas. On the other hand, it is only fair to remember that the practice was traditional in his early days; even Gluck adopted it, while no Italian composer would have dreamed of questioning its necessity. Rossini's fault lay in pushing it to an extreme. Even if the number of operas he wrote be discounted in proportion, however, there remains a sufficient quantity to absolve Rossini from anything that can possibly be called indolence. Rossini was not indolent; he was deficient in aesthetic conscientiousness. He needed, that is to say, to drive him into action, a definite stimulus like a contract or a desire to please some particular person, or even, occasionally, an enthusiasm for some particular subject.

THE COMPOSER

FRANCIS TOYE

It has been said that Rossini, despite the brilliance of his genius and the greatness of his popularity, exercised little influence on the main current of music, that his whole career was, in fact, a kind of backwater. . . . The various reasons for holding a contrary view may with advantage be summarized.

Curiously enough, it is not, I think, the Italian operatic stage where his influence was most felt except, of course, in the general sense. His young contemporary Vincenzo Bellini (1801–35) shows a marked reaction against Rossinian *fioriture* and, except in that

200

little gem *Don Pasquale*, there is not, perhaps, very much in common between Rossini and Gaetano Donizetti (1797–1848) beyond a certain conventional layout of arias and ensembles. Verdi owed him much more. Not to mention the early arias and ensembles, the spendid choruses of *Nabucco* and *I Lombardi* suggest the influence of *Mosè* (1818); the *Miserere* in *Il Trovatore* was clearly inspired by the finale of the first act of *Semiramide* (1823); various devices in the vocal parts of the early and middle-period operas had been anticipated by Rossini. Moreover, though Verdi, in *I Vespri siciliani, Don Carlo,* and perhaps *Aida,* indulged in a definite flirtation with Meyerbeer, he never quite forgot his *William Tell* (1829), while *Falstaff* is definitely a pendant for *The Barber* (1816).

A case might be made out, too, for considering *La Gazza ladra* (1817) as the ancestor of the realistic school of opera associated with Puccini, Pietro Mascagni (1863–1945), and company. Here, however, it is the subject rather than the musical treatment which is in question. The lighter operas of Ermanno Wolf-Ferrari (1876–1948) also derive to a large extent from Rossini.

As regards French opera, Rossini's great influence can scarcely be questioned. *William Tell* has been described as the foundation stone of French grand opera. This is incorrect, because the admirable *Masaniello* of Daniel-François-Ésprit Auber (1782–1871), though it may have been written about the same time, was in fact produced a year earlier. The era of grand opera was inaugurated by *Le Siège de Corinthe* (1826), closely followed by *Moïse* (1827). But it may truthfully be said, I think, that *William Tell,* owing to its great merit, standardized the form; without it Meyerbeer, the protagonist *par excellence* of French grand opera, could scarcely have written *Robert le diable* and *Les Huguenots;* while, incidentally, the influence of the earlier Rossini on Meyerbeer's Italian operas seems to have been far more potent than is usually supposed. . . .

Even in Germany and Austria Rossini left deeper traces than is sometimes thought. Wagner has himself told us how after conducting *William Tell* in Dresden, he could not get the tunes out of his head for days, and . . . he remembered one, if not two, of them to very good purpose. Professor Dent has further shown that Ros-

sini's influence on Schubert is by no means confined by the comparatively unimportant Schubertian operas, but is distinguishable in the
great C major Symphony, where, he says, the opening theme of
the Andante is reminiscent of *"Di tanti palpiti,"* and the rattle of
the rhythm in the last movement comes directly from Rossini. . . .
According to Dent, many characteristic devices in Weber, despite
his antagonism, are of Rossinian origin. . . .

It is not usually considered that Rossini achieved anything revolutionary in music, but such was by no means the opinion of his contemporaries. One of the principal reasons for the success of *Tancredi*
(1813) was that the public felt for the first time a new sense of ease
in the hitherto stilted opera seria. Indeed, Rossini, apart from a new
freshness in his style as a whole, may have the credit of having
grafted onto opera seria many of the more elastic conventions of
opera buffa, the employment of an important bass soloist being one
notable instance. Nor must it be imagined that Rossini's innovations
in this respect did not meet with opposition. Many cultured amateurs
shared Lord Mount Edgcumbe's dislike of the fusion of the two
styles; both courage and genius was necessary successfully to carry
through such a reform. Once started on the road, Rossini progressed
with rapidity, arriving not only at an unprecedented complexity in
ensemble-writing and at operatic Prayers with the backing of a full
chorus, but at the introduction of a military band on the stage.

Further . . . at the very outset of his career, Rossini had trouble
with his singers on account of the unprecedented importance he
attached to the orchestra. I am not concerned at the moment to
stress the orchestra progress shown in his Paris operas. . . . There
was nothing particularly remarkable in writing well for the orchestra
in a city familiar with Gluck and Weber. . . . But in Italy it was
different. There was no encouragement, rather the reverse, for
Rossini to take trouble with the orchestra, to enlarge, as he did,
the role played by the woodwind, especially the clarinets. To use
the orchestra for the accompaniment of recitatives, as was done for
the first time in *Elisabetta* (1815), must have seemed a veritable
revolution. Indeed, we know that the traditionalists of the Conservatory at Naples, where most of his important orchestral experiments were made, did regard him as a wanton and dangerous

revolutionary who, not content with allowing himself the use of consecutive fifths and other harmonic and contrapuntal licenses, actually wrote for a third and fourth horn and no less than three trombones! To them he was the apostle of noise and chaos. . . .

The question of Rossini's reform in the matter of writing down for the first time the actual *fioriture* to be performed by his singers is, needless to say, of the first importance. Here, too, it must not be imagined that the innovation commanded universal acceptance. Many of his contemporaries, including Stendhal, deplored the passing of the improvisations that had been the singer's prerogative. Rossini's method, they argued, tended to crystallize these ornaments; no scope was left for the singer to vary, as he or she used to do, the ornament or the cadenza according to the circumstances and his or her mood. It was not quite such a foolish attitude, I think, as is often assumed, particularly in view of the extreme musical and technical skill of many of the singers. . . . It must be emphasized that these ornaments were not merely what we call "fireworks." To contemporary audiences they possessed a definite expressive value, difficult though it may be for us to appreciate the fact.

Rossini, who beyond question understood the human voice as few others have understood it, appears to have thought that he could obtain the same results without the musical sense being endangered by some singer incompetent to grasp it. He took for granted the high level of technical ability usual in those days, and, be it remembered, he wrote less and very different *fioriture* when he had to deal with French singers whose technique was not so brilliant. . . .

. . . . .

The precise balance to be struck between the merits and defects of Rossini as a composer must always remain perforce a matter of opinion. His music will never appeal greatly to those who attach supreme value to profundity of feeling or intellect. The latter, at any rate, could scarcely be expected of him. Rossini was clearheaded, shrewd, urbane, but in no way intellectual. The extraordinary thing is rather, with an education so neglected, with a career during the first thirty years of his life so feverish and so vagabond, that he should have risen to the heights he did. Partly, no doubt, his lack of profound feeling can be ascribed to the same cause. Fétis observed with considerable perspicacity that, till he left Italy after *Semiramide*, Rossini never could have had the time to cultivate a genuine friendship. Thrown constantly into contact with thousands of people in one town after another, his life must have passed in a kind of delirium of sensations; and I think that this was reflected in his music. Doubtless, there was a great change in later life, when he made many real friends, but early habits leave an ineradicable mark, and, in any case, it must be remembered that he wrote very little music after the age of thirty-six.

Every student of Rossini has noticed, moreover, his comparative inability to portray the emotion of love in its more tender aspect. For my part, I doubt if he ever felt it. The countless amorous intrigues of his youth seem to have been nothing but the usual fleeting affairs of theatrical life. He must at one time have felt a certain amount of passion for Isabella Colbran and she, poor woman, certainly grew to love him, but one has an uneasy suspicion, that in that alliance material considerations counted at least as much as affection. In all probability he cared more deeply for Olympe Pélissier. By then, however, he had practically given up composition, and was, moreover, a sick man, full of self-pity, who needed protection and care, not stimulus to artistic creation. The most poignant emotion he ever knew was undoubtedly adoration of his mother, which some biographers have found reflected in certain pages of *William Tell*. It may be so. In any case, such filial devotion, however passionate, has nothing to do with the point.

To his faulty education, too, must be ascribed that indifference to the literary value of words and situations so noticeable in many of his operas. Any music would serve to express them provided it sounded agreeable in itself. His sluggishness and extraordinary facility combined further to induce in him a regrettable lack of self-criticism. Much of his subject-matter suffers from excessive similarity; he was far too easily satisfied with ideas as they first presented themselves, far too tolerant of repetitions and the continuous employment of stereotyped devices such as the famous crescendo. His excessive borrowings . . . were in reality part and parcel of the same attitude of mind.

Rossini's operatic career might be summarized as a tragedy of bad librettos, for only once, in fact, was he really well served. But he must bear some of the responsibility. Had he, like Verdi, possessed the character and the determination to insist on his own way and reject even one third of the fifteen librettos that he set to music in the space of four years; had he, like Beethoven, written three overtures for one opera instead of fitting one overture to three operas, there would have been a very different tale to tell. At the same time it must be remembered that the conditions of the Italian theater made any such proceeding exceedingly difficult. We should not so much blame Rossini as commiserate him on having been unable to rise above the handicaps of his life and circumstances. All things said and done, what he did in fact accomplish remains little less than a miracle.

Besides, as regards some of his defects, there is, to say the least, another side to the medal. His carelessness in the setting of words, for instance, proceeded to some extent from the remarkably pure musicality of his inspiration. Music as pure sound, rhythm as pure rhythm, meant everything to him; words very little. . . . He could, and did, compose music under any kind of conditions, amidst the chatter of friends, and clamor of copyists, out fishing, and in bed. Now this musicality is, perhaps, his principal attraction; to it must be ascribed the spontaneity, the vivacity, the charm that are characteristic of his work. He did not always make the best of his extraordinary natural gift in this respect, but he rarely allows us to forget that he possessed it. His music is never anything but indisputably musical, the precise reverse of Meyerbeer's, indeed, that is why most musicians have kept somewhere in their hearts a warm spot for Rossini, be his faults what they may. The "storms" in some half dozen of his operas provide a good instance of this musicality. They are never just imitative, but always translated into purely musical terms, often subtly attuned, as for instance in *Cenerentola* (1817), to the psychology of that particular score. In fact, one of the very few abstract principles which he laid down as a dogma, was that music should be "ideal and expressive," not imitative.

Generally speaking, however, Rossini never dogmatized; his approach to music was instinctive rather than intellectual. This is shown in his famous saying that there are only two kinds of music, the good and the bad; or that other, less known, where he states that every kind of music is good except the boring kind. These are scarcely the utterances of a man who attached any value to aesthetic theories as such. The fact of the matter is that Rossini regarded himself as an artist craftsman producing music when and where required, entirely devoid of the pretentions invented subsequently by the Romantic movement, which at no time affected Italy as it affected Germany, France, or England, and, before he went to Paris, had made no impression whatever south of the Alps. Besides, there is always a tendency to forget that for all practical purposes Rossini's musical career ended in 1829. To some extent, therefore, he remains in essence more akin to an 18th-century than to a 19th-century composer.

As regards Rossini's technical ability there can scarcely be two opinions. No man not a consummate technician could have written *William Tell*, while the wonderful ensembles in the earlier operas suffice by themselves to attest to his mastery. These ensembles lack as a rule the power of characterization later attained by Verdi, but as examples of skill and effectiveness in vocal part-writing they are supreme. Yet Rossini always professed indifference to scholastic ingenuity as such. *"Voilà du temps perdu,"* he added in pencil after writing some eight-part contrapuntal essay or other. He disliked the pedants as much as they disliked him, and I have a shrewd suspicion that many of the "irregularities" in his music were due as much to a wanton pleasure in annoying them as to carelessness and indifference.

His excellence in orchestration, too, has not, I think, been sufficiently emphasized. None of his Italian contemporaries, not even Verdi till the *Ballo in Maschera* period, scored as well as he did. It has been said, indeed, that with his retirement in 1829, Italian writing for the orchestra took a definite step backward. All through the Rossini operas we find instruments treated with great skill, with an unerring instinct for their potentialities of expression. The overtures, in particular, deserve the highest praise in this respect. Take, for instance, the writing for the cellos in the *William Tell* Overture. It is so masterly that the famous cellist Servais told Rossini that he had no need to be informed that the composer had himself studied the cello in his youth. As for sheer brilliance and effectiveness the rest of the orchestration is equally remarkable. Nor should the comparative simplicity of the effects in the earlier overtures such as *L'Italiana in Algeri* (1813), *The Barber of Seville, La Gazza ladra,* and *Semiramide* blind us to the surety of touch, the felicity of inspiration, that were necessary to invent them at that time. Everything "comes off" as well today as it ever did! . . . As a matter of fact, these overtures are little masterpieces from every point of view. In them we find displayed to the best advantage that rhythm in which Rossini so excelled, to which he attached so much importance, saying that in it resided all the power and expressiveness of music. The subject-material itself is nearly always excellent and highly individual; the form is as clear as the treatment. Possibly the very attractiveness of these overtures has led some of our musicians unduly to underrate them.

Finally, Rossini's exceptional knowledge and love of the human voice cannot be too strongly insisted upon. Himself a singer from childhood, he understood it as scarcely any other composer has understood it, and his writing for it sets a standard. There is no question here of demanding effects, as Verdi too often does, mainly from notes at the extremity of the singer's compass; the whole range of the voice is expected to pay its due contribution, while it is scarcely possible in all the operas and songs to find a vocal phrase that, granted the technique prevalent at the time, is not delightfully singable. It is not surprising that he should have excelled in this respect, for, of all forms of musical expression, Rossini loved singing the best. Inevitably, such enthusiasm on the part of so famous a composer produced its effect, particularly in France, where Rossini's influence is said to have altered for the better the whole style of French singing. The gradual decline of the art during the last thirty years of his life . . . filled him with dismay. He told Michotte, indeed, that his main ambition in the *Petite Messe* was to leave a final legacy that might serve as an example of how to write for the voice. Yet he never willingly suffered the tyranny of singers, and

207

he refused to allow that they had any share in the work of artistic creation. . . .

In view of all the reproaches that have been leveled at Rossini for writing solely to show off the virtuosity of his singers, this insistence is decidedly interesting. There is no reason to think that he did not in the main succeed in putting it into practice, though there were occasions in particular where Isabella Colbran was concerned, when he certainly did not. In fact, Isabella, quite unintentionally, did him definite harm, in that in all probability a desire to minister to her particular talents led him to write *opera seria* when, as Beethoven suggested and he himself admitted, he would have been better employed in writing *opera buffa*. A man of stronger character would have noted the pitfall, to bridge or avoid it, but once again it must be insisted that there was nothing grand or heroic about Rossini; for him the easiest path was the obvious, the only path. Can one imagine Verdi advising a young friend, as Rossini did, to get out of a difficulty by a lie, if necessary? His general attitude towards music has not been fairly described as indicative of a pronounced taste rather than passion or semi-religious veneration. His real justification is that he possessed in an exceptional degree the most essential attributes of a composer, melodic and rhythmical inventiveness, and that he brought into music a great healthy laugh that will always endear him to the artist if not to the educationalist. Wagner who . . . described him as the first man he had met in the world of art who was truly great and worthy of reverence, wrote after his death an epitaph that was alike kind, wise, and just: "Rossini can scarcely be handed to posterity in a more false guise than by stamping him as a hero of Art on the one hand, or degrading him to a flippant wag on the other. . . . No, Rossini will never be judged aright until someone attempts an intelligent history of the culture of our current century. . . . Were this character of our age correctly drawn, it would then be possible to allot to Rossini also his true and fitting station in it. And that station would be no lowly one, for with the same title as Palestrina, Bach, and Mozart belonged to their age, Rossini belongs to his. . . . Then and not till then will it be possible to estimate Rossini at his true and quite peculiar worth; for what fell short of full dignity would have to be accounted to neither his natural gifts nor his artistic conscience, but simply to his public environment, which made it difficult for a man of his nature to raise himself above his age and thereby share the grandeur of the veritable art-heroes."

ROSSINI SPEAKS

These are my opinions on the present state of music.

Formerly Haydn began to corrupt purity of taste by introducing into his works strange chords, artificial passages, and daring innovations. He still preserved so much sublimity and ancient beauty, however, that his errors could be forgiven. Then came Cramer and Beethoven with their compositions so lacking in unity and naturalness and so full of oddities and personal caprice that they completely corrupted the quality of instrumental music. In opera at the present time, Johann Simon Mayr has replaced the simple and majestic measures of Sarti, Paisiello, and Cimarosa with his ingenious though vicious harmonies, and the accompaniment drowning out the melody, and he is imitated by the young opera composers of the German school.

Many of our singers born outside of Italy have renounced purity of music (for which Italy has always been the center) to please the capitals of Europe and they have adopted the unwholesome style of the foreigners. When they returned to Italy they brought with them and spread the germ of bad taste. . . . Warblings, wild leaps and jumps, trills, misuse of semi-tones, notes all tangled up—this is the kind of singing that now holds sway. That is why the measure, the essential part of music, without which melody is unintelligible and harmony becomes disordered, is neglected and violated by singers. They arouse our astonishment rather than our emotion, and whereas in better times the performers tried to make their instruments sing, our singers now try to make their voices play. In the meantime the crowd, applauding such poor style, does to music what the Jesuits did to poetry and oratory when they preferred Lucan to Virgil and Seneca to Cicero.

· · · · ·

I maintain that in order to perform his part well, the singer must be nothing but an able interpreter of the ideas of the master, the composer, and he should try to express them with great skill and all the brilliance of which they are susceptible. Therefore the performers should be nothing but accurate executants of what is written down. In short, the composer and the poet are the only true creators. Sometimes a clever singer will burst into additional ornamentation and would like to call this his creation, but it often happens that this creation is false, and even more often that it ruins the composer's ideas, robbing them of the simplicity and expression they should have.

The French use the term *créer un rôle*—an example of French vanity—which should be applied to those singers who demand a leading part in a new opera, hoping to prove thereby that they will set the example to be followed later by other singers who perform the same part. Here, too, the word "create" seems rather inappropriate since to create means to dig up from nowhere. Instead the singer works with something already made, he follows the poetry with the music, which are not his creations.

GIACOMO MEYERBEER

1 7 9 1 – 1 8 6 4

GIACOMO MEYERBEER was a German-born composer who received much of his training in Italy and helped to create the traditions of French grand opera. He was born in Berlin on September 5, 1791, his name originally Jakob Liebmann Beer. His grandfather, Meyer Liebmann Wulf, left him a fortune as legacy on the condition he add the name "Meyer" to his own. Thus "Beer" became "Meyerbeer"; Jakob was changed to Giacomo when he initiated a career as composer of Italian operas.

Exceptionally gifted, he made an impressive public appearance as pianist when he was seven, and at ten wrote a cantata. He studied piano with Clementi and theory with Zelter, Anselm Weber and Abbé Vogler. While Vogler's student, Meyerbeer completed two operas, both dismal failures when introduced between 1812 and 1813. The second of these, *Alimelek*—accepted for performance in Vienna—brought Meyerbeer to the Austrian capital in 1813. There he became so impressed by Hummel's piano playing that he went into a ten-month period of retirement to perfect his technique, from which he emerged a remarkable virtuoso. But he did not lose his determination to succeed as a composer. On the advice of Salieri, court composer in Vienna, Meyerbeer went to Italy where he was caught in the then prevailing vogue for Rossini. Meyerbeer now assumed an Italian name and began writing operas in the Italian manner. The first such work—*Romilda e Costanza,* produced in Padua in 1817—was followed by several others of which *Il Crociato in Egitto*, given in Venice in 1824, proved a huge success.

In 1826, Meyerbeer came to Paris to help prepare a French production of the last-named work. For the next few years he devoted himself to the study of French opera, history, and culture. When he returned to composition he embarked upon the third, and most significant, phase of his creative evolution. His German and Italian experiences as composer were now merged with French backgrounds and traditions to help him evolve the spectacle opera. In this new manner he wrote *Robert le diable*, a sensation when introduced at the Paris Opéra on November 21, 1831. With *Les Huguenots* (February 29, 1836), and *Le Prophète* (April 16, 1849) he became celebrated as the foremost creator of French grand opera.

The last of his masterworks, *L'Africaine*, took him a quarter of a century to complete. He was still making revisions on this score when he died in Paris on May 2, 1864. It was produced posthumously, on April 28, 1865.

THE MAN

HEINRICH HEINE

Not long after the July Revolution, Meyerbeer appeared before the public with a new work, which had sprung from his heart during the storm of the Revolution. It was *Robert le diable*. . . . Meyerbeer was at that time rightly called a worried genius. He lacked triumphant confidence in himself. He was afraid of public opinion. The least reproof dismayed him. He flattered all the caprices of his public, and shook hands zealously everywhere, as if even in music he acknowledged the sovereignty of the people, and wanted to establish his preëminence by majority vote.

He is not yet free of this anxiety. He is still deeply concerned about public opinion. But the success of *Robert le diable* had the happy effect of freeing him from this anxiety while at work, and he composed with far greater assurance. He let the great will of his soul reveal itself in his creations. With this expansive freedom of soul he wrote *Les Huguenots* from which all his doubts have vanished.

Recently I stood in company of a friend before the cathedral of Amiens, and looked with awe and pity on the towering monument of giant strength and indefatigable dwarfish patience revealed in the stone-carving. How does it happen, he asked, that we no longer can build such piles? I said, "Dear Alphonse. In those days people had convictions. We moderns have opinions, but it takes more than opinions to build this Gothic dome."

That is the nub of the matter. Meyerbeer is a man of convictions. I am not referring to the social questions of the day, though here too Meyerbeer has more firm and settled opinions than other artists. Despite the fact that he has been overwhelmed by the princes of the earth with honors and decorations, for which distinctions he has a great weakness, Meyerbeer has a heart that glows for the sacred interests of humanity, and he openly avows his adoration of the heroes of the Revolution. . . . Yet his convictions are not really political, much less religious in character. Meyerbeer's true religion is that of Mozart, Gluck, Beethoven. It is music. He believes in it, in it alone does he find happiness. His convictions are here. In point of depth, passion, and duration they are like those of an earlier age. Yes, I would venture to say that he is the apostle of this faith. All that touches his music, he treats with apostolic zeal and passion. Other artists are content if they compose something beautiful; and often lose interest in their work the moment it is completed. With Meyerbeer, one might say, the more severe birth-pangs do not begin till after childbirth. He is not satisfied until the creation of his genius manifests itself to others in full splendor, until the whole audience is edified by his music, and the opera has poured its feelings into every heart—feelings which he wishes to preach to the whole world and to communicate to all mankind.

Music is Meyerbeer's conviction—and that may be the cause of all those worries and anxieties which the great master so often betrays and which so often makes us smile. One should see him at work while preparing an opera for production; he is the bane of all musicians and singers, whom he torments with endless rehearsals. He is never satisfied. A false note in the orchestra stabs him like the point of a dagger—and he takes it as a mortal blow. This anxiety follows him even after the opera has been produced and thunderously acclaimed. He is still worried; and I believe he remains discontented until some thousands of persons who have admired his

213

work have died and are buried. He does not have to fear that *they* will turn renegades. Their souls are secured for his cause.

On the day his opera is to be produced, not even God can satisfy him. If it rains or is chilly, he is worried lest Mademoiselle Falcon catch cold; if the evening is fine and warm, he is afraid that the good weather may keep people out in the open, and the theater will remain empty. Nothing is to be compared with the meticulous care with which Meyerbeer corrects the proofs of his printed music, for which he has become a byword among the artists of Paris. But one can keep in mind the fact that music is dearer to him than anything else on earth—certainly even than life itself. When the cholera broke out in Paris, I implored him to leave as soon as possible, but he had a few days' urgent business—he had to arrange for an Italian version of the libretto of *Robert le diable*.

THE COMPOSER

R. A. STREATFEILD

French music owes much to foreign influence, but very few of the strangers to whom the doors of Parisian opera houses were opened left a deeper impression upon the music of their adopted country than Meyerbeer. Giacomo Meyerbeer, to give him the name by which he is now best known, was in his youth intimate with Weber, and his first visit to Italy introduced him to Rossini, whose brilliant style he imitated successfully in a series of Italian works which are now completely forgotten. From Italy Meyerbeer came to Paris and there identified himself with the French school so fully that he is now regarded with complete propriety as a French composer pure and simple. Meyerbeer's music is thoroughly eclectic in type. He was a careful student of contemporary music, and the various phases through which he passed during the different stages of his career left their impress upon his style. It says much for the power of his individuality that he was able to weld such different elements into something approaching a harmonious whole. Had he done more than he did, he would have been a genius; as it is, he remains a man

214

of exceptional talent, whose influence on the history of music is still important, though his own compositions are now slightly super-annuated.

Robert le diable, the first work of his third or French period, was produced in 1831. The libretto, which, like those of all the composer's French operas, was by Eugène Scribe, is a strange tissue of absurdities, though from the merely scenic point of view it may be thought fairly effective. It was an immense success when first produced. The glitter and tinsel of the story suited Meyerbeer's showy style, and besides, even when the merely trivial and conventional had been put aside, there remains a fair proportion of the score which has claims to dramatic power.

The triumph of *Robert* militated against the success of *Les Huguenots* in 1836, which was at first rather coldly received. Before long, however, it rivalled the earlier work in popularity, and is now generally looked upon as Meyerbeer's masterpiece. The libretto certainly compares favorably with the fatuities of *Robert*. *Les Huguenots* shows Meyerbeer at his best. Even Wagner, his bitterest enemy, admitted the dramatic power of the great duet in the fourth act, and several other scenes are scarcely inferior to it in sustained inspiration. The opera is marred as a whole by Meyerbeer's invincible self-consciousness. He seldom had the courage to give his genius full play. He never lost sight of his audience, and wrote what he thought would be effective rather than what he knew was right. Thus his finest moments are marred by lapses from sincerity into the commonplace conventionality of the day. Yet the dignity and power of *Les Huguenots* are undeniable.

In *Le Prophète* (1849), Meyerbeer chose a subject which, if less rich in dramatic possibility than that of *Les Huguenots*, has a far deeper psychological interest. Unfortunately, Scribe, with all his cleverness, was quite the worst man in the world to deal with the story of John of Leyden. In the libretto which he constructed for Meyerbeer's benefit the psychological interest is conspicuous only by its absence, and the character of the young leader of the Ana-baptists is degraded to the level of the merest puppet. Meyerbeer's music, fine as much of it is, suffers chiefly from the character of the libretto. The latter is merely a string of conventionally effective scenes, and the music could hardly fail to be disjointed and scrappy. Meyerbeer had little or no feeling for characterizations, so that the opportunities for really dramatic effect which lay in the character of John of Leyden have been almost entirely neglected. Once only, in the famous *cantique*, *"Roi du ciel,"* did the composer catch an echo of the prophetic rapture which animated his youthful enthusiast. Meyerbeer's besetting sin, his constant search for the merely effective, is even more pronounced in *Le Prophète* than in *Les Huguenots*. The "Coronation Scene" (with its famous march) has nothing of the large simplicity necessary for the proper manipulation of mass of sound. The canvas is crowded with insignificant and confusing detail, and the general effect is finicking and invertebrate rather than solid and dignified.

Meyerbeer was constantly at work upon his last opera, *L'Africaine*, from 1838 until 1864, and his death found him still engaged in retouching the score. It was produced in 1865. With a musician of Meyerbeer's known eclecticism, it might be supposed that a work of which the composition extended over so long a period would exhibit the strangest conglomeration of styles and influences. Curiously enough, *L'Africaine* is the most consistent of Meyerbeer's works. This is probably due to the fact that in it the personal element is throughout outweighed by the picturesque, and the exotic fascination of the story goes far to cover its defects.

The characters of *L'Africaine*, with the possible exception of Selika and Nelusko, are the merest shadows, but the music, though less popular as a rule than that of *Les Huguenots*, or even *Le Prophète*, is undoubtedly Meyerbeer's finest effort. In his old age Meyerbeer seems to have looked back to the days of his Italian period, and thus, though occasionally conventional in form, the melodies of *L'Africaine*—and particularly the tenor aria, *O Paradiso* —have a dignity and serenity which are rarely present in the scores of his French period. There is, too, a laudable absence of that ceaseless striving after effect which mars so much of Meyerbeer's best work.

Besides the great works already discussed, Meyerbeer wrote two works for the *Opéra-Comique*, *L'Étoile du nord* (1854) and *Le Pardon de Ploërmel*, the latter better known as *Dinorah* (1859).

216

Meyerbeer was far too clever a man to undertake anything he could not carry through successfully, and in these operas he caught the trick of French *opéra-comique* very happily. *L'Étoile du nord* deals with the fortunes of Peter the Great. The lighter parts of this *opéra-comique* are delightfully arch and vivacious and much of the concerted music is gay and brilliant.

Dinorah shows Meyerbeer in a pastoral and idyllic vein. The music is bright and tuneful, and the reaper's and hunter's songs (which are introduced for no apparent reason) are delightful; but the libretto is so impossibly foolish that the opera has fallen into disrepute, although the brilliant music of the heroine—the "Shadow Song," for example—makes it a favorite role with coloratura sopranos.

Meyerbeer was extravagantly praised in his lifetime; he is now as bitterly decried. The truth seems to lie, as usual, between the two extremes. He was an unusually clever man, with a strong instinct for the theater. He took immense pains with his operas, often rewriting the entire score; but his efforts were directed less towards ideal perfection than to what would be most effective, so that there is a hollowness and a superficiality about his work which we cannot ignore, even while we admit the ingenuity of the means employed. His influence upon modern opera has been extensive. He was the real founder of the school of melodramatic opera.

MEYERBEER SPEAKS

Italy was enjoying the delights of a sweet ecstasy. The people had, so it seemed, found at last their longed-for paradise; all that was needed to complete their bliss was the music of Rossini. I was caught like the rest . . . in this fine web of sound. I was bewitched in a magic garden which I had no wish to enter, but which I could not avoid. All my thoughts, all my faculties became Italian; when I had lived there a year, I thought of myself as a native. I became completely acclimated to the splendid glory of nature, art, and the gay, congenial life, and could therefore enter into the thoughts, feelings, and sensibilities of the Italians. That so complete a transformation of my inner life must have had a radical effect upon the style of my music will readily be understood. I did not want, as is commonly supposed, to imitate Rossini or to write in the Italian manner, but I had to compose in the style which I adopted under the compulsion of my state of mind.

. . . . .

I am delighted at what you tell me of the good opinion which the Director of the Opéra [in Paris] has of my feeble talents. You enquire whether I would like to work for the French stage, I assure you that I should consider it a greater glory to have the honor of composing for the French Opéra than for all the theaters in Italy, in which, moreover I have given my works. Where else than in Paris should I find the immense resources which the Opéra affords to an artist who wishes to write really dramatic music? . . . You may ask me why, in view of these considerations, I have not tried so far to write for Paris. It is because I am told here that the Opéra is hedged about with difficulties and one must normally wait years and years before getting a hearing. That gives me pause. I confess that, perhaps, I have been spoiled on this score in Italy, where they have up to now sought me out.

. . . . .

No one will ever equal Gluck in simplicity, naturalness, and powerful dramatic expression. When I am enjoying his majestic works, I often feel so humiliated that I would like never again to write a note.

FELIX MENDELSSOHN

1 8 0 9 – 1 8 4 7

JACOB LUDWIG FELIX MENDELSSOHN-BARTHOLDY was born in Hamburg, Germany, on February 3, 1809. His grandfather was the celebrated philosopher, Moses Mendelssohn, and his father, Abraham, a banker, so Felix was raised in a setting of culture and wealth in which his formidable musical talent could flourish. In his boyhood, his immediate family was converted from Judaism to Protestantism, an occasion upon which it added the name "Bartholdy" to its own to distinguish themselves from the other Mendelssohns who had remained Jewish. Felix began music study early, first with his mother, then with Ludwig Berger and Karl Friedrich Zelter. He made his first public appearance as pianist when he was nine; at ten he made his debut as composer when the Berlin *Singakademie* performed one of his choral works; and by the time he was twelve he had completed numerous compositions, including symphonies and operas. In 1826 came his first masterwork, the *A Midsummer Night's Dream* Overture. A year after that, his opera *Die Hochzeit des Camacho* was introduced in Berlin.

Mendelssohn first made music history, as a conductor rather than as a composer, on March 11, 1829 when he directed Bach's *Passion According to St. Matthew* (the first performance since Bach's own time). The concert proved so successful that it was repeated, and became the first major event in the revival of Bach's long neglected music that swept Europe during the next half-century.

In the spring of 1829 Mendelssohn paid his first visit to England where he introduced some of his compositions; later the same year he was made honorary member of the Philharmonic Society. This marked the beginning of the vogue for Mendelssohn's music in England which continued throughout his life; indeed no foreign-

219

born musician since Handel had been so highly regarded. In 1830–32 Mendelssohn toured Germany and Austria, after which he paid his second visit to England, this time to introduce his *Fingal's Cave* Overture, the *Capriccio brilliant* for piano and orchestra, and the G minor Piano Concerto, and to publish the first volume of his *Songs Without Words.*

In 1833 Mendelssohn was appointed musical director in Düsseldorf, but he held this post only a few months. Between 1835 and 1840 he was the conductor of the Gewandhaus Orchestra in Leipzig which, through his efforts, became one of the most significant symphonic organizations in Europe. During this period, on March 28, 1837, he married Cécile Jeanrenaud, who bore him five children.

In 1841, Emperor Friedrich Wilhelm IV invited Mendelssohn to become head of the Academy of Arts then being projected in Berlin. Because of violent differences with the Court and fellow musicians, Mendelssohn resigned from this post in the fall of 1842; but the Emperor prevailed on him to accept an honorary appointment as General Musical Director. Mendelssohn now returned to Leipzig where he resumed his activity as conductor and where, in 1843, he helped found the Leipzig Conservatory.

In 1844, 1846, and 1847, Mendelssohn paid additional visits to England. On the first occasion he gave guest performances with the London Philharmonic; in 1846 he directed the première of his oratorio, *Elijah;* and in 1847, on his tenth and last visit, he gave a command performance for Queen Victoria. The death of his beloved sister, Fanny, on May 14, 1847, was a blow that shattered Mendelssohn's already delicate health. He died a few months after that, in Leipzig, on November 4, 1847.

THE MAN

EDUARD DEVRIENT

Of middle height, slender frame, and of uncommon muscular power, a capital gymnast, swimmer, walker, rider, and dancer, the leading feature of his outward and inner nature was an extraordinary sensitiveness. Excitement stimulated him to the verge of frenzy, from which he was restored only by his sound, deathlike sleep. This restorative he had always on hand; he assured me that he had but to find himself alone and unoccupied in a room where there was a sofa, to go straightway to sleep. His brain had from childhood been taxed excessively, by the university course, study of modern languages, drawing, and much else, and to these were added the study of music in its profoundest sense. The rapidity with which he mastered a score; his perfect understanding of the requirements of new compositions, the construction and complications of which were at once transparent to him; his marvelous memory, which placed under his hand the entire range of great works; these wondrous gifts filled me with frequent doubts as to whether his nervous power could possibly sustain him through the length of an ordinary life.

Moreover, he would take no repose. The habit of constant occupation, instilled by his mother, made rest intolerable to him. To spend any time in mere talk caused him to look frequently at his watch, by which he often gave offense; his impatience was only pacified when something was being done, such as music, reading, chess, and so forth. He was fond of having a leaf of paper and pen at hand when he was conversing, to sketch down whatever occurred to him.

His manners were most pleasing. His features, of the Oriental type, were handsome; a high, thoughtful forehead, much depressed at the temples; large, expressive, dark eyes, with drooping lids, and a peculiar veiled glance through the lashes; this, however, sometimes flashed distrust or anger, sometimes happy dreaming and expectancy. His nose was arched and of delicate form, still more so the mouth, with its short upper and full under lips, which was slightly protruded and hid his teeth when, with a slight lisp, he pronounced the hissing consonants. An extreme mobility about his mouth betrayed every emotion that passed within.

His bearing retained from boyhood the slight rocking of the head and upper part of the body, and shifting from foot to foot; his head was much thrown back, especially when playing; it was always easy to see whether he was pleased or otherwise when new music was

221

going on, by his nods and shakes of the head. In society his manners were . . . distinguished. The shyness that he still retained left him entirely during his subsequent travels, but even now, when he wished to propitiate, he could be most fascinating, and his attentions to young ladies were not without effect. In his affections filial love still held the foremost place; the veneration with which he regarded his father had in it something religious and patriarchal; with his sisters the fondest intimacy prevailed; from his brother, disparity of age still somewhat divided him. His elder sister, Fanny, stood musically most closely related to him; through her excellent nature, clear sense, and rich fund of sensibility (not perceptible to every one) many things were made clear to him. For his youngest sister, Rebecca, he had an unbounded admiration, sensitive as he was to all that was fair and lovely.

Felix's nature fitted him particularly for friendship; he possessed . . . a rich source of intimates, which increased as he advanced in life. To his friends he was frankly devoted, exquisitely tender; it was indeed felicity to be beloved by Felix. At the same time it must be confessed that his affection was exclusive to the utmost; he loved only in the measure that he was loved. This was the solitary dark speck in his sunny disposition. He was the spoiled child of fortune, unused to hardship or opposition; it remains a marvel that egotism did not prevail more than it did over his inborn nobleness and straightforwardness.

The atmosphere of love and appreciation to which he had been nurtured was a condition of life to him; to receive his music with coldness or aversion was to be his enemy, and he was capable of denying genuine merit in anyone who did so. A blunder in manners or an expression that displeased him, could alienate him altogether. . . . About small things he could be unforgiving, for he could not accustom himself to hearing what displeased him, and he never had been compelled to conform cheerfully to the whims of anyone.

But his irritability, his distrustfulness even toward his most intimate friends, were sometimes quite incredible. A casual remark, a stupid jest that he often accepted from me with perfect good temper, would sometimes suddenly cause him to drop his lids, look at me askance, and ask doubtfully: "What do you mean by that? Now I

222

want to know what you wish me to understand by that?" and it was difficult to restore his good humor. These peculiarities in Mendelssohn caused him, though much beloved, to be judged often unfavorably; but those who knew him intimately accepted these few faults, the natural product of his exceptional position, and prized none the less all that was excellent in him.

He was exquisitely kind-hearted and benevolent, even toward dumb animals. I recollect him, when a boy of thirteen, ardently pleading for the life and liberty of a small fish which had been given to his brother Paul, who wished to have it fried for himself. . . . I often thought of that fish when I later saw Felix take the part of those who were in trouble.

THE COMPOSER

SIR GEORGE GROVE

Mendelssohn's very early works show in certain points the traces of his predecessors—of Bach, Mozart, Beethoven, and Weber. But this is only saying what can be said of the early works of all composers, including Beethoven himself. Mendelssohn is not more but less amenable to this law of nature than most of his compeers. The traces of Bach are the most permanent, and they linger on in the vocal works even as late as *St. Paul* (1836). Indeed, Bach may be tracked still later in the solid construction and architectonic arrangement of the choruses, even of the *Lobgesang* (1840), the *Walpurgisnacht* (1843) and *Elijah* (1846), works in all respects emphatically Mendelssohn's own, not less than in the religious feeling, the union of noble sentiment with tender expression, and the utter absence of commonness or vulgarity which pervade all his music alike.

In the instrumental works, however, the year 1826 broke the spell of all external influence, and the Octet, the Quintet in A, and, above all, the *Midsummer Night's Dream* Overture, launched him upon the world at seventeen as a thoroughly original composer. The concert overtures *Fingal's Cave* (1832), *Meeresstille und glückliche Fahrt* (1832), and *Die schöne Melusine* (1833); the three great symphonies; the two piano concertos; and the Violin Concerto (1844) fully maintain this originality, and in thought, style, phrase, and clearness of expression, no less than in their symmetrical structure and exquisite orchestration, are eminently independent and individual works. The advance between the Symphony in C minor (1824)—which we call No. 1, though it is really No. 13—and the *Italian Symphony* (1833) is immense. The former is laid out quite on the Mozart plan, and the working throughout recalls the old world. But the latter has no model. The melodies and the treatment are Mendelssohn's alone, and while in gaiety and freshness it is quite unrivalled, it is not too much to say that the slow movement is as great a novelty as that of Beethoven's Piano Concerto in G. The *Scotch Symphony* (1842) is as original as the *Italian*, and on a much larger and grander scale. The opening Andante, the Scherzo, and the finale are especially splendid and individual. The concert overtures are in all essential respects as original as if Beethoven had not preceded them by writing *Coriolon*—as true a representative of his genius as *Fingal's Cave* is of Mendelssohn's. The *Midsummer Night's Dream,* which brought the fairies into the orchestra and fixed them there, and which will always remain a monument of the fresh feeling of youth; the *Fingal's Cave* with its intensely somber and melancholy sentiment, and the *Melusina* with its passionate pathos,—these also have no predecessors in sentiment, treatment, or orchestration. *Ruy Blas* (1839) is brilliant and as full of fire as the others are of sentiment, and does not fall a step behind them for individuality.

In these works there is little attempt at any modification of the established forms. Innovation was not Mendelssohn's habit of mind, and he rarely attempts it. The *Scotch Symphony* is directed to be played throughout without pause, and it has an extra movement in form of a long coda which appears to be a novelty in pieces of this class. There are unimportant variations in the form of the concertos, chiefly in the direction of compression. But with Mendelssohn, no more than with Schubert, do these things force themselves on the attention. He has so much to say, and says it so well, the music is so good and so agreeable, that it never occurs to the hearer to inquire if he has altered the external proportions of his discourses.

His Scherzos are still more peculiarly his own offspring, and really have no prototypes. That in a movement bearing the same name as one of Beethoven's most individual creations, and occupying the same place in the piece, he should have been able to strike out so entirely different a path as he did, is a wonderful tribute to his originality. No less remarkable is the variety of the many Scherzos he has left. They are written for orchestra and chamber, concerted and solo alike, in double and triple time indifferently; they have no fixed rhythm, and notwithstanding a strong family likeness—the impress of the gay and delicate mind of their composer—are all independent of each other. In his orchestral works Mendelssohn's scoring is remarkable not more for its grace and beautiful effect than for its clearness and practical efficiency. What the composer wishes to express comes out naturally, and each instrument has with rare exceptions the passages best suited to it. . . .

His great works in chamber music are on a par with those for the orchestra. The Octet, the two string quintets, the six string quartets are thoroughly individual and interesting, nothing far-fetched, no striving after effect, no emptiness, no padding, but plenty of matter given in a manner at once fresh and varied. Every bar is his own, and every bar is well said. The accusation which is sometimes brought against them that they are more fitted for the orchestra than the chamber, is probably to some extent well founded. Indeed, Mendelssohn virtually anticipates this charge in his preface to the parts of the Octet, which he desires may be played in a symphonic style; and in that noble piece, as well as in parts of the String Quintet in B-flat (1845) and the string quartets in D major (1838) and F minor (1847), many players have felt that the composer has placed his work in too small a frame, that the proper balance cannot always be maintained between the leading violin and the other instruments, and that to produce all the effect of the composer's ideas they should be heard in an orchestra of strings rather than in a quartet of solo instruments. On the other hand, the Piano Quartet in B minor (1825), the two piano trios in D minor (1839) and C minor (1845) have been criticized, probably with some justice, as not sufficiently concertante, that is as giving too prominent a part to the piano. Such criticism may detract from the pieces in a technical respect, but it leaves the ideas and sentiments of the music, the nobility of the style, and the clearness of the structure, untouched.

His additions to the technique of the piano are not important. Hiller tells a story which shows that Mendelssohn cared little for the rich passages of the "modern school"; his own were quite sufficient for him. But this is consistent with what we have just said. It was the music of which he thought, and as long as that expressed his feelings it satisfied him, and he was indifferent to the special form into which it was thrown. Of his piano works the most remarkable is the set of seventeen *Variations sérieuses* (1841); but the Fantasy in F-sharp minor (1830), the three great Caprices (1834), the Preludes and Fugues, and several of the smaller pieces, are splendid works too well known to need further mention. The *Songs Without Words* (1829–45) stand by themselves, and are especially interesting . . . on account of their great popularity. . . . It was some time before the *Songs Without Words* reached the public; but when once they became known, the taste for them quickly spread, and probably no pieces ever were so much and so permanently beloved. The piece, like the name, is virtually his own invention. Not a few of Beethoven's movements—such as the Adagio of the *Sonata pathétique*, or the Minuet of op. 10, no. 3—might be classed as "Songs Without Words," and so might the Nocturnes of John Field (1782–1837); but the former of these are portions of larger works, not easily separable, and the latter were little known; and neither of them possess that grace and finish, that intimate charm, and above all that domestic character, which have ensured the success of Mendelssohn's *Songs Without Words*. . . . His own feelings towards them was by no means so indulgent. It is, perhaps, impossible for a composer to be quite impartial towards pieces which make him so very popular, but he distinctly says, after the issue of Book III, that he does "not mean to write any more at that time, and that if such *animalculae* are multiplied too much no one will care for them." It is difficult to believe that so stern a critic of his own productions should not have felt the weakness of some of them, and the strong mannerism which, with a few remarkable exceptions, pervades the whole collection. We should not forget, too, that he is not answerable for the last two books, which were published after his death, without the great alterations which he habitually made before publication. One drawback to the excessive popularity of the *Songs Without Words* is, not that they exist—for we might as well quarrel with Goethe for the *Wanderers Nachtlied* or the *Heiden-röslein*—nor yet the number of imitations they produced, but that in the minds of thousands these graceful trifles, many of which were thrown off at a single sitting, are indiscriminately accepted as the most characteristic representatives of the composer of the Violin Concerto and the *Fingal's Cave* Overture.

His songs may be said to have introduced the German *Lied* to England, and to have led the way for the deeper strains of Schumann, Schubert and Brahms in English houses and concert auditoriums. No doubt the songs of those composers do touch lower depths of the heart than Mendelssohn's do; but the clearness and directness of his music, the spontaneity of his melody, and a certain pure charm pervading the whole, have given a place with the great public to some of his songs, such as *Auf Flügeln des Gesanges* (1834). Others, such as the *Nachtlied* (1847), the *Volkslied* (1839), and the *Schilflied* (1847) are deeply pathetic; others, as the *Lieblings-plätzchen* (1841) are at the same time extremely original; others, as *O Jugend*, the *Jagdlied* (1834), and *An die Entfernte* (1847) the soul of gaiety. He was very fastidious in his choice of words, and often marks his sense of the climax by varying the last stanza in accompaniment or otherwise, a practice which he was perhaps the first to adopt.

Ever since Handel's time, oratorios have been the favorite public music in England. Mendelssohn's works of this class, *St. Paul* (1836), *Elijah* (1846), the *Lobgesang* (1840) soon became well known. They did not come as strangers, but as the younger brothers of the *Messiah* and *Judas Maccabaeus* and we liked them at once. Not only liked them; we were proud of them, as having been produced or very early performed in England; they appealed to our national love for the Bible, and there is no doubt that to them is largely owing the position next to Handel which Mendelssohn occupies in England. *Elijah* at once took its place, and it is now on a level with the *Messiah* in public favor. Apart from the intrinsic quality of the music of his large vocal works, the melody, clearness, spirit, and

227

symmetry which they exhibit, are in common with his instrumental compositions. There is one thing which remarkably distinguishes them, and in which they are far in advance of their predecessors—a simple and direct attempt to set the subject forth as it was, to think first of the story and next of the music which depicted it. The thoughts and emotions are the first things, and the forms of expression second and subordinate. We may call this "dramatic" in as much as the books of oratorios are more or less dramas; and Mendelssohn's letters to Schubring in reference to *Elijah*, his demand for more "questions and answers, replies and rejoinders, sudden interruptions" etc., show how thin was the line which in his opinion divided the platform from the stage, and how keenly he wished the personages of his oratorios to be alive and acting, "not mere musical images, but inhabitants of a definite active world." But yet it was not so much dramatic in any conscious sense as a desire to set things forth as they were. Hauptmann has stated this well with regard to the three noble Psalms, "Judge Me, O God," "Why Rage Fiercely the Heathen?" and "My God, Why Hast Thou Forsaken Me?" (1844). He says that it is not so much any musical or technical ability that places them so far above other similar compositions of the time, as the fact that Mendelssohn has "just put the Psalm itself before him; not Bach, or Handel, or Palestrina, or any other style or composer, but the words of the Psalmist; and the result is not anything that can be classed new or old, but the Psalm itself is thoroughly fine musical effect; the music not pretending to be scientific, or anything on its own account, but just throwing life and feeling into the dry words. Any one who knows these Psalms will recognize the truth of this description. It is almost more true in reference to the 114th Psalm, "When Israel Out of Egypt Came" (1839). The Jewish blood of Mendelssohn must surely for once have beat fiercely over the picture of the great triumph of his forefathers, and it is only the plain truth to say that in directness and force his music is a perfect match for the spendid words of the unknown Psalmist. It is true of his oratorios also, but they have other great qualities as well. *St. Paul*, with all its great beauties, is an early work, the book of which, or rather perhaps the nature of the subject, does not wholly lend itself to forcible treatment, and it is an open question whether it can fully vie with either the *Lobgesang* or still more *Elijah*. These splendid compositions have that air of distinction which stamps a great work in every art, and which a great master alone can confer. As instances of this, take the scene of the Watchman, and the concluding chorus in the *Lobgesang*, "Ye Nations." Or in *Elijah* the double quartets; the arioso "Woe Unto Them" which might be the wail of a pitying archangel; the choruses, "Thanks Be to God," "Be Not Afraid," "He Watching Over Israel," "Behold! God the Lord Passed By"; the great piece of declamation for soprano which opens the second part; the unaccompanied trio, "Lift Thine Eyes"; the tenor air, "Then Shall the Righteous." These are not only fine as music, but are animated by that lofty and truly dramatic character which makes one forget the vehicle, but live only in the noble sentiment of the scene as it passes. . . .

. . . . .

We must now close this . . . attempt to set Mendelssohn forth as he was. Few instances can be found in history of a man so amply gifted with every good quality of mind and heart; so carefully brought up among good influences; endowed with every circumstance that would make him happy; and so thoroughly fulfilling his mission. Never perhaps could any man be found in whose life there were so few things to conceal and to regret.

Is there any drawback to this? Or, in other words, does his music suffer at all from what he calls his "habitual cheerfulness"? It seems as if there was a drawback, and that arising more or less directly from those very points which we have named as his best characteristics—his happy healthy heart, his single mind, his unfailing good spirits, his simple trust in God, his unaffected directness of purpose. It is not that he had not genius. The great works enumerated prove that he had it in large measure. No man could have called up the new emotions of the *Midsummer Night's Dream* Overture, the wonderful pictures of *Fingal's Cave*, or the pathetic distress of the lovely *Melusina*, without genius of the highest order. But his genius had not been subjected to those fiery trials which seem necessary to ensure its abiding possession of the depths of the human heart. "My music," says Schubert, "is the product of my genius and

229

my misery; and that which I have written in my greatest distress is that which the world seems to like best." Now Mendelssohn was never more than temporarily unhappy. He did not know distress as he knew happiness. Perhaps there was even something in the constitution of his mind which forebade his harboring it, or being permanently affected by it. He was so practical, that as a matter of duty he would have thrown it off. In this as in most other things he was always under control. At any rate he was never tried by poverty, or disappointment, or a morbid temper, or neglect, or the perfidy of friends, or any of the other great ills which crowded so thickly around Beethoven, Schubert, or Schumann. Who can wish that he had been? That that bright, pure aspiring spirit should have to be dulled by distress or torn with agony? It might have lent a deeper undertone to his songs, or have enabled his Adagios to draw tears where now they only give a saddened pleasure. But let us take the man as we have him. Surely there is enough of conflict and violence in life and in art. When we want to be made unhappy we can turn to others. It is well in these agitated days to be able to point to one perfectly balanced nature in whose life, whose letters, and whose music alike, all is at once manly and refined, clever and pure, brilliant and solid. For the enjoyment of such shining heights of goodness we may well forego for once the depths of misery and sorrow.

MENDELSSOHN SPEAKS

So much is said about music and yet so little is said! I am of the belief that words alone are inadequate for this purpose. Were I to find them adequate, I should probably no longer write music. People complain that music is too ambiguous, and that no one really knows how to interpret it, while words are readily comprehended. But the opposite holds true for me, not only an entire speech, but even with single words. These seem to hold for me many meanings, tend to become ambiguous, vague, and thus easily misinterpreted. Music, on the other hand, fills one's soul with a thousand nobler feelings and sentiments than words can ever do. Thoughts expressed to me by music I love are not too indefinite to be put into words, but on the contrary, too definite. I find that in every effort to express such thoughts something is right and at the same time something is lacking as well. . . . If you ask me what I was thinking of when I wrote it, I would say: just the song as it stands. And if I happen to have had certain words in mind for one or another of these songs [*Songs Without Words*], I would never want to tell them to anyone, because the same words never mean the same things to different people. Only the song can say the same thing, can arouse the same feelings in one person as in another, a feeling which is not expressed, however, by the same words.

Resignation, melancholy, the praise of God, a hunting song do not conjure up the same thoughts in everybody. What signifies melancholy to one may seem resignation to another, while a third person may perhaps be incapable of forming either conception. To anyone who is by nature a sportsman, a hunting song and the praise of God might come to pretty much the same thing, and to him the sound of a hunting horn would actually be praise of God, while to us it would be nothing more than a hunting song. However long we might discuss it with him we should not get very far. Words have meanings, but music we both can understand correctly.

. . . . .

As time goes by I think more and more sincerely of writing only as I feel, and less and less with regard to the outward results of my compositions. When I have produced a piece of music that has flowed from my heart, I am not at all concerned whether it will later bring me fame, honors, orders, or snuff boxes!

ROBERT SCHUMANN

1 8 1 0 – 1 8 5 6

ROBERT ALEXANDER SCHUMANN was born in Zwickau, Saxony, on June 8, 1810. He started studying the piano at six. At eight he wrote his first compositions, and by the time he was eleven had produced several ambitious choral and orchestral works. Between 1820 and 1828 he attended the Zwickau Gymnasium. In the latter year he entered the University of Leipzig to study law, continuing these studies in Heidelberg a year later. His musical activity, however, was not relaxed. His first published composition appeared in 1830: the *Abegg Variations,* for piano.

By fall of 1830, Schumann became convinced that music and not law was his goal. He began an intensive period of piano study with Friedrich Wieck in Leipzig, with the hopes of becoming an outstanding virtuoso. An attempt to make the fourth finger as flexible as the others—by means of an artificial device to keep it suspended—resulted in partial paralysis of the right hand in 1832. His dreams of a virtuoso career now shattered, Schumann directed his gifts and energies into creative channels. For a while he studied composition with Heinrich Dorn. Then, in 1832, he completed *Papillons* and the first set of the *Paganini Etudes,* both for the piano. The piano remained his principal medium for artistic self-expression until 1840. In that time he completed such masterworks as the *Carnaval,* the *Études symphoniques,* the *Fantasiestücke,* and the C major Fantasy.

While thus creating a new epoch in piano literature, Schumann also distinguished himself as a critic and editor. In 1833 he helped form a musical society of idealistic young musicians who called themselves the *Davidsbündler.* This society aimed to destroy philistinism in music. A year later, Schumann helped found a musical

232

journal, the *Neue Zeitschrift für Musik,* which he edited until 1844. Through its columns Schumann was able to introduce the then-unsung and unrecognized gifts of such young masters as Chopin and Brahms.

The years between 1836 and 1840 were turbulent ones. He had fallen in love with Clara, the sixteen-year-old daughter of his teacher, Wieck. The autocratic opposition of Clara's father put every possible obstacle in their way for four years. Finally, Schumann brought suit against Wieck and, winning his case, was able to marry Clara on September 12, 1840. It was a truly happy marriage, and it helped bring Schumann to new creative heights and to arouse in him an unprecedented artistic fertility.

During the first year of his marriage, Schumann turned to the *Lied,* creating about 140 songs. In 1841, he passed on to orchestral music by completing his first symphony, the first movement of the A minor Piano Concerto, and the first draft of the D minor Symphony. The year 1842 was mainly devoted to chamber music, with three string quartets, the Piano Quintet, and the E-flat major Piano Quartet as his principal works.

His health began deteriorating in 1844 when he was compelled to give up most of his activities outside of composition and live quietly in Dresden. Between 1850 and 1853 he was the municipal music director in Düsseldorf. While holding this post he became increasingly morbid. He began to hear voices and sounds that tortured him, and showed alarming signs of lapsing memory. After an unsuccessful attempt to commit suicide by drowning, he was committed to an insane asylum in Endenich, near Bonn, Germany, where he died on July 29, 1856.

THE MAN

GUSTAV JANSEN

His figure was stately, powerfully built, and his bearing was distinguished and aristocratic. He never tried to impress by outward appearances, never wore striking clothing. H. Truhn described him in the following way: "He had a large, spacious and truly German head, topped off with soft, dark blond hair; his face was full and beardless, with lips shaped in such a way that they almost seemed to begin a whistle. His eyes were a beautiful blue, but they were not large and suggested neither energy nor power; they appeared to be penetrating deep into and listening intently to his soul. He stood rigid and erect in posture, but walked with a soft and flexible step almost as if his strong, broad-shouldered body lacked bones. He was comparatively short, made much use of the lorgnette but without any trace of snobbery." In his conversation he was generally laconic, rarely displaying any kind of social sophistication. He was incapable of talking much and saying little.

After completing his day's work Schumann used to frequent Poppe's *Kaffeebaum* during the late hours of evening, a popular gathering place for young people of various professions. Schumann occupied no position of special importance in this circle. Not at all! Good cheer would prevail as far removed from any feeling of snobbishness nor cliques as it was from uninhibited revelry. Schumann preferred a hidden corner. "He used to sit at the table sideways," says Brendel, "so that he would be able to lean head on hand. From time to time he would stroke back his hair which would frequently fall over his forehead. Eyes half-shut, he would withdraw into himself and lapse into dreams. Then there would be something to inspire him to an interesting exchange of ideas with his companions. Suddenly he would become alive, talkative, animated. You could almost see him awaken from his dreams, returning from his inner to the outer world. You could almost see his eyes, a moment before turned backward and looking deep within himself, turn toward the world outside. He would then reveal a penetrating intelligence."

In the company of high-spirited people Schumann was always perfectly at ease. He would sit always in the same seat, at the end of the table, a cigar ever in his mouth. He never had to call for a fresh glass of beer, since he had taken care with the waiter to have fresh glasses of beer brought to him as soon as he had drained his glass. As soon as he was through with his beers he silently paid his bill and left a tip. Most evenings the company at *Kaffeebaum* was small, and Schumann never stayed past an hour usual for simple, middle-class people. Sometimes he left the place suddenly and precipitously, as if on military order, rushing out of the café without bidding anybody good night; and these were the times when his head was filled with music that he had to get down on paper at home.

For a number of years before 1836 Schumann often changed his rooms. Then in 1836 he rented a room situated agreeably, and he stayed here until his marriage. This room was in a house named "the red college," with a delightful court, and a view of a park, its window facing the woodiest section of the promenade that circles old Leipzig. His room was so quiet and peaceful that when the leaves rustled outside the window you could imagine yourself to be in some lonely castle in the woods. . . . Sitting in that room, it was impossible to believe you were in the very midst of busy Leipzig. . . . At the window, set off high above the floor, was a table on a kind of platform, with an inkstand and a hook on which a watch could hang. There was also a delightful miniature—the head of a pensive girl leaning against the inkstand. Schumann's watch also hung there. I was not allowed to ask him who the girl in the picture was. Although this little oblong room had only one window, it was sufficiently large to contain a grand piano and a sofa with an end table against the opposite wall. Here Schumann used to work.

THE COMPOSER

W. H. HADOW

Schumann's whole life was an endeavor to unite two ideals. In spirit he is a romantic of the romantics, directing his music towards the outside world with a hundred hints and explanations. In form he recognized Bach as his master, and strove to express his ideas in the most elaborate language of the old polyphony. He does not, like Berlioz, splash on his colors principally with an eye to effect. On the contrary, he pays the utmost attention to detail and finish. In a word, his Davidsbund, like the Pre-Raphaelite Brotherhood, was an attempt to adapt ancient methods to modern subjects, with this difference, that whereas the English Pre-Raphaelitism sometimes lost its hold of the theme in its attention to the treatment, Schumann regards the theme as paramount, and adapts the treatment to it as best he can. Hence the first requisite in estimating his work is to examine the character of his ideas, and especially to explain the contention, already advanced, that in forming them he was much influenced by the romantic movement in literature.

Now, as among the musicians of his time, Schumann was exceptionally well read. His classical attainments were probably allowed to rust during his long life as composer and journalist; but as late as 1854 he was ransacking Greek authors for passages about music, and, even if he took Voss's Homer instead of the original, must have gained some acquaintance with the spirit of the *Iliad* and the *Odyssey*. Among the English poets he was a thorough student of Byron and Shakespeare, and knew something at least of Burns and Scott. Of the Italians he certainly read Dante and Petrarch, and possibly others as well; while the romantic writers of his own country were almost as familiar to him as his own works. He knew his Richter as some Englishmen know Dickens, his Heine as some Frenchmen know Musset. He not only studied Goethe, but interpreted him. Of Rückert, Geibel, Eichendorf, Chamisso, and many other contemporary poets, he was the closest reader and the most valuable commentator. Further, he was himself endowed with some not inconsiderable talent for authorship.

In his earlier days music and literature divided his allegiance; at Heidelberg he could astonish his friend Rosen with verse translations of Petrarch's sonnets. During his Russian journey in 1844 he kept an intermittent "Poetical Diary," which must at least have implied some facility in meter. His projected romance on the Davidsbund never seems to have come into existence, but in the *Neue Zeitschrift* he treats that society in a manner which shows that he possessed something of the novelist's gift. Florestan, Eusebius, and Raro are distinct living characters, drawn, it may be, from life, but still "seen through a temperament," and contrasted with remarkable skill and consistency. To the last he retained his appreciation of style. The essay on Brahms which closed his career as a journalist is written with the same care as the essay on Chopin which began it. Throughout the whole course he uses his medium like an artist, and endeavors not only to say what he means, but to say it in accordance with the best literary traditions of his time.

Again he acknowledges the debt which his music owed to the study of his favorite author. "I learned more counterpoint from Jean Paul than from my music-master," he tells Simonin de Sire; and writing to Henrietta Voigt *à propos* of the *Papillons* (1832) he adds, "I might tell you a good deal about them had not Jean Paul done it so much better. If you ever have a moment to spare, please read the last chapter of the *Flegeljahre,* where you will find it all in black and white, down to the seven-league boot, in F-sharp minor. (At the end of the *Flegeljahre* I always feel as if the piece was over but the curtain still up.) I may further mention that I have adapted the text to the music and not vice versa. Only the last of all, which by a happy chance became an answer to the first, owes its existence to Jean Paul." It is difficult for us to see in the last number of the *Papillons* Wult's departure or Wult's fantastic dream, but the point is that Schumann saw it. The mind that conceived that dainty finale was brought into its particular mood by a literary influence.

Thirdly, in one important point Schumann's method of composition stands in closest relation to the earlier romantic movement in German poetry. "The plastic figures in antique Art," says Heine, "are identical with the thing represented. The wanderings of the *Odyssey* mean nothing more than the wanderings of the man called Odysseus, the son of Laetres and the husband of Penelope. It is otherwise in Romantic Art: here the wanderings of the knight have an esoteric signification; they typify, perhaps, the mazes of life in general. The dragon that is vanquished is sin: the almond tree that wafts its fragrance to the hero is the Trinity. . . . Classical Art had to portray only the finite, and its form could be identical with the artist's idea. Romantic Art had to represent, or rather to typify, the infinite and the spiritual, and therefore was compelled to have recourse to a system of traditional parabolic symbols." So it is with music. The tunes in a sonata of Mozart are satisfied to be beautiful melodies and nothing more: no question arises as to their meaning or character. The tunes of Schumann, like the colors of Rossetti, are always trembling on the verge of symbolism. Not, of course, that music

237

can be tied down to any definite signification: on this point the failure of Berlioz is complete and conclusive. But though it cannot work on the same lines as articulate thought, it may possibly work on parallel lines:—that is to say, it may express some broad generic type of emotion with which the articulate thought may be brought into sympathy. For instance, a great many of Schumann's pianoforte pieces have specific names—*Warum, Erster Verlust, Botschaft,* and so on. It would be impossible for us to supply the names from hearing the piece; but if we know the names already we shall recognize that the musical treatment is appropriate. This was precisely what Schumann intended. He writes to Dorn, "I have never come across anything more absurd than Rellstab's criticism of my *Kinderscenen.* He seems to imagine that I got hold of a crying child and sought for inspiration from its sobs. I don't deny that certain children's faces hovered before my mind while I was composing, but the titles were of course added afterwards, and are, as a matter of fact, merely hints as to the treatment and interpretation." At the same time his indications are curiously detailed. He distinguishes the *Kinderscenen* (1838) from the *Album für die Jugend* (1848) on the ground that the former are the recollection which a grown man retains of his childhood, while the latter "consists of imaginings and expectations of young people." He finds the story of Hero and Leander in the fifth of the *Fantasiestucke* (1837): he accompanies two of the *Davidsbundlertänze* (1837) with a running commentary of Florestan and Eusebius; while as climax he declares that in one of Schubert's pianoforte works he and a friend discovered exactly the same pageant, "down to the name of the town in which it was held." Even his directions for performance show something of the same tendency. In the ordinary indications of tempo he is notoriously careless; it is a well-known joke against him that the finale of the *Concerto without Orchestra* begins, *So schnell als möglich* and ends *piu presto,* while there is still a controversy whether the coda of the slow movement in his F major quartet should be marked *piu mosso* or *piu lento.* But on the other hand he often suggests the manner of interpretation by such phrases as *Etwas kokett,* or *mit humor,* or *mit innigkeit.* Once he gets as far as *Etwas hahnbuchen,* a hint which pianists must find some difficulty in taking. The great pianoforte

238

Fantasia in C (1836) has a motto from Schlegel, the fourth of the *Waldscenen* (1848–49) has one from Hebbel, and similar texts were appended to the earliest edition of the *Davidsbündlertänze* and of one of the *Novelletten* (1838). Everywhere we find the evident intention of establishing a parallelism between music and some influence from outside. In one word, Schumann did not wish his melodies to tell a definite story or paint a definite picture, but he did wish to bring his hearers into a condition of mind from which they could "go on romancing for themselves."

One example of this parallelism deserves a special word of comment, partly from its intrinsic importance, partly because hitherto it has been somewhat underrated. The *Kreisleriana* (1838) certainly owe more than their title to Hoffmann's fantastic sketches. Critics who tell us that Schumann "is expressing his own sorrows, not those of Dr. Kreisler," and that "he might just as well have called his pieces 'Wertheriana,' or any other name," have missed a point which it is of some moment to observe. Among Hoffmann's *Fantasiestücke in Callot's manier* there are two sets of Kreisleriana, loose, disconnected papers, dealing with music and musical criticism very much in the style which Schumann afterwards adopted for the *Neue Zeitschrift*. The essay on Beethoven might have been signed "R.S.," Florestan and Eusebius might have been members of the Musico-Poetical Club, the Musikfeind was a well-known figure in the editorial sanctum at Leipzig. Even Dr. Johannes Kreisler himself —"the little man in a coat the color of C-sharp minor with an E major colored collar"—is not far removed in spirit from the party who listened to Chopin's Opus 2, or tried experiments with the "psychometer." In short, of all German artists Schumann approaches most nearly to Hoffmann in standpoint. Both deserted law for music, both were at the same time composers and journalists, both employed the manner and phraseology of Richter to the advancement of the new school of composition. The differences between them, which no doubt are sufficiently wide, lie mainly outside the domain of the art: within that domain they fought for the same cause with the same weapons. Hence in calling his pieces *Kreisleriana* Schumann is expressing a real connection of thought, a real recognition of alliance. They are, in fact, *Fantasiestücke in Hoffmann's manier*, and bear

239

more intimate relation to the creator of Dr. Kreisler than all the copper-plates that ever issued from Callot's studio.

The connection is interesting because it illustrates the attempt to relate musical to literary influences under the most favorable of conditions. We have here two men possessed of somewhat similar gifts and united by a common aim. Hoffmann is enough of a composer to have a full understanding of music; Schumann enough of an author to be closely in touch with literature. Both desire to reconcile the two, so far as such reconciliation is possible; each sets himself to the work from his own side. Hence in estimating the result of their efforts we shall see once for all the limitations of musical romanticism. It is a unique opportunity for determining in what sense effects of tone and effects of word can be held to react upon one another.

Now in the second series of Hoffmann's *Kreisleriana* is described a meeting of the Musico-Poetical Club, a precursor of the Davidsbund, which assembled in the Kapellmeister's rooms to hear him play, and to profit by his instructions. Unfortunately at the outset there is an accident to the piano, attempts to remedy it only make matters worse, and at last so many of the strings are broken that the instrument becomes practically useless. But the doctor is equal to the occasion. He seats himself at the keyboard, and striking at intervals such notes as are still available, supplies the place of his fantasia with a long rhapsodical description of its poetical meaning. The performance, in fact, is the exact reverse of a song without words—it is a pianoforte piece without music. We may notice that Hoffmann is wise enough not to attempt any definiteness of outline. There is no portraiture of hero or heroine, no detailed description of incident, all is left vague, shadowy, indeterminate. Literature has become all but melodic, it is standing on the extreme verge and stretching out its hands over a gulf which it cannot cross. In like manner the *Kreisleriana* of Schumann are all but articulate. In no other of his piano works is the expression of emotion so clear and so intelligible; the voice is eloquent even though we cannot catch the precise words of its utterance. Here also is no attempt to depict any specific scene or occurrence; the music is suggestive, not descriptive; the end is attained purely and simply by the indication of broad general types of feeling. This, then, would seem to be the conclusion of the whole

240

matter. The most determinate effects of tone produce in the hearer a mental impression analogous to that caused by the least determinate effects of word. As language becomes more definite, as music becomes more abstract, so the two recede from one another until they arrive at poles, which have as little in common as a page of Macaulay with a melody of Mozart. At their nearest they can never be brought into contact, for music is in more senses than one a universal language, and cannot be adequately translated by the concrete particulars of our accustomed speech. But, near or far, their closest points of convergence are the two *Kreisleriana.*

So far we have considered the character of Schumann's ideas, and the external or literary influences by which his mind was trained for their conception. It would now follow to complete the account of his education by pointing out the influence exercised upon him by the work of previous composers. Among these, of course, Bach was paramount. Schumann almost passes over the great triumvirate to whom we owe the sonata, the quartet, and the symphony. Mozart and Haydn hardly affected him at all; Beethoven "mainly in his later compositions"; it is to Bach that he looks as the second fountain-head of his inspiration. "Bach and Jean Paul had the greatest influence upon me in former days," he writes to Kossmaly, and as late as 1851 he makes the same acknowledgment. "There are three to whom I always go for advice: the simple Gluck, the more intricate Handel, and the most intricate of all—Bach. Only study the last-named thoroughly and the most complicated of my works will seem clear." Half his admiration for Mendelssohn was devoted to "the master who was the first, by the strength of his own enthusiasm, to revive the memory of Bach in Germany"; almost the last work which occupied his failing powers was a set of pianoforte accompaniments to the violin and violoncello sonatas of the great Cantor. No doubt he gained something from Weber and Schubert, but his relation to them was far less intimate. From first to last his ideal in musical expression was "the great and lofty art of the ancestor of harmony."

Bach and Jean Paul—polyphony and romance—these are the two keys which unlock the mystery of Schumann's work as a composer. His own individuality remains unimpugned; all artists are in some degree indebted to the continuous growth and development of pre-

241

vious work; and Schumann's method is no more derivative than that of Beethoven or Handel. The formative conditions of genius are those by which it is trained, not those by which it is created, only in all cases the training must be efficient if creation is to lead to maturity. At the same time it is of considerable interest to notice three main points in which his education told upon his style. It may be impossible to explain the life; it is both possible and profitable to dissect the organism.

First, his career as a composer is unique in the history of music. There is no other instance of a musician who applies himself successively to each department of his art, masters it, and passes on to the next. Almost all his great piano works were written before 1840; then came a year of song writing, then a year of symphony, then a year of chamber music, then *Paradise and the Peri* (1841–43). Schubert's songs cover the whole period of his productive life; Beethoven's first piece of concerted music is Opus 1 and his last Opus 135; Haydn's symphonies extend over nearly half a century. The other great masters, in short, seem either to have had the forms always at hand, or, like Wagner and Berlioz, to have left some altogether untouched. Schumann employs every medium in turn; but he fetches it from outside, and puts it back when he has finished with it. No doubt he wrote songs after 1840, and orchestral compositions after 1841; but it is none the less noticeable that he devoted himself exclusively to the different forms when they first came under his hand, and that almost all his best work may be divided into a series of detached groups, each produced in one particular manner at one particular time. Surely we have here the indirect working of a logical, deliberative mind—a mind that has been trained into special habits of purpose and selection. In the very character of his method Schumann is actuated by psychological forces different from those of his predecessors in the art.

The second distinctive point is his system of melody. All tune implies a certain fundamental unity—otherwise it would be chaotic; and a certain variation of detail—otherwise it would be monotonous. This identity in difference can be attained in two ways, which we may call respectively the *continuous* and the *discrete*. In the former a series of entirely different elements is fused into a single whole:

242

no two of them are similar, yet all are so fitted together that each supplies what the others need. In the latter a set of parallel clauses are balanced antithetically: the same rhythmic figure is preserved in all, and the differences depend entirely upon qualities of tone and curve. The former is the typical method of Beethoven, the latter that of Schumann. Take, for instance, the opening subject of Beethoven's *Violoncello Sonata* in A. No two bars present the same figure, yet the whole is a unity. Take the longer melody which opens the slow movement of the *Sonata pathétique*. It contains almost as many figures as there are bars, yet the effect is of a single and perfect sentence. Of course Beethoven employed both methods, as he employed every other mode of musical expression, but it is incontestable that in the power of varying and developing his figures is to be found one of his greatest claims to supremacy as an artist. This power Schumann seldom or never brought into active operation. In the opening movement of his *Piano Quintet* (1842), to take an instance from the most familiar of all his works, the first four bars contain two clauses, upon which are built the whole of the first subject and the transition; while the first two bars of the second subject contain the clause upon which the whole of the succeding melody is constructed. In the last movement of the *D minor Piano Trio* (1847), in the cantabile tune of the first *Novellette*, in the well-known theme of the *Bilder aus Osten* (1848) and, in a hundred other examples we find a definite square-cut scheme, exactly analogous to the structure of a stanza of verse. There are very few of Beethoven's instrumental melodies to which it would be possible to adapt metrical words; there is scarcely one of Schumann's which could not be so treated. His relation to poetry extends even to the fact of versification.

Hence his melodies are much easier to analyze than those of Beethoven. Indeed it often happens that the melodic phrase is obvious—almost commonplace—and that the value of the tune depends upon the skill of its treatment, and especially the richness of its harmonization. The charming little waltz in the *Papillons* is simply an ascending and descending diatonic scale; the very effective opening subject in the slow movement of the *E-flat major Piano Quartet* (1842) is a series of sevenths; and similar instances may be found in the Scherzo of the *Piano Quintet* and in many of the songs. Sometimes, too, he took his theme from the "musical letters" in a word, witness the *Abegg Variations* (1830), the *Carnaval* (1834–35), and the fugues on the name of Bach (1845), and though this has been done by other composers, yet none have treated the matter so seriously or with such earnestness of purpose. The *Carnaval*, in particular, is an astonishing instance of the effects that can be produced out of five notes. But it is only very rarely that Schumann's tunes approach the "divine unconsciousness" of the *Appassionata* or the A major symphony. They have their own character, their own vitality, but the genius that gave them birth was to some degree affected by the preoccupations of an external interest.

The third point is Schumann's comparative indifference to what is technically known as musical form. When he writes about the constituent elements of music he almost always specifies them as melody and harmony—the "king and queen of the chess board"—without any mention of that relation of subjects and distribution of keys by which the laws of structure are constituted. This indifference is still more noticeable in his estimate of other men's work. Schubert's C major symphony, the *Piano Sonata* of Ludwig Schunke (1810–34), are discussed with little or no reference to their construction; while, strangest of all, Berlioz's *Symphonie Fantastique* is treated as the legitimate outcome of the system established by Mozart and Beethoven. So it is with his own compositions. Except the Symphony in B-flat (1841) all his orchestral works are in some degree experimental, and in one of them, the *Symphony in D minor* (1841–52), he practically abandons the old scheme altogether; his piano sonatas are only sonatas in the sense in which *Don Juan* is an epic; his quartets, although they keep the elementary laws, yet show that there is much difference between obeying rules and mastering them. His two finest examples of structure are the *Piano Quintet* and the overture to *Manfred* (1848–49); and even these exhibit a sense of effort which place them on a lower level than the concealed art of Beethoven or Brahms. No doubt it is perfectly admissible to seek after new forms. In this respect, as in every other, music must be allowed free permission to advance. But, if we are to acquiesce in a substitute for the earlier methods, we must be assured that it is at least as capable as they of satisfying our requirements. And at present it is not too much

244

to say that, except in the one detail of the "transference of themes," classical structure has not seen any discovery of importance since the publication of the Rasoumovsky quartets. It must be remembered that in this respect there is a marked difference between Schumann and Berlioz. The latter simply shows a want of acquaintance with the laws of construction. The former knows the laws, but underrates their importance. Schumann is far the greater musician of the two, but though his error is less apparent it is not less existent.

There are three possible reasons why a composer of such brilliant genius and such unwearied industry should have displayed this weakness. First, that Bach wrote before the great cyclical forms were established and could therefore give his devoted student little or no assistance in dealing with them. Second, that of all modes of musical expression form is the most abstract—the most essentially musical. Melody and harmony may have some rough analogues outside the limits of the art: the laws of structure have none. Hence they constitute an inner shrine to which only the most single-hearted musicians can penetrate; and he who visits the Temple with any other prepossession—even of poetry itself—must be content to worship among the people. Third, that the whole tone of Schumann's thought was lyric. A very large number of his works consist of short detached pieces, in which there is neither need nor scope for any elaborate system of construction. Hence he grew habituated to the methods of conciseness and concentration, and his sustained efforts were hardly more congenial than the tragedies of Heine or the historical dramas of Uhland.

In one further respect the character of his work was affected by his general habit of mind. No other composer has ever submitted his music to so much alteration and recension. The later editions of the *Davidsbündlertänze*, the *Etudes symphoniques* (1834), the *Impromptus on a Theme by Clara Wieck* (1833), and other of the piano compositions, are full of variant passages, which range in importance from the correction of a detail to the complete restatement of a whole number. No doubt this form of self-criticism has existed to some extent among artists of all ages: Handel rewrote part of the *Messiah*, Berlioz of the *Symphonie fantastique*, and Brahms, late in life, gave to the world a new version of his first piano trio; but in

no other case has the faculty manifested itself so persistently or attached itself so frequently to the printed page. Here again we have
evidence of a mind trained in a different school from that of Haydn
and Mozart. They made their point once for all with an unerring
certainty of intuition: Schumann weighs, deliberates, and finally
revises.

As a writer for the piano he may be said to rank beside Schubert.
He has less melodic gift, less sweetness, perhaps less originality, but he
appreciates far more fully the capacities of the instrument, and possesses more power of rich and recondite harmonization. His polyphony was a new departure in the history of piano music, based upon
that of Bach, but exhibiting a distinctive color and character of its
own. The beauty of his single phrases, the vigor and variety of his
accompaniments, the audacity of his "bitter sweet discords," are all
so many claims on immortality: hardly in the whole range of art
have we such intimate household words as *Warum,* and *Träumerei,*
Carnaval and *Humoreske, Kreisleriana* and *Novelletten.* His spirit,
too, is essentially human. No composer is more companionable, more
ready to respond to any word and sympathize with any emotion.

Among minute points may be mentioned his frequent use of synco-
pation, sometimes picking out the melody for emphasis, sometimes
retarding it to half-speed, oftener traversing the rhythm altogether;
his fondness for long sustained organ chords, as in the *Humoreske*
(1839) and at the end of the *Papillons;* and his peculiar habit of placing his theme in the middle of the harmony and surrounding it on
both sides with a "transparent fabric" of arpeggios. Of more importance is his employment of new lyric and narrative forms for the
piano: the former of which may be illustrated by the detached yet
interconnected numbers of the *Blumenstück* (1839), a Liederkreis
without words; the latter by the structure of the first *Novellette,* in
which the distribution of keys is based upon the interval of a major
third, instead of the old stereotyped relations of tonic and dominant.

A special word should be said on Schumann's position as a writer
of variations. There are two points of view from which this device
can be regarded. The composer may consider the melody as the
essential feature of the theme, and occupy himself solely with
embroideries and arabesques; or he may take his stand upon its

246

harmonic structure, and reproduce the thought that it contains in different modes of expression and phraseology. The one is, roughly speaking, the method of Mozart and Haydn—it is simpler, more rudimentary, more easily exhausted; the other, which is practically inexhaustible, is the method of Brahms. Beethoven represents the turning point between the two. In the slow movement of his *Piano Trio in C minor,* op. 1, no. 3, he gives us a developed example of the earlier form; in the Diabelli Variations we have the finest existing instance of the later. Schumann, of course, is an uncompromising exponent of the second system. Indeed he is sometimes over-zealous in his anxiety not to adhere too closely to the melody of his subject. The set of variations for two pianos (1843), though it atones for its freedom by its extraordinary beauty and charm, yet contains two episodes in which the theme is practically abandoned. It is in the *Études symphoniques* that his power of variation is shown at its best. They also push freedom to its utmost limit, but they never lose touch with their original text, and in richness, brilliance, and vitality they are almost worthy to rank beside the highest efforts of Schumann's great successor.

After the piano works come the songs. Here again Schumann's position can be stated by a single contrast. As absolute music his songs have less value than those of Schubert, as he has never given us a tune like the *Litanei* or *Sei mir gegrüsst;* as illustrations of lyric poetry they are unsurpassed in the whole history of art. With him the terms "words" and "setting," "melody" and "accompaniment" lose their distinctive meanings; all are fused into a single whole in which no part has the preëminence. He follows every shade of the poet's thought with perfect union of sympathy, he catches its tone, he echoes its phrase, he almost anticipates its issue. It is not too much to say that no man can understand Heine who does not know Schumann's treatment of the *Buch der Lieder.*

His songs are interesting also in certain matters of form. He was the first composer who ventured to end with an imperfect cadence, if the words were abrupt or inconclusive, as for instance *Im wunderschönen Monat Mai* (1840). Often, too, he ends his earlier verses with a half-close, and so makes the song continuous throughout, as in *Mondnacht* (1840), and the *Lieder der Suleika* (1840). Another

247

point is his curious use of declamatory passages, neither exact melody nor exact recitative, as in *Ich grolle nicht* (1840). But no analysis can do justice to the beauty, the variety, and the profusion of his lyrics. The composer of *Frühlingsnacht* (1840) and *Widmung* (1840), of *Die Löwenbraut* (1840) and *Die beiden Grenadiere* (1840) has assuredly some claim to be considered the most poetical of musicians.

The qualities required for a successful treatment of the orchestra are precisely those in which, comparatively speaking, Schumann was most deficient, and it is not therefore surprising that his orchestral compositions should be of less value than his works for the voice or the piano. The symphony stands to music as the epic to poetry; it is the broadest, most sustained, most heroic of all forms of expression. Hence it cannot easily be attained by a composer whose gift is for short flights and rapid movements, whose manner of thought is concrete, whose best writings are those which give most scope for the display of brevity and concentration. No doubt Schubert has left us one brilliant instance of a lyric symphony, but, apart from the difficulty of judging a work by two movements, it remains an exception. Schumann, at any rate, seems to lose his bearings among the "swelling and limitless billows." In the opening Allegro of his C major Symphony (1845–46), for instance, the exposition is vigorous and concise enough, but before the end of the movement his boat has refused to answer to the helm and gone drifting off into strange and unknown regions. Again, in the finale of the same work, he finds that the materials presented at the outset are inadequate, discards them half-way through, and introduces an entirely fresh subject. It is hardly unfair to say that the only thing which holds the movement together is a single two-bar phrase containing a diatonic scale. The same vagueness of outline is to be found in his Symphony in D minor, originally called by the more appropriate name of *Symphonische fantasie*. And it may be submitted that these are not really new forms, since they lack the organic unity which the form implies. If they are to be taken as experiments it must be in Bacon's sense of *mero palpatio*.

On the other hand the lyric movements—the Scherzos and Adagios—are always beautiful. Here Schumann was in his element, he was dealing with forces which he knew how to control, and his success was complete and indisputable. It is only necessary to recall the Larghetto of the first symphony, or the exquisite romance from the second, or the *Volkslied* from the third, the *Rhenish* (1850), to see that within the limits of a narrower form Schumann could well display his power of musical expression. Indeed his first symphony is almost a masterpiece throughout, and his others, even the most indeterminate, contain separate thoughts and phrases for which we may well be grateful. It is only when we compare him with the great symphonic writers, Brahms and Beethoven and Mozart, that we see evidence of weakness and imperfection.

It is usual to depreciate Schumann's power of orchestration, and indeed there can be little doubt that the general texture of his scoring is somewhat thick and heavy, and that he too frequently writes passages that seem to owe their inspiration to the piano. Still, he has supremely good moments—the bassoon in the Adagio of the C major Symphony, the trumpets in the *Manfred* Overture, the violin solo of the Symphony in D minor—and often what he loses in transparency he supplies in warmth and richness of color. Among his mannerisms may be mentioned a persistent habit of breaking up his string phrases into rapid repeated notes, and an almost restless change of pitch in his use of the transposing instruments.

Of his various concertos, that for piano in A minor (1841–45) is the best known and the most valuable. It consists of a brilliant opening fantasia, a light, graceful intermezzo in which the second subject is ingeniously developed out of a phrase in the first, and a stirring finale in Schumann's best style of composition. The *Concertstück for Four Horns* (1849) is seldom or never given, owing to the extreme difficulty and compass of its first solo part; but it may be noticed that the Allegro is more regular in form than the general run of Schumann's orchestral works, and that the romance is scored with unusual care. The *Violoncello Concerto* (1850) has a fine manly first movement, a very beautiful though very short Adagio, and a rather diffuse finale, in which, however, the capacities of the solo instrument are treated with considerable skill.

A composer who writes piano passages for the orchestra has but an ill augury in approaching the special technique of the string quartet. No form of composition demands more exact perfection of style, more intimate sympathy with the medium employed. Every phrase is salient; every note shows through; there is no possibility of covering weak places or condoning uncertainty of outline. Hence there is little wonder that Schumann's three essays in this field (1842) should rank among his comparative failures. The three opening Allegros have great charm of melody, and in two of them the structure is firm and solid; the sectional movements exhibit Schumann's usual power of dealing with lyric forms, but the rest show a continuous sense of effort which is inadequately repaid. Many passages, too, even in the more successful numbers, are alien to the style of the quartet, and recall methods of treatment which would be more appropriate to the orchestra. The case is very different in the concerted works for piano and strings. Here the medium is pastel in place of water-color; the new instrument brings with it an entirely new means of expression, and one, moreover, of which Schumann was a consummate master. At the keyboard he was once more at home, and his work in this department of the art may rank among the most genial of his inspirations. Indeed, this particular form lay most emphasis on the qualities of romance and least on the technical gifts of absolute music. Mozart's piano trios are weaker than his string quartets; Schumann, who is beaten by the strings alone, has only to add the piano and his victory is assured.

As a dramatic writer he displays the same strength and weakness as Byron, with whom he has often been compared. Both possessed a considerable gift of description; both were steeped in romanticism; both were too intensely subjective to succeed in that essential of the drama—characterization. In *Genoveva* (1847–50), for instance, the whole background of the opera is vividly depicted in the strong chivalrous overture, but the *dramatis personae* are drawn with an uncertain hand and even the situations are imperfectly presented. Golo's first song is far too beautiful to be wasted on a villain; the supernatural element is clumsily treated throughout; Siegfried, except for one moment, is a mere lay figure; and even the heroine fails to retain the interest which ought to center about a title-rôle. No doubt in this, as in Weber's *Euryanthe*, much allowance must be made for a weak libretto, but it may be remembered that Schumann

250

himself chose the subject and modeled the words. He treated it, in short, as a psychological study, than which the stage can follow no more fatal ideal.

Much may be said of *Manfred*. The incidental music is most successful where it deals with description, least so where it deals with action, and at best does not approach the superb force and splendor of the overture. In this Schumann's orchestral writing reaches its highest point. From the first note to the last, it is as magnificent as an Alpine storm, somber, wild, impetuous, echoing from peak to peak with the shock of thunder-clouds and the clamor of the driving wind.

In *Scenes from Goethe's Faust* (1844–53) we rise above the tempest. The overture and the earlier scenes need not here be considered, for they were written when Schumann's powers were beginning to fail under the stress of disease, and so cannot justly be estimated in relation to his normal work. But in the scene of Faust's salvation, we have an incontestable masterpiece. It may be, as some critics have asserted, that the last half of the *Chorus Mysticus* is something of anti-climax, that in neither of its two alternative versions does it "breathe the pure serene" of the other numbers. In any case the whole work is noble music, vast in scale, lofty in spirit, a worthy interpretation of the great poem that summoned it into being. The only fit analogue with which it may be compared is the third act of *Parsifal*, opening with the solemn quietude of the Hermitage and closing with the Eucharistic strains that ascend to the gate of Heaven itself.

Among Schumann's cantatas *Paradise and the Peri* stands pre-eminent. It is easy to see how readily he would be attracted by the subject, and how fully he would avail himself of the opportunities afforded by its warm imagery and its suggestions of Oriental color. The artificial glitter of Moore's verse is mercifully obscured in a translation: only the thought is left for the composer to decorate as he will. Nowhere is Schumann's treatment of a libretto more thoroughly characteristic. All his favorite devices are here—long rhetorical passages, hovering between tune and recitative, single melodic phrases of great beauty, rich, almost sensuous, harmonization, even the broad sustained chords which form such a distinctive feature in

251

his pianoforte music. It is, in short, an abstract and epitome of the romantic movement, a scene of fairyland admirably painted against a background of human interest and emotion. Of other choral works for the concert room two deserve special mention: the exquisite *Requiem for Mignon* (1849) and the bright, tuneful *Pilgrimage of the Rose* (1851). The rest belong to Schumann's period of exhaustion, and lie outside the limits of fair criticism.

At the same time no account of his compositions would be complete without some reference to the sacred music, which he declared to be the "highest aim of every true artist." Yet his own work in this field is singularly scanty. . . . We have only two works—the *Mass* (1852) and the *Requiem* (1852) left for examination.

Of these the *Requiem* is undoubtedly the finer. In the *Mass* Schumann is approaching too closely the unfamiliar region of absolute music; its style demands an austerity, a self-repression to which he had never grown accustomed. Further, with all his experience as a song writer, he had not concerned himself with the peculiar capacities of the voice, and hence was unprepared for the special treatment of counterpoint which all tradition has connected with the kyrie and the credo. Hence, although his *Mass* contains some good episodes, notably the Offertorium, which he added to the orthodox text, it cannot be regarded as certainly successful. In the *Requiem*, on the other hand, we have two of the finest things that Schumann ever wrote: the opening number, and the portion which contains the *Qui Mariam absolvisti*, the *Confutatis* and the *Lacrymosa*. It is hard to believe that the mind which conceived that wonderful music was already tottering to its fall.

It may be that much of his work will not survive the attack of time. There are few men who do not find that the greater part of their life's record is written in water. But something at least will remain. He is not only the best representative but the virtual founder of a distinct style in music; his sense of beauty is often exquisite; his feeling pure, manly and chivalrous. So long as melody possesses the power to soothe, to comfort, to sympathize, so long shall we turn in gratitude to one who could transmute the sorrows of his own heart into an elixir for the cure of others. After all we have no right to require that an artist's whole gift should consist of masterpieces. We do not judge . . . Shelley by his two attempts at burlesque; we take the ode and the sonnets, *Prometheus and Adonais,* and let the failures go. In like manner we can discard some of Schumann's compositions as uninspired, but when we have done so there will still be left a legacy that may enrich music to the end of the world. It matters little whether his monument be large or small; in either case it is imperishable.

SCHUMANN SPEAKS

People err if they think that a composer puts pen to paper with the predetermination of expressing or depicting some particular fact. Yet we must not estimate outward influences and impressions too lightly. . . . The more elements congenially related to music which the tone-picture contains within it, the more poetic and plastic will be the expression of the composition, and in proportion to the imaginativeness and receptivity of the composer will be the elevating and touching quality of his work.

The ill-educated man can scarcely believe that music possesses the power of expressing particular passions, and therefore it is difficult for him to comprehend the more individual masters. We have learned to express the finer shades of feeling by penetrating more deeply into the mysteries of harmony.

. . . . .

Everything that occurs in the world affects me—politics, literature, humanity. I ponder over everything in my own way until the thoughts then break forth and clarify themselves in music. But for this reason many of my compositions are so difficult to understand, because they are associated with remote interests. Often also they are significant because everything strange moves me, and I must then begin to express it musically.

. . . . .

There are moments when music possesses me so completely, when only sounds exist for me to such a degree that I am unable to write anything down.

. . . . .

Melody is the battle cry of amateurs. Naturally music without melody is nothing. But realize well what is meant by melody. An easily grasped rhythmically pleasing sweet tune is for some "melody." But there are melodies of a different character, and when you read Bach, Mozart, Beethoven, they gaze at you in a thousand varied ways. The scant monotony, particularly of modern Italian opera melodies will, I hope, soon tire you.

When you begin to compose, do it in your mind. The fingers must do what the mind wills, not the other way around.

If heaven has given you a vivid imagination, you will, in lonely hours, often sit at the piano, as though glued to it, ready to express your inmost feelings. These are the happiest hours of youth. But beware of yielding too often to a talent that may tempt you to waste time and energy, so to say, on shadowy pictures. The mastery of form, the power of clear creation, will be gained only by the firm symbol of script. Therefore write more and improvise less.

Get a good knowledge of all the other arts and disciplines.

The laws of life are also those of art.

There is no end to learning.

254

FRÉDÉRIC CHOPIN

1 8 1 0 – 1 8 4 9

FRANÇOIS FRÉDÉRIC CHOPIN, the foremost creator of music for the piano, was born in Zelazowa Wola, near Warsaw, Poland, on February 22, 1810. His musical studies began at six with piano lessons from Zwyny. One year later Chopin made a public appearance and completed several compositions, one of which (a polonaise) was published. For a three-year period, beginning with 1826, he received a comprehensive musical training from Joseph Elsner, director of the Warsaw Conservatory. After being graduated from the Conservatory in July 1829, Chopin paid a visit to Vienna where he gave two impressive concerts in which he introduced several of his own works. He was soon to leave his native land for good: in August 1831 he was touring Germany when he received the news in Stuttgart that Warsaw had fallen to the Russians. His first impulse was to rush back to Poland and join in the fight but, dissuaded by his mother and friends, he sublimated his patriotic feelings by writing the *Revolutionary Etude*.

He went on to Paris which, from then on, remained his permanent home. His first concert there, on February 26, 1832, established him as a preëminent pianist and composer. He moved as a notable figure in leading Parisian music circles and salons; aristocratic families sought him out as a teacher for their children. One Parisian critic described him as "the Ariel of the piano."

His personal life experienced a violent upheaval in 1837 when he was introduced by Liszt to the novelist, George Sand. At first he was repelled by her masculinity, brusque mannerisms, and lax morals. But before long he felt himself helplessly attracted to her dynamic personality and brilliant mind. The passionate liaison that ensued affected Chopin's nervous system profoundly; but it also stimulated him to write some of his greatest music. They spent the winter of 1838 in Majorca where the bad weather, poor food, and the suspicious antagonism of neighbors played havoc with Chopin's delicate health. Nevertheless he managed to complete his remarkable preludes during his stay.

Back in France, still involved emotionally with Sand, Chopin embarked upon the composition of some of his most ambitious works, including the B-flat minor Sonata (with the funeral march), the F minor Fantaisie, ballades, and impromptus. But his health was deteriorating, afflicted by tuberculosis. In addition, he suffered severely from the final and permanent rupture with Sand, which had taken place in 1847.

Despite his bad health, Chopin toured Great Britain in 1848 for seven months. By the time he returned to France it was obvious he did not have much longer to live. Unable to earn a living from concerts or teaching, he was compelled to live on the bounty of friends. During his last months he was a complete recluse. He died in Paris, on October 17, 1849, and was buried in the Père Lachaise cemetery.

THE MAN

GEORGE SAND

FRANZ LISZT

He was a man of the world *par excellence,* not of the too formal and too numerous world, but of the intimate world, of the salons of twenty persons, of the hour when the crowd goes away and the habitués crowd around the artist to wrest from him by amiable importunity his purest inspiration. It was then only that he exhibited all his genius and all his talent. . . . He visited several salons every day, or he chose at least every evening a different one as a milieu. He had thus by turns twenty or thirty salons to intoxicate or to charm with his presence.

He was modest on principle and gentle by habit, but he was imperious by instinct, and full of a legitimate pride that did not know itself. . . . He was the same in friendship [as in love], becoming enthusiastic at first sight, getting disgusted, and correcting himself incessantly, living on infatuations full of charms for those who were the object of them, and on secret discontents which poisoned his dearest affections. . . . When angry, Chopin was alarming, and as . . . he always restrained himself, he seemed almost to choke and die.

His creation was spontaneous and miraculous. He found it without seeking it, without foreseeing it. It came on his piano suddenly, complete, sublime, or it sang in his head during a walk, and he was impatient to play it himself. But then began the most heart-rending labor I ever saw. It was a series of efforts, of irresolutions, and of frettings to seize again certain details of the theme he had heard. . . . He shut himself up in his room for whole days, weeping, walking, breaking his pens, repeating and altering a bar a hundred times, writing and effacing it as many times, and recommencing the next day with a minute and desperate perseverance. He spent six weeks over a single page to write it at last as he had noted it down at the very first.*

．　．　．　．　．

The ensemble of his person was harmonious, and called for no special commentary. His blue eyes were more spiritual than dreamy, his bland smile never writhed into bitterness. The transparent delicacy of his complexion pleased the eye, his fair hair was soft and silky, his nose slightly aquiline, his bearing so distinguished and his manners stamped with so much high breeding that involuntarily he was always treated *en prince*. His gestures were many and graceful; the tone of his voice was veiled, often stifled; his stature was low, and his limbs slight.

His manners in society possessed that serenity of mood which distinguishes those whom no ennui annoys, because they expect no interest. He was generally gay, his caustic spirit caught the ridiculous rapidly and far below the surface at which it usually strikes the eye. He displayed a rich vein of drollery in pantomime. He often

---

* The paragraphs above are by George Sand; those below, by Franz Liszt.

257

amused himself by reproducing the musical formulas and peculiar tricks of certain virtuosos, in the most burlesque and comic improvisations, imitating their gestures, their movements, counterfeiting their faces with a talent which instantaneously depicted their whole personality. His own features would then become scarcely recognizable, he could force the strangest metamorphoses upon them, but while mimicking the ugly and the grotesque, he never lost his own native grace. Grimace was never carried far enough to disfigure him; his gaiety was so much the more piquant because he always restrained it within the limits of perfect good taste, holding at a careful distance all that could wound the most fastidious delicacy. He never made use of an inelegant word, even in moments of the most entire familiarity; an improper innuendo, a coarse jest would have been shocking to him. . . .

On some occasions, although very rarely, we saw him deeply agitated. We saw him grow so pale and wan, that his appearance was actually corpse-like. But even in moments of the most intense emotion, he remained concentrated within himself. A single instant for self-recovery always enabled him to veil the secret of his first impression. . . .

He could pardon in the most noble manner. No rancor remained in his heart toward those who had wounded him, though such wounds penetrated deeply into his soul, and festered there in vague pain and internal suffering, so that long after the exciting cause had been effaced from his memory, he still experienced the secret torture. By dint of constant effort, in spite of his acute and tormenting sensibilities, he subjected his feelings to the rule rather of what ought to be than of what is; thus he was grateful for services proceeding rather from good intentions than from a knowledge of what would have been agreeable to him. Nevertheless the wounds caused by such awkward miscomprehensions are, of all others, the most difficult for nervous temperaments to bear. . . .

The reserve which marked his intercourse with others extended to all subjects to which the fanaticism of opinion can attach. His own sentiments could only be judged by that which he did not do within the narrow limit of his activity. His patriotism was revealed in the course taken by his genius, in the choice of his friends, and in

258

the preferences given to his pupils, and in the frequent and important services which he rendered to his compatriots; but we cannot remember that he took any pleasure in the expression of this sentiment. If he sometimes entered upon the topic of political ideals, so violently attacked, so warmly defended, so frequently discussed in France, it was rather to point out what he deemed dangerous or erroneous in the opinions advanced by others than to win attention for his own. In constant association with some of the most brilliant political figures of the day, he knew how to limit his relations with them to a personal attachment entirely independent of political interests.

THE COMPOSER

OLIN DOWNES

It is no exaggeration to say that Chopin is the most popular and widely appreciated of the great masters. And not only this: he has left behind him less bad music—meaning less music which is immature, imperfect, or routine—than any other ranking composer. Moreover, a greater percentage of his music is alive in the repertory than that of any other significant composer. The fact is of course strongly conditioned by the reflection that Chopin wrote for the piano; that thousands can play a piano piece, well or badly, where communities may have to travel miles to hear an opera or a symphony. As for the Titans of music—the Bachs, Mozarts, Beethovens, and other towering few of their stature—they composed in practically all forms and for most instruments, taking the keyboard instruments in their stride as they did so. They loosed floods of tone which swept everything before them, overpowered every obstacle, inundated every channel. To them the piano was but a vehicle for their thought, accessory to their purpose. The fact emphasizes the lasting distinction and beauty of Chopin's expression, of his unparalleled realization of the true nature of the keyed instrument, and the depth and craftsmanship which usually go unrecognized because of the apparent simplicity and immediate sensuous appeal of his style. Indeed there are those

259

to whom such simplicity and such appeal are incongruous with greatness. They cannot believe that an art can be profound and yet attractive to the multitude. But art does not confine, or confide, its marvels to the estimates of snobs or academicians.

Chopin's existence was full of paradoxes. He was by nature exclusive in his life and his art, yet he proved to be the composer of composers for his fellow-beings. Because of the exceptionally personal and emotional character of his expression, he is a Romantic composer; yet he stands forth, through his perfection of form and proportion, the classic master of the romantic epoch. His music is national in its very essence, which lies much deeper than the quotation of folk melodies or other obvious insignia of race yet he speaks the passions of humanity with international, indeed universal, significance. He left Poland early in his career, never to return to his native soil. But the Polish earth was in his heart, and national memory and sensibility so deep in his nature that he remained creatively independent of every influence of European thought or aesthetic. The environment of the French capital was so sympathetic, indeed indispensable to him, that he remained there for the rest of his days—yet also remained, for all the future, the first great Slavic composer whose works became a part of and a profound element in European music. To that music he brought qualities which it had previously been without and which greatly enriched its substance. At the same time he was farthest from self-conscious nationalism and would have been the first to decry any such attitude on a musician's part. In this connection it is interesting to observe that in only one of Chopin's compositions is there the direct quotation of a Polish folk theme. It is the melody of the old Noël which makes the trio of the B minor Scherzo (1831–32).

Chopin, who distrusted democracy, was to outward appearances a most accomplished man of the world, who mingled almost instinctively and on equal terms with the "best society." To those unaware of his background and innermost purpose he could easily have appeared as something of a snob, which was in no sense his nature. Conditions propitious to his over-sensitivity, a regime which never violated the order he had to have about him, or the good taste which was a basic necessity of his environment, he craved, and established. Yet it is perceptible that among those eminent minds and personages who mingled in his salon, and to whom he was the perfect host, he was actually aloof and unapproachable. He observed in his daily existence precisely the selectiveness and the privacy of soul that he conveyed in his music. In both aspects of his life he was equally disdainful of verbal revelation. It was to his score paper, as Liszt put it, that he fully confided "those unexpressible sorrows to which the pious give vent in their communication with their Maker. What they never say except upon their knees, he said in his palpitating compositions."

Exclusivity, then, was an inalienable characteristic of this lonely artist. From everyone and everything, underneath his perfect manners and finished conversation, he kept his distance. His artistic independence remains almost unparalleled. With the exception perhaps of Berlioz there is no great composer who owes less to those who preceded him or who left fewer disciples after him. It appears as if Chopin could neither be prophesied nor imitated. And one may well ask how he achieved his mastery. By what steps of evolution did Chopin conceive his wholly individual approach to form? Where lay the secret, or conscious process, of his creative development? We know that he had as good a general education as was accessible in Poland to a young man of good family and breeding on general subjects, though this must have been a comparatively superficial aspect of his culture. We also know—though the fact has not been properly emphasized—that among the noble families and on the part of the Polish church and by a few individual composers who had cultivated the national dance forms, such as those of the mazurka and the polonaise, there were certain precedents for the nationalistic traits that appear in Chopin's art. But these are only partial explanations of his achievement, or of the fact that when he arrived in Paris as a youth of twenty-one he was already a composer of pronounced individuality, acknowledged as an artist to be reckoned with and not to be confused with any other musician of the day.

Chopin had as his birthright all that was requisite for the perfect musician: his Fortunatus's purse of melody, which is and always will remain the core of music; his rare harmonic imagination which summoned from the invisible world new vistas of tone, subtle colors, and discovered new relations of supposedly distant chords and keys; and qualities of rhythm, in part a racial attribute, obeying inner laws which are not those of the regimented down beat. And here we approach the matter of the Chopin *rubato,* and the free spacing of the beats—especially the almost imperceptible *Luftpause* which so frequently conditions the "two" and "three" of the mazurka, or sets at liberty the song with the wonderful exotic ornaments— sometimes with the imprint of Eastern cantillation upon them—of the nocturnes and other passages. These however are details of his work. Should we seek to find in some single aspect of this art one that epitomized the nature of his accomplishment, we would name Chopin's interpretation of form. The word is used in its broadest and most inclusive sense. It means not only of melodic form or harmonic form, but the artist's treatment, in his own creative image, of the form's innermost elements. In no case is the form treated by Chopin in a merely exterior manner. Thus, the dance forms which he variously selects with special objectives are never mere literal dances. They are dance spiritualizations. Chopin's sister, Isabelle, understood this well when she wrote him indignantly of the performance at a ball of the Zamoyskis, of the playing "almost throughout the evening" of the B-flat Mazurka (1832–33), the first of op. 17 for dancing. "What do you say," she writes to her brother, "to this profanation. Do write and tell me whether in your heart you wrote it as dance music. Perhaps we misunderstood you." As a matter of fact this happens to be a mazurka *dansant*—one that can be and often has been danced. But that is not the primary purpose of the music. There never have been such revelations of all the mazurka can mean and say to us as the pieces which Chopin composed in this form. In not a measure does he lose sight of the fundamental musical elements. Nor does he in a single measure merely repeat himself or fail to strike every emotional chord that this, the most popular of all the national Polish dances, permits. Each mazurka has the concision and concentration necessitated by seldom more than one to three minutes of music. In this space, short motives, often of disparate character, may be bound together in a manner which seems almost like an improvisation, yet achieves a remarkable unity. Among the means that Chopin employs here to achieve his swift transitions are the enharmonic modulations and the chromaticism which he so subtly developed, in pages prophetic of a whole period.

Contrast with this the grand lines and striding phrase-lengths of the polonaises, with their bardic evocations of the past, and battles heroically lost, and deathless ancestral glory. Everything is cut here to the grand pattern, whether it is the explosive outburst of the first of the polonaises in C-sharp minor (1834–35), or the trumpet-calls and visions of advancing hosts of the famous A-flat Polonaise (1842), or that great fresco of battle with the mournful interpolation of the mazurka danced by ghosts, in the Polonaise in F-sharp minor (1840–41). The polonaises, the scherzi, the great *Fantasy* (1840–41) are of the grander and most dramatic aspects of Chopin's genius. The scherzi are very far from the classic movement as conceived by Beethoven or the later Brahms. The triple rhythm is maintained but the form is vastly extended and dramatized. Of another concept are the two sets of etudes, op. 10 (1829–32) and 25 (1832–36), with the three supplementary pieces which Chopin contributed to the *Méthode des méthodes* of Moscheles and Fétis, wherein technical figures are so treated as to become tone poems. The nocturnes are free lyrical outpourings, dreams, *"Harmonies poétiques et réligieuses,"* as Liszt would have put it. They probably were suggested by the nocturnes of the gifted and eccentric Irishman, John Field (1782–1837), whom Chopin met and heard play in Paris in 1834. One has only to compare any two nocturnes by these respective composers to realize the transforming distinction which exists between talent and genius. The Preludes (1836–39), entirely free in form, and most strikingly contrasted in contents, are nevertheless no haphazard succession of pieces. Probably the title owes something to the free preludes which precede the fugues in all the twelve keys of Bach's *Well-Tempered Clavier*—Bach whom Chopin always practiced before a concert and whose keyboard music he so loved and admired. These pieces, beginning in the key of C, follow each other in the traditional fifth relationships upward through the sharp keys, downward through the flats, and establish a new interpretation, in Chopin's spirit, of the system of equal temperament! They are dramas of the spirit, in which, as George Sand truly remarked,

Chopin expressed in a few measures more than many composers in an act of an opera.

The form which Chopin elected for perhaps the freest and proudest expression of his imaginative genius, in which he is utterly liberated, comes with the four great ballades, no one of the four in the least like the others, each one a masterpiece from the legendary utterance in G minor (1831–35) which is the first of the set, to that supreme embodiment of lyrical development and variation, the fourth in F minor (1842).

One form, perhaps—at least in its academic interpretation—Chopin did not master. It is that of the sonata. Or it might be more just to quote the writer—he was Henry T. Finck—who remarked that if Chopin did not master this classic form, the form on the other hand never succeeded in mastering him! Certainly there is no traditional procedure to be discovered in the four movements of the Sonata in B-flat minor (1839), which in its implicit suggestions, at least, comes nearer a species of program music than Chopin attempted in any other instance. This is the sonata of an out and out romanticist, and not one who obeys formal dictates. The B minor Sonata (1844) on the other hand is as near so-called "absolute" and formal music as Chopin could come. It follows generally the accepted succession of movements, keys, themes, and developments, providing Chopin with a mold in which to pour some of his most interesting melodic ideas.

From all this there stands out a sovereign fact, namely, that Chopin was purely and only a musician! His expression has no relation whatever to literature, drama, philosophy, or ideologies of extramusical import. This is particularly remarkable when we compare his tendencies with those of all the other composers of his period. With Berlioz, Schumann, Weber, Wagner, Liszt, the boundaries of music cross over those of other arts. These typical musicians of their day wrote tone poems inspired by all sorts of subjects: piano pieces suggested by the novels of Jean Paul or the tales of E. T. A. Hoffmann, fantastic symphonies, vast symbolic operas, settings, often very eloquent ones, of romantic poetry in terms of song. They variously name their compositions to afford the listener an index to their expressive purpose and in order to stimulate the imagination. Of

264

such proclivities Chopin would have none, any more than he coun-
tenanced the realistic, crowd-stunning methods from which so few
of the romantics were willing to refrain. Their explosive accents,
their volcanos of sensation and passion for color and rhetoric, were
not sympathetic to the man who in his creative expression held his
impulses under iron control and to inexorable measurement demanded by his conception of art. Chopin comes within nearest distance of explicit "meaning" when he gives a work a generic title such
as "Berceuse," "Tarantella," "Barcarolle." Elsewhere he confines himself to the name of the form and the opus number. It is for us, if we
choose, to envision Venice and the night sky, amorous dialogue,
song and spray, when we listen to the matchless Barcarolle (1845–
46). Or, if our individual fancy should choose to do so, to think of
Poe's grisly tale of the fête interrupted by the apparition of the Red
Death, as we listen to the feverish gaiety, interrupted by the laconic
unisons and ending with the wild confusion of—*Valse brilliante,* op.
42 (1840)! What shall be said—what fittingly can be said in words—
of the soul-sickness of Mazurka, op. 17, no. 4 (1832–33); of the primitive scales, and thrummings and squealings of rude instruments of
op. 24, no. 2 (1834–35); of the gay Kermesse, interspersed with the
cry of the lonely spirit, op. 33, no. 3 (1837–38); of the great tragic
Mazurka, op. 41, no. 4 (1839) with the priceless D-natural, in the
C-sharp minor signature, the abandon which conceals despair, and
the transformation of the initial singsong melody into a war-chant
thundered out in octaves before the final relapse? One could speak
endlessly of the beauties, the intensities, the visions contained in
Chopin's music, but it would be a futile task, because we are at the
point where words are useless in music's presence. Chopin said once
that certain of the ballades had been inspired by the poems of his
contemporary and compatriot, Mickiewicz. But no one has found
in *Konrad Wallenrod* or in other of that great poet's writings any
tale which appears parallel to the musical narratives of the ballades.
The poems may possibly have served as a springboard for Chopin's
imagination, but it is difficult to believe that any music so liberated
and yet so completely obedient to its own organic laws could have
sprung from such exterior source. Or witness the composer's evasive
remark that the finale of the B-flat minor Sonata meant mourners

gossiping together after the ceremony! It is the very impersonality of this strange movement which makes it so impressive, so unparalleled in its time and so prophetic of tomorrow.

But this too is to be remembered and noted as one of the most important of Chopin's creative principles: he never wrote music uninhibited by emotion. He never conceived form as an artistic abstraction, as a matter of pure tonal design devoid of feeling. Yet he was the "purest" in the sense of uncontaminated artistic material and workmanship of perhaps all composers. The fact is suggestive. The beauty and lasting value of the music based upon these principles has perhaps a moral. We know that Chopin subjected his compositions to endless and self-torturing revision and that he did not wish some of the scores he left behind to be published. They were issued, however, some years after his death by his friend, Fontana, and on the whole the procedure is justified. Even somewhat inferior Chopin is valuable to us, and certain of these works are of a quality fully on a par with those published during his lifetime. The explanation of this lies in the fact that Chopin had the admirable habit of holding back works for publication till some time after he had written them, and that he usually submitted them to the test of public performance before making the final editorial revision. Some of the scores he left unpublished would in due course have been issued before his untimely end at the age of thirty-nine.

His purposes and convictions as an artist were never in doubt. He has been called weak, indecisive, capricious, neurotic, feminine, morbid, and other names. Physically frail, emotionally tortured, in his art he did not once falter. He is shown to have been a soul of purest purpose and indomitable courage in the face of obstacles which would have defeated a less heroic spirit. He burned himself out in approaching his goal. His reward is incontestable and still immeasurable, even by the world which knows his music so well and renders it homage today.

CHOPIN SPEAKS

In order to become a great composer, one needs an enormous amount of knowledge . . . which one does not acquire from listening only to other people's music, but even more from listening to one's own.

. . . . .

Every genius is a revolutionary who produces a good deal of commotion in the world. After he has abolished the old rules he writes his own, new ones, which no one even half understands; and after he has stupefied and bewildered everybody, he leaves the world neither understood nor regretted. When he is no more, the people breathe easier. Not always does the next generation comprehend and appreciate him properly. Sometimes it may even take a whole century.

It is a curious question: does the genius feel his own greatness? . . . Does he understand how far his echo will reach into the centuries? That only posterity can understand him is clear to me. When you are contemplating a colossal piece of sculpture you can see it well only from a certain distance because when standing near you can never see the whole object, and looking at it part by part, you will have a misshapen impression of it.

The genius is the strangest of men because he is so far ahead of his contemporaries that they lose sight of him. Moreover, nobody knows which generation is going to comprehend him.

Genius has a big nose and a splendid sense of smell which enable him to catch the direction of the wind of the future. Don't think that I am imagining that I am a genius, possessing as I do an enormous nose; you understand that I mean quite a different kind of nose.

. . . . .

Don't talk to me of composition; creation is not a thing one can learn. Every man sleeps, eats, and moves differently, and you wish

267

that all would create the same way. I am tormenting myself devilishly over every piece.

I seem to have a beautiful and finished thought in mind, but when I write it down, I realize that I have made a lot of holes in it. Everything looks different on paper so that it drives me to despair. And then begins the torture of remembering. Or I have several themes, and am always so undecided as to which to choose.

I cannot complain of lack of themes, but sometimes those little beasts drive me to tears when I have to make a choice. Often I throw ready things away for a long time, to let time decide and choose.

Ideas keep creeping into my head. Sometimes I write them down, sometimes I just play with them and throw them away for the future. One of them may be greater than the others; maybe I'll build a polonaise upon it, but I am leaving it for later.

I myself get tired very quickly, because creating is a serious matter to me; and when I am tired, things don't work out so well. As you know, I am very careful and do not like to toss off just anything into the world. Maybe I shall become more efficient in time, get less tired, indulge in shorter periods of rest, but I'll never reach the perfection of Mozart; that's a gift of nature.

A wise creator himself knows what is lacking in him. Whatever can be attained by dint of sweat, he should try; but what is beyond his possibilities, he would do better to leave alone, he will never reach it. While admiring the art of others, one must know enough to say to oneself: "Useless to climb, that's not my way."

He who has great aptitudes and talent but little knowledge is like a carpenter who has good materials, and plenty of them, but has no tools to work with. He who is very erudite' but has no talent is like a carpenter with a lot of the best tools but no material. Anyone can obtain knowledge, but talent you cannot buy even with diamonds.

What today is considered apostasy from the old rules, tomorrow may become original and great. It is even bad when people praise too much and understand too well, because it means that there is nothing in it that posterity alone could understand. Works which are perfectly clear to everybody are shallow and posterity will blow them off like soap bubbles.

I myself can never finish anything at once. I have too many themes and have rather an *embarras de richesse,* as the French say. But when I write them down on paper, selecting the best pieces, I find that the thing is full of holes. The best way out, then, is to throw such an unborn child into a corner and forget it.

After a certain time a theme falls suddenly as if from heaven which will fit exactly into one of those holes. Afterwards another one . . . finally the whole thing is composed like a mosaic. You would think that this is the happy ending. Not at all! Before I finish it at last I lose a terrible amount of time, and I have plenty of trouble, many tears, and sleepless nights. You women do not feel so weak after giving birth as I feel after finishing a composition.

CÉSAR FRANCK

1 8 2 2 – 1 8 9 0

CÉSAR-AUGUSTE FRANCK was born in Liège, Belgium, on December 10, 1822. He was a child-prodigy pianist, winning first prize at the Liège Conservatory when he was twelve, and giving concerts throughout Belgium. Between 1837 and 1842 he was a pupil at the Paris Conservatory, where he received many prizes in organ-playing and fugue. On March 17, 1843 there took place in Paris a concert of his chamber music, followed on January 4, 1846 by the première of his first significant work, the oratorio *Ruth*. After that he concentrated on composition, while earning his living teaching piano and solfeggio, and playing the organ. On February 22, 1848 he married an actress, Mlle. Desmousseaux. After holding several minor posts as organist and maître de chapelle, he assumed in 1858 the office he held for the rest of his life—that of organist at Ste. Clotilde. In 1872, he combined this activity with teaching, having been appointed professor of organ and composition at the Paris Conservatory. He was largely responsible for bringing about at the Conservatory a new interest in absolute as opposed to dramatic music. Through the years he gathered about him pupils inspired by his idealism, humility, creative integrity, and immense musical gifts. They carried on his own dedication to absolute instrumental music grounded in some of the contrapuntal principles of Bach's organ works, in preference to the prevailing vogue for the Wagner-Liszt school. These disciples included some of France's most distinguished musicians, including Vincent d'Indy (1851–1931), Ernest Chausson (1855–99), and Gabriel Pierné (1863–1937).

All the while Franck was teaching and playing the organ, he was completing masterpieces which were long ignored by both the general public and the critics. These included the oratorio *The Re-*

270

demption in 1874, the *Variations symphoniques* for piano and orchestra in 1885, and the Symphony in D minor. (The last was a fiasco when introduced in Paris on February 17, 1889.) Except in the eyes of his pupils and friends, Franck's importance rested more on his remarkable powers as an organ virtuoso than on his creative work. Partial recognition as composer came to him after his String Quartet was successfully introduced in Paris on April 19, 1890. Franck died of pleurisy the following winter, in Paris, on November 8, 1890.

THE MAN

VINCENT D'INDY

Physically, Franck was short, with a fine forehead and a vivacious and honest expression, although his eyes were almost concealed under his bushy eyebrows; his nose was rather large, and his chin receded below a wide and extraordinarily expressive mouth. His face was round, and thick gray side-whiskers added to its width. Such was the outward appearance of the man we honored and loved for twenty years; and—except for the increasing whiteness of his hair— he never altered till the day of his death. There was nothing in his appearance to reveal the conventional artistic type according to romance, or the legends of Montmartre. Any one who happened to meet this man in the street, invariably in a hurry, invariably absentminded and making grimaces, running rather than walking, dressed in an overcoat a size too large and trousers a size too short for him, would never have suspected the transformation that took place when, seated at the piano, he explained or commented upon some fine composition, or, with one hand to his forehead and the other posed above his stops, prepared the organ for one of his great improvisations. Then he seemed to be surrounded by music as by a halo, and it was only at such moments that we were struck by the conscious will power of mouth and chin, and the almost complete identity of the fine forehead and that of the creator of the Ninth Symphony. Then, indeed, we felt subjugated—almost awed—by the palpable presence of the genius that shone in the countenance of

271

the highest-minded and noblest musician that the 19th century has produced in France.

The moral quality which struck us most in Franck was his great capacity for work. Winter and summer he was up at half-past five. The first two morning hours were generally devoted to composition —"working for himself," as he called it. About half-past seven, after a frugal breakfast, he started to give lessons all over the capital, for to the end of his days this great man was obliged to devote most of his time to teaching the piano to amateurs, and even to take music classes in various colleges and boarding schools. All day long he went about on foot or by omnibus, from Auteuil to l'Île Saint Louis, from Vaugirard to the Faubourg Possonnière, and returned to his quiet abode on the Boulevard Saint-Michel in time for an evening meal. Although tired out with the day's work, he still managed to find a few minutes to orchestrate or copy his scores, except when he devoted his evening to the pupils who studied organ and composition with him, on which occasions he would generously pour upon them his most precious and disinterested advice.

In these two early hours of the morning—which were often curtailed—and in the few weeks he snatched during the vacation at the Conservatory, Franck's finest works were conceived, planned, and written.

The musical work which was his everyday occupation did not prevent him from taking an interest in all manifestations of art, and more especially of literature. During the holidays spent in the little house that he rented for the summer at Quincy, he set aside a certain time for reading books, both old and new, and sometimes very serious works. Once when he was reading in the garden with that close attention he gave to all his pursuits, one of his sons, seeing him smiling frequently, inquired what he was reading that amused him so much. "Kant's *Critique of Pure Reason*," answered the father, "it is really very amusing."

If Franck was an arduous and determined worker, his motive was neither glory, money, nor immediate success. He aimed only at expressing his thoughts and feelings by means of his art, for, above all, he was a truly modest man. He never suffered from the feverish ambition that consumes the life of so many artists in the race for worldly honor and distinction. It never occurred to him, for instance, to solicit a seat in the Institut; not because—like Degas or a Puvis—he disdained the honor, but because he innocently believed that he had not yet earned it.

This modesty, however, did not exclude that self-confidence which is so necessary to all creative artists, provided it is founded on a sound judgment and is free from vanity. In the autumn, when the classes were resumed and the master, his face lit up with a broad smile, used to say to us, "I have been working well these holidays; I hope you will all be pleased," we knew for certain that some masterpiece would soon blossom forth. On these occasions the great joy of his busy life was to keep an hour or two in the evening in which to assemble his favorite pupils around the piano while he played to them the work he had just finished, singing the vocal parts in a voice which was as warm as it was grotesque in quality. He did not even scorn to ask his pupils' advice on the new work, or, better still, to act upon it, if the observations they ventured to make seemed to him really well founded.

Untiring assiduity in work, modesty, a fine artistic conscientiousness—these were the salient features in Franck's character. But he had yet another quality—a rare one—namely, goodness: a goodness that was serene and indulgent.

The word most often used by the master was the verb "to love." "I love it," he would say of a work, or even of a detail which appealed to his sympathies; and in truth his own works are all inspired by love, and by the power of love and his high-minded charity he reigned over his disciples, over his friends, and over all the musicians of his day who had any nobility of mind; and it is out of love to him that others have tried to continue his good work.

We must not, however, infer from this that the master's temperament was cold and placid—far from it; his was a fervent nature, as all his works undoubtedly bear witness.

Who among us can fail to recall his indignation against bad music, his explosion of wrath when our awkward fingers went astray on the organ in some ugly harmonic combination, and his impatient gesture when the ball at the altar cut short the exposition of some promising offertory? But such displays of irritability on the part of "a South-

273

erner from the North" were chiefly directed to artistic principles, very rarely to human beings. Never during the long years I spent in his society did I hear it said that he had consciously given a moment's pain to anyone. How, indeed, could such a thing have happened to him whose heart was incapable of harboring an evil thought? He would never believe in the mean jealousy that his talent excited among his colleagues, not excluding those of some reputation, and to the day of his death he was always kindly in his judgments upon the works of others. . . .

This untiring force and inexhaustible kindness were drawn from the well-spring of his faith; for Franck was an ardent believer. With him, as with all really great men, faith in his art was blended with faith in God, the source of all art.

THE COMPOSER

LELAND HALL

The drift of romanticism toward realism is easy to trace in all the arts. There were, however, artists of all kinds who were caught up, so to speak, from the current into a life of the spirit, who championed neither the glory of the senses, as Wagner, nor the indomitable power of reason, as Brahms, but preserved a serenity and calm, a sort of confident, nearly ascetic rapture, elevated above the turmoil of the world, standing not with nor against, but floating above. Such an artist in music was César Franck, growing up almost unnoticed between Wagner and Brahms, now to be ranked as one of the greatest composers of the second half of the century. He is as different from them as they are from each other. Liszt, the omniscient, knew of him, had heard him play the organ in the church of Ste. Clotilde, where in almost monastic seclusion the greater part of his life flowed on, had likened him to the great Sebastian Bach, had gone away marvelling; but only a small band of pupils knew him intimately and the depth of his genius as a composer.

His life was retired. He was indifferent to lack of appreciation. When, through the efforts of his devoted disciples, his works were

274

at rare intervals brought to public performance, he was quite forgetful of the cold, often hostile, audience, intent only to compare the sound of his music as he heard it with the thought he had had in his soul, happy if the sound were what he had conceived it would be. Of envy, meanness, jealousy, of all the darker side of life, in fact, he seems to have taken no account. Nor by imagination could he picture it, nor express it in his music, which is unfailingly luminous and exalted. Most striking in his nature was a gentle, unwavering, confident candor, and in his music there is scarcely a hint of doubt, of inquiring, or of struggle. It suggests inevitably the cathedral, the joyous calm of religious faith, spiritual exaltation, even radiance.

He wrote in all forms, operas, oratorios, cantatas, works for piano, for orchestra, and chamber music. It is significant that in several fields his output was small: he wrote only one symphony, one string quartet, one piano quintet, one violin sonata.

With the exception of a few early pieces for piano all his work bears the stamp of his personality. Like Brahms, he has pronounced idiosyncrasies, among which his fondness for shifting harmonies is the most constantly obvious. The ceaseless alteration of chords, the almost unbroken gliding by half-steps, the lithe sinuousness of all the inner voices seem to wrap his music in a veil, to render it intangible and mystical. Diatonic passages are rare, all is chromatic. Parallel to this is his use of short phrases, which alone are capable of being treated in this shifting manner. His melodies are almost invariably dissected, they seldom are built up in broad design. They are resolved into their finest motifs and as such are woven and twisted into the close iridescent harmonic fabric with bewildering skill. All is in subtle movement. Yet there is a complete absence of sensuousness, even, for the most part, of dramatic fire. The overpowering climaxes to which he builds are never a frenzy of emotion; they are superbly calm and exalted. The structure of his music is strangely inorganic. His material does not develop. He adds phrase upon phrase, detail upon detail, with astonishing power to knit and weave closely what comes with what went before. His extraordinary polyphonic skill seems inborn, native to the man. Arthur Coquard said of him that he thought the most complicated things in music quite naturally. Imitation, canon, augmentation, and diminution, the most complex problems of the science of music, he solves without effort. The perfect canon in the last movement of the Violin Sonata (1886) sounds simple and spontaneous. The shifting, intangible harmonies, the minute melodies, the fine fabric as of a goldsmith's carving, are all the work of a mystic, indescribably pure and radiant. Agitating, complex rhythms are rare. The second movement of the Violin Sonata and the last movement of the *Prelude, Aria, and Finale* (1886–87) are exceptional. The heat of passion is seldom felt. Faith and serene light prevail, a music, it has been said, at once the sister of prayer and of poetry. His music, in short, wrote Gustave Derepas, "leads us from egoism to love, by the path of the true mysticism of Christianity; from the world to the soul, from the soul to God."

His form, as has been said, is not organic, but he gives to all his music a unity and compactness by using the same thematic material throughout the movements of a given composition. For example, in the first movement of the *Prelude, Chorale, and Fugue* (1884) for piano, the theme of the fugue which constitutes the last movement is plainly suggested, and the climax of the last movement is built up out of this fugue theme woven with the great movement of the chorale. In the first movement of the *Prelude, Aria, and Finale*, likewise for piano, the theme of the Finale is used as counterpoint; in the Aria again the same use is made of it; in the Finale the Aria theme is reintroduced, and the coda at the end is built up of the principal theme of the Prelude and a theme taken from the closing section of the Aria. The four movements of the Violin Sonata are most closely related thematically; the Symphony (1886–88), too, is dominated by one theme, and the theme which opens the String Quartet (1889) closes it as well. This uniting of the several movements of a work on a large scale by employing throughout the same material was more consistently cultivated by Franck than by any other composer. The Concerto for piano and orchestra in E-flat by Liszt is constructed on the same principle; the D minor symphony of Schumann also, and it is suggested in the first Symphony of Brahms, but these are exceptions. Germs of such a relationship between movements in the cyclic forms were in the last works of Beethoven. In Franck they developed to great proportion.

The fugue in the *Prelude, Chorale, and Fugue* and the canon in the last movement of the Violin Sonata are superbly built, and his restoration of strict forms to works in several movements finds a precedent only in Beethoven and once in Mozart. The treatment of the variation form in the *Variations Symphoniques* (1885) for piano and orchestra is no less masterly than his treatment of fugue and canon, but it can hardly be said that he excelled either Schumann or Brahms in this branch of composition.

Franck was a great organist and all his work is as clearly influenced by organ technique as the works of Sebastian Bach were before him. "His orchestra," Julien Tiersot wrote in an article published in *Le Ménéstrel* for October 23, 1904, "is sonorous and compact, the orchestra of an organist. He employs especially the two contrasting elements of strings (eight-foot stops) and brass (great-organ). The woodwind is in the background. This observation encloses a criticism, and his method could not be given as a model; it robs the orchestra of much variety of coloring, which is the richness of the modern art. But we ought to consider it as characteristic of the manner of César Franck, which alone suffices to make such use legitimate." Undeniably the sensuous coloring of the Wagnerian school is lacking, though Franck devoted himself almost passionately at one time to the study of Wagner's scores; yet, as in the case of Brahms, Franck's scoring, peculiarly his own, is fitting to the quality of his inspiration. There is no suggestion of the warmth of the senses in any of his music. Complete mastery of the art of vivid warm tone-coloring belongs only to those descended from Weber, and pre-eminently to Wagner.

The works for the piano (and those for strings as well) are thoroughly influenced by organ technique. The movement of the rich, solid basses, and the impracticably wide spaces call urgently for the supporting pedals of the organ. Yet they are by no means unsuited to the instruments for which they were written. If when played they suggest the organ to the listener, and the chorale in the *Prelude, Chorale, and Fugue* is especially suggestive, the reason is not to be found in any solecism, but in the religious spirit that breathes from all Franck's works and transports the listener to the shades of vast cathedral aisles. Among his most sublime works are three Chorales (1890) for organ, written not long before he died. These, it may safely be assumed, are among the few contributions to the literature for the organ which approach the inimitable master-works of Sebastian Bach.

There are three oratorios, to use the term loosely, *Ruth* (1843–46), *The Redemption* (1874), and *The Beatitudes* (1869–79), belonging respectively in the three periods in which Franck's life and musical development naturally fall. All were coldly received during his lifetime. *Ruth,* written when he was but twenty-four years old, is in the style of the classical oratorios. *The Redemption,* too, still partakes of the half dramatic, half epic character of the oratorio; but in *The Beatitudes,* his masterpiece, if one must be chosen, the dramatic element is almost wholly lacking, and he has created almost a new art form. To set Christ's sermon on the mount to music was a tremendous undertaking, and the great length of the work will always stand in the way of its universal acceptance; but here more than anywhere else Franck's peculiar gift of harmony has full force in the expression of religious rapture and the mysticism of the devout and childlike believer.

It is curious to note the inability of Franck's genius to express wild and dramatic emotion. Among his works for orchestra and for orchestra and piano are several that may take rank as symphonic poems, *Les Éolides* (1875–76), *Le Chasseur Maudit* (1882), and *Les Djinns* (1884), the last two based upon gruesome poems, all three failing to strike the listener cold. The symphony with chorus, later rearranged as a suite, *Psyche* (1886–88), is an exquisitely pure conception, wholly spiritual. The operas *Hulda* (1882–85) and *Ghisèle* (1888–90) were performed only after his death and failed to win a place in the repertory of opera houses.

It is this strange absence of genuinely dramatic and sensuous elements from Franck's music which gives it its quite peculiar stamp, the quality which appeals to us as a sort of poetry of religion. And it is this same lack which leads one to say that he grows up with Wagner and Brahms and yet is not of a piece with either of them. He had an extraordinarily refined technique of composition, but it was perhaps more the technique of the goldsmith than that of the sculptor. His works impress by fineness of detail, not, for all their length and remarkable adherence of structure, by breadth of design. His is intensely an introspective art, which weaves about the simplest subject and through every measure most intricate garlands of chromatic harmony. It is a music which is apart from life, spiritual and exalted. It does not reflect the life of the body, nor that of the sovereign mind, but the life of the spirit. By so reading it we come to understand his own attitude in regard to it, which took no thought of how it impressed the public, but only of how it matched in performance, in sound, his soul's image of it.

With Wagner, Brahms, and César Franck the romantic movement in music comes to an end. The impulse which gave it life came to its ultimate forms in their music and was forever gone. It has washed on only like a broken wave over the works of most of their successors down to the present day.

FRANCK SPEAKS

I think you will be impressed by *Ruth*. You will find in it no trace of the hand that wrote the trios, for it is extremely simple. Yet I have some affection for it myself, both for the ideas it contains, and for the individual atmosphere of the whole work. The choral and orchestral writing is designed for performance under the most ordinary conditions.

. . . . .

I finished the scoring [*Redemption*] but then I showed the piece to a pupil in whom I have great faith and who pointed out a number of other changes, I ought to make. So I have rewritten it, and now I fancy it is not too bad.

. . . . .

It [Symphony in D minor] is just music, nothing but pure music. At the same time, while I was composing the Allegretto, especially the first phrases, I did think—oh, so vaguely—of a procession of olden times. . . . The finale, just as in Beethoven's Ninth, recalls all the themes, but in my work they do not make their appearance as mere

279

quotations. I have adopted another plan and made each of them play an entirely new part in the music. It seems to me successful in practice. . . . I have been very daring, I know; but you wait till the next time. I shall go much farther in daring then.

. . . . .

You well know that I find it necessary to spend much time in thought over a work before putting the actual notes on paper. Up to now I have been casting around for the right colors. I have, so to speak, stocked my musical palette.

. . . . .

I, too, have written some beautiful things.

CHARLES GOUNOD

1 8 1 8 – 1 8 9 3

CHARLES FRANÇOIS GOUNOD, a dominant figure in the French lyric theater of the 19th century, was born in Paris on June 17, 1818. After completing his academic training at the Lycée St. Louis, he entered the Paris Conservatory in 1836 where he studied under Halévy, Lesueur, and Paër, and in 1839 received the Prix de Rome. During his three-year stay in Italy he became interested in both theology and church music and completed several ambitious choral compositions including a Mass and a Requiem, the former introduced in Rome, and the latter in Vienna. Upon returning to Paris, where for a while he was the organist of the Missions Etrangères, he plunged into a two-year period of study of theology, but finally decided against taking holy orders. His first attempt at writing for the stage was a *succès d'éstime:* the opera *Sapho,* introduced in Paris on April 16, 1851. A comic opera, *Le Médecin malgré lui,* on January 15, 1858, and his crowning masterwork, *Faust,* on March 19, 1859 brought him to the front rank of French composers for the theater. Among his later successful operas were *Mireille,* on March 19, 1864, and *Romeo and Juliet,* on April 27, 1867.

Between 1852 and 1860, Gounod conducted the Orpheon Choral Society in Paris. In 1870 he came to London where he founded and directed another society. He returned to Paris in 1874, and during the next decade wrote incidental music for several plays, and three unsuccessful operas. In the closing years of his life he devoted himself mainly to the writing of religious music. His most significant works included two choral trilogies: *Le Rédemption* and *Mors et Vita,* introduced at the Birmingham Festival in 1882 and 1885 respectively. Gounod died in Paris on October 18, 1893.

THE MAN

HOWARD PAUL

Despite the fact that he was a tall, compactly built, solid-looking man, with no suggestion of nerves, Gounod was singularly sensitive, with a proneness to devotion which was quite feminine in its manifestations.

He was always a late riser. He protested he could do with a great deal of sleep. He dressed with scrupulous care, and at home wore a black velvet cap and very finely made patent leather shoes. When his toilet was over, he repaired to his sanctum, drank a glass of milk, and sat down at a table to work in an immense room with vaulted ceiling suggesting a church, and principally furnished with an organ, two grand pianos, and a fine musical library. He sometimes smoked while he wrote. Then he received visitors, and at twelve o'clock he breakfasted with his wife. His afternoons, four days a week, were devoted to work. He was not a persistent diner out, though he received numerous invitations. He was fond of passing his evenings at the opera, occasionally the Boulevard theaters, and now and again, by way of what he termed a naughty spree, he went to see the broad farces at the Palais Royal, for with his constitutional seriousness of character he liked an occasional laugh. He was not by any means ascetic in temperament, but more like the monks of old, perhaps, who, if the French chansons are to be depended on, had a perfect appreciation of right good cheer. He was exceedingly fond of walking in the Bois, and most Sundays he attended the meetings of the Académie des Beaux Arts, where he fulfilled with assiduity his functions as president and member of a number of musical commissions and juries.

One day I dined with Gounod in the Place Malesherbes, at a family party; there was but one other stranger present, the poet, François Coppée, who at the time was discussing the subject of a libretto. The conversation of these two gifted men disclosed the fact that they were deeply read in religious history. The discussion

282

was too long to follow in detail, but Gounod's concluding words were eloquent and deserve recording. "It has been asserted," he said, "as a fundamental defect in Christianity, that the work of its founder was left unfinished, and that the system of Mohammed is simpler and more complete. Now to my mind, I detect in the simplicity of Islam the cause of its intellectual barrenness. Neither philosophy nor science has taken root in its thin soil. It possesses no principle of development but is monotonous and inflexible." And he wound up his observations with the remark that "Christianity is the richest of religions. It is the heir of all the ages and the nursing mother of all the higher forms of moral and spiritual life."

The dinner was a simple one of half a dozen courses, and we all paid profound attention to the conversation of the two *causeurs*, who were taking it at their best. When we joined the ladies in the salon, Gounod sat down at the piano, and at the request of his daughter, played the *Funeral March of a Marionette* and a lovely little fragment called *Ivy*. After coffee in the salon the conversation became more general, and it was evident the master could drop into a lighter vein.

THE COMPOSER

R. A. STREATFEILD

If one were set upon paradox, it would not be far from the truth to say that up to the middle of the 19th century the most famous French composers had been either German or Italian. Certainly if Jean-Baptiste Lully (1632–87), Gluck, Rossini, and Meyerbeer—to name only a few of the distinguished aliens who settled in Paris— had never existed, French opera would be a very different thing from what it actually is. Yet in spite of the strangely diverse personalities of the men who had most influence in shaping its destiny, French opera is an entity remarkable for completeness and homogeneity, fully alive to tendencies, the most advanced, yet firmly founded upon the solid traditions of the past.

Gounod was trained in the school of Meyerbeer, but his own sympathies drew him rather towards the serene perfection of Mozart. The pure influence of that mighty master, combined with the strange mingling of sensuousness and mysticism which was the distinguishing trait of his own character, produced a musical personality of high intrinsic interest, and historically of great importance to the development of music. If not the actual founder of modern French opera, Gounod is at least the source of its most pronounced characteristics.

His first opera, *Sapho* (1851), a graceful version of the immortal story of the Lesbian poetess's love and death, has never been really popular, but it is interesting as containing the germs of much that afterwards became characteristic in Gounod's style. In the final scene of Sappho's suicide, the young composer surpassed himself, and struck a note of sensuous melancholy which was new to French opera. *La Nonne sanglante* (1854), his next work, was a failure; but in *Le Médecin malgré lui* (1858), an operatic version of Molière's comedy, he scored a success. This is a charming little work, instinct with a delicate flavor of antiquity, but lacking in comic power.

The year 1859 saw the production of *Faust*, the opera with which Gounod's name is principally associated. The libretto, by Barbier and Carré, does not of course claim to represent Goethe's play in any way. The authors had little pretension to literary skill, but they knew their business thoroughly. They fastened upon the episode of Gretchen, and threw all the rest overboard. The result was a well-constructed and thoroughly comprehensible libretto, with plenty of love-making and floods of cheap sentiment, but as different in atmosphere and suggestion from Goethe's mighty drama as could well be imagined. . . .

A good deal of the first and last acts is commonplace and conventional, but the other three contain beauties of a high order. The life and gaiety of the Kermesse scene in the second act, the sonorous dignity of Valentine's invocation of the cross, and the tender grace of Faust's salvation—the last passage which might have been written by Mozart—are too familiar to need more than a passing reference. In the fourth act also there is much noble music. Gounod may be forgiven even for the soldiers' chorus, in consideration of the masculine vigor of the duel terzetto—a purified reminiscence of Meyerbeer—and the impressive church scene. But the most characteristic part of the work is, after all, the love music of the third act. The dreamy langor which pervades the scene, the cloying sweetness of the harmonies, the melting beauty of the orchestration, all combine to produce an effect which was at that time entirely new to opera, and had no little share in forming the then modern school. With all his admiration of Mozart, Gounod possessed little of his idol's genius for characterization. The types in *Faust* do not stand out clearly, Marguerite, for instance, is merely a sentimental school girl; she has none of the girlish freshness and innocence of Goethe's Gretchen, and Mephistopheles is much more of a tavern bully than a fallen angel. Yet with all its faults, *Faust* remains a work of a high order of beauty. Every page of the score tells of a striving after a lofty ideal, and though as regards actual form, Gounod made no attempt to break new ground, the aim and atmosphere of *Faust*, no less than the details of its construction, contrast so strongly with the conventional Italianism of the day, that it may well be regarded as the inauguration of a new era in French music.

Faust marks the zenith of Gounod's career. After 1859 he was content for the most part merely to repeat the ideas already expressed in his *chef d'oeuvre*, while in form his later works show a distinctly retrograde movement. He seems to have known nothing of the inward impulse of development which led Wagner and Verdi from strength to strength.

Philémon et Baucis (1860) is a charming modernization of a classical legend. . . . It adheres strictly to the conventional lines of opéra-comique, and has little beyond its tuneful grace and delicate orchestration to recommend it. Nevertheless it is a charming trifle, and has survived many of Gounod's more pretentious works. *La Reine de Saba* (1862) is now forgotten, but *Mireille* (1864), one of the composer's most delightful works, still enjoys a degree of popularity. . . . Gounod's music seems to have borrowed the warm coloring of the Provençal poet's romance. *Mireille* glows with the life and sunlight of the south. There is little attempt at dramatic force in it, and the one scene in which the note of pathos is attempted is perhaps the least successful in the whole opera. But the lighter portions of the work are irresistible. *Mireille* has much of the charm of Daudet's Provençal stories, the charm of warmth and color, independent of subject.

In 1867 was produced *Roméo et Juliette,* an opera which in the estimation of the majority of Gounod's admirers, ranks next to *Faust* in the catalogue of his works. The libretto, apart from one or two concessions to operatic convention, is a fair piece of work, and at any rate compares favorably with the parodies of Shakespeare which so often do duty for libretti . . . The composer of the third act of *Faust* could hardly fail to be attracted by *Romeo and Juliet.* Nevertheless Gounod was too pronounced a mannerist to do justice to Shakespeare's immortal love story. He is, of all 19th-century French composers, the one whose method varies least, and throughout *Roméo et Juliette* he does little more than repeat in an attenuated form the ideas already used in *Faust.* Yet there are passages in the opera which stand out in salient contrast to the monotony of the whole, such as the exquisite setting of Juliet's speech in the balcony scene beginning "Thou knowest the mask of night is on my face," which conveys something more than an echo of the virginal innocence and complete self-abandonment of Shakespeare's lines, or the more commonplace but still beautiful passage at the close of the act, suggested by Romeo's line, "Sleep dwell upon thine eyes." The duel scene is vigorous and effective, and the song allotted to Romeo's page—an impertinent insertion of the librettists—is intrinsically delightful. It is typical of the musician that he should put forth his full powers in the chamber duet, while he actually omits the potion scene altogether, which is the legitimate climax of the act. In the original version of the opera there was a commonplace cavatina allotted to Juliet at this point, set to words which had but a remote connection with Shakespeare's immortal lines, but it was so completely unworthy of the situation that it was usually omitted, and when the opera was revised for production at the Opéra in 1888, Gounod thought it wiser to end the act with the Friar's discourse to Juliet, rather than attempt once more to do justice to a scene which he knew to be beyond his powers. The last act is perhaps the weakest part of the opera. Barbier and Carré's version of Shakespeare's magnificent poetry is certainly not inspiring; but in any case it is difficult to believe that Gounod's suave talent could have done justice to the piteous tragedy of that terrible scene.

Gounod's last three operas—*Cinq-Mars* (1877), *Polyeucte* (1878), and *Le Tribut de Zamora* (1881)—did not add to his reputation. In *Cinq-Mars* much of the music is tuneful and attractive, though cast in a stiff and old-fashioned form, and the masque-music in the second act is as fresh and melodious as anything Gounod ever wrote. In *Polyeucte* he attempted a style of severe simplicity in fancied keeping with Corneille's tragedy. There are some noble pages in the work, but as a whole it is distressingly dull. *Le Tribut de Zamora*, like the other two, was also an emphatic failure.

Gounod's later works show a distinct falling off from the standard attained in *Faust* as regards form as well as in ideas. As he grew older he showed a stronger inclination to return to obsolete models. *Le Tribut de Zamora* reproduces the type of opera which was popular in the days of Meyerbeer. It is cut into airs and recitatives, and the accompaniment is sedulously subordinated to the voices. Without desiring to discredit the beauties of *Mireille* or *Roméo et Juliette*, one cannot help thinking that it would have been better for Gounod's reputation if he had written nothing for the stage after *Faust*.

GOUNOD SPEAKS

France is essentially the country of clean outlines, concision, moderation, taste: that is to say, the antithesis of excess, pretentiousness, disproportion, prolixity. A passion for the transcendental (I almost wrote " a passion for the bogus transcendental") may put us completely on the wrong track, by which I mean that it may make us mistake size for greatness, weight for worth, obscurity for depth, vagueness for sublimity.

·   ·   ·   ·   ·

Let us not touch the works of the great; it is an example of dangerous discourtesy and irreverence, to which there would never be an end. Let us not put our hands on the hands of that great race, for posterity should be able to view their noble lines and solid structure and majestic elegance without any veil. Let us remember that it is better to let a great master retain his own imperfections, if there be any, than to impose our own upon him.

. . . . .

It is hardly necessary to say that in permitting personal whims to replace obedience to the text, a gulf is created between the author and the auditor. What meaning is there, for example, in a prolonged pause on certain notes, to the detriment of the rhythm and the balance of the rhythm and the balance of the musical phrase? Do they reflect for an instant on the perpetual irritation caused to the listener—to say nothing of the insupportable monotony of the proceeding itself? And then what becomes of the orchestral design in this constant subordination to the singer's caprice? It is impossible to draw up a complete catalogue of abuses and licenses of all sorts which in the execution alter the nature of the sense, and compromise the impression of a musical phrase.

. . . . .

There are works that must be seen or heard in the places for which they were created. The Sistine Chapel is one of these exceptional places, unique of its kind in the world. The colossal genius who decorated its vaulted ceiling and the wall of the altar with his matchless conceptions of the story of Genesis and of the Last Judgment, the painter of prophets . . . will doubtless never have his equal, no more than Homer or Phidias. Men of this stamp and stature are not seen twice upon the earth; they are syntheses, they embrace a whole world, they exhaust it, they complete it, and what they have said no one can repeat after them.

The music of Palestrina seems to be a translation in song of the vast poem of Michelangelo, and I am inclined to think that these two masters explain and illustrate each other in the same light, the spectator developing the listener, and reciprocally, so that, finally one is tempted to ask if the Sistine Chapel—painting and music—is not the product of one and the same inspiration. Music and painting are found in a union so perfect and sublime that it seems as if the whole were the twofold expression of one and the same thought,

288

the double voice of one and the same hymn. It might be said that what one hears is the echo of what one sees.

.   .   .   .   .

The great geniuses suffer and must suffer, but they need not complain; they have known intoxication unknown to the rest of men and, if they have wept tears of sadness, they have poured tears of ineffable joy. That in itself is a heaven for which one never pays what it is worth.

JULES MASSENET

1 8 4 2 – 1 9 1 2

JULES-ÉMILE-FRÉDÉRIC MASSENET was born in Montaud, in the Loire, France, on May 12, 1842. Between 1851 and 1863 he attended the Paris Conservatory, a pupil of Laurent, Savard, Reber, and Ambroise Thomas. Massenet received first prizes in piano playing and fugue and, in 1863, the Prix de Rome. His first opera was written after his return from Rome. It was *La Grand' tante,* produced by the Opéra-Comique on April 3, 1867. Success came between 1872 and 1877, with the production of a comic opera, *César de Bazan,* at the Opéra-Comique on November 30, 1872; with the incidental music to Leconte de Lisle's *Les Érynnies,* which includes his popular *Élégie,* at the Odéon on January 6, 1873; and with *Le Roi de Lahore,* given by the Paris Opéra on April 27, 1877.

In 1878 Massenet became professor of composition at the Paris Conservatory, holding this post until the end of his life. His influence extended to an entire generation of French composers, including Alfred Bruneau, (1857–1934), Gabriel Pierné (1863–1937), Henri Rabaud (1873–1949), Florent Schmitt (1870–1958), and Gustave Charpentier (1860–1956). In 1879, Massenet became the youngest man elected to the Académie des Beaux-Arts, and in 1899 he was made Grand Officer of the Legion of Honor.

Massenet wrote his most famous operas between 1880 and 1900, achieving with them a preëminent position in the French lyric theater. The most significant were: *Hérodiade,* on December 19, 1881; *Manon,* on January 19, 1884; *Werther,* on February 16, 1892; *Thaïs,* on March 16,1894; and *Sapho,* on November 27, 1897. Though he created two significant operas after 1900—*Le Jongleur de Notre Dame* in 1902 and *Don Quichotte* in 1910—his significance and influence went into a sharp decline, as modern tendencies replaced the sentimental and romantic in French music. Massenet died in Paris on August 13, 1912.

THE MAN

HERBERT F. PEYSER

Massenet's dislike for the frequent intrusions of strangers, newspaper people, importuning artists, and so forth, led him to move from a more central part of Paris to 48 Rue de Vaugirard. The place (an apartment house, of course; the Parisian masters seem particularly partial to apartments however considerable their bank accounts) overlooks the picturesque gardens of the Luxembourg, and is situated within a few minutes' walk of the Cluny museum and the Pantheon. The exterior is bare and unpretentious, and, to the average American, about as uninviting as the majority of Parisian houses. The place is innocent of an elevator, but happily the premises of the master are located *au premier,* thus necessitating the ascent of only one flight of stairs.

The entrance hall and dining room are furnished with severe simplicity. The highly polished floors are uncarpeted. On the dining-room mantel some few simple pieces of bric-a-brac. In an opposite corner, a black upright piano with a brass handle on each side. The instrument is always closed, it appears, for Massenet's inspiration needs no piano to guide, stimulate, or otherwise invite it. A half-subdued light permeates the room, for its single window of leaded glass looks out upon a court, not the street. Yet this light only emphasizes the reposeful and consistently tranquil atmosphere of the place.

Massenet entered hastily from a side room where he had been busily composing (as he subsequently informed me) since the small hours of morning—his customary *modus operandi.*

Despite the fact that his face is thinner and more wrinkled and his cheeks far more sunken than is apparent in any of his published photographs, Massenet carries his seventy-odd years with surprising ease. His gray hair, sparse in front, but still falling in the approved

291

musician's mode over his ears, is yet liberally streaked with the black of earlier years. His eyes are luminous with a very youthful fire, and his varied play of features acts as a sort of incessant commentary on the import of his conversation. Massenet is loquacious, speaking with rapidity and directness; trenchantly, pointedly, yet with the utmost simplicity of expression. And the very polish of their simplicity makes the task of recording his words laborious. But though he fairly radiates geniality and *bonhomie* the observer is, nevertheless, immediately and indelibly impressed by his vivacity, animation, and supply of nervous energy. When particularly desirous of emphasizing some point he will unconsciously, as it were, grasp the listener's arm.

We sat close by the black piano with the brass handles, the master resting his left arm upon the lid (for he seems to hold armchairs in disdain). "You see," he said, "this is the most valuable usage I can get out of this instrument. I never think of composing at it, *voyez-vous!* There are many people who do not believe me when I tell them so, and therefore, their astonishment and amusement are great, when they come here and see this one. 'I know it,' they say. 'Massenet does compose with a piano after all!' '*Mais pas du tout!* Not at all!' I answer them. 'You see, I like to sit alongside it, *voila tout!*' I am most comfortable when I am resting against it like this, *vous comprenez?* That is what I use my piano for. But to compose on it—*jamais de la vie!*"

Massenet, with all his arduous work, is an indefatigable traveler. "Journeys do not interfere with my composing in the least, and I can write just as comfortably in a crowded hotel, regardless of the noise, as I can at home. Travel is one of the most essential elements to stimulate creative powers. We must have change, we must submit to new impressions, we must add new words to our artistic dictionaries. Not only do I travel considerably to quicken my imagination but I keep near me great numbers of photographs of other countries, which I often look at, and which help to put me in the right state of mind when I am composing a work dealing with some specific locality. Moreover, I find true artistic pleasure in seeing beautiful faces. Not long ago I was asked to go to America and one of the inducements held out to me was that the New York women were the most beautiful in the world. I replied, however, that I did not believe it, that the loveliest ones were right here in Paris."

Massenet has made it a practice to leave Paris when there is a première of one of his operas. "The reason for this," the master explains, "is not in the least nervousness, however much people may imagine that. When the time for the première is at hand my share of the work is finished. I have no further instructions to give. I have done my best. Why wait around any longer and be pestered with people rushing up to me in the *coulisses* and in the streets asking 'are you satisfied?' or 'are you happy?' and having to answer in some dreadfully banal terms myself?"

It has been claimed at various times that *Jongleur* was Massenet's favorite among his own creations. To the present writer, however, he would not confirm that opinion. "I have no favorite," he said, "or at least, I never can say which my favorite will be. For all I can tell it may be the one I shall write next; it may be the one I am writing now. It may, perhaps, be even the one I write after my next."

An instance of the kind-heartedness of Massenet was an incident which took place in Vichy, at the hotel where he was stopping. A band of street musicians came to play in the garden where the guests of the house, among whom was the composer, were drinking their after-dinner coffee. No one took note of them until suddenly the composer was struck by the fact that they played far better and with vastly more musicianly style and finish than the average organization of the kind. They were, as a matter of fact, graduates of the Conservatory, some of them even having been prize winners in their student days, whose fortunes had ultimately obliged them to eke out a scanty living in this nomadic fashion. Massenet, deeply struck by their work, went among them and complimented them with fervor, to the amazement of the other guests of the hotel who had not paid the faintest attention to the concert. The poor players were quite overcome at the honor paid them by their distinguished listener whose praise began to be echoed by all the rest of the audience as soon as the master's identity was learned. It goes without saying, moreover, that the composer was as liberal in his material donations to the musicians as he had been in his praise.

THE COMPOSER

MARTIN COOPER

Jules Massenet won the leading position as operatic composer in France in the late 19th century. . . . The soliciting of the audience during the 1880's was Massenet's specialty, brought by him to such a degree of perfection that in his best works it assumes the quality of an artistic gift. Of the four operas produced by Massenet between 1880–90, the first two, *Hérodiade* (1881) and *Manon* (1884) were by far the most successful. *Hérodiade* continues the tradition of *"l'erotisme discret et quasi-religieux"* of the oratorios of the 1870's. John the Baptist's love for Salome is at first mystical and half-paternal; his love-making is conducted through a religious medium and only becomes frankly human when in the last act he is faced with death. As usually happens with Massenet, he fails in the less emotional and intimate scenes, in the political action of the story; and the feeling between the Idumaean people and their Roman conquerors, Herod's vacillation, even Herodias's enmity and jealousy, are either coldly and conventionally treated or seen through the same haze of mystical eroticism. Massenet seemed then to be incapable of any musical expression except that which is concerned with erotic, or sub-erotic, personal relationships.

It was the fact that he could capitalize this weakness which makes *Manon* not only his finest work, but something very near a masterpiece. The whole of Prévost's story is set in an atmosphere of coquetry and amorous intrigue, which cries aloud for the accompaniment of music, such as Massenet's . . . "melodies which are delicate and caressing rather than deeply felt, an orchestration rich in pretty and clever filigree work but without any depth." From the opening scene, in which Manon flirts with her cousin Lescaut, the story is a succession of ambiguous erotic situations, none of which demands any real depth of emotion. The gentle, swaying phrase which depicts Manon's shyness and hesitation is brilliantly suggestive; and the burst of facile emotion in the phrase expressing des Grieux's passion for Manon is, of its kind, quite irresistible. . . . In the scenes of the Foire St. Germain and the gaming house, even in the seminary of St. Sulpice, Massenet can legitimately preserve the emotional atmosphere which was in reality the one string of his lyre, because Prévost's story is a perfect emotional unity and, whatever the scene may be, it is no more than the decor for Manon's amorous escapades. One may find this ceaseless harping on the erotic interest tedious and cloying, but it is admirably suited to Massenet's talent and called out the very best of which he was capable. After *Manon* Massenet produced *Le Cid* (1885) and *Esclarmonde* (1889), both inferior works. . . . Massenet did not repeat the outstanding success of Manon with any of his productions until *Werther* (1892) and *Thaïs* (1894). *Werther* is in some ways his masterpiece, one of the very few of his works with a male protagonist, though Werther is an hysterical boy rather than an adult. The structure of the work is conventional but the musical language has points of interest. There were already hints of a semi-Wagnerian use of the orchestra in *Manon,* and in *Werther* Massenet went further along the same path. Charlotte's soliloquy in Act III, for example, might also come from the *Meistersinger,* as far as the orchestral part is concerned, though the vocal line, with its tendency to monotone, is in the direct line from the recitative of Charles Gounod. Melodically, Massenet was moving away, with the fashion, from the enclosed and self-sufficient air, towards a freer and more fragmentary melody of the kind foreshadowed by Meyerbeer in Act IV of *Les Huguenots.* Thus Werther's monologue, *"O spectacle idéal d'amour"* starts informally, as it were. The final cadence is still purely traditional in the Gounod manner and this "tame" ending is even more noticeable in the theme which accompanies Werther's hopeless love throughout the opera. On the other hand, the orchestral music which introduces the scene of Werther's suicide in Act IV has an hysterical violence most apt in the circumstances, and closely resembles the music of Tchaikovsky.

Thaïs relies much more than *Werther* on external effect and on the popularity, even so late in the day, of the theme of the "good prostitute." Massenet obviously hoped to repeat the success of *Hérodiade,* and to exploit once again, in the relationship between

295

Thaïs and Athanaël, the *"erotisme discret et quasi religieux,"* which d'Indy had considered the distinguishing mark of Massenet's oratorio, *Marie Magdeleine,* twenty years earlier. The whole work is more old-fashioned than *Werther,* and it was already anachronistic in 1894 to make the climax of the ballet a ballroom waltz danced by La Perdition. Like Puccini after him, Massenet was adept at gleaning ideas from the methods of the modernists of the day; and so we find, separating the first two scenes of Act II, a small symphonic poem describing the loves of Venus and Adonis, while the famous *Meditation* is a transformation (in the Lisztian and Franckian sense) of the main theme from the orchestral interlude. It is interesting, too, to observe the naïve rhythmic associations—traceable to the opéra-comique of the 18th century—which make Massenet employ the voluptuous 12/8 or 9/8 rhythms for *Thaïs* before her conversion, whereas afterwards she sings in a simple 4/4 time or at most an occasional chaste 6/8 time (*"L'amour est une vertu rare"*). The famous song to her looking glass (*"Dis-moi que je suis belle"*) is a direct descendant of the *N'est ce plus ma main* in *Manon.*

Massenet's music has suffered from its fashionableness. No composer has been more whole-heartedly despised by one section of his contemporaries nor more popular with the general public. Massenet's whole nature was centered in the desire to please, and this has been enough to damn him in the eyes of intellectuals who, in every generation, provide a strong—and generally wholesome—puritan element in matters of taste. The desire to please creates prettiness, that facile and doubtfully bred poor relation of beauty. The appeal of the pretty is directly to the untrained senses, and, through them, to the surface emotions. Massenet's music resembles the pretty, superficial, and sentimental type of woman who relies on her charm, her feminine instinct, her dressmaker, and her hairdresser to carry her through life. It is an eternal feminine type and like all such types it has its biological and social justification; not certainly as the highest nor—as misogynists would say—as the basic type of woman, but simply as *a* type, despised by intellectuals and adored by the public, which has an unreasoning instinct for what *is* and remains indifferent to what ought to be. Massenet's operas, something like twenty of them, are a portrait gallery of women, most

296

of whom conform to this type. Each new work after *Hérodiade* is a variation of the same theme—the feminine character in the most striking point in which it differs from the masculine. Manon, Esclarmonde, Thaïs, La Navarraise, Sappho, Cinderella, Griselda, Ariadne, Thérèse are all *grand amoureuses* and they all, in different ways, conform to the feminine type, accepted in Latin countries until recently, for whom sexual love provides the central, and often the only meaning of existence. Long before Massenet died in 1912 this type had fallen into disrepute. . . . Beneath a new form of puritanism the love-obsessed woman has been progressively degraded. We find her in Strauss's *Salome* and again in *Elektra* where Chrysothemis is the mere woman and the foil to her virile sister; and she has sunk as low as it is possible to sink in Alban Berg's *Lulu.* In Puccini's *Turandot,* again, a woman's obsession with love has turned sour and taken the form of cruelty and craving for power: the wheel has gone full circle from the healthy, instinctive passion of Massenet's heroines with their clinging caresses and their simple philosophy of the world well lost for love. Love has been stripped of its idealistic glamor and reduced to sex alone.

No wonder that Massenet's operas have lost their popularity. What of their musical value? Massenet was an opportunist, as any purveyor of the pretty, the immediately catchy, must be; for prettiness varies with the fashion while beauty, to the trained and discerning eye, is immortal; but *Manon* must watch the fashions, in music as in everything else. After *Thaïs* Massenet was aware of the storm of realism which blew up from Italy with the appearance of *Cavalleria Rusticana* and had already caused a minor disturbance in France with Alfred Bruneau's *Le Rêve. La Navarraise* (1894) was an essay in the veristic manner—short, sharp, brutal, and designed to work by direct action on the spectators, to galvanize instead of to charm. This was not Massenet's true gift, but for a short time the opera had a success; and in his next, *Sapho* (1897), based on Alphonse Daudet's novel, he tried again in a full-length work—*La Navarraise* had only two acts—to portray the woman to whom love brings simply tragedy. The theme associated with the heroine, Fanny, is a direct descendant of the tragic theme in *Carmen,* and Act III, in which Fanny tries to get her lover back from his family,

297

is the nearest that Massenet ever approached to genuine tragedy. In the first two acts, on the other hand, he expressed better even than in *Manon* the precarious bliss of the clandestine affair, a Bohemianism with the perpetual hint of tragedy. The conflict between his mistress and his family in the young man's emotions, so natural and moving to a 19th-century Latin audience, would probably seem as unreal and exaggerated to a sophisticated modern audience as does the parallel situation in *Carmen*. The moral feeling on which the convention was based has, temporarily at least, been so weakened that the dramatic point is lost. Even so, the pleading of Fanny with Jean is irresistible, and the touching variation which follows is typical of Massenet at his best.

Cendrillon (1899) is treated frankly as a fairy story, with some excellent writing in the Italian buffo style. The music is largely decorative, written to entertain and only touching and sentimental here and there (the farewell to the old armchair in Act III, for example, in the same vein as Manon's farewell to the furniture in the room she had shared with des Grieux).

In *Grisélidis* (1901) and *Le Jongleur de Notre Dame* (1902) Massenet attempted a new field, medieval legend. . . . *Le Jongleur* is one of Massenet's best works—paradoxically, because there is not a single feminine character in the original version. It is the story of a wandering player turned monk, ashamed of his ignorance and lack of talent in the monastery and finally singing and dancing before the statue of Our Lady, who rewards his humility with a miracle. It was first published by Gaston Paris twenty-five years before, as *Le Tombeur de Notre Dame,* and was treated again later by Anatole France in *L'Étui de Nacre.* Massenet obtains the contrast, necessary to a work in which only male voices are used, by the underlining of the two elements which were at war in the Jongleur himself—the secular and the religious. The crowd scenes in Act I and the blasphemous *Alleluia du vin* are followed in Act II by the rehearsing of a new motet in the cloister, brilliantly done, and by the rival claims of the various monks for the supremacy of their various arts—sculpture, painting, poetry, and music. Boniface, the cook, a half-comic character and the only one who understands the Jongleur, in one of Massenet's best minor roles; and the musical quality of the whole work in which there is no hint of a love interest, shows that Massenet's lyre was not really one-stringed, and that circumstances of his own taste account to a large extent for the repetitiveness of his other librettos.

Both *Chérubin* (1905) and *Ariane* (1906) show signs of Massenet's age. He had always been industrious, and industry combined with a great natural facility had led him to exploit to the full for over thirty years a never very rich vein. After *Le Jongleur de Notre Dame* he became simply repetitive and *Thérèse* (1907) was his last success. This is an intimate two-act opera based on a story of the French Revolution and the conflict of two allegiances—love and duty—in the heart of the heroine. The old regime is characterized by a *menuet d'amour*, which is a charming piece of pastiche, and the Revolution by a simple march theme. Massenet had been able to adapt himself to the first minor operatic revolution which threatened his popularity—the appearance of lyrical realism. The school reached the zenith of its popularity in 1900 when Gustave Charpentier (1860–1956) produced his *Louise*, written in a skilfully modernized version of Massenet's own style. After that Massenet was too old to compete any more, and apart from his final success with *Don Quichotte* (1910), the remaining operas written before his death added nothing to his reputation.

MASSENET SPEAKS

I have made it a point to afford myself the necessary element of contrast in the style of my every succeeding work. If I write one in a lofty, passionate, tragic mood, I see to it that my next is in a comic or otherwise different vein. And after a less serious piece, again, something more exciting, more profound, more passionate. By thus constantly changing the emotional atmosphere in which I am immersed I avoid fatigue.

When I have completed a composition I experience a deep and poignant grief. I have loved the work. I have had untold joy at seeing it grow. I have lived with my characters, have been happy and have suffered with them. I have lost myself completely in my creation. I have totally merged my personality with the persons I have brought into being. They are so intensely real to me! And then, alas, when all is finished, I must tear myself away from them. I must give them to the public. And therewith the charm of the heartfelt intimacy is over. I have, it almost seems to me, given away my children in marriage and they have deserted me.

Fundamentally my style has not changed from year to year. But what does determine the general character of my music is the kind of subject it paints. This is a fact that one has often to explain to people, to critics in particular, before they understand a work. Critics do not take the time to study a composition intelligently before delivering their verdict.

I compose very easily, my ideas coming to me spontaneously and without effort. I believe that ideas that can only be brought into being by labor are worthless.

I have not been very deeply influenced by the developments among the composers in France at present. I have no confidence in the new scale which I feel sure has no future, and I still have a great deal in the old one, which is by no means played out in spite of all that may be said to the contrary. See all the chords you can build on the tones of our familiar scale! And then, when you turn to the other you find but one single chord—that of the augmented fifth! And how monotonous this chord becomes after a short while!

In a way I should feel thankful to this new music, for it benefits me. People turn to me all the more gratefully for what I have been able to give them and I therefore gain a larger number of admirers among the public.

. . . . .

Thoughts After Death
(Epilogue to Massenet's Autobiography)

I have departed from this planet and I have left behind my poor earthly ones with their occupations which are as many as they are useless; at last I am living in the scintillating splendor of the stars, each of which used to seem to me as large as millions of suns. Of old, I was never able to get such lighting for my scenery on the great stage of the Opéra where the backdrops were too often in darkness. Henceforth there will be no letters to answer; I have bade farewell to first performances and the literary and other discussions which come from them.

Here there are no newspapers, no dinners, no sleepless nights. Ah! if I could but counsel my friends to join me here; I would not hesitate to call them to me. But would they come?

Before I came to this distant place where I now sojourn, I wrote out my last wishes (an unhappy husband would have taken advantage of the occasion to write with joy, "my first wishes"). I had indicated that above all I wanted to be buried at Egreville, near the family abode in which I had lived so long. Oh, the good cemetery in the open fields, silent as befits those who live there! I asked that they should refrain from hanging black draperies on my door, ornaments worn threadbare by use. I expressed the wish that a suitable carriage should take me from Paris, the journey, with my consent, to begin at eight in the morning.

An evening paper (perhaps two) felt it to be its duty to inform its readers of my decease. A few friends—I still had some the day before—came and asked my concierge if the news were true, and he replied, "Alas, Monsieur went without leaving his address." And his reply was true for he did not know where that obliging carriage was taking me.

At lunch, acquaintances honored me among themselves with their condolences, and during the day here and there in the theaters they spoke of the adventure.

"Now that he is dead, they'll play him less, won't they?"

"Do you know that he left still another work?"

"Ah, believe me, I loved him well. I have always had such great success in his works." A woman's lovely voice said that.

They wept at my publishers, for there they loved me dearly.

At home, Rue de Vaugirard, my wife, daughter, grandchildren, and great-grandchildren gathered and almost found consolation in their sobs.

The family was to reach Egreville the same evening, the night before my burial.

And my soul (the soul that survives the body) listened to all these

301

sounds from the city left behind. As the carriage took me farther and farther away, the talking and the noises grew fainter and fainter, and I knew, for I had my vault built long ago, that the heavy stone once sealed would be a few hours later the portal of oblivion.

FRANZ LISZT

1 8 1 1 – 1 8 8 6

FRANZ LISZT was born in Raiding, Hungary, on October 22, 1811. After successful appearances as a prodigy pianist he came to Vienna in 1821 where he studied the piano with Czerny and theory with Salieri. He was acclaimed on his Vienna debut as pianist on December 1, 1822. He then went to Paris to enter the Conservatory, but was denied admission because he was a foreigner. For a short period he studied composition with Reicha and Paër. A Paris debut on March 8, 1824—followed by performances throughout Europe—established his reputation as a virtuoso.

Settling in Paris in 1827, where he was caught in the cross-currents of its intellectual and political life, he decided to abandon music for other endeavors. In turn he sought out philosophy, politics, literature, and religion. But by 1830, his personal associations with Chopin, Paganini, and Berlioz, carried him back to music-making. Paganini's genius with the violin inspired Liszt to become the foremost piano virtuoso of his time. For two years he worked slavishly on his piano technique, returning to the concert stage in 1833 one of the most idolized and widely acclaimed pianists of his generation.

His virtuoso career was temporarily interrupted by a turbulent love affair with Marie Countess d'Agoult. Though married and a mother, she went to live with Liszt in Geneva in 1835. They stayed together four years, in which time three children were born to them, one of these being Cosima, destined to become the wife first of Hans von Bülow and later of Wagner. When Liszt and the Countess separated in 1839, the former embarked on a series of triumphant concert tours.

In 1848, Liszt was appointed Kapelmeister to the Grand Duke of Weimar. He held this post over a decade, devoting himself with the highest artistic dedication to performances of opera and orchestral music, and to championing new music and unrecognized contemporary composers. In Weimar, Liszt formed a new liaison—with the brilliant though eccentric Princess Carolyne von Sayn-Wittgenstein. Her bent for religion and mysticism reawakened in Liszt his one-time religious ardor and eventually led him to seek out the spiritual comforts of the church. After leaving Weimar in 1859, Liszt achieved minor orders, submitted to the tonsure in 1865, then entered the Third Order of St. Francis of Assisi as abbé. The Princess also influenced his career as musician, inspiring him to devote more of his energies to creative work. Up to now, Liszt's compositions had been primarily for the piano, including such works as the *Années de pèlerinage,* first two series (1835–36, 1838–39), the *Paganini Etudes* (1838), the *Consolations* (1849–50), the extremely popular *Liebestraum* (1850), and the *Études d'exécution transcendante* (1851). Stimulated and encouraged by the Princess he now sought to write larger and more ambitious works: vast religious compositions for chorus; huge programmatic orchestral compositions like the *Faust* and *Dante* symphonies (1856–57); and twelve shorter programmatic works for orchestra, including the famous *Les Préludes* (1854), with which he devised the form henceforth known as the tone poem or symphonic poem. He also helped establish and popularize the rhapsody form with his *Hungarian Rhapsodies* (1846–85).

He broke off his friendship of many-years standing with Wagner in 1866 when his daughter, Cosima, deserted her husband Hans von Bülow to go to live with the genius of the music drama. Liszt and Wagner were not reconciled until six years later, when Liszt attended the ceremonies for the laying of the cornerstone of the Festspielhaus in Bayreuth and then to be present at the first Wagner festival there. But Cosima never forgave her father. She refused to permit him to attend Wagner's funeral in 1883 and would not have him as a guest at her home.

Liszt continued making spasmodic concert appearances as pianist until the end of his life, scoring a triumph in London in 1886. But his last years were spent in poverty and asceticism. He died of pneumonia in Bayreuth, Bavaria, on July 31, 1886.

THE MAN

AMY FAY

COUNTESS MARIE D'AGOULT

Liszt is the most interesting and striking looking man imaginable. He is tall and slight, with deep-set eyes, shaggy eyebrows, and long iron-gray hair, which he wears parted in the middle. His mouth turns up at the corners, which gives him a most crafty and Mephisto-phelean expression when he smiles, and his whole appearance and manner have a sort of Jesuitical elegance and ease. His hands are very narrow, with long and slender fingers that look as if they had twice as many joints as the other people's. They are so flexible and supple that it makes you nervous to look at them. Anything like the polish of his manner I never saw. When he got up to leave the box, for instance, after his adieus to the ladies, he laid his hand on his heart and made his final bow—not with affectation, or in mere gallantry, but with a quiet courtliness which made you feel that no other way of bowing to a lady was right or proper. It was most characteristic.

But the most extraordinary thing about Liszt is his wonderful variety of expression and play of feature. One moment his face will look dreamy, shadowy, tragic. The next he will be insinuating, amiable, ironical, sardonic; but always with the same captivating grace of manner. He is a perfect study. I cannot imagine how he must look when he is playing. He is all spirit, but half the time, at least, a mocking spirit. All Weimar adores him, and people say that women still go perfectly crazy over him. When he walks out he bows to everybody just like a king.

He is the most phenomenal being in every respect. All that you've heard of him would never give you an idea of him. In short, he represents the whole scale of human emotion. He is a many-sided prism and reflects back all the light in all colors, no matter how you look at him.

"When I play, I always play for the people in the gallery so that these people who pay only five groschen for the seat also hear something." Then Liszt began to play, and I wish you could have heard him! The sound didn't seem to be very loud, but it was penetrating and far-reaching. When he had finished, he raised one hand in the air, and you seemed to see all the people in the gallery, drinking in the sound. That is the way Liszt teaches you. He presents an idea to you, and it takes fast hold of your mind, and sticks there. Music is such a real, visible thing to him, that he always has a symbol, instantly, in the material world to express his idea.*

．　．　．　．　．

In politics, as in religion, he hated mediocrity, and his opinions were audaciously advanced. He despised the bourgeois monarchy of Louis Philippe and the government of the *juste milieu;* he cried out with all his being for the reign of justice, that is to say, a republic as he conceived it. With the same effervescence he gave himself up to the new movements in letters and the arts that were then menacing the old traditions. Childe Harold, Manfred, Werther, Obermann, all the proud or desperate revolutionaries of romantic poetry, were the companions of his sleepless nights. With their aid he rose to a haughty disdain of conventions; like them he quivered under the detested yoke of aristocracies that were founded on neither genius nor virtue; he cried out for an end to submission, an end to resignation, for a holy implacable hate that should avenge all iniquities. . . . The voice of the young enchanter, his vibrant speech, opened out before me a whole infinity, now luminous, now somber, forever changing, into which my thoughts plunged and were lost. . . .

---

* The paragraphs above are by Amy Fay; the one below, by the Countess d'Agoult.

THE COMPOSER

CECIL GRAY

The mere mention of Franz Liszt's name is enough to evoke in response a string of epithets such as fustian, tinsel, pinchbeck, rhodomontade, tawdry, shoddy, garish, bedizened, and so on; but you will generally find that those people who are most lavish in their employment of this vocabulary know little of Liszt's music. Even those who do know his work sufficiently well to be in a position to judge it for themselves almost invariably approach it with an adverse prejudice which is to a great extent quite unconscious, the outcome of several decades of steady vituperation of Liszt on the part of musicians of every conceivable creed and tendency. The inevitable result is that they find in it precisely what they expect to find, what they have been taught to find, what they subconsciously wish to find.

Now, it need hardly be said that such hard-and-fast, cut-and-dried, ready-made preconceived notions as these we have been examining have always a certain basis of justification. It is undeniable that at least some of the music of Liszt, and certainly most of it that is known and most frequently performed, thoroughly merits the denigratory epithets set forth above. Liszt's admirers, however, set little store by the greater part of the works by which he is commonly known; in fact, they might even agree with the conventional view of him in so far as it is based upon such works as the Piano Concerto No. 1 in E-flat (1849), the symphonic poem *Les Préludes* (1854), the etude *La Campanella* (1838), the *Hungarian Rhapsodies*, and the *Liebesträum* (1850), which are about all of Liszt that is familiar to the average concertgoer, and all of which are among his least successful productions. It is, or should be, a truism to say that a composer should be judged by his best work, but Liszt, up to the present time, has been condemned on account of his worst. It is true that the music public frequently displays a disconcerting propensity for taking to its heart the least significant productions of a great master; in our time, for example, Elgar first achieved recognition through *Salut d'amour* and *Pomp and Circumstance,* and Sibelius similarly through *Valse triste* and *Finlandia.*

In the course of time, however, their most important works have come to be appreciated at their proper value, but although Liszt has been dead over three-quarters of a century this consummation has not yet taken place with regard to his music; in concert programs he is still represented by works of the same order as those of Elgar and Sibelius mentioned above. *Les Préludes* is of all his large orchestral works the weakest; *La Campanella* is the least admirable of his studies in pianistic virtuosity; the *Hungarian Rhapsodies,* if hardly deserving the abuse to which they are habitually subjected, are quite unimportant; and the E-flat Concerto is admittedly a somewhat vulgar and flashy composition which, moreover, is played too often. Indeed, the only great and important works of Liszt which is comparatively well known to the ordinary concertgoing public is the Piano Sonata (1852–53), and the fact that this truly superb work should still elicit from many critical pens, whenever it is performed, the same stale old clichés that I quoted at the outset of this essay, provides the best illustration possible of my contention to the effect that the writers of such nonsense are listening to the music with a subconscious prejudice against the composer. To call such music as this "tinsel" or "pinchbeck"—the two favorite words in the anti-Lisztian vocabulary—is a critical aberration of the first magnitude. The Piano Sonata is pure gold throughout, probably the most outstanding achievement in piano music of the entire 19th century.

Whenever, then—and it is very often—one finds anyone giving vent to the customary clichés concerning the music of Liszt, one can be fairly sure that he is either totally ignorant of Liszt's work as a whole, or else so hidebound with prejudice that his reaction is not to the music itself but only to the associated idea. They may be applicable to a certain restricted number of his works, which happen unfortunately to be his best-known ones, but that is all. So far, indeed, are they from being true of his work as a whole that the exact opposite is very much nearer the truth, namely, that a chronological survey of his entire output reveals a steady and consistent diminution in brilliant externality, ending in a bareness and austerity of utterance almost without parallel in music. Moreover, even in many of those works which may seem to merit the opprobrious epithets habitually cast at them, the faults lie entirely on the surface and do not affect the sound core of the music.

In this respect there is a very close relation between the artist and the man. In the earlier part of his career, in particular, with all Liszt's splendor, brilliance, and generosity, one feels a certain element of ostentation and display in his character which are not entirely sympathetic, suggesting the artistic equivalent of a *nouveau riche*—he is altogether too conscious of his genius. Underneath this slightly vulgar exterior, however, there lay always the fineness and nobility of character which have perforce been recognized even by those who were, and are, most hostile to his art. In this connection there is an interesting and instructive anecdote told by his friend Legouvé, to the effect that on one occasion when Liszt was posing for his portrait, the French painter, Ary Scheffer, said to him rudely, "Don't put on the airs of a man of genius with me; you know well enough that I am not impressed by it." "You are perfectly right, my dear friend," replied Liszt quietly, "but you must try to forgive me; you cannot realize how it spoils one to have been an infant prodigy." The reply shows all the greatness and fineness of sensibility which underlay the superficial pose, involuntarily, unconsciously assumed, out of sheer force of habit and upbringing. Precisely the same phenomenon is to be observed in his art; the element of vulgarity and display in it which has always aroused such violent critical censure is just as superficial and skin-deep as it is with the man, and if his critics had reproached him with it to his face he no doubt would have replied to them as he replied to Ary Scheffer, saying that it was the inevitable outcome of having begun his artistic career as a piano virtuoso.

For this reason, the music of Liszt constitutes one of the most searching tests of critical acumen that the art presents. The hasty and superficial critic fails to penetrate through the frequently meretricious outer shell to the solid worth beneath, and only the most experienced and discerning assayer is able to determine correctly the proportion of pure metal to base in the complex alloys which many of his works are.

Even if one were to admit for the sake of argument that the brilliance and glitter of much of Liszt's music are intrinsically condemnable, the stricture only applies to a part of his work. For in the same way that Liszt began his career as a triumphant and opulent virtuoso and then gradually and progressively withdrew himself from the world until he finally took holy orders and died in poverty, so his work, viewed as a whole, exhibits precisely the same steady, unbroken process of recession from all that is superficial, decorative, external, until in the writings of his last years he arrives at a bareness and austerity of utterance which have no parallel in music. Needless to say, these later works are entirely unknown to those who prate so glibly of Liszt's flashiness and so forth. Not that I would necessarily suggest that they are his most important compositions, any more than his assumption of holy orders was the consummation of his earthly life. On the contrary, it is probable that the devout churchman in Liszt grew at the expense of the artist, and that the asceticism of the later works denotes a similar weakening and impoverishment of the genius exhibited in some of his earlier works. The fact remains that to ignore this process of development and its ultimate phase is to misunderstand Liszt entirely; to speak of him as an artist exclusively preoccupied with effects of superficial brilliance and showiness is as if one were to represent St. Augustine as the Don Juan of antiquity and St. Francis as the Casanova of the Middle Ages, simply because they lived loose and worldly lives in their youth. To concentrate almost exclusively on the early Liszt, or even the Liszt of complete maturity, and to ignore the latest works; to dwell at length on his dazzling triumphs as a virtuoso in his youth and to forget the twilight of his closing years and his tragic end, neglected and penniless, at Bayreuth of all places—this is to misunderstand him altogether. That the composer who, of all composers who have ever lived, has gone farthest in the direction of austerity and asceticism, and finally pushed the modern doctrine of the elimination of non-essentials to such an extreme pitch that he often ended by eliminating essentials as well—that he should invariably be held up to derision and contempt by musical historians and critics and represented as the supreme charlatan and trick showman of music—this is surely the most consummate stroke of ironic perversity in the history of music; for in such works as the symphonic poem *Von der Wiege bis zum Grabe* (1882), the third and last series of the *Années de pèlerinage* (1877), the later piano pieces such as *Nuages gris* (1881), *Sinistre* (c. 1882), *La lugubre gondole* (1882), and others, the last songs such as *J'ai perdu ma force* (1872), *Sei still* (1877), *Gebet* (c. 1878), *Einst* (c. 1878), *Verlassen* (1880), *Und wir dachten* (c. 1880)—in all these works with which he concluded his creative career one finds quite a disconcerting bareness of idiom and a complete sacrifice of every means of effect to the purposes of expression. The conceptions, moreover, to which expression is given in these later works are almost invariably of a gloomy and tragic order, and again in this respect also one finds merely the ultimate point of a constantly growing tendency throughout his entire creative activity. The real fundamental Liszt, indeed, is not the brilliant and facile rhetorician that he is invariably made out to be, delighting principally in grandiose sonorities and triumphant apotheoses; the essence of his art, on the contrary, consists in a sadness, a melancholy, a disillusion, a despair, of a depth and intensity unequalled, perhaps, in all music. No composer has ever ventured farther into that City of Dreadful Night of which the poet Thomson sings; none has expressed with greater poignancy "that all is vanity and nothingness."

This is the essential Liszt. It is here that his true greatness lies, here that he is original, unique, unsurpassed. Too often, however, as a dutiful son of the Church, he felt himself constrained to give the lie to his innermost convictions, of which, perhaps, he was not himself fully and consciously aware; hence his pompous, triumphant finales which are almost invariably the weakest sections of his works. Hostile criticism, in fact, is fully justified here in a sense; it rightly perceives in such things a certain hollowness, lack of conviction, and seeming insincerity, but errs in diagnosing the cause of them. Too often, indeed, Liszt went a long way toward spoiling his best works through his assumption of a facile and shallow optimism which is in opposition to his real self and stands in flagrant contradiction to what has gone before. The ending of the *Faust Symphony* (1854–57) is a case in point. The work should logically have concluded with the Mephistopheles movement, and I believe I am right in

311

saying that such was the original conception, but scruples of conscience and ethical considerations generally led him to tack on to
the end of it a choral epilogue, a kind of "happy ending" depicting
redemption, through womanly love, which not only impairs the profundity and originality of the conception as a whole, but also constitutes a blot upon the otherwise perfect form and musical logic
of the work. This fault, however, does not prevent the *Faust Symphony* from being probably, on the whole, his greatest work and
one of the highest achievements of the 19th century; for the rest,
however, his most completely satisfying compositions on a large
scale are those in which the sadness and despair which are at the
core of his thought and feeling are not thus contradicted, such as
the tone poems *Ce qu'on entend sur la montagne* (1848–49), *Héroïde
funèbre* (1849–50), *Hamlet* (1858), and the great Piano Sonata, the
closing page of which I never hear without thinking involuntarily of
that terrible little sentence of Pascal, *"Le silence éternel de ces es-
paces infinis m'effraie,"* of which it always seems to me to be the
perfect musical embodiment and equivalent. Even the finest of his
sacred music is not that wherein he celebrates the glories of the
Church militant and triumphant, as in so many grandiose pages of
the *Grand Festmesse* (1855), *Die Legende von der heiligen Elisabeth*
(1857–62), and *Christus* (1855–59), fine works though they are in
many ways, but in such things as his deeply moving setting of the
thirteenth Psalm, "How long wilt thou forget me, O Lord? For ever?
How long wilt thou hide thy face from me?" Here again, however,
the beauty of the work is somewhat impaired by the exultant conclusion, which does not seem to ring entirely true.

Another widely prevalent misconception regarding the music of
Liszt is that, in the words of Dannreuther in his volume on *The Romantic Period* in *The Oxford History of Music*, "he devoted extraordinary mastery of instrumental technique to the purposes of illus-
trative expression." All the tone poems, with the exception of
Orpheus, are, Dannreuther says, "impromptu illustrations, corresponding to some poem, or picture, or group of concepts expressed
in words. They are mere sketches arranged in accordance with some
poetical plan, extraneous, and more or less alien, to music. . . .
From the point of view of musical design, a lax and loose concep-

tion of art prevails more or less through all the *poèmes symphoniques*. . . . In lieu of musical logic and consistency of design, he is content with rhapsodical improvisation. The power of persistence seems wanting. . . . The musical growth is spoilt, the development of the themes is stopped or perverted by some reference to extraneous ideas. Everywhere the program stands in the way and the materials refuse to coalesce."

The two chief accusations made against Liszt here, namely, a lack of formal cohesion and a reliance on programmatic ideas alien to music, are both entirely untrue. Out of the twelve symphonic poems, which are the objects of these strictures, *Hungaria* (1854) and *Festklänge* (1853) have no program at all. *Hamlet* has no other than is contained in the title and makes no attempt to illustrate the drama. *Hunnenschlacht* (1857) is merely a battlepiece, also with no further indication than the title. *Tasso* (1849), *Mazeppa* (1851), and *Prometheus* (1850) are merely variants on the simplest of all possible musical formulas. The alleged programs of *Lamento e Trionfo* (1849), *Les Préludes* and *Héroïde funèbre* are the vaguest kind of romantic *schwärmerei* and contain no concrete images susceptible of illustration. *Orpheus* (1853–54) is specifically exempted by Dannreuther himself from the strictures quoted above. Only two of the twelve can be truly said to be program music in the strict sense of the words, namely the first and the last, *Ce qu'on entend sur la montagne* and *Die Ideale* (1857), to which may also be added the *Dante Symphony* (1855–56), which is only a gigantic tone poem in two movements. The first of these is based upon a poem of Victor Hugo, which it no doubt follows closely enough in general outline, but the poem itself is nothing more or less than a preliminary sketch for a musical composition. This is hardly a program that can be called "extraneous and more or less alien to music," it will be admitted. Rather it is true that Victor Hugo was guilty of writing a poem which is based upon a musical program that is extraneous and more or less alien to poetry.

In *Die Ideale* the composer followed an entirely different scheme from the poem of Schiller on which it was ostensibly based. The order of the verses inscribed in the score is not that of the poet, but an arbitrary arrangement made by the composer; even then he does not by any means follow the poem line by line, or even verse by verse. Still, it is true that the literary element in *Die Ideale* remains considerable, and without a knowledge of it the work is apt to seem somewhat unintelligible. The same is true of the *Dante Symphony*, but neither of these two works, though they are certainly among Liszt's most ambitious efforts, is among his best. Of them it may be admitted that the musical development is conditioned, and sometimes hindered, to a great extent by extraneous literary ideas, and that the form is, in consequence, loose and unsatisfactory. But to say of the rest of the large orchestral works, as Dannreuther and others do, that they are completely formless and consist chiefly of "rhapsodical improvisations" is entirely untrue, and can indeed be proved untrue. If Liszt is not one of the great masters of form —and he certainly is not—the reason is not that he relies on "rhapsodical improvisation" but precisely the opposite, namely, that his form is often, perhaps generally, too mechanical, precise, logical, and symmetrical, lacking the living, spontaneous, organic quality which is characteristic of the highest achievements in musical form. In some of his best works on a large scale, however, he does attain to formal perfection, notably in the Piano Sonata, *Hamlet,* and—apart from the slight flaw already indicated—the great *Faust Symphony* to name only three.

The immense quantity of fine music that Liszt wrote for the piano is almost entirely neglected by concert pianists, and is in consequence virtually unknown to the general public, apart from a few well-worn and hackneyed show pieces which are frequently included in the final groups of recital programs solely in order to display the technical accomplishments of the performer. Many of the best pieces, however, notably in the collections *Années de pèlerinage,* and *Harmonies poétiques et religieuses* (1847–52), are not exceptionally difficult but, on the contrary, for the most part well within the scope of the ordinarily proficient player, and among the finest in the pianist repertory. On the other hand, the difficult *Études d'exécution transcendante* are by no means mere virtuoso pieces, but works of intrinsic merit as well, and even many of the greatly abused operatic fantasias are in their way perfect masterpieces. Saint-Saëns has well said that such things are not necessarily any more negligible artistically than the overtures, which are generally little more than fantasias on the themes of the opera which is to follow. One might say that, while the overture prepares the listener's mind for the drama which is to come, the Lisztian fantasia is in the nature of an epilogue, a commentary or meditation upon the drama after it is over. The transfiguring imaginative power which Liszt brings to such things is seldom recognized criticism.

Two other neglected aspects of Liszt's phenomenally versatile genius are the few, but superb, works, which he wrote for the organ —probably the finest written for the instrument since Bach—namely, the *Fantasia and Fugue on the Theme B.A.C.H.* (1855–56), the *Evocation in the Sistine Chapel* (c. 1862) based upon Mozart's *Ave Verum*, the *Fantasia and Fugue on the Chorale Ad Nos, Ad Salutarem Undam* (1850); and the fifty or so songs with piano accompaniments, some of which, such as *Kennst du das Land?* (1842), *Es mus ein Wunderbares sein* (1857), *Kling leise* (1848), *Ein Fichtenbaum* (1855), *König im Thule* (1842), *Vatergruft* (1844), *Ich möchte hingehn* (1845), *Ich scheide* (1860), *Enfant, si j'étais roi* (1844), and many others too numerous to mention here, among the best songs written since Schubert. Above all, however, does Liszt excel in his settings of Heine, whose combination of sentimentality and irony, of lyricism and cynicism, was particularly congenial and akin to his own temperament.

This strain of irony and cynicism which so often underlies the suave and sentimental exterior of his music is the active aspect of the weariness and disillusionment which we have already noted in much of his best work, and particularly in his later years—the combination of medieval accidia and modern *Weltschmerz* which we find in his *Hamlet*, for example, and in the last songs and piano pieces. There it is, passive, despairing, almost resigned; in its more positive manifestations it takes the form of a withering and pitiless mockery of which the most perfect expression is to be found in the third movement of the *Faust Symphony*, the *Second Mephisto Waltz* (1880–81), the *Totentanz* (1849), and other similar essays in the musical macabre. It runs like a *Leitmotiv*, however, throughout his entire work.

315

Whatever one's opinion may be concerning the intrinsic merit, or the reverse, of Liszt's music, there can be no two opinions, concerning the immense influence his work has had, for good or evil, and possibly for both, on the history of the art—greater in all probability than that of any other composer who has ever lived. No musician has more generously lavished such superlative interpretative gifts, as pianist, as transcriber, as conductor (during the Weimar period), on his great predecessors and contemporaries; similarly none has more richly endowed his contemporaries and successors with the fruits of his creative activities. Liszt, indeed, quite simply is the father of modern music. There is no composer of any importance during the latter part of the 19th century, or the beginning of the 20th century, who has not been influenced by him in some way or another. The first and most important of all was, of course, Wagner. The Wagnerians have always attempted to minimize and gloss over this debt, but Wagner himself, greatly to his credit, never tried to do so but, on the contrary, openly proclaimed it. It is generally recognized today that the immense step forward that Wagner made between *Lohengrin* and *Das Rheingold* is in large part due to the influence of Liszt.

There is no need to mention the enormous extent of the debt that is owed to him by the most eminent modern German composers; it speaks for itself. The Richard Strauss (1864–1949) of the tone poems, for example, could not have existed without Liszt, and the same applied to innumerable others. Even Brahms himself, it is interesting and instructive to note, was influenced by Liszt in his early works such as the first and second piano sonatas, where he adopts the Lisztian device of thematic transformation, and in the clearly poetic elements of the third. In France, Saint-Saëns was, of course, one of the most fervent admirers and disciples of Liszt, and one of his most sedulous imitators. César Franck, is no less demonstrably and effectually indebted to him, not merely in his tone poems but in all his work, and the so-called Impressionists were anticipated by him in many of their most characteristic effects and procedures, sometimes by as much as half a century—see, for example, such things as *Au bord d'une source* and the *Jeux d'eaux a la Villa d'Este* in the *Années pèlerinage,* and the *Prédication aux oiseaux* of the *Légendes* (1863), also the augmented fifths and whole-tone scales encountered in works written as early as the 30's. Again, James Gibbons Huneker has described Liszt, not without justice, as "the first cosmopolitan in music," and as such he has numerous, if somewhat undistinguished, progeny in every country in Europe—the Moszkowskis, Glazunovs, Rachmaninoffs, Dohnányis, and so forth, are all direct descendants of Liszt; equally justly, however, he can be regarded as the first of the nationalists, not merely by virtue of his *Hungarian Rhapsodies* and other similar works, which were practically the first of their kind, but also on account of the encouragement and inspiration he gave to the formation of national schools in many countries. Mily Balakirev (1837–1910), the founder of the Russian nationalist school, Alexander Borodin (1833–87), to say nothing of Rimsky-Korsakov, were deeply influenced by Liszt; so also were the Bohemian nationalists, Smetana and Dvořák, Isaac Albéniz (1860–1909) and through him the modern Spanish nationalists, and even the Norwegian Grieg. Other eminent composers possessing no distinctively nationalist traits or anything else in common who have likewise been deeply influenced by him are Ferruccio Busoni (1866–1924), who is in many respects the very reincarnation of Liszt, Alexander Scriabin (1872–1915), whose witch's cauldron contains many ingredients stolen from him, and Sir Edward Elgar (1857–1934). Traces of his thought can even be perceived where no direct influence exists. For example, the passage of interlocking common chords of C natural and F sharp in *Petrouchka* by Igor Stravinsky (1882–   ) is basically identical with an episode in the posthumously published Concerto for Piano and Orchestra of Liszt entitled *Malédiction* (c. 1840)—a strange and arresting coincidence, this, by the way. Even Arnold Schoenberg (1874–1951) and the atonalists derive in many respects from Liszt. The perverse and ironic romanticism of *Pierrot Lunaire,* for example, is only a development of that in the amazing third movement of the *Faust Symphony,* and in his last works Liszt clearly foreshadows the principles of atonality.

There are many clear indications that the day is at last approaching when Liszt will be recognized not merely as the most potent

317

germinative force in modern music, but also, in his own right, as the inspired creator of some of the greatest and most original masterpieces of the 19th century.

LISZT SPEAKS

Music embodies feeling without forcing it—as it is forced in most other arts, and especially in the art of words—to contend and combine with thought. If music has an advantage over other media through which man expresses his soul, it owes this to its supreme capacity to make each inner impulse audible without the assistance of reason. . . . Music presents at one and the same time both the intensity and the expression of feeling. It is the embodied, the intelligible essence of feeling. Capable of being apprehended by our senses, this feeling permeates the senses, and fills the soul, like a ray of light, or like the dew. If music calls itself the supreme art, this supremacy lies in the hot flame of emotion that fires the heart without the aid of reflection, without having to wait upon accident for an opportunity for self assertion. . . . Only in music does actively and radiantly present feeling lift the ban which oppresses our spirit with the suffering of an evil earthly power and liberates us with the whitecapped floods of its free and warmth-giving might from "the demon of thought," brushing away for brief moments this yoke from our furrowed brows. Only in music does feeling . . . dispense with the help of reason and its means of expression—so inadequate in comparison with intuition, so incomplete in comparison with its strength, delicacy, and brilliance. On the towering, sounding waves of music, feeling lifts up to the heights that lie beyond the atmosphere of our earth, shows us cloud landscapes and world archipelagos that move about in ethereal space like singing swans. On the wings of the infinite art, it draws us with it to regions into which it alone can penetrate; where, in the ringing ether, the heart expands and, in anticipation, shares in an immaterial, incorporeal, spiritual life.

. . . . .

I prefer certain faults to certain virtues, the mistakes of clever people to the effects of mediocrity. In this sense there are failures which are better than many a success.

. . . . .

In the region of liberal arts they [authority and liberty] do not happily bring in any of the dangers and disasters that their oscillations occasion in the political and social world. In the domain of the Beautiful, genius alone is the authority. Hence, Dualism disappearing, the notions of authority and liberty are brought back to their original identity. Manzoni, in defining genius as "a stronger imprint of divinity" has eloquently expressed this very truth.

. . . . .

Come back to the Faith. It gives such happiness. It is the only, the true, the eternal. However bitterly you may scorn this feeling, I cannot help recognizing in it the way of salvation. I cannot help yearning for it, and choosing it.

. . . . .

Love is not justice. Love is not duty. It is not pleasure, either, but it mysteriously contains all these things. There are a thousand ways of experiencing it, a thousand ways of practising it, but for those whose heart is utterly and infinitely thirsty, there is one, eternally one, without beginning or end. If it manifests itself anywhere on earth, it is above all in the complete trust of one in the other, in this supreme conviction of our angelic nature, inaccessible to any saint, impenetrable to everything outside of it. . . . If love is at the bottom of our hearts, all has been said. If it has disappeared, there is nothing more to say.

RICHARD WAGNER

1813 – 1883

WILHELM RICHARD WAGNER, creator of the music drama, was born in Leipzig, Germany, on May 22, 1813. His musical training was spasmodic, with random instruction in piano, violin, theory, and composition. Before he was twenty he completed a piano sonata, string quartet, concert overture, and symphony; the last two were performed in Leipzig and Prague between 1830 and 1833. His first attempt at opera was *Die Hochzeit,* in 1832, which was never finished.

His first complete opera (for which, as was to be his practice, he wrote libretto as well as music), was *Die Feen,* in 1833; it remained unperformed until five years after the composer's death. In 1834, Wagner became conductor of the Magdeburg Opera where he completed *Das Liebesverbot,* his libretto based on Shakespeare's *Measure for Measure.* Its première, on March 29, 1836, proved such a fiasco that it helped send the company into bankruptcy. Wagner now found a new post as conductor in Königsberg.

After marrying Minna Planer, an actress, in 1836, Wagner served as conductor of the Riga Opera from 1837 to 1839. Heavily involved in debts, he had to flee the city by way of a smuggler's route to escape imprisonment. On September 17, 1839 he came to Paris, where he encountered little but frustration, poverty, and indifference. To survive, he had to accept hack work; at one period he was imprisoned for debts. Nevertheless, he managed to complete *Rienzi* and to work on *The Flying Dutchman (Der fliegende Holländer).* He also wrote a concert overture, *A Faust Overture (Eine Faust-ouvertüre).*

Rienzi was given on October 20, 1842, and *The Flying Dutchman* on January 2, 1843, both at the Dresden Opera. Their success led to

320

Wagner's appointment as director of the Dresden Opera in 1843 where, for six years, he maintained the highest artistic standards. During his tenure of this office he completed *Tannhäuser* and *Lohengrin,* the first of these introduced in Dresden on October 19, 1845.

Threatened again by arrest, this time for involvement in the revolutionary movement in Germany during 1848–49, Wagner was forced to flee Saxony. For a brief period he visited Liszt in Weimar. Then he settled in Zurich where, in pamphlets and essays, he started to propound his revolutionary concepts of opera—concepts which he was about to crystallize in his own dramas. Meanwhile, *Lohengrin* proved a major success when introduced in Weimar under Liszt's direction, on August 28, 1850, and soon thereafter was seen throughout Germany.

By 1852, Wagner had completed the text of a giant project: a trilogy of operas, with a prologue, based on the Nibelungen legends. The prologue, *The Rhinegold (Das Rheingold)* was completed in 1854. The first of the three dramas, *The Valkyries (Die Walküre)* came in 1856, followed by *Siegfried* in 1869, and *The Twilight of the Gods (Die Götterdämmerung)* in 1874. Thus, this Gargantuan task took him almost a quarter of a century to complete. Meanwhile he had written two more operas, both along the principles and aesthetics he had set for himself in the *Ring* cycle. One was *Tristan and Isolde* (1859), and the other, his only mature comic opera, *The Mastersingers (Die Meistersinger)* in 1867.

In the summer of 1860, an amnesty permitted Wagner to return to Germany. His wife, Minna, was no longer with him, their marriage having collapsed through a conflict of temperaments and because of Wagner's continual pursuit of other women. After his return to Saxony, Wagner fell in love with Cosima von Bülow, wife of the famous pianist-conductor and a passionate Wagnerite; she was also Liszt's daughter. In 1865, a daughter, Isolde, was born to Cosima and Wagner. After the birth of a second daughter, Cosima deserted von Bülow to live with Wagner in Triebschen, on Lake Lucerne, in Switzerland. There a son, Siegfried, was born to them in 1869. Only after that—on August 25, 1870—were Cosima and Wagner married.

321

In 1864, at a time when Wagner was in continual flight from creditors, he suddenly found a powerful patron in Ludwig II, King of Bavaria. Through the king's beneficence *Tristan and Isolde* was introduced on June 10, 1865, *The Mastersingers* on June 21, 1868, *The Rhinegold* on September 22, 1869, and *The Valkyries* on June 26, 1870—all in Munich. But still Wagner was not satisfied. He now had a new dream: a festival theater built to his own specifications and requirements where his music dramas could be performed according to his own exacting standards of staging and performance. The city of Bayreuth, in Bavaria, offered him a site for a building in 1872. Now settling in Bayreuth—where, in 1874, he built for himself a permanent home, the Villa Wahnfried—Wagner moved heaven and earth to realize his life's ambition. Most of the funds for his theater came from public subscription; some, from concerts conducted by Wagner. At long last, the festival theater (*Festspielhaus*) opened, and the first Wagner festival was inaugurated on August 13, 1876 with the world première of the complete *Ring of the Nibelungs* cycle. The last two of its operas (*Siegfried* and *The Twilight of the Gods*) were being performed for the first time anywhere, the former on August 16, the latter on August 17. Pilgrims from all parts of the world attended the event; since that time Bayreuth has remained a shrine of the Wagnerian music drama.

Wagner's last music drama was *Parsifal*, a "stage-consecrating festival play," introduced in Bayreuth on July 26, 1882. Wagner was on vacation with Cosima in Venice when he suffered a fatal heart attack. He died there on February 13, 1883. His body was brought back to Bayreuth and was buried in the garden of Villa Wahnfried where it still reposes.

THE MAN

DEEMS TAYLOR

He was an undersized little man, with a head too big for his body —a sickly little man. His nerves were bad. He had skin trouble. It was an agony for him to wear anything next to his skin coarser than silk. And he had delusions of grandeur.

He was a monster of conceit. Never for one minute did he look at the world or at people except in relation to himself. He was not only the most important person in the world to himself; in his own eyes he was the only person who existed. He believed himself to be one of the greatest dramatists in the world, one of the greatest thinkers, and one of the greatest composers. To hear him talk, he was Shakespeare, and Beethoven, and Plato rolled into one. And you would have had no difficulty in hearing him talk. He was one of the most exhausting conversationalists that ever lived. An evening with him was an evening spent in listening to a monologue. Sometimes he was brilliant; sometimes he was maddeningly tiresome. But whether he was being brilliant or dull, he had one sole topic of conversation: himself. What *he* thought and what *he* did.

He had a mania for being in the right. The slightest hint of disagreement from anyone, on the most trivial point, was enough to set him off on a harangue that might last for hours, in which he proved himself right in so many ways, and with such exhausting volubility, that in the end his hearer, stunned and deafened, would agree with him, for the sake of peace.

It never occurred to him that he and his doings were not of the most intense and fascinating interest to anyone with whom he came into contact. He had theories about almost any subject under the sun, including vegetarianism, the drama, politics, and music; and in support of these theories, he wrote pamphlets, letters, books . . . thousands upon thousands of words, hundreds and hundreds of pages. He not only wrote these things, and published them—usually at somebody else's expense—but he would sit and read them aloud for hours to his friends and family.

He wrote operas; and no sooner did he have the synopsis of a story, but he would invite—or rather summon—a crowd of his friends to his house and read it aloud to them. Not for criticism. For applause. When the complete poem was written, the friends had to come again, and hear *that* read aloud. Then he would publish the poem, sometimes years before the music that went with it was written. He played the piano like a composer, in the worst sense of what that implies, and he would sit down at the piano before parties that included some of the finest pianists of his time, and play for them, by the hour, his own music, needless to say. He had a composer's voice. And he would invite eminent vocalists to his house, and sing them his operas, taking all the parts.

He had the emotional stability of a six-year-old-child. When he felt out of sorts, he would rave and stamp, or sink into suicidal gloom and talk darkly of going to the East to end his days as a Buddhist monk. Ten minutes later, when something pleased him, he would rush out of doors and run around the garden, or jump up and down on the sofa, or stand on his head. He could be grief-stricken over the death of a pet dog, and he could be callous and heartless to a degree that would have made a Roman emperor shudder.

He was almost innocent of any sense of responsibility. Not only did he seem incapable of supporting himself, but it never occurred to him that he was under any obligation to do so. He was convinced that the world owed him a living. In support of this belief, he borrowed money from everybody who was good for a loan—men, women, friends, or strangers. He wrote begging letters by the score, sometimes grovelling without shame, at others loftily offering his intended benefactor the privilege of contributing to his support, and being mortally offended if the recipient declined the honor. I have found no record of his ever paying or repaying money to anyone who did not have a legal claim upon it.

What money he could lay his hands on he spent like an Indian rajah. The mere prospect of a performance of one of his operas was enough to set him to running up bills amounting to ten times the amount of his prospective royalties. On an income that would reduce a more scrupulous man to doing his own laundry, he would keep two servants. Without enough money in his pocket to pay his rent, he would have the walls and ceiling of his study lined with pink silk. No one will ever know—certainly he never knew—how much money he owed. We do know that his greatest benefactor gave him $6,000 to pay the most pressing of his debts in one city, and a year later had to give him $16,000 to enable him to live in another city without being thrown into jail for debt.

He was equally unscrupulous in other ways. An endless procession of women marches through his life. His first wife spent twenty years enduring and forgiving his infidelities. His second wife had been the wife of his most devoted friend and admirer, from whom he stole her. And even while he was trying to persuade her to leave her first husband he was writing to a friend to enquire whether he could suggest some wealthy woman—*any* wealthy woman—whom he could marry for her money.

He was completely selfish in his other personal relationships. His liking for his friends was measured solely by the completeness of their devotion to him, or by their usefulness to him, whether financial or artistic. The minute they failed him—even by so much as refusing a dinner invitation—or began to lessen in usefulness, he cast them off without a second thought. At the end of his life he had exactly one friend whom he had known even in middle age.

He had a genius for making enemies. He would insult a man who disagreed with him about the weather. He would pull endless wires in order to meet some man who admired his work, and was able and anxious to be of use to him—and would proceed to make a mortal enemy of him with some idiotic and wholly uncalled for exhibition of arrogance and bad manners. A character in one of his operas was a caricature of one of the most powerful music critics of his day. Not content with burlesquing him, he invited the critic to his house and read him the libretto aloud in front of his friends.

The name of this monster was Richard Wagner. Everything that I have said about him you can find on record—in newspapers, in police reports, in the testimony of people who knew him, in his own letters, between the lines of his autobiography. And the curious thing about this record is that it doesn't matter in the least.

Because this undersized, sickly, disagreeable, fascinating little man was right all the time. The joke was on us. He *was* one of the world's great dramatists; he *was* a great thinker; he *was* one of the most stupendous musical geniuses that, up to now, the world has ever seen. The world did owe him a living. People couldn't know those things at the time, I suppose; and yet to us, who know his music, it does seem as though they should have known. What if he did talk about himself all the time? If he had talked about himself twenty-four hours every day for the span of his life he would not

325

have uttered half the number of words that other men have spoken and written about him since his death.

When you consider what he wrote—thirteen operas and music dramas, eleven of them still holding the stage, eight of them unquestionably worth ranking among the world's great musico-dramatic masterpieces—when you listen to what he wrote, the debts and heartaches that people had to endure from him don't seem much of a price. Eduard Hanslick, the critic whom he caricatured in *Die Meistersinger* and who hated him ever after, now lives only because he was caricatured in *Die Meistersinger*. The women whose hearts he broke are long since dead; and the man who could never love anyone but himself has made them deathless atonement, I think, with *Tristan und Isolde*. Think of the luxury with which for a time, at least, fate rewarded Napoleon, the man who ruined France and looted Europe; and then perhaps you will agree that a few thousand dollars' worth of debts were not too heavy a price to pay for the *Ring* trilogy.

What if he was faithless to his friends and to his wives? He had one mistress to whom he was faithful to the day of his death: Music. Not for a single moment did he ever compromise with what he believed, with what he dreamed. There is not a line of his music that could have been conceived by a little mind. Even when he is dull, or downright bad, he is dull in the grand manner. There is greatness about his worst mistakes. Listening to his music, one does not forgive him for what he may or may not have been. It is not a matter of forgiveness. It is a matter of being dumb with wonder that his poor brain and body didn't burst with the torment of the demon of creative energy that lived inside him, struggling, clawing, scratching to be released; tearing, shrieking at him to write the music that was in him. The miracle is that what he did in the little space of seventy years could have been done at all, even by a great genius. Is it any wonder that he had no time to be a man?

THE COMPOSER

EDWARD J. DENT

Richard Wagner was not merely the most striking figure in the history of opera, but also one of the most vital forces in the cultural life of his century.

From childhood he was attracted to the theater, and he was already writing plays before he had any thought of devoting himself to music. Wagner is the first case of a composer who wrote all his own librettos. His first attempt at opera was *Die Feen* (*The Fairies*) based on a play of Gozzi; it was written in 1833–34 but never performed until after his death. Next followed *Das Liebesverbot* (*The Ban on Love*), performed only once at Magdeburg in 1836; this is a comic opera in the style of Daniel François Esprit Auber (1782–1871), based on the plot of *Measure for Measure*. It had the reputation of being very licentious, but there is nothing in it that would frighten a modern audience, and the chief tendency of its plot is to throw ridicule on pompous authority. *Rienzi* (1838–40) is an imitation of Meyerbeer, and is still performed fairly often in Germany. A more original style began to appear in *The Flying Dutchman* (1841), in which Wagner reverted towards the manner of Weber. The opera is a curious mixture of styles, and this is not surprising when we remember that Wagner had been a theatrical conductor for some years and was familiar with all the repertory of the day. French influences are still prominent in *The Flying Dutchman;* Auber was not yet forgotten, and Senta's famous ballad is obviously suggested by the "romance" indispensable to any French comic opera. Her leap from a high rock into the sea is another relic of French tradition.

Tannhäuser came out at Dresden in 1845; in 1849 Wagner became involved in a revolution and had to fly from Germany. He took refuge in Switzerland, and his next opera, *Lohengrin,* was performed for the first time at Weimar in 1850, conducted by Liszt in Wagner's absence. These are the two operas of Wagner best known to the general public, and it is difficult to realize now why there should

327

have been such an outcry against Wagner in those days and indeed throughout most of his life.

In these last three works Wagner began to discover the field that was to be peculiarly his own, that of old German legend; it is clear, too, what a difference was made to Wagner's whole outlook on opera by the fact that he was his own librettist instead of having to accept a libretto from someone else. One can see quite easily that Auber, like most of the composers of his time, is setting out to write *an opera,* not to give musical expression to a drama. Opera is already a going concern, with certain regular habitual features, such as songs, duets, choruses, ensembles, etc. The ordinary professional composer of that period did not want to achieve a new form of drama; he wanted success, and that meant doing what somebody else had done before. The problem of the librettist was to find a story that could be utilized to provide all the stock attractions, and the French librettists knew perfectly well how to set to work. So did the Italians on the whole, though when they took French plays as foundations, they found some difficulty in converting them into librettos without losing some vital link in the dramatic chain.

Wagner in his first attempts at opera followed traditional lines, and knew as well as any Frenchman what was wanted in the way of a libretto with all the conventionalities. His literary skill gave him a great advantage over other German musicians, for in the early history of German opera it is clear that composers were always severely hampered by the general incompetence of German librettists. In considering the rise of Wagner as an operatic composer we must remember that his career began at a time when Germany possessed an extraordinary wealth of literary genius. The two greatest poets, Goethe and Schiller, had chosen the theater to be the focus of their creative activity, and they, with the help of various other writers, made the German theater a temple consecrated to the highest ideals of the German nation, not merely a place of amusement as it was in England, or a battleground of literary cliques as in Paris. This religious devotion to the theater naturally affected the development of German opera, especially as all German Romanticism was inseparably bound up with music. In no other country was literature so conscious of music or music so closely associated with literature.

328

France can show but one outstanding figure—Berlioz, who is a writer as well as a musician; though we must not forget that in an earlier generation André Grétry (1741–1813) and Jean François Lesueur (1760–1837) had been men of letters. But in Germany almost every musician of eminence cherished literary ambitions—Weber, Ludwig Spohr (1784–1859), Schumann, Ernst Theodor Amadeus Hoffmann (1776–1822) are the conspicuous examples. Later on come Liszt and Peter Cornelius (1824–74), though Liszt as a rule preferred to write in French; and Mendelssohn, though never a journalist, was certainly a man of literary cultivation. Most of the German poets knew something of music, and it was only natural that the Romantic age should be at one and the same time the great period of German lyric poetry and the great age of German song.

Germany in those days was proud to call itself "the land of poets and thinkers," and Wagner may justly claim to belong to both these categories. A new spirit becomes perceptible in *Lohengrin* which was the fruit of solitude and meditation, whereas Wagner's previous operas had been written in the thick of professional life. *Lohengrin* looks forward to the last of Wagner's dramas, *Parsifal;* both are concerned with the story of the Holy Grail and Lohengrin actually informs us at the end of the opera that Parsifal is his father. The French composers of the Revolution had tried curious experiments in writing dramatic instrumental prologues to their operas instead of conventional overtures; but the prelude to *Lohengrin* showed an entirely new sort of theatrical imagination in its very first bars. It is supposed to describe the descent of the Holy Grail to earth and its return to Heaven. Most members of the audience probably knew nothing about that and would not much care if they did; but everyone must admit that it is one of the most beautiful pieces of music ever written, and it may well stand as the movement which most perfectly expressed that sense of "aspiration" which was characteristic of the whole life and thought of the 19th century.

From this moment onwards Wagner's whole life was dedicated to the accomplishment of an ideal—"the work of art of the future" that was to unite in itself all the arts in the service of the musical drama. Wagner never stopped to consider practicalities in the theater. His new dramas were to be full of things which were contrary to all tradition and had never been done before; these things have by now become more or less normal and accepted.

In his later operas Wagner goes his own way. Although he habitually wrote his libretto complete before composing the music, he certainly had a good many of his musical ideas germinating in his mind while putting the words into shape, so that we can regard these operas as simultaneous conceptions of poetry and music. And we must remember, too, that Wagner never lost contact with the concert room. Italian composers of the time seem to have gone on composing operas as if they never came across any other kind of music; one might easily imagine that Vincenzo Bellini (1801–35) and Gaetano Donizetti (1797–1848) never heard a classical symphony in their lives. Wagner on the other hand was keenly interested in concert conducting, and in fact it was he who started the outlook on orchestral music which has led to the modern idolization of the star conductor. Hence he was able to absorb into the technique of the theater the musical methods of Beethoven's symphonies and other classical works. Purely operatic experience might well teach him how to present characters on the stage and how to achieve obvious theatrical effects. From Beethoven, more than from anyone else, he learned what one might call the technique of rumination upon the events of the drama.

Beethoven, in *Fidelio*, often seems to forget the actual characters on the stage and lose himself in the contemplation of a moral idea. Wagner does the same thing, but with more deliberate intention and with a new technique of his own. This could not become possible until after Beethoven had perfected the process which in sonatas and symphonies is called "development"; it was only this technique which made it possible for Wagner to drop the old system of isolated songs with opportunities for applause at the end, and create a continuous style of music which allowed no thought of applause, not even a moment of respite, until the end of each act. This forced audiences, as Wagner was consciously determined to achieve, into a new attitude towards opera. It was no longer possible to drop in and go away just as one pleased, hear a particular singer and not bother about the rest; an opera had to be taken seriously, and the audience had to give themselves up to it, abandoning all independence of personality. . . . And this applied not only to the audience; the singers and the orchestra, the scene-shifters too, were compelled to make the same utter self-surrender and become no more than atoms absorbed into the one mighty stream of the composer's imagination. The doors are shut, the lights go down, the conductor raises the stick; and from that moment everyone is the slave of the music. There can be no waiting while a scene is being changed; lighting and machinery must function like instruments in the score, and with the same precision. We are so accustomed to all this nowadays that we can hardly imagine what operatic conditions were like before Wagner; yet those whose memories go back to the 1890's will not have forgotten the indignation of old habitués at Covent Garden when it was proposed to darken the auditorium for The Ring and close the doors to late arrivals. A German history of music gives a list of some six hundred German operas produced between 1830 and 1900; hardly a single one has remained in the ordinary German repertory, apart from a few comic operas and musical comedies of the 1840's which are still popular in their own country, though little known outside. Throughout the whole of Wagner's influence the German theaters were dependent mainly on French and Italian operas, just as they were in the days of Mozart, and indeed right up to 1900 and later certain old French comic operas survived in Germany, which had long been shelved in France. It is necessary to insist on this in order that the reader may realize the strength of the opposition to Wagner and the immensity of the conquest which he finally achieved.

The most important of Wagner's later works is the great tetralogy of The Ring (1853–74). Wagner's first idea was to write one drama only, to be called *Siegfried's Death,* founded on an episode from the ancient legendary epic of Germany, the *Nibelungenlied.* But he found that the story required so much explanation that he would have to write another opera as a prologue to it; and that led to another and yet another, so that the four dramas of The Ring came to be written in the inverse order of their natural sequence. During the years occupied in this work Wagner's mind underwent changes, so that the last of the four is much more like an old-fashioned opera than the first. The suicide of the heroine, by throwing herself (on horseback) on to the burning funeral pyre of her husband, at once reminds us of Auber's Fenella who jumps into the crater of Vesuvius and the Jewess of Jacques Halévy (1799–1862) who jumps into a cauldron of boiling oil; and the final destruction of the palace by fire looks back to *Lodoiska* of Luigi Cherubini (1760–1842), an opera quite often performed in Germany in Wagner's younger days. And Hagen's dive into the overflowing Rhine also has its parallel in various old French operas; Wagner, with his usual eye to grandiose stage effect, merely combined three stock operatic endings in one.

Apart from these relics of an earlier convention, *The Ring* breaks away from all traditional systems, though one can still find alternations of recitative and aria—that is, of passages which are mainly declamatory contrasted with lyrical episodes. Wagnerian music drama professes to follow the free form of the poem, but Wagner was far too good a musician to let his music become chaotic and formless, and he clearly laid out his poems with a view to their musical form. It was for this purpose that he adopted an entirely new metrical system, derived from early medieval German poetry, based on alliteration, and employing very short lines instead of the long rhymed lines which make *Lohengrin* so tedious in general effect. English poetry had made use of alliterative verse in the early 15th century (e.g. *Piers Plowman*), but it does not lend itself easily to modern English, and translations of Wagner have often provoked smiles.

It was a terrible shock to Wagner's early audiences to find that he had abolished not only separate airs and numbers but also practically all choruses and all ensembles. It is only in *The Mastersingers* (1862–67) and *Parsifal* (1877–82) that the chorus has a really important part. What Wagner wanted to get rid of was the conventionality of the old-fashioned chorus, who did nothing but stand in a row and bawl music that sounds like the middle parts of a brass band. In the days of Bellini and Donizetti no chorus singers were expected to read at sight; they learned everything by ear. They were miserably paid and amounted to little more than supers; and it is very noticeable that in all these old operas, French, German, or Italian, the chorus is almost always exclusively male. Women are not kept out altogether, but the amount they have to sing is very small compared with that of the male choruses; and we learn from Weber that in his day it was extremely difficult to obtain women chorus singers at all. When Weber conducted *La Vestale* by Gasparo Spontini (1774–1851) at Dresden, he had to get boys from a church choir school (the very school which Wagner attended as a boy) to take the parts of Vestal virgins.

Living for so many years in exile, away from all contact with the German theater, Wagner became more and more obsessed with the grandeur of his own ideas. In 1861, he had paid a visit to Paris, where he had had the humiliating experience of seeing his *Tannhäuser* hissed off the stage; this was quite enough to set him against France for many years, although in his last days he was very devoutly worshiped by a small group of French admirers, most of them extremely distinguished people. As *The Ring* grew ever larger in his conception, he began to see that this would never be realized unless he could build himself a theater of his own, a place set apart, a shrine of pilgrimage. Thanks to King Ludwig II of Bavaria, who took him under his protection in 1864, the idea of a Festival Theater became a practical possibility. The King's own wish had been to build it at Munich, but Wagner's position in Munich had become impossible in 1865 and he found it necessary to leave that city and go back to Switzerland. Wagner finally decided that his theater should be built at Bayreuth, a little town not very far from Nuremberg, which had formerly been the capital of a diminutive principality. The town authorities welcomed the scheme and the cost of the theater was defrayed mostly by private subscription among Wagner's friends and admirers. It was opened in August 1876, with the first complete performance of *The Ring*.

The Ring has now passed into the stock repertory of every large theater; it can be seen in Paris, London, Milan, or New York every year. But it was a long time before even the German theaters had the courage to undertake so vast a task, and in old days a performance even at Bayreuth was a rare event, and an unforgettable experience. If we see *The Ring* today, we see it just as one among many other operas, probably with the same singers, the same orchestra, and in the same theater—wherever it may happen to be—with its boxes and galleries all around and its invariable mass of gilding all about the proscenium, which even in a darkened house glitters in the light reflected from the desks of the orchestra. At Bayreuth, one was there to hear Wagner and for no other purpose. The theater stood apart from the town, on a hill by itself; before each act began, a group of brass instruments on the terrace sounded a fanfare from the opera. Inside the theater everything was as plain and neutral as possible; there were no galleries at the sides, only rows and rows of gradually rising seats, all facing the stage directly, so that one was hardly conscious of one's neighbors. The orchestra was in a sunken pit, so that the players—and the conductor, too, thank goodness— were completely invisible. There was nothing to see but the stage. The scenic designs of those days were too strictly realistic for modern taste, but they were executed with astonishing skill, and no other theater of that time could approach Bayreuth in stagecraft. Everything combined to take one away from the ordinary world, even from the ordinary world of music; one's whole receptive personality was concentrated on the stage and on the product of Wagner's imagination. Surrender was complete, not only to Wagner's work of art, but to every principle of Wagner's outlook on the relation of art to life.

At the present day there is a considerable feeling of reaction against Wagner and all that he stood for. Music has moved on and life has become filled with all sorts of new distractions. It is perhaps natural that many of us should say we have no time to listen to these slow-moving and interminable histories of primitive Teutonic gods and heroes. *The Ring* has ceased to be a rare experience, and producers take less and less trouble about it. But if you are young, and have never seen it, it may still be one of the great experiences of your life. If you have seen it so often that you are interested only in comparing one singer or conductor with another, or in criticizing divergences from orthodox tradition, then it is time you made up your mind to relegate *The Ring* to the museum of memory, and never go to see it again.

As regards *Tristan* (1857–59) and *The Mastersingers,* most people are inclined to love one and hate the other, whichever it may be; it is a question of personal temperament. *Tristan* is all chromatics, and there are many people who find it "morbid," "decadent" and utterly unbearable; *The Mastersingers* has always been the favorite of those clean-minded English people who want music to be "healthy" above everything. It is a testimony to Wagner's greatness that such criticisms should still be made now that Wagner has been dead over seventy-five years. Surely it would be better to let him pass over to the realm of the classics, and listen to *Tristan* simply as a work of beauty. The same applies to *The Mastersingers*. . . . In Germany this opera has become a national symbol.

In *Parsifal*, his last work, Wagner demanded an even more complete surrender of his audience than ever before, and it was his wish that *Parsifal* should never be performed outside his own theater in Bayreuth. As long as it was protected by copyright law, it did remain the exclusive possession of Bayreuth; but on December 24, 1903, a performance was given at the Metropolitan Opera House, New York. Paris heard it for the first time on January 1, 1914, and the first performance in England followed a month later. In Germany *Parsifal* is generally performed on Good Friday; in former times theaters were always closed on that day, but *Parsifal* is considered as a sufficiently sacred work, and it is sure to fill the house.

An opera which represented on the stage a ceremony that was practically the same thing as the Catholic Mass was naturally the subject of much discussion from the first. Some devout people thought it blasphemous, but the general trend of opinion has been to accept the work in the spirit in which it was supposed to have been written, and to regard it as a solemn confession of faith. Other people, perhaps not much concerned about faith, have felt offended by *Parsifal* as being an insincere exploitation of religion by a man whose whole life had stood for the very opposite of that doctrine of renunciation preached in the opera.

Wagner's literary works, and his interpretations of his own operas, may have been a valuable advertisement for them in his own time, but most people of today will feel that they prefer to think of him as a musician and as little else. The days of Wagnerian controversy are over; the "music of the future" has become the music of the past. We can enjoy *Parsifal* and derive spiritual benefit from it, whether we believe in these things or not, and it is a matter of no artistic moment whether Wagner himself believed in them. There can still be no doubt that *Parsifal*, like *Tristan*, is a work of extraordinary musical beauty; let us surrender to that and concentrate our minds upon it.

His political and philosophical views do not concern us, although he often believed that they were intimately connected with his music. As time passes on, all these things, once matters of acute controversy, become forgotten; they are manifestations of their own period, and the present age is content to leave them to the makers of research dissertations. Poetry and music remain, though we have to recognize that the heat of inspiration dies down, and the music of the romantics is no longer as exciting and overwhelming as it was in its own day.

Apart from the creation of these individual works of art, Wagner, through his writings and through his own personal influence, has converted the musical world, or a good part of it, to something like a new outlook on music in general. It may be that he was mistaken in supposing that the modern world could ever recover the attitude of ancient Greece to the religious aspect of musical drama, but he certainly induced it to take music, and especially opera, far more seriously than it had ever done before. When one looks back over the musical history of his century, and the developments which brought Germany the musical leadership of Europe, it is astonishing to think that opera played so small a part in them. What did Beethoven leave us in opera? One work, and that reserved for veneration rather than full-bloodedly enjoyed. Schubert? A dozen failures, the very existence of which is unknown to the millions who can hum the themes of the *Unfinished Symphony*. Schumann and Mendelssohn made timid experiments; and Brahms had not even the courage for that. Weber is the only name besides Wagner. . . . In the orthodox world of music, Weber was sometimes regarded as not quite on a level with the rest of the great German masters; his symphonies, concertos and sonatas were thought showy rather than profound, and his church music was considered operatic. "Operatic" was in fact always a word of disparagement, almost of moral disapproval; and if Wagner had been an Englishman, he would probably have used it himself in that sense.

The serious musicians of the 19th century turned away from opera as if it was an unclean trade; and there are music lovers who still maintain this point of view. Many hard things have been said about Wagner, and as far as his private life was concerned, he deserved a good many of them; but it could never be said of Wagner that he was not a serious-minded musician. He had faith in himself, and courage, which was what most of his contemporaries, however distinguished, had not. It was mainly owing to the influence of Wagner that a certain standard of artistic integrity has been brought into most of the great opera houses and many of the small ones; we owe to him the spirit of team-work and ensemble, of devotion to the work of art on the part of every single member of the company and staff. That was the spirit of Bayreuth, and from Bayreuth it has spread all over the world.

We owe it to Wagner that the auditorium is darkened as a matter of course during a performance, that the doors are shut and late-comers made to wait outside; we owe it to him that a soft prelude is heard in silence, and applause reserved for the end of an act. It may be replied that there are still many theaters where silence is not maintained, and that there are also many operas still in the repertory which suffer from uncomfortable moments when the applause which the composer expected is so reverently restrained. Nevertheless, the Wagnerian attitude to performance is on the whole an advantage to an opera of any style or period, for it gives us a chance of concentrating our attention on the drama itself.

These points of social observance are trivial compared with the fundamental principle which was at the base of all Wagner's doctrines and labors—that a work of art should be a spiritual experience, and that the summit of such experience could only be attained in the theater, where all the arts were united in this sublime act of worship. There can be no doubt that Bayreuth in the past did bring to many people of various nationalities a spiritual experience such as Wagner envisaged. It is obvious that such experiences can seldom be repeated, and it is hardly credible that any human being can live in a perpetual state of mystical ecstasy, especially in the modern world of practical life. Besides, our sense of humor . . . is always breaking in, and at the most enraptured moments the stage cat is sure to take the footlights. Every individual has to decide for himself whether skepticism or credulity is the preferable state of mind; but anyone who has ever known the complete surrender of the soul to music and drama in the theater will never enter an opera house without at least some faint hope that the experience may be renewed.

Many years passed before the next generation of German composers began to divide Wagner's heritage between them. Imitation Wagner was practicable only for theaters which had adopted the machinery of Bayreuth, and that sort of stage reform was naturally a long and gradual process, corresponding to the rate at which managers and conductors resolved to put *The Ring* on their own stages. The attempts to rival or surpass *The Ring* were none of them successful, and musicians soon realized that new directions must be taken. Wagner himself seemed to point many different ways, and his followers could be grouped in families, according as they pursued the "hearty" style of *The Mastersingers*, the erotics of *Tristan*, the morbid religiosity and exploitation of suffering derived from *Parsifal*, or attempted to scale the monumental heights of *The Ring*.

WAGNER SPEAKS

Can it possibly be doubted that in opera, music has actually been taken as the end, the drama merely as the means? Surely not! The briefest survey of the historic evolution of opera teaches us this quite past disputing; everyone who has busied himself with the account of that development has, simply by his historical research, unwillingly laid bare the truth. Not from the medieval folk plays, in which we find the traces of a natural cooperation of the art of tone with that of drama, did opera arise, but at the luxurious courts of Italy—notably enough, the great lands of European culture in which the drama never developed to any significance—it occurred to certain distinguished persons, who found Palestrina's church music no longer to their liking, to employ the singers engaged to entertain them at their festivals, on singing arias, *i.e.*, folk tunes stripped of their naïveté and truth, to which "texts" thrown together into a semblance of dramatic cohesion were added waywardly as underlay.

The dramatic cantata, whose contents aimed at anything but drama, is the mother of our opera; nay more, it is that opera itself.

The more it developed from this, its point of origin, the more consistently the purely musical aria, the only vestige of remaining form, became the platform for the dexterity of the singer's throat; the more plainly did it become the office of the poet, called in to give a helping hand to their musical diversions, to carpenter a poetic form which should serve for nothing further than to supply the needs both of the singer and of the musical aria with their verse requirements. Metastasio's great fame consisted in this, that he never gave the musician the slightest harass, never advanced an unwonted claim from the purely dramatic standpoint, and was thus the most obedient and obliging servant of the musician.

Has this relation of the poet to the musician altered by one hair's breadth to our present day? To be sure, in one respect: that which according to purely musical canons, is now held to be dramatic, and which certainly differs widely from the old Italian opera. But the chief characteristic of the situation remains unchanged. Today, as one hundred fifty years ago, the poet must take his inspiration from the musician, he must listen for the whims of music, accommodate himself to the musician's bent, choose his stuff by the latter's taste, mold his characters by the timbres and expedient for the purely musical combinations, provide dramatic bases for certain forms of vocal numbers in which the musician may wander at his ease—in short, in his subordination to the musician, he must construct his drama with a single eye to the specifically musical intentions of the composer—or else, if he will not or cannot do all this, he must be content to be looked on as unserviceable for the post of opera librettist. Is this true, or not? I doubt that any can advance one jot of argument against it.

The aim of opera has thus ever been, and still is today, confined to music. Merely so as to afford music with a colorable pretext for her own excursions, is the purposes of drama dragged on—naturally, not to curtail the ends of music, but rather to serve her simply as a means. . . . No one attempts to deny this position of drama toward music, of the poet toward the tone artist; only in view of the uncommon spread and effectiveness of opera, people have believed that they must make friends with a monstrosity, nay, must even credit its unnatural agency with the possibility of doing something

339

altogether new, unheard, and hitherto undreamed: namely, of erecting the genuine drama on the basis of absolute music. . . . By the collaboration of precisely *our* music with dramatic poetry a heretofore undreamed significance not only can but *must* be given to drama.

JOHANNES BRAHMS

1 8 3 3 – 1 8 9 7

JOHANNES BRAHMS was born in Hamburg, Germany, on May 7, 1833. He received music instruction from his father, a double bass player at the Hamburg Opera, Otto Cossel and Eduard Marxsen. At fourteen he made his public debut as pianist, after which he earned his living performing in taverns, teaching the piano, and doing hack work, all the while pursuing serious composition. In 1853 he became the piano accompanist for the Hungarian violinist, Eduard Reményi, with whom he toured Germany. He was now given the opportunity to come into personal contact with such eminent musicians as Joseph Joachim, Liszt, and Robert and Clara Schumann, all of whom were impressed by his gifts. Schumann hailed him in a now historic article in the *Neue Zeitschrift für Musik;* used his influence to get Brahms's three piano sonatas and some songs published; and arranged for Brahms to give a concert in the Gewandhaus in Leipzig. Brahms, in turn, became uniquely devoted to Schumann, and, after the composer's death, to Schumann's widow, Clara.

From 1857 to 1860, Brahms was music master for the Prince of Lippe-Detmold. During this period he completed his first piano concerto, which proved a failure when introduced in Hanover on January 22, 1859. For three years, beginning with 1860, he conducted a women's choir in Hamburg. Two piano quartets which he completed during this interval were first heard in Vienna in 1862, in a performance by the Hellmesberger Quartet, an occasion upon which Joseph Hellmesberger described the young Brahms as "Beethoven's heir."

In 1863, Brahms set his roots in Vienna where he conducted the Vienna *Singakademie,* taught piano, and from 1871 to 1874 directed orchestral concerts of the Gesellschaft der Musikfreunde. Meanwhile, he realized his first major public success with the first complete performance of *A German Requiem* in Bremen, on April 10, 1868. His first significant work for orchestra came in 1873, the *Variations on a Theme by Haydn;* his first symphony, in 1876. With three additional symphonies, between 1887 and 1894, he became the most significant symphonist since Beethoven. One of the foremost creative figures in music of his generation—the foremost living exponent of absolute music—he was honored throughout Europe. In 1877 and 1879 he received honorary doctorates from Cambridge and Breslau Universities; in 1886 he was made Knight of the Prussian *Ordre pour le merité* and elected a member of the Berlin Academy of Arts; in 1889 he was given the honorary freedom of the city of Hamburg; and in 1890, the Order of Leopold was conferred on him by the Austrian Emperor.

Through the years he expressed love for several women—and most of all for Clara Schumann—but he never married. Though comparatively affluent, he lived simply in modest bachelor quarters in Vienna for a quarter of a century, producing masterworks in all forms except the opera. He died in Vienna on April 3, 1897.

THE MAN

KARL GEIRINGER

Brahms had not a firm, self-contained, homogeneous character. A discord, a conflict of opposing forces, pervaded his whole existence. Two powers fought in him, which we may roughly call an "urge to freedom" and "a desire for subjection."

The simplicity that Brahms displayed in all matters of daily life may be regarded as an inheritance from his forefathers. Even when a famous man, he lived in a modest dwelling, dressed with greatest economy, ate in the cheapest restaurants, and took pride in spending little on his food. He had no extravagant tastes, and he devoted only comparatively small sums of money to his passion for collecting original manuscripts by great masters.

Nevertheless, Brahms was anything but a cynic or an ascetic. He loved to eat well and to drink well, and when he was invited to his friends' homes he was easily persuaded to exchange his ordinary plain fare for culinary delights on a higher plane.

Similar in origin was the pedantic love of order which Brahms displayed in everything connected with his work and his intellectual needs. He boasted that he could always instantly lay his hand on those books he valued—for example, the Bible—even in the dark. His manuscripts are covered with rapidly written script, which is, however, clearly and methodically arranged, and even his sketches can easily be deciphered. He was no less orderly in his reading: with him it was a matter of course to correct, with pedantic conscientiousness, every mistake he found in a printed book or music work.

Further, in all questions of money the bourgeois vein is apparent in Brahms. His letters to his publishers show remarkable commercial astuteness, and he insisted on being paid enormous fees for his works.

Most bourgeois of all was his ambition to occupy a permanent post, which would make it possible for him to settle down in his own home. The existence of a wandering virtuoso was abhorrent to him. He dreamed of a position as conductor that would keep him in one place, assure him a secure income, and enable him to marry and found a family. For Brahms this was by no means a vague desire. It took a very definite shape; where he had spent his childhood and youth, where he felt at home, there Brahms wanted to live. Had the fairy godmother of fiction stood before him, promising to fulfil a single wish, the master would not have hesitated for a moment before asking for the conductorship of the Hamburg Philharmonic Orchestra.

But all these traits of Brahms's character were opposed by others, which were directly antithetical, hence the peculiar duality of his character.

Brahms's love of order stopped short at his own person. He was accustomed to wander through the streets of Vienna in garments which were anything but the ideal of bourgeois respectability. His trousers were always pulled up too far, his clothes were hopelessly creased, an enormous safety pin held a plaid in place on his shoulders, and he always carried his hat in his hand instead of on his head. The cupboards containing his clothes and linen were in the most terrible confusion which was a constant source of grief to his landlady, Frau Truxa. His neglectfulness was too confined to superficialities. Brahms never attended to a matter which must have often occupied the mind of one who had from his youth kept his eyes fixed upon death: the drawing up of his will. He left his last will and testament half finished, and in a legally invalid form, although it was practically completed six years before his death. The meticulous love of order in everything that directly or indirectly concerned his art was balanced on the other hand by a definite carelessness and indifference in everyday affairs.

Once he had earned his money, Brahms, oddly enough, was as careless with it as he had been conscientious in its making. He left the management of his considerable fortune to his publisher Simrock, and was not in the least unhappy when his friend had to tell him that he had lost substantial sums belonging to Brahms in some Stock Exchange speculation. He left whole bundles of bank notes lying uncounted in his closet, and hardly ever took the trouble to check on his bank balance.

Brahms attributed his attitude to marriage to external events and especially to the grievous wrong done him at Hamburg. Again and again he declared that he had been unable to marry in his youth because he had not an adequate position and an assured income; but also because the sympathy of a loving wife in his fight against the hostility of the public would have shamed and hindered him far more than it would have strengthened him. This corresponds only to a certain extent with the external facts. For it was not long before Brahms was earning a respectable income, and after the success of his Requiem he was counted among the most highly esteemed German composers of his time. In a deeper sense, however, Brahms's explanation would seem to be justified. For that part of his nature which longed for bondage, a marriage was conceivable only on the basis of a fixed monthly income and the social esteem paid to the holder of a prominent position. The artist in Brahms might have been able to disregard such considerations had there

344

not been, on his side, far greater obstacles to marriage. Yet the composer was anything but a misogynist. He paid tribute to the charms of the fair sex by unconditional worship. And when physical beauty was coupled with intelligence and musical talent—and he was especially fascinated by a beautiful voice—he was only too ready to fall in love. He did so not once only, but again and again in the course of his life. And not only the passionate handsome youth, but also the mature artist, and even the master on the verge of old age, had reason to be confident that his love would be returned. Nevertheless he never formed a permanent connection; he always shrank from the last decisive step. The thought of sacrificing his personal liberty, his freedom from restraint, of adapting himself and surrendering part of his own being for the value of a new and higher unity, was entirely abhorrent to Brahms. Dimly he felt that he would be acting in defiance of his aim in life if he, who had dedicated himself wholly to art, were to belong to another.

We can at all events be sure that the renunciation of marriage was anything but easy for the composer. He had always longed for the comfort of a home, and further, he had ardently wished for children, in whom he hoped to see his own gifts more strongly and purely developed. As this was denied him, he bestowed his affection on the children of others. During his summer holidays Brahms quickly formed friendships with the young people of the village, and even in Italy he scraped up his knowledge of the foreign language in order to converse with the children. A great help in his advances were the sweets which he used to keep in his pockets for any little friend. . . . Brahms felt all the more drawn towards children, for he himself, like many a great artist, had much of the child in his nature. At the age of twenty, just when the blossoming friendship with the Schumanns was growing into an imperishable experience, he asked his mother to send his tin soldiers to Düsseldorf. Even in his last years, when he visited the little prodigy, the violinist Bronislaw Huberman, his attention was so held by the fascinations of a stamp album that the fourteen-year old boy had to spend over an hour initiating him into the secrets of his collection.

Brahms's life shows what an influence the abandonment of his hopes and dreams had on the development of his character. In his youth, Brahms, though modest and shy, was amiable, frank, and enthusiastic. There was a decisive change after his experience with Clara, and the changes became more and more marked after each disappointment in his career or his personal life. Qualities that slumbered in him but had rarely appeared, now came boldly to the fore. When, at the end of the 70's, Brahms hid his smooth and still boyish face behind a thick, full beard he seemed to have become a far different person. The careless inconsiderateness which had distinguished Brahms even as a young man (and had certainly helped him to achieve many of his artistic aims) increased alarmingly, and was often coupled with rudeness. The reputation that Brahms enjoyed in Vienna in this respect may be judged from the widely circulated anecdote to the effect that the master, on leaving a company in which he had found himself for the first time, took his departure with the words, "if there is anybody here whom I have forgotten to insult, I beg him to forgive me."

Thus Brahms clothed himself in an armor of irony and coldness, and this armor was so stout that sometimes even his best friends could not hear the warm heart of their Johannes beating behind it. When, on the other hand, help, sympathy, and advice were needed, no one was so quickly on the spot as the reserved composer. He who for months left letters unanswered forced himself, in the case of a request for help, to respond immediately.

We can thus discern two totally different elements of his character—irony and reserve, coupled with genuine kindness and readiness to help. The relations of those about him to the artist were determined by their ability to penetrate the uncouth shell. At first Brahms generally evoked timidity and embarrassment; a good judge of men, however, soon discovered the secret of his double nature, and those who gained an insight into the master's true character remained loyally attached to him for life.

346

THE COMPOSER

DANIEL GREGORY MASON

Of all the figures of Romantic music, brilliant and varied as they are, impressing one with the many-sidedness and wide scope of the art, there is perhaps only one, that of Johannes Brahms, which conveys the sense of satisfying poise, self-control, and sanity. Others excel him in particular qualities. Grieg is more delicate and intimate, Dvořák warmer and clearer in color; Saint-Saëns is more meteoric, Franck more recondite and subtle, and Tchaikovsky more impassioned; but Brahms alone has Homeric simplicity, the primeval health of the well-balanced man. He excels all his contemporaries in soundness and universality. In an age when many people are uncertain of themselves and the world, victims of a pervasive unrest and disappointment, it is solacing to find so heroic and simple a soul, who finds life acceptable, meets it genially, and utters his joy and his sorrow with the old classic sincerity. He is not blighted by any of the myriad forms of egotism—by sentimentality, by the itch to be effective at all costs, or to be "original," or to be Byronic, or romantic, or unfathomable. He has no "message" for an errant world; no anathema, either profoundly gloomy or insolently clever, to hurl at God. He has rather a deep and broad impersonal love of life; universal joy is the sum and substance of his expression.

It is hard to say whether the unique greatness of Brahms depends more on this emotional wholesomeness and simplicity or on the intellectual breadth and synthetic power with which it is combined. Probably the truth is that greatness requires the interaction of the two. At any rate, Brahms is equally remarkable, whether considered as a man or as a musician, for both. In his personal character frankness, modesty, simple and homely virtue were combined with the widest sympathy, the most far-ranging intelligence, extreme catholicity and tolerance. In music he prized the simplest elements, like the old German folk songs and the Hungarian dances, and the most complex artistic forms that are evolved from them by creative genius. Like Bach and Beethoven, he spanned the whole range of human interests; deep feeling fills his music with primitive expressiveness, and at the same time great intellectual power gives it the utmost scope and complexity. Lacking either trait he would not have been himself, he could not have performed his service to music.

His meeting with Schumann was one of the important events of his life. Probably no young composer ever received such a hearty welcome into the musical world as Schumann extended to Brahms in his famous article, "New Paths." "In sure and unfaltering accents," writes Mr. Hadow, "he proclaimed the advent of a genius in whom the spirit of the age should find its consummation and its fulfillment; a master by whose teaching the broken phrases should grow articulate, and the vague aspirations gather into form and substance. The five-and-twenty years of wandering were over; at last a leader had arisen who should direct the art into 'new paths,' and carry it to a stage nearer to its appointed place." It is not surprising that Schumann, whose generous enthusiasm often led him to praise worthless work, should have received the early compositions of Brahms so cordially. Their qualities were such as to affect profoundly the great romanticist. Although the essential character of his mature works is their classical balance and restraint, these first compositions show an exuberance, a wayward fertility of invention, thoroughly romantic. His first ten opuses, or at any rate the three sonatas (1852–53), and the four ballades for piano (1854), are frequently turgid in emotion, and ill-considered in form. The massive vigor of his later work here appears in the guise of a cyclopean violence. It is small wonder that Schumann, dazzled, delighted, overwhelmed, gave his ardent support to the young man. Brahms now found himself suddenly famous. He was discussed everywhere, his pieces were readily accepted by publishers, and his new compositions were awaited with interest.

But fortunate as all this was for Brahms, it might easily, but for his own good sense and self-control, have turned out the most unfortunate thing to happen to him. For consider his position. He was a brilliant young composer who had been publicly proclaimed by one of the highest musical authorities. He was expected to go on producing works; he was almost under obligation to justify his impressive introduction. Not to do so would be much worse than to remain a nonentity; it would be to become one. And he had meanwhile every internal reason for meeting people's demands. He was full of ideas, conscious of power, under inward as well as outward compulsion to express himself. Yet for all that, he was in reality immature, unformed, and callow. His work, for all its brilliancy, was whimsical and subjective. If he had followed out the path he was on, as any contemporary observer would have expected, he would have become one of the most radical of romanticists. At thirty he would have been a bright star in the musical firmament, at forty he would have been one of several bright stars, at fifty he would have been clever and disappointed. It required rare insight in so young a man, suddenly successful, to realize the danger, rare courage to avert it. When we consider the temptation it must have been to him to continue these easy triumphs, when we imagine the inward enthusiasm of creation with which he must have been on fire, we are ready to appreciate the next event of the drama.

That event was withdrawal from the musical world and the initiation of a long course of the severest study. When he was a little over twenty-one, Brahms imposed upon himself this arduous training, and commanded himself to forego for a while the eloquent but ill-controlled expression hitherto his, in order to acquire a broader, firmer, purer, and stronger style. For four or five years, to borrow Stevenson's expression, he "played the sedulous ape" to Bach and Beethoven, and in a minor degree to Haydn and Mozart. The complex harmonies of his first period gave place to simple, strong successions of triads; for an emotional and often vague type of melody he substituted clearly crystallized, fluent, and gracious phrases, frequently devoid of any particular expression; the whimsical rhythms of the piano sonatas were followed by the square-cut sections of the Serenade, op. 11 (1857). Yet Brahms knew what he was about, and his first large work, the Piano Concerto in D minor, op. 15 (1854–58), shows his individuality of expression entirely regained, and now with immensely increased power and resource.

Nothing could exhibit better than this dissatisfaction with his early work, and withdrawal from the world for study, that intellectual breadth which we have noted as characteristic of Brahms.

He was not a man who could be content with a narrow personal experience. No subjective heaven could satisfy him. His wide human sympathy and his passion for artistic passion alike, compelled him to study unremittingly, to widen his ideals as his powers increased. No fate could seem to him so horrible as that "setting" of the mind which is the aesthetic analogue of selfishness. Originality, which so often degenerates into idiosyncrasy, was much less an object to him than universality, which is after all the best means of being serviceably original. Dr. Deiters, in his reminiscences, after describing this period of study, continues: "Henceforth we find him striving, after moderation, endeavoring to place himself more in touch with the public, and to conquer all subjectiveness. To arrive at perspicuity and precision of invention, clear design and form, careful elaboration and accurate balancing of effect, now became with him essential and established his principles."

From this time until the end of his life, in fact, a period of only a little less than forty years, Brahms never departed from the modes of work and the ideals of attainment he had now set for himself. He labored indefatigably, but with no haste or impatience. He was too painstaking and conscientious a workman to botch his products by hurrying them. Thus laboring always with the same calm persistence, returning upon his ideas until he could present them with perfect clarity, caring little for the indifference or the applause of the public, but much for the approval of his own fastidious taste, he produced year by year an astonishing series of masterpieces.

A just conception of this broad scheme of Brahms's ideal and of his thoroughness in working it out is necessary, we must insist, not only to appreciation of the man himself, but to any true understanding of his relation and service to music. Brahms was enabled, by the tireless training to which he subjected his fertile and many-sided genius, to couch romantic feeling in classic form.

Without that severe training to which Brahms subjected himself in his youth, he would have gone on doing brilliant work of the romantic order, like his first compositions, but he would never have attained the grasp and self-control that raised him above all his contemporaries and that made possible his peculiar service to music. That period of training was the artistic counterpart of what many

350

men undergo when they discover how many sacrifices and how long a labor are necessary to him who would find a spiritual dwelling place on earth. Many pleasures must be renounced before happiness will abide; evil and suffering are opaque save to the steadfast eye. So, in music, effects and eloquences and crises must be the handmaids of orderly beauty, and tones are stubborn material until one has learned by hard work to make them transmit thoughts. Technique is in the musician what character is in the man. It is the power to stamp matter with spirit. Brahms's long apprenticeship was therefore needed in the first place to make him master of his materials; in the second place to teach him the deeper lesson that the part must be subordinated to the whole, or, in musical language, expression to beauty.

He achieved this subordination, however, not by the negative process of suppression, but by conquest and coordination. In his music emotion is not excluded, it is regulated; his work is not a reversion to an earlier and simpler type, it is the gathering and fusing together of fragmentary new elements, resulting in a more complex organism. Thus it is a very superficial view to say that he "went back" to Beethoven. He drew guidance from the same natural laws that had guided Beethoven, but he applied these laws to a material of novel thought and emotion that had come into being after Beethoven. Had he repudiated the new material, even for the reason that he considered it incapable of organization, he would have been a pedant, which is to say a musical Pharisee. One masters by recognizing and using, not by repudiating. And just as a wise man will not become ascetical merely because his passions give him trouble, but will study to find out their true relation to *him* and then keep them in it, so Brahms recognized the wayward beauties of romanticism, and studied how to make them ancillary to that order and fair proportion which is the soul of music.

To this great artistic service he was fitted by both the qualities which have been pointed out above as cooperating to form his unique nature. His deep and simple human feeling, which put him in sympathy with the aims of romanticists and enabled him to grasp their meaning would not have sufficed alone; but fortunately it was associated with an almost unprecedented scope of intellect and power of synthesis. Brahms's assimilative faculty was enormous. Like a fine tree that draws the materials of its beauty through a thousand roots that reach into the distant pockets of earth, he gathered the materials of his perfectly unified and transparent style from all sorts of forgotten nooks and crannies of medieval music. Spitta remarks his use of the old Dorian and Phrygian modes; of complex rhythms that had long fallen into disuse; of those means of thematic development, such as augmentation and diminution, which flourished in the 15th and 16th centuries; of "the basso ostinato with the styles pertaining to it—the passacaglia and the chaconne"; and of the old style of variations, in which the bass rather than the melody is the feature retained. "No musician," Spitta concludes, "was more well read in his art or more constantly disposed to appropriate all that was new, especially all newly discovered treasures of the past. His passion for learning wandered, indeed, into every field, and resulted in a rich and most original culture of mind, for his knowledge was not mere acquirement, but became a living and fruitful thing."

The vitality of his relation with the past is nowhere more strikingly shown than in his indebtedness to the two greatest masters of pure music, Bach and Beethoven. He has gathered up the threads of their dissimilar styles, and knitted them into one solid fabric. The great glory of Bach, as is well known, was his wonderful polyphony. In his work every voice is a melody, everything sings, there is no dead wood, no flaccid filling. Beethoven, on the other hand, turning to new problems, to problems of structure which demanded a new sort of control of key-relationship and the thematic development of single "subjects" or tunes, necessarily paid less attention to the subordinate voices. His style is homophonic or one-voiced rather than polyphonic. The interest centers in one melody and its evolutions, while the others fall into the subordinate position of accompaniment. But Brahms, retaining and extending the complexity of structure, the architectural variety and solidity, that was Beethoven's great achievement, has succeeded in giving new melodic life also to the inner parts, so that the significance and interest of the whole web remind one of Bach. His skill as a contrapuntist is as notable as his command of structure. Thanks to his wonderful power of assimilating methods, of adapting them to the needs of his own expression, so that he remains personal and genuine while becoming universal in scope, he is the true heir and comrade of Bach and Beethoven.

It was, perhaps, inevitable that in his great work of synthesis and formulation he should sometimes be led into dry formalism. One who concerns himself so indefatigably with the technique of construction naturally comes to take a keen joy in the exercise of his skill; and this may easily result, when thought halts, in the fabrication of ingenuities and Chinese puzzles. Some pages of Brahms consist of infinitely dexterous manipulations of meaningless phrases. And though one must guard against assuming that he is dry whenever one does not readily follow him, it certainly must be confessed that sometimes he seems to write merely for the sake of writing. This occasional over-intellectualism, moreover, is unfortunately aggravated by a lack of feeling for the purely sensuous side of music, for clear, rich tone-combination, to which Brahms must plead guilty. His orchestra is often muddy and hoarse, his piano style often shows neglect of the necessities of sonority and cleverness. Dr. William Mason testified that his touch was hard and unsympathetic, and it is rather significant of insensibility or indifference to tone color that his Piano Quintet (1864) was at first written for strings alone, and that the *Variations on a Theme of Haydn* (1873) exist in two forms, one for orchestra and the other for two pianos, neither of which is announced as the original version. There is danger of exaggerating the importance of such facts, however. Austere and somber as Brahms's scoring generally is, it may be held that so it should be in keeping with the musical conception. And if his piano style is novel it is not really unidiomatic or without its own pecular effects.

However extreme we may consider the weakness of sensuous perception, which on the whole cannot be denied in Brahms, it is the only serious flaw in a man equally great on the emotional and the intellectual sides. Very remarkable is the richness and at the same time the balance of Brahms's nature. He recognized early in life that feelings were valuable, not for their mere poignancy, but by their effect on the central spirit; and he labored incessantly to

353

express them with eloquence and yet with control. It is only little men who estimate an emotion by its intensity, and who try to express everything, the hysterical as well as the deliberate, the trivial and mischievous as well as the weighty and the inspiring. They imagine that success in art depends on the number of things they say, that to voice a temperament is to build a character. But great men, though they reject no sincere human feeling, care more to give the right impression than to be exhaustive; and the greatest feel instinctively that the last word of their art must be constructive, positive, upbuilding. Thoreau remarks that the singer can easily move us to tears or laughter, but asks, "Where is he who can communicate a pure morning joy?" It is Brahms's unique greatness among Romantic composers that he was able to infuse his music, in which all personal passion is made accessory to beauty, with this "pure morning joy." His aim in writing is something more than to chronicle subjective feelings, however various or intense. And that is why we have to consider him the greatest composer of his time, even though in particular departments he must take a second place to others. Steadily avoiding all fragmentary, wayward, and distortive expression, using always his consummate mastery of his medium and his sympathetic power of thought to subserve a large and universal utterance, he points the way for a healthy and fruitful development of music.

BRAHMS SPEAKS

There is no real creating without hard work. That which you would call invention, that is to say, a thought, is simply an inspiration from above, for which I am not responsible, which is no merit of mine. Yes, it is a present, a gift, which I ought even to despise until I have made it my own by right of hard work. And there need be no hurry about that either. It is as with the seed corn: it germinates unconsciously and in spite of ourselves. When I, for instance, have found the first phrase of a song, I must shut the book there and then, go for a walk, do some other work, and perhaps not think of it again for months. Nothing, however, is lost. If afterward

354

I approach the subject again, it is sure to have taken shape. I can now really begin to work at it.

· · · · ·

One should not venture to experience sublimer and purer emotions than the public. You can see from my case that if one dreams merely the same dreams as the public and puts them into music, one gets some applause. The eagle soars upwards in loneliness, but rooks flock together. May God grant that my wings grow thoroughly and that I belong at last to the other kind.

· · · · ·

[*Advice to a young composer.*] Let it rest, and keep going back to it and working it over and over again until it is completed as a finished work of art; until there is not a note too much or too little, not a bar you could improve upon. Whether it is beautiful also is an entirely different matter, but perfect it must be. You see I am lazy, but I never cool down over a work once begun until it is perfected, unassailable. One ought never to forget that by actually perfecting one piece one learns more than by beginning or half-finishing ten.

· · · · ·

I must go my way alone and in peace. I have never yet crossed the path of another.

· · · · ·

Once in my life I wish I could know the feeling of happiness that Schubert must have enjoyed when one of his melodies occurred to him.

· · · · ·

You have no idea how it feels to hear behind you the tramp of a giant like Beethoven.

BEDŘICH SMETANA

1 8 2 4 – 1 8 8 4

BIOGRAPHY

BEDŘICH SMETANA, Bohemia's first important nationalist composer, was born in Leitomischl on March 2, 1824. Though as a child he was exceptionally gifted in music, he did not begin formal study until he was nineteen. At that time he went to Prague to study piano and theory with Josef Proksch. Smetana's first post was as music teacher at the household of Count Thun. In 1848, with the help of Liszt, he founded in Prague a successful music school. One year later he married his childhood sweetheart, Katharina Kolař, and in 1850 he was appointed pianist to Ferdinand I, former Emperor of Austria.

Between 1856 and 1861, Smetana lived in Gothenburg, Sweden, where he taught and played the piano, and conducted the Philharmonic Society. There he wrote his first significant orchestral compositions, including the tone poem *Wallensteins Lager*. In 1861 he was back in his native land ready to assume an active part in its newly aroused nationalist movement after Austria had granted political autonomy to Bohemia. One of the consequences of this aroused nationalist feeling was the creation in 1862 of the National Theater in Prague for the presentation of Bohemian folk operas. For this theater Smetana created his first opera, *The Brandenburgers in Bohemia,* introduced on January 5, 1866.

Smetana's second opera came later the same year: his masterwork, *The Bartered Bride,* a comic opera that became the foundation of Bohemian musical nationalism. The first version, in 1866, was a spoken play with songs and dances. But in later revisions all spoken dialogue was replaced by recitatives, and new musical episodes (including two folk dances) were introduced. This definitive version was first given in Prague in 1870 and proved a sensation. It went on from there to conquer the world.

Smetana now assumed a place of first importance in the musical life of his country. He was active as conductor of the National Theater, as a music critic, teacher, and composer. In his compositions he continued to espouse the cause of Bohemian nationalism with numerous operas, the most important being *Dalibor* (1865–67) and *Libuša* (1869–72).

In the early 1870's, Smetana became afflicted with a serious nervous disorder which, in 1874, brought on deafness. Nevertheless, he continued producing important music, not only operas, but also an autobiographical string quartet—*Aus meinem Leben*, or *From My Life*, in 1876—and, between 1874 and 1879 a cycle of six national tone poems for orchestra collectively entitled *My Fatherland* (*Má Vlast*), the most popular of these being *The Moldau* (*Vltava*). The entire cycle received its première in Prague on November 2, 1882.

The severe criticisms encountered by his last opera, *The Devil's War*, in 1882, broke his spirit and precipitated a mental breakdown. In 1883, Smetana went insane and had to be confined to an asylum in Prague, where he died on May 12, 1884.

THE MAN

JOSEF SCHWARZ

Life in Jabkeniče [1876–84] was, as is usual, quiet, without great events. The master worked in his room on his compositions, often singing to himself under his breath—usually from 9:30 till lunch time, in the afternoon from two o'clock to 4:30.

After breakfast, around eight o'clock, and then in the evening, he liked to go out for a walk, swinging a thin cane, either to the game park surrounding the keeper's lodge where the old woods with their several ponds and long-legged deer provided a beautiful picture, or to the heights surrounding Jabkeniče from where there was a beautiful view of the Dobroviče valley in which clean villages framed by gardens nestle picturesquely, and speak eloquently of the fertility of the countryside.

In the park, Smetana enjoyed the sight of the game and various birds and often he would tell us how many huge stags and deer he had seen. He was altogether a great friend of nature.

Sometimes, hardly had he left home, [than] he would return to his room in great haste. In the beginning we could not imagine what had happened until we realized that he had run in to write down some new musical motive which had occurred to him during his walk or in order to add a few lines to his compositions.

He willingly joined in the excursions and amusements of his family, and if there was any dancing, he would smile at the "buffoonery" as he called it. For now, although he himself had been a passionate dancer in his youth, it seemed comic to him not to hear the music and to see the young people dancing around in such a variety of ways.

In the summer he would bathe in the nearby large fishpond in the same park in which the count's swimming pool had been built. In winter, if I was not occupied with business, I would play chess with Smetana. If I played badly, he would smile and sometimes break out into a hearty laugh, but he could also become very angry if I spoiled his plans. On such occasions he would say: "Even Franta can play as well as that," and then I had to take back as many chessmen as he would have me do. Only then did we continue with the game. Sometimes when he had no luck at all, he grew so angry that he swept all the chessmen off the board. But his outbursts of irritability soon passed.

He liked to sit on after supper, and if he was satisfied with his day's work, he would tell us amusingly of his experiences, adventures, thoughts. He always looked forward to his night's sleep for, as he often told us, he dreamed almost every night of the most beautiful landscapes imaginable.

He read the newspapers diligently and wrote down all memorable events in his diary, making shrewd comments the while. These

calendar-diaries of a popular size also did service as account books into which he wrote his receipts and expenditures.

He did not like to see strange guests in the house. But with acquaintances, of whom there were usually enough, he liked to spend the time in lively talk.

THE COMPOSER

KURT PAHLEN

In Bedřich Smetana Czechoslovakia had a bard who succeeded in attuning the richly flowing melodies of his native soil to European Romanticism. His works truly embody the soul of his land, a land which for centuries had been singing and had always been the home of gifted musicians.

The melodies of the Czech people are less melancholy than those of the Poles, less mystical than those of the Russians. In keeping with the landscape, its green hills, its crystal brooks, its fertile lands, and its lovely villages, the country's songs and dances, too, are more pleasant and cheerful, although now and then we may hear one of the nobly mournful airs which seem to be the common property of all Slavs.

Smetana, a simple son of his people, set to music the history, the legends, the joys and sorrows, of his fatherland. He was the composer of one of the finest comic operas in existence, *The Bartered Bride* (1866). In it, he managed to lift the folklike rhythms of the polka to the same artistic level that Chopin had found for the mazurka and Johann Strauss II for the waltz. Unfortunately his serious operas—like *Dalibor* (1865–67) and *Libuša* (1869–72)—are little known in other countries.

He poured forth all his love of home in the grandiose patriotic ode *My Fatherland* (*Má Vlast*), a work consisting of six symphonic poems (1874–79). The first, *Vysěhrad*, is a depiction of the times of Bohemia's ancient kings; the second, and best known, *The Moldau* (or *Vltava*) follows the course of the picturesque stream, gliding past festively decorated villages, listening to the nocturnal song of water sprites, and finally solemnly saluting the old Prague which, witness to a richly colored past, rises from its banks; *Šarka* takes us back to the legendary times of the bards; *From Bohemia's Fields and Groves* is a charming picturization of nature; *Tábor* gives sound to old Hussite motifs from the historical days of the religious wars; and *Blanik* gloriously rounds off the work like a hymn of victory and of faith in the rebirth of the Cezch nation.

A striking contrast to this work is formed by Smetana's beautiful string quartet, *From My Life* (*Aus meinem Leben*), in 1876, a deeply moving picture of the composer's soul. The first movement, in the words of the composer himself, "depicts the love of art in my youth . . . and also a kind of warning of future misfortune." The second movement, the composer adds, recalls "the joyful dance of my youth, when I composed dance music . . . and was known as a passionate lover of dancing." The third movement recollects "the bliss of a first love for the girl who afterward became my faithful wife." The finale describes "the discovery that I could treat the national element in music, and my joy in following this path until the catastrophe overwhelmed me, the beginning of my deafness."

Smetana's life was a sad one. All the more admirable was the energy which made him overcome all difficulties and enabled him unflinchingly to pursue his way. The nationalist tendencies of his early works aroused the suspicion of Austrian authorities who tried to suppress every symptom of Bohemian separatism. Outside of his country, there was but one man who did understand him, he who had a sense for everything that was great: Liszt.

Smetana left his home land and settled in Sweden in 1856. But it seemed as if his spirit continued to be active in his fatherland, for a change was taking place there: the whole people contributed towards the erection of a National Theater in Prague. And Smetana, who had dreamt of such a thing, became its first director. The solemn dedication of the house took place in 1866. But the years of Smetana's happiness were brief. Both the tragedy of Beethoven and that of Schumann befell him. Deaf since 1874, he died in a state of mental derangement in 1884.

Smetana's death, however, did not serve to extinguish the torch of

Bohemian music, as had happened in the case of Polish music when Chopin died.

SMETANA SPEAKS

If anyone ever asked me why I had written some passage or other in a particular way and not otherwise, and went into great detail, I could only say to him that I had to write it that way according to my feelings and my conscience.

. . . . .

My works do not belong to the category of "absolute music" where you can find your way about with the aid of musical signs and a metronome. These aids are not enough for my compositions. All my work has sprung from the inner moods of my soul, and the musician who is to play my work well must have a complete knowledge of it if he is to put the listener in the same frame of mind. It is, of course, quite certain, that this will not always be the case and lack of this may often be responsible for a completely erroneous interpretation of my compositions. And the consequence of this mistake will be that the public's verdict will be unfavorable.

. . . . .

If I now look at my youthful work, I have to say that I did not allow myself any short cuts, and that not even a finished artist would have to be ashamed of such thorough apprentice work. And whoever does not work through all the difficult forms in this way will remain a dilettante to his death.

. . . . .

I hope that if I have not reached the goal I set myself I am at least approaching it. And that goal is to prove that we Bohemians are not mere practising musicians as other nations nickname us, saying that our talent lies in our fingers, but not in our brains, but that we are also endowed with creative force, yes, that we have our own characteristic music.

. . . . .

[The height of original expression is] when it is possible to say after a few bars: this is Mozart—that is Chopin. Of other composers, less original, it is impossible to say as much often even after a hundred bars, indeed sometimes after the entire work. . . . If only one day it were possible to say after a few bars: this is Smetana!

ANTONIN DVOŘÁK

1 8 4 1 - 1 9 0 4

ANTONIN DVOŘÁK—who kept the fires of Bohemian national music burning bright—was born in Mühlhausen on September 8, 1841. When his father sent him to a nearby town to learn the German language in preparation for a business career, the boy took lessons in organ, piano, and viola from a local schoolmaster. Between 1857 and 1859, Dvořák attended the Prague Organ School.

For about a decade, beginning in 1861, Dvořák was the violist in the orchestra of the National Theater in Prague. Its conductor, Smetana, aroused Dvořák's national ardor and first encouraged him to write national music. In 1873, Dvořák became the organist of the St. Adalbert Church. That same year, on March 9, he attracted attention as a composer with *Hymnus.* Two years later one of his symphonies won the Austrian State Prize.

Now devoting more of his energies than heretofore to the writing of national music, he completed a comic opera in a folk idiom, and *Airs from Moravia,* a set of vocal duets. The latter received a prize from the Austrian State Commission, one of whose members was Brahms. Through Brahms's influence, the publishing firm of Simrock commissioned Dvořák in 1878 to write a set of *Slavonic Dances,* for piano four hands. They proved so successful throughout Europe that Simrock had Dvořák orchestrate them; Dvořák wrote a second set of these *Dances* in 1886.

In 1877, Dvořák left his organ post, and began filling invitations as guest conductor with major European symphony orchestras. In 1884 he was acclaimed in London for his performance of his *Stabat Mater.* He returned to England several times during the next few years to direct the premières of several major choral works at leading festivals. In 1891 he received an honorary doctorate from Cambridge.

Between 1892 and 1895 Dvořák served as director of the National Conservatory in New York. He now became deeply impressed with Negro spirituals, and the tribal songs and dances of the American Indian, and started to use some of these techniques and materials for major works. The Negro spiritual inspired his most famous symphony, *From the New World,* successfully introduced in New York on December 15, 1893, as well as the B minor Cello Concerto; with ideas derived from American Indian music he wrote the F major String Quartet, the E-flat Major String Quintet, and the Sonatina in G major for violin and piano.

After returning to Prague in 1895, Dvořák served for a while as professor at the Prague Conservatory, then, from 1901 until his death, as its director. Now the most celebrated musician in Bohemia, he was made life member of the Austrian House of Lords in 1901, the first musician thus honored. Dvořák died in Prague on May 1, 1904, a victim of Bright's disease. His funeral was, by government decree, a national day of mourning.

THE MAN

PAUL STEFAN

In New York Dvořák was surprised to find himself extraordinarily "at home": the life of the times and the cleanliness of the city both pleased him; he felt perfectly at ease with the unexacting democratic ways of Americans. He considered it an exemplary institution which permitted the laboring man to hear at popular prices the same concerts to which the middle class had to pay higher admission. "Why should not the ordinary citizen, hard at work all week, be able to make the acquaintance of Bach and Beethoven?" was the way he put it.

His daily life habits and hobbies remained as much as possible the same. True, his hobbies required much more attention and consumed more time than at home, but they brought him fresh revelations. Chief among these was his passion for locomotives. A locomotive was to him the highest achievement of the human inventive faculty, and he often said that he would give all his symphonies had he been able to invent the locomotive.

In the New York of those days it was not easy to get to the railway stations; they were inconveniently situated and only travelers were allowed on the platforms. There was slight sympathy for locomotive statisticians even when they were famous composers. He used to drive one whole hour to the 155th Street station in order to see the trains for Chicago go thundering by; Dvořák was tremendously impressed by their speed.

The harbor, however, lay close at hand and on sailing days anybody could go board ship. Dvořák did not wait to hear this twice. He fell into the habit of visiting each great vessel that left New York, making a thorough inspection of every feature from bow to stern, interviewing captain, officers and crew until it was sailing time. He remained on the pier until the last minute in order to see the liners with their attendant tugs sheer off into midstream. When he had to be at the Conservatory, he at least made every effort to see them sail.

Twice a week he went down to the docks, twice a week he visited a railway station, and the other two days he went walking in Central Park. Evenings were spent in fascinating speculation as to where a certain ship would be about that time and how many knots she could make. He knew to the day and hour what ships were arriving and departing, and prided himself on being able to address his letters to Bohemia, stating exactly on which ship they would be carried.

For the rest, his love of Nature had to be satisfied with Central Park. There were pigeons, too, in this extraordinary town, though you did not get to know them as well as in Vysoka.

He was always an early riser and persisted in going to bed at an early hour. Social gatherings, theaters, and concerts that interfered with bed time he avoided as much as possible. He and his family took all their meals at a nearby boarding house. Nervous about crossing the street, Dvořák never went for a walk except with a companion, usually Kovařík. In the afternoon, he liked to read the papers in the Café Boulevard on Second Avenue.

At home, in the evenings, he loved to play cards; Kovařík had to learn the game. But when Dvořák had lost several times in succession he would become very angry and toss the cards in the air. He soon got over it when Kovařík would propose to contribute his winnings towards the doll they were going to take home to his youngest daughter in Vysoka.

Dvořák's extreme sensibility was shown by his fear of thunderstorms: he would have all the window shutters closed, and play the piano as loud as he could. At meal times he always had a good appetite, drank a great deal of coffee, and smoked so-called Virginia cigars. . . . He loved window shopping, but always preferred to buy from peddlers and the market people, with whom he would pass the time of the day.

THE COMPOSER

VLADIMIR HELFERT

Antonin Dvořák enriched Bohemian music in several new directions. In him, Bohemian music produced a genius of spontaneous directness. In this he is related to Schubert, with whom he has much in common. Dvořák's wealth of inspiration is surely unique in Bohemian music. He is always full of fresh ideas and effervescent melodies. Such an elemental creative directness may well conceal some dangers under certain circumstances, especially where it becomes necessary to mold inspiration through creative work into a logical design and shape. The work of musical reflection may easily be set aside by his elemental directness. It is certain that this danger is not always absent from Dvořák's work, especially in instances where it is necessary to lead a work up to its logical culmination. The problem becomes most acute in the final movements of his cyclical works—symphonic and chamber music—and in operas. But even in such instances Dvořák knew how to counteract those dangers by means of a wealth of ideas and fascinating tone textures. In this respect, there can be little question but that Dvořák is the most gifted of all Bohemian composers, a typical example of a full-blooded musician.

Through Dvořák, Bohemian music gained in several important respects. In the first place, Dvořák was a man of the common people, natural in view of his humble origin; his music, therefore, has all the vigor and directness of folk music. Secondly, Dvořák had a passionate and lively temperament which had something elemental about it. It was the temperament of the joy and passion of the common man, often somewhat crude, but always spontaneous. Hence the characteristic Dvořák rhythms which never fail to create an immediate interest and impression and which are at their best in his *Slavonic Dances* (1878, 1886).

But this fierce joyousness is not the only trait of Dvořák's music, in which we also find an expression of piety—simple and sincere—such as only a deeply religious person is capable of. From this piety spring the touching Adagios and Lentos of his symphonies and chamber-music works. A new voice is thus introduced into Bohemian music, different from that, say, of Bedřich Smetana. As a true son of late Romanticism, Dvořák showed a keen understanding of the popular Romantic element, reflected in folk ballads and in the beauties of Nature. Such sources provided Dvořák with material enabling him to introduce new typical elements into Bohemian music. Foremost among such compositions are his symphonic poems based on the ballads of Erben (1896)—*The Water-Goblin, The Noonday Witch, The Golden Spinning Wheel,* and *The Wild Dove*—and particularly, the opera *Rusalka* (1900), which gives an excellent impression of the mysterious fairy-tale atmosphere of the forests.

It was also due to Romanticism that Dvořák conceived the idea of writing national Slavic music. Under the influence of Romantic theories regarding folk music, he saw in Russian and Ukranian folk songs a perfect example of native Slavic musical expression, untouched by Western civilization, and consequently purely racial. From these songs he derived many of his melodic and harmonic idioms. His efforts to create a Slavic music are reflected in the *Slavonic Dances* (a parallel to the *Hungarian Dances* of Brahms), and further in his *Slavonic Rhapsodies* in 1878 (this time a parallel to Liszt's *Hungarian Rhapsodies*); in the "dumky" introduced in his chamber-music compositions as separate movements; and finally in his opera, *Dimitrij* (1881–82), whose subject was taken from Russian history, thus supplying him with a suitable opportunity to what he regarded as Slavic music.

His prolific inspiration enabled Dvořák to write a great variety of compositions in which new forms in Bohemian music were exploited, previously avoided by Smetana. This applies in the first place to Dvořák's absolute music, in so far as this term may be used for other than program works. Smetana, raised on the neo-Romantic ideas of Liszt, found his proper sphere of creative activity in opera and symphonic poems, avoiding for the most part absolute music. For this reason he wrote only one symphony, and even this has a definite programmatic content. The same applies to his chamber music. On the other hand, Dvořák—as an intuitive, direct musician who allowed himself to be swept away by his ideas—sought out his proper sphere of activity everywhere his turbulent temperament could find full freedom of expression, as for example in his symphonies and chamber music. Thus Dvořák became the foremost Bohemian symphonic composer, a field in which he could prosper due to his natural gifts at orchestration, a gift which found its roots once again in popular and folk music.

Dvořák's symphonies provide an eloquent illustration of his artistic growth and development, of his gradual emancipation from the influence brought to bear on him (Wagner, Liszt, Schubert, Beethoven, and Smetana). His individuality found full expression in his beautiful Fourth Symphony in G major (1889), and even more so in the highly popular Fifth Symphony in E minor known as *From the New World* (1893). No less valuable is his chamber music, especially his Quartet in F major, known as the *"American"* (1893), the String Quintet in E-flat major (1893), the *Dumky Trio* for piano and strings (1891), and the Piano Quintet in A major (1887).

Dvořák further introduced for the first time the concerto into Bohemian music. His famous Violin Concerto in A minor (1880) and Cello Concerto in B minor (1895) are the foundations upon which rest the Bohemian traditions of instrumental concertos. Another

368

form of music new to Czech music of Dvořák's time is the oratorio. Smetana never wrote any works in this form, since it was foreign to his sense for the dramatic and the pictorial. On the other hand, Dvořák, a man of outstanding piety, found the oratorio a highly suitable medium for self-expression. His *Stabat Mater* (1877), the two secular oratorios, *The Spectre's Bride* (1884) and *St. Ludmilla* (1886), are among the best choral works of this type produced by 19th-century Bohemian music.

There is no doubt that such forms as the symphony, the concerto, the quartet, the quintet, and the oratorio gave Dvořák's genius an ample opportunity to sing his fluent, beautiful melodies, and to give vent to his elemental urges of self-expression. On the other hand, in less proscribed forms—guided not by conventional formulas, rules or procedures but by a poetic idea or a logic dictated in creative reflection—Dvořák was much less successful. This was true of his symphonic poems. Dvořák never could find a true balance between the purely musical logic of a work and the postulates of a program. He knew how to create a suggestive ballad atmosphere on writing his symphonic poems on subjects from Erben's ballads, but from the point of view of structural design he failed to solve the problem of the symphonic poem. Similarly in his operas Dvořák was unable to create a style of his own in the way Smetana had done. His operas are full of high purpose, sound musical values, but they lack uniformity of style. Some are written in the manner of French grand operas: *Dimitrij* and *Armida* (1902–3). Others are in the Wagnerian idiom: *Alfred* (1870), *The King and the Collier* (1871), and *Vanda* (1875). Still others are in the idiom of Smetana: *The Pigheaded Peasants* (1874), *Jakobin* (1887–88), and *The Devil and Kate* (1898–99). His best opera is probably *Rusalka,* a deeply poetic work which is also the most original and stylistically distinctive of his operas. Dvořák's manifold interest in varied forms also led him to write songs, choral music, and piano pieces, in all of which he reveals himself (as elsewhere) to be a master of melody.

Dvořák's life presents the story of a rapid rise to success, and continuous growth of fame and popularity. He was the first Bohemian composer of his age to become famous outside his native land. His music early gained success in Germany, then penetrated into England, and finally to the United States. If we were to attempt to uncover the reason for Dvořák's worldwide success, we might find it in the situation prevailing in European music at the close of the 19th century. Europe was sagging under the crushing weight of Wagner's music dramas. In France, the reaction against Wagner expressed itself in Impressionism, while Germany and England hailed Dvořák—who combined the utmost seriousness of artistic purpose with a spontaneous simplicity of melody—as a fresh and welcome relief from Wagnerism. This does not imply, of course, that Dvořák himself opposed Wagner. He was simply a different kind of composer, and he became a welcome complement to the music of his day, supplying a need strongly and often unconsciously felt by the music world around him.

DVOŘÁK SPEAKS

I am satisfied that the future music of this country [the United States] must be founded upon what are called the Negro melodies. These can be the foundation of a serious and original school of composition, to be developed in the United States. When first I came here I was impressed with this idea, and it has developed into a settled conviction. These beautiful and varied themes are the products of the soil. They are American. They are all the folk songs of America, and your composers must turn to them. All the great musicians have borrowed from the songs of the common people. . . . I have myself gone to the simple, half-forgotten tunes of the Bohemian peasants for hints in my most serious work. Only in this way can a musician express the true sentiment of a people. He gets in touch with the common humanity of a country. In the Negro melodies of America, I discover all that is needed for a great and noble school of music. They are pathetic, tender, passionate, melancholy, solemn, religious, bold, merry, gay, gracious, or what you will. It is music that suits itself to any mood or any purpose. There is nothing in the whole range of composition that cannot find a thematic source here.

· · · · ·

A while ago I suggested that inspiration for a truly national music might be derived from the Negro melodies or Indian chants. I was led to take this view partly by the fact that the so-called plantation songs are indeed the most striking and appealing melodies that have yet been found on this side of the water, but largely by the observation that this seems to be recognized, though often unconsciously, by most Americans. All races have their distinctively national songs, which they at once recognize as their own, even if they have never heard them before. . . .

What songs, then, belong to the American and appeal more strongly to him than any others? What melody could stop him on the street if he were in a strange land and make the home feeling well up within him, no matter how hardened he might be or how wretchedly the tune were played? Their number, to be sure, seems to be limited. The most potent as well as the most beautiful among them, according to my estimation, are certain of the so-called plantation melodies and slave songs, all of which are distinguished by unusual and subtle harmonies, the like of which I have found in no other songs but those of old Scotland and Ireland. The point has been urged that many of these touching songs, like those of Foster, have not been composed by the Negroes themselves, but are the work of white men, while others did not originate on the plantations, but are imported from Africa. It seems to me that this matters but little. . . . The important thing is that the inspiration for such music should come from the right source, and that the music itself should be a true expression of the people's real feelings. To read the right meaning the composer need not necessarily be of the same blood, though that, of course, makes it easier for him. The white composers who wrote the touching Negro songs, which dimmed Thackeray's spectacles so that he exclaimed, "Behold, a vagabond with a corked face and a banjo sings a little song, strikes a wild note, which sets the whole heart thrilling with happy pity!" had a . . . sympathetic comprehension of the deep pathos of slave life. If, as I have been informed they were, these songs were adopted by the Negroes on the plantations, they thus became true Negro songs. Whether the original songs which must have inspired the composers came from Africa or originated on the plantation mattered as little as whether Shakespeare invented his own plots or borrowed them from others. The thing to rejoice over is that such lovely songs exist and are sung at the present day. I, for one, am delighted with them. Just so it matters little whether the inspiration for the coming folk songs of America is derived from the Negro melodies, the songs of the Creoles, the red man's chant, or the plaintive ditties of the homesick German or Norwegian. Undoubtedly the germs for the best in music lie hidden among all the races that are commingled in this great country. The music of the people is like a rare and lovely flower growing amidst encroaching weeds. Thousands pass it, while others trample it under foot, and thus the chances are that it will perish before it is seen by the one discriminating spirit who will prize it above all else. The fact that no one has as yet arisen to make the most of it does not prove that nothing is there.

PETER ILITCH TCHAIKOVSKY

1 8 4 0 - 1 8 9 3

PETER ILITCH TCHAIKOVSKY was born in Votkinsk, Russia, on May 7, 1840. For nine years he attended the School of Jurisprudence in St. Petersburg, after which he worked for three years as clerk in the Ministry of Justice.

His early study of music had been spasmodic and without any demonstrations of unusual talent. In 1861 he resumed music study privately with Nicolas Zaremba. One year after that he resigned from the Ministry to enrol in the newly founded St. Petersburg Conservatory. There he proved a remarkable pupil, and was graduated in 1865 with a silver medal. In 1866 he became professor of harmony in the recently organized Conservatory in Moscow. In this post he applied himself industriously to composition, completed his first symphony, his first opera (*The Voyevode*), and in 1869 the first draft of his earliest masterwork, the orchestral fantasy, *Romeo and Juliet*.

On July 18, 1877, Tchaikovsky married Antonina Miliukova, a young, high-strung and neurotic Conservatory student who had come to him with avowals of adoration. Tchaikovsky did not love her, nevertheless he impulsively embarked upon marriage with her, in all probability to refute (or else to arrest) the mounting rumors about his sexual aberration. This marriage proved a disaster from the outset. Always hyperthyroid, morbid, and misanthropic, Tchaikovsky was now driven to such a state of mental torment by his marital experience that on one occasion he tried to commit suicide. After that he fled to St. Petersburg where his brother, a lawyer, arranged for a legal separation.

While this gruesome experience was sapping his health and

nervous energy, Tchaikovsky entered upon another, and far more beneficial relationship. In 1877, Nadezhda von Meck, a wealthy widow and art patroness, wrote expressing interest in his music and offering to be of financial assistance. Tchaikovsky replied gratefully, setting off a chain reaction of correspondence that continued for thirteen years. During a voluminous exchange of letters, Tchaikovsky confided to Mme. von Meck his most personal feelings, thoughts, and fears, as well as his artistic hopes and aspirations. At times his letters even gave voice to passionate expressions of love. Yet in all those years, Tchaikovsky and Mme. von Meck never met face to face—a stipulation the patroness had set down as a condition for their relationship. The reason for her strange request has never been satisfactorily explained.

Through Mme. von Meck's beneficence, Tchaikovsky was freed of all financial problems. In 1877–78 he traveled extensively throughout Europe, and in 1878 he resigned his post at the Moscow Conservatory to concentrate on composition. He now created a succession of masterworks with which he assumed leadership among the composers of his country and his time. His first ballet, *The Swan Lake*, was seen in Moscow on March 4, 1877. In 1878 came the Fourth Symphony; in 1879, his greatest opera, *Eugene Onegin;* and between 1880 and 1882, the Violin Concerto, the Piano Concerto No. 1, and the *Italian Caprice* and *Overture 1812* for orchestra. In 1884 the Czar conferred on him the Order of St. Vladimir, and in 1888 the government endowed him with a generous life pension.

While traveling in the Caucasus in 1890 he received word from Mme. von Meck that she was suddenly terminating both her correspondence and her subsidy. The reason for her decision was as mysterious and inexplicable as her earlier insistence that they never meet personally. The loss of his dearest friend—and for no apparent reason—was a blow from which Tchaikovsky never fully recovered.

In 1891, Tchaikovsky paid his only visit to the United States, making his debut in New York on May 5. After giving concerts in New York, Baltimore, and Philadelphia, he returned to Russia. In a mood of overwhelming depression he completed his last symphony, the *Pathétique,* whose première he conducted in St. Petersburg on

October 28, 1893. A victim of a cholera epidemic, Tchaikovsky died in St. Petersburg on November 6, 1893.

THE MAN

MME. ANATOL TCHAIKOVSKY

From the year 1882 to his death in 1893 I saw him constantly. He visited us regularly wherever he lived, and he stayed with us for three or four months. During the first three years of my married life, my husband had an appointment in Moscow. Every summer we took a house with Peter Ilitch in the country. In these surroundings, as he himself admitted, he became the "real Petya." He was free. He loved his brother, and he only saw his closest friends. He adored nature and for that reason we always chose a house situated in the beautiful country.

His capacity for labor was astonishing. There was even something pedantic in his manner of organizing his day's work. He rose at eight o'clock. At nine o'clock, after breakfast, he read Russian and foreign papers and wrote letters. His correspondence was enormous, for it was his principle to answer every letter, whether from Russian or other sources. He read all newly published books and reviews and played the piano. This occupied his morning. He dined at one o'clock. Afterward he took long solitary walks in the woods and fields. During these walks he thought out his compositions, making notes in a little book he always carried with him. At half-past four he came back for the tea which he so much adored. At five he retired to his rooms to set work upon the inspiration of his afternoon walk.

His generous nature laid him open to a kind of exploitation he particularly disliked. Young students sought him out hoping for advice and encouragement in the self-chosen career of composer or executant. With all his sensitiveness Tchaikovsky had to choose between kindly insincerity and a frank counsel to look elsewhere for a life's occupation. He had, again and again, to advise his visitors to leave music for some more suitable career. On one occasion kindli-

375

ness and integrity could meet. One interview and audition led him to interrupt the solitude of his late afternoon to proclaim in our presence the great name of Rachmaninoff. "For him," he said, "I predict a great future."

After supper we used to go for a stroll. He would talk with much animation about all kinds of things. He loved to speak of his childhood and early days, of people whom he liked and disliked. His admiration for his mother was almost a cult. Although he had lost her during his boyhood he still could not speak of her without tears coming to his eyes. On the anniversary of her birthday it was his custom to go to church where prayers were offered in her memory.

Neither in town nor in the country did he work during the evening. He played whist or went to theaters and concerts. His favorite pastime was to go mushrooming. This was how he would spend his Sundays in the country. When he found a mushroom he gave vent to his feelings like a child. He could walk for miles and miles in search of them.

He adored strong tea, saying that he could not play his hand at whist without it. I had heard somewhere that if a pinch of soda were added to the teapot the tea would look stronger than Russian tea usually does. I tried this one evening. At first sight he was delighted. He took one or two mouthfuls and then asked me what the concoction was. I did my best to reassure him. The next day I was up to the same trick. At the very moment when I was slipping the soda into the teapot someone sprang out from behind a curtain shouting, "Petya has caught Panya out," and waltzed me furiously around the kitchen.

These exuberant outbursts were nearly always followed by periods of intense depression. He then seemed completely unaware of his surroundings and bcame extremely absent-minded. One autumn day, when it was very cold and windy, he announced his intention of going to the chemist to buy me a pound of apples. To my great astonishment he returned with an enormous load of cotton wool. It appeared that the chemist had asked him whether a pound would be enough. This sufficed to make him forget his commission. He left his umbrella and the apples at the chemist's and was too shy to go and recover them.

376

He suffered to an almost incredible degree from an inferiority complex. He was nearly always dissatisfied with his compositions and thought they won more applause than they deserved. When Peter Ilitch left for America we learned through the press that his success was terrific. He was torn to pieces. He was carried shoulder high. Poetry was written about him. But when he came back he only told us his success was not deserved.

I used to tell him that he tried to conceal his age—actually he was only fifty-two—by lavish expenditure on clothes. And in fact in Paris he ordered far more clothes and hats than I did myself, and he had a special liking for expensive perfumes.

In one of the recent biographies there occurs the statement that Peter Ilitch loved money. This is not true. Certainly he liked to have it at his command, but only that he might be able to give it lavishly, right and left. Even when he was badly off he used to give it to those who still had less. In his days of affluence he was downright extravagant. I judge from my own experience, for he was constantly giving me unnecessary and very expensive presents. At restaurants it was always he who paid. He lent money to anyone who asked and never demanded it back. In his presence nobody was allowed to take out his purse.

Another legend will have it that he was so nervous as to be constantly crying. It is true that he was extremely nervous. Sometimes in the middle of an animated conversation his expression would change completely, a look of suffering would spread over his features and he would relapse into silence. It is possible that he cried when he was alone. He even mentioned it in his diary. But he never gave way in the presence of others, even of those nearest to him. I never saw him cry.

THE COMPOSER

RICHARD ANTHONY LEONARD

To Tchaikovsky must go the palm: He remains the most famous and most popular of all Russian composers. That fact alone is a distinction not easy to ignore, especially in view of the vicissitudes through which this composer's music has passed in the half century and more since his death. There has been no one in music quite like him, and certainly there has been no music with so remarkable a history of fortune and misfortune.

He remains for millions the arch-Russian nationalist, even though during his lifetime his work was disdained by the Five and their followers as too watery, a dilution of Russian and western European styles. The rest of the world took him up with avidity, until in the early decades of the present century the popularity of his music had reached the stages of a public craze. The institution of the all-Tchaikovsky program kept many a symphony orchestra out of the red, and many a conductor enjoyed an easy ride to fame on this composer's last three symphonies, his concertos, and his overtures.

Tchaikovsky, it is now quite evident, belonged among the most extreme manifestations of Romanticism in music, and when the entire movement threatened to collapse in the years following World War I, it seemed that his work might be buried forever under the ruins. By 1925, a large section of the public was utterly fed up with him, a natural result of an orgy of overplaying. Critics who had long preached against his excesses and his weaknesses redoubled their efforts, until it became a rare thing for anyone to say a good word for Tchaikovsky. There arose a new generation of modernist composers to whom sentiment and romance were so much mildew of an old age best forgotten, and for them the once-omnipotent Russian was an object only for ridicule. It seemed for a time that nothing was left for Tchaikovsky's music but to prepare the mortuary inscriptions.

Few of his detractors had reckoned with either the vitality of the man's music or the extent of the public's affection for the remnants of Romanticism itself. Romanticism may be dying, but it is not yet dead. Today the people have returned to Tchaikovsky; their regard for him is a sobered and more temperate one, it is true, but with all his faults they love him still. An accolade of a sort has even been accorded him by the special geniuses of Tin Pan Alley, who have made themselves several fortunes by vulgarizing some of his best-known melodies into popular songs. Thus the wheel turns full circle:

the work of a composer who freely availed himself of folk melodies is returned again to the mass of the people.

. . . . .

One of the first products of Tchaikovsky's early years in Moscow was his first symphony (1866). This was followed in 1872 by a second, and in 1875 by a third. The fate of these three works is unusual, considering the eminence which Tchaikovsky's music once attained. During the height of the Tchaikovsky craze, when his last three symphonies were played repeatedly all over the world, these first three were almost totally ignored. It began to seem as if they could not possibly be as bad as conductors implied by steadfastly refusing to exhume them. In recent years they have been brought to light, with isolated performances and on phonograph records. It transpires that they are not bad works at all, but what defeats them even more than lack of finished workmanship, is an absence of sustained melodic interest. Melody, as we now know, was Tchaikovsky's greatest single asset. It is interesting to note that in these early works—not only in the symphonies but in the operas and the piano pieces—he had not yet struck the vein of melodic gold which was to feed all the famous works of his maturity like ore from a bonanza.

The first work in which the composer definitely hit his stride came when he was twenty-nine years old. It was the overture-fantasy, *Romeo and Juliet* (1869)—one of the finest works in his entire catalogue. *Romeo and Juliet* is a score of passionate intensity, rich in melody, full of gorgeous harmonies, and making full use of the most glamorous orchestral sound. His colors are all purple and gold and crimson, the shadows are deep and dramatic, the highlights brilliant. In *Romeo and Juliet* we come upon one of the first of the famous melodies which have since sung their way around the world—the dark, richly ornate theme for English horn and muted violins. It is followed by another even finer—a theme of exquisite tenderness, scarcely breathed by the muted strings. Lawrence Gilman wrote, "Here Tchaikovsky outdid himself, here for a moment he captured the very hue and accent of Shakespearean loveliness." Not all of *Romeo and Juliet* achieves this inspirational level. There are sections representing the conflict between the Montagues and the Capulets which skirt close to bombast and mere noise, a failing which was to become unfortunately common with this composer. But on the whole the piece is one of the most successful of the tone-poem type. It is a work of musical cohesion, in which some fine romantic melodies are bound together with dramatic emphasis.

Five years elapsed before Tchaikovsky produced another large-scale work of similar caliber. Meanwhile he was hard at work—on several operas, various short piano pieces, two string quartets, his second symphony—and though many of these were adding to his reputation in Russia and abroad, the yield in comparison with his later efforts was not a rich one. In the first string quartet in D major (1871) another famous melody was born. Tchaikovsky made use of a folk tune which he heard from the lips of a carpenter working in his house. It appears in the movement marked Andante cantabile, which became one of his most successful advertisements as a composer of lush melodies, richly harmonized, gilded with sentiment and melancholy. Like certain less important works of Chopin, it has been played until it is now unbearable to many listeners. This is unfortunate, for despite its sentimentality it has the essential core of real melodic beauty.

Tchaikovsky was thirty-four years old when he composed his Piano Concerto in B-flat minor (1874–75). The style is derived, of course, from the piano concertos of Franz Liszt. The Russian simply took all the Hungarian wizard's tricks and went him one better. The soloist performs prodigies of dexterity and strength; at times the piano and the orchestra are antagonists in a roaring war, and on the next page they are lovers sighing out their hearts in close embrace. The whole piece is dramatically constructed to shock an audience to attention by a magnificently imposing opening and to keep them on an emotional edge to the last note of a frantic finale. The popularity of this concerto has been enormous, and even today after more than half a century of battle it retains its vitality to an astonishing degree. That it is bombastic and at times even meretricious is beyond question, and Tchaikovsky's failing for saying unimportant things in the grand manner is often perfectly exemplified. But again, he redeems himself by sheer force of his melodic material. His are seldom great themes in the noble sense that those of a Beethoven or a Brahms are, but they certainly have staying power.

The B-flat minor Piano Concerto spread the name of Tchaikovsky far and wide until western Europe and America became aware of a new phenomenon in music. Tchaikovsky had gotten the jump on the Five, and it was years before they caught up with him. One of the chief reasons for his popularity outside his native country was the fact that his music was Russian, but not too Russian. It was soon observed that he was eclectic in his procedures, and that he refused to subscribe to the dogmas of the Five in maintaining a strict nationalism. He mixed his Russian brew with a blend of German and even Italian ideas, and as a result of his compromise he gained a worldwide acceptance which was at first denied the others. His was the popularity of one who simplifies and conventionalizes a new and somewhat recondite movement to make it more immediately understandable to the general public.

. . . . .

The year 1877 had more significance in Tchaikovsky's life than the nightmare marriage. In the midst of this turmoil he had been at work on two major projects, the opera *Eugene Onegin* and his Fourth Symphony. The latter was the more enduring work. It was in fact the first of his three famous symphonies which were to form a crescendo of popularity, interest, and importance, as well as the inspirational climax of his entire career.

The Fourth Symphony in F minor is not one of Tchaikovsky's more nearly perfect scores, but it is surely one of his most effective. The opening bars are famous—a blaring of wind instruments, stirring and portentious, which seems to presage events of great moment. The movement which unfolds at length thereafter is melodious, colorful, and highly theatrical. Tchaikovsky himself described his "inner program" for this symphony in a letter to Mme. von Meck. The introductory fanfare, he said, represented the Fatum, "the inexorable force that prevents our hopes of happiness from being realized. . . . Despair and discontent grow stronger and sharper. Would it not be wiser to turn from reality and sink into dreams?"

The varying moods of this first movement are thus an alternation, as in life itself, between "hard reality and evanescent dreams."

The three remaining movements are less convincingly explained by the composer, but the truth is that his whole program is unnecessary. Musically the slow movement is a disappointment. There is a fine lyrical first theme, but the second is weak and repetitious. Depth and dignity, two requisites for a symphonic slow movement, are lacking. The third movement, on the other hand, is an instrumental *tour de force* which has delighted audiences from its first hearing. The movement is made up of three contrasting orchestral colors—strings (pizzicato throughout), woodwind, and brass. Each group plays separately until the end, when they are joined. The themes are not in themselves exceptional, but the scoring throughout is original and charming. The finale is a whirlwind of melodrama. At the height of the battle's fury the brasses interrupt with the ringing fanfare of the introduction. It is a moment of great dramatic effectiveness. Unfortunately, Tchaikovsky's surrounding melodic material is commonplace, unequal to the splendor and vigor of his bold design.

It was Tchaikovsky's lifelong ambition to write a successful opera and there was hardly a time when he was not occupied with some phase of the task. He finished eight operas in all, beginning with the abortive *Voyevode* in 1868 and ending with *Iolanthe* in 1891. Most of them represent only a huge waste of creative effort. Tchaikovsky's trouble was a common one. Whatever gifts he had for the musical side of the task were canceled out by his ignorance of dramaturgy. His pieces were usually all melody and no drama. As a result his efforts in this field caused him some of his worst embarrassments. Several were dismal failures; others enjoyed only a *succès d'estime*. All died quickly, with the exception of *Eugene Onegin* and *Pique Dame* (1890), which were real successes during the composer's lifetime. *Onegin* was especially a favorite both in Russia and abroad. Today both these operas have begun to wilt, although they get occasional performances outside of Russia. They are kept alive now by a few isolated excerpts of lyric beauty.

. . . . .

The years following Tchaikovsky's marriage and the creation of the Fourth Symphony were transitional, both in his life and in his art. He had achieved a technical assurance and a fluency of invention, but he knew that his inspiration had receded rather than advanced since the Fourth Symphony. The works of this period are seldom distinguished. The only exception is the Violin Concerto, which was written in Switzerland in 1878, immediately after the breakup of his marriage. The Concerto became one of the most popular works ever written for the violin. It was a typical work of the later 19th century, a period in which the repertory of the violin was degraded almost beyond recovery by sentimentality and display. That Tchaikovsky's Concerto could succeed in spite of its lopsidedness and its lack of formal beauty is both a tribute to the vitality of his melodies and an indictment of the entire trend of violin composition during a period of a hundred years.

In 1887 an event occurred which changed the later course of Tchaikovsky's life. He was finally persuaded to conduct a performance of one of his operas. The conducting experience of years before had seared his soul, and he undertook the task, suffering agonies of nervousness. To his astonishment he was able to acquit himself so creditably that he received an ovation from the audience. As a result, he made a tour of western Europe, conducting various noted orchestras in performances of his own works. Thereafter he made several international tours, one of which took him to America.

Shortly after his return to Russia from the first international tour, Tchaikovsky set to work on his Fifth Symphony in E minor (1888). The work is another laboratory specimen of the composer's mature style—which means a mixture of his virtues and faults in unexplainable juxtaposition. It has lyric richness almost to excess; it has brilliance, variety of mood, tremendous passion. It has also the composer's characteristic melancholia, at times so deep that it can be sopped up; and there is much of the throbbing rhythms which so befit his moods of desperate sadness. There is an orchestration of clarity, color, and resounding power; and finally, like pieces of glass set in a diadem, there are some classic examples of bad taste.

The symphony makes a good beginning, as Tchaikovsky so often does in his first movements. This one may be a patchwork of themes

383

instead of a logical piece of sonata construction, but it has melodic interest, well sustained. The motto theme with which the work begins is radically different from the Fatum of the Fourth Symphony, being not a brassy fanfare, but a soft, gloomily intoned melody for the clarinet. It runs through the whole symphony in various guises, becoming in the last movement the main declamation point of the entire work. The second movement presents another celebrated Tchaikovsky melody. It is given at first to the solo horn and is later entwined with an obbligato by the oboe. The movement is remindful of a Chopin nocturne, extended and intensified with all the swelling passions and colors of the great orchestra. It misses being one of the supreme nocturnes, for its chief blemish is two convulsive interruptions by the motto theme which are noisy and tasteless. The third movement is marked Waltz, and for this the composer has been doubly damned. The purists have said that a waltz has no place whatever in a symphony, and anyway this is not a real waltz at all. They may be right on both counts, but not many listeners would sacrifice this particular movement. It is unpretentious, melodious, and charming; and it serves to relieve the emotional tension of the surrounding movements.

It is hard to forgive Tchaikovsky for the last movement of the Fifth Symphony. Of all his lapses in taste and aesthetic judgment this blotch is very likely the worst. His purpose was to end his symphony with a resounding triumphal finale; his method in part was to take the gloomy motto theme, turn it from minor to major, and proclaim it to the skies. It so happens that this is one of the hardest tests to which a composer may subject a theme—to have it sung *fortissimo* by the brass. Better themes than Tchaikovsky's have failed under this ordeal. Here the record is lamentable. The tune takes on neither dignity nor beauty, only the banal trumpery of an operatic march by Meyerbeer. The entire movement degenerates into an orgy of noise and triviality.

·   ·   ·   ·   ·

With the Fifth Symphony out of the way, Tchaikovsky went on another international tour early in 1889. All over the Continent and in England he was received with acclaim, but he was homesick and depressed the entire time. During the next year he composed one of his most successful operas, *Pique Dame (The Queen of Spades)*, which created a sensation at its première in St. Petersburg. During the summer of 1891 he settled down in Russia to work on an opera and a ballet which had been commissioned by the Imperial Opera in St. Petersburg. The opera was *Iolanthe*, his last, and a failure. The ballet was one of his most treasured scores, the incomparable *Nutcracker* (1891–92). The suite which was drawn from this score has been deluged with performances for many years, so enormous has been its popularity.

Tchaikovsky had already written two ballets, *The Swan Lake* (1875–76) and *The Sleeping Beauty*, (1888–89), both melodious though not consistent scores. The *Nutcracker* music is much superior and is one of the best pieces of musical fantasy in existence. In a flash Tchaikovsky revealed a lightness of touch, a feeling for decoration and a sense of humor that would hardly be suspected of the writer of the big, gloom-ridden symphonies. Let no one imagine that because the music is "light" it is also easy. There is more melodic invention, more orchestral craftsmanship in these dainty miniatures than in many a symphonic movement. They are as charming and often as subtle as exquisitely made toys.

The last two years of Tchaikovsky's life were an odyssey of utter despair. In the autumn of 1892, the composer began to work on a new symphony. Before it was finished he lost interest, decided it was empty of inspiration, and destroyed the whole thing. Then late in the year, on the way to Paris, he began thinking about another symphony. "This time," he wrote, "a symphony with a program, but a program that will remain an enigma to all. Let them guess for themselves. . . . Often while composing it in my mind during the journey, I shed tears." This was the genesis of Tchaikovsky's Sixth Symphony in B minor (1893), the composer's masterpiece, and one of the most celebrated works in symphonic literature.

To this day no one knows what enigmatic program lies hidden under the notes of this score. Tchaikovsky had thought at first of calling it simply "A Program Symphony," but on the morning after its first performance he seized the suggestion of his brother, Modest, and called it *Pathetic* (*Pathétique*). Beyond that now famous title we know nothing.

In form the work is totally unorthodox. The first movement is almost as long as two full movements, the second is cast up in a curious waltz-like 5/4 rhythm, the third is a Scherzo which winds up like a finale, while the slow movement is placed at the end of the work. Schumann's remark about Chopin's B-flat minor Sonata might very well apply here: the composer "bound together four of his maddest children." Similarly what holds the four movements together is not a matter of technical device, or even of musical style; rather, it is a prevailing mood. The *Pathetic Symphony* is what its name indicates—an essay in pathos. Even the barbaric clamors of the third movement are an exultation that hides but does not obliterate a substratum of morbidity; it is a wild and desperate irony in the face of terrible grief.

The first movement has been called a "convulsion of the soul." It does not matter that the composer came not much closer than usual to the structure and organic growth of the true sonata form. He makes up for lack of strict form with emotional force. The development, with its long pedal point of the timpani on the low F sharp, the tortured writhing of the strings above and the relentless downward tread of the trombones, is like a descent into the inferno—and one of the most gripping pages in Romantic music. Tchaikovsky gave himself a huge span to fill in this long movement, but for once his melodic ideas have the breadth and the dignity to encompass it.

The second movement was long a novelty because of its unusual 5/4 rhythm. The graciousness, the felicity of the chief theme do not prevail. It is joined to a second theme poignant with repressed sorrow. The movement is interesting despite repetitiousness. The third movement, *Allegro molto vivace,* begins like a conventional Scherzo, but before long the racing, swirling figures have developed into headlong flight, likened to the sweep of Tartar hordes across the steppes. The furious energy, the Slavic violence of this music was hardly paralleled before Tchaikovsky's time.

The stunning climax at the end of the third movement would have meant the end of any conventional symphony; but Tchaikovsky, displaying the artistic growth that is one of the attributes of genius, had come to understand the emptiness of that kind of ending for a symphony which began as this one did. He rounded off this work with an *Adagio lamentoso*, an elegy which belongs with the noblest expressions of human grief.

That the composer was contemplating death in this closing effort of his life is almost certain. He found it intolerable; he protested and struggled against it with all the creative strength he could summon. Bruised and tormented by life, he was yet terrified and revolted by this iniquitous end of all man's striving. It is "death alone that can suddenly make man to know himself," said Raleigh. Tchaikovsky proved those words in his poignant *Adagio*. He came suddenly to know himself—a great artist whose powers had come at last to their flood. He had time for this single effort in which, for once, his grasp did not exceed his reach. After that, there was left only the indisputable truth of Raleigh's words: "O eloquent, just, and mightie Death! . . . . Thou hast drawne together all the farre stretchèd greatnesse, all the pride, crueltie, and ambition of man, and covered it all over with these two narrow words, *Hic jacet!*"

TCHAIKOVSKY SPEAKS

You want to know my methods of composing? It is very difficult to give a satisfactory answer to your question, because the circumstances under which a new work comes into the world vary considerably in each case. (1) Works which I compose on my own initiative—that is to say, from an invincible inward impulse. (2) Works which are inspired by external circumstances; the wish of a friend, or publisher, or commissioned works.

Here I should add that experience has taught me that the intrinsic value of a work has nothing to do with its place in one or the other of these categories. It frequently happens that a composition which owes its existence to external influences proves very successful, while one that proceeds entirely from my own initiative may, for

387

various indirect reasons, turn out far less well. These indirect circumstances, upon which depends the mood in which a work is written, are of the greatest importance. During the actual time of creative activity, complete quiet is absolutely necessary to the artist. In this sense every work of art, even a musical composition, is objective. Those who imagine that a creative artist can—through the medium of his art—express his feelings at the moment when he is moved, make the greatest mistake. Emotions—sad or joyful—can only be expressed retrospectively, so to speak. Without any special reason for rejoicing, I may be moved by the most cheerful creative mood, and vice versa, a work composed in the happiest surroundings may be touched with dark and gloomy colors. In a word, an artist lives a double life: an everyday human life and an artistic life, and the two do not always go hand in hand.

In any case, it is absolutely necessary for a composer to shake off all the cares of daily existence, at least for a time, and give himself up entirely to his art life. Works belonging to the first category do not require the least effort of will. It is only necessary to obey our inward promptings, and if our material life does not crush our artistic life under its weight of depressing circumstances, the work progresses with inconceivable rapidity. Everything else is forgotten, the soul throbs with an incomprehensible and indescribable excitement, so that, almost before we can follow this swift flight of inspiration, time passes literally unreckoned and unobserved.

There is something somnambulistic about this condition. *On ne s'entend pas vivre.* It is impossible to describe such moments. Everything that flows from one's pen, or merely passes through one's brain (for such moments often come at a time when writing is an impossibility) under these circumstances is invariably good, and if no external obstacle comes to hinder the creative flow, the result will be an artist's best and most perfect work. Unfortunately such external hindrances are inevitable. A duty has to be performed, dinner is announced, a letter arrives, and so on. This is the reason why there exist so few compositions which are of equal quality throughout. Hence the joints, patches, inequalities and discrepancies.

For the works in my second category, it is necessary to get into the mood. To do so, we are often obliged to fight indolence and

388

disinclination. Besides this, there are many other fortuitous circumstances. Sometimes the victory is easily gained. At other times
inspiration eludes us, and cannot be recaptured. I consider it, however, the duty of an artist not to be conquered by circumstances.
He must now wait. Inspiration is a guest who does not care to visit
those who are indolent.

. . . . .

What has been set down in a moment of ardor must be critically
examined, improved, extended, or condensed, as the form requires.
Sometimes one must do oneself violence, must sternly and pitilessly
take part against oneself, before one can mercilessly erase things
thought out with love and enthusiasm. I cannot complain of poverty
and imagination, or lack of inventive power; but on the other hand,
I have always suffered from my want of skill in the management of
form. Only after strenuous labor have I at last succeeded in making
the form of my compositions correspond more or less with their
contents. Formerly I was careless and did not give sufficient attention to the critical overhauling of my sketches. Consequently, my
"seams" showed; there was no organic union between my individual
episodes. This was a very serious defect, and I only improved gradually as time went on; but the form of my works will never be
exemplary, because although I can modify, I cannot radically alter
the essential qualities of my musical temperament.

. . . . .

I never compose in the abstract; that is to say, the musical thought
never appears otherwise than in a suitable external form. In this
way I invent the musical idea and the instrumentation simultaneously. Thus I thought out the Scherzo of our Symphony [Fourth
Symphony] at the moment of its composition—exactly as you heard
it. It is inconceivable except as pizzicato. Were it played with the
bow, it would lose all its charm and be a mere body without a soul.

As regards the Russian element in my works, I may tell you that
not infrequently I begin a composition with the intention of introducing some folk melody into it. Sometimes it comes of its own
accord, unbidden (as in the finale of our symphony). As to this

national element in my work, its affinity with the folk songs in some of my melodies and harmonies comes from my having spent my childhood in the country, and, from my earliest years, having been impregnated with the characteristic beauty of our Russian folk music. I am passionately fond of the national element in all its varied expressions. In a word, I am Russian in the fullest sense of the word.

MODEST MUSSORGSKY

1 8 3 9 – 1 8 9 1

Modest Petrovitch Mussorgsky was born in Karevo, Russia, on March 21, 1839. Planning a military career, he attended the Cadet School of the Imperial Guard and in 1856 became an officer. One year later, two prominent Russian composers—Alexander Dargomyzhsky (1813–69) and Mily Balakirev (1837–1910)—stimulated his interest in music. As Balakirev's pupil, Mussorgsky completed his first orchestral work, a Scherzo, introduced in St. Petersburg in 1860. Mussorgsky now joined with Balakirev, Rimsky-Korsakov, César Cui (1835–1918), and Alexander Borodin (1833–87) in a school of national composers henceforth identified as "The Russian Five" or "The Mighty Five." Following principles and aesthetics first established by Michael Glinka (1804–57) in two remarkable national operas, *A Life for the Czar* and *Ruslan and Ludmila,* the "Russian Five" dedicated itself to the creation of music freed of French and German influences: a Russian art inspired by native backgrounds, culture, and history, and deeply rooted in the styles and idioms of Russian folk songs, dances, and church music. Thus the first significant nationalist movement in music history was launched.

When serfdom was abolished in Russia in 1861, Mussorgsky lost his property and had to find a job. From 1863 to 1867 he was a clerk in the Ministry of Communications. Composition, however, was not neglected. In 1864 he finished the first act of *The Marriage;* between 1864 and 1865 he wrote his first song masterpieces; in 1866 came *A Night on Bald Mountain,* his first important work for orchestra. He was back in government service in 1869, in the department of forestry and remained there eleven years. In that time he completed

391

his crowning masterwork, the Russian folk opera *Boris Godunov*, first performed in St. Petersburg on February 8, 1874.

A drastic deterioration in his physical and mental health had begun to manifest itself by 1865. As the years passed he suffered increasingly from nervous disorders and melancholia. He became a helpless victim of alcoholism and often moved in the most disreputable company. Nevertheless, he did manage to produce some extraordinary music: the song cycles *Sunless* and *Songs and Dances of Death;* the suite for piano, *Pictures at an Exhibition;* and two operas, *Khovanchina* and *The Fair at Sorochinsk,* neither one of which he finished.

Mussorgsky died of an apoplectic stroke in St. Petersburg on March 28, 1881. After his death, his scores were revised by Rimsky-Korsakov to remove technical imperfections and awkwardness in harmony and orchestration. It was in Rimsky-Korsakov's editions that Mussorgsky's music first became known outside Russia.

THE MAN

NICOLAS SLONIMSKY

The image of Mussorgsky is fixed indelibly in our minds by Repin's famous portrait painted a few weeks before Mussorgsky's death: a heavy body, a bull's neck, a bulbous nose, an untrimmed beard coalescing with a moustache, a full head of unkempt hair. The large round eyes are averted and focused on some distant point. Mussorgsky is shown wearing an embroidered Russian shirt with a loose-fitting lounging robe over it. This robe was given to Mussorgsky especially for the portrait-sitting by César Cui; it was not uncommon for Mussorgsky's friends to lend him clothes to wear or buy second-hand suits for him when his own wearing apparel became too shabby.

Mussorgsky suffered from chronic alcoholism, which undermined his health and disrupted his work. Borodin wrote to his wife in 1873 about the thirty-four year old Mussorgsky: "He has begun to drink heavily. Almost every day he holds a session at the Maloyaroslavetz on Morskaya Street, and drinks himself to the point of total inebriation. What a pity! Why should a talented person like Mussorgsky debase himself so? Sometimes he vanishes from sight altogether, and when he reappears, he is sullen and uncommunicative, which is unusual for him. But after a while, he pulls himself together, and becomes his real self—genial, gay, friendly, witty. What a pity!"

Despite intense suffering and the most horrifying attacks of delirium tremens, Mussorgsky refused to stop drinking and managed to smuggle a bottle of wine even in the hospital during his last days of life. His end was remarkably similar to the scene of the death of Stepan Verkhovensky in Dostoyevsky's novel, *The Possessed:* The same exaltation of spirit, the same unconcern about death, the same rambling euphoria. Both Mussorgsky and the fictional Verkhovensky represented the same type of talented but disorganized Russians of the period.

Yet Mussorgsky possessed in his younger days all the graces necessary for social advancement. He was a good dancer. He spoke excellent French, the language of Russian aristocracy. He was convivial and had many friends. What was the fault in his character that drove him to ruin? As a youth he complained to Balakirev that his habit of self-abuse was driving him to nervous prostration. He idolized women, but his feminine associations seem to have been platonic. During the last year of his life he lived in the house of the contralto singer Leonova with whom he made a concert tour in Southern Russian as her accompanist. He enjoyed her company, but she was ten years older than he, and had a lover, a shady individual, who apparently exploited her.

Mussorgsky was perpetually in need of money. Yet he was not a pauper. He had some income from a family estate, and he earned a salary as a government clerk. But in his finances, as in his working habits, he was *bezalaberny,* a colorful Russian adjective which he applied to himself, and which connotes a complex of disorderly traits —inability to work methodically, habitual tardiness, procrastination, and plain irresponsibility. He was systematically delinquent in paying the meager rent for his lodgings in a furnished apartment in St. Petersburg, until one night, returning late, he found the door to his room locked and his suitcase with his belongings in the hall outside.

He picked it up and distractedly trudged along the embankment of the Neva River, his pocket empty, his mind vacant. In the early hours of the morning, he knocked at the door of one of his friends, Naoumov, who received him with characteristic Russian hospitality, and lodged him in his house for several years.

To the ravages of alcohol, there was added Mussorgsky's obsessive smoking habit. He was constantly beset by bronchial ailments, and his voice was hoarse much of the time. Yet, such was his enormous vitality that upon occasion he could entertain his friends by singing in a dramatic voice of great power, accompanying himself at the piano—and he was an excellent pianist.

Symptomatically, Mussorgsky's moods varied between humility and defiance. He launched the slogan "To the New Shores" out of his deep conviction that he was destined to initiate a new art of dramatic expression. He was enraged by Cui's contemptuous criticism of *Boris Godunov*, in which Mussorgsky was charged with "indiscriminate, self-satisfied, hasty scribbling of notes, the method that has led to such deplorable results in the works of Messrs. Rubinstein and Tchaikovsky." He wrote to Stassov in white heat: "This mad assault, this brazen falsehood makes me blind with rage. I can't see anything in front of me, as though a quantity of soap water were spread in the air obscuring the objects in the room."

In 1878, in a letter to Stassov, Balakirev reported a welcome change in Mussorgsky's manner: "I was pleasantly surprised by Mussorgsky. No trace of self-aggrandizement or self-adulation. Quite to the contrary, he behaved very modestly, listened attentively to what was being said, did not protest against the need of learning harmony, and did not even object to the idea of studying with Rimsky-Korsakov." And it is definitely known that during the last year of his life, Mussorgsky was seriously contemplating taking lessons from Rimsky-Korsakov's young pupil, Liadov!

Mussorgsky did not live long enough to improve his harmony. He was a genius, but he was also *bezalaberny*. Balakirev and Rimsky-Korsakov recognized his genius but believed that for the sake of Mussorgsky's survival in music history, his works had to be reharmonized and reorchestrated. This task was faithfully fulfilled by Rimsky-Korsakov. If in our modern age, Mussorgsky's uncouth, rough, but striking harmonies appear prophetic of the new musical vistas, this is something that no one, least of all Mussorgsky himself, could possibly imagine.

THE COMPOSER

GERALD ABRAHAM

Mussorgsky's art is essentially that of "a man of the 60's." The phrase conveys little, perhaps, to the average Western reader. But to a Russian it is as familiar and as precise in meaning as the words "Elizabethan" or "Victorian" to an Englishman. The 60's mark an epoch in Russian history; and the men of the 60's, alternately worshiped as heroes and derided as back numbers, seem a race apart. Coming after the appalling despotism of Nicholas I, the reign of Alexander II (at least in its first half) appeared almost millennial. With the freeing of the serfs, which altered so much and seemed to have altered so vastly much more, Russia took one of the greatest of all her clumsy strides from feudalism towards the modern Western state. The freed *mujik* was suddenly elevated to a pedestal and sentimentally worshiped—particularly by aristocrats like Tolstoy and Mussorgsky who saw that he was free from the vices of their class and were wilfully, happily blind to those of his own. To all that was young and generous and intelligent in Russia it was a dawn as blissful as that which intoxicated the young Wordsworth.

But the expression of this exuberant emotion took a surprising form. Just as the business-like Western, in such moments of spiritual intoxication, turns his back on harsh reality and kicks up his heels in the most fanciful antics, the enthusiasm of the dreamy Slav takes the form of fiery determination to be practical. He works himself up to the facing of facts and grappling with them, enthusiastically resolved to put behind him the seductions of mere sensuous beauty to which he is generally so susceptible. Mussorgsky's art is a manifestation of both the spiritual and the intellectual exuberance, the

395

intense aspirations of the period (toward the brotherhood of man, and so on), and a relentless determination to be truthful at all costs, a contempt for that which is merely beautiful. And at its best, when these two elements are in perfect equilibrium, as in *Boris Godunov* (1868–69), Mussorgsky transcends the 60's and rises to universality as completely as Shakespeare transcends the Elizabethan age. If Mussorgsky is in every fiber a Russian of the 60's, he is so only as Shakespeare is, through and through, an Elizabethan Englishman.

Leaving aside all technical, purely musical considerations, the head and front of Rimsky-Korsakov's offending against *Boris* is that he has completely altered its values. It is as if Rubens had repainted a Pieter Breughel. The "truth" is carefully toned down, the beauty made correspondingly luscious. It is all very splendid—but it is the negation of that which is Mussorgsky's special, and still unique, contribution to music in general and opera in particular. But if Rimsky-Korsakov is to be indicted for his well-intentioned crime, practically the whole of musical Russia must go in to the dock with him for aiding, abetting, and approving. For not only the rank and file of professional musicians and cultured amateurs, but critics of the high standing of Findeisen and Karatygin long agreed in preferring the Korsakov version to the original. The resuscitation and revaluation of the genuine *Boris* is principally due to the efforts of a few critics in France, Russia following suit only after the Revolution. Professor Paul Lamm of Moscow must be given the highest praise for his admirable edition of the authentic texts of Mussorgsky's complete works.

Apart from his harmonic forthrightness and his consistent refusal to "manufacture" music by conventional technical processes, the most striking of Mussorgsky's musical innovations are in the field of naturalism—truth to the spoken word, truth to the plastic movement: the "writing" themes in *Boris* and *Khovanschina* (1872–80); the "promenade" and the two Jews and so on in *Pictures at an Exhibition* (1874)—a naturalism equally effective in comedy and tragedy. In all this, particularly as regards the musical opportunities offered by humor, Mussorgsky was indebted to Dargomizhsky for a number of hints; he would hardly have taken quite the course he did, but for Dargomizhsky. Yet his actual musical style owes little to the older man, even in *The Marriage* (1868), or the most naturalistic of his songs. (And neither Dargomizhsky nor anyone else has possessed anything like Mussorgsky's ability to get inside the mind of children.)

Even if we object, on general aesthetic grounds, to Mussorgsky's musical prose in his less inspired moments, when he is content to give a mere literal translation of word and gesture into tone, we are left with an extraordinary wealth not only of inspired "translation," of sheer lyrical loveliness and of racy, vital melody but—the seal of Mussorgsky's genius—of dramatic points produced by non-naturalistic means: the moving innocence of the "Tsarevitch" *motif* at its first appearance in *Boris*, where it accompanies Pimen's words, "All steeped in blood and lifeless lay Dimitri"; the brass chords in the second scene of the Prologue, just before Boris's words "Now let us pay a solemn tribute to the tombs of Russia's rulers," chords (particularly the unexpected D major) almost as thrilling as those of Mozart's trombones in *Don Giovanni;* the music which accompanies Galitzin's departure into exile in *Khovanschina* (based on that of Marfa's divination), so simple and beautiful, yet loaded with an intolerable weight of tragic destiny; the irony of the lovely snatch of folk song sung by Shaklovity over the body of the murdered Khovansky; the equally effective, but more brutal, irony of the banal march of the Preobrazhensky Guards in the last act of the same opera. There is no end in these strokes of dramatic genius, astounding in their simplicity, each as definite and final as an overwhelming line of Shakespeare's.

What Mussorgsky's operas do on the large scale is done in miniature by his songs. They cover an even wider field of emotion and experience, and explore each corner with even greater daring. Things like *Savishna* (1866), *The Magpie* (1867), *The Peep-Show* (1872), and the *Nursery* cycle (1868) are unique in song literature; and each is an adventure along a different line from the others. A man who had written nothing but the *Songs and Dances of Death* (1875–77) and *Sunless* (1874) would have to be given an important place among the world's song composers. Nor have even 20th-century musicians given us anything quite like the *Pictures at an Exhibition* for piano, but better known to us in Ravel's orchestration. . . . And we owe all this to a poor, drink-sodden, inefficient little government clerk, more than half a child to the end of his life, a naughty child, vain, affectionate, lovable—a pitiable creature who happened also to be a genius.

MUSSORGSKY SPEAKS

What I want to do is to make my characters speak on the stage as they would in real life, and yet write music that will be thoroughly artistic.

. . . . .

I foresee a new kind of melody, which will be the melody of life. With great pains I have achieved a type of melody evolved from that of speech. Some day, all of a sudden, the ineffable song will arise, intelligible to one and all. If I succeed, I shall stand as a conqueror—and succeed I must.

. . . . .

The quest for artistic beauty for its own sake is sheer puerility— is art in its nonage. The goal of the artist should be to study the most subtle features of human beings and humanity in the mass. To explore and conquer these unknown regions, and find therein a healthy-giving pabulum for the minds of all men, that is the duty and the joy of joys.

. . . . .

If you forget all operatic conventions and admit the principle of musical discourse carried out in all simplicity, then *The Marriage* is an opera. If I have managed to render the straightforward expression of thoughts and feelings, as it takes place in ordinary speech, and if my rendering is artistic and musicianly, then the deed is done.

. . . . .

To seek assiduously the most delicate and subtle feelings of human nature—of the human crowd—to follow them into unknown regions, to make them our own: this seems to me the true vocation of the artist . . . to feed upon humanity as a healthy diet which has been neglected—there lies the whole problem of art.

. . . . .

Mussorgsky [in his *Memoirs* the composer speaks of himself in the third person] cannot be classed with any existing group of musicians, either by the character of his compositions or by his musical views. The formula of the artistic profession *de foi* may be explained by his view of the function of art: art is the means of communicating with people, not as an aim in itself. This guiding principle has defined the whole of his creative activity. Proceeding from the conviction that human speech is strictly controlled by musical laws, he considers the function of art to be the reproduction in musical sounds not merely of feelings, but first and foremost of human speech. Acknowledging that in the realm of art only artist-reformers like Palestrina, Bach, Gluck, Beethoven, Berlioz, and Liszt have created the laws of art, he considers these laws as not immutable but liable to change and progress, like everything else in man's inner world.

NIKOLAI RIMSKY-KORSAKOV

1 8 4 4 – 1 9 0 8

NIKOLAI RIMSKY-KORSAKOV was born in Tikhvin, Russia, on March 18, 1844. In 1862 he was graduated from the Naval School in St. Petersburg, and in the fall of the same year he went on a two-and-a-half year cruise as naval officer. Back in Russia in 1865, he settled in St. Petersburg where he began to devote himself seriously to composition, even though his previous training had been haphazard. In 1865 he completed a symphony (one of the earliest such works by a Russian), introduced in St. Petersburg on December 31. Fired by the nationalist ardor of Mily Balakirev (1837–1910), Rimsky-Korsakov joined forces with Mussorgsky, César Cui (1835–1918) and Alexander Borodin (1833–87), under Balakirev's leadership, to create the "Russian Five" or "Mighty Five," music history's first significant nationalist school. Like his colleagues, Rimsky-Korsakov set himself the mission of creating Russian music steeped in Russian history and backgrounds and influenced by the idioms of Russian folk songs and dances and church music. His first major works in such an idiom were the *Antar Symphony* (1868) and an opera, *The Maid of Pskov*, written between 1868 and 1872. The latter proved so successful when given in St. Petersburg on January 13, 1873, that Rimsky-Korsakov was able to give up his naval career for good and concentrate on music.

Meanwhile he was subjecting himself to a rigorous study of the theoretical aspects of music from which he emerged a consummate technician. In 1871 he embarked upon a long and distinguished career as teacher with an appointment as professor of composition and orchestration at the St. Petersburg Conservatory. With the exception of a few months in 1905, he held this post until the end of his life. The long roster of his pupils included some of Russia's

400

most renowned composers, including Alexander Glazunov (1865–1936), Anton Arensky (1861–1906), Anatol Liadov (1855–1914), Alexander Gretchaninoff (1864–1956) and Igor Stravinsky (1882–   ). Besides holding this post, Rimsky-Korsakov was Inspector of Military Orchestras from 1873 to 1884, an office created expressly for him; assistant director of the Court Chapel from 1883 to 1894; and from 1886 to 1900, conductor of the Russian Symphony concerts. He also made appearances as guest conductor in Paris and Brussels.

Between 1878 and 1881, Rimsky-Korsakov completed two important operas, *May Night* and *Snow Maiden*. Some of his best known works for orchestra were written between 1887 and 1890, including *Scheherazade, Russian Easter Overture*, and *Capriccio espagnol*. Opera was his principal medium after 1894, the most significant in this area being *Sadko* (1894–96), *The Tale of Tsar Saltan* (1898–1900), *The Invisible City of Kitezh* (1903–5), and *Le Coq d'or* (1906–7).

He made his last appearance as conductor outside Russia in 1907, directing two concerts of Russian music in Paris. He died of a heart attack in St. Petersburg on June 21, 1908.

THE MAN

NICOLAS SLONIMSKY

Among Russian composers who were grouped almost accidentally as the "Mighty Five," Rimsky-Korsakov was the most professional, and indeed professorial. The mentor of the group, Balakirev, stopped composing midway of his long life. Borodin was more preoccupied with teaching chemistry than with music; César Cui was a specialist in military fortification to whom music was a hobby. Mussorgsky was too erratic for a professional musician.

Tall, bespectacled, bearded, quiet in manner, friendly but not too convivial in company, a model husband, an affectionate father, Rimsky-Korsakov was the veritable personification of an old-fashioned Russian intellectual.

With the exception of an early sea voyage as a marine officer,

Rimsky-Korsakov led a sedentary life in St. Petersburg. He was a modest man. He declined the proffered doctorate of Cambridge University because he did not regard himself a scholar. But he was unyielding in matters of principle. His personal integrity was absolute. When the Czarist regime ordered the expulsion of a number of students of the St. Petersburg Conservatory accused of holding an unauthorized political meeting, Rimsky-Korsakov registered a vehement protest, and as a result was himself relieved of his position as director and professor. But he refused to abandon his pupils and continued to give them private lessons at home.

Another instance of Rimsky-Korsakov's quiet explosion occurred in connection with the production of his last opera, *Le Coq d'or*, based on a famous fairy tale by Pushkin. The censors took exception to the key line, "The tale is false but has a meaning, That may well be worth perceiving." The cockerel's cry, "Cock-a-doodle-doo, rule and sleep as some Czars do" seemed to be too pointedly apposite to the disastrous conduct of the Russo-Japanese War by the Czar's government. Rimsky-Korsakov fought furiously against this attempt to tamper with Pushkin's verses, and as the odds seemed against him, he wearily told his publisher: "So the *Cockerel* cannot be staged in Russia. I have no intention of making any alterations." The opera was produced posthumously with the incriminating verses altered to satisfy the censor. Not until the Revolution were Pushkin's lines restored in the stage performances of *Le Coq d'or*.

Rimsky-Korsakov was adamant against unauthorized cuts in his operas. When Diaghilev proposed drastic cuts in his Paris production of *Sadko,* because French audiences would not sit through a long opera, Rimsky-Korsakov wrote him in anger: "If to the dressed-up but feeble-minded Paris operagoers who are guided in their opinions by their venal press and their hired claque, my *Sadko* in its present state is too heavy, then I would rather not have it done at all."

Rimsky-Korsakov's musical conscience made him his own severest critic. Being human, he had his moments of creative fatigue, when he seemed unable to work productively, but he regarded such dereliction of duty as unwarranted self-indulgence. He was at his happiest in the final stages of orchestration. "What can be more satisfying than final scoring!" he wrote to a friend. "When I begin to orchestrate, everything becomes crystal clear and precise in harmony, rhythm, melodic line, even in secondary parts. The soul is calm, for the thread of the composition has been woven in, and in a way the work already exists. And what a pleasure to correct unsatisfactory passages and polish up the rough spots! As for the hopelessly bad sections, one simply gets used to them, and they cease causing irritation." This is, indeed, "an ode to professionalism and technique," as Rimsky-Korsakov's son, Andrei, described it.

Rimsky-Korsakov's musical personality conceals a paradox. How could this typical Russian music teacher, who led such an uneventful life, have produced such resplendent pageants of sensuous color as *Scheherazade* and *Le Coq d'or?* The answer is that Orientalism is a part of Russian musical heritage. Rimsky-Korsakov's Orient was the Near East, comprising countries with which Russia had a common frontier and carried on a flourishing trade.

The music of Rimsky-Korsakov is now, literally and figuratively, in the public domain. It is used and abused in pseudo-oriental shows and in popular songs, its carefully balanced harmonies filled with extraneous notes, its flowing melodies deformed and cut to meet the exigencies of the medium, its masterly instrumentation blatantly inspissated. What a cry of anguish would Rimsky-Korsakov have emitted at such ignominious treatment at the hands of musical barbarians! No wonder that in Rimsky-Korsakov's cinematic biography his life had to be distorted, too. In it he was made to compose *Scheherazade* not in a Russian country house where he actually wrote the score, but in an Algerian night club while watching the performance of a *danse du ventre* by a dark-eyed beauty.

THE COMPOSER

M. MONTAGU-NATHAN

Both the aims and the achievements of Rimsky-Korsakov were in sharp contrast to those of Mussorgsky. A man of regular habits, he

403

had a respect for tradition which was to lead him into the firm conviction that his own advancement in matters artistic was best to be secured by an evolutionary and not a revolutionary process. Thus it was that after having made his mark as a composer he was attacked by qualms that progress was impossible for him without a thorough grasp of that scientific knowledge which has been accumulated by successive observers of musical evolution. As to the actual effect upon Rimsky-Korsakov of this retarded grounding in musical theory, there are certain definite indications. We know that it did not choke the flow of his inspiration, but at the same time one cannot help feeling that it was these studies which awakened the latent academicism to be held accountable for want of appreciation of Mussorgsky's attempts to break down boundaries. Further, his adoption, fairly late in life, of that type of symphonic development, regarded by Russians as peculiarly non-Russian and typical of the Occidental and more especially of the German mind, seems likely to have sprung from the same origin. On more than one occasion, it is interesting to note, Mussorgsky expressed himself with considerable force concerning what seemed to him a thoroughly misguided step on his friend's part, and when it is borne in mind that the two composers lived together for some little time, one cannot but feel that the bond of friendship must have been fairly tough to have withstood the strain exerted upon it, not only by such a difference in temperament as their opposed views suggest, but by the difference in the views themselves.

The operatic precept of Alexander Dargomizhsky (1813–69) as fulfilled in *The Stone Guest* became something of a burden to the "group." A survey of his dramatic works shows that while Rimsky-Korsakov was not unmindful of his obligation to produce operas of the declamatory type, he could not settle down into an acceptance of the hard and fast canons of Dargomizhsky. Classification of his operas reveals a sort of wandering movement in search of a definite procedure, and towards the end of his life he showed a very marked sympathy with Wagner. But failure to render a consistent obeisance to *The Stone Guest* does not imply a total secession from the tents of Russian musical nationalism, and Rimsky-Korsakov is entitled to be regarded as an upholder of the Glinkaist tradition, since, in

404

addition to his fund of melodic inspiration, he was a determined advocate of folk music. He made a remarkable collection of popular melodies and drew heavily upon it in building up his operas. His persistent and felicitous employment of the elements of nationalism not only in his operas, but in his orchestra works and in some of his songs, seems to warrant our considering him as the culminating figure in the nationalistic movement.

. . . . .

In 1867, while perusing some of the legends in which Russian literature is so rich, Rimsky-Korsakov was so vividly impressed by that of Sadko that he decided to compose a symphonic version of the story. *Sadko,* op. 5 (1867), which is the first orchestral poem ever composed by a Russian, was one of the first fruits of the poetic inspiration. Its basis is an old legend concerning a merchant-minstrel whose impassioned performance on the "guslee" during a sojourn in a submarine kingdom causes storms and shipwrecks. *Sadko* is scored for a full orchestra with bass-drum, cymbals, and gong, and, as a piece of thorough-going program music is closely related to the subject illustrated. It reveals the composer's early power of brilliant orchestration, his feeling for splendid effects of color, and above all his humor.

Soon after the completion of *Sadko,* Rimsky-Korsakov began his orchestral fantasia on Serbian themes, op. 6 (1867). After that he began to turn his attention to the composition of operas—a sphere of work which was to form a permanent attraction for him and in which he became the most fertile of all the Russian school. Despite his vacillations in the matter of vocal writing, Rimsky-Korsakov will be found to have adhered to one of the most important axioms formulated by César Cui (1835–1918) in his manifesto, namely, that the music of an opera must have intrinsic value as music apart from its interpretative mission. Another feature of his operatic work is his faithfulness to Russian subject-matter. In his fifteen operas, there are but three exceptions. One treats of Polish life and is by a Russian librettist; the second is based upon a drama of ancient Rome; and the third takes as its libretto a famous work of Pushkin.

In *The Maid of Pskov,* Rimsky-Korsakov's first opera—begun in

1868—we find evidence pointing to an anxiety to produce a work thoroughly representative of the prevailing views as to operatic construction. The solo-vocal portions are cast in mezzo-recitative. The chorus is given great prominence, there is a liberal use of folk song, and the subject, which belongs to Russian history, is taken from a drama by a native poet, Lev Mey.

Meanwhile he had completed two symphonies and was working on a third. His first symphony (1861–65) was written entirely on classical lines—likewise his third (1866–73). But the work which we now have to mention, *Antar*, op. 9 (1868), he called a symphonic suite, adding a subtitle, "Second Symphony." In reality it is a symphonic picture in four sections. *Antar*, scored for full orchestra, is a remarkably fine piece of descriptive music. Its program, which prefaces the score, is derived from an Arab story by Sennkovsky. "In order to enhance the appeal of local color, Korsakov makes use of three Arab themes and the symphony is invested with a considerable cohesion by the circumstance that despite the dissimilarity in character of the four sections the Antar theme has been introduced into each" [César Cui].

For the subject of his second opera, *May Night*, finished in 1879, Rimsky-Korsakov went to one of Gogol's fantastically humorous tales which were written at the suggestion of Pushkin. The work is not, however, entirely comic in character, and, as a contrast to the fantastic element in the second act, the music of the first is couched in a vein of tender melancholy. In this opera, Rimsky-Korsakov's delicate and capricious humor is fully displayed, as well it might be, in the musical interpretation of such a master as Gogol.

Rimsky-Korsakov's next important venture was another opera begun in the summer of 1880. *The Snow Maiden* (*Snegourochka*), which is to be classified as a melodic opera, impresses one with the intensity of the composer's love of Nature and his earnest observation of its various phenomena. It is clear that the rustic surroundings of his youth must have engendered something more than a desire to picture the people in song, for in *The Snow Maiden,* we are face to face with a thoroughly poetic presentation of what may be called their background. The text is drawn from a piece by one of the greatest Russian dramatists, Ostrovsky. For the four acts and prologue, the composer has found an ample fund of incident and interest in the legend and the beliefs of pagan Russia, which are referred to from time to time in its pages. They help to create an atmosphere of nationality. There is quite a host of accessory characters: birds, flowers, nobles and their wives, the Czar's entourage, players of the guslee, the rebec, and the pipe, blind men, buffoons, shepherds, youths and maidens, all helping to make a striking pictorial effect.

In 1887, Rimsky-Korsakov completed that "colossal masterpiece of instrumentation" (Tchaikovsky), the *Capriccio espagnol*, op. 34. The work is thoroughly Spanish in character, brilliantly scored, and contains some epoch-making combinations of instruments—that of drums, tambourine, and cymbals, with the rest silent, following the violin cadenza in the fourth movement is sufficiently uncommon— and is a monument to the composer's remarkable flair for orchestral color.

Another orchestral work which now enjoys an equal esteem and an enhanced popularity was composed soon after the *Capriccio espagnol* (1887). *Scheherazade*, op. 35 (1888) is a symphonic suite written to a program based on stories from *The Arabian Nights*. The score is remarkable for certain successful experiments in instrumentation, and also for the employment of the various instruments as soloists, which procedure might well be supposed to have arisen out of the composer's intense satisfaction at the first performance of the preceding work. The interpretation of his program is carried out with all the power and resource which Rimsky-Korsakov has at his disposal, and which, together with his penchant for the Oriental, place him, in works of this class at least, far beyond his contemporaries.

That the purely symphonic was exerting a fascination upon the composer at this time is suggested by the appearance, shortly after *Scheherazade*, of the *Russian Easter Overture*, op. 36 (1888), which is based on Russian church tunes. Again there is an exceeding brilliance of orchestration; and the use of bell effects which accompany the appearance of the Easter hymn is at once characteristic, appropriate and masterly.

In 1889 began a remarkable series of operatic works which flowed from his pen with extraordinary rapidity. Of these the first was *Mlada* (1889–90) followed by *Christmas Eve* (1894–95). His next opera, on which he has been working since 1895, was *Sadko* (1894–96). Rimsky-Korsakov had drawn from his operas *The Snow Maiden*, *Mlada*, *Christmas Eve* and *Tsar Saltan*, the material for orchestral suites. Here he reverses the process and elaborates the scheme of a symphonic work to build up an opera. In *Sadko* the declamatory style of vocalization is given somewhat wider scope and the melodic element is less noticeable. Rimsky-Korsakov adopts a method of recitative which lends itself to the narration of legendary lore, but he indulges his gift for melody in many charming songs and dances, and gives scope to his flair for the picturesque by introducing a series of solos for three oversea merchants. Quite a feature of the opera is the wonderful variety of rhythm, one of the most original specimens being the song of Niejata, a minstrel from Kiev, in which the rhythms of 6/4 and 9/4 appear in alternate bars. Among the many beautiful numbers in the score may be mentioned the procession of the maidens (the king's daughters) and every kind of marine marvel in the penultimate tableau (there are seven), the Hindu chant better known as *The Song of India*, and Volkhova's slumber-song in the last tableau.

No sooner had he launched the operas *Boyarina Vera Sheloga* (1877) and *The Tsar's Bride* (1898), when Rimsky-Korsakov came forward with *The Tale of Tsar Saltan* (1898–1900), an opera in the melo-declamatory style which, by virtue of its subject, its manner, and its quality, is comparable to *Sadko*. *The Tale of Tsar Saltan* is a popular Russian folk story, but is to be found in the lore of other nations. The immediate source of Rimsky-Korsakov's libretto, which was made by Belsky, is Pushkin's version of the story, and in some portions of the text the original lines are preserved. With such a libretto, Rimsky-Korsakov could hardly fail to produce the best results of which he was capable. *The Tale of Tsar Saltan* contains in its many arias and ariosos some delightful music. These vocal pieces, it should be mentioned, are not divided off from the rest. Here again the composer dispenses with the overture and the preludial matter to each of the acts which is quite brief, with the exception of that preceding the second act. This, together with the introductions to the first act and the final tableau, form the material of a symphonic suite, which received performance before the opera itself.

The Invisible City of Kitezh (1903–5), Rimsky-Korsakov's last opera but one, has for its subject a religious-mystic legend which contains features recalling some of the stories from which certain of his earlier works are derived. The element of the allegorical to be found in *The Snow Maiden,* and the super-naturalistic phenomena of *Tsar Saltan,* each has its counterpart in the literary material of *Kitezh.* As to the significance of the work in relation to the aesthetic development of the composer, this may be determined more or less by reference to its resemblance, in virtue of its spiritual message, to *Parsifal.* The operatic style of *Kitezh* is on the whole lyrical or melodic, with occasional lapses into melo-declamation.

Le Coq d'or (1906–7), his last opera, cannot perhaps be considered as an impressive conclusion to the dramatic labors of its composer; one would rather have seen in that position such earlier and more thoroughly representative works as *Tsar Saltan, Sadko,* or *The Snow Maiden.* But viewed as a satire on human foibles, as a specimen of nationalistic art, or as a final chapter in the story of his musico-dramatic development, it is a work which deserves attention. If in *Le Coq d'or* we fail to discover the wealth of harmonic inspiration which we are accustomed to expect from this composer, we shall at least observe both that it contains the very essentials of Russian musical nationalism and that the firm hand of experience has been at work in tracing a steady course and thus overcoming the difficult and ever-present problems of construction. The melo-declamatory method has again been resorted to in the solo portions, the formal overture is dispensed with, the leading motive has been used with a lightness of touch that has contributed greatly to its effectiveness, and the comic aspect of the story has been translated into music in a fashion avoiding all appearances of undue emphasis. The story is derived from Pushkin and while, as its librettist points out, its subject is such as could win favor in any clime and at any period. Rimsky-Korsakov can be said to have given it a dress which is unmistakably Russian.

It has been said that Rimsky-Korsakov must verily have been created for the National Epos in Russian music. In him we see the

Russian who, though not by any means satisfied with the Russia as he finds it, does not set himself to hurl a series of passionate but ineffective indictments against things as they are, but who raises an ideal and does his utmost to show how best that ideal may be attained. He has been compared with his own Fevronia from *Kitezh*, seeking inspiration from Nature. His personality appears to have been reflected by his choice of subject in his operatic works, in which we find him so frequently glorifying the virtue of imagination, so plainly voicing the belief in the "fairies" which has been the theme of more than one of our modern British dramatists.

RIMSKY-KORSAKOV SPEAKS

One can learn by oneself. Sometimes one needs advice, but one has also to learn, that is, one must not neglect harmony and counterpoint and the development of a good technique and a clean leading subject. All of us—Borodin and Balakirev, and especially Cui and Mussorgsky—neglected this. I consider that I caught myself in time and made myself get down to work. Owing to such deficiencies in technique, Balakirev writes little; Borodin, with difficulty; Cui, sloppily; Mussorgsky, messily and nonsensically. And all this constitutes the very regrettable specialty of the Russian school.

. . . . .

Our post-Wagnerian epoch is the age of brilliance and imaginative quality in orchestral tone-coloring. Berlioz, Glinka, Liszt, Wagner, modern French composers—Delibes, Bizet and the others—those of the new Russian School (Borodin, Balakirev, Glazunov, and Tchaikovsky) have brought this side of musical art to its zenith; they have eclipsed as colorists, their predecessors, Weber, Meyerbeer, and Mendelssohn, to which genius they are nevertheless indebted for their own progress.

It is a great mistake to say: this composer scores well, or that composition is well orchestrated. Orchestration is part of the very soul of the work. A work is thought out in terms of the orchestra,

410

certain tone colors being inseparable from it in the mind of its creator and native to it from the hour of its birth. Could the essence of Wagner's music be divorced from its orchestration? One might as well say that a picture is well drawn in colors.

The power of subtle orchestration is a secret impossible to transmit, and the composer who possesses this secret should value it highly, and never debase it to the level of a mere collection of formulas learned by heart.

EDVARD GRIEG

1 8 4 3 – 1 9 0 7

EDVARD HAGERUP GRIEG, Norway's foremost composer and exponent of Norwegian musical nationalism, was born in Bergen, on
June 15, 1843. He studied the piano with his mother, then, beginning in 1858, he attended the Leipzig Conservatory for several years,
and after that studied privately with Niels Gade in Copenhagen.
In that city Grieg befriended Rikard Nordraak, a young Norwegian
composer profoundly interested in musical nationalism. Just as Gade
was to direct Grieg to the writing of large, serious works, Nordraak
was to turn him to national idioms and folk materials. With Nordraak, Grieg founded the Euterpe Society promoting national
Scandinavian music. At the same time, Grieg started writing compositions with a pronounced Norwegian identity, beginning with the
Humoresque, op. 6, for piano. When Nordraak died in 1866, Grieg
became fired with the ambition of carrying on his young friend's
mission. Returning to his native land, Grieg arranged concerts of
Norwegian music; helped found the Norwegian Academy of Music;
served as conductor of the Harmonic Society which presented works
of Norwegian composers. He, himself, proceeded further in his aim
to create authentic Norwegian music with the completion of the
first book of *Lyric Pieces,* for piano, in 1866.

On June 11, 1867, Grieg married his cousin, Nina Hagerup, a
singer. On April 3, 1869, Grieg realized his first significant success
as composer with the première of his famous Piano Concerto in
A minor, introduced in Copenhagen. In 1872 Grieg was appointed
to the Swedish Academy, and in 1873 to the Leyden Academy.

Successive works placed Grieg with the foremost composers of
his time, the leading figure in Scandinavian music: the incidental
music to *Peer Gynt,* introduced in Oslo on February 24, 1876; the

412

Norwegian Dances (1881), for orchestra and also for piano duet; the second and third books of the *Lyric Pieces* (1883, 1884); the *Holberg Suite*, for orchestra and also for piano solo (1884–85); the Violin Sonata in C minor (1886–87); the last seven books of the *Lyric Pieces* (1888–1901).

He was honored both at home and abroad. The Norwegian government endowed him with an annuity which made him financially independent; his sixtieth birthday, in 1903, was a national holiday. In 1890 he was made a member of the French Academy, and in 1894 and 1906 he received honorary doctorates from Cambridge and Oxford.

He spent the last thirty years of his life in a beautiful villa, Troldhaugen, outside Bergen. His last concert appearance took place in London, in May 1906, in a program of his works. A year and a half later, on September 4, 1907, he died of a heart attack in Bergen. Pursuant to his wishes, his remains were buried in a grotto on the grounds of Troldhaugen.

THE MAN

GERHARD SCHJELDERUP

PERCY GRAINGER

Grieg was of small stature, delicate but impressive. The fine serene forehead he had in common with many a creative artist. His light blue eyes under the bushy eyebrows sparkled like those of a child when listening to a fairy tale. They mostly had a joyful though gentle and dreamy expression, but when roused to sudden anger or indignation they could flash like lightning. For with his short stumpy nose, the fine flowing hair, the firm expressive mouth under the strong moustache, and the resolute chin, he had dynamic energy and an impatient and passionate temperament. As in Wagner's features there was in his a marked contrast between the upper and lower parts of the face. The forehead reveals the dreamer, the mouth and chin a strong determination to live a life of untiring

413

activity. Grieg's astounding energy gave to his frail body an elastic and impressive gait and more than once in his life he performed true feats of endurance.*

. . . . .

Often I am asked the question, "What kind of a man was Grieg?" And I think the simplest yet fullest answer is to say, "He was a United Nations type of man." For he was constantly striving in his life, his art, his thoughts for the same things as the United Nations are fighting today. Grieg consistently championed the Jews against their persecutors and supported the young, the unknown, the untried, in whatever struggle they had with the old, the famous, and the experienced. This was not because he was a rebel but because he was a true progressive, and because he realized that progress depends upon a reasonable degree of opportunity being granted to the forces of change, as against the forces of established authority. . . .

As protagonist for the Jewish cause in the Dreyfus case, Grieg's actions are probably known to most musicians; but I mention them briefly here for the benefit of those who may not have heard of this typical episode. In 1899, when Dreyfus was still a prisoner, the French conductor, Édouard Colonne, invited Grieg to conduct a program of Grieg music at the Châtelet Theater in Paris; to which invitation the composer replied, "Like all other non-Frenchmen I am shocked at the injustice in your country and do not feel myself able to enter into any relations whatsoever with the French public." In 1903 he again was approached by Colonne, and this time he accepted. But his pro-Dreyfus letter was remembered, and hissing and shouting, as well as applause, broke forth as Grieg appeared on the platform to conduct his music. Grieg (never a rabble-fearer) simply waited until the hostile demonstration had subsided somewhat, whereupon he embarked upon the loud opening of his *In Autumn* Overture, thereby drowning out what remained of the shouting and hissing. At the end of the concert, of course, he was

---

* The paragraph above is by Gerhard Schjelderup; those below, by Percy Grainger.

414

acclaimed with that frenetic applause which crowds reserve for those who are indifferent to them.

There was in Copenhagen a Danish opera composer who was well known for his plagiarisms. Shortly after the performance of one of his unoriginal operas, this composer dined with Grieg at the latter's hotel. During the dinner, Grieg, who was always a charming host, said nothing derogatory. But when the Dane had bid his host good-bye and was looking for his umbrella, which he could not find, Grieg heard him accuse one of the hotel bellhops of having stolen it. This was too much for Grieg, who always was on the side of the underdog. He burst forth from behind a curtain and thus admonished the surprised plagiarist: "You dare to call anyone a thief! You, who steal from us all!"

A few years before the master's death one of the world's greatest piano manufacturing houses offered him a lovely grand piano, an offer which Grieg accepted. But the piano firm, or its local agent, neglected to pay the import duty on the piano. This aroused in Grieg his typical Norwegian "independence," and also that blend of frugality and generosity that is so deliciously Scandinavian. "I wouldn't dream of paying import duty on a presentation piano," he declared. Forthwith he proceeded to write to a few of his friends, saying he would be glad to pass on the piano to the one who would care to pay the import duty. So his closest friend, Frantz Beyer, acquired the magnificent instrument. . . .

Grieg was impatient with needless authority. The little railroad that operated between Bergen and his summer villa, Troldhaugen, issued serial railroad tickets in a book, which tickets only the train conductor was supposed to tear out. But when the conductor drew near to collect the tickets, Grieg himself would ostentatiously tear the tickets out of the book and hand them to the conductor.

Grieg was much chagrined by his inability to identify himself with the Norwegian peasants and to feel at home with them in their daily life. By birth and association he was a middle-class man. The genius in Grieg (that heightened moral sense that drives a single man to feel responsible for the feeling and thinking of his whole nation or race) urged him to rise out of his middle-class beginnings into becoming an all-round Norwegian. So, as part of this all-roundness, he tried to mix with the peasants—to take part in their festivities. On such occasions the communal beer-bowl is passed around the table and every feaster is expected to drink from it. But here Grieg's middle-class squeamishness (his sense of "personal cleanliness") found him out. "When I saw the great bowl approach me, its rim dark with tobacco juice, my heart sank within me," he told me. This urge, "to feel at one with the peasants" is a more vital necessity for a Norwegian artist than a non-Norwegian might be able to guess; and it was a vital necessity with Grieg.

THE COMPOSER

KRISTIAN LANGE and ARNE ÖSTVEDT

For two generations Edvard Grieg was the central figure in the history of Norwegian music, symbolizing its very spirit and setting a standard by which other composers have been measured. Only in the last two generations have young Norwegian composers struck out in other directions and shown that other ways and means than those employed by Grieg can also be used to express the innately national sense of melody. Today their music is felt to be just as Norwegian as that of Grieg.

No one has hitherto attempted to define what exactly is covered by the term "Norwegian musical feeling," nor can we point to any specific factors which give us the immediate impression that a piece of music is peculiarly Norwegian. But it is a fact that both Grieg and more recent composers have been strongly influenced by Norwegian folk music. A typical Grieg interval, "Grieg's leading note"— octave, seventh and fifth—is a feature of many Norwegian folk tunes. In a letter to Johan Halvorsen written on December 1, 1901, Grieg writes: "This remarkable G-sharp and D major (in the *Slått* airs) was what drove me off my head in 1871. Of course I promptly stole it for my pictures of folk life." The Hardanger fiddle airs held an absorbing fascination for Grieg, though he did not discover the complete secret of their mystery until the last few years of his life. Every artist of genius sets his personal seal on the impulses he receives, and Grieg's music is just as much steeped in his own original personality as in the spirit of Norwegian folk music. In a way it is incorrect to consider Grieg as a prototype of Norwegian musical feeling, but his music enjoys such a strong position that until the last few years the term "Norwegian music" has been synonymous with his form of expression.

In his youth Grieg made it his aim to present Norwegian folk music, the Norwegian countryside and the Norwegian national characteristics in a musical language that would be understood throughout Europe. This Grieg achieved—in the Piano Concerto (1868) and the *Ballade* (1875), in many of the *Lyric Pieces* (1867–1901), in the songs, and in the String Quartet (1877–78). These have been played and sung in concert halls and homes all over the world. Few Norwegian names have spread so far abroad or made such a profound impression as that of Grieg.

His success as a composer of international status really began with a series of concerts which he gave in London in 1888, and ever since he has appealed greatly to the English and Americans, less to the Latins, and—in spite of good contracts with the publishing house of Peters in Leipzig—least to the Teutonic peoples, at any rate in his lifetime, though in the years after his death there have been signs of growing popularity in the Germanic countries.

At the time of his London concerts Grieg had already completed the bulk of his production—the Piano Concerto, the *Ballade*, the String Quartet, and the Ibsen and Vinje songs. A few years before these concerts he had arranged parts of the *Peer Gynt* music in two orchestral suites (1876), which more than any other of his compositions have made his name known and loved all over the world.

He maintained his popularity until the natural reaction against Romanticism set in. His works are still published in their thousands today, and the *Lyric Pieces* are stock favorites among amateur performers in every country. But his name is no longer found so often on concert programs. Opinion of the true worth of his achievement as a composer has had many ups and downs, both in Norway and abroad. But he still remains quite unchallenged as the dominant figure of Norwegian music.

Grieg's music wafted like a cool breeze over the musical life of

Europe during the last decades of the 19th century, with a new melodic approach and a harmonic language all his own. Their fascination lay in their Norwegian flavor as well as the composer's own bold personal touch. There was nothing new in exploiting a country's folk music. Chopin, Michael Glinka (1804–57), Mussorgsky, Smetana, Dvořák, Georges Bizet (1838–75) and many others had done it as well. Already in Norway, while Grieg was still a student at the Leipzig Conservatory, Otto Winter-Hjelm (1837–1931) had used a Norwegian folk tune in a symphony. Halfdan Kjerulf (1815–68) had made an attempt to weave country melodies into his songs and Rikard Nordraak (1842–66), with his inspiring visions of the possibilities of the native music, had shown Grieg the way he must go.

In Norway Grieg realized the ideas which during his youth were gaining ground in other European countries, on the same basis and overcoming the same difficulties as those facing contemporary composers abroad.

His music arrived at the right time: the musical public was just in the mood for the sentiments expressed in Grieg's music, on lines already pioneered by other composers. He was like a breath of fresh mountain air from the North, with his perfect blend of national feeling and love of Nature expressed with the emotional intensity demanded by the age.

In one sphere Grieg opened up fresh fields and influenced the trend of European music—that of harmony. Here too he borrowed from Norwegian folk music. . . . Grieg delighted in giving his harmonies new and surprising sound combinations. He often introduces a bass moving in diatonic or chromatic steps, combines different types of chords, uses parallel fifths and sevenths. In the major key he shows a predilection for a bi-triple chord, and blends major and minor most ingeniously. The chords are often used purely for their color effect. In many ways Grieg is a forerunner of Impressionism.

It is true that Debussy made strong personal attacks on Grieg. But his music owes a great deal to the Norwegian master. Maurice Ravel (1875–1937) declared that he never wrote a work that was not influenced by Grieg, and Grieg also meant a great deal to composers so diverse in their work as Frederick Delius (1862–1934), Edward MacDowell (1861–1908), and Vladimir Rebikov (1866–1920). And

418

even if Grieg is suffering a temporary eclipse, owing to the reaction against Romanticism, his pioneer work will remain an important and enduring contribution to the emancipation of harmony in the 19th century. Grieg seldom tackled the larger musical forms. A symphony written in his youth remained in manuscript form, with his own written instruction on the score, "Must never be performed."

In his thirties, in collaboration with Björnstjerne Björnson, he worked on the idea of writing an opera on the theme of the national hero Olav Trygvason. But poet and composer fell out, and all that came of the plan was a sketch describing the struggle between the old pagan worship of the Vikings and Christianity. One reason for his disagreement with Björnson was that Grieg had been asked by Henrik Ibsen to write the music for *Peer Gynt*. Grieg was not very enthusiastic; he considered *Peer Gynt* the most unlikely musical subject he could imagine. Nevertheless, he accepted, and after much toil the score was ready within a year and a half. The music was received with enthusiasm at its first public performance, and has since, in countless arrangements, achieved fame all over the world.

The Piano Concerto in A minor, op. 16, ranks highest of all Grieg's orchestral compositions. It was written during a stay at Sölleröd in Denmark in the summer of 1868. With its rhythmical flexibility, and the intense feeling for Nature that pervades it, it has become a favorite among pianists. The same lyrical freshness is expressed in the String Quartet which he composed while staying at Lofthus, Hardanger, in the winter of 1877–78. Here he breaks away from the traditional polyphonic style of quartet music, bursting the restricted dynamic range of chamber music with an almost orchestral sonority.

In the Piano Sonata, op. 7 (1865), Grieg adheres to the traditional sonata form, while the three violin sonatas, opp. 8, 13, 45 (1865, 1867, 1886–87), are more episodic in structure, and owe their cohesion to a single basic mood.

Grieg's main piano work is the *Ballade*, op. 24, written in the form of free variations on a folk tune from Valdres. It is a self-revealing work, testifying to an intense inner struggle. With great dramatic power he builds up to a climax; then the composer returns in resignation to the theme in its original simplicity. In ten volumes of

419

Lyric Pieces Grieg has given a lively panorama, mainly of Norwegian scenery and country life. These became exceedingly popular, and in the last years of his life Grieg was somewhat reluctantly compelled to produce more, to satisfy his public and his publisher. He rounded off the collection by taking the same melody for the last piece as for the first, harmonizing it in a new way that reveals the development he had undergone during the span of thirty-four years which separates the two pieces.

In his songs he puts his finger unerringly on the main thought and sentiment in each poem, and presents its essence in a simple melodic phrase. On his own confession he felt the urge to write his own feelings into his romances and his choice of text was always dependent on his personal experience. The early songs bear the mark of German Romanticism but soon, in op. 5, *The Heart's Melodies* (1864), written to the text of Hans Christian Andersen and including *I Love You,* we can note the influence of the Danish school of Niels Gade (1817–90). In his music written for Björnson's poems in the early 1870's we meet the real Norwegian touch. The high tide of his song compositions is reached in the Ibsen songs, op. 25 (1876), including *A Swan, With a Water Lily, A Bird Song* and the Vinje songs, op. 33 (1880). Once more he reached the highest level with the *Haugtussa* songs (1896–98) to the text of Arne Garborg, where Grieg has caught the soft subdued "underground" mood of the poet's words. In a class of its own stands *The Enchanted,* where the text is a folk poem describing a mortal who has lost his way into the enchanted forest and is trying in vain to find his way out again. It is one of Grieg's most gripping works. In it he interprets his own tragedy.

GRIEG SPEAKS

Artists like Bach and Beethoven erected churches and temples on the heights. I wanted, as Ibsen expressed it in one of his last dramas, to build dwellings for men in which they might feel at home and happy.

·　·　·　·　·

The artist is an optimist. Otherwise he would be no artist. He believes and hopes in the triumph of the good and the beautiful. He trusts in his lucky star till his last breath.

. . . . .

We are north-Teutons and in common with the Teutons have a tendency to dreaminess and melancholy. But we do not . . . feel the desire to pour out our souls in broad rivers of words; we have always cared only for what was clear and pregnant. . . . A study of French music will help [our young composers] to find their way back to themselves. It is French art, with its light, charming, and vivid composition, with its crystal clearness, which saves the Northern tone poet. . . . The Norwegian artist who has learned the secret of expressing what is in his heart will never forget that it is France which has taught him this secret and therefore we cherish a real and deep sympathy for the artists of France.

. . . . .

It's nonsense to talk so much about being faithful to the ideals of one's youth. There is room for development surely. I have always felt happiest in life when I thought I had added if only a little to the ideals of my youth. What is life more than a struggle for the realization of truths? How could one stop at the ideals of one's confirmation age? Today I love Schumann, but in a different way than when I was seventeen, and I love Wagner but differently from when I was twenty-seven. So one's love for music, like one's love for a woman, changes its character as time passes and it is not less beautiful for that but rather improves as wine does. Don't worry if you can't feel in the same way as when you were seventeen, as long as your feelings are true and sincere.

. . . . .

The realm of harmony has always been my dream-world, and my own sense of it has mystified even myself. I have found that the obscure depth of our folk tunes is due to their undreamed-of capacity for harmony. In my treatment of them I have tried to express my sense of the hidden harmonies of our folk airs.

421

GIUSEPPE VERDI

1813 - 1901

GIUSEPPE VERDI, foremost Italian opera composer, was born in Le Roncole, Italy, on October 10, 1813. As a child he received music instruction from a village organist and from Ferdinando Provesi in nearby Busseto. In 1832, Verdi went to Milan to enter the Conservatory, but failing the entrance examinations, he had to study privately with Vincenzo Lavigna. Between 1835 and 1838 he served as conductor of the Busseto Philharmonic and director of a Busseto music school. On May 4, 1836, he married Margherita Barezzi. Their marriage ended with Margherita's death in 1840, after their two children had died in infancy.

Verdi returned to Milan in 1838, and on November 17, 1839 his first opera, *Oberto,* was successfully introduced at La Scala. His second opera, a comedy—*Un giorno di regno*—was a failure in 1840, but a serious opera in 1842, *Nabucco,* proved such a triumph that Verdi became an idol in Milan overnight. The dozen or so operas he completed and had produced during the next decade made him one of the most famous and prosperous opera composers in Italy. The best were *I Lombardi* (1843), *Ernani* (1844), *Macbeth* (1847), and *Luisa Miller* (1849).

What we today recognize as the first of Verdi's unqualified masterworks, *Rigoletto,* was produced in Venice in 1851. With this opera a new and rich creative period opened for Verdi which yielded *Il Trovatore* and *La Traviata,* both in 1853, *Les vêpres siciliennes* or *I Vespri siciliani* (1855), *Simon Boccanegra* (1857), *Un Ballo in maschera* (1859), *La Forza del destino* (1862), *Don Carlo* (1867), and *Aida* (1871).

On August 25, 1859, Verdi married Giuseppina Strepponi, a singer who had appeared in *Nabucco.* In 1860 he was elected to the first

422

national Parliament when it was instituted by Cavour. But he detested politics and withdrew from this office five years later. In 1875 he accepted from the King an honorary appointment as Senator; but when the king offered to make him a Marquis in 1893 he declined the honor.

For fifteen years after *Aida*, Verdi wrote no more operas. His most significant work during this period was the *Requiem*, written in 1874 in memory of the Italian writer, Manzoni. Verdi returned to the stage with *Otello*, text by Boïto based on Shakespeare; its première at La Scala on February 5, 1887, attracted world attention. After that Verdi wrote one more opera, his first comic opera in half a century: *Falstaff*, again with a Shakespeare play adapted by Boïto, introduced at La Scala on February 8, 1893. This also proved to be a crowning masterwork.

The death of his wife in 1897 made him lose the will not only to work but also to live. After that he "vegetated," as he himself said, in a Milan hotel where he died on January 27, 1901. His passing was mourned officially in the Italian Senate and unofficially by millions of his admirers throughout Italy.

THE MAN

FRANZ WERFEL

At the same time of life when Giuseppe Verdi first came in contact with foreign countries, with the great world, with Paris, he bought a house, home, and fields on his native soil, not far from Roncole. This considerable country estate is named after the hamlet of Sant' Agata. Like the giant in the Greek myth, the Maestro now could touch the earth from which he sprang, renewing his strength from it. Though art and his own work might require long stays in Milan, Genoa, Rome, Naples, Paris, yes, even St. Petersburg and Madrid, though he had to violate his principles by making a European tour as conductor of his *Requiem* in 1875, he was everywhere an impatient guest; at Sant' Agata alone he was at home and under his own roof.

The author of almost thirty opera scores, the composer of the *Requiem* . . . was anything but the mere proprietor of a splendid estate and a handsome country retreat. He was a conscientious farmer, a large-scale agriculturist through and through, and this not in the ordinary but in the creative sense. He had his fair share of all the work, plans, schemes, alarms, troubles, cares, joys and pains of the real, serious landowner. The model estate of Sant' Agata brought about reforms in the agriculture of the whole district. Constant innovations and improvements surprised the conservative, skeptical peasants of the province. Verdi dug canals, introduced the threshing machine and the steam plow, started dairy farms round about, built roads.

He kept increasing his holdings. The soil of Sant' Agata swallowed a considerable part of the sums his operas earned. Music made Verdi a rich man. He was proud of the fortune he owed to his pen. No wonder that envy circulated every imaginable slander upon his person. Verdi they said, was greedy and miserly. But this greedy miser never worshiped money for a single hour of his life. He never put his money to work on the stock exchanges, in the world of shares and complicated interest. What he did not spend in living and farming, he invested in the more patriotic than profitable Italian funds. Verdi was never avaricious; he was the very opposite—he was thrifty. And he could think and act selflessly, like a patriarch, in a thrifty and constructive fashion, as the following episode shows.

About 1880, Italy went through a grave economic depression. Unemployment waxed from month to month. People in town and country, and particularly in the country, could no longer earn their bread. Emigration to America assumed alarming proportions. While the romantic artists of the time simply took no notice of such things, the Italian operatic composer Verdi immediately turned to his own locality with a vigorous hand. In the middle of the winter he left the comfortable Palazzo Dorio and went to Sant' Agata. There he not only started a long-planned remodeling of the house, but had three large dairy farms and agricultural establishments set up on his own land, so that he could give work and bread to two hundred unemployed peasants and their numerous families. Soon he could explain with satisfaction: "Nobody is emigrating from my village now!"

Verdi was no friend of socialists, as indeed he was no friend of any one political party. But his was a resolutely responsible social spirit like that of no other musician in his day. And he saw not the slightest contradiction between speech and action. He showed the same integrity and purity of character in all questions of public welfare. He hated it when it was only the alms to ease the consciences of the well-to-do. He refused to participate in anything that smelled of "benevolence" of "charity." He would take any burden upon himself, even that of doing good. For instance he not only built the hospital in the neighboring town of Villanova out of his own pocket, but supervised the administration of the place, looked after the wine, milk, and meat, and made sure the patients were not stinted in any way.

. . . . .

Here is the everyday routine of Sant' Agata. Giuseppe Verdi rises early. Like most Italians, he takes nothing but a cup of unsweetened black coffee. Then he goes out on horseback—in later years he has the carriage hitched up—to inspect the work in the fields, barnyards, and at the dairy farms, or to call on some of his tenants. He is the squire, not the maestro. Between nine and ten he comes home. Meanwhile, the mail has arrived. The mail is of course the great daily event at any country house. Signora Giuseppina has sorted the letters, separating the nuisances attendant on a celebrity from the important correspondence. Some time is spent every day in dealing with this. If guests come, they generally arrive about noon. Verdi's equipage usually fetches them from the nearest railway station, Firenzuola-Arda. His circle of friends is small, and grows no larger despite the vast number of connections formed in the course of a long, brilliant life. Only seldom does an outsider come in, like Monsieur du Locle, the director of the Paris Grand Opéra, who asks Verdi in vain for a new work for his institution. After 1870, the group of friends consists chiefly of the singer Teresina Stolz, a Czech with a superb voice who created *Aida* at La Scala, Giulio Ricordi, and Arrigo Boïto, the poet-composer of *Mefistofele,* a vigorous talent

425

and more vigorous intellect who writes the masterly librettos of *Otello* and *Falstaff* for Verdi.

The main meal comes at about six in the evening. Verdi has the reputation of a lover and connoisseur of good cooking; though he does not compare with Rossini in that respect, he sets a splendid table. He loves the light wines of Italy and heavy Havana cigars, nor does he disdain a game of cards after the evening meal.

Music seems to cut no great figure in the house. Verdi is not fond of musical discussions. He warns some of his visitors that they will find no scores in his house, and a piano with broken strings.

THE COMPOSER

F. BONAVIA

Verdi's last opera when first performed won a very qualified success. Indeed, when it was known that he was writing *Falstaff* (1893) the general impression was one of surprise not so much because of the composer's age—he was nearly eighty years old—but because of the comic subject chosen by the author of *Il Trovatore* (1853). *Otello* (1887) had been eminently successful; but popular opinion still held to the belief that the secret of the good fortune that attended Verdi's operas lay in an almost inexhaustible vein of rich, flowing melody. *Falstaff* was received with every outward sign of favor. Congratulations poured in from every part of the world, the press published enthusiastic eulogies, but the public showed a curious disinclination to go to the theater. With that marvelous sense of reality found only in the perfect idealist, Verdi soon discovered how things stood and answered his admirers by pointing to the box-office returns—"the true barometer of success." Time did justice to *Falstaff* and confounded those who had suggested that its composition had been undertaken merely to solace an old man's leisure. The freshness of this great comedy, its tenderness and good humor, not only cleared away prejudices but opened the way for closer and more sympathetic study of an art as simple and as difficult as that of Mozart.

There is, of course, nothing more bewildering than simplicity for the very good reason that no one can gauge its depth. It may be shallow, it may be profound—only time and temperamental affinities can help us discriminate. Complexity, on the other hand, inevitably attracts both the thoughtful and the thoughtless, since the former can exercise their ingenuity, and the latter, profiting by the other's researches [can] lay claim to a knowledge they do not possess.

The slow but certain rehabilitation of *Falstaff* led to a revision of former opinion and vindicated critics who . . . had made no secret of their profound admiration. But earlier operas also profited by the favorable atmosphere thus created. Performances became less casual than they had been. Singers could not easily be weaned from the affectations and abuses which had gone so long unchecked, but a more earnest and thoughtful attitude came to be expected and the possibility of revising earlier works was seriously considered.

In time the movement culminated in the revival of *Macbeth* (1847) in Germany—a significant move since it could not be mistaken for a passion for those sometimes coarse but full-blooded melodies of the early Verdian period—and pointed to a new appreciation of qualities not generally supposed to be characteristic of Verdi's work. A gift for vigorous, popular melody was never denied him any more than it had been denied to Vincenzo Bellini (1801–35) and Gaetano Donizetti (1797–1848), whom he was held to have beaten at their own game. The charge most frequently profferred against him was of having allowed lyrical expression a greater and more important share than musical drama can stand—if it is to be a drama and not a succession of songs. It was admitted that his melodies had greater vitality than those of his predecessors; but it was urged, and with truth, that melody alone could not support the weight of dramatic action.

Macbeth, produced three years before *Lohengrin* and forty before *Otello,* shows clearly and unmistakably how quick Verdi's mind was in appreciating the needs of the music drama and how well he knew that, if trills and flourishes do not make a melody, sweet or impetuous tunes do not make an opera. It was characteristic of him that he revealed it not in a manifesto but casually, in a letter protesting against the choice of a singer who seemed to him unlikely

427

to understand what he required of Lady Macbeth. "Mme. Tadolini," he wrote, "whom you have chosen, sings to perfection and I prefer the interpreter of Lady Macbeth not to sing at all." Rather significant, this demand for a singer to refrain from singing in an age when singers did not scruple to ask composers to add another aria or two and refused a part like that of Senta if they thought it unworthy of their talents.

One wonders how many who heard *Macbeth* when it was first produced, or even later when it was revived in Paris in 1865, realized all it meant to Verdi. There is authority for asserting that the dilettanti of the time cherished above all else the baritone aria—probably the least individual and interesting piece in the whole opera. Verdi, however, knew well where its strength lay. He pinned his faith on the duet between Macbeth and Lady Macbeth and the sleep-walking scene; if these failed in their effect, the whole opera, he said, must collapse. And, it is important to note, in the aria which "was not to be sung"—the sleep-walking scene—the orchestra becomes the protagonist. The whole musical interest is there.

We need go no further to see where Verdi differed from his Italian contemporaries. With them it was the eloquence of melody that counted; with him its dramatic fitness. Before Verdi a melody could be transported from one situation to another without seeming irrelevant. With him and after him music acquired richer but also more definite expression. There could be never again a question of adapting, and still less of "borrowing." A melody such as that in which Gennaro reveals himself to Lucrezia Borgia in Donizetti's opera could fit equally well and equally vaguely any other occasion. Lady Macbeth's aria cannot be translated elsewhere without making nonsense of it.

Not all in *Macbeth* is of a piece with the sleep-walking scene. Passages and whole pages, if scored with greater ability, yet recall the earlier manner. But once the principle of dramatic fitness had begun to dominate Verdi's mind, it never again allowed him to stray from it. The operas which immediately followed in rapid succession, *I Masnadieri* (1847), and *Il Corsaro* (1848), are less important in this respect. But dramatic aptness is well in evidence in *Luisa Miller* (1849), in *La Battaglia di Legnano* (1849), and gives all their force

428

to the finest pages of *Rigoletto* (1851). Once the critical world accepted without scandal the substitution of one mistress for another; the true marriage of words and music allowed no such latitude.

. . . . .

Donizetti and others who, like him, revelled in the new liberty and range which the romantic impulse had given to music were apt to overrate the value of a melodic style. It could not alone provide sufficient contrast; it could not depict some degrees in the gamut of passion; it could not discriminate with sufficient clearness between different characters. That is what, of all the Italians, Verdi was the first to learn.

He was not very well equipped by fortune for such a task. Born and bred mostly in a small community where, we may be sure, no one ever thought of questioning the existing order either in music or in the drama, nothing could be further from his mind than to challenge it. But he had, apart from his musical genius, two immensely valuable qualities—artistic honesty and an unusual amount of common sense. His honesty prevented him from pandering to what was thought to be public taste. His common sense showed him where reform was needed and how far it could be carried out. Paradoxical as it may seem, this composer who so early won popular applause had never to compromise with his own conscience . . . and passed the greater part of his life away from the masses who acclaimed him. When an opera was ready he appeared in public, trained his singers, perhaps conducted and certainly supervised the first performance, and then disappeared. Such a naturally modest and retiring disposition does not suggest the eagerness of the born reformer. If he came to carry out reforms it was because common sense showed that they were indispensable. Nothing is more significant than the answer he gave to a singer who asked for another aria: "I cannot; for I have already done my best. It may be little; but I can do nothing better." Verdi's whole character is summed up in those brief sentences. He was strengthened in the conviction that sincerity is the best policy by an almost superstitious reverence for "inspiration," for those moments of exaltation in which new ideas flashed into his mind. This criterion is not wholly sound; mediocre ideas may also be conceived in moments of unnatural excitement. The minor composer, even the unknown composer, may think of a new idea, believe it excellent, and continue so to do, unless he happens to be one of those exceptional men who accept the world's verdict. But in Verdi's case this belief was confirmed by success, and helped to steel the determination never to listen to the advice of outsiders. . . . Undoubtedly the system suited his genius to perfection. His own revisions were seldom happy, and operas which were completed in the shortest time have survived many a revolutionary period in the history of music—the revelation of Wagner's genius, the recognition of Brahms, the new Impressionism of Debussy, the invasion of the picturesque art of Russia—and have lived into an era when the really advanced discuss, like Milton's fallen angels,

> Fix'd fate, free-will, foreknowledge absolute,
> And found no end, in wand'ring mazes lost.

We speak of Verdian reform, but it would be more accurate to speak of development. It is true that in comparing the formal divisions into which the acts of the early operas fall with the later operas, where the only law is that of dramatic development, one is struck by the difference of shape, outlook, and craftsmanship. But his reform was as gradual a growth as his technique—even more, since at no time did he take up a position from which he later found it desirable to withdraw. The development was as gradual and as continuous as that of the child into the man. It was, above all, a deepening of the understanding, a widening of sympathies, a quicker and more generous, more intelligent response to the appeal of whatever passion sways the *dramatis personae* of the plays.

The unequal quality of the early operas was due partly, no doubt, to a conventional conception of musical theory, but also to Verdi's inability to conceal the fact that some situations did not quicken his genius as well as others. There is no sin in this, since when Verdi began writing, recitative was still in use—long stretches of which were never meant to be treated otherwise than in a conventional fashion. In *Nabucco* (1842), as in *Oberto* (1839), his finer powers are awakened by situations meant to appeal to a warm and generous rather than a very sensitive nature. Only occasionally does he prove

430

to us that his nature was highly sensitive as well as generous, that his musical instinct could be equal to subtlety of expression. Neither *La Battaglia di Legnano* nor *Luisa Miller* shows anything like the range and the sure touch of the later operas. Yet if we consider them together—they were both produced in the same year (1849)—we cannot but marvel that two such different subjects should appeal to him in exactly the same degree, that the hand which wrote the scene in Sant' Ambrogio of the former opera (outshining the once famous conspiracy in *Les Huguenots*) should also have written the delicate, sensitive arias of *Luisa Miller*.

These operas suffer today from the somewhat unadventurous nature of the harmonies, which frequently repeat a more or less conventional pattern and set limits to the melodic invention. To appraise them it is necessary to approach them by different ways and bear in mind the limitations of analysis and criticism so clearly defined by Saint-Beuve: "However well the net is woven, something always remains outside and escapes; it is what we call genius, personal talent. The learned critic lays his siege to attack this like an engineer. He trenches it about and hems it into a corner, under color of surrounding it with all the outward conditions that may prove necessary. And these conditions really do serve personal originality; they incite it, they tempt it forth, they place it in a position to act and react, more or less; but they do not make it. This particle which Horace entitles divine and which in the primitive, natural sense of the term really is such, has never yet surrendered to science, and abides unexplained. That is no reason for science to throw down her weapons and renounce her daring enterprise. The siege of Troy lasted ten years; and there are problems which perhaps may last as long as human life itself."

Verdi's genius is all in that particle which abides unexplained. He is not the great grammarian whose discoveries may be analyzed and discussed; nor is he the symphonic composer whose essays in form can be made the subject of profound study. His harmony is always controlled by that more personal factor, taste. His conception of symphonic form is evident only in the String Quartet (1873), which, admirable work as it is in many ways, pales in importance by the side of the operas. Nor is our task made easier by the curious standard applied by those who deny the name of music to anything which does not conform to a preconceived pattern and make extravagant claims for the easy melodies of the early period because they are more extended in form. These fail to see what Verdi himself saw as clearly as Monteverdi—the essential difference between the dramatic and the lyrical style. As long as the subject of opera was a mere excuse for music, when the heroes were traditional figures of mythology, Achilles or Alexander, the treatment did not matter very much. The action was entirely conventional, and all the musician was expected to do was to choose from the text those situations he thought best adapted to his talents and temperament. When, however, the theme is Othello or Lear, the lengthening effects of music at once become apparent; thoughts which should move quickly are arrested by lyrical treatment and a mean must be struck between the aria and the recitative; the gulf must be bridged somehow if a constantly recurring anti-climax is to be avoided. The only alternative to Verdi's is the Wagnerian plan, with its deliberate cutting down of the action to its bare essentials so as to make full allowance for the expansion of music. In choosing a different way Verdi was wise since in all his operas the action is swift and better suited to his temperament.

Admittedly the expediency of a system is no proof of its worth. The more dramatic style of *Otello* (1887) would be inferior to the more lyrical style of *Aida* (1871) if its only justification lay in aptitude to express more fittingly certain emotions. But if there is a beauty of lyrical there is also a beauty of dramatic expression, even though the apostles of lyricism or "pure music" may not agree to it. They differ as the song of Schubert differs from that of Hugo Wolf; but they both have beauty and their character is essentially "musical." The one moves us with the wonder of a single perfect idea, the other with a succession of thoughts more brief but not less poignant. The old operatic style with its subdivisions of the scene into set pieces, arias, duets, and the like, favored the first form; the second is exemplified by the love duet in *Otello* where the music changes with every new image that flashes in the mind of the characters.

Are the love duets of *Ernani* (1844) or *Rigoletto* or even *Aida* finer musically than that of *Otello?* No one can seriously suggest it. In part, the superiority of *Otello* can be traced to finer workmanship—greater wealth of technical resources, surer and more masterly touch in exploiting them. But its chief merit rests mainly in a lyrical impulse which, controlled, gains immeasurably in vigor and originality, in depth and swiftness. It is not in the least necessary to deny virtue and beauty to the melodies which enrich the scores of *Ernani* or *Trovatore* (1853) in order to establish the claims of the later operas. But the essence of the Verdian reform is just this schooling of the lyrical instinct; and its evolution led to the fullest development of a genius who began his career amongst the arrangements for brass band found in the library of his patron, Barezzi.

No wonder Verdi was at first reluctant to leave the safe path of the plainest of harmonic gambits. And perhaps today we are apt to give too much importance to "freedom" of harmony; at any rate some modern composers, for all their airs of independence and dexterous camouflage, have already gone back a considerable way towards simpler formulas. However this may be, it should be remembered in attempting to gauge the extent of Verdian reforms that amongst Verdi's immediate predecessors and contemporaries there was no one to stimulate his genius, no one akin to him in temperament. Rossini, who should have taken the place in Verdi's mind and heart which Beethoven had in Wagner's, was of a temperament so different as to preclude the possibility of intimate understanding. Thus he [Verdi] had to work out his own salvation and go step by step, from the buoyant but undistinguished *Nabucco* to *Macbeth*, where first he searched and found a dramatic effect removed from lyricism; to *Rigoletto*, conceived, as he said, "without arias, without final tableaux, just as an endless succession of duets" because this form alone satisfied his dramatic instinct; to *Traviata* (1853) with its glow of romantic passion; to the splendor and pathos of *Aida;* to the most terrible of tragedies, *Otello*, and the most sparkling of comedies, *Falstaff*.

The last, indeed, embodies the experience of a lifetime. An artist's view of life, however rich, of its pleasures and sorrows, nobilities and futilities, does not constitute a philosophy. But it has the detachment which philosophers, who are bound to justify their ways, affect but do not always possess. The composer, like the poet, needs

433

no other justification than excellence. In *Falstaff* there is philosophic detachment, a sense of pity, of finality, of complete harmony; foibles and wits, vanities and love-making are blended together and have a common factor—humanity. It is comedy in which no one is wiser than his fellow. In an odd way it recalls not only Shakespeare's Falstaff but also Shakespeare's rustic philosopher, Jaques, for behind the comedy a more thoughtful spirit broods. The delicacy of the fairy music composes the mind to such thoughts as become night and the silence of a forest. When the uproarious fun of the last fugue is past we feel as if we had seen a mighty ship slipping from its mooring to make her way to unknown seas. The more serious mood is evident even in the idyll of Fenton and Ann Page, for the gentle sweetness of their songs hints that even their love-dream can lead but to an awakening.

To seek in the character of the man traits which might explain his art may be a hopeless venture in the cast of most musicians, who often show their muse a countenance very different from that with which they face the world. Verdi, in this respect, was the exception. His life does not explain his genius but, at least, it was not at variance with his practice of the art of music. A conviction of fairness and honesty inspired them both. The instinct which bade him keep a strict account of every commercial transaction made him scrupulous in keeping faith with the public and give his best in all circumstances—sometimes against his better judgment, as when he sought to meet the taste of the Parisians by planning *Don Carlo* (1867) on the scale of a Meyerbeerian "grand" opera. Another trait evident in the man and in the artist was his inborn conservatism which made him suspicious of new-fangled ideas and thus resulted in the carrying out of important reforms in so smooth a way that no one realized at the time either how important or how very much his own they were. Yet another is provided by the simplicity of his mode of life and of his tastes, matching the directness of a style profound in expression but never involved in texture. Most important perhaps is the generosity of a nature always ready to champion the cause of the weak. Unversed in the ways of statesmanship and political expediency, he resented bitterly what he conceived as the betrayal of Italy by France after the peace of Villafranca (1859), but when

434

France was beaten in 1870 he would have preferred to share in the defeat than enjoy the advantages of what seemed to him a dishonorable neutrality. He chose the heroes and heroines of his operas in the same spirit. Simon Boccanegra, Manrico the Troubadour, Violetta, Rigoletto, Don Alvaro—what a gallery of unfortunates! It may be thought perhaps that in this choice he was inspired by a romantic ideal which together with the "grace of childhood and dignity of the untaught peasant" showed a new pity and a new understanding of the poor and lowly. But opera lagged behind the drama, and when Verdi began to write phantoms from the classical or biblical age were still considered capable of firing a composer's imagination. Verdi's *Nabucco* was one of the four operas of that name produced in the 19th century while nine of his contemporaries found the ideal heroine in Judith. No wonder the censors of the time suspected Rigoletto to be a revolutionary propagandist and took exception to *Traviata* (long after *La Dame aux camélias* had been produced) on both moral and aesthetic grounds.

Verdi stood well another test to which not a few men—distinguished and undistinguished—have succumbed: the test of success. Indeed, he seems to have looked upon success with distrust. Perhaps he learned its worth when, after all the praise that had been bestowed on *Nabucco*, he found himself without the means of satisfying his landlord—a trifle which his scruples magnified into a mountain. Perhaps the loss of his first wife and two children within a few weeks impressed him with the utter futility of human hopes and wishes. At any rate the applause of the public, the eulogies of the critics, never affected his development in the slightest. He was one of the few composers who learned early to take critical buffets and rewards with equal thanks.

To assign to him his place amongst famous men is difficult while his works are still performed by those who have not the necessary technique or intelligence, who never hesitate to deal arbitrarily with his directions, by singers who turn every high note into an occasion to display their endurance. But most of those who have taken the trouble to clear away from his music the incrustations accumulated during years of license, and have discovered how many moments there are even in the earlier operas in which everything earthly has

435

been fused away and only the fire of passion remains, will not hesitate to place him amongst the great epic poets of music.

VERDI SPEAKS

I cannot tell what the outcome of the present [1875] movements is likely to be. One man wants to be a melodist like Bellini; another wants to specialize in harmony like Meyerbeer. I want neither the one nor the other. I should like the young composer to resist any desire to be a melodist, harmonist, realist, idealist, or futurist—may the devil take all these pedantries! Melody and harmony are the means the artist has at hand to write music. If a day should come when there will be no more talk of melody, of harmony, of schools, of past and future, then the kingdom of art will perhaps begin. Another mischief of the present time is that these young men are afraid. No one lets himself go; when they write they are afraid of public opinion; they want to court the critics. You tell me that my success is due to the blending of two schools. No such thought has ever entered my head.

. . . . .

I am under the impression that an art, for which one has to beat a drum, is not art at all, but a craft; that an artistic event sinks to the level of a hunting party, to something after which one runs to gain, not success, but notoriety.

I always like to remember the joys of my early days when I, almost without friends, without anyone having spoken to me, without any influence, offered my work to an audience, and was happy if I had made a good impression. But now—what a show! Journalists, artists, choristers, directors, professors, and so on—they all must add their little stone to the building up of my publicity, and to help form a picture of little miseries that add nothing to the worth of an opera but cover up its true significance. This is to be regretted, deeply to be regretted.

. . . . .

436

I know perfectly well that success is impossible for me if I cannot write as my heart dictates, free of any outside influence whatsoever, without having to keep in mind that I'm writing for Paris and not for the inhabitants of, say, the moon. Furthermore, the singers would have to sing as I wish, not as they wish, and the chorus which, to be sure, is extremely capable, would have to show the same good will. A single will would have to rule throughout: my own. That may seem rather tyrannical to you, and perhaps it is. But if the work is an organic whole, it is built on a single idea and everything must contribute to the achievement of this unity.

. . . . .

I should have said to young pupils: "Practice the fugue constantly and persistently until you are weary of it and your hands are supple and strong enough to bend the music to your will. Thus you will learn assurance in composition, proper part-writing, unforced modulations. Study Palestrina, and some few of his contemporaries. Then skip everything up to Marcello, and pay particular attention to the recitatives. Attend but few performances of contemporary opera, and don't be seduced by the profusion of harmonic and instrumental beauties, or by the chord of the diminished seventh, that easy subterfuge for all of us who can't write four measures without half a dozen sevenths."

When they have gone thus far and achieved a broad literary background, I would finally say to these young students: "Now lay your hands on your heart and go ahead and write. If you have the stuff of artists in you, you will be composers. In any case, you will not swell the legion of modern imitators and neurotics who seek and seek but never really find, although they may do some good things." In singing I would have modern declamation taught along with time-honored studies. But to apply these few deceptively simple principles, it would be necessary to supervise the instruction so closely that twelve months a year would be almost too little.

. . . . .

Opera is opera, symphony is symphony; and I don't think it is a

437

good idea to insert a symphonic piece into an opera just for the pleasure of letting the orchestra cut loose once in a while.

.   .   .   .   .

I would be willing to set even a newspaper or letter to music, but in the theater the public will stand for anything except boredom.

.   .   .   .   .

Please don't think that when I speak of my extreme musical ignorance I'm merely indulging in a little *blague*. It's the truth, pure and simple. In my home there is almost no music. I've never gone to a music library, or to a publisher, to look at a piece of music. I keep up with a few of the best operas of our day, not by studying them, but only by hearing them now and then in the theater. In all this I have a purpose that you will understand. So I repeat to you: of all past or present composers I am the least erudite. Let's understand each other. I tell you again that this is no *blague* with me: I'm talking about erudition not about musical knowledge. I should be lying if I denied that in my youth I studied long and hard. That is why my hand is strong enough to shape the sounds as I want them, and sure enough for me generally to succeed in making the effect I have in mind. And when I write something that doesn't conform to the rules, I do it because, in that case, the strict rule doesn't give me what I need.

.   .   .   .   .

The artist must yield himself to his own inspiration, and if he has a true talent, no one knows and feels better than he what suits him. I should compose with utter confidence a subject that set my blood going, even though it were condemned by all other artists as antimusical.

GIACOMO PUCCINI

1 8 5 8 - 1 9 2 4

GIACOMO PUCCINI, who was, next to Verdi the most successful and significant of Italian opera composers, was born in Lucca, on December 22, 1858. Since his family had been professional musicians for several generations, he was early directed to a musical career. After some study at the Istituto Musicale of Lucca, he served as organist in two local churches and began composing choral music. A stipend donated by Queen Margherita then enabled him to complete his musical education at the Milan Conservatory in 1883. One of his teachers there, Amilcare Ponchielli (1834–86), the composer of *La Gioconda,* directed him towards writing for the stage and encouraged him to enter a competition for one-act operas conducted by the publishing house of Sonzogno. Puccini's entry, *Le Villi,* did not win the prize but it was successfully introduced in Milan in 1884. Ricordi, Italy's foremost publishers, now became interested in him and commissioned him to write *Edgar,* which proved only passingly successful when given by La Scala in 1889. Puccini's first real triumph came immediately after that: *Manon Lescaut,* introduced in Turin on February 1, 1893. With *La Bohème* (1896) and *Tosca* (1900) Puccini achieved world-wide recognition as the foremost creative figure in Italian opera since Verdi.

In 1903, though seriously incapacitated by an automobile accident and confined for many months to an invalid's chair, Puccini completed a new opera, *Madama Butterfly.* Its first production, at La Scala on February 17, 1904, was a dismal failure. He revised it extensively, and the new version of *Madama Butterfly,* introduced in Brescia on May 28, 1904, went on to capture the enthusiasm of the music world.

In 1907, Puccini visited the United States to assist in the production of the American première of *Madama Butterfly* by the Metropolitan Opera Company. On this occasion, the Metropolitan Opera commissioned him to write a new work. For this assignment, Puccini chose a text with an American setting, *The Girl of the Golden West*, based upon a Broadway play by David Belasco. The première on December 10, 1910, attracted world interest, but *The Girl of the Golden West* never proved one of Puccini's popular works. Puccini followed this with *La Rondine* in 1917; a trilogy of one-act operas in 1918 collectively entitled *Il Trittico* and comprising *Il Tabarro*, *Suor Angelica*, and *Gianni Schicchi*; and *Turandot*, which he did not complete. He died in Brussels of a heart attack following an operation for cancer of the throat, on November 29, 1924.

THE MAN

RICHARD SPECHT

It was about the beginning of the Twenties, in 1921 or 1923—I cannot recall which—in the resplendently illuminated hall of one of the great hotels on the Ringstrasse, Vienna. A brilliant gathering had assembled, and intellectual Vienna was present to a man, especially all which that city contains in the way of musicians and singers. . . . They had come to do honor to the Maestro, Giacomo Puccini, who had arrived for the first performance of his *Trittico*. . . . He was now resting in an arm-chair, a little weary, with a happy sparkle in his fine, dark eyes, veiled from time to time by their heavy lids, and with a pleasant smile on his fastidious mouth, often drawn into an expression of melancholy irony, and scarcely concealed by the soft, full moustache. . . . On this occasion, I was permitted to hold his slender, powerful hand in mine and listen to his cordial voice, observing from its slightly veiled tones that on good days it was a *voce bruna* (deep voice), a cheerful, ringing baritone, though capable on occasion of a harsh abruptness. Even during an animated conversation, however, its full, healthy ring was dampened by a huskiness foreshadowing the insidious disease that, within so terribly short a time, was to snatch him, all unaware, from his equally unsuspecting friends. It may be observed in passing that his finely shaped, thoroughly manly hand, with its long, musical fingers, though very well kept, was not altogether irreproachable, but suggested the suspicion that, like so many of his fellow-musicians, he bit his nails during moments of nervous impatience or tormenting doubt while meditating over composition—a surmise in which I was correct. Any one who desires to call up the image of a striking personality at some subsequent time knows that such a handclasp, together with the characteristic timbre of the voice, however irrelevant the words uttered by it, bring one closer to the magic of the living being, and, without any rational explanation, throw more light upon the secret of his work, than all critical analysis or the fullest accounts of him derived from hearsay. Such a statement admits of no proof; but, not for the first time, I felt the indisputable truth of it as I listened to Puccini's voice and was able to look into his frank, noble countenance, only occasionally clouded by a distressing languor, with the vigorous chin and bold brow round which lustered the thick brown hair slightly touched with gray. It was a face that need not necessarily have belonged to an artist, though it was unquestionably that of a man of breeding, with an active brain, easily kindled sensibilities, and an eager receptivity, at once shy and conscious of his own worth, full of strong vitality, sensuous curiosity, and an instinctive repugnance for all that is vulgar; a man, too, in whom primitive, popular elements were combined with a subtle culture, an unconstrained naïveté with the acquired exterior of a man of the world and a dash of eternal youthfulness that made an enchanting mixture.

Those who saw Puccini on that evening, at a time when death had already sealed him as its own, carried away an impression of a highly luxurious dweller in great cities, inordinately spoiled by the ladies, somewhat capricious, and rather indifferent to his own fame, though not in the least blasé, who associated on the same easy footing with kings and peasants, and had long since lost the power of being astonished, whether at the marvels of life or at those of nature. Even when young he had never had the sun-clear, seeing eye for these, in spite of his passion for sport and the fact that he simply could not bear to live anywhere but in the country.

He was never fond of society; shy to the core and essentially helpless as he was, he always felt constrained and ill at ease among the bourgeoisie, and even in artistic circles in the town. In particular when he had to appear at a banquet, and especially when he had to make an after-dinner speech—which he found the greatest difficulty in stammering out, even when he had notes, jotted down with the utmost brevity—his annoyance and despair knew no bounds. He loved to mix with his friends and with simple men in an atmosphere of unpretentious jollity, and in such company he could feel quite at his ease. Here, among the uncultured residents of Torre del Lago and Viareggio, his two beloved retreats, he was the best and most carefree of companions, for he had escaped from the "great Puccini," the part that he had to play outside in the world—though, as a matter of fact, he did not do so. Here he took part in every prank, nor did these spare even his own person; he smoked like a chimney, indulged in strong language to his heart's content, helped the needy, and felt quite at home. Yet amid all this fraternal simplicity and easy jollity he was alone, thanks to his insuperable melancholy and the artist's life that isolated him; but it was only here that he could breathe, and only here that he could create. Life in the great artistic centers would have been the ruin of him; here, among his intimates, either shooting water fowl, a sport for which he had what almost amounted to a monomania, or fishing, or making excursions in his motor boat, he was entirely himself, and managed to endure even those periods which he execrated so furiously, when the lack of a suitable libretto condemned him to enforced and despairing inaction. He insisted that his friends, whom he formed into a "La Bohème Club" at Torre del Lago, and a "Gianni Schicchi Club" at Viareggio, should appear at his house every evening, there to smoke, drink, and play cards. Curiously enough these hours were his favorite time for work. He did not feel the presence of his friends in the least disturbing; on the contrary, it was a stimulus to him, and if by chance they suddenly became aware that he was in a creative mood, and fell into an awed silence, hanging upon some chord struck by the Master on the little cottage piano, he would fly into a rage, hurl some vigorous epithet at them, and ask them to go on arguing and talking without bothering about him; "otherwise," he would say, "I feel as if you were listening to me, and that makes me ill!" Whereupon the squabble over politics, or a game of cards that had got into a muddle would be resumed, and those engaged in it would once more disappear amid heavy clouds of tobacco. Puccini had, moreover, a curious habit: in spite of his unusually thick hair, he almost always kept his hat on, even in the house, and while working at the piano or his writing table. One might almost have thought that he went to bed in his favorite felt hat, whose dented form is now gradually fading into oblivion: but I feel sure that during those hours when he was committing to paper the heart-rending orchestral epilogue to *La Bohème* or the ominous strains that accompany the execution in the third act of *Tosca,* he bared his head.

He would never have been able to create all those touching, and often, in my opinion, sentimental feminine figures in his operas, with their striking ardor and animation, had he not himself been the lover and slave of feminine fascination throughout his whole life. He was the type of the *homme à femmes,* and in some ways surpassed the type. He never lost himself in adventures; but he always sought them and found them. To quote his own avowal: "I am always in love," and once, when he was taken to task for his love of the chase, he answered calmly, "Yes I am a passionate hunter of water fowl, good libretti, and women." . . . It is small wonder that an artist with his winning, manly exterior and aureole of world fame —which he wore, be it said, as unconcernedly as he did his inevitable felt hat—and with a melancholy reserve and noble bearing that promised a still further attraction, and who was, moreover, a lover of beauty with inflammable passion, should have had feminine favors showered upon him without any effort on his part. It is not surprising that he hardly ever had to waste much time in wooing a woman whom he desired, and that he accepted without any serious qualms of self-reproach every tribute paid, equally unrepentantly, by feminine charm to this operatic composer accustomed to love and raised to eminence by success—the "male siren" as Alfred Kerr called him. Nor is it any wonder that Donna Elvira, his chosen companion, did not have an easy life with such an inflammable person, who regarded the slightest constraint as a wrong. She had to preserve her own dignity and that of her home, and in spite of all her loving indulgence, she had to overcome much vexation and jealousy as a result of the escapades of the man whom she loved; nor did she always do so in silence. Perhaps indeed she did not always go the right way to work to attach "Monsieur Butterfly" to his home for good, and suffered bitterly in consequence; though perhaps she made him suffer, too, for forcing her to play Donna Elvira, whose name she bore, to his Don Juan. Yet, in spite of all, she loved him as no other woman did in his life, filled though it was with all that was rich and exquisite.

THE COMPOSER

DONALD JAY GROUT

The chief figure in Italian opera of the late 19th and early 20th centuries was Giacomo Puccini, who resembles Massenet in his position of mediator between two eras, as well as in many features of his musical style. Puccini's rise to fame began with his third opera, *Manon Lescaut* (1893), which is less effective dramatically than Massenet's opera on the same subject (1884) but rather superior in musical interest—this despite occasional reminiscences of *Tristan*, which few composers in the '90's seemed able to escape. Puccini's worldwide reputation rests chiefly on his next three operas: *La Bohème* (1896), *Tosca* (1900), and *Madama Butterfly* (1904). *La Bohème* is a sentimental opera with dramatic touches of realism, on a libretto adapted from Henri Murger's *Scènes de la vie de Bohème* (*Scenes of Bohemian Life*); *Tosca*, taken from Victorien Sardou's drama of the same name (1887) is a "prolonged orgy of lust and crime" made endurable by the beauty of the music; and *Madama Butterfly* is a tale of love and heartbreak in a Japanese setting.

The musical characteristic of Puccini which stands out in all these operas is the intense, concentrated, melting quality of expressiveness in the vocal melodic line. It is like Massenet without Massenet's urbanity. It is naked emotion, crying out, and persuading the listener's feelings by its very earnestness. For illustrations the reader need only recall the aria *Che gelida manina* and the ensuing duet in the first

444

act of *La Bohème,* the closing scene of the same work, or the familiar arias *Vissi d'arte* in *Tosca* and *Un bel di* in *Butterfly.*

The history of this type of melody is instructive. In Verdi we encountered from time to time a melodic phrase of peculiar poignancy which seemed to gather up the whole feeling of a scene in a pure and concentrated moment of expression, such as the *Amami, Alfredo* in *La Traviata,* the recitative *E tu, come sei pallida* of *Otello,* or the kiss motif from the same work. For later composers, lacking the sweep and balance of construction found in Verdi at his best but perceiving that the high points of effectiveness in his operas were marked by phrases of this sort, naturally became ambitious to write operas which should consist entirely (or as nearly so as possible) of such melodic high points, just as the *"Verismo"* composers had tried to write operas consisting entirely of melodramatic shocks. Both tendencies are evidence of satiety of sensation. These melodic phrases in Verdi are of the sort sometimes described as "pregnant"; their effect depends on the prevalence of a less heated manner of expression elsewhere in the opera, so that they stand out by contrast. But in Puccini we have, as an apparent ideal if not always an actuality, what may be called a kind of perpetual pregnancy in the melody, whether this is sung or entrusted to the orchestra as a background for vocal recitative. The musical utterance is kept at high tension almost without repose, as though it were to be feared that if the audiences were not continually excited they would go to sleep. This tendency towards compression of language, this nervous stretto of musical style, is characteristic of the *fin de siecle* period.

The sort of melody we have been describing runs through all of Puccini's works. In the early operas it is organized in more or less balanced periods, but later it becomes a freer lien, often skilfully embodying a series of *Leitmotifs.* The *Leitmotifs* of Puccini are admirably dramatic in conception and effectively used either for recalling earlier moments in the opera or, by reiteration, to establish a mood, but they do not serve as generating themes for musical development.

Puccini's music was enriched by the composer's constant interest in the new harmonic developments of his time; he was always eager to put current discoveries to use in opera. One example of striking harmonic treatment is the series of three major triads (B-flat, A-flat, E-natural) which opens *Tosca* and is associated throughout the opera with the villainous Scarpia. The harmonic tension of the augmented fourth outlined by the first and third chords of this progression is by itself sufficient for Puccini's purpose; he has created his atmosphere with three strokes, and the chord series has no further use but to be repeated intact whenever the dramatic situation requires it. There is no use in making comparisons between Puccini's procedure and that, for example, of Vincent d'Indy in *Istar* or Sibelius in the Fourth Symphony, both of which works are developed largely out of the same augmented fourth interval; but no contrast could show more starkly the difference between good opera on the one hand and good symphonic music on the other.

One common trait of Puccini's found in all his operas from the early *Edgar* (1889) down to his last works, is the "side-slipping" of chords; doubtless this device was learned from Verdi (compare the passage *Oh! come è dolce* in the duet at the end of Act I of *Otello*) . . . but it is based on a practice common in much exotic and primitive music and going back in European music history to medieval *organum* and *faux-bourdon*. Its usual purpose in Puccini is to break up a melodic line into a number of parallel strands, like breaking up a beam of white light by a prism into parallel bands of color. In a sense it is a complementary effect to that of intensifying a melody by duplication at the unison and octaves—an effect dear to all Italian composers of the 19th century and one to which Puccini also frequently resorted. Parallel duplication of the melodic line at the fifth is used to good purpose in the introduction to Scene 3 of *La Bohème* to suggest the bleakness of a cold winter dawn; at the third and fifth, in the introduction to the second scene of the same opera, for depicting the lively, crowded street scene (a passage which may or may not have been in the back of Stravinsky's mind when he wrote the music for the first scene of *Petrouchka*); and parallelism of the same sort, extended sometimes to the chords of the seventh and ninth is found at many places in the later operas.

The most original places in Puccini, however, are not dependent on any single device; take for example the opening scene of Act III of *Tosca*, with its broad unison melody in the horns, the delicate descending parallel triads over a double pedal in the bass, the Lydian melody of the shepherd boy, and the faint background of bells, with the veiled, intruding threat of the three Scarpia chords from time to time—an inimitably beautiful and suggestive passage, technically perhaps owing something to both Verdi and Debussy, but nevertheless thoroughly individual.

An important source of color effects in Puccini's music is the use of exotic materials. Exoticism in Puccini was more than a mere borrowing of certain details but rather extended into the very fabric of his melody, harmony, rhythm, and instrumentation. It is naturally most in evidence in the works on oriental subjects, *Madama Butterfly* and *Turandot*. *Turandot*, based on a comedy of the 18th-century Carlo Gozzi, was completed after Puccini's death by Franco Alfano; it is "so far the last world success in the history of opera." It shows side by side the most advanced harmonic experimentation (compare the bitonality at the opening of Acts I and II), the utmost development of Puccinian expressive lyric melody, and the most brilliant orchestration of any of his operas.

Puccini did not escape the influence of *Verismo*, but the realism in his operas is always tempered by, or blended with, romantic and exotic elements. In *La Bohème*, common scenes and characters are invested with a romantic halo; the repulsive melodrama of *Tosca* is glorified by the music; and the few realistic details in *Madama Butterfly* are unimportant. A less convincing attempt to blend realism and romance is found in *La Fanciulla del West* (*The Girl of the Golden West*) taken from a play by David Belasco, and first performed at the Metropolitan Opera in 1910. Though enthusiastically received by the first American audiences, *La Fanciulla del West* did not attain as wide or enduring popularity as the preceding works. The next opera, *La Rondine*, or *The Swallow* (1917) was even less successful. A return was made, however, with the *Trittico*, or triptych, of one-act operas performed at the Metropolitan in December 1918: *Il Tabarro* (*The Cloak*), a Veristic melodrama; *Suor Angelica* (*Sister Angelica*), a miracle play; and *Gianni Schicchi*, the most popular of the three, a delightful comedy in the spirit of 18th-century *opera buffa*. Puccini's comic skill, evidenced also in some parts of *La Bohème* and *Turandot*, is here seen at its most spontaneous, incorporating smoothly all the characteristic harmonic devices of his later period. Only the occasional intrusion of sentimental melodies in the old vein breaks the unity of effect.

Puccini was not one of the great composers, but within his own limits (of which he was perfectly aware) he worked honorably and with mastery of technique. Bill Nye remarked of Wagner's music that it "is better than it sounds"; Puccini's music, on the contrary, often sounds better than it is, owing to the perfect adjustment of means to ends. He had the prime requisite for an opera composer, an instinct for the theater; to that he added the Italian gift of knowing how to write effectively for singers, an unusually keen ear for new harmonic and instrumental colors, a receptive mind to musical progress, and a poetic imagination excelling in the evocation of dreamlike, fantastic moods. Even *Turandot,* for all its modernistic dissonance, is essentially a romantic work, an escape into the exotic in both the dramatic and the musical sense.

PUCCINI SPEAKS

That which I have dreamed is always very far from that which I am able to hold fast and write down on paper. An artist seems to me to be a man who looks at beauty through a pair of glasses which, as he breathes, becomes clouded over and veils the beauty he sees. He takes out his handkerchief. He cleans his glasses. He sees clearly again. But at the first breath the absolute disappears. It is only the veil, the approximation, that we can perceive.

. . . . .

These are the laws of the theater: to interest, to surprise, to move. Musical drama must be "seen" in its music as well as heard.

We must appreciate the astounding conquests and the courage of foreign composers in the technical field. We must be nourished by them so that they can become a part of us, but we must never lose sight of the fundamental characteristics of our art.

. . . . .

448

I have the greatest weakness of being able to write only when my puppet executioners are moving on the scene. If only I could be a purely symphonic writer! I should then at least cheat time . . . and my public. But that was not for me. I was born so many years ago— oh, so many, too many, almost a century . . . and Almighty God touched me with His little finger and said: "Write for the theater —mind, only for the theater." And I have obeyed the supreme command.

When fever abates, it ends by disappearing, and without fever there is no creation. Emotional art is a kind of malady, an exceptional state of mind, over-exciting of every fiber and every atom of one's being, and so on, *ad aeternam*. For me, the libretto is nothing to trifle with. . . . It is a question of giving life that will endure, to a thing which must be alive before it can be born, and so on till we make a masterpiece.

ANTON BRUCKNER

1 8 2 4 - 1 8 9 6

ANTON BRUCKNER was born in Ansfelden, Austria, on September 4, 1824, the son of the village schoolmaster. As a boy he taught himself to play the organ. Directed to teaching, he completed his academic studies at the St. Florian School in Linz, and then for several years served there as a teacher. In 1853, deciding to embrace a career in music, he left Linz to go to Vienna where he studied counterpoint with Simeon Sechter. In 1856 he became organist of the Linz Cathedral, holding this post about a dozen years. He also conducted a choral society in Vienna from 1860 on, with which group he made his official debut as composer on May 12, 1861, by directing the première of his *Ave Maria*.

The impact of Wagner's music dramas upon him at this time proved overpowering. He not only became one of the master's most dedicated disciples, but in his symphonic compositions he began assimilating Wagner's stylistic mannerisms and artistic methods.

In 1867, Bruckner was appointed court organist in Vienna, and a year after that he became teacher of theory and organ at the Conservatory. Between 1869 and 1871 he scored major successes in France and England as a virtuoso of the organ. In 1871 he rose to the rank of professor at the Conservatory, and in 1875 he became a lecturer on music at the University.

Despite his varied activities he continued to be a productive composer. His first symphony was introduced in Linz on May 9, 1868; his second, in Vienna on October 26, 1873; his third, dedicated to Wagner, in Vienna on December 16, 1877. All were failures. He continued to write his music in obscurity and neglect—at times in the face of the most violent opposition on the part of the anti-Wagner clique in Vienna. A small measure of success came with his Fourth

450

Symphony, the *Romantic,* whose première was conducted in Vienna by Hans Richter on February 20, 1881. His Seventh Symphony enjoyed something of a triumph, not only upon its introduction in Leipzig by Arthur Nikisch on December 30, 1884, but also in many other cities of Germany and Austria under such distinguished conductors as Karl Muck, Felix Mottl, and Hermann Levi. Now enjoying the limelight of recognition, Bruckner became the recipient of many honors. In 1891 he received an honorary degree from the University of Vienna, and in 1894 the Emperor of Austria bestowed on him an imperial insignia. Bruckner died in Vienna on October 11, 1896. Since his death his symphonies have been widely performed (usually in versions edited by Ferdinand Loewe or Franz Schalk) and acclaimed, mainly through the efforts of Bruckner Societies in Vienna and New York. The publication of a Bruckner journal between 1929 and 1939, and the issue of a monumental edition of Bruckner's symphonies in their original orchestrations, further helped to propagandize the gospel of Bruckner.

THE MAN

GABRIEL ENGEL

He was a little above the average in height; but an inclination to corpulency made him appear shorter. His physiognomy, huge-nosed and smooth-shaven, as he was, was that of a Roman emperor; but from his blue eyes beamed only kindness and childish faith. He wore unusually wide white collars, in order to leave his neck perfectly free; and his black loose-hanging clothes were obviously intended to be above all comfortable. He had even left instructions for a roomy coffin. The only thing about his attire suggestive of the artist was the loosely arranged bow tie he always wore. About the fit and shape of his shoes he was, according to his shoemaker, more particular than the most exactingly elegant member of the fair sex. As he would hurry along the street swinging a soft black hat, which he hardly ever put on, a colored handkerchief could always be seen protruding from his coat pocket.

He lived in a small, simple apartment of two rooms and kitchen which were kept in order by an old faithful servant, Kathi, who for twenty years had spent a few hours each day attending to the bachelor's household. In the blue-walled room where he worked stood his old grand piano, a harmonium, a little table and some chairs. The floor and most of the furniture were littered with music. On the walls hung a large photograph and an oil painting of himself. From this room a door led to his bedroom, the walls of which were covered with pictures of his "beloved Masters." On the floor stood a bust of himself which he was pleased to show his friends, who relate that he would place his hand upon its brow, smile wistfully, and say, "Good chap!" Against the wall stood an English brass bed presented to him by his pupils. This he called "my luxury." At home he would go dressed even more comfortably than on the street, merely donning a loose coat if a guest was announced. Kathi knew exactly at what hours guests were welcome. If the Master was composing no one was permitted to disturb him. At other times he went in person to meet the caller at the door.

Bruckner worked, as a rule, only in the morning; but sometimes he would get up during the night to write down an idea that had suddenly occurred to him. Possessing no lamp, he did this night work by the light of two wax candles; but if Kathi saw traces of these in the morning she scolded him severely, warning him to be more careful about his health. When she insisted that he compose only in the daytime, he would say contemptuously: "What do you know about such things? I have to compose whenever an idea comes to me."

Sometimes, other answers failing him, he tried naïvely to impress her with his importance, crying: "Do you know whom you are talking to? I am Bruckner!" "And I am Kathi," she retorted; and that was the end of his argument. After his death, she said of him: "He was rude, but good!"

. . . . .

Once, a maid in a Berlin hotel pressed a note into his hand on his departure for Vienna, in which she expressed great concern for the bodily welfare of her "dear Mr. Bruckner." Naturally, he re-

sponded at once to the call, but insisted (this was a matter of principle with him) upon being introduced to the girl's parents. With them
an understanding was arrived at and a lively correspondence entered upon, until Bruckner, despite the admonition of his horrified
friends, had made up his mind to marry the girl. He insisted, however, that she be converted to Catholicism (she being Protestant)
and this proved in the end the only stumbling block to one of the
weirdest matches on record. The girl simply would not sacrifice
her religion even for the privilege of nursing her "beloved Mr.
Bruckner." He was seventy-one years old when this adventure with
Ida Buhz, the solicitous maid, came to an end.

Then there was also the affair with the young and pretty Minna
Reischl. Add to a pair of roguish eyes a thoroughly musical nature
and it is easy to see why the aged lover lost his heart in this case.
The girl, of course, must have been amusing herself at Bruckner's
expense, because when she went so far as to bring the composer
home to her parents, these sensible people of the world at once
awakened him out of his December dream. When he came to Linz
shortly after, his acquaintances, guessing the truth, teased him
saying: "Aha! So you have been out marrying again!" With Minna,
however, who soon married a wealthy manufacturer, Bruckner
remained very friendly until his death.

THE COMPOSER

H. C. COLLES

Anton Bruckner was untroubled by any of the misgivings in undertaking the task of symphonic composition that beset his chief contemporary in Vienna, Brahms. Bruckner had, in fact, written four
symphonies for orchestra, though only two had attained a public
performance, before Brahms' No. 1 appeared in Karlsruhe in 1876.
Brahms once expressed a sense of thankfulness for having been preserved from the sin of spilling notes on to music paper; Bruckner's
life might be described as one long act of thanksgiving for the power
to do so. From the time of his Second Symphony in C minor (1872)

onwards, he was never without a large-scale work on the stocks. When he died he left eight completed symphonies, and three movements of a Ninth which surpasses all predecessors in length and elaboration.

Bruckner's First Symphony in C minor, first played under his own direction in his native town of Linz on May 9, 1868, was scored for the normal symphonic orchestra with two trumpets, three trombones (but no bass tuba), but this body was increased with nearly every work. He used three trumpets in the Third Symphony in D minor (1873–88), dedicated to Wagner *"in tiefster Ehrfurcht,"* and subsequently the constitution of his orchestra followed Wagnerian precedent. A "stage" band of brass (three trumpets, three trombones, bass tuba, and four horns additional to the same instruments in the orchestra proper) was engaged to add weight to the peroration of his Fifth Symphony in B-flat (1875–78). In the Seventh Symphony in E major (1881–83) he employed a quartet of tenor and bass tubas as devised by Wagner for *The Ring,* and in the Eighth Symphony in C minor (1884–90) and the Ninth in D minor (1895–96), he revelled in the full panoply of the Bayreuth orchestra, with triple woodwind, eight horns (four to interchange with the tubas), and harps.

Bruckner's known admiration for Wagner and these externals of his style labelled him a Wagnerian and brought him a certain amount both of the obloquy and the admiration which belonged to such an adherence, but while the technical influence of Wagner appears in these externals of orchestration as well as in certain idiosyncrasies of harmony, the spiritual one is chiefly discernible as an urge towards magniloquence. It cannot be said of Bruckner that there is any of that close fusion of color with line, making his orchestration an integral part of a symphonic scheme, in the way that Wagner's was essential to a dramatic one. Bruckner did not gravitate towards the program symphony which was Liszt's counterpart to the Wagnerian music drama. He did not construct his movements on an elaborate system of leading themes reappearing through the several movements, which was César Franck's application of the *Leitmotive* principle to symphonic form. To only one, the Fourth in E-flat (1873–74), did he give a title *Romantic,* and that a term of such general significance that one wonders at it having been appropriated by one rather than by all his nine. He was indeed a Romantic of the Romantics, too deeply imbued with a sense of vision in the act of creation to submit it to any intellectual principles such as Franck's, or to confine it with verbal explanations in the manner of the programmists.

Bruckner, a simple soul, whose career began as a country schoolmaster and organist, used the orchestra as he had been wont to use the organ. When he found that Wagner had built a larger instrument than the one he knew, he took the country organist's pleasure in pulling out all the stops. What he played on this ever-increasing instrument, too, was like an organist's improvisation. Each symphony begins softly and each ends in a blazing fortissimo. The customary opening is a soft pedal-point of some kind, a string tremolando, a reiterated note or rhythmic figure; in the Fifth, a basso ostinato (pizzicato) replaces the pedal-point. Whatever the device may be, it seems to suggest the organist's habit of listening to the tone of his instrument before beginning to do something with it. Presently some more positive feature is added, and so the music gets under way. Once started Bruckner gives full rein to his fertile, if not distinguished, inventiveness. He is never at a loss for something to do next, and he keeps just so much check on his wayward fancy as to adhere to the old plan of a periodic recapitulation. This is a very different thing from . . . Beethoven's method of building up from nothing, or of giving life to the dry bones. There is indeed a notable absence of bony matter from Bruckner's structures. . . .

Professor Tovey, in his essay on Schubert full of pregnant ideas about the aesthetic principles of sonata form, pointed out that "there is no surer touchstone of Schubert's, as of Mozart's, Beethoven's, and Brahms's, treatment of form than the precise way in which their recapitulations differ from their expositions," and he suggests that the genius for form may be shown in the identity of the two sections as much as in their differences. If we attempt to apply this "touchstone" to any one of Bruckner's sonata-form movements we get no reaction at all. Neither identity nor difference in the recapitulation of his ideas appears to be of the least consequence, because the ideas have acquired little or no additional significance as a result of their preceding development. This it is which puts Bruckner right outside

455

symphony in the sense in which the classics have defined the term for us. At the same time he cannot be said to be conspicuous as an inventor of self-contained tunes, as so many minor composers, who have mistaken themselves for symphonists, have been. Bruckner falls between the two schools of the symphonic and lyrical styles.

To say this is not to deny that he had genius of a kind. He pursued his art with religious devotion. He had a soaring imagination which led him to project vast designs in orchestral tones which have compelled admiration; he excelled in subtle effects of harmony heightened by the instrumental colors with which he clothed them.

Appreciation of Bruckner was slow in coming. Three of his symphonies, the Fifth, the Sixth, and the unfinished Ninth were not performed until several years after his death, even though in later years, as professor of the organ and musical theory at the Vienna Conservatory, he was the center of an admiring circle, and enjoyed the affectionate support of pupils in well nigh as full a measure as did César Franck in Paris. Foreign musicians, especially English ones, have felt some surprise at his posthumous fame. Allowing something for that extravagant insistence on nationalism which has deflected musical judgment in all countries since the beginning of the 20th century, and remembering that "Bruckner can only be fully understood through his own country, Upper Austria, much as Schubert can only be completely understood through his own country, Lower Austria, and through his attributes as a devout Catholic" [Alfred Einstein], we still have to find a cause for the prevalence of his works in the concert rooms of Europe outside Austria.

That cause is the establishment in the last generation of virtuoso orchestras commanded by virtuoso conductors. The conductors found that they could "make something" of Bruckner, indeed that he required them to make his music articulate. The classical symphony having life in itself allows comparatively little scope for the impress of the virtuoso conductor's personality. Bruckner's symphonies became to the virtuosi of the baton what the concertos of Henri Vieuxtemps (1820–81), Heinrich Wilhelm Ernst (1814–65), and Henri Wieniawski (1835–80) had been to the virtuosi of the bow. His successor in this line of composition was himself one of the greatest of these virtuosi, Gustav Mahler, whose nine symphonies lie on the border-line of the two centuries.

BRUCKNER SPEAKS

It was sometime about the beginning of 1873 (for the Crown Prince Frederick was just then at Bayreuth) that I asked the master's [Richard Wagner's] permission to lay before him the scores of my Second and Third Symphonies. He complained of the press of time (theater construction, etc.) saying that it was not only impossible for him to examine my music at that moment, but that he could not even give the score of *The Ring* any attention. I said, "Master, I know I have no right to deprive you of even a quarter of an hour, but I thought that for you an instant's glance would be sufficient to grasp the quality of my work." Then he tapped me on the shoulder and said, "Well, then, come on in." We entered the salon together and he opened the Second Symphony. "Yes, yes," he remarked, glancing through it hastily, and I could see that it seemed too tame to him (for they had at first succeeded in intimidating me at Vienna). Then he began to look at the Third (in D minor) and at once exclaimed, "Look! Look! Now this is surprising!" And so he went carefully through the whole opening passage (he particularly remarked the trumpet theme). Then he said, "Leave this score here; I want to look through it more thoroughly after dinner." (It was twelve o'clock.) "Shall I tell him now?" thought I, and Wagner, sensing my hesitation, gazed inquiringly at me. Then with pounding heart, and trembling voice, I said, "Master, there is something on my heart which I hardly dare to tell!" And he said quickly, "Out with it! Don't be afraid! You know how much I think of you." Thereupon I revealed my longing, adding that I wished permission for the dedication only if the master was really willing to grant it, for I feared above all to cast any unworthy reflection upon his sacred name. He replied, "Come and see me at Wahnfried at five this evening. Meanwhile I shall have examined your D minor Symphony carefully and we shall then be able to decide this matter." At five sharp I entered Wahnfried

457

and the master of all masters hurried forward to greet me, embracing me, while he exclaimed, "Dear friend, the dedication is truly appropriate; you have given me great joy with this symphony." For two and a half hours thereafter I had the happiness of sitting beside him while he spoke of the musical conditions in Vienna and continuously served me with beer. Then he led me into the garden and showed me his grave! I left Bayreuth the next day, and he wished me a pleasant journey, reminding me, "Remember, where the trumpet sounds the theme!"

During the years that followed, in Vienna and in Bayreuth, he would often ask me, "Has the symphony been performed? It must be performed. It must be performed."

In 1882, when he was already suffering from severe illness, he once took my hand, saying, "Don't worry. I myself will perform the symphony and all your works." Moved, I could only exclaim, "O master!" Then he asked, "Have you heard *Parsifal?* How do you like it?" And then, while he still held my hand, I knelt before him and, pressing it to my lips, said, "O master, I worship you!" Then he said, "Be calm, Bruckner," and a moment later, "Good night," and he left me. On the following day he sat behind me during the *Parsifal* performance and scolded me for applauding too loud.

GUSTAV MAHLER

1 8 6 0 – 1 9 1 1

Gustav Mahler was born in Kalischt, Bohemia, on July 7, 1860. After attending the Vienna Conservatory, and completing courses in history and philosophy at the University, he received his first appointment as conductor. Several more engagements in various small German opera houses prepared him for the significant post of principal German conductor of the Prague Opera in 1885. From 1886 to 1888 he was assistant to Artur Nikisch at the Leipzig Opera; from 1886 to 1891, he was music director of the Royal Opera in Budapest; and from 1891 to 1897, he held a similar post with the Hamburg Opera. In 1897 he was appointed music director of the Vienna Royal Opera which, under his exacting and uncompromising leadership, became one of the world's foremost opera companies. While holding this post he married Alma Maria Schindler in 1902; they had two daughters, one of whom died in infancy.

Despite his world renown as conductor, Mahler placed a considerably greater importance on his creative work. His first major composition was a song cycle, *Songs of a Wayfarer* (*Lieder eines fahrenden Gesellen*), in 1885. Three years after that came his first symphony, a failure when introduced in Budapest on November 20, 1889. He wrote eight more complete symphonies after that. These, together with his remarkable song cycles with orchestra—the *Kindertotenlieder* in 1904 and *Das Lied von der Erde* in 1910—gave him leadership in the post-Romantic movement in Germany and Austria.

Confronted by continual obstruction placed in his way by rivals, and incapable of maintaining the lofty standards he had established, Mahler resigned from the Vienna Royal Opera in 1907. In 1908 he became the principal conductor of German operas at the Metropolitan Opera in New York, and from 1909 to 1911 he was the music

459

director of the New York Philharmonic. He broke down physically in 1911 and was brought back to Vienna where he died on May 18, a victim of pneumonia.

Mahler's reputation as composer grew formidably after his death. This was mainly due to the indefatigable efforts of some of his disciples, among whom were Bruno Walter, Richard Strauss, and Otto Klemperer. In 1955, the International Gustav Mahler Society was formed in Vienna with Bruno Walter as honorary president.

THE MAN

ALMA MAHLER WERFEL

Mahler's daily program during the next six summers [1902–8] at Maiernigg never varied. He got up at six or half-past six and rang for the cook to prepare his breakfast instantly and take it up to the steep and slippery path to his hut, which was in the woods nearby, two hundred feet higher than the villa. The cook was not allowed to take the usual path, because he could not bear the sight of her, or indeed of anyone whatsoever, before setting to work: and so, to the peril of the crockery, she had to scramble up a slippery, steeper one. His breakfast consisted of coffee (freshly roasted and ground), bread and butter, and a different jam every day. She put the milk on a spirit-stove, matches beside it, and then beat a hasty retreat by the way she had come in case she might meet Mahler climbing up. He was not long about it; he was very quick in all he did. First he lit the spirit-stove, and nearly always burned his fingers—not so much from clumsiness as from a dreamy absence of mind. Then he settled down comfortably at the table and bench in front of the hut. It was simply a large stone building with three windows and a door. I was always afraid it was unhealthy for him, because it was surrounded by trees and had no drainage; but he was so fond of this retreat that I could do nothing about it.

He had a piano there and a complete Goethe and Kant on his shelves; for music, only Bach. At midday he came noiselessly down to the villa and went up to his rooms to dress. Up in the woods he delighted in wearing his oldest rags. After that he went down to the boathouse, where he had two beautiful boats. On each side of it there was a bathing hut with a platform of planks in front. The first thing he did was to swim far out and give a whistle, and this was the signal for me to come down and join him. Once I had both little children with me in the bathing hut. Mahler went off with one under each arm and then forgot all about them. I was just in time to catch one of them as she was falling into the water.

I usually sat down on the boathouse steps. When he came out of the water we talked and he lay sun-bathing, until he was baked brown; then he jumped into the water again. As I watched this procedure I always felt a terrible anxiety about his heart. I was ignorant in those days, but I knew at least that it could not be good for him. But nothing I could say could induce him to give it up, and he persisted in heating himself up and cooling himself down, often four or five times running. After this he felt invigorated and we went home for lunch, making a tour of the garden on the way. He loved the garden and knew every tree and plant in it. The soup had to be on the table the moment we got in, and the food had to be simple, even frugal, but perfectly cooked, and without tempting the appetite or causing any sensation of heaviness. In fact he lived all his life on an invalid's diet. Burckhard's opinion was that it was enough to ruin a man's stomach for good and all.

We sat and talked for half an hour afterwards. Then up and out, however hot or however wet it might be. Sometimes our walk was on our side of the lake; sometimes we crossed to the other side by the steamer and then set off on our walk—or run, rather. I see now that his restless energy after meals was his way of escape from the pressure of a full stomach on an overworked heart. It was purely instinctive. He could not bear lying down after meals, but he never knew the real reason.

Our expeditions were fairly long. We walked for three or four hours, or else we rowed over the dazzling water, which reflected the glare of the sun. Sometimes I was too exhausted to go on. We invented a hypnotic cure for my collapse: he used to put his arm around me and say, "I love you." Instantly I was filled with fresh energy and on we tore.

461

Often and often he stood still, the sun beating down on his bare head, and taking out a small notebook ruled for music, wrote and reflected and wrote again, sometimes beating time in the air. This lasted very often for an hour or longer, while I sat on the grass or a tree trunk without venturing to look at him. If his inspiration pleased him he smiled back at me. He knew that nothing in the world was a greater joy to me. Then we went on or turned for home if, as often happened, he was eager to get back to his studio with full speed.

His remarkable egocentricity was often betrayed in amusing little incidents. Sometimes he liked to break off work for a day or two in order to go back to it with his mind refreshed. On one such occasion we went to Misurina. My mother was with us and we had three rooms next to each other. My mother was in my room and we were whispering cautiously as our habit was, for Mahler's ears detected the slightest sound and the slightest sound disturbed him. Suddenly my door flew open and was banged shut and there stood Mahler in a fury. "Do you hear that? Someone banging a door again along the passage. I shall make a complaint." For a moment we looked duly horrified and then burst out laughing.

"But, Gustav, you've just done the same thing yourself."

He saw the absurdity.

One of his favorite quotations was from *The World as Will and Imagination:* "How often have the inspirations of genius been brought to naught by the crack of a whip!"

His life during the summer months was stripped of all dross, almost inhuman in its purity. No thoughts of fame or worldly glory entered his head. We lived on peacefully from day to day undisturbed in mind, except for an occasional letter from the Opera which was sure to bring trouble.

Soon after this our holidays came to an end and we returned to Vienna. . . . Up at seven, breakfast, work. At nine, to the Opera. Punctually at one, lunch. His servant telephoned from the Opera as soon as he left, and as soon as Mahler rang the bell on the ground floor, the soup had to be on the table on the fourth. The door had to be open to avoid the slightest delay. He stormed through all the rooms, bursting open unwanted doors like a gale of wind,

462

washed his hands, and then we sat down to lunch. Afterwards, a brief pause, just as at Maiernigg; and then either a race four times round the Belvedere or the complete circuit of the Ringstrasse. Punctually at five, tea. After this he went every day to the Opera and stayed there during part of the performance. I picked him up there nearly every day and we hastened home to dinner. If he was still busy in the office, I sometimes looked in at whatever opera was on, but never stayed on after he was free.

Mahler lived the life of a Stoic—a small flat, no luxuries of any sort. His one aim was to be unconscious of the body, so as to concentrate entirely on his work.

THE COMPOSER

BRUNO WALTER

The fundamental element in Mahler's work is the simple fact that he was a genuine musician. At first he was a Romantic at heart—witness *Das klagende Lied* (1880–99) and the *Lieder eines fahrenden Gesellen* (1885)—but his later development shows conflict between and blending of Romantic and Classical elements. Classical is the determination to give form to the music that gushed from him, to control and master his virile power, imagination, and sensibility. Romantic, in the wider sense, is the bold and unbounded range of his fantasy: his "nocturnal" quality, a tendency to excess in expression, at times reaching the grotesque; above all, the mixture of poetic and other ideas in his musical imagination. His was a turbulent inner world of music, impassioned humanism, poetic imagination, philosophic thought, and religious feeling. As he had both a feeling heart and the urge and power of ardent expression, he was able to subject his individual musical language to the tyranny of symphonic form. This form came to dominate his creative activity; he was to expand a content, at first rich, various, and dispersed, to the point of chaos, to the creation of works ever richer and more novel.

His First Symphony (1888), although conceived as a personal

463

credo, already showed how completely he was dedicated to the symphonic idea. From the Second Symphony (1894) on, his advance along the symphonic path was more and more conscious and determined, and was characterized by the steady developments from a thematic core whose musical completeness is deflected by no poetic idea or musical interjection sacrificing the principle of organic coherence. He was to develop symphonic form and expand its scale immensely, above all in his development sections, where he heightened the use of the motif as created and employed by Beethoven—always keeping the idea of the whole structure in mind when forming the single parts. Here he simply follows in Beethoven's tracks. The glorious, singing quality of many of his themes, like the happy-go-lucky Austrian coloration of his melodies, shows traces of the influence of Schubert and Anton Bruckner. The choral theme in the Second Symphony, the breadth of its layout, and the traces in it of solemnity, also recall Bruckner. There are echoes of Berlioz, too, in the daring use of bizarre and grotesque means for the purpose of reaching the utmost keenness of expression; he perhaps learned more from the great French genius than from anyone else.

· · · · ·

Has his rich personality given us music of equal stature? I put the question fairly and squarely: did Mahler possess a "genuine faculty of musical invention?"

In Mahler's symphonies the thematic materials reveals the inspiration of an authentic musician, genuine and sound: one who could not work out a major thematic construction from motifs in themselves paltry or artificial. For the sustained development of his symphonic works he required the continuous stimulus of the inspired idea, of the theme given in blessed moments of insight. In music, in the broad sense of the word, everything depends on invention: both the "material" and its symphonic development. Mahler's inventive faculty carries, in the first place, the stamp of a personality whose originality no one can deny.

I attach importance to recognition of the mingling of Classical and Romantic in his thematic material, as in his nature. But where he draws on themes from the sphere of folklore, he never merely imitates, let alone adapts; it is the genuine voice of the people with which he speaks, and which comes from deep within his own being. . . .

In general, Mahler made happy use of the Austrian musical dialect. It sounds in the trio of the second movement of the First, with echoes of Schubert, and with some of Haydn in the main theme of the first movement of the Fourth (1901); there are Styrian touches in the country dance in the Ninth (1910), to which I have already referred. The traditional opening bar of the Austrian military band, played by drums and cymbals, is wittily reproduced in the March of the Third, and its Scherzo "sounds off" in true military fashion. There are echoes of Vienna's folk songs in the secondary theme of the Fourth and even a Viennese waltz in the Scherzo of the Fifth (1902); one of the variations in the Andante of the Fourth behaves very Austrian indeed. Austrian military music, of which he was very fond, permeates his marches. When he was a two-year old, his nurse used to leave him in a barracks yard while she enjoyed the company of a soldier friend: he listened to drums and trumpets, and watched soldiers marching; the romantic aspect of the military, often present in his work, may perhaps derive from these infantile barracks impressions. The reveille sounds twice; the *Grosser Appell* in the last movement of the Second symbolizes the call to the dead to rise for the Last Judgment; the first movement of the Fourth completes the picture, with the finely modulated *Kleiner Appell,* as he called it. Military, again, are the repeated trumpets in the introduction to the first movement of the Third (1896), the wild music of the "charge," and the closing march-rhythms on the drums. Military romance also colors songs like *Der Schildwache Nachtlied* (1888), *Der Tambourg'sell* and *Revelge* (c. 1909).

Marches recur in Mahler's work. In his First and Fifth symphonies, the funeral march carries a singular, tragic-ironic meaning; in the finale of his Second, a vigorous quick march plays an important part. A fiery march—*Der Sommer marschiert ein*—occupies a large portion of the first movement of his Third. There are march rhythms in the first movement of the Sixth (1905), the second movement of the Seventh (1906), and the last movements of the Fifth and Seventh.

465

With his Second Symphony, Mahler begins to think in contrapuntal terms. Its polyphonic structure and artful formation and transformation of motifs show the work's classical affiliation. Mahler's absorption in problems of technique grew steadily right up to his Ninth; by the time of the Fifth they had produced a radical change in style. Far from being a poet setting poetic visions to music, he was . . . a musician *pur sang*. As such, he was primarily concerned to achieve his aim by the plastic use of thematic material. This aim governs the shape of every movement, the development of every theme: the use of counterpoint, the molding of rondo, fugue, and so forth, in the sonata form. His first four symphonies are infiltrated with ideas, images, and emotions. From the Fifth to the Seventh inclusive, purely musical forms dominate. Between these two periods, he was absorbed in Bach: *The Art of the Fugue* had a profound influence on his counterpoint. This is plain in the rondo-fugue of the Fifth, in which a tendency to imaginative deepening of the rondo itself is also evident. The exalted *Veni, Creator Spiritus* of the Eighth (1907), like the contrapuntal mastery of the third movement of the Ninth, dedicated to the "Brothers in Apollo," shows immense advance in his polyphony. He was also particularly interested in the art of variations. He was a passionate admirer of Brahms' *Variations on a Theme of Haydn* and loved to explain how high a standard Brahms in this composition had given the whole concept of variations. Mahler's use of variations is confined to the Andante of his Fifth, but the "variant"—the transformation and elaboration of a given theme, lying, as it does, at the basis of variation—is a significant element in development, and one by which he was constantly preoccupied. In each of his later symphonies, the art of variation is progressively used, and enriches both recapitulation and coda.

There was, also, a notable advance in instrumentation, based in his case on an unrivaled capacity for vivid sound-imagination and on an intimate knowledge of the orchestra. Yet his imaginative mastery of sound never seduced him into attaching too great importance to coloration. He used his rare aural gifts to achieve the utmost orchestral lucidity. Where special color was needed to fulfill his intentions, he mixed it on his own palette, as only one of his amazing sensibility could do. The heightening of his polyphony, with its complex interweaving of vocal effects, taxed even his instrumental mastery: in his Fifth he himself had difficulty keeping pace with the growing complications of the structure. . . .

. . . . .

Mahler's first four symphonies reveal a significant part of his inner history. In them the power of the musical language responds to the force of the spiritual experience. They also have in common a continuous interchange between the world of sound and the world of ideas, thoughts, and feelings. In the First the music reflects the stormy emotions of a subjective experience; beginning with the Second, metaphysical questions demand answers and solutions. The reply is threefold, and is given from a fresh standpoint each time. The Second is concerned with the meaning of the tragedy of human life: the clear reply is its justification by immortality. Assuaged, he turns in the Third, to Nature, and after traversing its cycle, reaches the happy conviction that the answer is in "omnipotent love, all-forming, all-embracing." In the Fourth he assures himself and us through a lofty and cheerful dream of the joys of eternal life, that we are safe.

Now the struggle to achieve a new vision of the universe in terms of music is suspended. Now full of strength and equal to life's demands, he is ready to write music as a musician. His Fifth Symphony is a work full of power and sane self-confidence which turns its face toward life and reality. Its movements are a powerful funeral march leading into the agitated first movement; a Scherzo of imposing scale; an Adagietto, and a rondo-fugue. Nothing in my talks with Mahler, not a single note in the work, suggests that any extrinsic thought or emotion entered into its composition. Here is music. Passionate, wild, heroic, exuberant, fiery, solemn, tender, it covers the whole gamut of feeling. But it is "merely" music. And not even from afar do metaphysical questions cross its purely musical course. But the musician in him tried all the more eagerly to develop his symphonic craft, even to create new and higher forms. The Fifth demanded, in its heightened polyphony, a renewing of his style of orchestration. Here begins a new phase of his development, and we now have in the Fifth a masterpiece that shows its composer at the

467

zenith of his life, his powers, and his craft. There is a certain sense in which the Fifth, Sixth, and Seventh belong together. Both of the latter are as unmetaphysical as music can be; in them the composer is concerned to expand the symphonic idea. However, the Sixth is bleakly pessimistic; it reeks of the bitter taste of the cup of life. In contrast with the Fifth, it says "No," above all in its last movement, where something resembling the inexorable strife of "all against all" is translated into music. "Existence is a burden; death is desirable and life hateful," might be its motto. Mahler called it his "Tragic." The mounting tension and climaxes of the last movement resemble, in their grim power, the mountainous waves of a sea that will overwhelm and destroy the ship; the work ends in hopelessness and the night of the soul. *"Non placet"* is his verdict on this world; the "other world" is not glimpsed for a moment.

The Seventh likewise falls into the absolutely musical, purely symphonic, group. These three works needed no words to clarify their conceptual ideas, and consequently no voices are used. For this reason, I cannot discuss them. I could never talk about the music itself, and there is no need to analyze it; analysis on these lines has long been available. Note, however, the reappearance of the seemingly long-buried Romantic, significant and humanly illuminating, in the three central movements of the Seventh. These three nocturnal pieces, steeped in the emotions of the past, reveal that the master of the superb first movement and of the brilliant rondo is again involved in that longing for fulfillment, that search for answers to his questions about life, which always haunted him.

At this crucial juncture, he came upon the *Hymn of Maurus* and turned all his highly developed symphonic powers to giving an answer to the most heart-searching of all questions, by placing in a full-scale musical context the *Veni, Creator Spiritus* and the belief in immortality voiced by Goethe in the final scene of *Faust*. This was his Eighth Symphony. No other work expresses so fully the impassioned "Yes" to life. "Yes" resounds here in the massed voices of the hymn wrought by a master hand into the temple-like structure of a symphonic movement; it peals from the *Faust* words and from the torrent of music in which Mahler's own emotion is released. Here, advanced in years, the seeker after God confirms, from a higher plane, the assurance which his youthful heart had poured out in the passion of the Second Symphony. In the later work the relation between idea and music is absolutely clear; from the first, the word is integral; from the first, eternity is the issue of which the symphony is born, to which it is the reply.

Can the man who reared the structure of the Eighth "in harmony with the Everlasting," be the same as the author of the *Trinklied vom Jammer der Erde (Drinking Song of Earthly Woe)*—the man who slinks alone, in autumn, to the trusty place of death in search of comfort, who looks at youth with the commiserating eyes of age, at beauty with muted emotion, who seeks to forget in drink the senselessness of life and finally leaves it in deep melancholy? Is it the same master who, after his gigantic symphonies, constructs a new form of unity out of the six songs? He is scarcely the same as a man or as a composer. All his previous work had grown out of his sense of life. Now the knowledge that he had serious heart trouble was, as with the wounded Prince Andrei in Tolstoy's *War and Peace*, breaking his inner hold on life. The loosening of all previous ties altered his entire outlook. *Das Lied von der Erde* (1910) is, in terms of the sentence of Spinoza already quoted, written *sub specie mortis*. Earth is vanishing; he breathes in another air, a new light shines on him—and so it is a wholly new work that Mahler wrote: new in its style of composition, new in invention, in instrumentation, and in the structures of the various movements. It is more subjective than any of his previous works, more even than his First. There, it was the natural "I" of a passionate youth whose personal experience obstructed his view of the world; here, while the world slowly sinks away, the "I" becomes the experience itself—a limitless range of feeling opens for him who soon will leave the earth. Every note carries his individual voice; every word, though based on a poem a thousand years old, is his own. *Das Lied von der Erde* is Mahler's most personal utterance, perhaps the most personal utterance in music. His invention, which from the Sixth on had been significant less in itself than as material for his formative hand, here achieves a highly personal stamp. In this sense, it is accurate to call *Das Lied* the most Mahlerian of his works.

469

Der Abschied (Farewell), title of the last song in *Das Lied,* might serve as rubric for the Ninth Symphony. Its first movement is derived from the mood of *Das Lied,* though in no sense musically related to it. It develops from its own thematic material into the kind of symphonic form which he alone could now create. It is a noble paraphrase of the *Abschied,* shattering in its tragedy. The movement floats in an atmosphere of transfiguration achieved by a singular transition between the sorrow of farewell and the vision of the radiance of Heaven—an atmosphere derived not from imagination, but from immediate feeling. Its invention is as Mahlerian as that of *Das Lied.* The second movement, the old, familiar Scherzo in a new form —this time the main tempo is broad—reveals a wealth of variations, with a tragic undertone sounding through the happiness: "The dance is over." The defiant *agitato* of the third movement shows once more Mahler's stupendous contrapuntal mastery; the last voices a peaceful farewell: with the conclusion, the clouds dissolve in the blue of Heaven. In design, movement, technique, and polyphony, the Ninth continues the line of the Fifth, Sixth and Seventh symphonies. It is, however, inspired by an intense spiritual agitation: the sense of departure. And although it is also purely orchestral music, it differs from the middle group, is nearer to the earlier symphonies in its deeply subjective emotional mood.

· · · · ·

In our art the new, challenging, revolutionary, passes, in the course of time, over into the known, accepted, familiar. The lasting validity of Faust's great idea is not owing to the fact that he wrested new territory from the encroaching sea; only when the new becomes the old do thoughts and actions reveal their importance. Mahler, an adventurer of the mind, left behind him in music a certain stretch of newly conquered territory, but as the decades pass, his works should no longer be expected to sound sensational. Yet, strangely enough, they still generate excitement; Mahler's feeling and unrestricted drive for self-revelation were far too elemental in his music for it to become cozily familiar and be taken for granted. The daring spirit flames high whenever the notes are heard. But should not the interpreter be distrusted whose performance of the works of Bach,

Beethoven or Wagner conveys an impression of easy possession? Have we not learned from Mahler's conducting that it is possible to make such works always sound as if they were being performed for the first time? Adequate performances of Mahler's own works today will surely reveal a Titan. Anything new in music and the drama needs the protection of congenial interpretation.

There is, however, a gradual fading of the sound, and as time passes, the daring is bound to pale, to lose its edge, especially in lesser interpretations. This raises the question on how much daring and adventurousness really signify in a work of art. Mere daring, aimed at challenge and novelty, is certain to wear off; only together with profound and permanent values is it assured of lasting effect. If the works of these Promethean masters are rewarded with immortality, the reason lies in their creative power, depth of feeling, and, above all, beauty. For beauty is immortal; it can preserve the mortal charm of the merely "interesting" from decay.

So the supreme value of Mahler's work lies not in the novelty of its being intriguing, daring, adventurous, or bizarre, but rather in the fact that this novelty was transfused into music that is beautiful, inspired, and profound; that it possesses the lasting values of high creative artistry and a deeply significant humanity. These keep it alive today, these guarantee its future.

MAHLER SPEAKS

I know that as long as I can express an experience in words, I would certainly not express it in music. The need to express myself in music, that is symphonic music, only comes when *indefinable* emotions make themselves felt—when I reach the threshold that leads to the other world—the world in which things are no longer subject to time and space.

Just as I consider it trivial to invent music to a program, so I think it unsatisfactory and futile to add to it a program. That does not alter the fact that the *incentive* for a composition may have been an experience in the life of the author, something real and tangible

471

enough to be clothed in words. We have now arrived—and I am sure of it—at the crossroads where everybody who understands the nature of music will see that the two divergent paths of symphonic and dramatic music are able to separate forever.

If you compare a Beethoven symphony with a music drama by Wagner, you will already see the essential differences between the two. True, Wagner assimilated the *devices* of symphonic music just as the symphonic writer of today will be fully entitled to borrow, consciously, some of his means from a style of expression that was developed by Wagner. In that sense all arts are linked with one another, and even art with Nature. But as yet we have not thought enough about this problem because we still lack the perspective for it. I have not constructed this "system" and composed accordingly. It was rather that, after writing a few symphonies and constantly coming up against the same questions, I began to see the whole matter. It is, therefore, just as well if the listener to whom my style is unfamiliar is given, to begin with, signposts and milestones on his journey, or, if you like, a chart of the stars so that he may find his bearing in the night sky. That is all a program can be. The human mind must start with familiar things, otherwise it goes astray.

.   .   .   .   .

Only when I experience do I compose—only when I compose do I experience! . . . A musician's nature can hardly be expressed in words. It could be easier to explain how he is different from others. What it is, however, perhaps he least of all would be able to explain. It is the same with his goals, too. Like a somnambulist he wanders towards them—he does not know which road he is following (it may skirt dizzy abysses) but he walks towards the distant light, whether this be the eternally shining stars or an enticing will-o'-the-wisp.

HUGO WOLF

1 8 6 0 – 1 9 0 3

HUGO WOLF, probably the foremost composer of the art-song
(Lied) since Schubert, was born in Windischgraz, Austria, on March
13, 1860. He began music study early, first with local teachers, then
from 1875 to 1877, at the Vienna Conservatory. Impatient with the
discipline imposed on him there, and severely critical of some of his
teachers, he became a rebellious student and was expelled in 1877.
For a while he earned his living teaching music to children. At the
same time he started writing Lieder to texts by Goethe, Heine, and
other poets. In 1881 he worked as chorusmaster in Salzburg. Two
years after that he was appointed music critic of a Vienna music
journal where his passionate espousal of Wagner and "the music of
the future"—together with his bitter denunciation of Brahms—gained
him both enemies and disciples. For a while the enemies were
stronger than the friends. The Rosé Quartet turned down his String
Quartet, completed in 1884; and while the Vienna Philharmonic
under Hans Richter did perform his *Penthesilea Overture* in 1886,
the severe public and critical reaction resulted in a fiasco. In 1887
Wolf gave up music criticism to devote himself completely to composition. In 1888 he completed the Moerike songs. His first published
volume of art songs appeared in 1889. In 1891 came the Spanish
songs, the *Alte Weisen*, and the first part of the Italian songs.

Performances of his most important songs by the Wagner Verein
in Vienna—and subsequently by various artists and groups in many
major music centers in Germany—soon brought him to a place of
preëminent importance among German writers of vocal music. In
1896 a Hugo Wolf Society was formed in Berlin to promote his
music in Germany, and a similar organization appeared in Vienna
a year later. On June 7, 1896, there took place in Mannheim the

473

world première of his opera, *Der Corregidor*—a *succès d'estime*, thanks to the presence of many of his admirers. With his creative energies and gifts at their peak—and success apparently at hand— Wolf suffered a nervous breakdown in 1897 and had to be institutionalized. By early 1898 he had recovered sufficiently to be allowed to travel in Austria and Italy. But his mental condition again deteriorated alarmingly. After an unsuccessful attempt at suicide, Wolf requested that he be readmitted into an asylum in October 1898. He died there, in Vienna, on February 22, 1903.

THE MAN

DAVID AND FREDERIC EWEN

He was small, of mean build, thin, and undernourished. His eyes looked out wild and feverish. He seemed always on the brink of hysteria. He was excitable in gesture and expression, his heart always pounding—either in admiration or hatred. The small body was an inexhaustible storehouse of energy, of fiercely burning hysterical energy. The poet Kleist had been like that. And Hugo Wolf understood Kleist.

When he read his favorite poet, "his hands trembled . . . his eyes lit up, and he appeared transfigured, as if at the sight of higher, brighter regions, the gates of which had suddenly sprung open. He gasped for air." He responded to poetry with vehemence; a beautiful line would enchant him; a bad one would bring on an almost physical disorder.

With equal passion he worshiped his musical gods. "Gluck, Mozart, Wagner, these be our divine trinity—which Holy Three become one in Beethoven." But he had other gods—in a lesser Pantheon —whom he espoused no less ardently: Berlioz, Schumann, and, later, Bruckner.

He was poor, most of the time penniless. But when he had a book in his hand or a copy of a Beethoven sonata, which he would take with him to the Prater, he was unassailable. "Restlessly, I am driven to improve my weak talents, to extend my horizon, to endow my

474

thoughts, my actions, my feelings with as ripe an expression as possible."

When he was eighteen years old he was still a bohemian. For the ordinary ways of living he was unfitted. He loved freedom above all, and the life of a music teacher (which he tried for a while) galled him. When he was employed, he earned something like thirty-six gulden during the month, and could scarcely allow himself more than one full meal a day. But his intemperate rages, and his honest dread of mediocrity, lost him many students, so that most of the time he was close to starvation. In 1881 he was recommended as an assistant to Karl Muck at Salzburg, but here he lasted no more than a few months. His fiery temper made intercourse impossible.

But he did not care. No bread; no roof; no bed. Somehow he would survive. Already he was composing his own songs. By 1885 he had no less than fifty, and a symphonic poem, *Penthesilea*, based on Kleist's tragedy.

The storm-tossed vagrant made friends who were glad to give him a home. Edmund Lang offered him an attic in the Trattnerhof. The poet, Hermann Bahr, who lived in the same house and had come home very early one morning after a student *Schmaus*, has described Wolf as he appeared at this time. "Heavy with drink and the enthusiasm of youth, we sought rest. Suddenly, the door opened, and from another room appeared Hugo Wolf, dressed in a very long shirt, and carrying a candle; very pale, and strange to look at, in the gray, gloomy light; gesticulating now mysteriously, now scurrilously. He laughed shrilly and mocked us. . . . Then he began reading, mostly passages from *Penthesilea*. He did this with such power, that we became silent and dared hardly utter a word. When he spoke, he was great. I have never in my life heard anyone read like him."

In moments of lagging inspiration he replenished his spirit with Wagner. He went to Bayreuth, and for a time was completely undone by *Parsifal*. An acquaintance of his, Dr. Zweybrücken, saw him after the night of the performance, sitting on a bench in the open, his head buried in his hands. "He seemed completely removed from the world and shaken to the very depths."

The failure to obtain a hearing at the Royal Opera upset him. His nervous organism—sustained, it seemed, even to this time, by a miracle, but almost always on the point of breaking—now gave way completely. On September 19, 1897 he began his aimless wandering at three o'clock in the morning. The friends, whom in turn he sought out, failed at first to gauge the symptoms. They had seen him distraught before. He spoke of himself as the director of the Vienna Opera, raved in anger at his "subordinates." In the evening he sat down at the piano and played a portion of *Die Meistersinger*. Suddenly his memory gave way. He became hysterical and violent.

He was brought to a sanatorium. . . . Here he lived his last years, in heart-breaking solitude. In the world outside his fame grew—but the little man with the pale, thin face and the blazing eyes was past understanding or caring about it.

THE COMPOSER

ERNEST NEWMAN

Hugo Wolf, a remarkable musician in general and the most remarkable of song writers, is to song what Beethoven is to the symphony, Wagner to the opera, and Richard Strauss (1864–1949) to the symphonic poem.

We get the key to Wolf's own tastes and ideals in his sharp criticism of the songs of Robert Franz (1815–92). Of these he liked only the *Gewitternacht*. "He made it a reproach against Franz," says one of his friends, "that through his archaic leaning towards the four-part structure he had forced back into narrower fields the song-form that Schubert and Schumann had so greatly enlarged." The criticism may, in its haste, pass over the real charm and beauty of Franz, but, like all Wolf's criticisms, it is true and incisive; and it throws a light on his own attitude towards the song. With him there was to be no harking back to the past, no hampering reverence of the great masters, no attempt to see things through the eyes of other men, no matter how big they might be. He brings to bear upon the song the same weight of *contemporary* thinking that Wagner brought upon the opera and Strauss brought upon the symphonic poem; that is, while admiring to the fullest the expression that Schubert and Schumann and the others were able to find for their own conception of life, he realizes that his own conceptions are different from theirs, that he lives in a different intellectual and emotional and social world, and that to give natural expression to the life of this world he must break the mold of the older form and recast the thing from top to bottom, as Wagner and Strauss and Ibsen have all had to do. And, as in the case of these other men, the sufficient justification of the new manner is simply the newness of the outlook.

The central point of Wolf's system is that the whole song—voice part and piano part—is conceived in a piece. He does not write "songs with piano accompaniment," any more than Wagner wrote vocal scenes with orchestral accompaniment. In Wagner at his best the conception is homogeneous throughout—the voice, the orchestra, the gesture, the stage-setting, are all inseparable parts of an indissoluble whole; take one of them away and the full effect of the others is lost. The aesthetic and psychological unity that Wagner achieved in the music-drama has been achieved by Hugo Wolf in the song. His work, indeed, is grounded on Wagner's—not by way of imitation, but by way of assimilation of certain principles of which Wagner was the first to see the main possibilities. It used to be said by some of the older school of critics that Wagner had made the orchestra more important than the voice. They had been used to the singer being the center of attraction, and the orchestra "accompanying" him, as Wagner said, like a big guitar. When they found that not only the vocal part but the orchestral part was full of music, they foolishly assumed that because there was more than usual in the orchestra there must be less than usual on the stage; it never occurred to them that they were actually getting no less but more melody in opera than they had ever had before. I have no doubt that a number of people will say of Hugo Wolf what their fathers used to say of Wagner. For in Wolf's songs the piano part (it is an error to call it the accompaniment: he himself, indeed, always styles his works "songs for voice and piano") acquires a pregnancy of meaning to which there is no parallel in any previous or contemporary song writer. Time after time you can ignore the vocal part, and the piano part still constitutes a lovely piece of music, quite coherent in itself and apparently quite complete: see, for example, *Im Frühling, An*

477

den Schlaf, and *Lebe wohl,* all in the Moerike volume (1889). Here the hasty man may feel inclined to say that in this case the voice part must be superfluous—that Wolf must have conceived his songs as piano pieces, and added the vocal portion afterwards as best he could. It is not so, however, as you will find when you combine the vocal part with the piano part. You will then see that while formerly the piano part seemed to be completely satisfying in itself, its meaning is enormously intensified by the verbal current that flows along with it, and that henceforth the two are inconceivable in separation. Here and there in Wagner we feel that, whatever he might say to the contrary, the composer had in the first place written a certain thing as an orchestral piece, afterwards forcing the words to go along with it—which is the impression a great many of us have of Isolde's *Liebestod,* for example. This is a feeling we rarely get with Hugo Wolf. Examine such a song as *Was für ein Lied soll dir gesungen werden* in the *Italienisches Liederbuch* (1896) and you will see how absolutely organic is the connection between voice part and piano part. The one is not simply plastered on the other and induced to fit where it will; the whole conception is one and indivisible. In *Nun bin ich dein,* again, in the *Spanisches Liederbuch* (1891) or *Auf einer Wanderung* in the Moerike volume, though the one figure is kept going more or less persistently in the piano, the vocal melody is never the slave of it. Now and then, perhaps, one suspects that Wolf adheres too closely to the figure with which he begins—does not vary it and break it up sufficiently; but I doubt whether the criticism really holds good. His plan, in songs of this kind, is to fix the general atmosphere of the words, as it were, in a suggestive piano phrase, to keep this going practically all through the song with comparatively little change, and to throw various lights upon it by an exceedingly skilful and delicate manipulation of the voice part. Look at the piano part alone, and you may possibly feel, at times, that it is capable of more development than Wolf gives it; but I think Wolf's reply to a criticism of this kind would have been that he was perfectly aware of it, but that he chose to fix it as he did as a kind of permanent background, across which there flit the infinitely subtle nuances of feeling expressed by the voice.

It is only after a long familiarity with his songs that we realize

478

how new and how consummate was his sense of vocal rhythm. Recall the flexibility of the plastic shapes into which Richard Strauss fashioned his orchestral speech, transport these to the voice in combination with the piano, and you get the art of Hugo Wolf. I once suggested that in Strauss the poetry of music had given place to the prose of music; in place of the old, regular, even structure and rectangular balancing of phrases we have a mode of speech that flows on more continuously, halts where it likes, takes up the rhythm again where it likes, substituting a more complex and a more daring beauty of line for the simpler and more timid line of classical music. We have the same phenomenon in Hugo Wolf. Strauss's avoidance of the square-cut musical paragraph is matched by the absolute freedom and ease of Wolf's sentences. Again I can only compare the change from the methods of his predecessors to a transition from the rhymed stanza of set shape and dimensions to natural and flexible prose, or to the free verse-structure that we have in some of Henley's poems, in Whitman, in some of Traherne's work, or in Gabriele D'Annunzio's *Francesca da Rimini*. I do not for a moment mean to try to discredit the other kind of writing; it also has its beauties, and the palate that would be insensitive to the charm of the rhymed stanza would, of course, be a most imperfect poetical or musical organ. I only wish to point out that the evolution from the regular to the irregular sentence is as perfectly natural a one in music as in poetry, accounting as well for the change from Mozart to Strauss or Wolf as for the change from Popean neatness to the blank verse of Shelley, Wordsworth, and Keats. It may be that before long there will be a reaction from this irregularity, as there has been from the previous regularity; and that just as later poets like Tennyson have shown what subtly gradated and varied rhythms can be got out of the rhymed stanza, so some later musician may intoxicate us with the new beauties he can evoke from the set and balanced musical phrase. If this should come, well and good; meanwhile it is our duty to appreciate the rich and copious effects that the present day men are drawing from the supple rhythms they employ.

I have mentioned two points in which Hugo Wolf makes a quite exceptional figure in the history of the song—the unusually intimate connection he has established between the voice part and the piano part, and the wonderful rhythmic ease and naturalness of his speech. It only remains to say that on the purely expressive side his art is extremely emotional and extraordinarily wide in its range. No other song writer has composed anything like so wide a circle of interests as he. Strauss ran him close with his hundred songs, many of which are among the most original and most beautiful things the world has ever seen; but Strauss's songs, though they would represent a decent life's achievement for another man, are after all only a by-product of his amazing fertility, little overflows of feeling that he did not know where else to use. The greatest volume and whitest heat of Strauss's thoughts went into his orchestral works and operas. Wolf, concentrating all that is best of him upon the song, packs it with a wealth and variety of thinking and feeling that in other men would have sought expression in the larger forms. Hence the power of his singing, its grip, its range. A ballad like *Prometheus* (1889) or *Der Feuerreiter* from the Moerike set contains such a volume of mental energy as was never put into any ballad before; while even in the smaller things—yes, even the smallest of them—we feel that we are watching the cerebration of a man of extraordinary psychological insight. He greatly widened the scope of the song by showing triumphantly how it can mate itself with the most unpromising subject; and, with the rarest of exceptions, whatever he takes up he treats with incisive convincingness. In *Das verlassene Mägdlein,* in the Moerike volume, he has painted a singularly pathetic picture of a poor little maidservant getting up in the cold morning to light the fire, and thinking of the faithless lover of whom she had dreamt in the night. Examine this song carefully and you will realize the consummate art of it—its faultless suggestion of the cold gray atmosphere of the poem, its subtle gradations of feeling, its pure pathos and big humanism. Who else could set such a song—but Strauss—I do not know; I am quite certain no one else could make of it what Wolf made of it. But indeed this volume of his is the richest treasury of song bequeathed to us since Schubert—the charming and profound and passionate reflections upon life of a great artist and a great man. His rare faults—of which the chief is an occasional tortuosity of harmonic sequence—are, at this time of day, not worth dealing upon. It is much more to the point that those who realize what changes Wagner and Strauss have made in the map of music should also realize that the name of Hugo Wolf is inseparable from theirs.

WOLF SPEAKS

What I write now, I write for the future. . . . Since Schubert and Schumann there has been nothing like it.

.   .   .   .   .

I am so happy—oh, happier than the happiest of kings. Another new Lied! If you could hear what is going on in my heart! . . . the devil would carry you away with pleasure! . . . Another two new Lieder! There is one that sounds so horribly strange that it frightens me. There is nothing like it in existence, Heaven help the unfortunate people who will one day hear it! . . . If you could only hear the last Lied I have just composed, you would have only one desire left —to die.

.   .   .   .   .

A man is not taken away, before he has said all he has to say.

.   .   .   .   .

For the last four months [August 13, 1891] I have been suffering from a sort of mental consumption, which makes me think very seriously of quitting the world forever. . . . Only those who truly live should live at all. I have been for some time like one dead. I only wish it were an apparent death; but I am really dead and buried though the power to control my body gives me a seeming life. It is my inmost, my only desire, that the flesh may quickly follow the spirit that has already passed. For the past fifteen days I have been living at Traunkirchen, the pearl of Traunsee. . . . All the comforts that a man could wish for are here to make life happy—peace, solitude, beautiful scenery, invigorating air, and everything that could suit the tastes of a hermit like myself. And yet—and yet, my friend, I am the most miserable creature on earth. Everything around me

481

breathes peace and happiness, everything throbs with life and fulfills its functions. . . . I alone, oh God! . . . I alone live like a beast that is deaf and senseless. Even reading hardly serves to distract me now though I bury myself in books in my despair. As for composition, that is finished; I can no longer bring to mind the meaning of a harmony or a melody, and I almost begin to doubt if the compositions that bear my name are really mine. Good God! What is the use of all this fame? What is the end of these great aims of misery, what lies at the end of it? . . . Heaven gives a man a complete genius or no genius at all. Hell has given me everything by halves.

CAMILLE SAINT-SAËNS

1 8 3 5 – 1 9 2 1

CHARLES-CAMILLE SAINT-SAËNS was born in Paris, France, on October 9, 1835. He was remarkably precocious in music, making a concert appearance before his fifth birthday and starting composition at six. After a period of piano study with Camille-Marie Stamaty, Saint-Saëns made a highly successful formal debut as pianist in Paris on May 6, 1846. From 1848 to 1852 he attended the Paris Conservatory where he received many honors. His first successes as composer came between 1852–53 when he won the Award of the Société Sainte-Cécile for his *Ode à Sainte-Cécile* and had his first symphony performed. From 1853 to 1857 he was organist at the Saint-Merry Church in Paris, and from 1858 to 1877 at the Madeleine, where he received recognition as one of France's most eminent organ virtuosos. His impressive career as teacher began in 1861 with an appointment as professor of piano at the École Niedermeyer. In 1871 he helped found the Société nationale de musique in Paris to promote the works of French composers. In 1875 he married Marie Truffot who bore him two sons, both of whom died in infancy. They were permanently separated in 1881, but never divorced.

All the while Saint-Saëns continued writing music prolifically in every possible form and medium, establishing his reputation as one of France's most significant 19th-century composers. His tone poem *Le Rouet d'Omphale* was introduced in 1871, followed in 1874 by his popular *Danse macabre*. His fourth piano concerto in 1875, his opera *Samson and Delilah* (introduced in Weimar on December 2, 1877), and his third symphony in 1886 added further to his stature. He was honored as the *grand'homme* of French music in 1881 through his election to the Institut de France. In 1913 he attained the highest possible rank in the Legion of Honor, that of Grand-Croix.

Saint-Saëns traveled extensively throughout the world as conductor and pianist in performances of his own works. In 1906 and 1915 he paid visits to the United States. He was eighty-one when he embarked on an extended tour of South America, and in his eighty-fifth year he performed in Greece and Algiers. He was on a holiday in Algiers when he died there on December 16, 1921.

THE MAN

PHILIP HALE

An enemy of Saint-Saëns—and Saint-Saëns made enemies by his barbed words—might have applied to him the lines of Juvenal:

> Grammarian, painter, augur, rhetorician,
> Rope-dancer, conjuror, fiddler, and physician,
> All trades his own, your hungry Greekling, counts,
> And bid him mount the sky—the sky he mounts.

For Saint-Saëns was not satisfied with the making of music, or the career of a virtuoso. Organist, pianist, caricaturist, dabbler in science, enamored of mathematics, and astronomy, amateur comedian, feuilletonist, critic, traveler, archaeologist—he was a restless man.

He was of less than average height, thin, nervous, sick-faced; with great and exposed forehead, hair habitually short, beard frosted. His eyes were almost level with his face. His eagle-beak would have excited the admiration of Sir Charles Napier, who once exclaimed: "Give me a man with plenty of nose." Irritable, whimsical, ironical, paradoxical, indulging in sudden changes of opinion, he was faithful to friends, appreciative of certain rivals, kindly disposed toward young composers, zealous in practical assistance as well as in verbal encouragement. A man that knew the world and sparkled in conversation; fond of society; at least on equal terms with leaders in art, literature, fashion. A man whose Monday receptions were long famous in Paris, eagerly anticipated by *tout Paris;* yet never so happy as when acting Calchas to Bizet's or Regnault's Helen in

Offenbach's delightful *La Belle Hélène,* or impersonating in an extraordinary costume Gounod's Marguerite surprised by the casket of jewels. An indefatigable student of Bach, he parodied the Italian opera of the 30's, 40's, 50's, in *Gabriella di Vergi.*

Then there is his amusing *Carnaval des animaux* which was written, as was his *Gabriella di Vergi,* without intention of publication. A Parisian from crown of head to sole of foot; yet a nomad.

THE COMPOSER

ROMAIN ROLLAND

Saint-Saëns had the rare honor of becoming a classic during his lifetime. His name, though it was long unrecognized, commands universal respect. No artist had troubled so little about the public or had been more indifferent to criticism whether popular or expert. As a child he had almost a physical revulsion for outward success. Later on, he achieved success by a long and painful struggle in which he had to fight against the kind of stupid criticism that condemned him "to listen to one of Beethoven's symphonies as a penance likely to give him the most excruciating torture." And yet after this, and after his admission to the Academy, after *Henry III* (1883) and the Third Symphony With Organ (1886), he still remained aloof from praise or blame and judged his triumphs with sad severity.

The significance of Saint-Saëns in art is a double one, for one must judge him from the inside as well as the outside of France. He stands for something exceptional in French music, something which was almost unique until lately: that is, a great classical spirit and a fine breadth of musical culture—German culture, we must say, since the foundations of all modern art rests on the German classics. French music of the 19th century is rich in clever artists, imaginative writers of melody, and skilful dramatists; but it is poor in true musicians and in good solid workmanship. Apart from two or three splendid exceptions, our composers have too much the character of gifted amateurs, who compose music as a pastime and regard it not

485

as a special form of thought but as a sort of dress for literary ideas. Our musical education is superficial: it may be got for a few years in a formal way at a conservatory, but it is not within the reach of all; the child does not breathe music as, in a way, he breathes the atmosphere of literature and oratory; and although nearly everyone in France has an instinctive feeling for beautiful writing, only a very few people care for beautiful music. From this arise the common faults and failings in our music. It has remained a luxurious art; it has not become, like German music, the poetical expression of the people's thought.

To bring this about we should need a combination of conditions that are very rare in France, though such conditions went to the making of Camille Saint-Saëns. He had not only remarkable natural talent, but came of a family of ardent musicians who devoted themselves to his education. At five years of age he was nourished on the orchestral score of *Don Giovanni;* as a little boy he "measured himself against Beethoven and Mozart" by playing in a public concert; at sixteen years of age he wrote his First Symphony. As he grew older he soaked himself in the music of Bach and Handel and was able to compose at will after the manner of Rossini, Verdi, Schumann, and Wagner. He wrote excellent music in all styles—the Grecian style and that of the 16th, 17th, and 18th centuries. His compositions were of every kind: Masses, grand operas, light operas, cantatas, symphonies, symphonic poems, music for the orchestra, the organ, the piano, the voice, and chamber music. He was the learned editor of Gluck and Rameau and was thus not only an artist but an artist who could talk about art. He was an unusual figure in France—one would have thought rather to find his home in Germany.

In Germany, however, while he was alive, they made no mistake about him. There the name of Camille Saint-Saëns stood for the French classical spirit and was thought worthiest to represent us in music from the time of Berlioz until the appearance of the school of César Franck. Saint-Saëns possessed, indeed, some of the best qualities of a French artist, and among them the most important quality of all—perfect clearness of conception. It is remarkable how little this learned artist was bothered by his learning and how free he was

486

from all pedantry. . . . "Saint-Saëns is not a pedant," wrote Gounod; "he has remained too much of a child and become too clever for that." Besides, he had always been too much of a Frenchman.

Sometimes Saint-Saëns reminds me of one of our 18th century writers. Not a writer of the *Encyclopédie*, nor one of Rousseau's camp, but rather of Voltaire's school. He had a clarity of thought, an elegance and precision of expression, and a quality of mind that made his music "not only noble, but very noble, as coming of a fine race and distinguished family."

He had also excellent discernment, of an unemotional kind; and he was "calm in spirit, restrained in imagination, and keeps his self-control even in the midst of the most disturbing emotions." This discernment is the enemy of anything approaching obscurity of thought or mysticism; and its outcome was that curious book, *Problèmes et mystères*—a misleading title, for the spirit of reason reigns there and makes an appeal to young people to protect "the light of a menaced world" against "the mists of the North, Scandinavian gods, Indian divinities, Catholic miracles, Lourdes, spiritualism, occultism, and obscurantism."

His love and need of liberty was also of the 18th century. One may say that liberty was his only passion. "I am passionately fond of liberty," he wrote. And he proved it by the absolute fearlessness of his judgments on art; for not only had he reasoned soundly against Wagner but dared to criticize the weaknesses of Gluck and Mozart, the errors of Weber and Berlioz, and the accepted opinions about Gounod; and this classicist, who had nourished on Bach, went so far as to say: "The performance of works by Bach and Handel today is an idle amusement," and that those who wish to revive their art are like "people who would live in an old mansion that has been uninhabited for centuries." He went even further; he criticized his own work and contradicted his own opinions. His love of liberty made him form, at different periods, different opinions of the same work. He thought that people had a right to change their opinions, as sometimes they deceived themselves. It seemed to him better to admit an error boldly than to be the slave of consistency. And this same feeling showed itself in other matters besides art: in ethics . . . and in metaphysics also, where he judges religions, faith, and the Gospels with a quiet freedom of thought, seeking in Nature alone the basis of morals and society.

His most characteristic mental trait seemed to be a languid melancholy, which had its source in a rather bitter feeling of the futility of life; and this was accompanied by fits of weariness which were not altogether healthy, followed by capricious moods and nervous gaiety, and a freakish liking for burlesque and mimicry. It was his eager, restless spirit that made him rush about the world writing Breton and Auvergnian rhapsodies, Persian songs, Algerian suites, Portuguese barcarolles, Danish, Russian, or Arabian caprices, souvenirs of Italy, African fantasias, and Egyptian concertos; and in the same way, he roamed through the ages, writing Greek tragedies, dance music of the 16th and 17th centuries, and preludes and fugues of the 18th. But in all these exotic and archaic reflections of times and countries through which his fancy wandered, one recognizes the gay, intelligent countenance of a Frenchman on his travels who idly follows his inclinations and does not trouble to enter very deeply into the spirit of the people he meets but gleans all he can and then reproduces it with a French complexion—after the manner of Montaigne in Italy, who compared Verona to Poitiers, and Padua to Bordeaux, and who, when he was in Florence, paid much less attention to Michelangelo than to "a strangely shaped sheep, and an animal the size of a large mastiff, shaped like a cat and striped with black and white, which they called a tiger."

From a purely musical point of view there is some resemblance between Saint-Saëns and Mendelssohn. In both of them we find the same intellectual restraint, the same balance preserved among the heterogeneous elements of their work. These elements are not common to both of them because the time, the country, and the surroundings in which they lived are not the same; and there is also a great difference in their characters. Mendelssohn is more ingenuous and religious; Saint-Saëns is more of a dilettante and more sensuous. They are not so much kindred spirits by their science as good company by a common purity of taste, a sense of rhythm, and a genius for method, which gave all they wrote a Neo-Classic character.

As for the things that directly influenced Saint-Saëns, they are so numerous that it would be difficult and rather bold of me to pretend to be able to pick them out. His remarkable capacity for assimilation had often moved him to write in the style of Wagner or Berlioz, of Handel or Rameau, of Jean-Baptiste Lully (1632–87), or Marc-Antoine Charpentier (1634–1704), or even of some English harpsichord and clavichord player of the 16th century, like William Byrd (1543–1623)—whose airs are introduced quite naturally in the music of *Henry VIII;* but we must remember that these are deliberate imitations, the amusements of a virtuoso, about which Saint-Saëns never deceived himself. His memory served him as he pleased, but he was never troubled by it.

As far as one can judge, Saint-Saëns' musical ideas were infused with the spirit of the great classics belonging to the end of the 18th century—far more, whatever people might say, with the spirit of Beethoven, Haydn, and Mozart than with the spirit of Bach. Schumann's seductiveness also left its mark upon him, and he has felt the influence of Gounod, Georges Bizet (1838–75), and Wagner. But a stronger influence was that of Berlioz, his friend and master, and, above all, that of Liszt. We must stop at this last name.

Saint-Saëns had good reason for liking Liszt, for Liszt was also a lover of freedom and had shaken off traditions and pedantry and scorned German routine; and Saint-Saëns liked him, too, because his music was a reaction from the stiff school of Brahms. He was enthusiastic about Liszt's work and was one of the earliest and most ardent champions of that new music of which Liszt was the leading spirit—of that "program" music which Wagner's triumph seemed to have nipped in the bud but which suddenly and gloriously burst into life again in the works of Richard Strauss. . . . This influence seems to me to explain some of Saint-Saëns' work. Not only is this influence evident in his symphonic poems—some of his best work—but it is to be found in his suites for orchestra, his fantasias, and his rhapsodies, where the descriptive and narrative element is strong. . . .

And so we find that Saint-Saëns had taken part in the vigorous attempt of modern German symphony writers to bring into music some of the power of the other arts: poetry, painting, philosophy, romance, drama—the whole of life. But what a gulf divided them and him! A gulf made up not only of diversities of style but of the difference between two races and two worlds. Besides the frenzied

489

outpourings of Richard Strauss (1864–1949), who flounders uncertainly between mud and debris and genius, the Latin art of Saint-Saëns rises up calm and ironical. His delicacy of touch, his careful moderation, his happy grace, "which enters the soul by a thousand little paths," bring with them the pleasures of beautiful speech and honest thought; and we cannot but feel their charm. Compared with the restless and troubled art of today, his music strikes us by its calm, its tranquil harmonies, its velvety modulations, its crystal clearness, its smooth and flowing style, and an elegance that cannot be put into words. Even his classic coldness does us good by its reaction against the exaggerations, sincere as they are, of the new school. At times one feels oneself carried back to Mendelssohn, even to Spontini and the school of Gluck. One seems to be traveling in a country that one knows and loves; and yet in Saint-Saëns' works one does not find any direct resemblance to the works of other composers; for with no one are reminiscences rarer than with this master who carried all the old masters in his mind—it is his spirit that is akin to theirs. And that is the secret of his personality and his value to us; he brings to our artistic unrest a little of the light and sweetness of other times. His compositions are like fragments of another world.

"From time to time," he said in speaking of *Don Giovanni*, "in the sacred earth of Hellene we find a fragment, an arm, the debris of a torso, scratched and damaged by the ravages of time; it is only the shadow of the god that the sculptor's chisel once created; but the charm is somehow still there, the sublime style is radiant in spite of everything."

And so with this music. It is sometimes a little pale, a little too restrained; but in a phrase, in a few harmonies, there will shine out a clear vision of the past.

SAINT-SAËNS SPEAKS

Music should charm unaided, but its effect is much finer when we use our imagination and let it flow in some particular channel, thus imagining the music. It is then that all the faculties of the soul are brought into play for the same end. What art gains from this is not greater beauty but a wider field for its scope—that is, a greater variety of form and a larger liberty.

. . . . .

He who does not take delight in a simple well-constructed chord, beautiful in its arrangement, does not love music. He who does not prefer the first Prelude in the *Well-Tempered Clavier* played without nuances, even as the composer wrote it for the instrument, to the same prelude embellished with a passionate melody, does not love music. For who does not prefer a folk tune of simple, lovely character, or a Gregorian chant without any accompaniment, to a series of dissonant and pretentious chords, does not love music.

. . . . .

I take very little notice of either praise or censure, not because I have an exalted idea of my own merits (which would be foolish) but because in doing my work and fulfilling the function of my nature, as an apple tree grows apples, I have no need to trouble myself with other people's views.

. . . . .

Having tried to release lyric drama from the fetters which caused all clear-sighted spirits to sigh—one now has gone so far as to declare all other music outside of modern lyric drama as unworthy of the attention of intelligent people. Furthermore one has distorted music by completely suppressing singing in favor of declamation, and by placing the real element into an orchestra developed to excess. Whereby the latter has been robbed of balance, equilibrium, it has gradually been shorn of all beauty of form and has transformed it into a liquid, unfathomable pulp, which is intended to arouse sensations, to affect the nervous system. And now they are even trying to make us believe that, too, is already a standpoint of the past. We are presented with a picture of a musical drama (the term lyric drama is no longer adequate) as it should be conditioned to reach perfection. A subject, essentially of a symbolic order, little action, the persons regarded as personified ideas rather than acting beings of flesh and blood. And from one deduction to another, they have finally come to the conclusion that the ideal drama is a chimera not to be realized, and it is no longer proper to write for the theater—meaning the stage as it now exists—but for an ideal stage alone, after the pattern of Bayreuth. With such exaggerations, we should arrive at feeling nothing for the old Italian opera but a deep pity. That was a poor flat thing, but it was nevertheless a finely chiselled, more or less gay golden frame, in which appeared from time to time wonderful singers who had an excellent schooling. That, at any rate, was better than nothing. If we have no ambrosia, it is better to eat dry bread than to die of starvation.

CLAUDE DEBUSSY

1 8 6 2 – 1 9 1 8

ACHILLE-CLAUDE DEBUSSY, father of musical Impressionism, was born in St. Germain-en-Laye, France, on August 22, 1862. For six years, beginning in 1874, he attended the Paris Conservatory. Though often impatient with academic routines and textbook rule, he proved a brilliant student, winning many prizes. After graduating in 1880, he worked for two summers as household pianist for Mme. von Meck, Tchaikovsky's patroness and "beloved friend." In 1884, Debussy received the Prix de Rome for the cantata, *L'Enfant prodigue*. He was not happy in Rome—partly because he disliked Italy, but mainly because the compositions (*"envois"*) he submitted to the Prix de Rome authorities were severely criticized for their unusual style and techniques. Returning to Paris without completing the three years prescribed by the Prix, he became influenced by the then flourishing Symbolist movement in literature and Impressionist movement in painting, and also by the avant-garde tendencies and iconoclastic approaches of the provocative French composer Erik Satie (1886–1925). Such ideas, theories, and progressive viewpoints helped Debussy to clarify his own aims as a composer. He soon arrived at the style and technique of Impressionism with which he achieved full maturity as a creative artist and with which he revolutionized French music.

The first significant compositions in which this new manner was fully crystallized were the *Suite bergamasque* for piano, in 1890 (in which the popular *Clair de lune* is found), the String Quartet in G Major in 1893, and the orchestral tone poem *The Afternoon of a Faun (L'Après-midi d'un faun)* in 1894. After that came the masterworks with which Debussy became one of the most significant composers of his generation: the opera, *Pelléas et Mélisande*, introduced at the Opéra-Comique on April 30, 1902; the three *Nocturnes* for orchestra, in 1899; the three symphonic sketches collectively entitled *La Mer,* in 1905; the two series of *Images* for piano, between 1905 and 1907; the two books of piano preludes between 1910 and 1913.

In 1899 Debussy married Rosalie Texier. He abandoned her in 1904 to elope with Emma Bardac, wife of a banker, whom he married later the same year after her divorce had been finalized. They had one child, a daughter who died when she was fourteen.

During the last years of his life, Debussy was a victim of cancer. Physical pain was combined with serious financial problems brought on by World War I and with the bitter disappointment at failing to gain a seat at the Académie de France. He died in Paris on March 25, 1918, a man broken in health and spirit. Due to the war, his passing went unnoticed except by a meager handful of those who had been closest to him.

THE MAN

OSCAR THOMPSON

Something feline in his nature was noted again and again by those who knew Achille-Claude Debussy. He was catlike and solitary, as he was artistic and amorous. . . . Feline . . . is the adjective most used to suggest his walk, his manner, his particular kind of acrid wit, his playfulness, his sulks and, most of all, the voluptuousness that colored his whole relation to life and art. He was a hedonist, a sybarite, a sensualist. But his career was one of toil and narrow means. The prodigal in him got him into difficulties he might otherwise have avoided, but his extravagances were small, like the opportunities therefor. Successive affairs of the heart, each of the irregular order that the French condone readily enough . . . were the chief of these extravagances, so far as any or all of them may have affected his career. Plainly there was no want of virility in Debussy's attitude towards the affections. The man who set the *Chansons de Biltis* of Pierre Louÿs and who conceived the Prelude to Mallarmé's

L'Après midi d'un faun was an epicure, but no epicene. Physically, said Georgette Leblanc, who described him as he appeared at the time of his first meeting with Maurice Maeterlinck, he gave the impression of having been built for strength—a strength he had no occasion, and no incentive, to acquire. Debussy was lazy in all except his art. Until sickness sapped his vitality and weakened his will, he worked steadily and conscientiously at composition. Otherwise, life was nothing for a display of energy. He was no great reader. He was much less an athlete, a sportsman, or a soldier. . . . Debussy's life was sedentary and altogether civilian.

As for cats, he liked them and they were his house pets during the successive liaisons that preceded and attended his two marriages. His friend René Peter is authority for the statement that the cats were always Angoras, and always gray. Moreover, since they were taken in one at a time, the name of any cat encountered in the Debussy domicile was always Line.

A natural bohemian, a man of Montmartre by instinct and habit, it was inevitable that Debussy should be one of the celebrities who frequented the famous café that in its title paid public tribute to the dignities of catship, the historic Chat Noir. With the Brasserie Pousset, the Chez Weber, and the Reynolds bar, it supplied the kind of background that many remember when they think of "Claude de France." There was sobriety in his conduct, as in his music. But he relished late hours in places where painters, writers, stage folk, and musicians congregated. He could be solitary as well as catlike there, too. But he knew well many of the notables who frequented such places and he was similarly well known.

The Debussy of the cafés, the mature Debussy, was the Debussy of the black beard and mop of curly black hair that fell over one eyebrow. Henri Lerolle has said that he looked exactly like a Syrian. His rather delicate nose was sufficiently aquiline to comport with the Levantine swarthiness. But his huge forehead dominated his face. Of medium height, he was short-legged and large of trunk. His shoulders were wide. His voice was low, but as Lerolle remembered it, of a marked nasal quality. (Elsewhere it is described as "sepulchral.") At forty, though still not a celebrity as a composer, Debussy was a figure to be recognized in the surroundings of his choice. Strangers would ask who the *"grand noir"* was—the dark fellow with the familiar faunlike beard, the cowboy hat, and the Macfarlane overcoat, the wings of which sometimes gave him a batlike appearance as he moved among the tables or on the streets. . . .

André Suarès has spoken of a sort of patina over his face. It is a choice figure to describe the peculiar pallor that others found there —a swarthy pallor—even in the days when he was assumed to be in the best of health. According to Henri Régnier, Claude walked with heavy, muffled tread. His figure was flabby and suggested indolence. From the dull pastiness of his face shone his keen black, heavy-lidded eyes. Over the huge head with its curious bumps drooped his wayward, fuzzy hair. He was feline in movement, and something gypsy-like, with a passionate strain discoverable under his lethargic manner.

In manner Debussy was a being of many contradictions. One description refers to him as "that very materially minded fellow," "that sleep-heavy creature," "always taciturn unless he wanted to get good addresses for procuring caviar, for which he was on the lookout and of which he was inordinately fond." An interviewer for *Le Figaro* found he smiled readily and spoke quietly in a soft, melodious voice (not "nasal" or "sepulchral" this time) but was almost monastic in his reserve. Raymond Bonheur noted a certain brusqueness in his speech. Often it was hesitating, "as often happens with people who are not content with commonplace remarks and who think for themselves." Moreover, he spoke with a slight lisp. Rarely on first meeting would he disclose anything of himself. While others talked, Claude would turn the leaves of a book or examine an engraving, listening but apparently not concentrating on what was said. Yet his eyes would take on a look of singular intensity when he was really interested, and it was clear that although he was master of his comportment he had difficulty in controlling his emotions.

The virtuosity with which he rolled a cigarette in paper always devoid of glue without spilling the slightest speck of tobacco was a source of wonder and admiration to great and humble alike among the Parisians he encountered day by day. The opera he endured— if only now and then. But the circus! There he would gladly have gone every day. He could admire Mary Garden or Maggie Teyte. But the clowns! Debussy was like a child in his relish of their time-honored slapstick. The card game he most enjoyed was called bezique—Chinese bezique. When he played, Debussy would put his pipe beside him, as a cowboy of American frontier times might have placed his six-shooter. He would cheat, more or less openly, turning down the tip of a card he might want to put in his hand later. Consultation of an English dictionary brings a reminder that bezique is a game similar to pinochle, save that it is played with piquet packs in number equal to the players. Whether, with his training, Debussy would have made an incomparable pinochle player is something not to be determined by analysis of any of his chord sequences and subtle evasions of settled tonalities.

Financially, Debussy was never out of difficulties. . . . If he had possessed more of the business acumen of Richard Strauss, and another well-known Straussian characteristic which may be referred to here as thrift, perhaps, he would have been a more comfortable, even a happier man. But Debussy was too fond of life to stint himself where his sort of modest pleasures were concerned; he could no more live primarily for money than he could write for it. His was the art aesthetic applied to life. Both life and art were governed by the same bent for the sensuous, the select, the rare, the different. He was fond of books, and bibelots—fonder of possession, in the case of the former, than he was of reading—but, as Henri Régnier said, he always got back to music. It was there he really lived his life and, as has been true of others who had a really seminal mission to fulfil, he lived it largely in the music that was his own.

THE COMPOSER

PAUL ROSENFELD

Debussy's music is our own. All artistic forms lie dormant in the soul, and there is no work of art actually foreign to us, nor can such a one appear, in all the future ages of the world. But the music of Debussy is proper to us, in our day, as is no other, and might stand before all time our symbol. For it lived in us before it was born, and after birth returned upon us like a release. Even at a first encounter the style of *Pelléas* (1902) was mysteriously familiar. It made us feel that we had always needed such rhythms, such luminous chords, such limpid phrases, that we perhaps had even heard them, sounding faintly, in our imaginations. The music seemed as old as our sense of selfhood. It seemed but the exquisite recognition of certain intense and troubling and appeasing moments that we had already encountered. It seemed fashioned out of certain ineluctable, mysterious experiences that had budded, ineffably sad and sweet, from out our lives, and had made us new, and set us apart, and that now, at the music's breath, at a half-whispered note, at the unclosing of a rhythm, the flowering of a cluster of tones out of the warm still darkness, were arisen again in the fullness of their stature and become ours entirely.

For Debussy is of all musicians the one amongst us most fully. He is here, in our midst, in the world of the city. There is about him none of the unworldliness, the aloofness, the superhumanity that distances so many of the other composers from us. We need not imagine him in exotic singing robes, nor in classical garments, nor in any strange and outmoded and picturesque attire, to recognize in him the poet. He is the modern poet just because the modern civilian garb is so naturally his. He is the normal man, living our own manner of life. We seem to know him as we know ourselves. His experiences are but our own, intensified by his poet's gift. Or, if they are not already ours, they will become so. He seems almost ourselves as he passes through the city twilight, intent upon some errand upon which we, too, have gone, journeying a road which we ourselves have travelled. We know the room in which he lives, the windows from which he gazes, the moments which come upon him there in the silence of the lamp. For he has captured in his music what is distinguished in the age's delight and tragedy. All the fine sensuality, all the Eastern pleasure in the infinite daintiness and warmth of nature, all the sudden, joyous discovery of color and touch that made men feel as though neither had been known before, are contained in it. It, too, is full of images of the "earth of the liquid and slumbering trees," the "earth of departed sunset," the "earth of the

498

vitreous pour of the full moon just tinged with blue." It is full of material loveliness, plies itself to innumerable dainty shells—to the somnolence of the Southern night, to the hieratic gesture of temple dancers, to the fall of lamplight into the dark, to the fantastic gush of fireworks, to the romance of old mirrors and faded brocades and Saxony clocks, to the green young panoply of spring. And just as it gives again the age's consciousness of the delicious robe of earth, so, too, it gives again its sense of weariness and powerlessness and oppression. The 19th century had been loud with blare and rumors and the vibration of colossal movements, and man had apparently traversed vast distances and explored titanic heights and abysmal depths. And yet, for all the glare, the earth was darker. The light was miasmic only. The life of man seemed as ever a brief and sad and simple thing, the stretching of impotent hands, unable to grasp and hold; the interlacing of shadows; the unclosing, a moment before nightfall, of exquisite and fragile blossoms. The sense of the infirmity of life, the consciousness that it had no more than the signification of a dream with passing lights, or halting steps in the snow, or an old half-forgotten story, had mixed a deep wistfulness and melancholy into the very glamour of the globe, and become heavier itself for all the sweetness of earth. And Debussy has fixed the two in their confusion.

He has permeated music completely with his Impressionistic sensibility. His style is an image of this our pointillistically feeling era. With him Impressionism achieves a perfect musical form. Structurally, the music of Debussy is a fabric of exquisite and poignant moments, each full and complete in itself. His wholes exist entirely in their parts, in their atoms. If his phrases, rhythms, lyric impulses, do contribute to the formation of a single thing, they yet are extraordinarily independent and significant in themselves. No chord, no theme, is subordinate. Each one exists for the sake of its own beauty, occupies the universe for an instant, then merges and disappears. The harmonies are not, as in other compositions, preparations. They are apparently an end in themselves, flow in space, and then change hue, as a shimmering stuff changes. For all its golden earthiness, the style of Debussy is the most liquid and impalpable of musical styles. It is forever gliding, gleaming, melting; crystallizing for an instant in some savory phrase, then moving quiveringly onward. It is well-nigh edgeless. It seems to flow through our perceptions as water flows through fingers. The iridescent bubbles that float upon it burst if we but touch them. It is forever suggesting water—fountains and pools, the glistening spray and heaving bosom of the sea. Or, it shadows forth the formless breath of the breeze, of the storm, of perfumes, or the play of sun and moon. His orchestration invariably produces all that is cloudy and diaphanous in each instrument. He makes music with flakes of light, with bright motes of pigment. His palette glows with the sweet, limpid tints of a Monet or a Pissarro or a Renoir. His orchestra sparkles with iridescent fires, with divided tones, with delicate violets and argents and shades of rose. The sound of the piano, usually but the ringing of flat colored stones, at his touch becomes fluid, velvety, and dense, takes on the properties of satins and liqueurs. The pedal washes new tint after new tint over the keyboard. *Reflets dans l'eau* (1905) has the quality of sheeny blue satin, of cloud pictures tumbling in gliding water. Blue fades to green and fades back again to blue in the middle section of *Hommage à Rameau* (1905). Bright, cold moonlight slips through *Et la lune descend sur le temple que fut* (1907); ruddy sparks glitter in *Mouvement* (1905) with its Petrouchka-like joy; the piano is liquid and luminous and aromatic in *Cloches à travers les feuilles* (1907).

Yet there is no uncertainty, no mistiness in his form, as there is in that of some of the other Impressionists. His music is classically firm, classically precise and knit. His lyrical, shimmering structures are perfectly fashioned. The line never hesitates, never becomes lost nor involved. It proceeds directly, clearly, passing through jewels and clots of color, and fusing them into the mass. The trajectory never breaks. The music is always full of its proper weight and timbre. It can be said quite without exaggeration that his best work omits nothing, neglects nothing, that every component element is justly treated. His little pieces occupy a space as completely as the most massive and grand of compositions. A composition like *Nuages*, the first of the three *Nocturnes* for orchestra (1893–99), while taking but five minutes in performance, outweighs any number of compositions that last an hour. *L'Après-midi d'un faun* (1892–94) is inspired and new, marvelously, at every measure. The three little pieces that comprise the first set of *Images* for piano (1905) will probably outlast half of what Liszt has written for the instrument. *Pelléas* will some day be studied for its miraculous invention, its classical moderation and balance and truth, for its pure diction and economical orchestration, quite as the scores of Gluck are studied to-day.

For Debussy is, of all the artists who have made music in our time, the most perfect. Other musicians, perhaps even some of the contemporary, may exhibit a greater heroism, a greater staying power and indefatigability. Nevertheless, in his sphere he is every inch as perfect a workman as the greatest. Within his limits he was as pure a craftsman as the great Johann Sebastian in his. The difference between the two is the difference of their ages and races, not the difference of their artistry. For few composers can match with their own Debussy's perfection of taste, his fineness of sensibility, his poetic rapture, and profound awareness of beauty. Few have been more graciously rounded and balanced than he, have been, like him, so fine that nothing which they could do could be tasteless and insignificant and without grace. Few musicians have been more nicely sensible of their gift, better acquainted with themselves, surer of the character and limitations of their genius. Few have been as perseverantly essential, have managed to sustain their emotion and invention so steadily at a height. The music of Debussy is full of purest, most delicate poesy. Perhaps only Bach and Mussorgsky have as invariably found phrases as pithy and inclusive and final as those with which *Pelléas* is strewn, phrases that with a few simple notes epitomize profound and exquisite emotions, and are indeed the word. There are moments in Debussy's work when each note opens a prospect. There are moments when the music of *Pelléas*, the fine fluid line of sound, the melodic moments that merge and pass and vanish into one another, become the gleaming rims that circumscribe vast darkling forms. There are portions of the drama that are like the moments of human intercourse when single syllables unseal deep reservoirs. The tenderness manifest here is scarcely to be duplicated in musical art. And tenderness, after all, is the most intense of all emotions.

A thousand years of culture live in this fineness. In these perfect gestures, in this grace, this certainty of choice, this justice of values,

501

this simple, profound, delicate language, there live on thirty generations of gentlefolk. Thirty generations of cavaliers and dames who developed the arts of life in the mild and fruitful valleys of "the pleasant land of France" speak here. The gentle sunlight and gentle shadow, the mild winters and mild summers of the Ile de France, the plentiful fruits of the earth, the excitement of the vine, contributed to making this being beautifully balanced, reserved, refined. The instruction and cultivation of the classic and French poets and thinkers, Virgil and Racine and Marivaux, Catullus and Montaigne and Chateaubriand, the chambers of the Hôtel de Rambouillet, the gardens and galleries of Versailles, the immense drawing-room of 18th century Paris, helped form this spirit. In all this man's music one catches sight of the long foreground, the long cycles of preparation. In every one of his works, from the most imposing to the least, from the String Quartet (1893) and *Pelléas* to the gracile, lissome little waltz, *La plus que lent* (1910), there is manifest the Latin genius nurtured and molded and developed by the fertile, tranquil soil of France.

And in his art, the gods of classical antiquity live again. Debussy is much more than merely the sensuous Frenchman. He is the man in whom the old Pagan voluptuousness, the old untroubled delight in the body, warred against so long by the black brood of monks and transformed by them during centuries into demoniacal and hellish forms, is free and pure and sweet once more. They once were nymphs and naiads and goddesses, the Quartet and *L'Après-midi d'un faun* and *Sirènes*. They once wandered through the glades of Ionia and Sicily, and gladdened men with their golden sensuality, and bewitched them with the thought of "the breast of the nymph in the brake." For they are full of the wonder and sweetness of the flesh, of flesh tasted deliciously and enjoyed not in closed rooms, behind secret doors and under the shameful pall of the night, but out in the warm, sunny open, amid grasses and scents and the buzzing of insects, the waving of branches, the wandering of clouds. The Quartet is alive, quivering with light, and with joyous animality. It moves like a young fawn; spins the gayest, most silken, most golden of spider webs; fills one with the delights of taste and smell and sight and touch. In the most glimmering, floating of poems, *L'Après-midi d'un faun,* there is caught magically by the climbing, chromatic flute, the drowsy pizzicati of the strings, and the languorous sighing of the horns, the atmosphere of the daydream, the sleepy warmth of the sunshot herbage, the divine apparition, the white wonder of arms and breasts and thighs. The lento movement of *Ibéria* is like some drowsy, disheveled gypsy. Even *La plus que lent* is full of the goodness of the flesh, is like some slender young girl with unclosing bosom. And in *Sirènes,* something like the eternal divinity, the eternal beauty of woman's body, is celebrated. It is as though on the rising, falling, rising, sinking tides of the poem, on the waves of the glamorous feminine voices, on the aphrodisiac swell of the sea, the white Anadyomene herself, with her galaxy of tritons and naiads, approached earth's shores once more.

If any musical task is to be considered as having been accomplished, it is that of Debussy. For he wrote the one book that every great artist writes. He established a style irrefragably, made musical Impressionism as legitimate a thing as any of the great styles. That he had more to make than that one contribution is doubtful. His art underwent no radical changes. His style was mature already in the Quartet and in *Proses lyriques* (1892–93), and had its climax in *Pelléas,* its orchestral deployment in *Nocturnes* and *La Mer* (1903–5) and *Ibéria* (1906–9), its pianistic expression in the two volumes of *Images* for pianoforte. Whatever the refinement of the incidental music to *Le Martyre de Saint-Sébastien* (1911), Debussy never really transgressed the limits set for him by his first great works. And so, even if his long illness caused the deterioration, the hardening, the formularization, so evident in his most recent work, the Sonatas (1915–17), the *Épigraphes* (1915), *En blanc et noir* (1915), and the *Berceuse héroïque* (1914), and deprived us of much delightful art, neither it nor his death actually robbed us of some radical development which we might reasonably have expected. The chief that he had to give he had given. What his age had demanded of him, an art that it might hold far from the glare and tumult, an art into which it could retreat, an art which could compensate it for a life become too cruel and demanding, he had produced. He had essentially fulfilled himself.

The fact that *Pelléas* is the most eloquent of all Debussy's works and his eternal sign does not, then, signify that he did not grow during the remainder of his life. A complex of determinants made of his music-drama the fullest expression of his genius, decreed that he should be living most completely at the moment he composed it. The very fact that in it Debussy was composing music for the theater made it certain that his artistic sense would produce itself as its mightiest in the work. For it entailed the statement of his opposition to Wagner. The fact that it was music conjoined with speech made it certain that Debussy, so full of the French classical genius, would through contact with the spoken word, through study of its essential quality, be aided and compelled to a complete realization of a fundamentally French idiom. And then Maeterlinck's little play offered itself to his genius as a unique auxiliary. It, too, is full of the sense of the shadowiness of things that weighed upon Debussy, has not a little of the accent of the time. This *"vieille et triste légende de la forêt"* is alive with images, such as the old and somber castle inhabited by aging people and lying lost amid sunless forests, the rose that blooms in the shadow underneath Mélisande's casement, Mélisande's hair that falls farther than her arms can reach, the black tarn that broods beneath the castle-vaults and breathes death, Golaud's anguished search for truth in the prattle of the child, that could not but call a profound response from Debussy's imagination. But, above all, it was the figure of Mélisande herself that made him pour himself completely into the setting of the play. For that figure permitted Debussy to give himself completely in the creation of his ideal image. The music is all Mélisande, all Debussy's love-woman. It is she that the music reveals from the moment Mélisande rises from among the rocks shrouded in the mystery of her golden hair. It is she the music limns from the very beginning of the work. The entire score is but what a man might feel toward a woman that was his, and yet, like all women, strange and mysterious and un-known to him. The music is like the stripping of some perfect flower, petal upon petal. There are moments when it is all that lies between two people, and is the fullness of their knowledge. It is the perfect sign of an experience.

And so, since Debussy's art could have no second climax, it was in the order of things that the works succeeding upon his masterpiece should be relatively less important. Nevertheless, the ensuing poems and songs and piano pieces, with the exception of those written during those years when Debussy could have said with Rameau, his master, "From day to day my taste improves. But I have lost all my genius," are by little less perfect and astounding pieces of work. His music is like the peaks of a mountain range, of which one of the first and nearest is the highest, while the others appear scarcely less high. And they are some of the bluest, the loveliest, the most shining that stretch through the region of modern music. It will be long before humankind has exhausted their beauty.

DEBUSSY SPEAKS

For a long time I sought to compose music for the theater. But the form I wished to employ was so unusual that after various efforts I had almost abandoned the idea. Previous research in pure music led me to hate classical development, whose beauty is merely technical and of interest only to the highbrows of our class. I desired for music that freedom of which she is capable perhaps to a greater degree than any other art, as she is not confined to an exact reproduction of Nature, but only to the mysterious affinity between Nature and the imagination.

After several years of passionate pilgrimage to Bayreuth, I began to entertain doubts as to the Wagnerian formula; or, rather, it seemed to me that it could serve only the particular case of Wagner's genius. He was a great collector of formulas. He assembled them all into one, which appears individual to those who are ill acquainted with music. And without denying his genius one may say that he placed a period to the music of his time in much the same way as Victor Hugo did for poetry. The thing, then, was to find what came after Wagner's time but not after Wagner's manner.

The drama of *Pelléas* which, in spite of its fantastic atmosphere, contains much more humanity than the so-called documents on life, appeared to me to be admirably suited to my purpose. The sensitiveness of the suggestive language could be carried into the music and orchestral setting. I have also tried to obey a law of beauty which appears to be singularly ignored in dealing with dramatic music. The characters of this drama endeavor to sing like real persons, and not in an arbitrary language built on antiquated traditions. Hence the reproach levelled at my alleged partiality for the monotone declamation in which there is no trace of melody. . . . To begin with, this is untrue. Besides, the feelings of a character cannot be continually expressed in melody. Then, too, dramatic melody should be totally different from melody in general. . . . The people who go listen to music at the theater are, when all is said and done, very like those one sees gathered around a street singer! There, for a penny, one may indulge in melodic emotions. . . . One even notices greater patience than is practised by many subscribers to our state-endowed theaters and even a wish to understand which, one might even go so far as to say, is totally lacking in the latter public.

By a singular irony, this public, which cries out for something new, is the very one that shows alarm and scoffs whenever one tries to wean it from old habits and the customary humdrum noises. . . . This may seem incomprehensible; but one must not forget that a work of art or an effort to produce beauty are always regarded by some people as a personal affront.

I do not pretend to have discovered everything in *Pelléas;* but I have tried to trace a path that others may follow, broadening it with individual discoveries which will, perhaps, free dramatic music from the heavy yoke under which it has existed so long.

· · · · ·

Music is a mysterious form of mathematics whose elements are derived from the infinite. Music is the expression of the movement of the waters, the play of curves described by changing breezes. There is nothing more musical than a sunset. He who feels what he sees will find no more beautiful example of development in all that book which, alas, musicians read too little—the book of Nature.

We do not listen to the thousand sounds with which Nature surrounds us. We are not sufficiently on the alert to hear this varied music which she so generously offers. It envelops us, and yet we have lived in its midst until now, ignoring it. This, to my mind, is the new path. But, believe me, I have but caught a glimpse of it. Much remains to be done and he who does it . . . will be a great man.

. . . . .

Art is the most beautiful deception: and no matter how much a man may wish to make it the setting for his daily life, he must still desire that it remain an illusion lest it become utilitarian, and as dreamy as a workshop. Do not the masses as well as the select few seek therein oblivion, which is in itself a form of deception? The smile of Mona Lisa probably never really existed—still its charm is eternal. Let us then avoid disillusioning any one by clothing the dream with too much reality. Let us be satisfied with interpretations that are the more consoling because of their undying beauty.

APPENDICES

APPENDIX I

Principal Works of the Great Composers

GIOVANNI PIERLUIGI DA PALESTRINA

Choral Music: 93 Masses, including *Papae Marcelli* (1567), *Assumpta Es* (1567), *Aeterna Munera Christi* (1590), and *Ecco ego Joannes;* 256 motets, including the *Canticle of Solomon* (1584); 4 books of madrigals; 3 books of litanies; 3 books of lamentations; 2 books of madrigali spirituali; *Stabat Mater* (1595); hymns, offertories, psalms.

CLAUDIO MONTEVERDI

Choral Music: 8 books of madrigals (1587, 1590, 1592, 1603, 1605, 1614, 1619, 1638); canzonette, scherzi musicali, motets, Masses, magnificats.

Operas: La Favola d'Orfeo (1607); *L'Arianne,* from which only the "Lament" has survived (1608); *Il Combattimento di Tancredi e Clorinda* (1624); *Proserpina rapita* (1630); *Il Ritorno di Ulisse* (1641); *Le Nozze di Eneo con Lavinia* (1641); *L'Incoronazione di Poppea* (1642).

JEAN-BAPTISTE RAMEAU

Chamber Music: Pièces de clavecin en concert, for harpsichord, violin or flute, and viol or second violin (1741).

Choral Music: Motets, cantatas.

Harpsichord Music: Pièces de clavecin (1706, 1724); *Nouvelle suite de pièces de clavecin.*

Operas and Opera-Ballets: Hippolyte et Aricie (1733); *Les Indes galantes* (1735); *Castor et Pollux* (1737); *Les Fêtes d'Hébé* (1739); *Dardanus* (1739); *Les Fêtes de Polimnie* (1745); *Platée* (1745); *Les Fêtes de l'Hymen et de l'amour* (1747); *Zoroastre* (1749); *Acante et Céphise* (1751); *Zéphire* (1754); *Anacréon* (1754); *Les Paladins* (1760).

ANTONIO VIVALDI

Chamber Music: 73 sonatas.

Choral Music: 2 oratorios: *Moyses Deus Pharaonis* (1714), *Juditha triumphans* (1716); cantatas; *Gloria Mass.*

Operas: Nerone fatto Cesare (1715); *Arsilda regina di Ponto* (1716); *L'Incoronzione di Dario* (1716); *Armida al campo d'Egitto* (1718); *L'Inganno trionfante in amore* (1725); *Farnace* (1726); *La Fida Ninfa* (1732); *Motezuma* (1733); *L'Olimpiade* (1734); *Griselda* (1735); *Feraspe* (1739).

Orchestral Music: 23 sinfonias; about 500 concertos including *L'Estro armonico,* op. 3 (c. 1712), *La Stravaganza,* op. 4, and *Il Cimento dell' armonia e dell' inventione,* op. 8 (1725); various concertos for solo instruments and orchestra.

Vocal Music: 24 secular cantatas; 43 arias; *Stabat Mater.*

JOHANN SEBASTIAN BACH

Chamber Music: 3 sonatas for unaccompanied violin (c. 1720); 3 partitas for unaccompanied violin (c. 1720); 6 sonatas, or suites, for unaccompanied cello (c. 1720); 3 sonatas for cello and clavier (1717–23); 3 sonatas for flute and clavier (1717–23); *Das musikalisches Opfer* (1747).

Choral Music: About 190 religious cantatas; secular cantatas including the *Trauer-Ode* (1727), *Phoebus and Pan* (c. 1732), *Coffee Cantata* (1732); and *Peasant Cantata* (1742); 2 magnificats (1723); *Passion According to St. John* (1723); motets for unaccompanied voices (1723–29); *Passion According to St. Matthew* (1729); Mass in B Minor (1733–1738); *Christmas Oratorio* (1734); *Easter Oratorio* (1736); *Lutheran Masses* (1737–40).

Orchestral Music: 6 Brandenburg Concertos (1721); 4 suites; various concertos for solo instruments and orchestra (1717–36).

Organ Music: Passacaglia and Fugue in C Minor (1717); *Orgelbüchlein* (1717); chorale preludes, toccatas, preludes, fugues, fantasias.

Piano (Clavier) Music: Clavierbüchlein vor Anna Magdalena (1720); *Chromatic Fantasy and Fugue* (1720–23); 6 *French Suites* (c. 1722); *The Well-Tempered Clavier* (1722–44); 6 *English Suites* (c. 1725); inventions (1725); 6 partitas (1731); *Italian Concerto* (1735); *Goldberg Variations* (1742); *Die Kunst der Fuge,* for an unspecified instrument but usually played on the harpsichord or piano (1748–50); fantasias, little preludes, fughettas, fugues.

Vocal Music: Songs for voice and clavier including *Bist du bei mir, Komm süsser Tod, Ich halte treulich still* and *O Jesulein süss.*

GEORGE FRIDERIC HANDEL

Chamber Music: Various sonatas for solo instruments and accompaniment; trio-sonatas.

Choral Music: 19 oratorios, including: *Esther* (1732); *Saul* (1739); *Israel in Egypt* (1739); *Messiah* (1742); *Samson* (1743); *Belshazzar* (1745); *Judas Maccabaeus* (1747); *Joshua* (1748); *Susanna* (1749); *Solomon* (1749); *Theodora* (1750); and *Jephtha* (1752).

Chandos Anthems (1717–20); *Alexander's Feast* (1736); *Ode for St. Cecilia's Day* (1739); *L'Allegro ed Il Penseroso* (1740); *Dettingen Te Deum* (1743).

Operas: About 40 Operas, including: *Almira* (1705); *Agrippina* (1709); *Rinaldo* (1711); *Radamisto* (1720); *Acis and Galatea* (1720); *Floridante* (1721); *Giulio Cesare* (1724); *Tamerlano* (1724); *Rodelina* (1725); *Admeto* (1727); *Partenope* (1730); *Ezio* (1732); *Arianna* (1734); *Alcina* (1735); *Atalanta* (1736); *Berenice* (1737); *Faramondo* (1738); *Serse* (1738).

Orchestral Music: Water Music (1717); 6 *concerti grossi,* op. 3 (1734); 12 *concerti grossi,* op. 6 (1739); *Royal Fireworks Music* (1749); various concertos for solo instruments and orchestra; overtures.

Piano (Harpsichord) Music: Fugues, sonatas, sonatinas, suites.

Vocal Music: 72 Italian cantatas for voice and accompaniment; other cantatas for various voices and instruments; 22 Italian duets with accompaniment; German songs; French songs; English songs.

CHRISTOPH WILLIBALD GLUCK

Ballets: Don Juan (1761); *Semiramide* (1765).

Chamber Music: 6 sonatas for two violins and accompaniment.

Choral Music: Frühlingsfeier (1767); *De Profundis* (c. 1782).

Operas: Over 40 operas including: *Semiramide riconosciuta* (1748); *Ezio* (1750); *Il re pastore* (1756); *L'Ivrogne corrigé* (1760); *Le Cadi dupé* (1761); *Orfeo ed Euridice* (1762); *Il Trionfo di Clelia* (1763); *La Rencontre imprévue* (1764); *Alceste* (1767); *Iphigénie en Aulide* (1774); *Paride ed Elena* (1770); *Armide* (1777); *Iphigénie en Tauride* (1779); *Écho et Narcisse* (1779).

Orchestra: Overtures.

JOSEPH HAYDN

Chamber Music: 82 string quartets including: 6 *Sun Quartets,* op. 20 (1772); 6 *Russian Quartets,* op. 33 (1781); 6 *Prussian Quartets,* op. 50 (1785–87); 6 *Tost Quartets,* op. 54–55 (1788); 6 *Quartets,* op. 64 (1790); 6 *Apponyi Quartets,* op. 71, 74 (1793); 6 *Erdödy Quartets,* op. 76 (1799); 2 *Lobkowitz Quartets,* op. 77 (1799).

35 piano trios; 18 string trios; 125 trios for other instrumental combinations; sonatas, duos, quintets, sextets, divertimenti, nocturnes, cassations.

Choral Music: Mariazeller Mass (1782); *Missa in tempore belli* (1796); *Die Schöpfung,* or *The Creation* (1798); *Nelson* Mass (1798); *Theresien* Mass (1799); *Missa solennis* (1801); *Die Jahreszeiten,* or *The Seasons* (1801); *Harmoniemesse* (1802).

Operas: Lo Speziale (1768); *Il Mondo della luna* (1777); *L'Isola disabitata* (1779); *Armida* (1784); *Orfeo ed Euridice.*

Orchestral Music: 104 symphonies, including: No. 6, D Major, *Le*

Matin (1761); No. 7, C Major, *Le Midi* (1761); No. 8, G Major, *Le Soir* (1761); No. 45, F-sharp Minor, *Farewell* (1772); No. 82, C Major, *L'Ours* (1786); No. 83, G Minor, *La Poule* (1785); No. 85, B-flat Major, *La Reine* (1786); No. 88, G Major (1787); No. 92, G Major, *Oxford* (1788); 12 "London" Symphonies, op. 93–104 (1791–95).

15 piano concertos, including Concerto in D Major, op. 21 (1783); 2 cello concertos, including Concerto in D Major (1783); 3 violin concertos; 2 horn concertos; *Seven Last Words of Christ* (1785); marches, notturnos, German dances, divertimenti, overtures, cassations.

Piano Music: 52 sonatas, including: No. 35, C Major (1780); No. 37, D Major (1780); No. 43, A-flat Major (1785); No. 51, D Major (1794); No. 52, E-flat Major (1794).

Andante con variazioni (c. 1774); Fantasia in C Major (1789); Variations in F Minor (1793); various shorter pieces.

Vocal Music: 12 English canzonets (1794–95), including *My Mother Bids Me Bind My Hair, The Sailor's Song,* and *She Never Told Her Love;* various other songs for voice and piano, including the Austrian National Anthem, *Gott erhlate Franz den Kaiser* (1797), *Liebes Mädchen, The Spirit's Song,* and *Heller Blick;* arias, solo cantatas, vocal duets, vocal trios, vocal quartets, canons, rounds, and arrangements of folk songs.

WOLFGANG AMADEUS MOZART

Chamber Music: 26 string quartets including the 6 *Haydn Quartets,* K. 387, 421, 428, 458, 464, 465 (1782–85) and 3 *Prussian Quartets,* K. 575, 589, 590 (1789–90).

5 string quintets including Quintet in G Minor, K. 516 (1787) and Quintet in E-flat Major, K. 614 (1791).

42 violin sonatas, including Sonata in G Major, K. 379 (1781), and Sonata in E-flat Major, K. 481 (1785).

7 piano trios; quintets for a wind instrument and strings; quintet for piano and winds; flute quartets; oboe quartet; string trios; duets.

Choral Music: 15 Masses including the *Credo Mass,* K. 257 (1776),

Coronation Mass, K. 317 (1799), and the *Great Mass,* K. 427, (1783).

Ave Verum, K. 618 (1791); *Requiem,* K. 626 (1791); 9 offertories, 4 litanies, magnificat.

Operas: Bastien and Bastienne, K. 50 (1768); *La Finta semplice,* K. 51 (1768); *Mitridate, Rè di Ponte,* K. 87 (1770); *Ascanio in Alba,* K. 111 (1771); *Il Sogno di Scipione,* K. 126 (1772); *Lucio Silla,* K. 135 (1772); *La Finta giardiniera,* K. 196 (1774); *Il Rè pastore,* K. 208 (1775); *Thamos, König in Aegypten,* K. 345 (1779); *Idomeneo, Rè di Crete,* K. 366 (1781); *Die Entführung aus dem Serail,* K. 384 (1782); *Der Schauspieldirektor,* K. 486 (1786); *Le Nozze di Figaro,* K. 492 (1786); *Don Giovanni,* K. 527 (1787); *Così fan tutte,* K. 588 (1790); *Die Zauberflöte,* K. 620 (1791); *La Clemenza di Tito,* K. 621 (1791).

Orchestral Music: 49 symphonies including: No. 29, A Major, K. 201 (1774); No. 31, D Major, *Paris,* K. 297 (1778); No. 34, C Major, K. 338 (1780); No. 35, D Major, *Haffner,* K. 385 (1782); No. 36, C Major, *Linz,* K. 425 (1783); No. 38, D Major, *Prague,* K. 504 (1786); No. 39, E-flat Major, K. 543 (1788); No. 40, G Minor, K. 550 (1788); No. 41, C Major, *Jupiter,* K. 551 (1788).

25 piano concertos including: F Major, K. 459 (1784); D Minor, K. 466 (1785); C Major, K. 467 (1785); A Major, K. 488 (1786); C Minor, K. 491 (1786); D Major, *Coronation,* K. 537 (1788); B-flat Major, K. 595 (1791).

6 violin concertos including: No. 4, D Major, K. 218 (1775) and No. 5, A Major, K. 219 (1775).

Various other concertos for solo instrument or instruments and orchestra: 2 pianos; 3 pianos; flute and harp; flute; bassoon; clarinet; horn.

Sinfonia concertante in E-flat major, for violin, viola and orchestra, K. 364 (1779); divertimenti, cassations, serenades, minuets, German dances, contredanses, marches, sonatas for organ and orchestra.

Organ Music: 14 sonatas for organ and strings; 3 sonatas for organ and orchestra.

Piano Music: 17 sonatas for solo piano including: A Major, K. 331, with the "Turkish March" movement (1778); C Minor, K. 457 (1785); D Major, K. 576 (1789).

Sonata for Two Pianos, in D Major, K. 448 (1781); Sonata for Piano Four Hands in F Major, K. 497 (1786); 3 fantasias, 3 rondos, minuets, fugues, allegros.

Vocal Music: About 30 Songs for voice and piano including *Das Veilchen,* K. 476 (c. 1786) and *An Chloe,* K. 524 (1787).

27 arias for soprano and orchestra; various other arias and duets for solo voices and orchestra; canons, trios, quartets.

LUDWIG VAN BEETHOVEN

Ballet: Die Geschöpfe des Prometheus, op. 43 (1800–1).

Chamber Music: 16 string quartets: 6 *Lobkowitz Quartets,* op. 18 (1798–1800); 3 *Rasoumovsky Quartets,* op. 59 (1806); E-flat Major, *Harp,* op. 74 (1809); F Minor, op. 95 (1810); E-flat Major, op. 127 (1824); B-flat Major, op. 130 (1825); C-sharp Minor, op. 131 (1826); A Minor, op. 132 (1825); F Major, op. 135 (1826).

9 piano trios including: Trio in D Major, op. 70, no. 1 (1808) and Trio in B-flat Major, *Archduke,* op. 97 (1811).

4 piano quartets; 5 string trios; 2 wind octets; 3 string quintets; Septet in E-flat Major, op. 20 (1800); *Grosse Fuge* in B-flat Major, for string quartet, op. 133 (1825).

10 violin sonatas including: F Major, *Spring,* op. 24 (1801); C Minor and G Major, op. 30, nos. 2 and 3 (1802); A Major, *Kreutzer,* op. 47 (1803).

5 cello sonatas including: Sonata in A Major, op. 69 (1808) and Sonatas in C Major and D Major, op. 102, nos. 1 and 2 (1815).

Choral Music: Piano Fantasy, with chorus and orchestra, op. 80 (1808); *Christus am Ölberge,* or *Christ on Mt. Olives,* op. 85 (1802); *Missa Solemnis,* op. 123 (1818–23); cantatas.

Opera: Fidelio, op. 72 (1805).

Orchestral Music: 9 symphonies: No. 1, C Major, op. 21 (1800); No. 2, D Major, op. 36 (1802); No. 3, E-flat Major, *Eroica,* op. 55 (1803); No. 4, B-flat Major, op. 60 (1806); No. 5, C Minor, op. 67 (1805–7); No. 6, F Major, *Pastoral,* op. 68 (1807–8); No. 7, A Major, op. 92 (1812); No. 8, F Major, op. 93 (1812); No. 9, D Minor, *Choral,* op. 125 (1823).

5 piano concertos: No. 1, C Major, op. 15 (1797); No. 2, B-flat, op. 19 (1795); No. 3, C Minor, op. 37 (1800); No. 4, G Major, op. 58 (1806); No. 5, E-flat Major, *Emperor,* op. 73 (1809).

Triple Concerto in C Major, for piano, violin, cello and orchestra, op. 56 (1805); Violin Concerto in D Major, op. 61 (1806).

2 Romances, for violin and orchestra, opp. 40, 50 (1802, 1803); *Coriolon Overture,* op. 62 (1807); *Ah, Perfido!,* for voice and orchestra, op. 65 (1796); *Fidelio Overture,* op. 72c (1814); *Leonore* Overtures, Nos. 1, 2, and 3, opp. 138, 72a, and 72b (1805, 1806, 1807); *Egmont,* incidental music to a play, including a famous overture, op. 84 (1810); *Wellingtons Sieg,* op. 91 (1813); *König Stephan,* incidental music to a play including overture, op. 117 (1811); *Die Weihe des Hauses* Overture, op. 124 (1822); Deutsche Tänze, ecossaises, Ländler, minuets, waltzes.

Piano Music: 32 sonatas including: No. 7, D Major, op. 10, No. 3 (1796–98); No. 8, C Minor, *Pathétique,* op. 13 (1798); No. 12, A-flat Major, *Funeral March,* op. 26 (1801); No. 14, *Quasi una fantasia,* C-sharp Minor, *Moonlight,* op. 27, No. 2 (1801); No. 15, D Major, *Pastoral,* op. 28 (1801); No. 17, D Minor, op. 31, No. 2 (1802); No. 21, C Major, *Waldstein,* op. 53 (1804); No. 27, F Minor, *Appassionata,* op. 57 (1804); No. 26, E-flat Major, *Les Adieux,* op. 81a (1809); No. 28, A Major, op. 101 (1816); No. 29, B-flat Major, *Hammerklavier,* op. 106 (1818); No. 30, E Major, op. 109 (1820); No. 31, A-flat Major, op. 110 (1821); No. 32, C Minor, op. 111 (1822).

33 Variations on a Waltz by Diabelli, op. 120 (1823); *Andante Favori,* op. 170 (1804); 32 Variations in C minor, op. 191 (1806); bagatelles, ecossaises, minuets, preludes, rondos, waltzes, various variations.

Vocal Music: 6 *Gellert Lieder,* op. 48 (1803); *An die ferne Geliebte,* op. 98 (1816); *Irish Songs,* opp. 223, 224, 255 (1813–15); *Scottish Songs,* op. 108, 227 (1815); *Welsh Songs,* op. 226 (1817); 12 Songs of Various Nationalities, op. 228 (1815).

Numerous individual songs for voice and piano including: *Adelaide,* op. 46 (1795); *Andenken,* op. 240 (1819); *Ich liebe dich,* op. 235 Canons. (1803); *In questa tomba obscura,* op. 239 (1807).

CARL MARIA VON WEBER

Chamber Music: Piano Quartet, op. 18 (1809); *Nine Variations on a Norwegian Air,* for violin and piano, op. 22 (1808); 6 sonatas, or sonatinas, for violin and piano (1810); Clarinet Quintet, op. 34 (1815); *Grand Duo Concertant,* for clarinet and piano, op. 48 (1816); Flute Trio, op. 63 (1819).

Choral Music: 6 cantatas; 3 Masses; 2 offertories; part songs.

Operas: Peter Schmoll und seine Nachbarn (1803); *Silvana* (1810); *Abu Hassan* (1811); *Der Freischütz* (1821); *Euryanthe* (1823); *Oberon* (1826); *Die drei Pintos* (completed by Gustav Mahler).

Orchestral Music: 2 piano concertos: C Major, op. 11 (1810); E-flat Major, op. 32 (1812).

2 clarinet concertos: F Minor, op. 73 (1811); E-flat Major, op. 74 (1811).

Sinfonia No. 2 in C (1807); Andante in D Minor and Variations in F Major for cello and orchestra (1810); Clarinet Concertino in C Minor-E-flat Major, op. 26 (1811); *Andante e rondo ongarese* in C Minor, for bassoon and orchestra, op. 35 (1813); *Tedesco* in D Major (1816); *Jubel Overture,* op. 59 (1818); *Konzertstück* in F Minor-F Major for piano and orchestra, op. 79 (1821).

Piano Music: 4 sonatas; *Momento capriccioso* in B-flat Major, op. 12 (1808); *Grande Polonaise* in E-flat Major, op. 21 (1808); 18 *Favorit Walzer* (1812); *Air russe and Variations,* op. 40 (1815); *Seven Variations on a Gypsy Song,* op. 55 (1817); *Aufforderung zum Tanz,* or *Invitation to the Dance,* rondo brilliante in D-flat Major, op. 65 (1819); ecossaises; variations; pieces for piano duet.

Vocal Music: Songs, with piano or guitar; songs for several voices; canons; solfeggi; duets; trios; quartets.

FRANZ SCHUBERT

Chamber Music: 15 string quartets including: No. 11, E-flat Major, op. 125, No. 1 (1813); No. 12, *Quartetsatz* in C Minor (1820); No. 13, A Minor, op. 29 (1824); No. 14, D Minor, *Tod und das Mädchen* (1826).

519

2 piano trios: B-flat Major, op. 99 (1827); E-flat Major, op. 100 (1827).

String Trio in B-flat Major (1816); Rondo brilliant in B Minor, for violin and piano, op. 70 (1826); Piano Quintet in A Major, *Die Forelle,* op. 114 (1819); 3 violin sonatinas, op. 137 (1816); Fantasy in C Major, for violin and piano, op. 159 (1827); Violin Sonata in A Major, op. 162 (1817); Sonata in A Minor, for arpeggione and piano (1824); String Quintet in C Major, op. 163 (1828).

Choral Music: 7 Masses including: No. 1, in F (1814); No. 2, G Major (1815); *Deutsche Messe* in F Major (1827).

Offertories, Salve Reginas, Stabat Maters, cantatas, psalms, Tantum Ergos, part songs.

Operas: About 10 operas and operettas including: *Die Zwillingsbrüder* (1819); *Alfonso und Estrella,* op. 69 (1822); *Fierrabras,* op. 76 (1823); *Der häusliche Krieg* (1823).

Orchestral Music: 8 symphonies including: No. 4, C Minor, "Tragic" (1816); No. 5, B-flat Major (1816); No. 7, sometimes also designated as No. 9, C Major, *The Great* (1828); No. 8, B Minor, *Unfinished* (1822).

7 overtures, including two in Italian style; incidental music to *Rosamunde,* including famous overture (1823); *Konzertstück* for violin and orchestra (1816); Rondo in A Major, for violin and orchestra (1816); German dances, minuets.

Piano Music: 22 sonatas including: No. 9, A Major, op. 120 (1819); C Minor, A Major, B-flat Major (posthumous).

Wanderer Fantasy in C Major, op. 15 (1822); Grand Duo, for piano duet, op. 140 (1824); 8 impromptus, opp. 90, 142 (1827); 6 *Moments musicaux,* op. 94 (1823–27); ecossaises, German dances, Ländler, minuets, waltzes, piano duets.

Vocal Music: Die schöne Müllerin, op. 25 (1823); Songs from *Lady of the Lake,* op. 52 (1825); *Die Winterreise,* op. 89 (1827); *Schwanengesang* (1828).

Over 500 individual songs for voice and piano including: *Die Allmacht,* op. 79, No. 2 (1825); *Am See* (1814); *An die Leier,* op. 56, No. 2 (1822); *An die Musik,* op. 88, No. 4 (1817); *Auf dem Wasser zu singen,* op. 72 (1823); *Du bist die Ruh',* op. 59, No. 3 (1823); *Der Erlkönig,* op. 1 (1815); *Die Forelle,* op. 32 (1817); *Gretchen am*

Spinnrade, op. 2 (1814); *"Hark, Hark, the Lark"* (1826); *Heiden-röslein,* op. 3, No. 3 (1815); *Im Abendrot* (1824); *Die junge Nonne,* op. 43, No. 1 (1825); *Der Tod und das Mädchen,* op. 7, No. 3 (1817); *Der Wanderer,* op. 4, No. 1 (1816); *Who Is Sylvia?,* op. 106, No. 4 (1826); *Wiegenlied,* op. 98, No. 2.

Vocal duets, vocal trios, vocal quartets.

HECTOR BERLIOZ

Choral Music: Requiem, *Messe des morts,* op. 5 (1837); *Te Deum,* op. 22 (1849); *La Damnation de Faust,* op. 24 (1846); *L'Enfance du Christ,* op. 25 (1850–54).

Operas: Benvenuto Cellini, op. 23 (1834–38); *Les Troyens:* I. *La Prise de Troie,* II. *Les Troyens à Carthage* (1856–59); *Béatrice et Bénédict* (1860–62).

Orchestral Music: Waverly, op. 2 bis (c. 1827); *Les Francs-juges,* op. 3 (c. 1827); *King Lear,* op. 4 (1831); *Rob Roy* (1832); *Rêverie et caprice,* for violin and orchestra, op. 8 (1839); *Le Carnaval romain,* op. 9 (1844); *Symphonie fantastique,* op. 14 (1830–31); *Harold en Italie,* with solo viola, op. 16 (1834); *Roméo et Juliette,* with soloists and chorus, op. 17 (1839); *Le Corsaire,* op. 21 (1855).

Vocal Music: Nuits d'été, for voice and piano or orchestra, op. 7 (1834–41, 1843–56); *La Captive,* for voice and piano or orchestra, op. 12 (1832).

GIOACCHINO ROSSINI

Chamber Music: 5 string quartets (1808); theme and variations, for woodwind quartet (1812).

Choral Music: Mass (1808); Stabat Mater (1832, revised 1842); Saul (1834); *Petite messe solennelle* (1863); cantatas, hymns.

Operas: About 40 operas including: *La Scala di Seta* (1812); *Il Signor Bruschino* (1813); *Tancredi* (1813); *L'Italiana in Algeri* (1813); *Elisabetta* (1815); *Il Barbiere di Siviglia* (1816); *Otello* (1816); *Cenerentola* (1817); *La Gazza ladra* (1817); *Mosè in Egitto* (1818); *Semiramide* (1823); *Le Comte Ory* (1828); *Guillaume Tell* (1829).

Piano Music: Péchés de vieillesse, 186 pieces.

GIACOMO MEYERBEER

Ballet: Der Fischer und das Mildmädchen (1810).

Choral Music: Gott und die Natur (1811); cantatas, psalms, Pater Noster, *Festal Hymn.*

Operas: 16 operas including: *Semiramide riconosciuta* (1819); *Margherita d'Anjou* (1820); *Il Crociato in Egitto* (1824); *Robert le diable* (1831); *Les Huguenots* (1836); *Ein Feldlager in Schlesien* (1844); Le *Prophète* (1849); *L'Étoile du nord* (1854); *Dinorah* (1859); *L'Africaine* (1865).

Orchestral Music: 3 *Torch Dances* (1846–1853); *Coronation March* (1863).

Vocal Music: Quarante mélodies.

FELIX MENDELSSOHN

Chamber Music: 6 string quartets including: No. 1, E-flat Major, op. 12 (1829).

Violin Sonata in F Minor, op. 4 (1825); String Octet in E-flat Major, op. 20 (1826); Piano Sextet in D Major, op. 110 (1824); 3 piano quartets; 2 piano trios; 2 cello sonatas.

Choral Music: St. Paul, op. 36 (1836); *Lobgesang,* op. 52 (1840); *Die erste Walpurgisnacht,* op. 60 (1832, revised 1843); *Elijah,* op. 70 (1846); Psalms, anthems, church pieces, sacred pieces, sacred choruses, part songs.

Operas: Die Hochzeit des Camacho, op. 10 (1825); *Die Heimkehr aus der Fremde,* op. 89 (1829).

Orchestral Music: 5 major symphonies including: No. 3, A Minor, *Scotch,* op. 56 (1842); No. 4, A Major, *Italian,* op. 90 (1833); No. 5, D Major, *Reformation,* op. 107 (1830).

2 piano concertos: No. 1, G Minor, op. 25 (1831); No. 2, D Minor, op. 40 (1837).

A Midsummer Night's Dream, overture and suite, op. 21, 61 (1826, 1842); *Capriccio brilliant* in B Minor, for piano and orchestra, op. 22; *Fingal's Cave,* or *Hebrides,* op. 26 (1830, revised 1832); **Meeresstille und glückliche Fahrt,** or **Calm Sea and Prosperous**

Voyage, op. 27 (1832); *Rondo brilliant* in E-flat Major, for piano and orchestra (1834); *Ruy Blas,* op. 95 (1839).

Organ Music: 6 sonatas, op. 65 (1844–45); preludes and fugues.

Piano Music: Lieder ohne Worte, or *Songs Without Words,* 8 books: op. 19 (1829); op. 30 (1833–34); op. 38 (1837); op. 53 (1841); op. 62 (1843–44); op. 67 (1843–45); op. 85 (1834–45); op. 102 (1842–45).

3 sonatas; *Seven Characteristic Pieces,* op. 7; *Rondo capriccioso* in E Major, op. 14; *Variations sérieuses* in D Minor, op. 54 (1841); 6 *Kinderstücke,* op. 72 (1842); Capriccio in E Major, op. 118 (1837); caprices, fantasies, Clavierstücke, preludes and fugues, etudes, scherzos, variations, preludes.

Vocal Music: About 75 individual songs for voice and piano including: *Auf flügeln des Gesanges* (1834); *Jagdlied* (1834); *Volkslied* (1834); *Das Schiffeln* (1845); *Nachtlied* (1847); *An die Entfernte* (1847).

ROBERT SCHUMANN

Chamber Music: 3 string quartets, op. 41 (1842); No. 1, A Minor; No. 2, F Major; No. 3, A Major.

3 piano trios: No. 1, D Minor, op. 63 (1847); No. 2, F Major, op. 80 (1847); No. 3, G Minor, op. 110 (1851).

2 violin sonatas: No. 1, A Minor, op. 105 (1851); No. 2, D Minor, op. 121 (1851).

Piano Quintet in E-flat Major, op. 44 (1842); Piano Quartet in E-flat Major, op. 47 (1842); *Fantasiestücke,* for piano trio, op. 88 (1842); *Drei Romanzen,* for oboe, op. 94 (1849).

Choral Music: Das Paradies und die Peri, op. 50 (1841–43); *Scenen aus Goethe's Faust* (1844–53); *Requiem für Mignon,* op. 98b (1849); *Der Rose Pilgerfahrt,* op. 112 (1851); Mass, op. 147 (1852); Requiem, op. 148 (1852); part songs for women's voices; part songs for mixed voices.

Opera: Genoveva, op. 81 (1847–1850).

Orchestral Music: 4 symphonies; No. 1, B-flat Major, *Spring,* op. 38 (1841); No. 2, C Major, op. 61 (1845–46); No. 3, E-flat Major,

Rhenish, op. 97 (1850); No. 4, D Minor, op. 120 (1841–1852).

Overture, Scherzo and Finale, op. 52 (1840); Piano Concerto in A Minor, op. 54 (1841–45); Overture to *Die Braut von Messina,* op. 100 (1850–51); Incidental music to *Manfred,* including famous overture, op. 115 (1848–49); Overture to *Julius Caesar,* op. 128 (1851); Cello Concerto in A Minor, op. 129 (1850); Fantasy in C Major, for violin and orchestra, op. 131 (1853); *Introduction and Allegro,* in D Minor, for piano and orchestra, op. 134 (1853); Overture to *Hermann und Dorothea,* op. 136 (1851); Violin Concerto in D Minor (1853).

Organ Music: Six Fugues on the Name of B.A.C.H., op. 60 (1845).

Piano Music: 2 Sonatas: No. 1, F-sharp Minor, op. 11 (1833–35); No. 2, G Minor, op. 22 (1833–38).

Variations on Abegg, op. 1 (1830); *Papillons,* op. 2 (1832); *Paganini Etudes,* two sets, op. 3, 10 (1832, 1833); 6 Intermezzi, op. 4 (1832); *Impromptus on a Theme by Clara Wieck,* op. 5 (1833); *Davidsbündlertänze,* op. 6 (1837); Toccata in C Major, op. 7 (1832); *Carnaval,* op. 9 (1834–35); *Fantasiestücke,* op. 12 (1837); *Études symphoniques,* op. 13 (1834); *Kinderscenen,* op. 15 (1838); *Kreisleriana,* op. 16 (1838); Fantasy in C Major, op. 17 (1836); *Arabeske* in C Major, op. 18 (1839); *Blumenstück,* in D-flat Major, op. 19 (1839); *Humoreske* in B-flat Major, op. 20 (1839); 8 *Novelletten,* op. 21 (1838); 4 *Nachtstücke,* op. 23 (1839); *Faschingsschwank aus Wien,* op. 26 (1839); 3 Romances, op. 28 (1839); 4 *Clavierstücke,* op. 32 (1838–39); *Album für die Jugend,* op. 68 (1848); *Waldscenen,* op. 82 (1848–49); *Bunte-Blätter,* op. 99; *Fantasiestücke,* op. 111 (1851); *Albumblätter,* op. 124 (1832–1845).

Vocal Music: Myrthen, op. 25 (1840); *Gedichte aus Liebesfrühling,* op. 37 (1840); *Liederkreis,* op. 39 (1840); *Frauenliebe und Leben,* op. 42 (1840); *Dichterliebe,* op. 48 (1840); *Lieder und Gesänge aus Wilhelm Meister,* op. 98a (1849).

Many individual songs for voice and piano including: *Abendlied,* op. 107, No. 6 (1851–52); *Alte Laute,* op. 35, No. 12 (1840); *Aufträge,* op. 77, No. 5 (1841–50); *Die beiden Grenadiere,* op. 49, No. 1 (1840); *Die Kartenlegerin,* op. 31, No. 2 (1840); *O ihr Herren,* op. 37, No. 3 (1840); *Wanderlied,* op. 35, No. 3 (1840).

Vocal duets, vocal trios, vocal quartets.

FRÉDÉRIC CHOPIN

Chamber Music: Introduction and Polonaise, for cello and piano, op. 3 (1829–30); Piano Trio in G Minor, op. 8 (1828–29); Cello Sonata in G Minor, op. 65 (1845–46).

Orchestral Music: 2 piano concertos: No. 1, E Minor, op. 11 (1830); No. 2, F Minor, op. 21 (1829).

Variations on "Là ci darem" from Mozart's Don Giovanni, op. 2 (1827); *Andante spianato and Grande Polonaise brilliante,* in E-flat for piano and orchestra, op. 22 (1830–31).

Piano Music: Ballades, op. 23 (1835), op. 38 (1839), op. 47 (1841), op. 52 (1842); Barcarolle in F-sharp Minor, op. 60 (1846); Berceuse in D-flat, op. 57 (1843); Bolero in C Major, op. 19 (1834); Ecossaises, op. 72 (1826); Etudes, op. 10 (1829–1832), op. 25 (1832–36); Fantaisie in F Minor, op. 49 (1840–41); Impromptus, op. 29 (1837); op. 36 (1839), op. 51 (1842), op. 66 (1842); Mazurkas, op. 6 (1830–31), op. 7 (1830–31), op. 17 (1832–33), op. 24 (1834–35), op. 30 (1836–37), op. 33 (1837–38), op. 41 (1839), op. 50 (1841), op. 56 (1843), op. 59 (1845), op. 63 (1846), op. 67 (1855), op. 68 (1849); Nocturnes, op. 9 (1830–31), op. 15 (1830–31), op. 27 (1834–35), op. 32 (1836–37), op. 37 (1838), op. 48 (1841), op. 55 (1843), op. 62 (1846), op. 72 (1827); Polonaises, op. 26 (1834–35), op. 40 (1838–39), op. 44 (1840–41), op. 53 (1842), op. 61 (1845–46), op. 71 (1829); Preludes, op. 28 (1836–39), op. 45 (1841); Rondo in E-flat, op. 16 (1832); Rondo in C Major, for two pianos, op. 73 (1828); Scherzos, op. 20 (1831–32), op. 31 (1837), op. 39 (1839), op. 54 (1842).

3 sonatas: No. 1, C Minor, op. 4 (1827); No. 2, B-flat Minor, with the Funeral March, op. 35 (1839); No. 3, B Minor (1844).

Tarantelle in A-flat, op. 43 (1841); Waltzes, op. 18 (1831), op. 34 (1838), op. 42 (1840), op. 64 (1846–47), op. 69 (1835), op. 70 (1829–1835); *Variations brilliantes,* op. 12 (1833); Variations in F Major, for piano duet (1826).

Vocal Music: 17 Polish songs (1829–31).

CÉSAR FRANCK

Chamber Music: Piano Quintet in F Minor (1878–79); Violin Sonata in A Major (1886); String Quartet in D Major (1889).

Choral Music: Ruth (1843–46); *Ave Maria* (1863); *Les Béatitudes* (1869–1879); *Trois Offertoires* (1871); *Rédemption* (1871–72, revised 1874); *Psyché* (1886–88); *Psalm CL* (1888).

Operas: Le Valet de ferme (1851–52); *Hulda* (1882–85); *Ghisèle* (1888–90).

Orchestral Music: Ce qu'on entend sur la montagne (c. 1846); *Les Éolides* (1875–76); *Le Chasseur maudit* (1882); *Les Djinns,* for piano and orchestra (1884); *Variations symphoniques,* for piano and orchestra (1885); Symphony in D Minor (1886–88).

Organ Music: Six Pièces pour grand orgue (1860–62); 44 *Petites Pièces* (1863); *Trois Pièces pour grand orgue* (1878); *L'Organiste,* 55 pieces for harmonium (1889–90); *Trois Chorals* (1890).

Piano Music: Prélude, choral et fugue (1884); *Danse lente* (1885); *Prélude, aria, et final* (1886–87).

Vocal Music: Individual songs for voice and piano including: *Le Mariage des roses* (1871); *Nocturne* (1884). Six vocal duets (1888).

CHARLES GOUNOD

Chamber Music: 3 string quartets; piano quintet (c. 1841); *Petite symphonie,* for winds (1888).

Choral Music: Requiem (1873); *La Rédemption* (1881); *Mors et Vita* (1884); *Te Deum* (1886); *La Contemplation de Saint François au pied de la croix* (1890); *Messe breve* (1890); *Tantum Ergo* (1892); Masses, motets, Stabat Maters, psalms.

Operas: Sapho (1851); *La Nonne sanglante* (1854); *Le Médecin malgré lui* (1858); *Faust* (1859); *Philémon et Baucis* (1860); *La Colombe* (1860); *La Reine de Saba* (1862); *Mireille* (1864); *Roméo et Juliette* (1867); *Cinq-Mars* (1877); *Polyeucte* (1878); *Le Tribut de Zamora* (1881).

Orchestral Music: 2 symphonies (1855); *Saltarello* (1871); *Marche romaine* (1872); *Marche funèbre d'une marionette* (1873); *Marche religieuse* (1878); *Les Rendezvous,* waltzes for piano and orchestra (1887).

Piano Music: 8 *Mélodies* (1864); 5 *Romances sans paroles;* wedding marches, valses, pieces.

Vocal Music: Italian songs (1872–73); English songs (1873); *Quinze melodies enfantines* (1878).

Individual songs for voice and piano including: *Au printemps* (1865); *Ave Maria* (1859); *Ou voulez-vous aller?* (c. 1855); *Serenade* (1855).

Vocal duets.

JULES MASSENET

Ballets: Le Carillon (1892); *La Cigale* (1904); *Espada* (1908).

Choral Music: Marie-Magdeleine (1873); *Ève* (1875); *La Terre promise* (1900).

Operas: About 25 operas including: *Le Roi de Lahore* (1877); *Hérodiade* (1881); *Manon* (1884); *Le Cid* (1885); *Werther* (1892); *Thaïs* (1894); *Sapho* (1897); *Cendrillon* (1899); *Grisélidis* (1901); *Le Jongleur de Notre Dame* (1902); *Don Quichotte* (1910); *Cléopâtre* (1914).

Orchestral Music: Incidental music to numerous plays by Leconte de Lisle, Hugo, Sardou, Racine and others including: *Les Érynnies* (1873) which embraces the popular "Élégie"; *Notre Dame de Paris* (1879); *Phèdre* (1900).

7 suites including: *Scènes pittoresques* (1874); *Scènes alsaciennes* (1881).

3 concert overtures including *Phèdre* (1873).

Visions (1890); *Marche solennelle* (1897); *Fantaisie,* for cello and orchestra (1897); piano concerto (1903).

FRANZ LISZT

Choral Music: Grand Festmesse (1855); *Christus* (1855–59); *Die Legende von der heiligen Elisabeth* (1857–62); *Requiem* (1867–68);

527

Die heilige Cäcilia (1874); *Via Crucis* (1878–79); Psalms, Pater Nosters, Te Deums, responses and antiphons, chorales.

Orchestral Music: 12 tone poems including: *Tasso* (1849); *Mazeppa* (1851); *Orpheus* (1853–54); *Les Préludes* (1854); *Hungaria* (1854) and *Hamlet* (1858).

2 piano concertos: No. 1, E-flat Major (1849); No. 2, A Major (1839, subsequently revised several times).

Totentanz, for piano and orchestra (1849); *Hungarian Fantasy,* for piano and orchestra (1852); *A Faust Symphony* (1854–57); *Dante Symphony* (1855–56); *Two Episodes from Lenau's Faust* (1860); *Second Mephisto Waltz* (1880–81).

Organ Music: Fantasie and Fugue on the Chorale "Ad Nos, ad salutarem undam (1850); *Prelude and Fugue on the Name B.A.C.H.* (1855–56); *Evocation in the Sistine Chapel,* based on Mozart's *Ave Verum* (c. 1862); *Requiem* (1883); *Am Grabe Richard Wagners* (1883); *Zwei Vortragstücke* (1884).

Piano Music: 19 Hungarian rhapsodies (1846–1885) including: No. 2, C-sharp Minor; No. 9, E-flat Major, *Carnaval de Pesth;* No. 12, C-sharp Minor; No. 13, A Minor, also for piano and orchestra as *Hungarian Fantasy;* No. 15, A Minor, *Rakóczy March.*

Années de pèlerinage, three series (1835–36, 1838–39, 1877).

3 *Liebesträume,* including popular one in A-flat Major (1850).

2 concert etudes (1862): I. *Waldesrauschen;* II. *Gnomenreigan.*

2 legends (1863): I. *St. François d'Assise, La Prédiction aux oiseaux;* II. *St. François de Paule marchant sur les flots.*

Album d'un voyageur (1835–36); *Paganini Etudes* (1838); *Harmonies poétiques et religieuses* (1847–1852); *Consolations* (1849–1850); *Etudes d'exécution transcendante* (1851); Sonata in B Minor (1852–53); *Weihnachtsbaum* (1874–76); *Nuages gris* (1881); *La lugubre gondole* (1882); *Sinistre* (c. 1882); Albumblätter, ballades, caprices, Ländler, mazurkas, and numerous transcriptions.

Vocal Music: Numerous songs for voice and piano including: *Einst* (1878); *Enfant, si j'étais roi* (1844); *Es muss ein wunderbares sein* (1857); *Ein Fichtenbaum* (1855); *Gebet* (c. 1878); *Ich möchte hingehn* (1845); *Ich scheide* (1860); *J'ai perdu ma force* (1872); *Kennst du das Land?* (1842); *Kling leise* (1848); *König in Thule* (1842); *Sei still* (1877); *Verlassen* (1880).

RICHARD WAGNER

Operas: Die Feen (1833–34); *Das Liebesverbot* (1835–36); *Rienzi* (1838–40); *Der fliegende Holländer* (1841); *Tannhäuser* (1843–44); *Lohengrin* (1846–48); *Der Ring des Nibelungen:* I. *Das Rheingold* (1853–54), II. *Die Walküre* (1854–56), III. *Siegfried* (1869–74), IV. *Götterdämmerung* (1869–74); *Tristan und Isolde* (1857–59); *Die Meistersinger von Nürnberg* (1862–67); *Parsifal* (1877–82).

Orchestral Music: Symphony in C Major (1832); *Eine Faust Ouvertüre* (1840); *Huldigungsmarsch* (1864); *Siegfried Idyll* (1870); *Kaisermarsch* (1871).

Piano Music: 2 sonatas (1829, 1831); *Lied ohne Worte* (1840); *Album-Sonata* in E-flat Major (1853); 3 *Albumblätter* (1861).

Vocal Music: 5 *Gedichte von Mathilde Wesendonk:* I. *Der Engel* (1857); II. *Stehe still* (1858); III. *Im Treibhaus* (1858); IV. *Schmerzen* (1857); V. *Träume* (1857).

Other songs for voice and piano; vocal duets.

JOHANNES BRAHMS

Chamber Music: 3 piano quartets; No. 1, G Minor, op. 25 (1861); No. 2, A Major, op. 26 (1862); No. 3, C Minor, op. 60 (1874).

3 string quartets: No. 1, C Minor, op. 51, No. 1 (1873); No. 2, A Minor, op. 51, No. 2 (1873); No. 3, B-flat Major, op. 67 (c. 1875).

3 piano trios: No. 1, B Major, op. 8 (1853–54, revised 1890); No. 2, E-flat Major, op. 40 (1865); No. 3, C Major, op. 87 (1882).

3 violin sonatas: No. 1, G Major, *Rain,* op. 78 (1879); No. 2, A Major, *Thun,* op. 100 (1886); No. 3, D Minor, op. 108 (1886–88).

2 string sextets: No. 1, B-flat Major, op. 18 (1859–60); No. 2, G Major, op. 36 (1865).

2 string quintets: No. 1, F Major, op. 88 (1882); No. 2, G Major, op. 111 (c. 1890).

2 cello sonatas: No. 1, E Minor, op. 38 (1862–63); No. 2, F Major, op. 99 (1886).

2 clarinet (or viola) sonatas, op. 120 (1894): No. 1, F Minor; No. 2, E-flat Major.

Piano Quintet in F Minor, op. 34 (1864); Clarinet Trio in A Minor, op. 114 (1891); Clarinet Quintet, in B Minor, op. 115 (1891).

Choral Music: Ein deutsches Requiem, op. 45 (1857–68); *Rinaldo,* op. 50 (1863–68); *Alto Rhapsody,* op. 53 (1869); *Schicksalied,* op. 54 (1868–71); *Triumphlied,* op. 55 (1870–71); *Gesang der Parzen,* op. 89 (1882); sacred choruses, motets, part songs, romances, psalms, canons.

Orchestral Music: 4 symphonies: No. 1, C Minor, op. 68 (1876); No. 2, D Major, op. 73 (1877); No. 3, F Major, op. 90 (1883); No. 4, E Minor, op. 98 (1885).

2 serenades: No. 1, D Major, op. 11 (1857–58); No. 2, A Major, op. 16 (1859, revised 1875).

2 piano concertos: No. 1, D Minor, op. 15 (1854–58); No. 2, B-flat Major, op. 83 (1881).

Variations on a Theme by Haydn, op. 56a, also for two solo pianos (1873); Violin Concerto in D Major, op. 77 (1878); *Akademisches Festouvertüre,* op. 80 (1880); *Tragische Ouvertüre,* op. 81 (1880); Double Concerto, for cello and violin and orchestra, op. 102 (1887); Hungarian Dances, Nos. 1, 3, and 10, also for piano duet.

Organ Music: 11 Chorale Preludes, op. 122 (1896); preludes and fugues.

Piano Music: Ballades, op. 10 (1854), op. 118 (1893); Capriccios, op. 76 (1878), op. 116 (1891–92); *Hungarian Dances,* four sets, for piano duet (1858–80); Intermezzi, op. 76 (1878), op. 116 (1891–92), op. 117 (1892), op. 118 (1893), op. 119 (1893); Rhapsodies, op. 79 (1879), op. 119 (1893).

3 sonatas: No. 1, C Major, op. 1 (1852–53); No. 2, F-sharp Minor, op. 2 (1852); No. 3, F Minor, op. 5 (1853).

Variations on a Theme by Handel, op. 24 (1861); *Variations on a Theme by Paganini,* op. 33 (1862–63); Waltzes, for piano duet, op. 39 (1865).

Vocal Music: 16 *Romances from Magelone,* op. 33 (1861–68); *Liebeslieder* Waltzes, for vocal quartet and piano duet, op. 52a (1868–69); *Neue Liebeslieder* Waltzes, for vocal quartet and piano duet, op. 65a (1874); *Zigeuenerlieder,* for vocal quartet and piano, op. 103 (1887); *Vier ernste Gesänge,* op. 121 (1896).

Numerous individual songs for voice and piano including: *Am*

530

Sonntag Morgen, op. 49, No. 1 (c. 1868); *An die Nachtigall,* op. 46, No. 4 (c. 1868); *Auf dem Kirchhofe,* op. 105, No. 4 (c. 1886); *Die Botschaft,* op. 47, No. 1 (c. 1868); *Feldeinsamkeit,* op. 86, No. 2 (1877–78); *Der Gang zum Liebchen,* op. 48, No. 1 (c. 1868); *Gestillte Sehnsucht,* op. 91, No. 1 (c. 1884); *Immer leiser wird mein Schlummer,* op. 105, No. 2 (c. 1886); *Der Jäger,* op. 95, No. 4 (1884); *Die Mainacht,* op. 43, No. 2 (c. 1868); *Nicht mehr zu dir zu gehen,* op. 32, No. 2 (c. 1864); *O wüsst ich doch den Weg zurück,* op. 63, No. 18 (1873–74); *Sappische Ode,* op. 94, No. 4 (1884); *Der Schmied,* op. 19, No. 4 (1858–59) *Sonntag,* op. 47, No. 3 (c. 1868); *Ständchen,* op. 106, No. 1 (c. 1886); *Der Tod das ist die kühle Nacht,* op. 96, No. 1 (c. 1884); *Vergebliches Ständchen,* op. 84, No. 4 (c. 1878); *Von ewiger Liebe,* op. 43, No. 1 (c. 1866) *Wie bist du, meine Königen,* op. 32, No. 9 (c. 1864); *Wiegenlied,* op. 49, No. 1 (c. 1868).

Canons, vocal duets, vocal quartets, arrangements and settings of folk songs.

BEDŘICH SMETANA

Chamber Music: 2 string quartets: No. 1, E Minor, *Aus meinem Leben* (1876); No. 2, D Minor (1882).

Piano Trio in G Minor (1855); two pieces, for violin and piano (1878).

Choral Music: Three Horsemen (1863); *The Farmer* (1868); *Czech Song* (1868, revised 1878); *Festive Chorus* (1870); *Sea Song* (1877); *Prayer* (1880); *Our Song* (1883).

Operas: The Brandenburgers in Bohemia (1862–63); *The Bartered Bride* (1863–66); *Dalibor* (1865–67); *Libuša* (1869–1872); *Two Widows* (1873); *The Kiss* (1875–76); *The Secret* (1877–78); *The Devil's Wall* (1879–1882).

Orchestral Music: Richard III (1858); *Wallensteins Lager* (1858–59); *Haakon Jarl* (1860–61); *Solemn Prelude* (1868).

Má Vlast, a cycle of six tone poems (1874–79): I. *Vyšehrad;* II. *Vltava,* or *The Moldau;* III. *Šárka;* IV. *From the Fields and Groves of Bohemia;* V. *Tábor;* VI. *Blanik.*

The Prague Carnival (1883).

Piano Music: Six Characteristic Pieces, two books (1848); *Sonata in One Movement* (1849); *Memories of Bohemia,* two books (1861); *Dreams* (1875); *Czech Dances* (1877–78); Bagatelles, impromptus, polkas, waltzes.

Vocal Music: The Song of Liberty (1848); *Evening Songs* (1879).

ANTONIN DVOŘÁK

Chamber Music: 13 string quartets, including Quartet in F Major, *American,* op. 96 (1893); 4 piano trios, including *Dumky Trio,* op. 90 (1891); 3 string quintets, including Quintet in E-flat Major, op. 97 (1893); 2 piano quintets, including Quintet in A Major, op. 81 (1887).

String Sextet in A Major, op. 48 (1878); Violin Sonata in F Major, op. 57 (1880); *Four Romantic Pieces,* for violin and piano, op. 75 (1887); Violin Sonatina in G Major, op. 100 (1893).

Choral Music: Stabat Mater, op. 58 (1877); *Amid Nature,* op. 63 (1882); *The Spectre's Bride,* op. 69 (1884); *St. Ludmilla,* op. 71 (1886); Mass in D Major, op. 86 (1887); *Requiem,* op. 89 (1890); *The American Flag,* op. 102 (1893); Te Deum, op. 103 (1892); Slavic folk songs, part songs, choral songs.

Operas: King Alfred (1870); *The King and the Collier,* op. 14 (1871, revised 1874, 1887); *The Pigheaded Peasants,* op. 17 (1874); *Vanda* (1875); *The Cunning Peasant,* op. 37 (1877); *Dimitrij,* op. 64 (1881–82, revised 1883, 1894); *The Devil and Kate,* op. 112 (1898–99); *Rusalka,* op. 114 (1900); *Armida,* op. 115 (1902–3).

Orchestral Music: 7 published symphonies including: No. 1, D Major, op. 60 (1880); No. 4, G Major, op. 88 (1889); No. 5, E minor, *From the New World,* op. 95 (1893).

Piano Concerto in G Minor, op. 33 (1876); 3 *Slavonic Rhapsodies,* op. 45 (1878); *Slavonic Dances,* two series, also for piano duet, opp. 46, 72 (1878, 1886); Violin Concerto in A Minor, op. 53 (1880); *10 Legends,* op. 59, also for piano duet (1881); *My Home,* op. 62 (1881); *Scherzo capriccioso,* op. 66 (1883); *Symphonic Variations,* op. 78 (1877); *Nature, Life and Love,* three overtures, opp. 91–93 (1891–92): I. *In Nature's Realm,* II. *Carnival,* III. *Othello.* Cello Concerto in B Minor, op. 104 (1895).

532

4 tone poems based on ballads by K. J. Erben, opp. 107–10 (1896): I. *The Water Sprite;* II. *The Midday Witch;* III. *The Golden Spinning Wheel;* IV. *The Wood Dove.*

Heroic Song, op. 111 (1897).

Piano Music: Silhouettes, op. 8 (1879); Theme and Variations in A-flat, op. 36 (1876); *From the Bohemian Forest,* for piano duet, op. 68 (1884); *Poetic Pictures,* op. 85 (1889); Suite in A Major, *American,* op. 98 (1894); 8 *Humoresques,* op. 101 (1894); Dumky, waltzes, mazurka.

Vocal Music: Evening Songs, op. 3, 31 (1876); *Four Serbian Songs,* op. 6 (1872); *Three Sacred Duets,* op. 19 (1879); *Moravian Duets,* op. 32 (1876); *Gypsy Songs,* op. 55 (1880), including "Songs My Mother Taught Me"; *Biblical Songs,* op. 99 (1894).

PETER ILITCH TCHAIKOVSKY

Ballets: Swan Lake, op. 20 (1875–76); *The Sleeping Beauty,* op. 66 (1888–89); *The Nutcracker,* or *Casse-Noisette,* op. 71 (1891–92).

Chamber Music: 3 string quartets including, Quartet in D Major, op. 11 (1871) with the famous Andante Cantabile; *Souvenir d'un lieu cher,* for violin and piano, op. 42 (1878), with the famous *Melody in E-flat;* Piano Trio in A Minor, op. 50 (1881–82); *Souvenir de Florence,* string sextet, op. 70 (1887–90, revised 1891–92).

Choral Music: Liturgy of St. John Chrysostom, op. 41 (1878); *Vesper Service,* op. 52 (1881–82); *Six Church Songs* (1885); Cantatas, Choral Pieces.

Operas: The Voyevode, op. 3 (1867–68); *Undine* (1869); *The Oprichnik* (1870–72); *Vakula the Smith,* op. 14 (1874, revised 1885); *Eugene Onegin,* op. 24 (1877–78); *The Maid of Orleans* (1878–79, revised 1882); *Mazeppa* (1881–83); *The Sorceress* (1885–87); *Pique Dame,* or *The Queen of Spades,* op. 68 (1890); *Iolanthe,* op. 69 (1891).

Orchestral Music: 6 symphonies: No. 1, G Minor, *Winter Dreams,* op. 13 (1866, revised 1874); No. 2, C Minor, *Little Russian* op. 17 (1872, revised 1879); No. 3, D Major, op. 29 (1875); No. 4, F Minor, op. 36 (1877); No. 5, E Minor, op. 64 (1888); No. 6, B Minor, *"Pathé-tique,"* op. 74 (1893).

4 suites: No. 1, D Minor, op. 43 (1878–79); No. 2, C Major, op. 53 (1883); No. 3, G Major, op. 55 (1884); No. 4, *Mozartiana,* op. 61 (1887).

3 piano concertos including No. 1, B-flat Minor, op. 23 (1874–75).

Tempest, op. 18 (1873); *Romeo and Juliet* (1869, revised 1870, 1880); *Swan Lake Suite,* op. 20 (1876); *Sérénade mélancolique,* for violin and orchestra, op. 26 (1875); *Marche slave,* op. 31 (1876); *Francesca da Rimini,* op. 32 (1876); *Variations on a Rococo Theme,* for cello and orchestra, op. 33 (1876); Violin Concerto in D Major, op. 35 (1878); *Capriccio italien,* op. 45 (1880); Serenade in C, for strings, op. 48 (1880); *Ouverture solennelle, 1812,* op. 49 (1880); *Manfred,* op. 58 (1885); *Sleeping Beauty Suite,* op. 66 (1889); *Hamlet,* op. 67a (1888); *Nutcracker Suite,* op. 71a (1892).

Piano Music: Souvenir de Hapsal, op. 2 (1867), including *Chant sans paroles; The Months,* op. 37b (1875–76); *Children's Album,* op. 39 (1878); *Twelve Pieces of Moderate Difficulty,* op. 40 (1876–78), including *Chanson triste; 18 Pieces,* op. 72 (1893); Sonata in C-sharp Minor, op. 80 (1865).

Vocal Music: 16 *Children's Songs,* op. 54 (1883); 6 *French Songs,* op. 65 (1888).

Many individual songs for voice and piano including: "Again, as Before, Alone," op. 73, No. 6 (1893); *At the Ball,* op. 38, No. 3 (1878); *Don Juan's Serenade,* op. 38, No. 1 (1878); *I Bless You Forests,* op. 47, No. 5 (1880); *It Was in Early Spring,* op. 38, No. 2 (1878); *None But the Lonely Heart,* op. 6, No. 6 (1869); *Only Thou,* op. 57, No. 6 (1886); *Pimpinella,* op. 38, No. 6 (1878); *Why?,* op. 6, No. 5 (1869). Vocal duets.

MODEST MUSSORGSKY

Choral Music: Shamil's March (1859); *The Destruction of Senna-cherib* (1867, revised 1874); *Joshua* (1874–77); 3 *Vocalises* (1880); 5 *Russian Folksongs* (1880).

Operas: Salammbô, unfinished (1863–66); *The Marriage,* first act only (1868); *Boris Godunov* (1868–69, revised 1871–72); *Khovan-china*, unfinished (1872–80); *The Fair at Sorochinsk*, unfinished (1874–80).

Orchestral Music: A Night on Bald Mountain (1867); *Intermezzo symphonique in modo classico* (1867); *Triumphal March* (1880).

Piano Music: From Memories of Childhood (1865); *Duma* (1865); *La Capricieuse* (1865); *The Seamstress* (1871); *Pictures at an Exhibition* (1874); *On the Southern Shore of Crimea* (1880); *Album Leaf* (1880); *Une Larme* (1880).

Vocal Music: The Nursery (1868); *Sunless* (1874); *Songs and Dances of Death* (1875–77).

Individual songs for voice and piano including: *Forgotten* (1874); *Hopak* (1866); *Night* (1864); *Savishna* (1866); *The Magpie* (1864); *The Peep Show* (1872); *Song of the Flea* (1879); *Song of the Old Man* (1863).

NIKOLAI RIMSKY-KORSAKOV

Chamber Music: 3 string quartets (1875, 1879, 1897); String Sextet in A Major (1876); Piano Trio in C Minor (1897); *Serenade*, for cello and piano, op. 37 (1903).

Choral Music: 4 Variations and Fughetta on a Russian Folksong, op. 14 (1875); 15 *Russian Folksongs*, op. 19 (1879); *Dragon-Flies*, op. 53 (1897); *Switezianka*, op. 44 (1897); *Song of Oleg the Wise*, op. 58 (1899); *Dubinushka*, op. 61 (1905–6); Three-Part Choruses.

Operas: The Maid of Pskov (1868–72, revised 1877, 1891); *May Night* (1877–79); *Snegourchka*, or *Snow Maiden* (1880–81); *Mlada* (1889–90); *Christmas Eve* (1894–95); *Sadko* (1894–96); *Mozart and Salieri*, op. 48 (1897); *The Tsar's Bride* (1898); *The Tale of Tsar Saltan* (1898–1900); *Kastchei the Immortal* (1901–2); *Pan Voyevoda* (1902–3); *The Invisible City of Kitezh* (1903–5); *Le Coq d'or* (1906–7).

Orchestral Music: 3 symphonies: No. 1, E-flat Minor, op. 1 (1861–65); No. 2, *Antar*, op. 9 (1868); No. 3, C Major, op. 32 (1866–73).

Sadko, op. 5 (1867); *Fantasia on Serbian Themes*, op. 6 (1867); *Overture on Russian Themes*, op. 28 (1866); Piano Concerto in C-sharp Minor, op. 30 (1882–83); *Sinfonietta on Russian Themes,* op. 31 (1879); *Fantasy on Russian Themes,* for violin and orchestra, op. 33 (1886); *Capriccio espagnol,* op. 34 (1887); *Scheherazade,* op. 35 (1888); *Russian Easter Overture,* or *Grande pâque russe,* op. 36 (1888); 2 Ariosos for Bass and Orchestra, op. 49 (1897); 2 Songs for Soprano and Orchestra, op. 56 (1898); Suites from *Le Coq d'or, Mlada, Christmas Eve.*

Piano Music: 6 Variations on the Theme of B.A.C.H., op. 10 (1878); various pieces, fugues, variations.

Vocal Music: In Spring, op. 43 (1897); *To the Poet,* op. 45 (1897–99); *By the Sea,* op. 46 (1897).

Individual songs for voice and piano including: *It Is Not the Wind,* op. 43, No. 2 (1897); *The Rose and the Nightingale,* op. 2, No. 2 (1865).

EDVARD GRIEG

Chamber Music: 3 violin sonatas: No. 1, F Major, op. 8 (1865); No. 2, G Minor, op. 13 (1867); No. 3, C Minor, op. 45 (1886–87).

String Quartet in G Minor, op. 27 (1877–78); Cello Sonata in A Minor, op. 36 (1883).

Choral Music: At a Southern Convent's Gate, op. 20 (1871); *Album,* op. 30 (1877); *Landsighting,* op. 31 (1872); *Four Psalms,* op. 74 (1906).

Orchestral Music: In Autumn, op. 11 (1865, revised 1888); Piano Concerto in A Minor, op. 16 (1868); *Two Elegiac Melodies,* for strings, op. 34 (c. 1880); *Norwegian Dances,* op. 35 (1881), also for piano duet; *Holberg Suite,* for strings, op. 40 (1884–85), also for piano solo; *Peer Gynt,* two suites, op. 46, 55 (1876); *Sigurd Jorsalfar Suite,* op. 56 (1872, revised 1892); *Two Norwegian Melodies,* op. 63 (1894–95); *Symphonic Dances,* op. 64 (1898); *Lyric Suite* (1891).

Piano Music: Lyric Suite, ten volumes, opp. 12, 38, 43, 47, 54, 57, 62, 65, 68, 71 (1867–1901).

Humoresque, op. 6 (1865); *Sonata in E Minor,* op. 7 (1865); *Norwegian Dances and Songs,* op. 17 (1870); *Scenes from Peasant Life,* op. 19 (1872); Ballade, op. 24 (1875); *Album Leaves,* op. 28, (1875); *Improvisations on Norwegian Folk Songs,* op. 29 (1878); *Norwegian Folk Melodies,* op. 66 (1896); *Norwegian Peasant Dances,* op. 72 (1902); *Moods,* op. 73 (1906).

Vocal Music: German Songs, opp. 2, 4, 48 (1862, 1863–64, 1889); *Danish Songs,* opp. 5, 10 (1862–64); *From Mountain and Fjord,* op. 44 (1886); *Norway,* op. 58 (1894); *Elegiac Poems,* op. 59 (1894); *Children's Songs,* op. 61 (1894–95); *Haugtussa,* op. 67 (1896–98).

Individual songs for voice and piano including: *A Dream,* op. 48, No. 6 (1889); *Eros,* op. 70, No. 1 (1900); *I Love Thee,* op. 5, No. 3 (1864); *Spring,* op. 33, No. 2 (1880); *A Swan,* op. 25, No. 2 (1876); *While I Wait,* op. 60, No. 3 (1894); *The Wounded Heart,* op. 33, No. 3 (1880).

GIUSEPPE VERDI

Chamber Music: String Quartet in E Minor (1873).

Choral Music: Inno alle nazione (1862); *Manzoni Requiem* (1874); *Pater Noster* (1880); *Ave Maria* (1889); *Stabat Mater* (1898); *Te Deum* (1898); *Laudi alla Vergine Maria* (1898); 2 secular cantatas.

Operas: About 30 operas including: *Un giorno di regno* (1840); *Nabucco* (1842); *I Lombardi* (1843); *Ernani* (1844); *Macbeth* (1847); *Luisa Miller* (1849); *Rigoletto* (1851); *Il Trovatore* (1853); *La Traviata* (1853); *I Vespri siciliani,* or *Les Vêpres siciliennes* (1855); *Simon Boccanegra* (1857); *Un Ballo in maschera* (1859); *La Forza del destino* (1862); *Don Carlo* (1867); *Aida* (1871); *Otello* (1887); *Falstaff* (1893).

Vocal Music: Sei romanze (1838); *Album di sei romanze* (1845); *Ave Maria,* for soprano and strings (1880); various individual songs for voice and piano; vocal trio.

GIACOMO PUCCINI

Chamber Music: Scherzo, for string quartet (1880–83); String Quartet in D Major (1880–83); Fugues, for string quartet (1883); *I Crisantemi,* for string quartet (1889).

Choral Music: I Figli d'Italia bella (1877); Mass in A Major (1880).
Operas: Le Villi (1884); *Edgar* (1889); *Manon Lescaut* (1893); *La Bohème* (1896); *Tosca* (1900); *Madama Butterfly* (1904); *La Fanciulla del West,* or *The Girl of the Golden West* (1910); *La Rondine* (1917); *Il Trittico* (1918): I. *Il Tabarro,* II. *Suor Angelica,* III. *Gianni Schicchi; Turandot* (completed by Franco Alfano after Puccini's death).
Vocal Music: Several songs for voice and piano.

ANTON BRUCKNER

Chamber Music: Aequali, for three trombones (1847); *Abendklänge,* for violin and piano (1866); String Quintet in F Major (1878–79); intermezzo, for string quintet (1879).
Choral Music: Requiem in D Minor (1848–49, revised 1854, 1894); *Missa Solemnis* (1854); Mass in D Minor (1864, revised 1876, 1881–82); Mass in E Minor (1866, revised 1885); Mass in F Minor, *Grosse messe* (1867–68, revised 1871, 1890); Te Deum in C Major (1881–84) Ave Marias, cantatas, chorales, choruses for male voices, graduals, offertories, Psalms.
Orchestral Music: 9 symphonies including: No. 3, D Minor, "Wagner (1873, revised 1876–77, 1888); No. 4, E-flat Major, "Romantic" (1874, revised 1878–80); No. 7, E Major (1881–83); No. 9, D Minor (1887–96).
March in D Minor (1862); *Three Pieces* (1862); Overture in G Minor (1862–63).
Organ Music: Preludes, pieces, fugue.
Piano Music: Three Pieces, for piano duet (1852–54); *Klavierstück* in E-flat Major (c. 1856); *Errinerung* (1866); Fantasy in E-flat Major (1868).
Vocal Music: Several songs for voice and piano.

GUSTAV MAHLER

Orchestral Music: 9 symphonies including: No. 1, D Major, *Titan* (1888); No. 2, C Minor, *Resurrection* (1894); No. 4, G Major (1901); No. 5, C-sharp Minor (1902); No. 7, E minor (1906); No. 8, E-flat

Major, *Symphony of a Thousand Voices* (1907); No. 9, D major (1910); Symphony No. 10 (unfinished).

Das klagende Lied, for soprano, contralto, tenor, chorus and orchestra (1880–99); *Lieder eines fahrenden Gesellen,* for voice and orchestra (1885); *Kindertotenlieder,* for voice and orchestra (1904); *Das Lied von der Erde,* for contralto, tenor, and orchestra (1910).

Vocal Music: Lieder und Gesänge aus der Jugendzeit (1882); *Des Knaben Wunderhorn* (1888), also for voice and orchestra; Five Songs to Poems by Rückert (1902); *Revelge* (c. 1909); *Der Tambourg'sell* (c. 1909).

HUGO WOLF

Chamber Music: String Quartet in D Minor (1878–84); Intermezzo in E-flat Major, for string quartet (1886); *Italienische Serenade,* also for orchestra (1887).

Choral Music: Compositions for unaccompanied male-voices; unaccompanied mixed chorus, male-voices and orchestra, and mixed-chorus and orchestra.

Operas: Der Corregidor (1896); *Manuel Venegas* (unfinished).

Orchestral Music: Penthesilea (1883–85).

Piano Music: Variations (1875); Rondo capriccioso in B-flat Major (1876); *Humoreske* (1877); *Aus der Kinderzeit* (1878); Canon (1882).

Vocal Music: Sechs Lieder für eine Frauenstimme (1888); *Sechs Gedichte von Scheffel, Moerike, Goethe und Kerner* (1888); *Moerike Lieder* (1889); *Eichendorff Lieder* (1889); *Goethe Lieder* (1890); *Spanisches Liederbuch* (1891); *Alte Weisen* (1891); *Italienisches Liederbuch,* two parts (1892, 1896); *Drei Gedichte von Robert Reinick* (1897); *Drei Gesänge aus Ibsens Das Fest auf Solhaug* (1897); *Vier Gedichte nach Heine, Shakespeare und Lord Byron* (1897); *Drei Gedichte von Michelangelo* (1898).

CAMILLE SAINT-SAENS

Ballet: Javotte (1896).

Chamber Music: 2 string quartets: No. 1, E Minor, op. 112 (1899); No. 2, G Major, op. 153 (1919).

2 piano trios: No. 1, F Major, op. 18 (1869); No. 2, E Minor, op. 92 (1892).

2 violin sonatas: No. 1, D Minor, op. 75 (1885); No. 2, E-flat Major, op. 102 (1896).

2 cello sonatas: No. 1, C Minor, op. 32 (1873); No. 2, F Major, op. 123 (1905).

Various other sonatas for solo instruments and piano; Piano Quartet in B-flat Major, op. 41 (1875); Romance in D Major, for cello and piano, op. 51 (1877); Septet, for trumpet, strings and piano, op. 65 (1881); *Havanaise,* for violin and piano, op. 83; *Triptyque,* for violin and piano, op. 136 (1912); *Élégie,* for violin and piano, op. 143 (1915).

Choral Music: Messe solennelle, op. 4 (1856); Psalm 18, op. 42 (1865); *Le Déluge,* op. 45 (1876); *Requiem,* op. 54 (1878); *La Lyre et la harpe,* op. 57 (1879); *La feu céleste,* op. 115 (1900); *La Gloire,* op. 131; *Le Printemps,* op. 165; canticles, motets, other Psalms.

Operas: 12 operas including: *La Princess jaune,* op. 30 (1872); *Samson et Dalila,* op. 47 (1877); *Henry VIII* (1883); *Ascanio* (1890); *Phryné* (1893); *L'Ancêtre* (1906); *Déjanire* (1911).

Orchestral Music: 3 symphonies: No. 1, E-flat Major, op. 2 (1855); No. 2, A Minor, op. 55 (1878); No. 3, C Minor, with organ and two pianos, op. 78 (1886).

5 piano concertos: No. 1, D Major, op. 17 (1858); No. 2, G Minor, op. 22 (1868); No. 3, E-flat Major, op. 29 (1869); No. 4, C Minor, op. 44 (1875); No. 5, F Major, op. 103 (1895).

3 violin concertos: No. 1, A Minor, op. 20 (1859); No. 2, C Major, op. 58 (1879); No. 3, B Minor, op. 61 (1880).

2 cello concertos: No. 1, A Minor, op. 33 (1873); No. 2, D Minor, op. 119 (1902).

Le Rouet d'Omphale, op. 31 (1871); *Marche héroïque,* op. 34 (1871); 3 Romances for solo instruments and orchestra, opp. 36, 37, 48 (1874, 1876); *Phaëton,* op. 39 (1873); *Danse macabre,* op. 40 (1874); Suite, op. 49 (1877); *La Jeunesse d'Hercule,* op. 50 (1877); *Suite Algérienne,* op. 60 (1879); *Une Nuit à Lisbonne,* op. 63 (1881); *Jota aragonesa,* op. 64 (1881); *Rapsodie d'auvergne,* for piano and orchestra, op. 73 (1884); *Le Carnaval des animaux,* for two pianos and orchestra (1886); *La Fiancée du timbalier,* for mezzo-soprano and orchestra, op. 82 (1887); *Sarabande et rigaudon,* for strings, op. 93 (1892); *Pallas Athène,* for soprano and orchestra, op. 98 (1894); *Lola,* for soprano and orchestra, op. 116 (1900); *Ouverture de fête,* op. 133 (1910).

Incidental music to various plays including: *Andromque* (1903); *On ne badine pas avec l'amour* (1917).

Organ Music: Fantasies, improvisations, preludes and fugues.

Piano Music: Variations on a Theme by Beethoven, for two pianos, op. 35 (1874); *Album,* op. 72 (1884); Suite, op. 90 (1892); *Thème varié,* op. 97 (1894); *Valse mignonne,* op. 104; *Caprice héroïque,* for two pianos, op. 106 (1897); 6 Etudes, for left hand, op. 135 (1912); *Feuillet d'album,* op. 169 (1921); Bagatelles, etudes, mazurkas.

Vocal Music: Mélodies persanes, op. 26 (1870); *La Cendre rouge,* op. 146 (1915).

Individual songs for voice and piano including: *La Bonheur est un chose légère, La Cloche, Danse macabre,* and *La Pas d'armes.* Vocal duets, vocal quartets.

CLAUDE DEBUSSY

Ballets: Jeux (1912); *Khamma* (1912); *La Boite à joujoux* (1913).

Chamber Music: String quartet in G Minor (1893); *Rapsodie,* for saxophone and piano (1903–5); *Rapsodie,* for clarinet and piano, also clarinet and orchestra (1909–10); Cello Sonata (1915); Flute, Viola, and Harp Sonata (1916); Violin Sonata (1916–17).

Choral Music: L'Enfant prodigue (1884); *La Damoiselle élue* (1887–88); *Trois chansons de Charles d'Orléans* (1908).

Opera: Pelléas et Mélisande (1902).

Orchestral Music: Printemps (1887); *Fantaisie,* for piano and orchestra (1889); *L'Après midi d'un faun* (1892–94); *Nocturnes* (1893–99): I. *Nuages,* II. *Fêtes,* III. *Sirènes; La Mer* (1903–5); *Danse sacrée et danse profane,* for harp and strings (1904); *Images* (1906–9): I. *Gigues,* II. *Ibéria,* III. *Rondes de printemps;* Incidental music to *Le Martyre de Saint-Sébastien* (1911).

Piano Music: Deux Arabesques (1888); *Petite suite,* for piano duet

(1888); Ballade (1890); *Suite bergamasque,* including *Claire de lune* (1890–95); *Pour le piano* (1896–1901); *Estampes* (1903); *L'Isle joyeuse* (1904); *Masques* (1904); *Images,* two sets (1905, 1907); *Children's Corner* (1906–8); *La plus que lente,* also for orchestra (1910); 24 preludes, two books (1910–13); 24 etudes, two books (1915); *Six Épigraphes antiques,* for piano duet (1915); *En blanc et noir,* for two pianos (1915).

Vocal Music: Cinq poèmes de Baudelaire (1887–89); *Ariettes oubliées* (1888); *Deux Romances* (1891); *Trois Mélodies* (1891); *Fêtes galantes,* two sets (1892, 1904); *Proses lyriques* (1892–93); *Chansons de Bilitis* (1897); *Trois Chansons de France* (1904); *Le Promenoir des deux amants* (1904–10); *Trois Ballades de François Villon* (1910); *Trois Poèmes de Stéphane Mallarmé* (1913).

Individual songs for voice and piano including: *L'Angelus* (1891); *Beau soir* (1878); *Les Cloches* (1887); *Mandoline* (1880); *Noël des enfants qui n'ont pas de maisons* (1915); *Romance* (1887); *Voici que le printemps* (1887).

APPENDIX II

A Select Bibliography in English

COLLECTIVE BIOGRAPHIES

Bacharach, A. L. (editor): *The Music Masters*. Four volumes. London. Pelican. 1942, 1957.

Blom, Eric. *Some Composers of Opera*. London. Oxford. 1952.

Blom, Eric. *Some Great Composers*. London. Oxford. 1944.

Brockway, Wallace, and Weinstock, Herbert. *Men of Music*. Second revised edition. New York. Simon and Schuster. 1950.

Calvocoressi, M. D., and Abraham, Gerald. *Masters of Russian Music*. New York. Knopf. 1936.

Cardus, Neville. *A Composer's Eleven*. London. Jonathan Cape. 1958.

Ewen, David. *Composers of Yesterday*. New York. H. W. Wilson. 1937.

Ewen, David, and Cross, Milton. *Encyclopedia of Great Composers*. Revised edition. New York. Doubleday. 1962.

Foss, Hubert (editor). *The Heritage of Music*. Two volumes. London. Oxford. 1927, 1951.

Horton, John. *Some Nineteenth Century Composers*. London. Oxford. 1950.

Leonard, Richard Anthony. *The Stream of Music*. New York. Doubleday. 1946.

Mason, Daniel Gregory. *Beethoven and His Forerunners*. Revised edition. New York. Macmillan. 1940.

Mason, Daniel Gregory. *The Romantic Composers*. New York. Macmillan. 1930.

Mason, Daniel Gregory. *From Grieg to Brahms*. New York. Macmillan. 1927.

543

Parry, C. Hubert. *Studies of Great Composers.* New York. Dutton. Date unknown.

Rolland, Romain. *Musicians of Today.* New York. Holt. 1915.

Rolland, Romain. *Some Musicians of Former Days.* New York. Holt. 1915.

Zoff, Otto (editor). *Great Composers Through the Eyes of Their Contemporaries.* New York. Dutton. 1951.

INDIVIDUAL BIOGRAPHIES

PALESTRINA

Coates, Henry. *Palestrina.* New York. Pellegrini and Cudahy. 1949.

Pyne, Zoë Kendrick. *Giovanni Pierluigi Palestrina.* London. John Lane, The Bodley Head. 1922.

MONTEVERDI

Prunières, Henri. *Claudio Monteverdi.* New York. Norton. 1926.

Redlich, Hans F. *Claudio Monteverdi.* London. Oxford. 1952.

Schrade, Leo. *Monteverdi: Creator of Modern Music.* New York. Norton. 1950.

RAMEAU

Girdlestone, Cuthbert. *Jean-Philippe Rameau.* London. Cassell. 1957.

VIVALDI

Pincherle, Marc. *Vivaldi.* New York. Norton. 1957.

J. S. BACH

David, Hans T., and Mendel, Arthur (editors). *The Bach Reader.* New York. Norton. 1945.

Dickinson, A. E. F. *The Art of Bach.* Revised edition. London. Hinrichson. 1950.

Forkel, Johann Nikolaus. *Johann Sebastian Bach: His Life, Art and Work.* London. Boosey. 1820.

Parry, C. Hubert. *Johann Sebastian Bach.* Revised edition. New York. Putnam. 1934.

Pirro, André. *Johann Sebastian Bach.* New York. Orion. 1957.

Schweitzer, Albert. *Bach.* London. Breitkopf and Hartel. 1911.

Spitta, Philipp. *Johann Sebastian Bach.* London. Novello. 1947.

Terry, Charles S. *Bach: A Biography.* London. Oxford. 1928.

Terry, Charles S. *Bach: The Historical Approach.* London. Oxford. 1930.

HANDEL

Abraham, Gerald (editor). *Handel: A Symposium.* London. Oxford. 1954.

Dent, Edward J. *Handel.* New York. Wyn. 1949.

Deutsch, O. E. *Handel: A Documentary Biography.* New York. Norton. 1955.

Flower, Newman. *George Frideric Handel.* Revised edition. New York. Scribner. 1948.

Rolland, Romain. *Handel.* New York. Holt. 1916.

Streatfeild, R. A. *Handel.* London. Methuen. 1909.

Weinstock, Herbert. *Handel.* Revised edition. New York. Knopf. 1959.

Young, Percy M. *Handel.* New York. Pellegrini and Cudahy. 1947.

GLUCK

Berlioz, Hector. *Gluck and His Operas.* London. Reeves. 1914.

Cooper, Martin. *Gluck.* London. Oxford. 1935.

Einstein, Alfred. *Gluck.* London. Dent. 1936.

Rolland, Romain. *Some Musicians of Former Days.* New York. Holt. 1915.

HAYDN

Brenet, Michel. *Haydn.* London. Oxford. 1926.

Geiringer, Karl. *Haydn: A Creative Life in Music.* New York: Norton. 1946.

Hadden, J. Cuthbert. *Haydn.* New York. Dutton. 1931.

Hughes, Rosemary. *Haydn.* New York. Pellegrini and Cudahy. 1950.

Jacob, H. E. *Haydn: His Art, Times, and Glory*. New York. Rinehart. 1950.

MOZART
Anderson, Emily (editor). *The Letters of Mozart*. New York. Macmillan. 1938.

Biancolli, Louis (editor). *The Mozart Handbook*. New York. World. 1954.

Blom, Eric. *Mozart*. New York. Pellegrini and Cudahy. 1949.

Burk, John N. *Mozart and His Music*. New York. Random House. 1959.

Einstein, Alfred. *Mozart, His Character and His Work*. New York. Oxford. 1945.

Jahn, Otto. *W. A. Mozart*. London. Novello, Ewer. 1889.

King, A. Hyatt. *Mozart in Retrospect*. London. Oxford. 1955.

Landon, H. C. Robbins and Mitchell, Donald (editors). *The Mozart Companion*. New York. Oxford. 1956.

Turner, W. J. *Mozart: The Man and His Works*. New York. Knopf. 1945.

BEETHOVEN
Bekker, Paul. *Beethoven*. New York. Dutton. 1925.

Burk, John N. *The Life and Works of Beethoven*. New York. Random House. 1943.

Hamburger, Michael. *Beethoven: Letters, Journals, and Conversations*. New York. Anchor. 1960.

Rolland, Romain. *Beethoven the Creator*. New York. Harper. 1929.

Schauffler, Robert Haven. *Beethoven: The Man Who Freed Music*. New York. Tudor. 1947.

Specht, Richard. *Beethoven as He Lived*. New York. Macmillan. 1936.

Sullivan, J. W. N. *Beethoven: His Spiritual Development*. New York. Knopf. 1927.

Thayer, A. W. *The Life of Beethoven*. New York. Beethoven Association. 1921.

Turner, W. J. *Beethoven: The Search for Reality*. London. Dent. 1927.

WEBER

Saunders, William. *Weber*. London. Dent. 1940.

Stebbins, Lucy Poate and Stebbins, Richard Poate. *Enchanted Wanderer*. New York. Putnam. 1940.

Weber, Max Maria von. *Carl Maria von Weber*. Boston. Ditson. 1865.

SCHUBERT

Abraham, Gerald (editor). *Schubert: A Symposium*. New York. Norton. 1947.

Bie, Oscar. *Schubert: The Man*. New York. Dodd, Mead. 1928.

Brown, M. J. E. *Schubert*. New York. St. Martin's Press. 1958.

Deutsch, Otto Erich (editor). *Schubert: Memoirs of His Friends*. New York. Macmillan. 1958.

Deutsch, Otto Erich (editor). *Franz Schubert's Letters and Other Writings*. New York. Knopf. 1928.

Einstein, Alfred. *Schubert: A Musical Portrait*. New York. Oxford. 1951.

Flower, Newman. *Franz Schubert: The Man and His Circle*. New York. Scribner. 1928.

Kobald, Karl. *Franz Schubert and His Time*. New York. Knopf. 1928.

Schuaffler, Robert Haven. *Franz Schubert: The Ariel of Music*. New York. Putnam. 1949.

BERLIOZ

Barzun, Jacques. *Berlioz and the Romantic Century*. Boston. Little, Brown. 1950.

Barzun, Jacques (editor). *Berlioz, New Letters*. New York. Columbia University. 1954.

Berlioz, Hector. *Memoirs of Hector Berlioz*. Edited by Ernest Newman. New York. Knopf. 1948.

Elliott, J. H. *Berlioz*. London. Dent. 1938.

Hadow, W. H. *Studies in Modern Music*. London. Seeley. 1893.

Rolland, Romain. *Musicians of Today*. New York. Holt. 1915.

Turner, W. J. *Berlioz: The Man and His Work*. London. Dent. 1934.

Wotton, Tom S. *Berlioz*. London. Oxford. 1935.

ROSSINI

Toye, Francis R. *Rossini: A Study in Tragi-Comedy*. New York. Knopf. 1934.

MEYERBEER

Hervey, Arthur. *Meyerbeer*. New York. Stokes. 1913.

MENDELSSOHN

Devrient, Eduard. *Reminiscences of Mendelssohn*. London. Bentley. 1869.

Kaufman, Schima. *Mendelssohn*. New York. Crowell. 1934.

Radcliff, Philip M. *Mendelssohn*. London. Dent. 1954.

Seldon-Goth (editor). *Mendelssohn's Letters*. New York. Pantheon. 1945.

Young, Percy M. *Introduction to the Music of Mendelssohn*. London. Dobson. 1949.

SCHUMANN

Abraham, Gerald (editor). *Schumann: A Symposium*. London. Oxford. 1952.

Basch, Victor. *Schumann: A Life of Suffering*. New York. Knopf. 1931.

Bedford, Herbert. *Schumann*. New York. Harper. 1925.

Chissell, Joan. *Schumann*. London. Dent. 1948.

Harding, Bertita. *Concerto: The Glowing Story of Clara Schumann*. New York. Bobbs-Merrill. 1961.

Niecks, Frederick. *Robert Schumann*. New York. Novello, Ewer. 1888.

Schauffler, Robert Haven. *Florestan: The Life and Works of Robert Schumann*. New York. Holt. 1945.

CHOPIN

Bidou, Henri. *Chopin*. New York. Knopf. 1927.

Hadden, J. Cuthbert. *Chopin*. New York. Dutton. 1934.

Hedley, Arthur. *Chopin*. New York. Pellegrini and Cudahy. 1949.

Liszt, Franz. *Chopin*. London. Reeves. 1913.

Maine, Basil. *Chopin*. New York. Wyn. 1949.

Mizwa, Stephen P. (editor). *Chopin*. New York. Macmillan. 1949.

Murdoch, William. *Chopin: His Life*. New York. Macmillan. 1935.

Porte, John F. *Chopin: The Composer and His Music*. New York. Scribner. 1935.

Pourtalès, Guy de. *Chopin*. New York. Holt. 1927.

Weinstock, Herbert. *Chopin*. New York. Knopf. 1949.

Wierzynski, Casimir. *The Life and Death of Chopin*. New York. Simon and Schuster. 1949.

FRANCK

Demuth, Norman. *César Franck*. New York. Philosophical Library. 1949.

d'Indy, Vincent. *César Franck: A Study*. New York. Dodd Mead. 1931.

Vallas, Léon. *César Franck*. London. Harrap. 1951.

GOUNOD

Demuth, Norman. *Introduction to the Music of Gounod*. London. Dobson. 1950.

Gounod, Charles. *Autobiographical Reminiscences*. London. Heinemann. 1896.

MASSENET

Cooper, Martin. *French Music*. London. Oxford. 1951.

Finck, Henry T. *Massenet and His Operas*. New York. Lane. 1910.

Massenet, Jules. *My Recollections*. Boston. Small, Maynard. 1919.

LISZT

Hill, Ralph. *Liszt*. New York. Wyn. 1950.

Huneker, James Gibbons. *Liszt*. New York. Scribner. 1911.

Newman, Ernest. *The Man Liszt*. New York. Alfred A. Knopf. 1935.

Pourtalès, Guy de. *Franz Liszt.* Holt. 1926.

Searle, Humphrey. *The Music of Liszt.* London. Williams and Norgate. 1954.

Sitwell, Sacheverell. *Franz Liszt.* New York. Houghton Mifflin. 1934.

Westerby, Herbert. *Liszt, Composer and His Piano Works.* London. Reeves. 1936.

WAGNER

Bekker, Paul. *Richard Wagner.* New York. Norton. 1931.

Burk, John N. (editor). *Letters of Wagner: The Burrell Collection.* New York. Macmillan. 1950.

Gilman, Lawrence. *Wagner's Operas.* New York. Farrar and Rinehart. 1937.

Henderson, W. J. *Richard Wagner: His Life and His Dramas.* New York. Putnam. 1901.

Neumann, Angelo. *Personal Recollections of Wagner.* New York. G. Schirmer. 1915.

Newman, Ernest. *The Life of Richard Wagner.* 4 Volumes. New York. Knopf. 1933–1946.

Newman, Ernest. *Wagner As Man and Artist.* New York. Vintage. 1960.

Turner, W. J. *Wagner.* New York. Wyn. 1948.

Wagner, Richard. *Prose Works.* London. Reeves. 1892, 1899.

BRAHMS

Geiringer, Karl. *Brahms: His Life and Work.* Second Revised edition. New York. Oxford. 1947.

Latham, Peter. *Brahms.* New York. Pellegrini and Cudahy. 1949.

May, Florence. *The Life of Brahms.* London. Reeves. 1948.

Niemann, Walter. *Brahms.* New York. Knopf. 1947.

Pulver, Jeffrey. *Johannes Brahms.* New York. Harper. 1926.

Schauffler, Robert Haven. *The Unknown Brahms.* New York. Dodd, Mead. 1933.

Specht, Richard. *Brahms.* New York. Dutton. 1930.

SMETANA

Bartos, F. and Ocadlik, M. (editors). *Letters and Reminiscences of Smetana*. Prague. Artea. 1955.

DVOŘÁK

Robertson, Alec. *Dvořák*. New York. Pellegrini and Cudahy. 1949.
Sourek, Otakar. *Dvořák*. New York. Philosophical Library. 1954.
Stefan, Paul. *The Life and Work of Anton Dvořák*. New York. Greystone. 1941.

TCHAIKOVSKY

Abraham, Gerald (editor). *The Music of Tchaikovsky*. New York. Norton. 1946.
Abraham, Gerald. *Tchaikovsky: A Short Biography*. New York. Norton. 1946.
Bowen, Catherine D., and Meck B. von. *Beloved Friend*. New York. Dover. 1946.
Evans, Edwin. *Tchaikovsky*. New York. Pellegrini and Cudahy. 1949.
Lakond, Wladimir. *The Diaries of Tchaikovsky*. New York. Norton. 1945.
Shostakovich, Dimitri, and others. *Russian Symphony: Thoughts About Tchaikovsky*. New York. Philosophical Library. 1947.
Weinstock, Herbert. *Tchaikovsky*. New York. Knopf. 1946.

MUSSORGSKY

Calvocoressi, M. D. *Mussorgsky*. London. Rockliff. 1956.
Leyda, Jay, and Bertenson, S. *The Mussorgsky Reader*. New York. Norton. 1947.
Reisemann, Oskar von. *Mussorgsky*. New York. Knopf. 1935.

RIMSKY-KORSAKOV

Abraham, Gerald. *Rimsky-Korsakov: A Short Biography*. New York. Wyn. 1949.
Rimsky-Korsakov, Nikolai. *My Musical Life*. Third edition. New York. Knopf. 1942.

GRIEG

Abraham, Gerald (editor). *Grieg: A Symposium.* Norman. University of Oklahoma. 1950.

Finck, Henry T. *Grieg and His Music.* New York. Dodd, Mead. 1909.

Horton, John. *Grieg.* London. Duckworth. 1950.

Johansen, D. M. *Edvard Grieg.* New York. Tudor. 1945.

VERDI

Bonavia, F. *Verdi.* London. Dobson. 1947.

Gatti, Carlo. *Verdi, The Man and His Music.* New York. Putnam. 1955.

Hussey, D. *Verdi.* New York. Pellegrini and Cudahy. 1949.

Toye, Francis. *Giuseppe Verdi: His Life and Works.* New York. Knopf. 1946.

Werfel, Franz, and Stefan, Paul (editors). *Verdi: The Man in His Letters.* New York. L. B. Fischer. 1942.

Ybarra, T. R. *Verdi, Miracle Man of Opera.* New York. Harcourt, Brace. 1955.

PUCCINI

Adami, Giuseppe (editor). *Letters of Giacomo Puccini.* Philadelphia. Lippincott. 1931.

Carner, Mosco. *Puccini.* New York. Knopf. 1959.

Marek, George R. *Puccini: A Biography.* New York. Simon and Schuster. 1951.

Specht, Richard. *Giacomo Puccini.* New York. Knopf. 1933.

BRUCKNER

Engel, Gabriel. *The Life of Bruckner.* New York. Roerich Museum. 1931.

Newlin, Dika. *Bruckner–Mahler–Schoenberg.* New York. Kings Crown. 1947.

Wolff, Werner. *Anton Bruckner: Rustic Genius.* New York. Dutton. 1942.

MAHLER

Engel, Gabriel. *Mahler: Song Symphonist.* New York. Bruckner Society. 1932.

Mahler, Alma Maria. *Gustav Mahler: Memories and Letters.* New York. Viking. 1946.

Stefan, Paul. *Gustav Mahler: A Study of His Personality and His Work.* New York. G. Schirmer. 1913.

Walter, Bruno. *Gustav Mahler.* Revised edition. New York. Knopf. 1957.

HUGO WOLF

Newman, Ernest. *Hugo Wolf.* London. Methuen. 1907.

Walker, Frank. *Hugo Wolf: A Biography.* Knopf. 1952.

SAINT-SAËNS

Cooper, Martin. *French Music.* London. Oxford. 1951.

Hervey, Arthur. *Saint-Saëns.* New York. Dodd, Mead. 1922.

Lyle, Watson. *Camille Saint-Saëns: His Life and Art.*

DEBUSSY

Debussy, Claude. *Monsieur Croche, the Dilettante Hater.* New York. Lear. 1948.

Dumesnil, Maurice. *Claude Debussy: Master of Dreams.* New York. Washburn. 1940.

Lockspeiser, Edward. *Debussy.* New York. Pellegrini and Cudahy. 1949.

Myers, Rollo, H. *Debussy.* New York. Wyn. 1949.

Seroff, Victor. *Debussy: Musician of France.* New York. Putnam. 1956.

Thompson, Oscar. *Debussy, Man and Artist.* New York. Dodd, Mead. 1937.

Vallas, Léon. *Claude Debussy: His Life and Works.* London. Oxford. 1933.

APPENDIX III

CONTRIBUTORS

Abraham, Gerald, eminent English musicologist, is the author of a biography of Rimsky-Korsakov, *A Hundred Years of Music,* and (with M. D. Calvocoressi) *Masters of Russian Music,* and editor of various symposiums on composers of past and present.

D'Agoult, Countess Marie, who played such a prominent role in Liszt's life, was a celebrated authoress under the pen-name of Daniel Stern. Her personal portrait of Liszt is derived from her *Mémoires* (1833–54).

Apthorp, William Foster, for many years the music critic of the Boston *Evening Transcript,* was the author of *The Opera, Past and Present* and other books.

Bekker, Paul, the German musicologist who resided in New York from 1934 until his death, was the author of distinguished biographies of Beethoven and Wagner, and penetrating studies and surveys of symphonic music and the opera.

Bonavia, Ferruccio, Italian-born critic and composer, was for many years the music critic of *The Manchester Guardian* and the London *Daily Telegraph.* His books include biographies of Verdi, Mozart, and Rossini.

Burney, Charles, eminent 19th-century musical historian, was the author of a monumental four-volume history of music, published in England between 1776 and 1789.

Chabanon, Michel-Paul-Guide, distinguished 18th-century French writer, was an intimate friend of Rameau. As a member of the French Academy he delivered a eulogy of Rameau, a portion of which is used in the personal portrait of that composer.

Champigneulle, Bernard, French musicologist, is the author of *Histoire de la musique* among other volumes.

Coeuroy, André, pen name of Jean Belime, was a distinguished French critic and musicologist. His books include biographies of Weber, Schumann, and Chopin, and studies of French and contemporary music.

Colles, H. C., English music scholar, was the editor of the third and fourth editions of Grove's *Dictionary of Music and Musicians* and the author of numerous books, including the seventh volume (*Symphony and Drama: 1850–1900*) of the *Oxford History of Music.*

Cooper, Martin, is the music critic of the London *Daily Telegraph,* and for several years was the editor of the *Musical Times.* He is the author of *French Music* and biographies of Gluck and Bizet.

Dent, Edward J., one of England's foremost music scholars, is Professor of Music at Cambridge, president of the International Society of Musicology, and the author of several significant books including biographies of Alessandro Scarlatti and Handel, *Mozart's Operas, Music of the Renaissance in Italy,* and *The Opera.*

Devrient, Eduard, German writer, singer, playwright, and librettist, was a friend of Mendelssohn, about whom he wrote a valuable volume of personal reminiscences (1869).

Dies, Albert Christoph, an 18th-century German painter, knew Haydn well and recorded his impressions and conversations with that master in *Biographische Nachrichten von Joseph Haydn* (1810).

Downes, Olin, was the music critic of the *New York Times* from 1924 until his death in 1955.

Einstein, Alfred, one of Germany's outstanding musicologists, was a member of the music faculty at Smith College until his retirement in 1950. His many valuable contributions to musicology include biographies of Gluck and Schubert, *Music in the Romantic Era, A Short History of Music,* and a revision of the Köchel catalogue of Mozart's works.

Engel, Gabriel, American writer, was the author of brief biographies of Bruckner and Mahler.

Ewen, Frederic, is the co-author of *Musical Vienna,* and the editor of *The Poetry and Prose of Heinrich Heine.*

Fay, Amy, American pianist, studied with Liszt in Weimar. Some of her impressions of the composer are found in her book, *Music Study in Germany* (1905).

Flower, Sir Newman, is the author of biographies of Handel, Schubert, and Sir Arthur Sullivan.

Forkel, Johann Nikolaus, celebrated German music historian, was the author of the first full-length biography of Johann Sebastian Bach (1802), based on material provided him by Bach's sons.

Geiringer, Karl, is Professor of Music at Boston University and for several years was president of the American Musicological Society. His books include biographies of Brahms, Haydn, and the Bach family.

Grainger, Percy, eminent Australian-born and American pianist-composer, received valuable counsel and encouragement from Grieg early in his career. Grainger described his personal impressions of Grieg in two articles for *Etude.*

Gray, Cecil, distinguished English musicologist, was the author of biographies of Sibelius, Gesualdo and Peter Warlock, of a history of music and a survey of contemporary music.

Grillparzer, Franz, is the distinguished 19th-century Austrian poet and playwright who was personally associated with Beethoven and Schubert.

Grout, Donald Jay, is Professor of Music at Cornell University and author of *A Short History of Opera* and *A History of Western Music.*

Grove, Sir George, was a distinguished English musicographer, and editor of the monumental *Dictionary of Music and Musicians* (1879–89).

556

Hadow, Sir William Henry, English musicologist and educator, was the author of several important books including *Studies of Modern Music,* the fifth volume in the *Oxford History of Music* (*The Viennese Period*), and biographies of Beethoven and William Byrd.

Hale, Philip, was the eminent music critic of the *Boston Herald* and program annotator for the Boston Symphony Orchestra.

Hall, Leland, was a member of the music faculties of the University of Wisconsin and Columbia University and, for several years, program annotator for the New York Symphony Society.

Heine, Heinrich, is the world-famous 19th-century German lyric poet.

Helfert, Vladimir, Czech musicologist, was a noted professor of musicology and editor in Prague, who wrote valuable essays and books on many aspects of Czech music.

Hüttenbrenner, Anselm, an eminent Viennese musician, was a close friend of Beethoven and Schubert. His personal impressions of Schubert appeared in *Errinerungen an Schubert* (1906).

D'Indy, Vincent, distinguished French composer and conductor, was first a pupil, then a devoted disciple, of César Franck. He was the author of a notable biography of that master.

Jansen, Gustav, was a German musician who knew Schumann intimately in Leipzig, and reported his impressions and recollections of that master in *Die Davidsbündler: Aus Robert Schumanns Sturm und Drang Periode* (1883).

Kelly, Michael, an Irish singer, was a close friend of Mozart in Vienna, and recalled this association in *Reminiscences* (1826).

Lange, Kristian, and *Östvedt, Arne,* are the authors of *Norwegian Music.*

Leichtentritt, Hugo, distinguished German music scholar, was for many years lecturer on music at Harvard University. His books include *Music, History and Ideas, Musical Form, Music of the Western Nations,* and biographies of Chopin, Handel, and Busoni.

Leonard, Richard Anthony, is the author of *The Stream of Music* and *A History of Russian Music.*

Liszt, Franz, the world-famous composer discussed within the text of this volume, was the author of a biography of Chopin.

Mason, Daniel Gregory, eminent American educator and composer, was the author of *The Chamber Music of Brahms, Beethoven and His Forerunners, The Romantic Composers, From Grieg to Brahms,* and other books.

Montagu-Nathan, M., English writer on music, is an authority on Russian music. His books include *A History of Russian Music, Contemporary Russian Composers,* and a biography of Scriabin.

Newman, Ernest, one of England's foremost music critics and musicologists, was the author of a monumental four-volume biography of Wagner, among numerous other books. His critical essay on Wolf appeared in *The Contemporary Review* of London (May 1904).

Pahlen, Kurt, Viennese-born musicologist, has been active in Buenos Aires for many years as educator and writer on musical subjects. He is the author of *Music of the World: A History.*

Paul, Howard, was an American writer on musical subjects whose articles have appeared in leading journals.

Peyser, Herbert F., was for many years, a music critic on various American newspapers and journals, and a program annotator for the New York Philharmonic Orchestra.

Pincherle, Marc, distinguished French musicologist, has been professor at the École Normale in Paris and president of the French Society of Musicology. His books include biographies of Corelli, Vivaldi, and Albert Roussel.

Prunières, Henri, outstanding French musicologist, was the founder and for many years editor of *La Revue musicale.* He has written valuable studies of various aspects of French music and opera, together with a significant biography of Monteverdi.

Pyne, Zoë Kendrick, was the author of the *Palestrina: His Life and Times.*

Rolland, Romain, who received the Nobel Prize for literature in 1915, was one of France's most eminent musical scholars. He wrote a biography of Handel, several volumes on Beethoven, and numerous penetrating studies of the music of the past gathered in *Some Musicians of Former Days* and *A Musical Tour Through the Land of the Past,* among other books.

Rosenfeld, Paul, American author and music critic, was a penetrating commentator on the contemporary scene. His books include *Musical Portraits, Musical Chronicle* and *Discoveries of a Music Critic.*

Sand, George, French novelist whose real name was Amadine Aurore Dupin, played a significant role in Chopin's life. She has written about Chopin and her turbulent love affair with him, in several books including *Les Lettres d'un voyageur* (1836), *Un Hiver en Majorca* (1841), *Consuelo* (1842), and *Histoire de ma vie* (1855).

Schindler, Anton, was one of Beethoven's most intimate friends, and the author of a significant biography of that master (1840).

Schjelderup, Gerhard, was a distinguished Norwegian composer and writer, who was a personal friend of Grieg. He wrote a valuable biography of that composer (1903), and a monograph on Wagner.

von Schlichtegroll, Adolph Heinrich, writer, historian and librarian, was the author of the first extended biography of Mozart (in English, 1839).

Schwarz, Josef, is a Czech writer on musical subjects whose articles have appeared in leading European journals.

Schweitzer, Albert, is the world-famous humanitarian, organist, and physician who received the Nobel Peace Prize in 1952. As an organist he distinguished himself as one of the world's foremost interpreters of Bach's organ music. He also wrote a definitive Bach biography (1905).

Slonimsky, Nicolas, eminent American musicologist, is the author of *Music Since 1900,* and *Music of Latin America,* editor of the fifth edition of Baker's *Biographical Dictionary,* and compiler of the *Thesaurus of Scales and Melodic Patterns.*

Specht, Richard, Austrian writer on music, was the founder, and for many years editor, of *Der Merker.* His books include biographies of Mahler, Johann Strauss II, Brahms, Richard Strauss, and Puccini.

Stefan, Paul, was the author of biographies of Mahler, Schoenberg, Schubert, Dvořák, Toscanini, and Bruno Walter.

Streatfeild, Richard Alexander, was for many years the music critic of the *Daily Graphic* in London. His books include *The Opera, Modern Music and Musicians,* and a biography of Handel.

Strunk, W. Oliver, American musicologist, is Professor of Music at Princeton University and the editor of *Source Readings in Music History.*

Taylor, Deems, is one of America's most eminent music critics, composers, and program annotators. He was the music critic of the *New York World* and *New York American* and editor of *Musical America.* Among his books are *Of Men and Music, The Well Tempered Listener* and *Music to My Ears.*

Tchaikovsky, Mme. Anatol, was the sister-in-law of the celebrated composer, the wife of Anatol, twin brother of Modest.

Terry, Charles Sanford, eminent English musicologist, was an outstanding authority on Bach. His books on the master and his family include *The Origins of the Family of Bach Musicians, Bach: The Historical Approach, Bach's Orchestra, The Music of Bach,* and *Bach: A Biography.* He also translated Forkel's biography of Bach, the German texts of all Bach cantatas, and edited a three-volume work on Bach's chorales.

Thompson, Oscar, was the music critic of the *New York Sun* and editor of *Musical America.* He was the author of an important biography of Debussy and editor of the *International Cyclopedia of Music.*

Tovey, Sir Donald Francis, distinguished English musicologist

560

and pianist, was Professor of Music at Edinburgh University and the author of a monumental six-volume opus analyzing the orchestral repertory, *Essays in Musical Analysis*.

Toye, Francis, English music critic, was the author of important biographies of Verdi and Rossini.

Turner, Walter James, English poet and writer on music, was for many years the music critic of *The New Statesmen* in London. His books on music include *Mozart: The Man and His Work, Beethoven: The Search for Reality, Wagner,* and *Berlioz: The Man and His Work.*

Walter, Bruno, one of the world's foremost conductors, has written a significant biography of Mahler.

Werfel, Alma Mahler, widow first of Gustav Mahler and then of Franz Werfel, is the author of *Gustav Mahler: Memories and Letters.*

Werfel, Franz, one of the outstanding literary figures of the 20th century, wrote *Verdi: A Novel of the Opera,* and with Paul Stefan edited *Verdi: The Man in His Letters.*

LIST OF COPYRIGHTS
AND SOURCES

For permission to reprint copyright material, the editor wishes to express his gratitude to the following:

Alfred A. Knopf, Inc.: critical essay on Mahler reprinted from *Mahler* by Bruno Walter, copyright 1957 by Alfred A. Knopf, Inc.; critical essay on Mussorgsky, reprinted from *Masters of Russian Music,* by M. D. Calvocoressi and Gerald Abraham, copyright 1936 by Alfred A. Knopf, Inc.; personal portrait of Puccini, from *Giacomo Puccini: The Man, His Life and His Work,* by Richard Specht, by permission of Alfred A. Knopf, Inc., published in 1933 by Alfred A. Knopf; the critical and personal essays on Rossini, reprinted from *Rossini: A Study in Tragi-Comedy,* published in 1934 by Alfred A. Knopf; and the critical essay on Weber, reprinted from *A Short History of Music,* by Alfred Einstein, copyright 1937 by Alfred A. Knopf, Inc.

Bradley, Mrs. W. A., and the proprietors of the copyright, for the critical essay on Monteverdi, from *A New History of Music,* by Henri Prunières, published by the Macmillan Company, 1943.

Charles Scribner's Sons, for personal portrait of Handel reprinted with the permission of Charles Scribner's Sons, from *George Frideric Handel: His Personality and His Times,* pages 149–50, and 244–45, by Newman Flower, copyright 1948, Charles Scribner's Sons.

Citadel Press, for personal portrait of Meyerbeer by Heinrich Heine, reprinted by permission of the publishers, from *The Poetry and Prose of Heinrich Heine,* selected and edited by Frederic Ewen, 1948.

Columbia University Press for critical essay on Puccini, from *A Short History of Opera,* by Donald Jay Grout, 1947.

Crown Publishers, for critical essay on Smetana, reprinted, from

essay on Mozart by W. J. Turner, and on Schubert by Sir Donald Francis Tovey, from *The Heritage of Music,* edited by Hubert J. Foss, Vol. 1 (1927); the critical essay on Liszt by Cecil Gray and on Verdi by F. Bonavia, from *The Heritage of Music,* edited by Hubert J. Foss, Vol. 2 (1946).

Oxford University Press, Inc. (New York), for personal portrait of Brahms, from *Brahms: His Life and Work,* by Karl Geiringer, copyright 1947, by Oxford University Press, Inc., reprinted by permission.

Penguin Books, Ltd., for critical essay of Wagner, from *The Opera,* by Edward J. Dent, 1940.

Presses Universitaires de France, for critical essay on Rameau, from *L'Histoire de la Musique,* by Bernard Champigneulle (1951), translated into English by George Reese.

Simon and Schuster for personal portrait of Wagner, copyright 1937 by Deems Taylor and reprinted from *Of Men and Music,* by permission of Simon and Schuster, Inc., New York.

Strunk, Oliver W., for permission to reprint critical essay on Haydn which he wrote originally for *From Bach to Stravinsky,* edited by David Ewen, and published by W. W. Norton, 1931.

Viking Press, Inc., for personal portrait of Gustav Mahler, reprinted from *Gustav Mahler: Memories and Letters,* by Alma Mahler Werfel, copyright 1946 by Alma Mahler Werfel, reprinted by permission of the Viking Press, Inc.

W. W. Norton, for critical essay on Vivaldi by Donald Jay Grout, reprinted from *A History of Western Music,* copyright 1960 by W. W. Norton & Co.; and personal portrait of Vivaldi by Marc Pincherle reprinted from *Vivaldi,* copyright 1957 by W. W. Norton & Co.

Essays, not listed above, were derived from the following sources: Personal portrait of Palestrina from *Giovanni Pierluigi da Palestrina; His Life and Times,* by Zoë Kendrick Pyne (1922). Personal portrait of Monteverdi from *Pioneers of Music,* by David Ewen (1940). Personal portrait of Bach by Forkel from *The Life of Johann Sebastian Bach,* by Johann Nikolaus Forkel (1820), and that by Schweitzer from *Bach,* by Albert Schweitzer (1911). Personal portrait of Handel by Charles Burney from *An Account of the Musical Performances in Westminster Abbey and the Pantheon Commemoration of Handel* (1785). Critical essay on Handel is a condensation by David Ewen of material from Romain Rolland's biography (1916) authorized and approved by Rolland and first used in *From Bach to Stravinsky*, edited by David Ewen (1933). Personal portrait of Gluck from *Some Musicians of Former Days*, by Romain Rolland (1915), and the critical essay on Gluck from *The Opera, Past and Present*, by William Foster Apthorp (1905). Critical essay on Haydn by W. Oliver Strunk was written on commission from David Ewen and used in *From Bach to Stravinsky*, edited by David Ewen (1933). Personal portrait of Mozart by Kelly from *Reminiscences of Michael Kelly* (1826), and that by Schlichtegroll from *The Life of Mozart* (1839). Personal portrait of Beethoven by Schindler from Beethoven biography by Anton Schindler (1840), and that by Franz Grillparzer from *Recollections of Beethoven*, by Grillparzer, reprinted in *Music and Letters* (London), January 1923. Personal portrait of Weber by André Coeuroy appeared in *The Sackbut* of London. Personal portrait of Schubert from *Recollections of Schubert*, by Anselm Hüttenbrenner (1906). Critical essays of Berlioz and Schumann from *Studies in Modern Music*, by W. H. Hadow (1893). Critical essays on Meyerbeer and Gounod from *The Opera*, by R. A. Streatfeild (1909). Personal portrait of Mendelssohn from *Recollections of Mendelssohn* by Eduard Devrient (1869). Critical essay on Mendelssohn by Sir George Grove from *Dictionary of Music and Musicians* (1907). Personal portrait of Chopin from *Histoire de ma vie*, by George Sand quoted in Frederick Niecks' biography *Chopin As Man and Musician* (1888). Critical essay on Chopin by Olin Downes from a brochure prepared by Mr. Downes for Alexander Brailowsky's all-Chopin cycle of concerts in New York. Personal portrait of Franck from biography by Vincent d'Indy (1931). Critical essay on Franck by Leland Hall was commissioned by David Ewen and used in *From Bach to Stravinsky*, edited by David Ewen (1933). Personal portrait of Gounod by Howard Paul appeared in *The Musician*, New York. Personal portrait of Massenet by Herbert F. Peyser appeared in *Musical America*, New York, August 17, 1912. Personal portrait of Liszt by Amy Fay from *Music Study in Germany* (1905), and by

Countess Marie d'Agoult from *Memoires* (1927). Personal portrait of Smetana by Josef Schwarz appeared in *Letters and Reminiscences of Smetana,* edited by Bartos and Ocadlik (1933). Personal portrait of Dvořák from *Anton Dvořák,* by Paul Stefan (1941). Critical essay on Dvořák by Vladimir Helfert was commissioned by David Ewen but never before published. Critical essay of Rimsky-Korsakov by M. Montagu Nathan from *History of Russian Music* (1918). Personal portraits of Rimsky-Korsakov and Mussorgsky by Nicolas Slonimsky were written expressly for this book. Personal portrait of Grieg by Gerald Schjeldrup from his biography of Grieg (1903), and that by Percy Grainger appeared in *Etude,* Philadelphia, May–June 1943. Personal portrait of Verdi by Franz Werfel from *Verdi: The Man in His Letters,* edited by Franz Werfel and Paul Stefan (1942). Personal portrait of Bruckner by Gabriel Engel from *The Life of Anton Bruckner* (1931). Personal portrait of Hugo Wolf from *Musical Vienna,* by David and Frederic Ewen (1939). Critical essay on Wolf by Ernest Newman was published in *Contemporary Review* of London, May 1904.

INDEX

ABRAHAM, GERALD, 395, 554, 562
Académie de France, 413, 494
Accadémia degli Invaghiti, 13
Albéniz, Isaac, 317
Albert, Heinrich, 48
Albinoni, Tomaso, 29
Albrechtsberger, Johann, 122
Alfano, Franco, 447
Allegri, Gregorio, 110
Amati, Andrea, 43
Andersen, Hans Christian, 420
Apthorp, William F., 77, 554, 565
Arabian Nights, The, 407
Arensky, Anton, 401
Argentina Theatre Rome, (Rome), 195
Aria, 13-14
Arnaud, Abbé, 80
Arnould, Sophie, 82
Artusi, Giovanni, 10, 11, 80
Atonalists, 317
Auber, Daniel, 201, 327, 328, 332
BACH, CARL PHILIPP, 35, 84, 99, 101
Bach, Johann Cristoph, 34, 38
Bach, Johann Michael, 48
Bach, Johann Sebastian, 5, 20, 25, 26, 28, 34-53, 59, 98, 223, 228, 235, 241, 245, 274, 277, 399, 460, 501; *Art of the Fugue*, 466; biography, 34-35, 544-45; Brahms, 349, 352-53; *Brandenburg Concertos*, 34; cantatas, 48; characteristics, 35-38, 39; chorales, 47; church music, 5; composer, 38-52; death, 97; "English Suites," 45; fingering, 45; "Forty-Eight," 44-45; fugues, 50-51; Handel, 38-39, 40, 45, 55, 58; *Magnificat*, 41, 48; Mahler, 460, 466; Mass in B minor, 34, 48; Masses, 48-49; Overture in B minor, 45; Passions, 47, 49-50; principal works, 512-13; quoted, 52-53; *St. John Passion*, 49; *St. Matthew Passion*, 34, 219; Saint-Saëns, 485, 486, 487, 489; spiritual faith, 116-18; status, 51; universality, 348; Vivaldi, 33; *Well-Tempered Clavier*, 51, 263, 491
Bach, John Christian, 35, 44
Bach, Wilhelm Friedemann, 35
Bahr, Hermann, 475
Balakirev, Mily, 317, 410; "Five, The," 391, 400, 401; Mussorgsky, 391, 393
Barbaja, Domenico, 147, 195
Barbier, Jules, 284, 286
Bardac, Emma, 494
Bardi, Giovanni, 43
Barezzi, Antonio, 433
Barezzi, Margherita, 422
Baroque, 4, 9, 25, 29, 30
Bartered Bride, The, 356-57, 359

Bayreuth (*see under* Wagner)
Beethoven, Ludwig van, 34, 38, 67, 75, 92, 96, 97, 102, 111, 121-45, 150, 156, 157, 161, 163, 167, 205, 208, 209, 213, 223, 230, 241, 242, 244, 399, 472, 474, 489; A-flat Major Piano Sonata, 136; *Appassionata*, 123, 129, 244; biography, 115-16, 122-23, 126, 546; Brahms, 349, 351, 352-53, 355; characteristics, 124-27, 140-41; C minor Symphony, 67; codas, 170; composer, 127-41, 243, 247, 330, 455, 464; *Consecration of the House*, 129; *Coriolon*, 133, 224; deafness, 123, 142; *Egmont*, 133, 138; *Emperor Concerto*, 137; *Eroica*, 123, 133, 135, 136, 168; *Fidelio*, 123, 133, 151, 330; Fifth Symphony, 138, 157; form, 174; Handel, 67-68, 70, 73; *Heiligenstadt Testament*, 123, 142-44; hero, 131-32; intellectual curiosity, 45; *Leonore Overture*, 133; Mass in C major, 157; melancholy, 115; *Missa Solemnis*, 123, 134, 184; *Moonlight Sonata*, 123; Mozart, 114, 116-17, 118, 122, 183-84; Nature, 175; Ninth Symphony, 11, 117, 123, 134, 279; *Ode to Joy*, 134; *Pastoral Symphony*, 32, 123, 130-31; *Pathétique*, 226, 243; Piano Concerto in B-flat major, 122; Piano Concerto in G, 224; power, 169; principal works, 517-18; program music, 129-31, 135; quoted, 141-45; *Rasoumovsky quartets*, 123; *Ritter-ballet*, 71; *Seventh Symphony*, 114, 189; sonatas, 50, 129, 139-40, 164-66; songs, 159; spiritual faith, 116, 117, 118, 134-35; status, 51; String Quartet in E minor, 171; symphony, 249, 476; universality, 348; variations, 139; *Violoncello Sonata in A*, 243; *Waldstein Sonata*, 123
Beggar's Opera, The, 54
Bekker, Paul, 127, 546, 554, 563
Belasco, David, 440, 447
Bellaigue, Camille, 66
Bellini, Vincenzo, 200, 330, 332, 427, 436
Berg, Alban, 297
Berger, Ludwig, 219
Berlin: Academy of Arts, 220, 342; *Singakademie*, 219
Berlioz, Hector, 67, 148, 179-94, 235, 238, 242, 245, 261, 303, 329, 399, 410, 464, 474, 486, 487, 489; *Béatrice et Bénédict*, 186, 189, 190; *Benvenuto Cellini*, 179, 186, 189; biography, 181-82, 547-48; *Captive, La*, 186, 189; *Carnaval romain, Le*, 179, 186; characteristics, 180-83; composer, 183-92, 264; *Damnation of Faust*, 179-80, 184, 185, 186, 189, 190, 194; *Élégie*, 183, 185; *Enfance du Christ*, 184, 189, 190,

567

194; *Feuillets d'album*, 189; *Harold in Italy*, 179, 183, 184, 185, 188, 189, 190; *Invitation to the Dance*, 191; *Judex crederis*, 193; *King Lear*, 189; *Lachrymosa*, 183, 185, 189, 191; Mass, 179; *Musée Wiertz*, 184; principal works, 521; quoted, 192-94; *Rakóczy March*, 191; religion, 185; *Requiem*, 183, 184, 186, 189, 191, 193, 194; *Rêverie et caprice*, 188; *Romeo and Juliet* symphony, 179, 181, 185, 189; *Symphonie fantastique*, 179, 181, 182, 183, 184, 185, 187-88, 189, 244, 245; *Symphonie funèbre et triomphale*, 186, 193; *Te Deum*, 185, 190, 191, 193; *Tempest Fantaisie*, 191; *Troyens, Les*, 181, 185, 186, 189; Wagner, 181
Beyer, Frantz, 415
Birmingham Festival, 281
Bizet, Georges, 410, 489, 555; *Carmen*, 297, 298; nationalism, 418
Björnson, Björnstjerne, 419, 420
Bohème, La, 429, 443, 444-45, 446, 447
Böhm, Georg, 39, 50
Boïto, Arrigo, 423; *Mefistofele*, 425
Bologna: Accademia Filarmonica, 110; Conservatory, 195, 196
Bonavia, Ferruccio, 426, 554, 564
Bonheur, Raymond, 496
Bononcini, Giovanni, 54, 63, 81
Borodin, Alexander, 317, 410; "Five, The," 391, 400, 401; Mussorgsky, 392
Brahms, Johannes, 163, 233, 236, 244, 279, 316, 341-55, 363, 453, 473, 489; biography, 341-42, 550; characteristics, 199, 342-46; 347; composer, 245, 247, 274, 275, 347-54; First Symphony, 276; *German Requiem*, 342, 344; *Hungarian Dances*, 367; melancholy, 115; Piano Concerto in D minor, 349; Piano Quintet, 167, 353; principal works, 529-31; quoted, 354-55; *Song of Fate*, 184; songs, 173; study, 349-51; universality, 347-48; *Variations on a Theme of Haydn*, 342, 353, 466
Brandt, Caroline, 146, 147, 148-49
Breslau, Theater, 146
Breuning, Frau von, 122
Brosses, Charles de, 28
Bruckner, Anton, 450-58, 464; *Ave Maria*, 450; biography, 450-51, 552; characteristics, 451-53; composer, 453-57; principal works, 538; quoted, 457-58; symphonies: First, 454; Second, 453, 457; Third, 454, 457; Fourth (*Romantic*), 451, 545-55; Fifth, 454, 455, 456; Sixth, 456; Seventh, 451, 454; Eighth, 454; Ninth, 454, 456; Wagner, 450, 454, 455, 457-58
Bruneau, Alfred, 290; *Le Rêve*, 297
Budapest Royal Opera, 459
Bülow, Hans von, 167, 303, 304, 325; wife, 321, 325
Burney, Charles, 46, 55, 56n, 75, 554, 565
Busoni, Ferruccio, 317, 557
Busseto Philharmonic, 422
Buxtehude, Dietrich, 39, 50

Byrd, William, 489, 557
Byron, Lord, 117, 236, 250, 347
CACCINI, GIULIO, *Euridice*, 14
Caldara, Antonio, 29, 39
Calzabigi, Raniere de, 74, 78-79
Carissimi, Giacomo, 47
Carré, Albert, 284, 286
Cavalieri, Emilio del, 43
Cavalli, Pier Francesco, 72, 83
Chabanon, Michel-Paul, 19, 554, 563
Chamisso, Adelbert von, 236
Champigneulle, Bernard, 20, 555, 564
Charpentier, Gustave, 290; *Louise*, 299
Charpentier, Marc-Antoine, 489
Châtelet Theater (Paris), 414
Chausson, Ernest, 270
Cherubini, Luigi, 125, 161; *Deux journées*, 152; *Lodoiska*, 332
Chopin, Frédéric, 233, 236, 255-69, 303; ballades, 264, 265; *Barcarolle*, 265; biography, 255-56, 548-49; characteristics, 256-61; composer, 257, 259-68, 361, 362; *Fantasy*, 256, 263; mazurka, 261, 262-63, 265, 359; melancholy, 115; nationalism, 418; nocturnes, 384; Polonaise, 261, 262, 263; Preludes, 256, 263-64; principal works, 525; quoted, 267-69; *Revolutionary Étude*, 255; Scherzo, 260; Sonata in B-flat minor (*Funeral March*), 256, 264, 265-66, 386; *Valse brillante*, 265
Cimarosa, Domenico, 209
Clementi, Muzio, 211
Coeuroy, André (Jean Belime), 147, 555, 556
Colbran, Isabella, 195, 196, 204, 208
Colles, H. C., 453, 455
Colonne, Édouard, 414
Cooper, Martin, 545, 549, 553, 555
Coppée, François, 282-83
Coquard, Arthur, 273
Corelli, Arcangelo, 26, 29, 32, 44, 60, 69-70, 558
Cornelius, Peter, 329
Cossel, Otto, 341
Couperin-le-Grand, François, 39, 44, 45
Covent Garden, 331
Creation, The, 88, 92, 95, 96, 97, 172
Cui, César, 405, 406, 410; "Five, The," 391, 400, 401; Mussorgsky, 392, 394
Czerny, Karl, 303
D'AGOULT, COUNTESS MARIE D', 303, 305, 306n, 554, 566
Damnation of Faust, The (see Berlioz)
Dannreuther, Edward, 312-14
D'Annunzio, Gabriele, 479
Danse macabre, 483
Dante Symphony, 304, 313, 314
Danzi, Franz, 147
Dargomyzhsky, Alexander, 391, 396-97; *Stone Guest*, 404
Davidsbundlertänze, 238, 239, 245
Debussy, Claude, 23, 418, 447, 493-507; *Afternoon of a Faun*, 493, 500, 502-3; biography, 493-94, 553; characteristics, 199, 494-97; *Clair de lune*, 493; composer,

568

497-505; *L'Enfant prodigue*, 493; *Hommage à Rameau*, 500; *Ibéria*, 503; *Images*, 494, 501, 503; Impressionism, 430; *La plus que lent*, 502, 503; *Martyre de Saint-Sébastien*, 503; *Mer, La*, 494, 503; *Nocturnes*, 494, 500, 503; *Nuages*, 500; *Pelléas and Mélisande*, 493, 498, 501, 502, 503-4, 505-6; principal works, 541-42; *Proses lyriques*, 503; quoted, 505-7; *Reflets dans l'eau*, 500; *Sirènes*, 502, 503; *Sonatas*, 503; String Quartet, 493, 502, 503; *Suite bergamasque*, 493

Delibes, Léo, 410

Delius, Frederick, 418

Dent, Edward J., 201-2, 327, 545, 555, 564

Derepas, Gustave, 276

Devrient, Eduard, 220, 555, 565

Diaghilev, Sergei, 402

Dies, Albert Christoph, 88, 555

Dietricshtein, Moritz, 126

Don Giovanni, (*see* Mozart)

Donizetti, Gaetano, 201, 330, 332, 427-29

Dorn, Heinrich, 232, 238

Downes, Olin, 259, 555, 563, 565

Dresden Opera, 320, 321

Durante, Francesco, 78

Durazzo, Giacomo, 74

Dvořák, Antonin, 318, 347, 363-72; *Airs from Moravia*, 363; "American" quartet, 368; biography, 363-64, 551; Cello Concerto, 364, 368; characteristics, 364-67; composer, 366-70; *Dimitrij*, 368, 369; *Dumky Trio*, 368; *Fourth Symphony*, 368; *Hymnus*, 363; nationalism, 418; *New World Symphony*, 364, 368; principal works, 532-33; quoted, 370-72; *Rusalka*, 367, 369; *St. Ludmilla*, 369; *Slavonic Dances*, 363, 367; *Spectre's Bride*, 359, 369; *Stabat Mater*, 363, 369; Violin concerto, 368

Egmont Overture, 133, 138

Einstein, Alfred, 150, 456, 555, 562

Elgar, Edward, 317; *Salut d'amour*, 308

Elijah, 220, 223, 227, 228, 229

Elsner, Joseph, 255

Emperor Concerto, 137

Encyclopedists, 19, 77

Enfance du Christ, 184, 189, 190, 194

Engel, Gabriel, 109, 451, 556, 566

England: 18th century, 66-67, 72; Handel, 59, 60, 63, 66-67, 70; Haydn, 95-96; "Lessons," 44; music, 45-46

Erben, Karel, 367, 369

Erlkönig, 155, 159-60, 161, 171

Ernst, Heinrich Wilhelm, 456

Eroica Symphony, 123, 133, 135, 136, 168

Eugen Onegin, 374, 381, 382

Euryanthe, 147, 151-52, 153, 250

Euterpe Society, 412

Ewen, David, 9, 474, 543, 564-66

Ewen, Frederic, 474, 556, 562, 566

Falstaff, 201, 423, 426-27, 433-34

Fantasiestücke, 232, 238

Farewell Symphony, 101

Faust (Gounod), 281, 284-85, 286, 287

Faust Overture, 320

Faust Symphony, 304, 311-12, 314, 315, 317

Fay, Amy, 305, 306n, 556

Festspielhaus (*see* Bayreuth)

Fétis, François, 204, 263

Fidelio, 123, 133, 151, 330

Field, John, 226; Nocturnes, 263

Finck, Henry T., 264, 549, 552

Fingal's Cave Overture (*see under* Mendelssohn)

Finlandia, 308

Fireworks Music, 68, 71

"Five, The Russian," 378, 381, 391, 400, 401

Flower, Newman, 55, 56n, 556, 562

Flying Dutchman, The, 320, 327

Forellen Quintet, 162, 163, 167, 171

Forkel, Johann, 35, 37n, 45, 50, 556, 560, 564

Forza del destino, 422

Foster, Stephen, 371

Fouqué, Friedrich, 151

France: Bach, 44-45; Handel, 63, 66; musical renaissance, 44; 19th century, 485-86; opera, 18-19, 22, 65, 72, 84, 201, 211, 283-84; opéra-comique, 217; "ordres," 44; "suites," 44

France, Anatole, 298

Franck, César, 270-80, 316, 347, 456, 486; *Beatitudes, The*, 278; biography, 270-71, 549; characteristics, 271-75; composer, 274-79; *Ghisèle*, 278; *Hulda*, 278; *Leitmotive*, 454; *Prelude, Aria, and Finale*, 276; *Prelude, Chorale and Fugue*, 276, 277; principal works, 526; quoted, 279-80; *Redemption, The*, 270-71, 278, 279; religion, 274, 275, 277-78; *Ruth*, 270, 278, 279; String Quartet, 276; Symphony in D minor, 271, 275, 276, 279; *Variations symphoniques*, 271, 277; Violin Sonata, 276, 277

Frankh, Johann, 87

Franz, Robert, 476

Frescobaldi, Girolama, 50

Freischütz, Der, 147, 148, 151, 152, 153

Fürnberg, Karl Joseph von, 87, 99

Fux, Johann Josef, 50-51; *Gradus ad Parnassum*, 50

Gabrieli, Andrea, 50

Gade, Niels, 412, 420

Garborg, Arne, 420

Gasparini, Francesco, 29

Gay, John, *The Beggar's Opera*, 54

Geibel, Emanuel von, 236

Geiringer, Karl, 342, 545, 550, 556, 564

Geminiani, Francesco, 69

Genzinger, Marianne von, 91

German Requiem, 342, 344

Germany: chorale, 47; geniuses, 58-59; Mannheim school, 32; motet, 48-49; music, 46, 49, 485-86 (*see* Wagner and Weber); painting in music, 66; "Partitas," 44; Reformation, 46-47; Renaissance, 46; Romanticism, 328-29; theater, 328

569

Gewandhaus Orchestra (Leipzig), 220, 341
Ghezzi, P. L., 26
Gilman, Lawrence, 379, 550
Girl of the Golden West, 440, 447
Glazunov, Alexander, 317, 401, 410
Glinka, Michael, 404, 410; *Life for the Czar*, 391; nationalism, 418; *Ruslan and Ludmilla*, 391
Gluck, Christoph Willibald, 38, 45, 72, 73, 74-86, 150, 152, 154, 184, 190, 200, 202, 213, 218, 241, 283, 399, 474, 486, 487, 490, 501; *Alceste*, 74, 79, 81, 83, 85; *Armide*, 81; *Artaserse*, 74, 77; biography, 74-75, 545; characteristics, 75-77; *Clemenza di Tito*, 78; composer, 77-85; controversy, 80-81; death, 105; *Écho et Narcisse*, 82, 83; Handel, 63, 64, 75-76; *Iphigénie en Aulide*, 74-75, 76, 79, 80, 81; *Iphigénie en Tauride*, 64, 75, 82, 84; Marie Antoinette, 80; opera, 22, 77-84; *Orfeo ed Euridice*, 74, 75, 78-79, 81, 84; *Paride e Elena*, 74, 79; Piccini, 81-82; principal works, 514; quoted, 84, 85-86; *Semiramide riconosciuta*, 74
Goethe, Wolfgang von, 59, 95, 135, 159, 175, 227, 236, 328, 460, 473; on Beethoven, 67; *Faust*, 160, 284, 285, 468; songs, 172; Weber, 149
Gogol, Nikolai, 406
Gonzaga, Vincenzo, 12
Gounod, Charles, 281-89, 295, 485; biography, 281, 549; characteristics, 282-83; *Cinq-Mars*, 287; composer, 283-87; *Faust*, 281, 284-85, 286, 287; Mass, 281; *Médecin malgré lui, Le*, 281, 284; *Mireille*, 281, 285-86, 287; Mozart, 281; *Mors et Vita*, 281; *Nonne sanglante, La*, 284; *Philémon et Baucis*, 285; *Polyeucte*, 287; principal works, 526-27; quoted, 287-89; *Rédemption, Le*, 281; *Reine de Saba, La*, 285; religion, 281, 283; *Requiem*, 281; *Romeo and Juliet*, 281, 286, 287; Saint-Saëns, 487, 489; *Sapho*, 281, 284; *Tribut de Zamora, Le*, 287
Gozzi, Carlo, 327, 447
Grainger, Percy, 413, 414n, 556, 566
Gray, Cecil, 307, 556, 564
Gretchaninoff, Alexander, 401
Gretchen am Spinnrade, 155, 159, 160, 161
Grétry, André, 329
Grieg, Edvard, 317, 347, 412-21; *Ballade*, 417, 419; biography, 412-13; characteristics, 413-16; composer, 416-20; *Holberg Suite*, 413; *Humoresque*, 412; Ibsen songs, 417, 420; *In Autumn*, 414; *Lyric Pieces*, 412, 413, 417, 420; *Norwegian Dances*, 413; *Peer Gynt*, 412, 417, 419; Piano Concerto, 412, 417, 419; Piano Sonata, 419; principal works, 536-37; quoted, 420-21; String Quartet, 417, 419; Vinje songs, 417, 420; Violin Sonata, 413, 419
Griesinger, Georg, 95, 97
Grigny, Nicholas de, 39
Grilparzer, Franz, 124, 125n, 128, 556, 565

Grimm, Friedrich, 22, 80
Grout, Donald Jay, 28, 444, 556, 562, 564
Grove, George, 156, 169, 223, 556, 565
Gyrowetz, Adalbert, 183
HADOW, W. H., 183, 235, 348, 557, 565
Hagerup, Nina, 412
Hale, Philip, 484, 557, 563
Halévy, Jacques, 281, 332
Hall, Leland, 274, 557, 565
Halvorsen, Johan, 416
Hamburg Opera, 341, 459
Hamlet, 312, 313, 314, 315
Hammerschmidt, Andreas, 48
Handel, George Frideric, 28, 29, 44, 46, 54-73, 75-76, 98, 102, 135, 157, 220, 227, 228, 241, 242, 486, 487, 489; *Alcina*, 63; *Acis and Galatea*, 67; *Admeto*, 64; *Agrippina*, 63; *Alexander Balus*, 60, 65, 67, 68; *Alexander's Feast*, 66; *Almira*, 54; *Arianna*, 72; *Ariodante*, 63; *Athalia*, 66; Bach, 38-39, 40, 45, 55, 58; Beethoven, 67-68, 73; *Belshazzar*, 65, 66; *Berenice*, 72; biography, 54-55, 57, 545; blindness, 55, 60; *Chandos Anthems*, 65; characteristics, 55-57; *Cleopatra*, 67, 68; Commemoration, 1791, 96; composer, 58-73; Concerti Grossi, 68, 69-70; *Deborah*, 66; *Deidamia*, 63, 77; *Esther*, 65, 66; *Fireworks Music*, 68, 71; *Giulio Cesare*, 63, 67, 68; Haydn, 95-96; *Hercules*, 60, 65; *Hornpipe*, 70; *Israel in Egypt*, 61, 64, 65, 66, 67, 72; *Jephtha*, 55, 66, 96; *Joshua*, 65, 96; *Judas Maccabaeus*, 55, 72, 227; *L'Allegro ed Il Pensoroso*, 60, 64, 66, 67; material, 131; *Messiah*, 55, 60, 62, 67, 73, 157, 184, 227, 245; *Nero*, 54; *Ode for St. Cecilia's Day*, 64; open-air music, 70-72; operas, 63-64, 65, 72; oratorios, 55, 64-68, 72; *Orlando*, 63, 64; *Ottone*, 54, 72; *Pifferari*, 60; principal works, 513-14; quoted, 73; *Radamisto*, 54, 56; *Resurrection*, 68; *Rinaldo*, 54; *Samson*, 64, 65; *Saul*, 60, 64, 65; *Scipione*, 72; *Semele*, 55, 64, 68; *Serse*, 63; *Solomon*, 55, 65, 67; *Susanna*, 65; *Tamerlano*, 63, 64; *Te Deum*, 62; *Theodora*, 55, 65, 66; *Triumph of Time*, 68; *Water Music*, 68, 71
Hanslick, Eduard, 93, 326
Harold in Italy (see Berlioz)
Hasse, Johann Adolph, 60, 61, 183
Haydn, Joseph, 38, 84, 85, 87-103, 122, 157, 159, 161, 167, 184, 209, 241, 349, 465, 489; "Apponyi" quartets, 92, 96; biography, 87-88, 95, 545-56; characteristics, 88-90; composer, 91-102, 246, 247; *Creation*, 88, 92, 95, 96, 97, 172; *Farewell Symphony*, 101; Handel, 95-96; *Harmoniemesse*, 92; *Il Ritorno di Tobia*, 96; *Krumme Teufel, Der*, 99; *London Symphonies*, 87, 92, 94, 96; *Midi, Le*, 99; Mozart, 87, 91, 93, 100, 101, 105; *Oxford Symphony*, 101; "Paris" symphonies, 101; principal works, 514-15; quoted, 94-95, 96, 97, 101-3; *Representation of Chaos*, 96; "Russian" quar-

tets, 101; *Schöpfungsmesse,* 92; *Seasons, The,* 88, 92, 95, 96, 97; sonata, 94, 164-65; *Surprise Symphony,* 93; Te Deum, 92; *Trauersymphonie,* 101
Haydn, Michael, 146
Haymarket Theater (London), 54
Heine, Heinrich, 147, 175, 188, 212, 236, 237, 245, 247, 473, 557; Liszt, 315
Helfert, Vladimir, 366, 557, 566
Hellmesberger, Joseph, 341
Herder, Johann von, 59
Heuschkel, J. P., 146
Hoffmann, E.T.A., 239-40, 264, 329; *Undine,* 151
Holzbauer, Ignaz, 150
Holzer, Michael, 155
Homer, 172, 236, 288
Huberman, Bronislaw, 345
Hugo, Victor, 313, 505; *Cromwell,* 83
Huguenots, Les (see Meyerbeer)
Hummel, Johann, 211
Huneker, James Gibbons, 317, 549
Hungarian Rhapsodies (see Liszt)
Hüttenbrenner, Anselm, 156, 557, 565
IBSEN, HENRIK, 419, 420, 477; Grieg songs, 417, 420
Impressionism, 370, 418, 430, 493, 499-500, 503
Indy, Vincent d', 270-71, 296, 557; *Istar,* 446
Ingegneri, Marc' Antonio, 9, 11
Institut de France, 180, 273, 483, 485
Iphigénie en Aulide, 74-75, 76, 79, 80, 81
Israel in Egypt, 61, 64, 65, 66, 67, 72
Italy: Handel, 59, 60, 69; opera, 22, 29, 43, 49, 65, 74, 85; "sonatas," 44; violin playing, 44
JAHN, OTTO, 92, 546
Jansen, Gustav, 233, 557, 563
Joachim, Joseph, 341
Jonson, Ben, 185
Julian Choir, 1, 3
KANT, IMMANUEL, 272, 460
Karatygin, Vyatcheslav, 396
Keats, John, 479
Keiser, Reinhard, 49, 63
Kelly, Michael, 106, 106n, 557, 565
Kerr, Alfred, 443
Kjerulf, Halfdan, 418
Kleist, Heinrich von, 474, 475
Klemperer, Otto, 460
Kolař, Katharina, 356
"Konvict" School, 155, 158
Kozeluch, Leopold, 93
Kretzschmar, August, 65, 70
LA CAVE, François Morellon de, 26, 27
La Harpe, 76, 80
"Lament of Arianna," 15
Lamm, Paul, 396
Lange, Kristian, 416, 557, 563
La Scala, 110, 422, 423, 425, 439
Lavigna, Vincenzo, 422
Leblanc, Georgette, 495
Legouvé, Ernest, 180, 183, 309

Legrenzi, Giovanni, 25, 39
Leibnitz, Gottfried von, 59
Leichtentritt, Hugo, 4, 557, 563
Leipzig: Conservatory, 220, 412, 418; Opera, 459
Leonard, Richard A., 377, 558, 563
Lerolle, Henri, 495
Le Roux, Gaspard, 39
Lesueur, Jean François, 281, 329
Levi, Hermann, 451
Leyden Academy, 412
Liadov, Anatol, 394, 401
Liège Conservatory, 270
Lippi, Fra Filippo, 6
Lisle, Leconte de, 290
Liszt, Franz, 166, 180, 255, 274, 303-19, 329, 341, 356, 360, 399, 410, 454, 489, 501, 558; *Années de pèlerinage,* 304, 311, 314, 317; biography, 303-4, 549-50; *Campanella, La,* 307, 308; characteristics, 305-6, 309; Chopin, 256, 257n, 261, 263, 558; *Christus,* 312; composer, 264, 307-18; Concerto in E-flat, 276; *Consolations,* 304; *Dante Symphony,* 304, 313, 314; *Études d'exécution transcendante,* 304, 314; *Faust Symphony,* 304, 311-12, 314, 315, 317; *Grand Festmesse,* 312; *Hamlet,* 312, 313, 314, 315; *Harmonies poetiques et religieuses,* 314; *Héroïde funèbre,* 312, 313; *Hungarian Rhapsodies,* 304, 307, 308, 317, 368; *Ideale, Die,* 313-14; *Légendes,* 317; *Liebestraum,* 304, 307; *Malédiction,* 317; modern music, 316; nationalism, 317; *Paganini Études,* 304; piano concertos, 307, 308, 380; Piano Sonata, 308, 312, 314; *Préludes, Les,* 304, 307, 308, 313; principal works, 527-28; quoted, 318-19; religion, 304, 309, 311; *Second Mephisto Waltz,* 315; songs, 311, 315; *Totentanz,* 315; Wagner, 304, 316, 321, 327
Locatelli, Pietro, 69
Locle, M. du, 425
Loewe, Ferdinand, 451
Loewe, Karl, 159-60
Lohengrin (see Wagner)
London Symphonies, 87, 92, 94, 96
Lotti, Antonio, 29, 39
Louÿs, Pierre, 494
Lucca, Instituto Musicale, 439
Lully, Jean-Baptiste, 18, 21, 44, 45, 72, 81, 84, 283, 489
Luther, Martin, 46, 47, 49
MACDOWELL, EDWARD, 418
Madame Butterfly (see Puccini)
Maeterlinck, Maurice, 495, 504
Magdeburg Opera, 320
Magic Flute, The (see Mozart)
Mahler, Gustav, 457, 459-72; Bach, 460, 466; biography, 459-60, 553; characteristics, 460-63; composer, 463-72; *Kindertotenlieder,* 459; *Klagende Lied, Das,* 463; *Lied von der Erde, Das,* 459, 469-70; principal works, 538-39; quoted, 471-72; songs, 465,

571

469-70; *Songs of a Wayfarer*, 459, 463; symphonies, 459, 464: First, 463-64, 465, 466, 467; Second, 464, 465, 466, 467, 469; Third, 465, 466, 467; Fourth, 465, 466, 467; Fifth, 465, 466, 467-68, 470; Sixth, 465, 466, 468, 469, 470; Seventh, 465, 466, 468, 470; Eighth, 466, 468-69; Ninth. 465, 466, 470
Malherbe, Charles, 23
Mallarmé, Stéphane, 494-95
Mannlich, Christian von, 75, 76
Manzoni, Alessandro, 319, 423
Marcello, Benedetto, 437
Marchand, Louis, 18, 39, 45
Marenzio, Luca, 11
Marie Antoinette, and Gluck, 80
Marivaux, Pierre, 502
Marmontel, Antoine-François, 80
Marpurg, Friedrich, 98
Marriage of Figaro (*see* Mozart)
Marxsen, Eduard, 341
Mascagni, Pietro, 201; *Cavalleria Rusticana*, 297
Mason, Daniel Gregory, 347, 558, 563
Mason, Dr. William, 353
Massenet, Jules, 290-302, 444; *Ariane*, 299; biography, 290-91, 549; *Cendrillon*, 298; *César de Bazan*, 290; characteristics, 291-93; *Chérubin*, 299; *Cid, Le*, 295; composer, 291, 294-300; *Don Quichotte*, 290, 299; *Élégie*, 290; *Esclarmonde*, 295; *Grand' tante, La*, 290; *Grisélidis*, 298; *Hérodiade*, 290, 294, 297; *Jongleur de Notre Dame*, 290, 293, 298-99; *Manon*, 290, 294-95, 297, 298, 444; *Marie Magdeleine*, 296; *Navarraise, La*, 297; principal works, 527; quoted, 299-302; *Sapho*, 290, 297; *Thaïs*, 290, 295-96, 297; *Thérèse*, 299; *Werther*, 290, 295, 296
Mayr, Johann Simon, 209
Mayrhofer, Johann, 155, 156, 172; *Auflösung*, 175
Mazurka (*see* Chopin)
Meck, Nadezhda von, 374, 381, 493
Meistersinger, Die (*see* Wagner)
Mendelssohn, Felix, 62, 219-31, 241, 329, 410, 488, 490; biography, 219-20, 548; Caprices, 226; *Capriccio brillant*, 220; characteristics, 220-23, 229; composer, 223-30; *Elijah*, 220, 223, 227, 228, 229; *Fingal's Cave Overture*, 220, 223, 224, 227, 229; G minor Piano Concerto, 220; *Italian Symphony*, 224; *Lohgesang*, 223, 227, 229; *Melusina*, 224, 229; *Midsummer Night's Dream Overture*, 219, 223, 224, 229; principal works, 522-23; quoted, 230-31; *Ruy Blas*, 224; *St. Paul*, 223, 227, 228-29; *Scotch Symphony*, 224; songs, 227; *Songs Without Words*, 220, 226-27, 231; *Variations sérieuses*, 226; Violin Concerto, 227; *Walpurgisnacht*, 223
Mendelssohn, Moses, 219
Messiah (*see* Handel)
Metastasio, Pietro, 74, 78-79, 106, 339

Metropolitan Opera, 335, 440, 447, 459
Mey, Lev, 406
Meyerbeer, Giacomo, 84, 201, 205, 211-18, 283, 327, 410, 436; *Africaine, L'*, 212, 216; *Alimelek*, 211; biography, 211-12; characteristics, 212-14; composer, 214-17; *Crociata in Egitto, Il*, 211; *Dinorah*, 216, 217, *Étoile du nord, L'*, 216, 217; *Huguenots, Les*, 201, 212, 215, 216, 295, 431; principal works, 522; *Prophète, Le*, 212, 215-16; quoted, 217-18; *Robert le diable*, 201, 212, 214, 215; *Romilda e Costanza*, 211; Rossini, 197-98, 217-18
Michelangelo, 4, 288, 488
Mickiewicz, Adam, 265
Milan Conservatory, 439
Milton, John, 95, 430
Moke, Camille, 182
Molière, Jean Baptiste, 148, 284
Monet, Claude, 500
Monn, Georg Matthias, 99
Montagu-Nathan, M., 403, 558, 566
Montaigne, Michel, 488, 502
Monteverdi, Claudio, 9-17, 80, 83, 432; *Arianna*, 9, 15; biography, 9, 544; characteristics, 9-10; composer, 10, 11-16; *L'Incoronazione di Poppea*, 9, 15; *Lament of Arianna*, 17; madrigals, 11-12, 13; motets, 9; *Orfeo*, 9, 12-14; principal works, 511; quoted, 16-17; religious works, 15-16; *Ritornello*, 13, 14; *Ritorno di Ulisse*, 15
Morzin, Count, 87, 99
Moscheles, Ignaz, 263
Moscow Conservatory, 373, 374
Mottl, Felix, 451
Mozart, Leopold, 107
Mozart, Wolfgang Amadeus, 5, 38, 51, 61, 104-21, 151, 157, 161, 162, 163, 167, 184, 191, 213, 223, 224, 241, 249, 284, 349, 426, 474, 479, 487, 489; arioso, 64; *Ave Verum*, 105, 315; Beethoven, 114, 116-18, 122; biography, 92, 104-5, 110, 546; chamber music, 225-26; characteristics, 106-8, 112; composer, 108-19, 246, 247, 362; death, 25, 91; *Don Giovanni*, 64, 105, 108, 112, 114, 115, 116, 150, 157, 397, 486, 490; *Finta Semplice, La*, 110; form, 111-12, 113, 174; G minor Quintet, 118-19; *God Is Our Refuge*, 110; *Haydn*, 87, 93, 100, 101; *Idomeneo*, 104, 108; *Magic Flute, The*, 105, 113-14, 115, 116, 150; *Marriage of Figaro*, 105, 109, 111, 113, 114; melancholy, 115-16; *Mitridate Rè di Ponto*, 110; motifs, 152; principal works, 515-17; quoted, 119-21; *Requiem*, 105, 114, 116, 157; *Seraglio*, 104, 110, 111; sonatas, 118, 159, 164-65, 166, 237; spiritual faith, 116-17, 118, 119; superiority, 117-18; *Twelfth Mass*, 116
Muck, Karl, 451, 475
Muffat, Georg, 69
Müller, Wilhelm, 172
Murger, Henri, 444

Music: 15th century, 11; 16th century, 12; 17th century, 12, 42; 18th century, 12, 28, 32, 97-98; Baroque, 32; Classical, 32-33; religion and, 40

Musset, Alfred de, 148, 236

Mussorgsky, Modest, 391-99, 410, 501; biography, 391-92, 551; *Boris Godunov*, 392, 394, 396, 397; characteristics, 392-95; composer, 395-98; "Five, The Russian," 400, 401; *Khovanschina*, 392, 396, 397; *Marriage, The*, 391, 397, 398; nationalism, 418; *Night on Bald Mountain*, 391; *Pictures at an Exhibition*, 392, 397, 397; principal works, 534-35; quoted, 398-99; Rimsky-Korsakov, 403-4; songs, 397; *Songs and Dances of Death*, 392, 397; *Sunless*, 392, 397

NABUCCO (*see* Verdi)

Naples Conservatory, 202

Napoleon, 117, 130, 135, 192, 326

Nationalism, in music, 356, 359, 363, 367-68, 378, 381, 390, 400, 404-5, 412, 416, 417, 418, 456 (*see* "Five, The Russian")

Neefe, Christian Gottlieb, 122, 128

Neue Zeitschrift für Musik, 233, 236, 239, 341

Newman, Ernest, 476, 549, 550, 553, 558, 566

New York: National Conservatory, 364, 365; Philharmonic, 460 (*see* Metropolitan Opera)

Nikisch, Artur, 451, 459

Nocturnes (John Field), 226, 263

Nordraak, Rikard, 412, 418

Norwegian Academy of Music, 412

ODÉON (Paris), 290

Offenbach, Jacques, *La Belle Hélène*, 485

Orpheon Choral Society (Paris), 281

Ortigue, Joseph d', 180

Ospitale della Pieta (Venice) , 25, 28, 30

Ostrovsky, Alexander, 406

Östvedt, Arne, 416, 557, 563

Otello (*see* Verdi)

Ottoboni, Cardinal, 68

PACHELBEL, JOHANN, 50

Paër, Ferdinando, 281, 303

Paganini, Niccolò, 179, 303; *Études*, 232, 304

Pahlen, Kurt, 558, 563

Paisiello, Giovanni, 195, 209

Palestrina, Giovanni Pierluigi, 1-8, 39, 41-42, 49, 228, 288, 338, 399, 437; biography, 2-3, 544; *Canticle of Solomon*, 6, 7; composer, 4-7; death, 43, 47; Masses, 1; *Missa Assumpta Es*, 6; *Missa Papae Marcelli*, 1, 6; Motets, 6, 7; principal works, 511; quoted, 7-8; *Stabat Mater*, 6, 41

Paris: Académie des Beaux Arts, 282, 290; Académie de Musique, 79, 80, 81; Conservatory, 179, 180, 270, 281, 290, 303, 483, 493; Opéra, 18, 21, 75, 179, 197-98, 218, 286, 290, 425; Opéra-Comique, 290, 494

Parry, Hubert, 46, 160, 544, 545

Parsifal (*see* Wagner)

Pascal, Jean Louis, 312

Pastoral Symphony, 32, 123, 130

Paul, Howard, 282, 558, 565

Paul, Jean, 237, 241, 264

Pélissier, Olympe, 196, 204

Pelléas and Mélisande (see Debussy)

Pepys, Samuel, 70

Pergolesi, Giovanni: *La serva padrona*, 18

Peri, Jacopo: *Eurydice*, 14, 43, 83

Peter, René, 495

Petrarch, 236

Peyser, Herbert F., 291, 553, 565

Piccini, Niccolò, 75, 80-81; *Iphigénie en Tauride*, 82; *Roland*, 82

Pierné, Gabriel, 270, 290

Pincherle, Marc, 26, 558, 564

Pisendel, Johann, 26

Pissarro, Camille, 500

Planer, Minna, 320, 321, 325

Plato, 10, 17, 323; *Rhetoric*, 16

Polonaises (*see* Chopin)

Ponchielli, Amilcare: *La Gioconda*, 439

Pontifical Choir, 1, 3

Pope, Alexander, 172, 479

Porpora, Niccolò, 68, 99

Pouplinière, Riche de la, 18, 21

Prague: Conservatory, 364; National Theater, 356, 357, 360, 363; Opera, 112, 459

Prévost, Abbé, 294, 295

Proksch, Josef, 356

Provesi, Ferdinando, 422

Prunières, Henri, 11, 558, 562

Puccini, Giacomo, 43, 201, 296, 439-49; biography, 439-40, 552; *Bohème, La*, 439, 443, 444-45, 446, 447; characteristics, 440-44; composer, 444-48; *Edgar*, 439, 446; *Gianni Schicchi*, 440, 447-48; *Girl of the Golden West*, 440, 447; Leitmotifs, 445; *Madama Butterfly*, 439, 440, 444, 445, 447; *Manon Lescaut*, 439, 444; principal works, 537-38; quoted, 448-49; *Rondine, La*, 440, 447; *Suor Angelica*, 440, 447; *Tabarro, Il*, 440, 447; *Tosca*, 439, 443, 444, 445, 446-47; *Trittico, Il*, 440, 447; *Turandot*, 297, 440, 447, 448; Verdi, 446, 447; *Villi, Le*, 439

Purcell, Henry, 45-46, 66

Pushkin, 402, 406, 408, 409

Pyne, Zoë Kendrick, 2, 559, 564

QUINAULT, PHILIPPE, 81; *Roland*, 81

RABAUD, HENRI, 290

Rachmaninoff, Sergei, 317, 376

Racine, Jean Baptiste, 79, 502

Radiciotti, Giuseppe, 197, 198

Raison, André, 39

Raleigh, Sir Walter, 387

Rameau, Jean-Philippe, 18-24, 74, 78, 84, 486, 489, 505; biography, 18-19, 544; *Castor et Pollux*, 18, 19, 22; characteristics, 19-20, 21, 22; composer, 20-23; *Dardanus*, 22; *Fêtes d' Hébé*, 22; harmony, 18, 21, 23, 24; *Hippolyte et Aricie*, 18, 21-22; *Indes Galantes*, 22; *Nouveau*

système de musique théorique, 21; *Pièces de clavecin,* 18, 21; *Platée,* 22; *Princesse de Navarre,* 22; principal works, 511-12; quoted, 23-24; *Surprises de l'amour,* 22; *Traité de l'harmonie,* 12, 18, 21
Raphael, 6
Ravel, Maurice, 397, 418
Reber, Napoléon-Henri, 290
Rebikov, Vladimir, 418
Recio, Maria, 180, 182, 183
Régnier, Henri, 496, 497
Reicha, Anton, 303
Reichardt, Johann, 75
Reinken, Johann, 39, 50
Remenyi, Eduard, 341
Renoir, Pierre, 500
Repin, Ilia, 392
Reutter, Johann von, 98-99
Richter, Hans, 451, 473
Richter, Jean Paul, 236, 239
Ricordi, Giulio, 425
Riga Opera, 320
Rimsky-Korsakov, Andrei, 403
Rimsky-Korsakov, Nikolai, 317, 400-411; *Antar Symphony,* 400, 406; biography, 400-1, 551-52; *Boyarina Vera Sheloga,* 408; *Capriccio espagnol,* 401, 407; characteristics, 401-3; *Christmas Eve,* 408; composer, 403-10; *Coq d'or, Le,* 401, 402, 403, 409; "Five, The," 391, 400, 401; *Invisible City of Kitezh,* 41, 409, 410; *Maid of Pskov,* 400, 405-6; *May Night,* 401, 406; *Mlada,* 408; Mussorgsky, 392, 393, 394, 396, 403-4; principal works, 535-36; quoted, 410-11; *Russian Easter Overture,* 401, 407; *Sadko,* 401, 402, 405, 408, 409; *Scheherazade,* 401, 403, 407; *Snow Maiden,* 401, 406-7, 408, 409; *Song of India,* 408; *Tsar Saltan,* 401, 408-9; *Tsar's Bride,* 408
Rinuccini, Ottavio, 13
Rochefoucauld, La, 116
Rolland, Romain, 58, 75, 180, 485, 559, 565
Romanticism, 150-51, 206, 279, 378, 417, 419
Rosenfeld, Paul, 497, 559, 563
Rossini, Gioacchino, 195-210, 211, 214, 283, 433, 486; *Barber of Seville,* 111, 195, 201, 207; biography, 195-96, 197, 204, 548; *Cambiale di matrimonio,* 195; *Cenerentola,* 205; characteristics, 196-200, 203-4, 208, 426; composer, 200-9; *Don Pasquale,* 201; *Elisabetta,* 202; "great renunciation," 196, 197, 198, 199; *Italiana in Algeri,* 195, 207; *Mosé,* 201; *Petite Masse,* 207; principal works, 521; quoted, 209-10; *Semiramide,* 201, 204, 207; singing, 207-10; *Tancredi,* 195, 202; Wagner, 208-9; *William Tell,* 195, 196, 197, 201, 204, 206, 207
Roubliliac, L. F., 55
Rousseau, Jean-Jacques, 19, 22, 77, 80, 130, 487
Royal Academy of Music (London), 54, 55
Rückert, Friedrich, 236
Ruskin, John, 6

SAINT-BEUVE, CHARLES, 431
St. Petersburg: Conservatory, 373, 400, 402; Imperial Opera, 385
Saint-Saëns, Camille, 23, 314, 316, 347, 483-92; biography, 483-84, 486, 553; *Carnaval des animaux,* 485; characteristics, 484-85; composer, 485-90; *Danse macabre,* 483; First Symphony, 486; Fourth Piano Concerto, 483; *Gabriella di Vergi,* 485; Handel, 66, 67; *Henry III,* 485; *Henry VIII,* 489; *Ode à Sainte-Cécile,* 483; organist, 483, 484; principal works, 539-41; quoted, 490-92; *Rouet d'Omphale,* 483; *Samson and Delilah,* 483; Third Symphony, 483, 485
Salieri, Antonio, 105, 122, 211, 303
Salomon, Johann Peter, 87
Sammartini, Giovanni Battista, 74, 77, 99
Sand, George, 189, 255-56, 257n, 263, 559, 565
Sardou, Victorien, 444
Sarti, Giuseppe, 209
Satie, Erik, 493
Scarlatti, Alessandro, 29, 63, 555
Schalk, Franz, 451
Schiller, Fredrich von, 95, 175, 313, 328
Schindler, Alma Maria, 459
Schindler, Anton, 124, 125, 125n, 129, 559, 565
Schjelderup, Gerhard, 413, 414n, 559, 566
Schlegel, Friedrich von, 239
Schlichtegroll, Adolph von, 106, 106n, 559, 565
Schmitt, Florent, 290
Schober, Franz von, 155
Schoenberg, Arnold, 317, 560
Schubert, Franz, 113, 155-78, 189, 224, 230, 241, 246, 355, 456; *Allmacht, Die,* 172; A major Piano Sonata, 171; Beethoven, 161, 170, 171, 174, 175; biography, 155-56, 547; characteristics, 156-58; C major Symphony, 167, 170, 171, 202, 244; composer, 158-75; *Doppelgänger, Der,* 175; E-flat Piano Trio, 165, 168-69; *Erlkönig,* 155, 159-60, 161, 171; *Forellen Quintet,* 162, 163, 167, 171; *Gretchen am Spinnrade,* 155, 159, 160, 161; *Hagars Klage,* 155, 158-59; Mahler, 464, 465; Mass in F, 161; Mozart, 112-13, 161, 162; Piano Sonata in B-flat, 163-64, 165, 166, 167, 169; principal works, 519-21; quoted, 175-78, 229-30; *Rosamunde,* 155; *Schwanengesang,* 174; sonatas, 164-66, 167, 168, 455; songs, 159-61, 172-75, 242, 247, 315, 432, 476-77, 480; String Quartet; in C major, 165, 169, 171, in G major, 163-64; *Symphony in D minor,* 244; *Trockne Blumen,* 173; *Unfinished Symphony,* 113, 167, 169, 170, 336; *Wanderer Fantasy,* 166; *Winterreise, Die,* 173, 174; *Zauberharfe, Die,* 155; *Zwillingsbrüder, Die,* 155
Schumann, Clara, 233, 341, 342, 345, 346
Schumann, Robert, 52, 156, 230, 232-54, 329, 341, 345, 348, 386, 474, 486, 489;

Abegg Variations, 232, 244; *Album für die Jugend*, 238; *Bilder aus Osten*, 243; biography, 232-33, 548; *Blumenstück*, 246; *Buch der Lieder*, 247; *Carnaval*, 232, 244, 246; characteristics, 233-35; C major Symphony, 248; composer, 235-53, 264; *Concerto without Orchestra*, 238; *Davidsbundlertänze*, 238, 239, 245; D minor Piano Trio, 243; D minor Symphony, 276; E-flat major Piano Quartet, 243; *Études symphoniques*, 232, 245, 247; Fantasia in C, 232, 239; *Fantasie-stücke*, 232, 238; *Genoveva*, 250; *Humoreske*, 246; *Impromptus on a Theme by Clara Wieck*, 245; *Kinderscenen*, 238; *Kreisleriana*, 239-41, 246; *Manfred*, 244, 249, 251; *Novelletten*, 239, 243, 246; *Paganini Études*, 232; *Papillons*, 232, 237, 243, 246; *Paradise and the Peri*, 242, 251-52; *Piano Quintet*, 168, 243, 244; principal works, 523-24; quoted, 253-54; *Requiem*, 252; *Scenes from Goethe's Faust*, 251; songs, 247-48, 476-77; Symphony in D minor, 248; *Violoncello Concerto*, 249; *Waldscenen*, 239
Schunke, Ludwig, 244
Schütz, Heinrich, 48, 49
Schwarz, Josef, 357, 559, 566
Schweitzer, Albert, 35, 37n, 559, 564
Schweitzer, Anton, 150
Scott, Sir Walter, 236
Scriabin, Alexander, 317, 558
Scribe, Eugène, 215
Sechter, Simeon, 156, 450
Shakespeare, William, 168, 236, 286, 396, 423, 434; *Measure for Measure*, 320, 327; power of, 169; *Tempest*, 129
Shaw, George Bernard, 108
Shelley, Percy Bysshe, 253, 479
Sibelius, Jean: *Finlandia*, 308; Fourth Symphony, 446; *Valse triste*, 308
Simrock, Nikolaus, 344, 363
Sire, Simonin de, 237
Slonimsky, Nicolas, 392, 401, 559-60, 566
Smetana, Bedřich, 318, 356-62, 363, 367, 368, 369; *Bartered Bride*, 356-57, 359; biography, 356-57, 551; *Brandenburgers in Bohemia*, 356; characteristics, 357-59; composer, 359-61; *Dalibor*, 357, 359; *Devil's War*, 357; *From My Life*, 357, 360; *Libuša*, 357, 359; *My Fatherland*, 357, 359-60; nationalism, 418; principal works, 531-32; quoted, 361-62; *Wallensteins Lager*, 356
Smithson, Harriet, 179, 181-83
Sonnleithner, Joseph, 125
Spaun, Joseph von, 155
Specht, Richard, 440, 560, 562
Spinoza, Baruch, 135, 469
Spitta, Philipp, 352, 545
Spohr, Ludwig, 329; *Jessonda*, 151; *Witches' Dance*, 151
Spontini, Gasparo, 148, 183, 333, 490
Stamaty, Camille-Marie, 483

Stanford, Charles, 47, 109
Starzer, Josef, 98
Stassov, Vladimir, 394
Stefan, Paul, 364, 560, 561, 566
Steffani, Agostino, 63
Stolz, Teresina, 425
Stradella, Alessandro, 61
Stradivari, Antonio, 43
Strauss, Johann II, 359, 560
Strauss, Richard, 316, 460, 489-90, 497, 560; *Elektra*, 297; *Salome*, 297; songs, 480; symphonic poem, 476-77, 479
Stravinsky, Igor, 401, 564, 565; *Petrouchka*, 317, 446
Streatfeild, R. A., 214, 283, 560, 565
Strepponi, Giuseppina, 422, 425
Striggio, Alessandro, 12, 13
Strunk, W. Oliver, 91, 560, 564, 565
Sturm und Drang, 68, 127
Suarès, André, 496
Sullivan, Arthur, 156, 556
Süssmayr, Franz, 105
Swedish Academy, 412
Sweelinck, Jan Pieterzoon, 50
TARTINI, GIUSEPPE, 44
Tasso, Torquato, 16
Taylor, Deems, 322, 560, 564
Tchaikovsky, Mme Anatol, 375, 560, 563
Tchaikovsky, Modest, 385, 560
Tchaikovsky, Peter Ilitch, 295, 347, 373-90, 410, 493; biography, 373-75, 551; characteristics, 375-77; composer, 377-90; *Eugene Onegin*, 374, 381, 382; First String Quartet, 380; *Iolanthe*, 382, 385; *Italian Caprice*, 374; melancholy, 115; *Nutcracker*, 385; *Overture 1812*, 374; Piano Concerto, B-flat minor, 380-81, No. 1, 374; *Pique, Dame*, 382, 385; principal works, 533-34; quoted, 387-90; *Romeo and Juliet*, 373, 379-80; *Sleeping Beauty*, 385; *Swan Lake*, 374, 385; symphonies, 379, 381, 383, 385-86: Fourth, 374, 381-82, 383, 384, 389; Fifth, 383-84; Sixth (*Pathétique*), 374, 385-87; Violin Concerto, 374, 383; *Voyevode*, 373, 382
Telemann, Georg Philipp, 66
Terry, C. Sanford, 38, 560, 563
Texier, Rosalie, 494
Teyte, Maggie, 497
Théâtre Italien (Paris), 195
Thomas, Ambroise, 290
Thompson, Oscar, 494, 560, 563
Tiersot, Julien, 181, 277
Tolstoy, Leo, 395; *War and Peace*, 469
Torelli, Giuseppe, 25, 29-31, 43-44
Tovey, Donald, 110, 118, 119, 158, 455, 560-61, 564
Toye, Francis, 196, 200, 548, 552, 561
Truffot, Marie, 483
Turner, Walter J., 546, 548, 550, 561, 564
UHLAND, LUDWIG, 245
VERDI, GIUSEPPE, 5, 43, 201, 205, 206, 207, 422-38, 486; *Aïda*, 201, 422, 423, 425, 432, 433; *Ballo in maschera*, 206, 422; *Bat-*

taglia di Legnano, 428, 431; biography, 422-23, 552; characteristics, 208, 423-26; composer, 285, 426-36; *Corsaro, Il*, 428; *Don Carlo*, 201, 422, 433; *Ernani*, 422, 432, 433; *Falstaff*, 201, 423, 426-27, 433-34; *Forza del destino*, 422; *Giorno di regno*, 422; *Lombardi, I*, 201, 422; *Luisa Miller*, 422, 428, 431; *Macbeth*, 422, 427, 433; *Masnadieri*, 428; *Nabucco*, 201, 422, 430, 433, 435; *Oberto*, 422, 430; *Otello*, 423, 426, 427-28, 432, 433, 445, 446; principal works, 537; quoted, 436-38; *Requiem*, 423, 424; *Rigoletto*, 422, 429, 432, 433; *Simon Boccanegra*, 422; String Quartet, 431; *Traviata*, 422, 433, 435, 445; *Trovatore*, 201, 422, 426, 433; *Vespri siciliana*, 422

Vienna: Burgtheater, 74, 79, 105; Conservatory, 450, 456, 459, 473; Court Theater, 74; Opera 459, 462, 463, 475, 476; Philharmonic, 473; *Singakademie*, 341

Vieuxtemps, Henri, 456

Vitali, Giovanni, 43

Vivaldi, Antonio, 25-33, 39, 44, 69; biography, 25-26, 544; characteristics, 26-28; composer, 25-33; *Concerto de' Cucchi*, 27; *Concerto in A*, 26-27; *Coro delle Monache*, 27; *Primavera, La*, 30; principal works, 512; *Quattro stagione*, 30, 32; quoted, 33; *Tito Manlio*, 28

Vogl, Johann Michael, 155, 175

Vogler, Abbé, 125, 146, 211

Volbach, Fritz, 37, 68

Voltaire, 19, 23, 80, 487

Volterra, Daniel da, 4

WAGENSEIL, GEORG CHRISTOPH, 98

Wagner, Cosima, 303, 304, 321, 322, 325

Wagner, Richard, 5, 67, 147, 152, 173, 181, 198, 201, 208-9, 215, 242, 279, 320-40, 370, 410, 411, 433, 472, 486, 487, 489; Bayreuth, 304, 322, 333-34, 335, 337, 338, 454, 492, 505; biography, 320-22, 550; Bruckner, 450, 454, 455, 457-58; characteristics, 322-26, 413; composer, 264, 274, 277, 285, 327-38, 432; Debussy, 504, 505; *Faust Overture*, 320; *Feen, Die*, 320, 327; Festspiel (*see* Bayreuth); *Flying Dutchman*, 320, 327; *Gotterdämmerung*, 321,

322; *Hochzeit, Die*, 320; *Liebestod*, 478; *Liebesverbot, Das*, 320, 327; Liszt, 304, 316, 321, 327; *Lohengrin*, 191, 316, 321, 327, 329, 332, 427; *Meistersinger, Die*, 295, 321, 322, 326, 332, 334-35, 338, 476; opera, 22, 337, 476-78; *Parsifal*, 322, 329, 332, 335-36, 338, 409, 458, 475; principal works, 529; quoted, 338-40; *Rheingold*, 316, 321, 322; *Rienzi*, 320, 327; *Ring* cycle, 115, 322, 326, 331-32, 333, 338, 454, 457; *Siegfried*, 321, 322; *Tannhaüser*, 321, 327, 333; *Tristan and Isolde*, 321, 322, 326, 333, 335, 338, 444; *Valkyries*, 321, 322; Wolf, 473, 474, 475, 477

Walter, Bruno, 460, 463, 561

Warsaw Conservatory, 255

Weber, Anselm, 211

Weber, Karl Maria von, 96, 146-54, 198, 202, 223, 241, 328, 329, 332-33, 336, 410, 487; *Abu Hassan*, 146; biography, 547; characteristics, 147-50; composer, 150-53, 264, 277; *Ein steter Kampf ist unser Leben*, 148; *Euryanthe*, 147, 151-52, 153, 250; *Freischütz*, 147, 148, 151, 152, 153; *Oberon*, 147, 149, 153; opera, 146-47, 153-54; *Preciosa*, 153; principal works, 519; quoted, 153-54; *Silvana*, 146, 149, 150

Werfel, Alma Mahler, 460, 561, 564

Werfel, Franz, 423, 552, 561, 566

Wieck, Friedrich, 232, 233

Wieniawski, Henri, 456

Winter-Hjelm, Otto, 418

Wolf, Hugo, 173, 473-82; *Alte Weisen*, 473; biography, 473-74, 553; characteristics, 474-76; composer, 476-81; *Corregidor*, 474; *Lied*, 473, 481; Moerike songs, 473, 477-78, 480; *Penthesilea Overture*, 473, 475; principal works, 539; *Prometheus*, 480; quoted, 481-82; songs, 432, 473 ff.; String Quartet, 473; Wagner, 473, 474, 475, 477

Wolf-Ferrari, Ermanno, 201

Wordsworth, William, 175, 395, 479

ZACHAU, FRIEDRICH, 54, 59

Zaremba, Nicolas, 373

Zelter, Karl Friedrich, 95, 96, 211, 219

Zumsteeg, Johann Rudolf, 158-59

576